Witchcraft in Europe: 400–1700

D1297224

WITCHCRAFT

IN EUROPE,

400–1700

A Documentary History

SECOND EDITION

Edited by Alan Charles Kors and Edward Peters

Revised by Edward Peters

University of Pennsylvania Press   Philadelphia

Copyright © 2001 University of Pennsylvania Press
Printed in the United States of America on acid-free paper

10 9 8 7 6 5 4 3 2 1

Published by

University of Pennsylvania Press

Philadelphia, Pennsylvania 19104-4011

Library of Congress Cataloging-in-Publication Data

Witchcraft in Europe, 400–1700 : a documentary history / edited by Alan Charles Kors and
    Edward Peters ; revised by Edward Peters. — 2nd ed.

    p.   cm.

Includes bibliographical references.

ISBN 0-8122-1751-9 (pbk. : alk. paper)

    1. Witchcraft—Europe—History—Sources.   I. Kors, Alan Charles.   II. Peters, Edward.

BF1566 .W739 2001

133.4′3′094—dc21   00-064934

Contents

III

THOMAS AQUINAS ON SORCERY AND THE NATURE OF EVIL   87

IV

POPES, THEOLOGIANS, PREACHERS, LAWYERS, AND JUDGES   112

V

THE SECT OF DIABOLICAL WITCHES   149

VI

THE HAMMER OF WITCHES   176

VII

HUMANISTS, SORCERERS, PREACHERS, AND POPES   230

Preface to the Second Edition

To revise a popular and useful book after nearly thirty years requires three things: a sense that the project is still useful, a careful look at the virtues and shortcomings of the original, and an appreciation of what a new edition might need in order to take adequate account of the scholarly research that has been published since its first appearance in 1972.

The first edition of this book contained forty-four texts, a third of which dealt with the period between 1140 and 1376, illustrating some of the medieval antecedents and developments of the beliefs about diabolical sorcery that coalesced into a new ensemble in the second quarter of the fifteenth century. The remaining two-thirds of the book traced both trial records and demonological theory through the seventeenth century and also the growth of expressions of skepticism, doubt, and disbelief through some of the eighteenth. One-third of the whole was newly translated. The book also contained seventy-two illustrations, some of them difficult to find, and all of them linked to the texts and headnotes.

In 1975 and 1976 Norman Cohn and Richard Kieckhefer independently proved that one of our texts (No. 15) was in fact a nineteenth-century forgery. We indicated the forgery in subsequent printings of the book, and we also later added a slight bibliographical addendum on scholarship up to 1990. Enough time and scholarship have passed to rethink the entire subject and offer what is essentially a new book with an older book wrapped up inside it, one with sixty-nine texts over a longer period, a new set of forty-one illustrations, all of which are closely tied to the texts translated, with all translations, headnotes, and the introduction completely redone and new suggestions for further reading indicated with each text.

This edition takes into account the achievements of the past three decades of scholarship in North America and Europe, particularly its overall effect of having made the subject of witchcraft an important component in the study of early modern European history. The new texts have been chosen in order to illustrate that process, and we are deeply indebted to those scholars in the United States and Europe whose work has done so much to illuminate our understanding of the subject.

Although I have assumed the responsibility for this new edition, Alan Charles Kors has read and commented on all the revisions and additions. In this edition, as in the original, the co-authorship still stands.

For discussing the project with us, checking and correcting our translations, and giving me opportunities to examine the sources and literature more deeply, occasionally in public lectures, I owe particular thanks to Bengt Ankaarloo, Jodi Bilinkoff, Kathleen Brown, Kevin Brownlee, Stuart Clark, Jonathan Elukin, Erica Gelser, Gustav Henningsen, Richard Kieckhefer, Armando Maggi, Frank Menchaca, John Pollack, Larry Silver, David Warner, and Liliane Weissberg.

Illustrations

Abbreviations

Anglo, *The Damned Art*
Sydney Anglo, ed., *The Damned Art: Essays in the Literature of Witchcraft*
(London and Boston, 1977)

Burr, *The Witch-Persecutions*
George Lincoln Burr, *The Witch-Persecutions, Translations and Reprints from
the Original Sources of European History*, vol. 3, no. 4, Department of History,
University of Pennsylvania (Philadelphia, 1907; rprt. New York, 1971)

Clark, *Thinking with Demons*
Stuart Clark, *Thinking with Demons: The Idea of Witchcraft in Early Modern
Europe* (Oxford, 1997)

Cohn, *Europe's Inner Demons*
Norman Cohn, *Europe's Inner Demons: An Enquiry Inspired by the Great
Witch-Hunt* (New York, 1975)

Colish, *Medieval Foundations*
Marcia L. Colish, *Medieval Foundations of the Western Intellectual Tradition,
400–1400* (New Haven, 1997)

Flint, *The Rise of Magic*
Valerie I. J. Flint, *The Rise of Magic in Early Medieval Europe* (Princeton, 1991)

Hansen, *Quellen*
Joseph Hansen, *Quellen und Untersuchungen zur Geschichte des Hexenwahns
und der Hexenverfolgung im Mittelalter* (Bonn, 1901)

Kieckhefer, *Magic in the Middle Ages*
Richard Kieckhefer, *Magic in the Middle Ages* (Cambridge, 1990)

Lea, *Materials*
Henry Charles Lea, *Materials Toward a History of Witchcraft*, ed. Arthur C. Howland, 3 vols. (Philadelphia, 1939; rprt. New York, 1957)

Peters, *The Magician, the Witch, and the Law*
Edward Peters, *The Magician, the Witch, and the Law* (Philadelphia, 1978)

Russell, *Satan*
Jeffrey Burton Russell, *Satan: The Early Christian Tradition* (Ithaca and London, 1981)

Russell, *Witchcraft*
Jeffrey Burton Russell, *Witchcraft in the Middle Ages* (Ithaca and London, 1972)

Veenstra, *Magic and Divination*
Jan Veenstra, *Magic and Divination at the Courts of Burgundy and France* (Leiden-New York-Cologne, 1998)

Witchcraft and Magic in Europe
Witchcraft and Magic in Europe, ed. Bengt Ankarloo and Stuart Clark, 6 vols. (Philadelphia, 1999–2001)

Witchcraft in Early Modern Europe
Witchcraft in Early Modern Europe: Studies in Culture and Belief, Jonathan Barry, Marianne Hester, and Gareth Roberts, eds. (Cambridge, 1996)

Introduction:

The Problem of European Witchcraft

A Historical Problem and Its Components

Western minds, when confronted by the problem of what we term sorcery or witchcraft in primitive or non-Western cultures, assume most comfortably the attitudes and categories of formal or informal cultural anthropology. We know, and we find nothing unusual in this, that in a number of worldviews men and women, when they are fearful and helpless before the awesome forces of the visible world, traditionally seek to reach normally inaccessible forces beyond that world in order to increase their meager human powers and their abilities to control their own destinies. They then assign to other men and women, or acknowledge in them, the extraordinary role of causing events not normally within the province of human determination. We regard the beliefs, rites, and institutions of such "magic" as purposeful, whatever our views on their legitimacy and efficacy, and we speculate freely on the psychological, social, and explanatory functions which they serve. We understand, with varying degrees of satisfaction, why it is that the recognized holders of such magical powers— the witches, sorcerers, and shamans of other cultures—should be among the most feared and revered members of any society and why people's behavior toward them should take intensely particular and peculiar forms. Our orderings and explanations of "magic" may seem to us still inchoate or insufficient, but on the whole we preserve a sense of the final comprehensibility and clarity of such phenomena.

Confronted with the problem of "witchcraft" in Western culture, however, we feel ourselves faced with a much more complex problem. It seems to us far less comprehensible that *after* our own alleged period of primitive experience in the West, after our "Dark Ages," during the centuries of dynamic intellectual experimentation, the Renaissance, the Reformations, and, more perplexing still, during that seventeenth century which we continue to consider the "Age of Reason" and the "Age of Scientific Revolution," Europeans engaged in a systematic and furious assault upon men and women believed to be diabolical sorcerers and witches manipulating the forces of the supernatural to effect evil in the world and bring Satan's kingdom to a complete and terrible fulfillment. The otherwise calm and analytic language of the social sciences suddenly appears inadequate to the task even of description alone, and the terms "craze," "mania," "superstition," and "aberration" record our recoil from our culture's past far more than they clarify and explain that part of the past.

It is precisely those techniques of investigation and description so useful to the study of other cultures that we generally fail to apply to the most puzzling and unsettling parts of the past of our own: the suspension of current criteria of "truth" and "falsehood," of "sanity" and "insanity," of "logic" and "illogic," and the impartial schematization of a people's entire worldview upon which so many aspects of its beliefs and behavior depend. If we are ever to understand or explain the phenomenon of European witchcraft, we must begin by appreciating Europeans' sense of the ontology of a world with demons and witches in it and the character of the participants (both accusers and accused) involved.

This collection of sources has been assembled to offer the reader significant examples of the European view of that reality and those participants. During the period from 1100 to 1750 the concern of European (and some North and South Americans) over the nature, activities, and numbers of diabolical sorcerers and witches became a major intellectual and juridical preoccupation of people from all walks of life and culminated in the widespread fears, accusations, trials, and executions that so arrest our attention. Our work focuses on this period, from the development of integral components of a systematic theory of witchcraft to the end of the major persecutions and the formulation of criteria for skepticism, ridicule, and eventual outright disbelief.

The Problem of the Past

Some elements of witch beliefs, of course, antedate the period of pandemic fear and active persecution, roughly from 1430 to 1660. Historians of late antiquity and early medieval Europe, folklorists, and anthropologists, in fact, have long debated the exact sources from which they were drawn and the diverse methods of their continuing existence. Celtic and Germanic religion and folklore, biblical and patristic speculation on the nature of evil, Neoplatonism and the related philosophical and subphilosophical spiritualism of late antiquity, and even the postulated survival of "underground" ancient pre-Christian cults have all been identified at one time or another as major contributors. Some of the essential strands of late antique and early medieval normative thought on these subjects are traced in Part I of this volume (Texts 1–4).

From 1100 on, however, indistinct and often idiosyncratic strains of belief were organized in western Europe into an increasingly coherent and generally uniform system of theological and juridical dogma, the logical implication of which was the obligation of churchmen and the secular courts actively to seek out and extirpate the witches and their protectors and defenders.[1] In the pages of the texts under consideration in this volume, one can trace the transformation of individual sorcerers, shamans, and "cunning" men and women of earlier centuries into the diabolical sorcerer and witch of the period of persecutions (Texts 5–12).[2] Two phenomena whose causal interaction with other social and intellectual circumstances constitutes one of the great problems of European history become increasingly clear around 1100: attention to the ensemble of beliefs about sorcerers and witches centering on the universal greed, malevolence, and diabolic connection of sorcerers and witches, and the growing aware-

1. The sources and scholarship on antiquity and the pre-Christian Celtic and Germanic worlds are vast and are not addressed in this book. The best introductions to these problems are the first three volumes of the series edited by Bengt Ankarloo and Stuart Clark, *Witchcraft and Magic in Europe* (Philadelphia, 1999–). Individual works include Georg Luck, *Arcana Mundi: Magic and the Occult in the Greek and Roman Worlds* (Baltimore, 1985), an extensive collection of annotated sources in English translation; Fritz Graf, *Magic in the Ancient World*, trans. Franklin Philip (Cambridge, Mass., 1997); and Peter Schäfer, "Jewish Magic Literature in Late Antiquity and Early Middle Ages," *Journal of Jewish Studies* 41 (1990): 75–91. On Byzantine and Islamic magic, also not treated here, see Henry Maguire, ed., *Byzantine Magic* (Washington, D.C., 1995), and Charles Burnett, *Magic and Divination in the Middle Ages: Texts and Techniques in the Islamic and Christian Worlds* (Aldershot, Brookfield, Vt., 1996). On Celtic and Germanic practices, see Kieckhefer, *Magic in the Middle Ages*, 43–55; Flint, *The Rise of Magic*; Edward Peters, "The Medieval Church and State on Superstition, Magic, and Witchcraft," in *Witchcraft in Europe*, vol. 3, *The Middle Ages* (Philadelphia, 2001); Ramsay MacMullen, *Christianity and Paganism in the Fourth to Eighth Centuries* (New Haven and London, 1997); and Thomas A. DuBois, *Nordic Religions in the Viking Age* (Philadelphia, 1999).

2. On pagan survivals and shamanism see Gabor Klaniczay, *The Uses of Supernatural Power: The Transformation of Popular Religion in Medieval and Early Modern Europe* (Princeton, 1980); Ludo Milis, ed., *The Pagan Middle Ages* (Woodbridge, Suffolk, 1998); Wolfgang Behringer, *Shaman of Oberstdorf: Chonrad Stoeckhlin and the Phantoms of the Night*, trans. H. C. Erik Midelfort (Charlottesville, 1998); Éva Pócs, *Between the Living and the Dead: A Perspective on Witches and Seers in the Early Modern Age*, trans. Szilvia Rédey and Michael Webb (Budapest, 1999). See also Carlo Ginsburg, *Ecstasies: Deciphering the Witches' Sabbath*, trans. Raymond Rosenthal (New York, 1991), and Michael Bailey, "The Medieval Concept of the Witches' Sabbath," *Exemplaria* 8 (1996): 419–39. On the midwife problem, see David Harley, "Historians as Demonologists: The Myth of the Midwife-Witch," *Social History of Medicine* 3 (1990): 1–26, and Hilde De Ridder-Symoens, "Intellectual and Political Backgrounds of the Witch-Craze in Europe," in *La Sorcellerie dans les Pays-Bàs sous l'Ancien Régime: Aspects juridiques, institutionnels et sociaux*, ed. S. Dupont-Bouchat (Courtrai, 1987), 37–64.

ness of the active and horrific dangers posed by the ever-increasing numbers of sorcerers and witches at large.

Before 1100 or so, churchmen generally professed skepticism concerning the alleged activities and magical powers of witches, although they strongly condemned certain kinds of activities as deviant practice from their concept of normative religious life. Churchmen, after all, by 1100 had virtually disarmed the last bastion of pagan beliefs by convincing men and women that "the gods of the pagans were demons in disguise" (Psalm 95 [96]: 5), that all pagan religious practices (whether Mediterranean or northern European) were superstitions (a much stronger word then than now), and that some pagan religious practices constituted forbidden magic. Churchmen also argued convincingly for a long time that belief in the Christian god and normative religious practice protected the faithful from the inept assaults of malevolent, but increasingly ineffective demons.

As the intellectual synthesis of beliefs about magic and sorcery continued, however, it was precisely churchmen and, among them, theologians and other educated clergy who were to shape and channel much European opinion. As awareness of the theological and juridical ramifications of the reality of diabolical sorcery and witchcraft spread, so did people's perceptions of the nature of magical activity; as the latter grew, so did the demand for further theological and juristic clarification and response.

From 1100 on one can observe (and sometimes even date rather precisely) the appearance of certain common elements of both sorcery and witchcraft and the emerging realization that the victory of Christianity had not, after all, been complete and that something new and dreadful in the history of Christendom had appeared. Many contemporary observers from the fourteenth century on looked upon manifest diabolical sorcery and witchcraft as quantitatively and qualitatively the single greatest threat to Christian European civilization.

At the height of these fears in the sixteenth and seventeenth centuries, churchmen and others speculated on when and why the concerted and terrible assault of the diabolical sorcerers and witches had begun. Some dated the crisis from the later fourteenth century, others from around 1500. In the sixteenth century Protestants accused the Roman Catholic clergy of fostering witchcraft through "popish blasphemies," and Catholics in turn proceeded to identify witchcraft, first, with traditional and recognized heresy and later with Protestantism itself. Almost all agreed, however, that intensive witchcraft was essentially a new danger and a particularly urgent one. This perception of the novelty and historical uniqueness of witchcraft by people of the fifteenth through the seventeenth centuries suggests the value of studying European witchcraft as a peculiarly time-bound phenomenon.

The time-bound character of witch beliefs and persecutions from the second quarter of the fifteenth century to the last quarter of the seventeenth is illustrated by two apparently incompatible features of the literature of the period. On the one hand, thinkers cited Jewish and Christian scripture, classical Greek and Latin literature, and the writings of some church fathers as evidence that the ideas of witchcraft that they themselves held were the same—and indicated the same thing—as those of Hebrew, Christian, and classical antiquity. On the other hand, they also argued on the basis of texts from the eighth through the eleventh and early twelfth centuries that before their own time witchcraft had apparently not been the extensive threat that it later became. Earlier ecclesiastical injunctions against belief in diabolical sorcery and witchcraft were regarded as legitimately applicable only to the time of their original utterance, before the magnitude of the witches' assault had reached its current epidemic proportions. The development of theories concerning the witch prepared Europeans for the identification of certain empirical phenomena as diabolical witchcraft. Once that identification had been made, people were bound by their own worldview to the consequent necessity of persecution.[3] In this sense, the problem of European witchcraft demands less the study of magic as pure folklore and the useful, but incomplete, results of anthropology than the study of the intellectual, perceptual, and legal processes by which "folklore" was transformed into and understood as systematic demonology that required systematic prosecution.

Cosmology and Ontology
When the problem of historical witchcraft is seen in this light, it becomes essential to consider particular social, intellectual, and legal phenomena chronologically. Before the twelfth century, Christian cosmology had not become the detailed common frame of reference—the literal and articulated blueprint of God's creation—which it became between 1100 and 1700.[4] Before the thirteenth century, there had existed no systematic and comprehensive universal ontology as elaborate and thorough in its description of the interrelations among the elements of creation as was that of St. Thomas Aquinas and other scholastic

3. The most influential study of the process of persecution as a component of early European society is that of R. I. Moore, *The Formation of a Persecuting Society: Power and Deviance in Western Europe, 950–1250* (Oxford and New York, 1987).

4. On the beginnings of Christian interpretations and representations of the universe, see Gerhart B. Ladner, *God, Cosmos, and Humankind: The World of Early Christian Symbolism* (Berkeley and Los Angeles, 1995). On the twelfth-century origins, see Brian Stock, *Myth and Science in the Twelfth Century: A Study of Bernard Sylvester* (Princeton, 1972), and the essays in Peter Dronke, ed., *A History of Twelfth-Century Western Philosophy* (Cambridge, 1988). On the problem of the organization of knowledge, see the excerpt from Hugh of St. Victor, Text 7 in this volume.

philosophers (Texts 13–17).[5] Scholastic ontology gave to both demons and witches a logically consistent place within the Christian schema.

Before the fourteenth century, there had existed no regular body of investigators and judges whose sole duty was to uncover and uproot theological error, eventually including that of the witches, such as was at the disposal of the "inquisitors of heretical depravity," however ill-understood and distorted their activities were in common depictions.[6] Before the fifteenth century there had been no widespread, literate, and concentrated public subjected to widespread social strains and capable of mutually reinforcing that acute awareness of shared vulnerability and helplessness, danger, and pervasive fear which was an essential ingredient of any substantial and continuing witch scare or persecution (Texts 18–24).[7] Furthermore, and perhaps most important, once the diabolical sorcerer and the witch had been irrefutably identified as the visible agents of Satan upon the earth, then the social, political, and economic turmoils of the late medieval and early modern European world, the agonizing disintegration of Christendom into warring religious camps, and the brutalizing and disheartening recurrence of plague and famine all served to heighten that sensibility to the power of evil, to demonic powers, upon which the persecutions largely depended (Texts 25–60).

The History of Satan

At an intellectual and systematic theological level, the clarification of the ontological status and purposeful activities of Satan and his host of demons was essential to a changed perception of the witch, whose nature and fate were increasingly linked to those of the diabolical power.[8] The early Christians had inherited an eclectic, unorganized body of theory about the power of evil in the world.[9] Satan had appeared infrequently in Hebrew scripture, where he was depicted occasionally as a tempter of mankind, but more usually as an obedient, accusing angel in particular service to God. In Jewish apocrypha, however, more imbued

5. See the excerpt from Aquinas and the discussion in the Introduction in Part III, Texts 13–16 in this volume, and Richard Kieckhefer, "The Specific Rationality of Medieval Magic," *American Historical Review* 99 (1994): 813–36.

6. Edward Peters, *Inquisition* (New York, 1988; rprt. Berkeley and Los Angeles, 1989).

7. The seminal work is Richard Kieckhefer, *European Witch Trials: Their Foundations in Popular and Learned Culture, 1300–1500* (London, 1976).

8. See Russell, *Satan*; Russell, *Lucifer: The Devil in the Middle Ages* (Ithaca and London, 1984); Alan E. Bernstein, *The Formation of Hell: Death and Retribution in the Ancient and Early Christian Worlds* (Ithaca and London, 1993). Particularly useful and informative in terms of the history of both Satan and the conceptualization of dissent is Elaine Pagels, *The Origin of Satan* (New York, 1995).

9. Kieckhefer, *Magic in the Middle Ages*, 19–42; Peters, "The Medieval Church and State on Superstition, Magic, and Witchcraft"; Flint, *The Rise of Magic*.

as it was with the themes of Eastern dualism, the Devil was often presented as the causal agent of all that is evil, a spirit in active rebellion against God. It is this latter concept that emerged as dominant in Christian scripture—coupled, to be sure, with the unswerving promise of Christ's ultimate triumph over him. The book of Revelation, or the Apocalypse, the last book of the Christian bible, referred to "that ancient serpent, who is called the Devil and Satan, the deceiver of the whole world," thus revealing Eve's tempter and Satan to be one and the same.

In this role Satan tempted both Judas and Jesus Christ, and later theorists of witchcraft repeatedly pointed to Satan's transport of Jesus to the top of the Temple (Matthew 4) as proof of Satan's power to move witches from one place to another. St. Paul logically warned the Christian congregations against the powers and wiles of the archfiend, and the Epistle to the Ephesians became the fundamental scriptural proof of both diabolical character and intentions.

By the fourth century, when St. Augustine (354–430) was drawn to discuss the problem of the source and nature of evil in his dispute with the Manichaeans, the notion of the Devil as the enemy of God and man was firmly enshrined in Christian belief. Augustine was to systematize this concept and place it in a meaningful context. By stressing to so great a degree the climactic effects of the fall from Eden and the continuing efforts of Satan to prey upon sinful human nature for the perdition of souls, Augustine heightened the Christian awareness of the Devil's powers so that they seemed second only to those of God.[10] When Thomas Aquinas turned to the codification of Christian theology in the thirteenth century, he thus found a clear source of dogma concerning Satan in the works of Augustine, and he cited Augustine continually in his defense of the theory of Satan as the pinnacle of the hierarchy of evil spirits, working for the temporal and eternal suffering of mankind through the inscrutable will— and with the permission—of God. The dualism of the Manichaeans, it is true, had been defeated in the area of normative Christian belief, but the influence of these and similar dualist beliefs, particularly as they further contributed to illuminating the role of Satan in the world, were to remain a part of Christian awareness for centuries to come.

That Satan commanded a host or army of subordinate demons was an essential part of late antique and medieval folklore and both positive and normative theological doctrine. The major Christian attack on the pagan gods had anathematized them as evil spirits who deluded mankind. The systematization and elaboration of these beliefs beginning about 1100 gave the myriads of subdemons an essential place in the development of ideas of witchcraft. The book of Genesis had told of the "sons of God" who descended to earth and had intercourse with women, producing a race of giants, an idea greatly elaborated in the apocryphal Book of Enoch. The book of Revelation had described a rebellion in

10. Elaine Pagels, *Adam, Eve, and the Serpent* (New York, 1988).

Heaven in which Satan waged war with the forces led by the archangel Michael and had been cast down to earth with his rebel angels. From these and other scriptural and apocryphal references later theologians deduced two important concepts: that the earth was infested with a myriad legion of powerful demons (fallen evil spirits), and that these demons could have sexual intercourse with human beings, with men as *succubi* and with women as *incubi*. In the New Testament, Christ often demonstrated his divine powers specifically by exorcising demons, and Scripture held that Christ gave the ability to drive out demons directly to the Apostles as proof of the divine sanction of their mission. The power of exorcism became an essential tool of the later missionary Church:

> However many sound social and cultural reasons the historian may find for the expansion of the Christian Church, the fact remains that in all Christian literature from the New Testament onwards, the Christian missionaries advanced principally by revealing the bankruptcy of men's invisible enemies, the demons, through exorcisms and miracles of healing.[11]

Before the work of the scholastic philosophers and systematic theologians in the twelfth and thirteenth centuries, however, the role of the demons in the affairs of men and women was part of a variegated and inconsistent folk- and clerical lore in which demonic activities ranged from the horrific and utterly diabolical to mere impishness and mischievousness, often betraying a whimsical humor. In the increasingly systematic thought of Aquinas and his contemporaries, however, this folklore became complex and rigorous ecclesiastical doctrine. The demons were evil angels who had the ability to unite themselves to bodies and to communicate their knowledge and commands to men and women. They were a hierarchically organized army in the service of Satan working collectively for the perdition of the faithful. Satan and his hosts could tempt human beings into their service, thereby making them commit the twin sins and crimes of apostasy and idolatry. They also could secure both present and future service by written contracts with humans, leave distinguishing marks as tokens of that service on the bodies of their human servants, gather their servants into nocturnal assemblies called "sabbats" to pay homage to the devil and plan new assaults on the human community, have sexual relations with humans, and give humans the powers of flight and morphological change. Such human servants of Satan became the witches of the theologians and inquisitors, the visible agents of demonic power. Once the diabolical sorcerer and the witch had come to be understood in this new context, the logic of the witch-hunt and execution of the convicted sorcerer or witch became manifest and compelling. There could no longer be simple superstition or simple magic per-

---

11. Peter Brown, *The World of Late Antiquity* (London, 1971), 55. See also Henry Ansgar Kelly, *The Devil at Baptism: Ritual, Theology, and Drama* (Ithaca and London, 1985).

formed by self-proclaimed cunning-folk, wizards, wisewomen, or magicians, even if such rites were aimed to relieve human suffering and anguish—there could only be the diabolical sorcerer or witch.[12]

Fear of the devil and fear of the witch, thus linked by scholastic ontology, increased in importance together from the thirteenth century on. The changing European perception of the power and triumphs of the devil clearly became a major factor in the movement toward more intensive witch fears. In one sense, at least, the formulation of beliefs in active witchcraft and the ensuing persecution of accused witches may be said to have coincided with a new emphasis on the suffering of Christ and a "strengthening" of the devil that emerged in literature and art between the thirteenth and the sixteenth centuries. Historians of art, popular culture, and devotional forms in this period have long noted that the image of the divinity in the early Middle Ages was that of the ever powerful and ever triumphant majestic judge—the Father of the Old Testament. Before 1100 the devil was the greatest source of evil, but his power never threatened the power of God in an absolute way: the disproportion between them was clear and unquestionable. After 1100, however, the humanity and suffering of the Christ-God began to receive more emphasis as part of the emotionalizing of the relationship between God and humans. With a new emphasis on the suffering of Christ came also a sense of the fearsomeness of the powers of the devil. No longer was Satan the unsuccessful tempter in the desert who ignorantly tried to entice Christ into becoming his servant in return for mere earthly rewards. No longer was Satan the lord who extended a legitimate claim for the service of death over all men—in this sense, his "vassals"—until he mistakenly extended that claim to Christ himself, thinking Him to be only human, and with this irreparable mistake lost forever his absolute power over the afterlife and inadvertently opened to humans the gates of heaven. Satan became once again, as he had been for St. Augustine, the Great Devourer, the archenemy against whose numerous and awesome powers man was utterly helpless without a suffering God's alert and loving aid through the ministry of the church.[13]

---

12. See the excellent study by Jean-Claude Schmitt, *The Holy Greyhound: Guinefort, Healer of Children Since the Thirteenth Century*, trans. Martin Thom (Cambridge, 1982), and Willem de Blécourt, "Witch Doctors, Soothsayers and Priests: On Cunning Folk in European Historiography and Tradition," *Social History* 19 (1994): 285–303.

13. For the beginning of the process, see R. W. Southern, *The Making of the Middle Ages* (New Haven, 1961); and for the later period Richard Kieckhefer, "Main Currents in Late Medieval Devotion," in *Christian Spirituality: High Middle Ages and Reformation*, ed. Jill Raitt (New York, 1987), 75–108. See also R. N. Swanson, *Religion and Devotion in Europe, c. 1215–c. 1515* (Cambridge, 1995); Henk van Os, with Hans Nieuwdorp, Bernhard Ridderbos, Eugène Honée, *The Art of Devotion in the Late Middle Ages in Europe, 1300–1500* (Princeton, 1994); Ruth Mellinkoff, *The Devil at Isenheim: Reflections of Popular Belief in Grünewald's Altarpiece* (Berkeley and Los Angeles, 1988).

The Servants of Satan

This shift in the human conception of God and Satan is a critical force in the growth of the phenomenon of witch beliefs, because witch beliefs and persecutions of witches were all based on the doctrine of the malevolence, strength, cunning, and ubiquity of an absolutely hostile, ruthless, and relentless devil whose capacity for harming mankind had increased greatly. Moreover, all doctrinal authorities agreed that in some mysterious way this was taking place with the permission of God himself, probably because of failures in the practice of Christian life and the growth of what many reformers called "superstitious practices and beliefs." The early fifteenth-century theologian and reformer Jean Gerson explained God's permission to the demons in four ways: to achieve the damnation of the obstinate, to punish sinners, to test the faithful, and to manifest God's own glory.

In the face of a clumsily brutal, occasionally stupid, and often bungling Satan, the erring but controlled servant of God, churchmen and the faithful could maintain a mutual confidence in their ability to ward off the most serious attacks of the powers of darkness by traditional and unexceptional means: repentance for sin, increased individual moral righteousness and faithful observance of the sacraments in normal times, and exorcisms, particular specialized liturgies (such as protected against storms, crop failures, and plague), and the invocation of saints' aid in abnormal times. The veneration of relics, the wearing of blessed objects, and particular forms of devotion to the earthly "expertise" of individual patron saints all constituted an effective and durable bridge between high theology and lived Christian beliefs. With the emergence of a more powerful and increasingly effective Satan, however, both ordinary and extraordinary devotional forms and practices often seemed pitiably ineffective. Moreover, the growth of religious reform movements—both inside the church of the fourteenth and fifteenth centuries and also in the dramatic reform movements of the sixteenth—further weakened much devotional piety by declaring it mere superstition. In the light of these changes, a stronger and more determined response to Satan's threats was necessary.

With the new intensification of the power and fear of Satan, the figures of the diabolical sorcerer and the witch, now Satan's visible earthly servants, became increasingly vile and fearsome. Scholastic philosophers, systematic theologians, and demonologists reached a gradual consensus on the nature and activities of diabolical sorcerers and witches, and passed their conclusions on to inquisitors of heretical depravity and conscientious lay lawmakers and magistrates. The diabolical sorcerer and the witch, according to this consensus, had succumbed of his or her own will to Satan's temptation and had entered into a contract or pact with the Devil, one which usually was said to be sealed by an act of carnal intercourse with Satan or one of the demons and by Satan's placing of a mark on the body of his new servant. These acts themselves entailed the

terrible offenses of apostasy from the Christian religion—and hence the breaking of an inviolable contract with fellow Christians and with God—and idolatry,
the worship of a false god. Several historians have argued that from the late
thirteenth century on the conventional list of seven deadly sins as a guide for
confession and repentance had been gradually displaced by the Ten Commandments, in which idolatry is the first and greatest sin.[14]

As a new agent of Satan, the witch was given the power to exceed all human
capabilities in working harm upon—or illicitly influencing—the persons, families and servants, and property of the faithful by occult ("hidden") and preter-
natural means. Witches were portrayed as congregating in covens (a ritual inversion of appropriate Christian assemblies), feasting on obscene foods, and flying
through the night air on brooms, distaffs, or beasts to the blasphemous sabbats
at which they met their master.[15] To be sure, this was only the ideal typology of
the witches' activities constructed by learned men whose primary attention
had been concentrated on Satan and his assault on humankind in general, not
upon the intermittent complaints of villagers and townspeople who were apprehensive about the supposed malevolence of individual neighbors, and many
theologians expressed considerable doubts about many of the aspects of the
type, particularly night flight. The various activities of witches throughout
most of Europe thus came to be made homogeneous in the eyes of theologians,
preachers, and inquisitors of heretical depravity, and, whatever the specific accusations against later witches, this ecclesiastical typology soon made its appearance in nearly every case. Once the ideal schema of witch activities had
taken shape—by 1450 at the latest—the learned inquisitors and secular judges,
particularly on the Continent, continued to conceive the fundamental crime of
the witch as devil worship, the necessary act that empowered the witch to
commit *maleficia*, evil acts against other humans.[16]

The evil and suffering believed to be inflicted upon humans by witches' *male-*

---

14. See John Bossy, "Moral Arithmetic: Seven Sins into Ten Commandments," *Conscience and
Casuistry in Early Modern Europe*, ed. Edmund Leites (Cambridge and Paris, 1988), 214–34.

15. On the sabbat, see the too wide-ranging study by Ginzburg, *Ecstasies: Deciphering the
Witches' Sabbath*, and the more precise study by Bailey, "The Medieval Concept of the Witches'
Sabbath." The most exhaustive work is the collection of essays edited by Nicole Jacques-
Chacquin and Maxime Préaud, *Le sabbat des sorciers en Europe (XVe–XVIIIe siècles)* (Gren-
oble, 1993).

16. On the regional character of both concepts and persecutions, see Bengt Ankarloo and Gustav
Henningsen, eds., *Early Modern European Witchcraft: Centres and Peripheries* (Oxford, 1990).
On the synthetic type of the witch—and the dangers of applying it indiscriminately—see Robin
Briggs, *Witches and Neighbors: The Social and Cultural Context of European Witchcraft* (New
York and London, 1996), Chap. 1, "Myths of the Perfect Witch," 17–59, and James Sharpe,
Instruments of Darkness: Witchcraft in Early Modern England (Philadelphia, 1997). See also the
works of Wolfgang Behringer cited throughout this book.

ficia soon became a catalogue of all those calamities people most deeply dreaded, and the witch was seen increasingly as a necessary efficient agent of those events. Intensive anxiety regarding the witches and the nature of the threat they constituted grew and spread through many regions, orders, and conditions of men and women. Both the most and the least coherent writers on the subject assigned to the witch an increasingly broad spectrum of crimes that covered the deepest traumatic fears of mankind: the power to cause sudden illness or death; sexual impotence, frigidity, or barrenness; crippling or painful and uncurable illness; unpredictable and malevolent climatic or meteorological changes, crop failures, and losses or barrenness of livestock; involuntary physical actions, rapid personality changes, and loss of friends; finally, a "demonic possession," in which the individual personality lost its ability to order itself and felt itself given over to all it had once believed to be evil and degrading (Text 56). If mental health may be said to consist of people's confident reliance on the knowledge and experience of the real world which they are certain they possess, the utilization of mental and moral energy to eliminate the causes of trauma and dread, and the attempt to control those forces that most effect our lives, then the witchcraft persecutions, whatever our estimation of their conceptual and noetic components, represented, not an insane "aberration," but a desperate attempt to apply a system of putative knowledge toward restoring order in the world.

Sorcerer to Witch
The terms "diabolical sorcery" and "witchcraft" used in this book designate the behavior of someone, man or woman, who has acquired extraordinary powers to harm others through a pact, or agreement, with the Devil. Those humans who acquired knowledge or power without committing apostasy and idolatry, however, were technically not guilty of either offense (Text 22). From the late fourteenth century on, however, the line between the two kinds of magic became harder and harder to draw.[17] As European vernacular languages came more and more into general use, they usually distinguished between magic and witchcraft: *magie* and *sorcellerie* in French, *Zauberei* and *Hexerei* (after 1419) in German, *hechicería* and *brujería* in Spanish. In English there are *magic* and *witchcraft*—the former from Latin via the Romance languages, and the latter from the Old English word *wiccecræft*, which once meant only divination—foretelling the future. These linguistic distinctions do not, however, always indicate two distinct things. When defined as diabolical, both *magician* and *witch* often mean the same thing.

Although the early Christian writers condemned the magic of the pagan world wholesale, and later writers followed them (Text 7), not all thinkers

---

17. Richard Kieckhefer, "The Holy and the Unholy: Sainthood, Witchcraft, and Magic in Late Medieval Europe," *Journal of Medieval and Renaissance Studies* 24 (1994): 355–85.

agreed, especially after the twelfth century, when a growing familiarity with Arabic magical literature, the rise of the universities and the challenging explosion of new subjects of learning, and the Christian discovery of cabbalistic literature in the fifteenth century seemed to describe a neutral magic having nothing to do with diabolism. The subject of learned magic is important, but it must be remembered that magic existed along a dangerous spectrum, in which some magic might indeed sincerely claim to be free of any taint of diabolism, but other kinds shaded off more and more toward diabolism. It is these latter kinds, often described as *necromancy* (Text 36), that link the diabolical sorcerer and the witch after the fourteenth century.[18]

The Reaction

From the late thirteenth to the late fifteenth century, ecclesiastical pronouncements and judicial decisions reflect both old defenses and, increasingly, an awareness of new dangers. In 1258 Pope Alexander IV issued the first papal letter empowering the inquisitors of heretical depravity to deal with witchcraft, but only when they determined that it "savored of heresy" (Text 19). Pope Alexander's letter was later reissued by other popes and became an official text of canon law. As late as 1310 churchmen proposed the withdrawal of the sacraments from those convicted of sorcery and, for those who nevertheless remained unrepentant, excommunication.[19] The formal structure of scholastic

---

18. Learned magic is not the subject of this book, except in those instances when it is grouped with diabolical sorcery and witchcraft. The bibliography on the subject is vast. The best recent studies are those of Clark, *Thinking with Demons*, and William Eamon, *Science and the Secrets of Nature* (Princeton, 1994). Classic works remain Frances Yates, *Giordano Bruno and the Hermetic Tradition* (Chicago, 1964), and her *The Occult Philosophy in the Elizabethan Age* (London and Boston, 1979), as well as D. P. Walker, *Spiritual and Demonic Magic from Ficino to Campanella* (rprt. Notre Dame, 1975). On the learned magician Agrippa of Nettesheim, see Charles G. Nauert, *Agrippa and the Crisis of Renaissance Thought* (Urbana, 1965). There are good collections of studies in Brian P. Copenhaver, ed., *Occult and Scientific Mentalities in the Renaissance* (Cambridge, 1984), and Ingrid Merkel and Alan G. Debus, eds., *Hermeticism and the Renaissance: Intellectual History and the Occult in Early Modern Europe* (London and Toronto, 1988). On the connections with witchcraft theories, see Brian Easlea, *Witch Hunting, Magic, and the New Philosophy: An Introduction to the Debates of the Scientific Revolution* (Atlantic Highlands, N.J., 1980), and Wayne Shumaker, *The Occult Sciences in the Renaissance* (Berkeley and Los Angeles, 1972). For the earlier period, Kieckhefer, *Magic in the Middle Ages*, and idem, *Forbidden Rites: A Necromancer's Manual of the Fifteenth Century* (University Park, 1997), and Claire Fanger, ed., *Conjuring Spirits: Texts and Traditions of Medieval Ritual Magic* (University Park, 1998). For the early modern period there is a useful collection of texts in translation: P. G. Maxwell-Stuart, *The Occult in Early Modern Europe: A Documentary History* (New York, 1999).

19. On the punishment of exclusion, see Elizabeth Vodola, *Excommunication in the Middle Ages* (Berkeley and Los Angeles, 1986).

ontology, however, offered the inquisitors little choice but to inquire whether the witches were indeed guilty of heresy, and by 1376, the date of publication of Nicolau Eymeric's *Directorium inquisitorum* (Text 22), the connection between witchcraft and heresy was drawn sharply and inflexibly.

Once this association was established and the inquisitors were juridically armed against witches as well as heretics, the persecutions followed quickly.[20] As churchmen fulfilled their duty to protect the faithful from evil, those witches they discovered and convicted were remanded to civil authorities for execution, with a purely pro forma recommendation for mercy.[21] By 1398, supported by selective and derivative scholastic thought and papal and conciliar decisions were based on it, the intricate judicial theology of writers like Eymeric, and the evidence of trials, confessions, and recantations of witchcraft, the faculty of theology of the University of Paris professed to silence nearly all doubters with its proof, contained in a twenty-eight-article statement, that witchcraft and diabolical sorcery, in all their manifestations, could only be heretical (Text 23).

The juridical and doctrinal developments of the fourteenth century generated a new interest in formal demonology which manifested itself in a number of new treatises on diabolical sorcery and witchcraft, some of which were discussed and others written at the Council of Basel around 1437 during the pontificate of Eugenius IV, himself convinced of the pressing danger (Text 26). One of the most influential of these treatises was the *Formicarius* (The Ant-Colony) by Johannes Nider, provost of the Dominican convent at Basel, which brought to bear on any skeptics who might remain the full weight, not only of scriptural, patristic, and scholastic authorities, but of accounts of recent trials and convictions for witchcraft in nearby places, by known judges (Text 27). In the mid-fifteenth century yet more specialized treatises appeared, all of them stressing urgently and cogently the case for vigorous prosecution and punishment (Texts 28–31).

In 1487 there appeared the single most detailed treatise of all, the *Malleus Maleficarum* (The Hammer of Witches, or, more precisely, of Women Who Commit Maleficia), written by two Dominican inquisitors from the upper Rhineland, Heinrich Kramer (Institoris) and Jacob Sprenger (Texts 33–34). The

---

20. See Richard Kieckhefer, "The Office of the Inquisition and Medieval Heresy: The Transition from Personal to Institutional Jurisdiction," *Journal of Ecclesiastical History* 46 (1995): 36–61.

21. On the techniques, see James B. Given, *Inquisition and Medieval Society: Power, Discipline, and Resistance in Languedoc* (Ithaca and London, 1997); Scott L. Waugh and Peter Diehl, eds., *Christendom and Its Discontents: Exclusion, Persecution and Rebellion, 1000–1500* (Cambridge, 1996); and Alberto Ferreiro, ed., *The Devil, Heresy and Witchcraft in the Middle Ages: Essays in Honor of Jeffrey Burton Russell* (Leiden, Boston, Cologne, 1998). On the changes in legal practice, see Manlio Bellomo, *The Common Legal Past of Europe, 1000–1800* (Washington, D.C., 1995), and Edward Peters, *Torture* (Oxford and New York, 1985; expanded edition Philadelphia, 1996).

Malleus not only closed the question in favor of the prosecution, but virtually silenced all opposition as well with its rigor and irrefutable weight of cited authority, offering a ringing affirmative answer to the very first problem which it took up: "Whether the belief that there are such beings as witches is so essential a part of the Catholic faith that obstinately to maintain the opposite opinion manifestly savors of heresy."

Making disbelief, skepticism, or doubt concerning the very reality of witchcraft heretical in itself not only enlarged the scope of possible heretical behavior, but understandably fettered discussion of the nature of witchcraft. Although the *Malleus* was not binding on other churchmen, it was influential, and it became a common reference in most subsequent demonological literature and a common source for judges at witchcraft trials. Some of its influence, as well as other ideas concerning the danger of contemporary witchcraft, even before the confessional reformations of the sixteenth century, may be seen in works of otherwise quite diverse early sixteenth-century humanists and preachers (Texts 36–39).

The religious reformations of the sixteenth century, with their strong emphasis on the scriptural Satan and their insistence on a strict, literal reading of such injunctions as that of Exodus 22: 18, which they translated as "Thou shalt not suffer a *witch* to live," although neither the original Hebrew nor the Greek Septuagint compelled the use of the term, only strengthened the already present fear of diabolism and witchcraft in the lands that reformed their churches and translated scripture into the vernacular languages.[22] From the mid-fifteenth to the mid-seventeenth centuries, the witch beliefs of theologians, philosophers, lawyers, and secular magistrates found a progressively larger and more receptive audience.

The "craze" deeply touched the daily life of every European. Rural villages, remote mountain farms, and the greatest and most economically complex cities—with, to be sure, many exceptions and varieties—equally expressed ever greater evidence of shared helplessness and terror. The ensuing malevolence among neighbors and families sustained suspicion, accusation, and persecution, sometimes over a period of two or three generations in a single place. No

---

22. There are excellent discussions of the problem of reformed confessions in Clark, *Thinking with Demons*, 526–45, and Euan Cameron, "For Reasoned Faith or Embattled Creed? Religion for the People in Early Modern Europe," *Transactions of the Royal Historical Society* 6th ser. 8 (1998): 165–87. Substantial material is also in Julio Caro Baroja, "Witchcraft and Catholic Theology," and Stuart Clark, "Protestant Demonology: Sin, Superstition and Society (c. 1520–c. 1630)," both in *Early Modern European Witchcraft*, 19–43, 45–81. There is an excellent description and perceptive analysis of the confessional spectrum in William Monter, *Ritual, Myth, and Magic in Early Modern Europe* (Athens, Ohio, 1983), and a specialized study by Johathan L. Pearl, "French Catholic Demonologists in the Late Sixteenth and Early Seventeenth Centuries," *Church History* 52 (1983): 457–67.

estate, no order, no class, no group, however conceived, was completely exempt from the pervasiveness of belief in witchcraft and the even more dangerous belief that anyone could be a witch and that witches could strike anywhere. The theological and judicial portrait of the witch responded to and inspired in its turn an ever-widening public consensus, until scholar and peasant, jurist and artisan, priest and layman, king and merchant, all believed, and believing, feared and called for even more intensive persecution. Indeed, the prosecution of those at the highest ranks of local societies is striking testimony to the range to which the beliefs could drive a particular prosecution (Texts 47, 53).

In brief, the new intellectual zeal of the fifteenth-century demonologists was more than matched by the increasing anxiety of the general public, and both were reinforced by the increasingly widespread activities of—and discoveries of witches by—the ecclesiastical and secular courts. Churchmen had originally taken the lead in seeking out and prosecuting witches, once witchcraft and heresy had been firmly linked. At the outset of the prosecutions, churchmen often had to threaten to excommunicate or otherwise discipline those secular authorities who proved reluctant to carry out the sentence of death on convicted witches. Soon, however, the ecclesiastical courts found that civil authorities had grown more cooperative and had even begun to bring witches to trial independently of ecclesiastical procedure. While skepticism was suppressed or dissipated by the general fear inspired by widely circulating horrific tales, by confessions of witchcraft (usually obtained by the more widespread use of torture, itself a legal instrument of the romano-canonical inquisitorial judicial procedure that spread across continental Europe in the late fifteenth and sixteenth centuries), and by the spectacular convictions of unsuspected and sometimes highly placed citizens and subjects, the number of trials increased at a rapid rate.

The first trials in any number were a group of political trials involving relatives and servants of the royal houses of France and England, and the papacy, shortly after 1300.[23] Other individual trials also occurred, but without triggering outbreaks of either fear or prosecutions. Such a trial was the isolated case of Alice Kyteler in Kilkenny, Ireland, in 1324–25.[24] A cluster of trials for diabolical sorcery took place in Paris in the 1390s.[25] In the fifteenth century they spread slowly across parts of Europe: Rome in 1424 (Text 24); western Switzerland,

23. William R. Jones, "Political Uses of Sorcery in Medieval Europe," *Historian* 34 (1972): 670–87; H. A. Kelly, "English Kings and the Fear of Sorcery," *Medieval Studies* 39 (1977): 206–38; Edward Peters, *The Magician, the Witch, and the Law* (Philadelphia, 1978); Jan Veenstra, *Magic and Divination*.

24. L. S. Davidson and John O. Ward, eds. and trans., *The Sorcery Trial of Alice Kyteler* (Binghamton, 1993; rprt. Asheville, N.C., 1998).

25. See Veenstra, *Magic and Divination*.

southeastern France, and northwestern Italy around the same time (Texts 27–31); then down the Rhine to Heidelberg (1446), Cologne (1456), Arras (1460), and Metz (1488). By the sixteenth century Europeans were convinced that the continent was increasingly plagued with witches, and later in the century "burning courts"—courts operated by specialists in witch-finding—were established in many areas well into the first half of the seventeenth century. Between 1590 and 1650 England and Scotland experienced their most intensive, if intermittent, witch prosecutions. It was not uncommon for scores and occasionally hundreds of witches, contemporaries claimed, to be executed in a single city or district during a period of terror lasting several years. The cases of Trier between 1581 and 1593 (Text 47) and Bamberg in 1628 are striking examples (Text 53).

Numbers

It is impossible to calculate exactly the total number of convicted witches, women and men, who were executed between the fifteenth and the eighteenth centuries by burning at the stake or hanging. Historians have been astonishingly casual with their estimates in the past (some of the least competent estimating as high as nine million victims), but the most recent scholarship rarely allows more than a total of 50,000 victims over the entire period, a number that must, of course, be compared wherever possible with local rates of conviction and execution for other capital crimes. However great the actual count of victims was, witnesses all convey the impression that the witches existed in incalculable numbers and that convictions and executions consumed them in great numbers.

Gender

Both diabolical sorcerer and witch could be male or female. Since diabolical sorcerers were thought to use learning—or the diabolical illusion of learning—to achieve their wicked ends, sorcerers tended to be male. Learned magicians who claimed to use "natural" magic rather than diabolical sorcery were also predominantly male, since formal learning was usually a male prerogative.

Witches might be male or female, and the average difference throughout Europe generally was a preponderance of women accused, convicted, and executed at a ratio of about four to one. The one exception, France, shows more males than females executed. These figures certainly raise the problem of gender distribution in the offense of witchcraft. The "gender-debate" among historians of witchcraft has taken many twists and turns and is not, even today, settled.[26]

26. A critical review article from a feminist perspective is that of Elspeth Whitney, "The Witch 'She'/The Historian 'He': Gender and the Historiography of the European Witch-Hunts," *Journal of Women's History* 7 (1995): 77–101. From another perspective, Diane Purkiss, *The Witch in*

Although there had been a long tradition of generic misogyny in both antiquity and early Christian Europe, there is little evidence that traditional misogyny necessarily *had* to erupt into the particular witch concepts and witch persecutions of late medieval and early modern Europe without other elements being involved, not even in the furiously misogynistic *Malleus Maleficarum*. Heide Dienst has shrewdly asked whether or not the *Malleus*, particularly in its instrumental use of traditional misogyny, can be considered representative for all of Europe in its period.[27] As Christina Larner pointed out, "Witchcraft was not sex-specific but it was sex-related."[28]

How? One approach is not to assume a uniform set of ideas equally applicable across continental Europe and the British Isles, but to look at particular sets of trials and what they may reveal. Susanna Burghartz, in a comparative study of trials before secular courts at Lucerne and before ecclesiastical courts at Lausanne, has found that,

> In Lausanne . . . ecclesiastical inquisitors, whose views doubtless conformed to the misogynistic traditions of the Church, and whose image of the witch conformed to the classic pattern [of the prosecution of the alleged heretical behavior of both men and women—see Texts 11 and 18] from the very beginning, directed their persecuting zeal mainly towards men. In Lucerne, by contrast, demonologically illiterate secular judges concentrated their attentions on the persecution of women. Thus, the traditional hostility of the medieval Church towards women, though it has been repeatedly adduced in the general context of witchcraft persecutions, can only be accredited with a part in the creation of the classic, stereotypical image of the witch as a female being: it is certainly not enough to explain the realities of the persecutions themselves.[29]

The witches studied by Burghartz in Lucerne were generally mature women, often poor, who came from elsewhere or had long been suspected by their neighbors, and who also exhibited disliked traits, such as insolence, quarrelsomeness,

---

History: Early Modern and Twentieth-Century Representations (London and New York, 1996).

27. Heide Dienst, "Zur Rolle von Frauen im magischen Vorstellungen und Praktiken—nach ausgewählten mittelalterlichen Quellen," in, *Frauen in Spätantike und Frühmittelalter: Lebensbedingungen—Lebensnormen—Lebensformen*, ed. Werner Affeldt (Sigmaringen, 1990), 173–94, at 176.

28. Christina Larner, *Enemies of God: The Witch Hunt in Scotland* (London, 1981), 91.

29. Susanna Burghartz, "The Equation of Women and Witches: A Case Study of Witchcraft Trials in Lucerne and Lausanne in the Fifteenth and Sixteenth Centuries," in *The German Underworld: Deviants and Outcasts in German History*, ed. Richard J. Evans (London and New York, 1988), 57–74, at 64–65. Burghartz's study also critically rehearses most of the traditional arguments concerning gender distribution in witchcraft cases, and she raises the equally important question of accusations against women in other crimes than witchcraft.

or aggressive behavior, who spoke publicly about sexual matters—their own or others'—and who had a bad reputation. Unmarried or widowed older women whose neighbors had suspected them, often for a long time, of causing harm to people or property by particular means—weather-magic, for example, or love-magic—seem to have been the most frequently accused, tried, and convicted. Witchcraft was also thought to run in families, especially from mother to daughter, and to be more likely in some occupations—lower domestic servants, for example—than in others.[30] Similar investigations must be made across larger sets of tribunals like those examined by Burghartz before any final conclusion for all of Europe and the Americas can be reached.[31]

Skepticism to Unbelief
Voices opposed to persecutions, however, were never entirely silenced. Earlier ecclesiastical insistence, like that of John of Salisbury in the twelfth century (Text 10) or Jean de Meung in the late thirteenth, that night rides and carnal pacts with the devil were illusory found individual echoes in, for example, the treatise *Le songe du vergier* in the fourteenth century and the sixteenth-century bishop of Cuenca, Fray Lope de Barrientos, who bluntly remarked that:

> Nor should anyone believe such an absurd thing as that these supposed events really take place other than in dreams or in the imagination. Anyone who believes such things is an infidel and worse than a pagan, to judge the way they conceive this.[32]

In the mid-sixteenth century the physician Johann Weyer (Text 44) caused a major scandal by publicly denying, not, to be sure, that diabolical sorcerers

30. Among the most reliable discussions are those of Merry E. Wiesener, *Women and Gender in Early Modern Europe* (Cambridge, 1981); Lyndal Roper, *Oedipus and the Devil: Witchcraft, Sexuality, and Religion in Early Modern Europe* (London, 1994); Briggs, *Witches and Neighbors*, 257–86; Sharpe, *Instruments of Darkness*, 169–99; Clark, *Thinking with Demons*, 106–33. Strong feminist positions are represented in Deborah Willis, *Malevolent Nature: Witch-Hunting and Maternal Power in Early Modern England* (Ithaca and London, 1995); Marianne Hester, "Patriarchal Reconstruction and Witch Hunting," in *Witchcraft in Early Modern Europe*, 288–306; Gerhild Scholz Williams, *Defining Dominion: The Discourses of Magic and Witchcraft in Early Modern Europe* (Ann Arbor, 1995); Sigrid Brauner, *Fearless Wives and Frightened Shrews: The Construction of the Witch in Early Modern Germany* (Amherst, 1995).
31. Except for the Salem Village trials in 1692 the Americas are not represented in this book. See Sabine MacCormack, *Religion in the Andes: Vision and Imagination in Early Colonial Peru* (Princeton, 1991); Fernando Cervantes, *The Devil in the New World: The Impact of Diabolism in New Spain* (London, 1994); and Cervantes, "The Devil's Encounter with America," in *Witchcraft in Early Modern Europe*, 119–44; Irene Silverblatt, *Moon, Sun, and Witches: Gender Ideologies and Class in Inca and Colonial Peru* (Princeton, 1987).
32. P. S. Lewis, *Later Medieval France: The Polity* (New York, 1968), 16–27; Julio Caro Baroja, *The World of the Witches*, trans. O.N.V. Glendinning (Chicago, 1965), 276–79; cf. 99–111.

existed, but that the particular activities of which witches were commonly accused were anything but illusions. Weyer found few followers—and he triggered a considerable outburst of opposition—but his work is generally regarded as the beginning of extensive theological and legal speculation critical of the existence of witches. In the later sixteenth century, Michel de Montaigne (Text 61) maintained a philosophical skepticism concerning the certainty of human beliefs which culminated in his dramatic observation that, "after all, it is putting a very high price on one's conjectures to have a man roasted alive because of them."

It was, in fact, as unproven (and unprovable) "conjectures" that witchcraft beliefs were challenged by many of these early opponents of the witch persecutions. The intentions of the inquisitors (many of whom were skeptical themselves—Text 63) and civil courts, the excessive use of torture, the unremitting concentration of most of the trials upon the poor and the defenseless, and the sophisticated psychological techniques of interrogation vitiated for the skeptics much of the theoretical structure of witch beliefs and reduced them to the status of mere conjectures, still subject to other tests of veracity than those to which they had been customarily submitted. By the end of the sixteenth century the Englishman Reginald Scot's *Discoverie of Witchcraft* (Text 60) took up the thread of criticism where Weyer's work had left it and constituted a major attack on both the literal existence of witches as men depicted them and the means employed to find them.

Whenever critics of the beliefs and persecutions appeared, however, learned clerics, philosophers, and jurists rushed vigorously to their refutation, and a vast body of literature about witchcraft, pro and con, appeared in the seventeenth century and continued into the eighteenth—as did the beliefs themselves, not only among the learned but among the unlearned as well.[33] King James VI & I wrote his treatise *Daemonologie*:

> against the damnable opinions of two principally in our age, whereof the one called SCOT an Englishman, is not ashamed in publike print to deny, that ther can be such a thing as Witch-craft: and so maintieines the old error of the Sadducees, in denying of spirits. The other called WIERUS, a German Phisition, set out a publick apologie for al these craftes-folkes.[34]

Yet from the beginning of the seventeenth century, when the witch beliefs and persecutions appeared to be reaching new heights, their foundations had already

33. The best accounts are those of Ian Bostridge, *Witchcraft and Its Transformations, c. 1650–c. 1750* (Oxford, 1997); and Sharpe, *Instruments of Darkness*; and Texts 44, 60–69 below. See also the essays in *Witchcraft and Magic in Europe*, vol. 5, *The Eighteenth and Nineteenth Centuries*.

34. *King James the First* Daemonologie *(1597) Newes from Scotland . . . (1591)*, Bodley Head Quartos, vol. 4, ed. G. B. Harrison (rprt. London and New York, 1924), xi–xii.

begun to crumble. The erosion of what had been a major intellectual and social force in the life of Europe for three centuries occurred so rapidly that few at the time were aware of the momentous changes in conceptions and attitudes that underlay the decline. Such philosophical spiritualists as Henry More and Joseph Glanvill (Text 59) correctly identified them in part as the consequence of a decline of belief in spiritual agency and scripturalist explanations of earthly phenomena and in the authenticity and value of spectral evidence in trials for capital crimes.

In a society undergoing accelerated and fundamental change, almost all the major new intellectual currents pointed away from an active fear of and belief in witches and the widespread activities of Satan. Anti-scholasticism (and its attendant anti-Aristotelianism); skepticism of and snobbery toward what learned and respectable people considered to be purely popular traditions; increasing theological optimism concerning the providence of God; mechanistic explanations of material causality; empiricism, naturalism, and a critical rationalism all began to pervade the realm not only of philosophy and theology, but of the jury and the bench as well.[35] Further, they were expressed not only in academic and confessional debates among the learned, but in a broad and widely read literature that included satire and ridicule, in pictures as well as texts.

To be sure, defenders of witchcraft beliefs were neither wholly silent nor wholly absent from the ranks of people who supported these new strains of thought, but the cumulative impact of the new ideas of natural philosophy and theology was to undermine the conceptions, traditions, and authorities upon which witchcraft beliefs and persecutions had stood. The new patterns of social organization which emerged in the late sixteenth and seventeenth centuries altered or eliminated many of the social relationships, social antagonisms, and social pressures which had contributed to the emergence of many of the witch beliefs. The civil community, no longer the churches or individuals, became responsible for the care of the sick, poor, or insane, and the civil community, abstract and impersonal, was far better able to absorb the fear, hostility, and, perhaps, guilt generated by numbers of displaced or useless individuals.

The late seventeenth century, then, witnessed both the most intensive expression and the virtual death of witchcraft belief and persecution—at least among the more respectable orders of society. Accusations and occasional persecutions certainly lived on—and, indeed, erupted briefly in Salem Village (now Danvers), Massachusetts Bay Colony in North America in 1692 (Texts 58, 67). Although the last witches were legally burned in Europe as late as the 1780s, there was ultimately no body of educated people able or willing to lead or even

---

35. On the rejection of popular opinion, see the classic essay by Natalie Zemon Davis, "Proverbial Wisdom and Popular Errors," in Davis, *Society and Culture in Early Modern France* (Stanford, 1975), 227–67. See also the headnotes to Texts 60–69 in this volume.

to defend such practices. By the dawn of the eighteenth century the question was no longer whether Christian belief demanded a belief in witchcraft, but whether the system that had generated and compelled such beliefs could continue to hold any authority over the minds and hearts of thinking people.[36]

In the course of a debate that was begun by the publication in 1749 of Girolamo Tartarotti's controversial demonological treatise *Del Congresso Notturno delle Lammie* (On the Nocturnal Meeting of Witches), which had asserted, as had Weyer two centuries before, that diabolical sorcery existed but that witchcraft did not, a critic asked, "Does not the denial of the existence of demons open the way and lead directly to the denial of the existence of God?"[37] The Jesuit priest Georg Gaar went further. Unsettled by the kind of arguments now being deployed against witchcraft beliefs, Gaar complained in 1751, "We seem to have a new heaven, new elements, a new system of the world, while those old opinions which before our times were scarce the subject of doubt are laughed at and exploded with an unjust sentence of error." Against that complaint, thinkers of the eighteenth century led European civilization into another age, one in which, as Voltaire remarked, the witches and exorcists both, if they remained quiet, would be left in peace.

Sources and Studies

There are three general kinds of sources, and three only, that inform us about the nature of the beliefs and persecutions for the offenses of diabolical sorcery and witchcraft from the fourteenth century to the mid-eighteenth.

The first and most reliable of these, when we have it, is *archival*—the actual court records and reports of accusations, arrests, investigations, depositions, confessions, court procedures and costs, verdicts, and punishments that were made and kept by regional judicial authorities that tried witches and everybody else for all other crimes (Texts 32, 46–48, 52, 56–57). These are preserved in regional and national archives all across Europe and in a few places in North and

---

36. There has been a growing scholarly interest in the survival of witchcraft beliefs, if not of prosecutions, from the eighteenth century to the twenty-first. The most recent survey is Owen Davies, *Witchcraft, Magic and Culture, 1736–1951* (Manchester and New York, 1999). See also Willem de Blécourt, "On the Continuation of Witchcraft," in *Witchcraft in Early Modern Europe*, 335–51; *Witchcraft and Magic in Europe*, vol. 6, *The Twentieth Century*. A classic modern study is Jeanne Favret-Saada, *Deadly Words: Witchcraft in the Bocage* (Cambridge, 1990). On continuity of beliefs in the United States, see Richard Godbeer, *The Devil's Dominion: Magic and Religion in Early New England* (Cambridge, 1992), 223–32, and Herbert Leventhal, *In the Shadow of the Enlightenment: Occultism and Renaissance Science in Eighteenth-Century America* (New York, 1976).

37. The controversy is discussed in Lea, *Materials*, 3: 1441–59.

South America. Because they are part of an official record that includes all other court activities, they can be extracted and studied only with great care and caution. Not all procedures and rules of evidence were identical in all of these territories, and to understand a court archive it is essential to know how these courts did their other business besides witchcraft. Archives are also difficult to extract from the jurisdictional contexts in which they are preserved, because the records of witchcraft trials are part of a court's entire work and need to be interpreted in the context of all of its work. Particular moments of prosecution and particular offenses must be linked to local social and political stress faults and to the full spectrum of local practice of criminal law.

Archival material also sometimes appears in the extensive pamphlet literature, especially of the sixteenth and seventeenth centuries, although here, too, it must be used with caution, because pamphlet writers were often perfectly willing to distort official records in the interests of a more dramatic story or a particular point of view.[38] Sometimes archival material was also extracted and quoted or paraphrased by writers of longer treatises on witchcraft and other forms of demonology. Here, too, the same caution must apply.

The second and more wide-ranging kind of source may be called the *literary* sources. Diaries, narrative records of various organizations, public and private newsletters, the annual reports submitted by different religious orders or agents to their superiors, larger histories that mention witchcraft incidentally, books of prodigies and wonders, literary works in prose or verse (including drama), sermons, and works of demonology proper. Some works of demonology focus exclusively on witchcraft, others on witchcraft as (an often small) part of a larger and more ambitious moral or theological subject. Often, the archival material extracted in pamphlets or longer treatises and other literary sources suggests a direct relationship between a particular literary work and a particular group of trials in a single place or in the writer's own experience as a judge or inquisitor (Text 49). The literature of witchcraft has also been integrated into the larger dimension of early modern European thought and culture, characterized in this respect as "a complex of interrelated magical ideas which informs many aspects of medieval and Renaissance thought."[39]

These first two kinds of sources may best be used together, at least when we know enough about a particular group of trials and a particular literary work to make a plausible connection between them. As in the case of archival material,

---

38. Marion Gibson, *Reading Witchcraft: Stories of Early English Witches* (London and New York, 1999) is an excellent introduction to the problems of the pamphlet literature.

39. Sydney Anglo, "Evident Authority and Authoritative Evidence: The *Malleus Maleficarum*," in Anglo, *The Damned Art*, 1–21, at 3. Anglo's collection was a pioneering effort in bringing the literary sources of witchcraft theory to the attention of historians.

it is useful to know who these writers were, what their experience and interests were, and what else they wrote. Also together they have helped to inform other disciplines: women's studies and gender history, legal history—particularly that of crime and punishment—theology, the study of both normative and lived religion, art history, folklore, historical anthropology, sociology, and literature.

The third kind of source is *pictorial*—visual representations of the activities and sometimes the trials of sorcerers and witches. Although many of these were produced by well-known and immensely gifted artists and hence fall under the demanding and rigorous discipline of art history, many of them are crude and often copied, in a process of standardization of related images that is particularly prominent from the late sixteenth century on.[40]

Just as legislation against witchcraft was being repealed and trials stopped in the eighteenth century, and when skepticism about witchcraft had turned into ridicule—at least among the politer classes—a few scholars undertook to describe the history of the phenomenon of the persecutions. The most impressive of these was the work of the Lutheran pastor Eberhard David Hauber (1695–1765), whose *Bibliotheca Acta et Scripta Magica* appeared at Lemgo between 1738 and 1745. But the modern study of European witchcraft really began in 1843, when Wilhelm Gottlieb Soldan (1803–1869) published in Stuttgart his *Geschichte der Hexenprozesse*, and Johann Georg Theodor Grässe (1814–1872) published in Leipzig his monumental, annotated bibliography, *Bibliotheca Magica et Pneumatica*. Soldan's study was revised by his son-in-law Heinrich Heppe in 1879, and the combined work of Soldan-Heppe was re-edited and published by Max Bauer in 1911. Just as the Soldan-Heppe history constituted the first major history of witchcraft in Europe, that of Grässe was the first modern attempt to assemble a bibliography of witchcraft materials, basing his work on the earlier bibliography of Hauber. Grässe's work is still of considerable value; no one since has systematically added to it.

With few exceptions, other nineteenth-century studies of witchcraft betray either a distinct rationalist and anachronistic disapproval of the ecclesiastical and secular mentality that had encouraged witchcraft beliefs to flourish, or a Romantic fascination with social oppression and the imagined revolutionary character of those accused of witchcraft. In some instances witchcraft was included in local and regional nineteenth-century studies of German and French history. Both rationalist historians and their critics helped to revive American interest in the Salem Village witch trials around the middle of the nineteenth century. Two rationalist historians, however, W. G. H. Lecky, and the American Henry Charles Lea, seriously undertook to consider historical witchcraft broadly as an integral part of early European culture.

40. The pictorial material in this book will be considered in the next section of this Introduction.

In 1889 George Lincoln Burr, an American historian at Cornell, published a path-breaking survey of the literary sources for the history of witchcraft in his essay, "The Literature of Witchcraft," and, often in academic debate with George Lyman Kitteridge of Harvard, restored the subject to the standards of professional historiography. Lea spent the last years of his long life (1825–1909) compiling materials for a proposed history of witchcraft on the massive scale of his earlier histories of the medieval and Spanish inquisitions, but he died before he could complete his work, which was later edited and published in 1939 as *Materials Toward a History of Witchcraft*, edited by Arthur C. Howland with an introduction by George L. Burr, in three volumes [Philadelphia, 1939; reprt. New York, 1957]. Lea's volumes contain a mine of information, quotations, translations, and Lea's reading notes on hundreds of often rare original sources and are still indispensable to the historian.

Around the turn of the twentieth century several works of scholarship included extracts from or summaries and discussions of individual works in the literature. The most important of these are two works by the great archivist of Cologne Joseph Hansen (1862–1943): *Zauberwahn, Inquisition und Hexenprozess im Mittelalter* (Munich, 1900), and *Quellen und Untersuchungen zur Geschichte des Hexenwahns und der Hexenverfolgung im Mittelalter* (Bonn, 1901). In 1910 the great Catholic historian Nicholas Paulus published his confessionally partisan but extremely learned study *Hexenwahn und Hexenprozess, vornehmlich im 16. Jahrhundert* at Freiburg-im-Breisgau. And in 1911 the young American historian Wallace Notestein published his *A History of Witchcraft in England from 1558 to 1718* (Washington, D.C., 1911; rprt. New York, 1965). The highly original and wide-ranging study by the Dutch historian Johan Huizinga, *The Autumn of the Middle Ages*, first published in 1919, also drew sorcery and witchcraft into the cultural history of France and the Burgundian Low Countries in the fourteenth and fifteenth centuries.[41] Stuart Clark's *Thinking with Demons* (Oxford, 1997) is the most recent and comprehensive study of the entire range of literary discussions of witchcraft in the sixteenth century.

Interested readers should also, of course, refer to the relevant sections of the massive work of Lynn Thorndike, *A History of Magic and Experimental Science*, 8 vols. (New York, 1923–58), which contains many texts and important discussions of the topic of magic and witchcraft in the context of the history of science. Rossell Hope Robbins, *The Encyclopedia of Witchcraft and Demonology* (New York, 1959) is extensive and often very useful for particular individuals and topics. The opinions of Hansen, Lea, Burr, Robbins (especially useful for identifications, if not Robbins's judgments), and Thorndike on particular

---

41. On Huizinga, see Edward Peters and Walter P. Simons, "The New Huizinga and the Old Middle Ages," *Speculum* 74 (1999): 587–620.

matters today need to be read with caution in the light of more recent scholarship.[42] Most of the authors and subjects dealt with in the present book will also usually be found in the index to Clark, whose bibliography and index are exhaustive.

In the case of England and North America several of the older surveys also remain valuable: Wallace Notestein's work remains valuable and intelligent. Others include George L. Kitteridge, *Witchcraft in Old and New England* (Cambridge, Mass., 1929); C. L'Estrange Ewen, *Witch Hunting and Witch Trials: The Indictments for Witchcraft from the Records of 1373 Assizes Held for the Home Circuit, A.D. 1559–1736* (London, 1929), and C. L'Estrange Ewen, *Witchcraft and Demonianism: A Concise Account Derived from Sworn Depositions and Confessions Obtained in the Courts of England and Wales* (London, 1933).[43]

The archival and literary basis of the study of European witchcraft was substantially modified by later historians' adoption of the new methods of cultural anthropology in the 1960s. In 1937 E. E. Evans Pritchard published his seminal work, *Witchcraft, Oracles and Magic Among the Azande* (Oxford, 1937), which set the question on a new footing. Evans Pritchard's legacy is best approached through the work of Mary Douglas, particularly the essays in her *Witchcraft Confessions and Accusations* (London, 1970). Several historical studies that appeared around the turn of the 1970s used much of the new anthropological method: Alan Macfarlane, *Witchcraft in Tudor and Stuart England* (London, 1970), and Keith Thomas, *Religion and the Decline of Magic* (New York, 1971).[44] A few years earlier the great Spanish scholar Julio Caro Baroja had published his *The World of the Witches*, translated by O. N. V. Glendinning (Chicago, 1965), also a model of the use of anthropological methods for the social hisory of pre-modern Europe. In France Robert Mandrou, in *Magistrats et sorcières en France au 17e siècle* (Paris, 1968) examined the changing mentality of French judges in cases of witchcraft. Several collections of sources in translation and volumes of collected essays helped to circulate these new views: E. William Monter, *European Witchcraft* (New York, 1969); Barbara Rosen,

---

42. The most recent survey of the entire scholarly tradition, far broader than the title suggests, is Wolfgang Behringer, "Witchcraft Studies in Austria, Germany and Switzerland," in *Witchcraft in Early Modern Europe*, 64–95, and Behringer, *Witchcraft Persecutions in Bavaria: Popular Magic, Religious Zealotry and Reason of State in Early Modern Europe*, trans. J. C. Grayson and David Lederer (Cambridge, 1997), 1–17. There is a broad and informative review article dealing with a number of recent studies by Alison Rowlands, "Telling Witchcraft Stories: New Perspectives on Witchcraft and Witches in the Early Modern Period," *Gender and History* 19 (1998): 294–302.

43. There is a set of summaries and additions/corrections to Ewen in Alan Macfarlane, *Witchcraft in Tudor and Stuart England* (London, 1970), 254–309.

44. There is a good essay on Thomas: Jonathan Barry, "Keith Thomas and the Problem of Witchcraft," in *Witchcraft in Early Modern Europe*, 1–45.

Witchcraft (London, 1970), and the bibliographical essay by H. C. Erik Midelfort, "Recent Witch-Hunting Research, or Where Do We Go from Here?" in *Papers of the Bibliographical Society of America* 62 (1968).[45] This was essentially the state of the field when the first edition of this book was published in 1972.

At the turn of the millennium, the field has again been transformed as dramatically as it had been at the turn of the twentieth century and again around the turn of 1970.[46] Although much of the recent scholarship has been written originally in English and some of it translated into English, there is considerable activity and a growing literature, especially in German, French, Dutch, Italian, and Spanish, although sources and studies not in English are usually not listed here.

Several general surveys of the subject, either focusing on the medieval period or covering the entire history, appeared in the 1970s. Jeffrey Burton Russell, *Witchcraft in the Middle Ages* (Ithaca and London, 1972), exhaustively established the relationship between earlier and changing ideas of heresy and the emergence of the crime of witchcraft. In 1975 Norman Cohn, *Europe's Inner Demons: An Enquiry Inspired by the Great Witch-Hunt* (New York) performed two considerable services to scholarship: first, Cohn identified several formerly key texts as forgeries, thereby changing the chronology of both the concept and the persecutions; second, he linked witchcraft and diabolical sorcery in a way that supplemented the approach of Russell. Richard Kieckhefer's remarkably precise study, *European Witch Trials: Their Foundations in Learned and Popular Culture, 1300–1500* (London, 1976), not only independently proved one long-used text a nineteenth-century forgery and established a firm chronology for the early trials, but also offered a useful model for distinguishing the ideas of those who brought the initial accusations from the judges and magistrates who evaluated the offense. Edward Peters, *The Magician, the Witch, and the Law* (Philadelphia, 1978), looked closely at the problem of the relationship among sorcerers and witches from late antiquity to the early sixteenth century in terms of their classification in different legal and social systems, a subject part of which is more specifically treated in Richard Kieckhefer, *Magic in the Middle Ages* (Cambridge, 1990). There is also the useful collection of documents dealing with both magic and witchcraft translated into English by P. G. Maxwell-Stuart, *The Occult in Early Modern Europe* (New York, 1999). A comparable volume of translated texts from Greek and Roman antiquity is that of Georg

---

45. Other bibliographical accounts were those of Donald Nugent, "Witchcraft Studies 1959–1971: A Bibliographical Survey," *Journal of Popular Culture* 5 (1971): 711–12; Midelfort followed his 1968 bibliographical essay with another: "Witchcraft and the Occult," in Steven Ozment, ed., *Reformation Europe: A Guide to Research* (St. Louis, 1982), 183–209.

46. There is an excellent introduction to recent scholarship in the superb study by Behringer, *Witchcraft Persecutions in Bavaria*, esp. 1–33.

Luck, *Arcana Mundi: Magic and the Occult in the Greek and Roman Worlds* (Baltimore, 1985).[47]

With the appearance of Brian Levack, *The Witch-Hunt in Early Modern Europe* (London and New York, 1987; 2nd ed. 1995), the subject found its best general survey in English, one which contains an extensive bibliographical guide.[48] Robin Briggs, *Witches and Neighbors* (New York, 1996), is the best general survey written directly from the archival sources. In French, there is also the ambitious general survey by different scholars edited by Robert Muchembled, *Magie et sorcellerie en Europe du Moyen Age à nos jours* (Paris, 1994). Brian Levack has also edited a twelve-volume collection of useful scholarly essays, *Articles on Witchcraft, Magic, and Demonology: A Twelve-Volume Anthology of Scholarly Articles* (New York, 1992).

There are also a number of research centers and publication series devoted to the subject. One of the most impressive is the series *Cahiers lausannois d'histoire médiévale* at the University of Lausanne, Switzerland. In Germany there is the AKIH (Arbeitskreis Interdiszipläre Hexenforschung), founded at Stuttgart in 1985 and productive of conference volumes and individual studies since then. For the Low Countries see M. Gijswijt-Hofstra, "Recent Witchcraft Research in the Low Countries," in *Historical Research in the Low Countries*, edited by N.C.F. van Sas and E. Witte (The Hague, 1992). In France there is the group Histoire critique de la sorcellerie, directed by Nicole Jacques-Chaquin and Maxime Préaud, part of the research center, Formation Histoire des Idées et des Lettres of the École Normale Supérieur de Fontenay/Saint-Cloud, which has produced the volume *Les sorciers du carroi de Marlou: Un procès de sorcellerie en Berry (1582–1583)*, edited by N. Jacques-Chaquin and Maxime Préaud (Grenoble, 1996). The Pennsylvania State University Press in conjunction with the *Societas Magica* is issuing a series of older and new studies of the subject under the series title *Magic in History*, under the editorship of Richard Kieckhefer. The University of Pennsylvania Press is issuing the series *Witchcraft and Magic in Europe*, edited by Bengt Ankarloo and Stuart Clark, in six volumes, of which volumes 3 and 4 especially deal with the period of this book.[49] Primary Source Media, in its series Rare Books On Line, has opened the site *Witchcraft in Europe and America*, ed. Mark Dimunation and Edward Peters: ⟨http://www.psmedia.com/witchcraft.htm⟩. For the Salem Village trials, see the website ⟨http://etext.Virginia.edu/salem/witchcraft⟩.

47. In addition to the translations by Luck, there is a useful survey by Fritz Graf, *Magic in the Ancient World* (Cambridge, Mass., 1997) and detailed studies on the period in *Witchcraft and Magic in Europe*, vol. 1, *Ancient Greece and Rome*.

48. Joseph Klaits, *Servants of Satan: The Age of the Witch Hunts* (Bloomington, 1985) is also a very good survey of the scholarship process itself.

49. Most recently, see vol. 3, *The Middle Ages*, and vol. 4, *The Sixteenth and Seventeenth Centuries* (Philadelphia, 2001).

Among the most important and accessible archival and regional studies (most of which also treat the relevant literary sources in conjunction with archival material) are those of H.C. Erik Midelfort, *Witch Hunting in Southwestern Germany, 1562–1684* (Stanford, 1972); E. William Monter, *Witchcraft in France and Switzerland: The Borderlands During the Reformation* (Ithaca and London, 1976); Hans Sebald, *Witchcraft: The Heritage of a Heresy* (New York and Oxford, 1978), dealing with Franconian Switzerland, a triangular land in Germany bounded by Nuremberg, Bamberg, and Bayreuth;[50] Gustav Henningsen, *The Witches' Advocate: Basque Witchcraft and the Spanish Inquisition (1609–1614)* (Reno, 1980); Christina Larner, *Enemies of God: The Witch-Hunt in Scotland* (Baltimore and London, 1981); Gabor Klaniczay, *The Uses of Supernatural Power: The Transformation of Popular Religion in Medieval and Early Modern Europe* (Princeton, 1990), especially useful for central and eastern Europe; W. F. Ryan, *The Bathhouse at Midnight: An Historical Survey of Magic and Divination in Russia* (University Park, 1999); Wolfgang Behringer, *Witchcraft Persecutions in Bavaria: Popular Magic, Religious Zealotry and Reason of State in Early Modern Europe*, trans. J. C. Grayson and David Lederer (Cambridge, 1997). The best study of the subject in England is that of James Sharpe, *Instruments of Darkness: Witchcraft in Early Modern England* (Philadelphia, 1997). Current research often first appears in individual scholarly articles or in collections of scholarly articles, two of the best of which are *Witchcraft in Early Modern England*, edited by Jonathan Barry, Marianne Hester, and Gareth Roberts (Cambridge, 1996), and *The Devil, Heresy and Witchcraft in the Middle Ages: Essays in Honor of Jeffrey Burton Russell*, edited by Alberto Ferreiro (Leiden, Boston, and Cologne, 1998).

For the transition from late antiquity to eleventh-century Europe, see Valerie I. J. Flint, *The Rise of Magic in Early Medieval Europe* (Princeton, 1991), a controversial but consistently stimulating study, and Ramsay MacMullen, *Christianity and Paganism in the Fourth to Eighth Centuries* (New Haven and London, 1997).

A pioneering collection of essays that inaugurated the modern study of the literary sources for the history of witchcraft was that edited by Sydney Anglo, *The Damned Art: Essays in the Literature of Witchcraft* (London and Boston, 1977). Subsequent literature on particular texts is indicated in the headnotes to those texts in this volume. The most important recent works are those of Stuart Clark, *Thinking with Demons: The Idea of Witchcraft in Early Modern Europe* (Oxford, 1997), and Jan R. Veenstra, *Magic and Divination at the Courts of Burgundy and France: Text and Context of Laurens Pignon's "Contre les devineurs" (1411)* (Leiden-New York-Cologne, 1998). Two of the most important literary sources have been translated, those of Johann Weyer (Text 44) and Jean

---

50. Sebald has also written a study of the role of children in witchcraft prosecutions: *Witch-Children from Salem Witch-Hunts to Modern Courtrooms* (Amherst, 1995).

Bodin (Text 45). P. G. Maxwell-Stuart is presently translating the work of Martín Del Rio (Text 50).[51]

"Everything that happens visibly in this world can be done by demons": The Pictorial Sources

At the mention of "witchcraft" at the turn of the twenty-first century, our most common reaction is to conjure up a visual image, usually of a woman, old and ugly or young and beautiful, dressed in a characteristically defining costume, or nude—that is, we think first of visual images and only later of documents and court records. And when we think of the latter two things we generally do so while at the same time visualizing the figures involved. We do this in part because of the large number of pictorial sources produced between the late fifteenth and the eighteenth centuries, from the illuminators of fifteenth-century manuscripts to William Hogarth and Francisco Goya. As Charles Zika has pointed out, "late medieval religiosity was fundamentally a religion of seeing."[52] Zika's observation certainly also applies in many respects to the sixteenth and early seventeenth centuries. We also visualize the subject because of the heavy investment during the second half of the twentieth century in the visual representation of sorcerers and witches in movies and on television—from the master of the sorcerer's apprentice Mickey Mouse in Walt Disney's *Fantasia* (or the sequence of the sabbat in the "Night on Bald Mountain" episode that begins the conclusion of the film), the wicked queen in *Snow White*, or the wonderful Margaret Hamilton in *The Wizard of Oz*. More recently Cher and others in *The Witches of Eastwick*, Bette Midler in *Hocus Pocus*, Sandra Bullock and Nicole Kidman in *Practical Magic*, or *The Blair Witch Project*. The fact

51. There is already a Spanish translation of Del Rio: Martín Del Río, *La Magia demoníaca*, trans. Jesús Moya, Intro. Julio Caro Baroja (Madrid, 1991).

52. Charles Zika, "The Devil's Hoodwink: Seeing and Believing in the World of Sixteenth-Century Witchcraft," in *No Gods Except Me: Orthodoxy and Religious Practice in Europe, 1200–1600* (Melbourne, 1991), 153–96, at 154. One of the most important themes in Johan Huizinga's brilliant 1919 study *Autumn of the Middle Ages*, trans. Rodney Payton and Ulrich Mammitzsch (Chicago, 1996), is that of "religious thought crystallizing into images," and Huizinga cites as an example the extraordinary verbal imagery of the Dominican theologian Alain de la Roche, one of the teachers of Jacob Sprenger—one of the authors of the *Malleus Maleficarum*—"The sexual element also has a place in the satanic fantasies. Alain de la Roche sees the monsters of sin with disgusting genitals from which a fiery and sulphur-like cloud is emitted that darkens the earth with smoke. He sees the [prostitute of apostasy] who devours the apostates, vomits them up and devours them again, kisses and cuddles them like a mother, and from her womb gives birth to them over and over again. This is the dark side of the 'sweetness' of the devotees. As an inevitable complement to the sweet heavenly fantasy, the mind harbored a black cesspool of hellish notions that were expressed in the fiery language of earthly sensuality" (232–33).

that in recent films, with few exceptions, the witches are young and attractive rather than old and ugly, also has roots in an old pictorial tradition. The fact that in that tradition most of the witch-figures depicted are women—far more than in historical trials—may also tell us something about our ideas concerning witchcraft and gender differences in history and the role of illustrations in shaping our—and their—ideas.

The first edition of this book contained seventy-two illustrations, all relevant to the texts and introductions, in two series. The first series (Figures 1–26) depicted relevant themes in the Christian view of history and the world, from the fall of Satan, through demonic temptation, incubi, exorcisms, the moment of death, judgment, and the torments of the damned. The second series (Figures 27–72) depicted thematically a broad range of activities attributed to witches, from the invocation of the devil to satirical pictorial critiques of witch beliefs. At the time, few students could have been expected to know the pictorial traditions of either series, since the discipline of art history had until then paid little attention to the subjects of sorcery and witchcraft.

This second edition has only two-thirds the number of pictures of the first for several reasons. First, there is much more pictorial material and discussion readily available concerning the themes of our first series, and we have eliminated this series. Second, the work of art historians over the past several decades has made it possible to illustrate the subject of our second series with fewer, but more extensively discussed illustrations, each of them tied closely to a particular text, activity, or pictorial theme. Developments in art historical scholarship thus parallel the remarkable developments in archival and literary studies since the early 1970s. The forty-one illustrations in this edition represent almost the same number as the second series in the first edition. Of those original forty-six pictures, however, fifteen were from a single work, Francesco Maria Guazzo's *Compendium Maleficarum*, the 1610 Milan edition. By reducing the number of Guazzo illustrations (they are artistically undistinguished and the activities are represented elsewhere in the present illustrations, although Guazzo is meticulous and therefore important in depicting men and children as well as women as witches) and narrowing our choice of representational subjects, we have been able to print more important and influential illustrations. We have also arranged the pictures (with a few exceptions) to follow a chronological time line, rather than the thematic sequence of the first edition. This rearrangement allows the reader to see the historical development of pictorial themes and the expansion of media in which those themes were represented.

The pictures here are not decorations, as they so often are, even in otherwise good books.[53] They constitute a source that is parallel to the archival and liter-

---

53. This is true even of such excellent collections of scholarly texts as Muchembled, *Magie et sorcellerie*, and the richly illustrated work of Hans-Jürgen Wolf, *Geschichte der Hexenprozesse*.

ary materials, are usually closely linked to them, and often derive from textual sources, although the very media in which illustrators worked gave them sufficient freedom of design and execution to allow for considerable originality. The ability of illustrators both to preserve and to change pictorial traditions over time makes the pictorial history a valid third type of source, along with archival and literary textual sources.

As an example, consider the earliest and latest depictions of witches preparing to leave for the sabbat, an extremely popular subject (depicted much earlier than pictorial representations of the sabbat, with which it is often confused), of which there are hundreds of variations between the late fifteenth and late seventeenth centuries. The earliest versions show the witches—usually both old and young, and always women—outdoors, often in wild landscapes, surrounded by their *materia magica* and human and animal bones and skulls, some already in the air riding sticks or beasts, others using flaming jars of loathsome ointments to prepare themselves for flight (Fig. 15). Later depictions in the seventeenth century, however, without any textual justification that we know of, move the scene indoors, usually to a kitchen with a chimney, and thereby transform the comfortable, familiar genre of the domestic interior, very popular in seventeenth-century northern European art, into a subversive setting for the most feared and most fascinating of female activities, especially fascinating because the action takes place in a familiar setting while it consists of chillingly unfamiliar role-changes (Fig. 33). This pictorial change in setting for the same activity may also suggest its usefulness in indicating an increased fear of the subversion of the household by certain forms of female socializing. The transfer of scene suggests a dark side to the well-known genre of *opera muliebria*, "women's work," and women's space—that of masterless women who socialize in unholy activities in the normally benevolent, pious, and secure household.[54]

Many of the pictorial components that came to be particular to witchcraft had long been represented in Christian art. The figure of Satan as rebel angel and

---

Holocaust und Massenpsychose vom 16.–18. Jahrhundert (Erlensee, 1995). There are some astute remarks in Clark, *Thinking with Demons*, 11–30. The only book-length study of the subject is that of Jane P. Davidson, *The Witch in Northern European Art, 1470–1750* (Freren, 1987). Individual studies will be cited in the notes below. Exhibition catalogs, when carefully done, are also useful for the pictorial history. Excellent examples are Maxime Préaud, ed., *Les sorcières* (Paris, 1973); *Hexen und Hexenverfolgung im deutschen Südwesten*, ed. Sönke Lorenz, 2 vols. (Karlsruhe, 1994), and *Bibliotheca Lamiarum: Documenti e immagini della stregoneria dal Medioevo all' Età Moderna* (Pisa, 1994). On the related topic of inquisitorial imagery, see Francisco Bethencourt, "The *Auto da fé*: Ritual and Imagery," *Journal of the Warburg and Courtauld Institute* 55 (1992): 155–68.

54. On the pictorial representation of masterless women, see Charles Zika, "Fears of Flying: Representations of Witchcraft and Sexuality in Early Sixteenth-Century Germany," *Australian Journal of Art* 8 (1989/90): 19–47.

tempter of humans, the vices and virtues, exorcism, the Last Judgment and the torments of the damned all appeared in manuscript illuminations, frescoes, and sculpture before they circulated even more widely with the appearance of woodcuts and engravings during the print revolution of the late fifteenth and sixteenth centuries. Both flying women and the later witches' dismemberment of children at the sabbat, for example, had pictorial antecedents in depictions of legendary figures like the fairy Melusine and the biblical account of the slaughter of the innocents.[55] Thus, the original principles that governed and inspired the depiction of witchcraft beliefs were not generically different from those which governed the depiction of other spiritual phenomena. The concrete representation of demons, diabolical sorcerers, and witches did not differ from the attempts to portray artistically and dramatically the spiritual population of the Christian universe, terrestrial and celestial, demonic, divine, and human. Medieval and early modern artists alike sought to bring to the eyes of their audiences the hand of God, the rebellion of Satan, the struggle of the rebel angels, and the temptation and perdition of fallen humans. The pictorial illustration of such phenomena in no way lessened their spiritual reality for the viewer, although it also gave these images a greater familiarity. In Romans 1: 20 St. Paul has said that "Ever since the creation of the world [God's] eternal power and divine nature, invisible though they are, have been understood and seen through things he has made." Gregory the Great had called such representations "the scriptures of the unlettered." A twelfth-century theologian had remarked that "the sluggish mind reaches spiritual truths through material objects." Indeed, the vivid imagery enhanced the drama and awesomeness of such forces and events for those unable to read or comprehend the difficult language of the schools. No text illustrates this capacity of religious art in the later Middle Ages more vividly than does the prayer which the poet François Villon put into the mouth of his illiterate mother:

> I am an old woman, and poor,
> I know nothing—I know not one letter.
> In my parish church, there I can see
> Paradise painted, with harps and lutes,

55. On Melusine, see Jacques Le Goff, *Time, Work, and Culture in the Middle Ages*, trans. Arthur Goldhammer (Chicago, 1980), 205–24. Even the varieties of the human figure possessed a rich and varied pictorial vocabulary. See Ruth Mellinkoff, *Outcasts: Signs of Otherness in Northern European Art of the Late Middle Ages*, 2 vols. (Berkeley and Los Angeles, 1993). A most stimulating study of the relation of some of these elements to ordinary experience in even a strictly defined and scripturally based context is that of Mitchell B. Merback, *The Thief, the Cross and the Wheel: Pain and the Spectacle of Punishment in Medieval and Renaissance Europe* (Chicago, 1998). On the role of child victim, see Richard Kieckhefer, "Avenging the Blood of Children: Anxiety over Child Victims and the Origins of the European Witch Trials," in Ferreiro, *Devil, Heresy, and Witchcraft*, 91–110.

> And the damned boiling in Hell.
> One makes me fear, one gives me joy, delight.
> Make that joy mine, O Virgin Goddess,
> To you all sinners have recourse,
> All filled with faith and no hesitation:
> In that faith may I live, may I die.

"That faith," for most Christian Europeans, as for Villon's mother, was forged as much through the pictorial representation of doctrinal truths and the vivid verbal images of preachers as through the much more formalized written texts of high theology. When these two powerful media came to be joined, as they were in the printed sermons of Johann Geiler von Kaysersberg, the great Strassburg cathedral preacher, in 1516 (Figs. 20–21, Text 37), ideas and images both swept across Europe faster and faster.

The illustrations in this book begin with the association of magic with idolatry and diabolism represented in the textual sources of hagiography (Text 12) and in apocryphal piety respectively in the figures of the clerk Theophilus, who acquired magical powers by signing a contract with the demon (Fig. 1), and with the magician Hermogenes, whose early depiction by a follower of Hieronymous Bosch (Fig. 2) in the late fifteenth century originally echoed that of Theophilus, but whose depiction by Pieter Bruegel the Elder around 1565 (Figs. 3–4) constituted a virtual encyclopedia of all the forms of diabolical magic known to sixteenth-century Europe. Sexual congress between demons and human women is represented in an illustration of the begetting of the Antichrist (Fig. 5) upon his mother by a demon, an image which parallels, for example, the legendary begetting of the magician Merlin and of Alexander the Great by a similar process, a scene also illustrated in manuscripts of the Alexander romances.[56]

The medium of preaching is represented by the painting by Sano di Pietro of Bernardino of Siena delivering his sermons in 1427 (Fig. 6, Text 24). Many of the most important texts in this volume, including those by San Bernardino, Geiler von Kaysersberg, Martin Luther (Text 40), and John Calvin (Text 41), as well as the collection of exemplary stories for preachers by Johannes Nider (Text 27) all illustrate the power of the spoken word in connecting the ideas and imagery of learned theologians with the understanding of a public well beyond the reach of the schools.

One of the earliest illustrations of humans adoring Satan in the form of a goat is found in a 1460 treatise by Johannes Tinctoris (Fig. 7), dealing with a case of heretical sorcery in Arras, and of women riding on broomsticks to the sabbat in

---

56. There are a number of useful scenes from late medieval manuscripts depicting these and other themes reprinted in Christa Habiger-Tuczay, *Magie und Magier im Mittelalter* (Munich, 1992).

a marginal manuscript illustration of the poem by Martin Le Franc, *The Defender of Ladies*, copied and illustrated around 1450 (Fig. 8, Text 30). A 1486 treatise on vices and virtues by Johannes Vintler contained the earliest illustration of a witch performing weather magic, one of the great concerns of the early formulation of witch beliefs (Fig. 9), and also one of the earliest depictions of the kinds of harm that witches were believed to cause. The realism of these and later pictures reflected the charges made against witches, and the realistic depiction of those charges, just as later in the century the representation of witches on the dramatic stage—in *Macbeth*, for example—brought the reality of the charges graphically home to the visual or theater audience (Text 51). In 1487 there appeared a pictorial and textual warning against all forms of magic in a German woodcut.[57] Perhaps surprisingly, the *Malleus Maleficarum* (Texts 33– 34), printed in the same year, contained no illustrations and was not illustrated in any later edition. But its own verbal imagery very quickly had an impact.

Before the end of the fifteenth century, such images were usually isolated, illustrating one aspect or another of early witchcraft beliefs, and some of the scenes would not necessarily be identifiable as scenes of witchcraft without the accompanying text. With the appearance of Ulrich Molitor's *On Witches* in 1488–89, the arguments of the *Malleus* were repeated in the literary format of a conversation among Molitor, Duke Sigismund of the Tyrol, and Sigismund's minister Conrad Schatz, with a suite of seven remarkable woodcuts that for the first time offered related pictorial images of witches' activities (Figs. 10–12), although the illustrations simply depict selected instances of witches' activities without any identifying physical or costume features attributed to witches— that is, some of the illustrations seem to depict ordinary women doing ordinary things. The work was often reprinted and was translated from Latin into German in 1545, with the same suit of woodcuts redone for contemporary tastes. At least one printer quickly modified the Molitor illustration of the witch's transformation and flight to the sabbat to illustrate a short *Treatise Against Evil Women Called Witches*, published at Ulm in 1490 (Fig. 13). Although not many witchcraft treatises contained entire series of illustrations, the work of Molitor and the 1608 treatise by Francesco Maria Guazzo (Fig. 30), the most extensively illustrated of all witchcraft treatises, suggest the transition from a limited number of illustrations to a complete set that depicted every conceivable activity of witches.

Around the turn of the sixteenth century a number of accomplished artists, including Albrecht Dürer (Fig. 14) and some of his students and copyists took up the theme with remarkable results. Dürer's *Witch Riding* drew upon both popular beliefs (weather magic and the inversion of the witch's reality) and images

---

57. The picture is reproduced and discussed in Kieckhefer, *Magic in the Middle Ages*, 177–79.

from classical art (Aphrodite Pandemos, the goddess of lust, mounted on the goat, the zodiacal sign of Capricorn).[58]

Dürer also suggested the theme of the eroticism of witches' activities. Although the *Malleus Maleficarum* and much earlier misogynistic literature had gone into extraordinary detail on the subject of women's proneness to lust and therefore to demonic temptation, and Molitor had included a rather reserved depiction of the witch and her demon lover, from Dürer on, the erotic dimension of witchcraft—and the figure of the nude witch—became an invariable and attractive pictorial subject. It is in the work of Dürer's pupil Hans Baldung Grien, however, that the full force of eroticism in relation to witchcraft makes it appearance in European art.[59] Between 1510 and 1514 Baldung executed several drawings in chiaroscuro (see Figs. 15–18), not, like Molitor, of various sorts of witches' activities, but with a narrow focus on the erotic activities and psychological inversions of the witches' reality.[60] Baldung's chiaroscuro drawing of 1510 (Fig. 15) became the basis for all later depictions of preparations for the sabbat, a new theme more prominent in pictorial than in textual sources. Baldung's other drawings resemble the tone and emphases of the 1510 drawing, although he produced the much more ambitious painting *Weather Witches* in 1523 (Fig. 16) and later, far different from his earlier interests in eroticism and inversion, and portraying this time an old and ugly witch and the victim she has harmed, the much more somber and mysterious *Bewitched Groom* in 1544 (Fig. 17).[61]

Instead of an expensive series of illustrations, early in the sixteenth century some printers began to use the composite picture—virtually all the activities of witches depicted simultaneously in a single illustration, as in Hans Schäuffe-

58. Charles Zika, "Dürer's Witch, Riding Women, and Moral Order," in *Dürer and His Culture*, ed. Dagmar Eichberger and Charles Zika (Cambridge, 1998), 118–40.

59. The large literature includes Dyan Elliott, *Fallen Bodies: Pollution, Sexuality, and Demonology in the Middle Ages* (Philadelphia, 1999), and Michael Goodich, ed., *Other Middle Ages: Witnesses at the Margins of Medieval Society* (Philadelphia, 1998). Margaret A. Sullivan, "The Witches of Dürer and Hans Baldung Grien," *Renaissance Quarterly* 53 (2000): 333–401, makes a powerful argument that their illustrations of witches derive more from classical art and literature than from sixteenth-century witchcraft theories. Although there was more concern in the period than Sullivan allows, her thesis is important and well-documented.

60. Comprehensive is the study by Linda C. Hults, "Baldung and the Witches of Freiburg," *Journal of Interdisciplinary History* 18 (1987): 249–76, with extensive further references, particularly to Dale Hoak, "Art, Culture, and Mentality in Renaissance Society: The Meaning of Hans Baldung Grien's *Bewitched Groom* (1544)," *Renaissance Quarterly* 38 (1985): 488–510. See also Clark, *Thinking with Demons*, 11–30; Jane P. Davidson, *The Witch in Northern European Art*; and Davidson, "Great Black Goats and Evil Little Women: The Image of the Witch in Sixteenth-Century German Art," *Journal of the Rocky Mountain Medieval and Renaissance Association* 6 (1985): 45–61.

61. On the bewitched groom, see the essays by Hoak and Hults.

lein's illustration in the 1511 edition of Ulrich Tengler's *The New Mirror for Layfolk*, a revision of an earlier work with substantial additions from the *Malleus Maleficarum* (Fig. 19).[62] Baldung, or more likely someone from his workshop, produced the illustrations for the printed edition of the sermons of Johann Geiler von Kaysersberg in 1516–17 (Figs. 20–21), including the depiction of the witch drawing milk from an axe-handle, a discussion of which is found in Geiler's sermons (Text 37).

Dürer was not the only artist to use images and themes from classical antiquity, the mythographic tradition, or scripture. In his 1526 painting illustrating the biblical subject of *Saul and the Witch of Endor* (Fig. 22), Jacob Cornelisz van Oostsanen explicitly connected the biblical story in 1 Samuel 28: 3–20 with early sixteenth-century alleged activities of witches, including the newly introduced erotic component.[63] Around 1530 Lucas Cranach the Elder portrayed a troop of witches riding to the sabbat in a detail in his allegorical painting *Melancholia* (Fig. 23), identifying witches and diabolical sorcerers as children of Saturn, since theologians had long argued that melancholic women were especially prone to demonic temptation.[64] Sixteenth-century printed editions of the *Metamorphoses*, or *The Golden Ass*, by Apuleius of Madaura—a novel about female sorcerers and their incompetent apprentices among many other things—also illustrated the book with sixteenth-century-looking depictions of witches' activities, implying that Apuleius and other earlier Greek and Roman writers, like the Bible, were discussing the same kind of sorcery that people knew in the sixteenth century. Even such a work as Cicero's *De officiis* in an edition published at Augsburg in 1531 depicted the activities of sixteenth-century witches.[65]

Something similar happens in sixteenth-century depictions and discussions of "witches" in Greek and Roman literature: those of Circe and Medea in Ovid's *Metamorphoses*, for example, or the vile sorceresses in the poems of Horace and Lucan's *Pharsalia*. One great sixteenth-century poet, Torquato Tasso, in his epic poem on the First Crusade, *Jerusalem Delivered*, written in 1575, created the

---

62. It is important to recognize the composite picture for what it is, both in illustrations like this one and in illustrations of torture chambers, which do not represent reality, but rather a composite of the kinds of torture that could be used at different times. See Peters, *Inquisition*, plates 10 and 11.

63. The best discussion is Charles Zika, "Les parties du corps, Saturne et le cannibalisme: Représentations visuelles des assemblées des sorcières au XVIe siècle," in Jacques-Chaquin and Préaud, *Le sabbat des sorciers*, 389–418. Zika's important study also emphasizes the conjunction of Saturn, the theme of melancholy, and cannibalism that occurred in late sixteenth- and early seventeenth-century depictions of the witches' sabbat, which had only been represented infrequently before the late sixteenth century.

64. The association with Saturnian melancholy was first noted by Norman Cohn, *Europe's Inner Demons*.

65. The picture is reproduced in Behringer, *Witchcraft Persecutions in Bavaria*, 93.

first great witch as a major literary figure.[66] In 1587, the first Faust-book was published in Germany, bringing the Faust-story into conjunction with the problem of diabolical sorcery in an echo of the older stories of Theophilus, Cyprian the Magician, and Gerbert (Text 12).[67]

The increasingly rich and diverse vocabulary of witchcraft images that had been developed by Molitor and then greatly expanded by Hans Baldung Grien was further expanded by the widely circulating *History of the Northern Peoples* by the Swedish cleric Olavus Magnus, published at Rome in 1555 and reprinted at Basel with the original illustrations redone by a Master C. G. in 1567 (Fig. 24).[68]

At the same time, newsletters and printed single broadsheets, new kinds of media in which images of witchcraft now circulated, began to depict the punishments of convicted witches, part of the policy of exemplary public executions that was prominent in most of the states of early modern Europe. The illustration of the execution of three witches at Derneburg in 1555 (Fig. 25) was one of the earliest of many of this type, which came to include illustrations of the witch subjected to the water ordeal known as "swimming the witch" (Fig. 26).[69]

Another location for images was the title page or the frontispiece of treatises on witchcraft, a significant number of which appeared around the turn of the seventeenth century (Text 50). One of the most widely circulating was the 1591 treatise of Peter Binsfeld, suffragan bishop in the archdiocese of Trier, whose work discussed the prosecutions at Trier in 1581–93 and was reprinted in Munich in 1592 (Fig. 27, also a composite picture).[70] Another was the *Disquisitiones magicarum* by Martín Del Rio of 1603, whose title page illustrated all the biblical texts allegedly condemning witchcraft (Fig. 28, Text 50). The famous illustration of the full sabbat in 1613 by Jan Ziarnko, a Polish printmaker working in Paris, for Pierre de Lancre's large treatise was later reproduced with few changes, but with wholly different intent, in 1710 in a successful work that

---

66. For illustrations of sorcery in editions of Tasso, see Davidson, *The Witch in Northern European Art*, 84–85.

67. Elizabeth M. Butler, *The Fortunes of Faust* (Cambridge, 1952; rprt. University Park, 1998).

68. On the work, see Davidson, "Great Black Goats," 52–56.

69. Further examples of this type may be found in Behringer, *Witchcraft Persecutions in Bavaria*, 231, 302, 329, 332, 335. On the subject of illustrating public punishments, see the works of Merback and Mellinkoff cited above, and Samuel Y. Edgerton, Jr., *Pictures and Punishment: Art and Criminal Prosecution During the Florentine Renaissance* (Ithaca, N.Y., and London, 1985); Pieter Spierenburg, *The Spectacle of Suffering: Executions and the Evolution of Repression from a Preindustrial Metropolis to the European Experience* (Cambridge and New York, 1984); Richard van Dülmen, *Theater of Horror: Crime and Punishment in Early Modern Germany*, trans. Elizabeth Neu (Cambridge, 1990).

70. Discussion in Behringer, *Witchcraft Persecutions in Bavaria*, 141.

parodied witchcraft beliefs, the comic novel by Laurent Bordelon, *The Extravagant Imaginations of Monsieur Oufle.*

By the early seventeenth century, the ensemble of pictorial scenes had largely become standardized and was exhaustively recapitulated in Francesco Maria Guazzo's richly but uninspiringly illustrated *Compendium Maleficarum* of 1610 (Fig. 30) and the approximately contemporary composite picture by Jasper Isaac (Fig. 31). On the least interesting level, illustrators simply copied already existing pictures, displaying little if any originality, but also leaving conventional images that still echo in the twenty-first century, as in an early nineteenth-century depiction of a witch that might have been the model for those in *The Wizard of Oz.*

On a more interesting level, however, seventeenth-century artists also seem to have been stimulated by the opportunities offered by the subject for artistic virtuosity, and they introduced new contexts for conventional scenes. In 1607 Frans Francken the Younger depicted a lush, detailed sabbat, richly colored and designed to show a considerable variety of activities (Fig. 32).[71] In 1624 (or so it is often dated, although it looks more like a late seventeenth-century style) Jan van de Velde depicted a sensuous young witch, an image and style taken up more and more frequently later in the century and into the eighteenth, as in Saint-Aubert's early eighteenth-century treatment of a similar scene (Fig. 34). The preparation for the sabbat was domesticated in David Teniers the Younger's painting (Fig. 33), later reproduced in an engraving by Jacques Aliamet.[72] With Michael Herr's late seventeenth-century sabbat (Fig. 36), the standardization of the scene has been completed, and the viewer can go from Herr to the "Night on Bald Mountain" sequence in Disney's *Fantasia.*

Just as skepticism, doubt, and eventual disbelief in witchcraft can be studied in literary texts, so can they be in pictures, which often add the visual dimension of ridicule and satire. The illustration for Bordelon's novel about Monsieur Oufle is simply a slightly reworked version of Ziarnko's illustration of de Lancre's furious book attacking witches, but the same image is now suggested as ridiculous in the satirical context of the novel. Satire and ridicule also show up in the frontispiece for the 1703 edition of Christian Thomasius's work against witches (Fig. 37, Text 69), whose inscription reads:

> My reader! Do you still deny the reality of the Magic
> Mountain? This page shows it to you clearly. You see
> the witches' choir stand out upon it plainly. Ah, how
> I fool myself, for it exists only on paper.

71. Discussion in Davidson, *The Witch in Northern European Art,* 39–45.
72. Discussion in Davidson, *The Witch in Northern European Art,* 48–57.

In 1762 William Hogarth published his *Credulity, Superstition, and Fanaticism: A Medley* (Fig. 38), a brutally satirical cartoon that was meticulously referenced to several dozen contemporary and recent outbursts of belief in witchcraft and superstition.[73] At the end of the century Francisco Goya's *Caprichos*, based on the trials at Logroño in 1610–14, satirized what he considered the surviving popular beliefs in witchcraft in Spain, "the destruction of false beliefs."

The subject even served to provide new pictorial elements in the area of political cartoons. As had Hogarth before them, both Thomas Rowlandson and James Gillray around the turn of the nineteenth century adapted some of the traditional pictorial elements to satirize elements of the British government as well as popular beliefs, as in Gillray's *Weird Sisters* of 1791 (Fig. 39)

With the turn of the nineteenth century, pictures dealing with witchcraft thus ceased to reflect beliefs and led the pictorial elements developed between 1450 and 1750 to serve the artistic styles and subjects of Romanticism and "Decadence," the latter abundantly evident in the work of the Belgian painter Felicien Rops. But the best example of the process that we know of is an early nineteenth-century painting by Anton Wierz (Fig. 40), whose subject—the initiation of the young witch by the old witch—had long been conventional, but whose execution has no interest in witchcraft ideas or beliefs, finding instead only eroticism and perhaps in the process inventing what would later be called the centerfold.

Some of the imagery has found a new life in the past century, and the reader will be familiar with much of it. Perhaps less known, however, is the final picture, an engraving by John Buckland-Wright to illustrate a poem in the volume *Yew-leaf and Lotus Petal* by John Evelyn Barlas (a pseudonym for Evelyn Douglas), in which an entirely de-Satanized young and beautiful witch (Fig. 41) becomes an image of feminine power and grace, new life and purpose given here to an older and more lethal image.

---

73. Discussion in Bostridge, *Witchcraft and Its Transformations*, 170–79.

I

Christianizing the Traditions,

400–900

THE GREEK, LATIN, AND HEBREW ideas and terms designating various kinds of what may generally be called magic, whether practiced by men or women, reach back into a distant past and were all transformed by the Christianization of the Roman world and the later experience of early Europe. The official Christianization of the Roman Empire late in the fourth century A.D., and indeed of virtually the whole world of Mediterranean Hellenistic culture by the sixth century, required Christians to come to terms with—and define themselves as different from—both Greco-Roman and Jewish religions as well as to take into Christian account the diverse Greco-Roman and Jewish ideas of magic and sorcery. Much of the energy and effort of Christian thinkers from Origen to St. Augustine and later to Isidore of Seville was expended on these problems, and the solutions reached by influential Christian thinkers between the late fourth and the seventh centuries were then applied to the next phase of the expansion of Christianity—into the world of late Iron Age northern Europe, with its very different cultural practices of both religion and magic.

The Greco-Roman and Jewish texts dealing with magic and sorcery in their various forms that were most frequently cited by later Christian thinkers are noted below. One of the most distinctive features of Latin Christianity was its successful appropriation of an already existing Latin vocabulary to define itself and to characterize those beliefs and practices that it characterized as "pagan"—Christians assumed for their faith the Latin term *religio*, which had designated the proper relationship between the Romans and the gods, and they designated both earlier and contemporary religious practices as *superstitio*, for Romans the abominable opposite of *religio* (and a much stronger word than the modern "superstition"). To both Roman religion and the various forms of magic that the Romans themselves had condemned, Christians applied the terms *ma-*

leficia and *magia*. This appropriation was deliberate—the second-century Roman author Suetonius had termed Christianity itself as a *malefica superstitio*. As later Christian writers asserted, *religio* is the true cult paid to God; *superstitio* is the false.

Early Christian writers defended their practices against accusations of the worst and most disgusting practices that their opponents imagined as taking place in their own religious world.[1] The early third-century work by Minucius Felix, the *Octavius*, is a convenient and accessible example of such anti-Christian polemic.[2] In chapters 6–11 of the *Octavius*, Caecilius, the pagan opponent of Christianity, accuses Christians of rejecting ancestral beliefs and of failing to imitate the piety of the Romans (chap. 6), of failing to understand the communication of gods with humans (chap. 7), of denying the existence of many gods and accepting only the dregs of society, the most shameful people, into their assemblies and organizing dreadful, nocturnal, secret meetings (chap. 8). They practice indiscriminate sexual activity, worship the head of an ass, worship the genital organs of their priests, and initiate novices by making them kill infants and cannibalize them (chap. 9). Their rites are held in secret, and they have no temples (chap. 10). Finally, they are a subversive sect that threatens the stability of the whole world (chap. 11).

This kind of polemic was later adapted by Christian writers themselves to describe the imagined activities of some dissenting Christians (below, Texts 11, 18, 24). Little of this diatribe against Christianity had anything in particular to do with classical accounts of sorcery (these expressed revulsion of equal intensity but of a different kind), but the combination of late antique condemnations of sorcery and of unnatural religious practices remained a powerful model for later formulations of religious dissent.

By the end of the fourth century, when the empire had become officially and exclusively Christian, Augustine the theologian had his work cut out for him.

1. There is an excellent, readable survey in Robert L. Wilken, *The Christians as the Romans Saw Them* (New Haven and London, 1984); cf. Ramsay MacMullen, *Christianity and Paganism in the Fourth to Eighth Centuries* (New Haven and London, 1997), 74–102, and Peter Brown, *The Rise of Western Christendom: Triumph and Diversity, A.D. 200–1000* (Malden and Oxford, 1996).
2. *The Octavius of Marcus Minucius Felix*, trans. G. W. Clarke (New York and Ramsey, 1974), 62–70; also, *Tertullian, Apologetical Works and Minucius Felix, Octavius*, trans. Rudolph Arbesmann, Emily Joseph Daly, Edwin A. Quain (New York, 1950), chaps. 9–11.

I
Augustine: *On Christian Teaching*, Book II (395–98, 426)

The most original and influential Latin Christian theologian was Augustine (354–430), bishop of Hippo Regius in North Africa. Augustine's skill as a rhetorician, his familiarity with both late antique philosophy and literature, as well as the early Latin versions of Jewish and Christian scripture, his intensive and literal reading of the epistles of St. Paul in the 390s, and his voluminous and authoritative writings gave him a position of preeminence among Latin Christian theologians. His influence can be traced through most of the texts in this volume.

One of Augustine's earliest discussions of a form of magic was his consideration of the Christian understanding of the struggle between Moses and Aaron and the "magicians" of Pharaoh in Exodus 7–8, in question 79 of a work called *On Eighty-Three Diverse Questions*, written around 396. There, Augustine lays out his arguments concerning demonology and the weakness of humans when their pride and sinful curiosity leads them to worship demons instead of God. Around the same time, in the *Diverse Questions to Simplicianus*, Book II, question 3, Augustine considered the problem of whether or not the "witch" of En-dor had actually raised the spirit of Samuel for Saul (1 Samuel 28), an argument repeated and slightly expanded, with Augustine's original opinion changed, in the *Eight Questions to Dulcitius* written in 422. Augustine's most important discussion of the subject occurs in his treatise *On Christian Teaching*, begun in 395–98 and completed in 426, several sections of which are printed below. He elaborated extensively on the nature and effects of demonic power in the treatise *On the Divination of Demons* of 406, as well as in *On the Trinity* of 419, especially in Book XV, and he reviewed many of the historical arguments for pagan religion and demonology in Books IV–V and VIII–X (especially X.9–11) of *The City of God*, written in 425, as well as extensive reflections on shape-shifting and demonic power in Book XVIII, Chapters 17–18 (texts that later were included in canon law). Generally Augustine laid out four arguments that continued to influence European thought throughout the period treated in this book: the gods of the pagans were demons in disguise (Ps. 95 [96]: 5); pagan religious practices were superstitious abominations (*City of God* IV.30–34); demons and humans entered agreements (pacts), each for private glorification (Isa. 28:15); the difference between demonic magic and legitimate miracle was clear and could not be mistaken by any Christian who was properly instructed—"Magicians perform wonders of one kind, good Christians of another kind, and bad Christians of yet another: those of magicians by means of a private contract [with demons], those of good Christians by public [divine] justice [or righteousness], those of bad Christians by the signs [or imitations] of divine righteousness." The later influence of Augustine's demonology, his dismissal of any independent validity to magic, however learned its practitioners and defenders claimed it to be, without recourse to demons, his refusal to recognize acceptable and unacceptable levels of magic, and his emphasis on the pride, sinful curiosity, and self-centeredness of those who practice magic was enormous and is echoed in most of the texts cited in this volume.

SOURCE: Augustine, *De Doctrina Christiana*, ed. and trans. R. P. H. Green (Oxford, 1995), 91–95, 97–101.

FURTHER READING: Peter Brown, *Augustine of Hippo: A Biography* (Berkeley and Los Angeles, 1969); Robert A. Markus, "Augustine on Magic: A Neglected Semiotic Theory," *Revue des études augustiniennes* 40 (1994): 375–88; Peter Brown, "Sorcery, Demons, and the Rise of Christianity: From Late Antiquity into the Middle Ages," in Brown, *Religion and Society in the Age of Saint Augustine* (New York and Evanston, 1972), 119–46; John O. Ward, "Witchcraft and Sorcery in the Later Roman Empire and the Early Middle Ages: An Anthropological Comment," *Prudentia* 12 (1980): 93–108; Russell, *Satan*, 186–218; Cohn, *Europe's Inner Demons*, 1–15; Flint, *The Rise of Magic*, 13–35.

A PERSON WHO IS a good and a true Christian should realize that truth belongs to his Lord, wherever it is found, gathering and acknowledging it even in pagan literature, but rejecting superstitious vanities and deploring and avoiding those who "though they knew God did not glorify him as God or give thanks but became enfeebled in their own thoughts and plunged their senseless minds into darkness. Claiming to be wise they became fools, and exchanged the glory of the incorruptible God for image of corruptible mortals and animals and reptiles."

73. But to analyse this whole matter more closely—and it is something of the greatest importance—there are two kinds of learning pursued even in pagan society. One comprises things which have been instituted by humans, the other things already developed, or divinely instituted, which have been observed by them. Of those instituted by humans, some are superstitious, some not.

74. Something instituted by humans is superstitious if it concerns the making and worshipping of idols, or the worshipping of the created order or part of it as if it were God, or if it involves certain kinds of consultations or contracts about meaning arranged and ratified with demons, such as the enterprises involved in the art of magic, which poets tend to mention rather than to teach. From this category—only their vanity is even more reckless—come the books of

haruspices and augurs. 75. To this category belong all the amulets and remedies which the medical profession also condemns, whether these consist of incantations, or certain marks which their exponents call "characters," or the business of hanging certain things up and tying things to other things, or even somehow making things dance. The purpose of these practices is not to heal the body, but to establish certain secret or even overt meanings. They call these "physical" matters, using this bland name to give the impression that they do not involve a person in superstition but are by nature beneficial. So, for example, ear-rings on the tip of one ear, or rings of ostrich bone on the fingers, or the advice given you when hiccuping to hold your left thumb with your right hand. 76. Besides all this there are thousands of utterly futile practices—do this if a part of your body suddenly twitches, do that if a stone or a dog or a slave comes between you and a friend as you walk together. The habit of treading on a stone as if it were a threat to one's friendship is less offensive than cuffing an innocent boy who happens to run between people walking together. But it is nice to record that such boys are sometimes avenged by dogs: some people are so superstitious that they go as far as striking a dog who comes between them, but they do so to their cost, because as a result of this inane remedy the dog sometimes sends its assailant straight to a real doctor. 77. Other examples are these: treading on the threshold when you pass in front of your own house; going back to bed if you sneeze while putting on your shoes; returning inside your house if you trip up while leaving it; or, when your clothing is eaten by mice, worrying more about the premonition of future disaster than about the present damage. Cato had a witty saying about this: when approached by someone who said that mice had been nibbling his slippers he replied that this was not an omen, but would certainly have been if the slippers had been nibbling the mice.

78. We must not omit from this category of deadly superstition the people called *genethliaci* because of their study of natal days, or now in common parlance *mathematici* (astrologers). Although they investigate the true position of the stars at a person's birth and sometimes actually succeed in working it out, the fact that they use it to try to predict our activities and the consequences of these activities is a grave error and amounts to selling uneducated people into a wretched form of slavery. 79. When free people go to see such an astrologer, they pay money for the privilege of coming away as slaves of Mars or Venus, or rather all the stars to which those who first made this error and then offered it to posterity gave either the names of animals, because they resembled animals, or the names of people, in order to honour particular people. It is no surprise that even in relatively recent times the Romans tried to consecrate the star we call Lucifer in the name of, and in honour of, Caesar. . . .

87. In this way it happens that, by some inscrutable divine plan, those who have a desire for evil things are handed over to be deluded and deceived according to what their own wills deserve. They are deluded and deceived by corrupt

angels, to whom in God's most excellent scheme of things this lowest part of the world has been subjected by the decree of divine providence. As a result of these delusions and deceptions it has come about that these superstitious and deadly kinds of divination actually do tell of past and future things, which happen exactly as predicted; many things happen to observers in accordance with their observations, so that as they are caught up in them they may become ever more inquisitive and entrap themselves more and more in the manifold snares of this most deadly error. 88. This is a kind of spiritual fornication, and in the interests of spiritual health scripture has not failed to mention it. It did not warn the soul by forbidding the practice of these things on the grounds that its teachers utter falsehoods; it has actually said, "If they tell you and it happens in that way, do not trust them." The fact that the ghost of the dead Samuel prophesied the truth to King Saul does not make the wickedness of summoning that ghost any less abhorrent. Nor did the fact that (in Acts) a soothsayer bore true testimony to the Lord's apostles lead Paul to spare that spirit rather than cleanse the woman by rebuking the demon and driving it out.

89. So all the specialists in this kind of futile and harmful superstition, and the contracts, as it were, of an untrustworthy and treacherous partnership established by this disastrous alliance of men and devils, must be totally rejected and avoided by the Christian. "It is not," to quote the apostle, "because an idol is something, but because whatever they sacrifice they sacrifice it to devils and not to God that I do not want you to become the associates of demons." 90. What the apostle said about idols and the sacrifices made in their honour must guide our attitude to all these fanciful signs which draw people to the worship of idols or to the worship of the created order or any parts of it as if they were God, or which relate to this obsession with remedies and other such practices. They are not publicly promulgated by God in order to foster the love of God and one's neighbour, but they consume the hearts of wretched mortals by fostering selfish desires for temporal things. So in all these teachings we must fear and avoid this alliance with demons, whose whole aim, in concert with their leader, the devil, is to cut off and obstruct our return to God. 91. Just as there are deceptive human ideas of human origin about the stars, which God created and ordered, so there are many ideas, committed to paper by many writers, apparently derived systematically from human surmises, about everything which is born or somehow comes into being by the workings of divine providence—I mean things which happen abnormally, like a mule giving birth or something being struck by lightning.

92. The influence of all these things varies in proportion to the extent of the agreement with demons achieved by presumptuous minds through such kinds of common language. But they are all brimful of dangerous curiosity, agonising worry, and deadly bondage. They were not observed as a result of their influence, but they gained their influence as a result of being observed and recorded.

This is how they came to have different effects on different people, according to their particular thoughts and fancies. Spirits who wish to deceive someone devise appropriate signs for each individual to match those in which they see him caught up through his speculations and the conventions he accepts.

2
Caesarius of Arles: Sermon 54 (ca. 530)

Caesarius of Arles (469/70–542) was born into a noble Gallo-Roman family at Chalon-sur-Saône and lived as a monk at the important island monastery of Lérins. In 501/2 he succeeded his relative Aeonius as bishop of the *civitas* of Arles, where he remained until his death. It was not uncommon for members of Roman aristocratic families to become bishops in Roman Gaul in the troubled fifth and sixth centuries, when the Roman cities needed powerful protectors against both political unrest and spiritual uncertainty. Nor was it unusual in Gaul for monks to become bishops. One of the earliest in Gaul was St. Martin at Tours. The monastery of Lérins had already provided a number of bishops when Caesarius left it for Arles. It had also provided Caesarius with an excellent education and an extensive familiarity with the work of Augustine as well as a decidedly pastoral bent as bishop. Caesarius's pastoralism was directed at bringing a provincial and localized Gallo-Roman religious culture into line with earlier Christian traditions and with the practices of other respected regional churches. Caesarius also represents what may be termed an "ascetic turn" in sixth-century Gallic Christianity—the movement of the ascetic, world-rejecting values of monastic communities from the fringes of Gallo-Christian culture to the social forefront, partly through the influence of aristocratic sympathy, and a consequent marginalization of the secular accommodation with religion that had characterized other regional Christian communities. In effect, the "secular" was marginalized, and many of its aspects were now denounced as "pagan," that is, as falling outside the new code of ideal Christian conduct, but always threatening to reappear in the minds of weak Christians. The proper aim of learning was now the study of scripture, and the purpose of the bishop as preacher was to instill these values into his congregation. Thus, the aim of Sermon 54 is to correct a "lived religion" into a new "normative religion" based on the ideals of aristocratic, ascetic Christianity.

SOURCE: *Saint Caesarius of Arles: Sermons, Volume I (1–80)*, trans. Sister Mary Magdalene Mueller (New York, 1956), 265–70.

FURTHER READING: Robert A. Markus, *The End of Ancient Chris-*

tianity (Cambridge, 1990), 181–229, and Markus, "From Caesarius to Boniface: Christianity and Paganism in Gaul," in *The Seventh Century: Change and Continuity*, ed. Jacques Fontaine and J. N. Hillgarth, Studies of the Warburg Institute 42 (London, 1992), 154–72; William E. Klingshirn, *Caesarius of Arles: The Making of a Christian Community in Late Antique Gaul* (Cambridge, 1994) and *Caesarius of Arles: Life, Testament, Letters* (Liverpool and Philadelphia, 1994), esp. 1:55, pp. 37–38, and 2:18, pp. 52–53); Giselle de Nie, "Caesarius of Arles and Gregory of Tours: Two Sixth-Century Gallic Bishops and 'Christian Magic,'" in *Cultural Identity and Cultural Integration: Ireland and Europe in the Early Middle Ages*, ed. Doris Edel (Dublin, 1995), 170–96; Peter Brown, *The Rise of Western Christendom: Triumph and Diversity, A.D. 200–1000* (Malden and Oxford, 1997), 99–102.

An Admonition to Those Who Not Only Pay Attention to Omens, but, What Is Worse, Consult Seers, Soothsayers, and Fortune-Tellers in the Manner of Pagans

1. You well know, dearly beloved, that I have frequently exhorted you with paternal solicitude, advising and proclaiming that you should by no means observe those wicked practices of the pagans. However, as I hear reported of many, our admonition has not profited some individuals. If I do not speak about it I will have to render an evil account on judgment day for both of us, and I, together with you, will have to endure eternal punishments. Therefore, I acquit myself before God if I admonish you repeatedly and assert that none of you should consult sorcerers, seers, or soothsayers, questioning them for any reason or infirmity. No one should summon charmers, for if a man does this evil he immediately loses the sacrament of baptism, becoming at once impious and pagan. Unless generous almsgiving together with hard, prolonged penance saves him, such a man will perish forever. Likewise, do not observe omens or pay attention to singing birds when you are on the road, nor dare to announce devilish prophecies as a result of their song. No one should set any store on certain days for leaving home and certain days for returning again, because God made all the days. As Scripture says: "And there was made the first day," also a second and a third in like manner, then a fourth, a fifth, a sixth, and a sabbath; and "God made all very good." And do not pin any faith on or pay any attention to the both impious and ridiculous [interpretation of] sneezes. As often as there is need for you to hurry, sign yourself in the name of Christ, devoutly recite the Creed or Lord's Prayer, and go on your way secure in God's help. . . .

3. Perhaps someone says: What are we to do, for the magicians and seers often announce true omens to us? Concerning this the Scriptures warn and advise us:

Even if they tell you the truth, do not believe them, "For the Lord your God trieth you, whether you fear him, or not." Again you say: Sometimes many would run the risk even of death from the bite of a snake or some infirmity if there were no magicians. It is true, dearly beloved, that God permits this to the Devil, as I already mentioned above, to try Christian people. Thus, when they sometimes are able to recover from sickness by these impious remedies, men see some truth in them and afterwards more readily believe the Devil. However, if a man wants to practice the Christian religion with all his heart, he should despise all these things with all the strength of his soul, fearing the Apostle's rebuke: "You are observing days and seasons; I fear for you, lest perhaps I have labored among you in vain." Behold, the Apostle says that one who observes omens receives his teaching to no purpose. Therefore, avoid the Devil's tricks as much as you can.

4. Above all, brethren, know that the Devil cannot injure you, those who belong to you, your animals, or the rest of your earthly substance even in small matters, unless he receives his power from God. Just as he did not dare to destroy the wealth of holy Job without the Lord's permission, so we read in the Gospel that when the demons were driven out of men they asked to be allowed to enter swine. I beseech you to consider this, brethren. If the demons did not dare to enter swine without receiving the Lord's permission, who would be so perfidious as to believe they can harm good Christians in any way unless God allows it in His providence? God permits this for two reasons: either to try us, if we are good, or to punish us, if we are sinners. However, if a man patiently endures the dispensation of the Lord—and, as I already said, when he loses something says: "The Lord gave, and the Lord hath taken away. As it hath pleased the Lord, so is it done; blessed be the name of the Lord"—he will receive a crown for his patience that is pleasing to God if he is just, and forgiveness if he is a sinner. Notice, brethren, that when the Devil had destroyed all the earthly substance of blessed Job, Job did not say: The Lord gave, the Devil hath taken away, but "The Lord gave, and the Lord hath taken away." That holy man was unwilling to give the Devil the glory of being able to take away anything that the Lord had not permitted him to remove. Since the Devil could not have injured the children, youths, camels, asses, or sheep of blessed Job before the Lord gave His permission, why do we think that he can do to Christians more than the divine power allows in its just and secret judgment?

5. Therefore, since we believe most certainly that we can lose nothing but what God allows to be taken away, let us cling to His mercy with all our heart, and after faithfully abandoning impious observances let us always presume upon His help. If a man believes in the aforementioned evils—magicians, seers, soothsayers, phylacteries, and other omens—it profits him nothing even if he fasts, prays, continually runs to church, gives generous alms, and afflicts his

body with every sort of mortification, as long as he does not abandon those impious practices. That impious, wicked observance ruins and destroys all those good actions to such an extent that they cannot profit men when they wish to exercise good works along with those evils. What the Apostle says is true: "A little leaven ferments the whole lump," and "you cannot drink the cup of the Lord and the cup of devils; you cannot be partakers of the table of the Lord and of the table of devils."

6. . . . If a man signs himself on the lips and puts a sword into his heart, then, just as the body is slain with a sword, so the soul is killed by that evil food. However, we trust in God's mercy that He will deign to inspire you to do what is right, so that the wickedness of the Devil may never overtake you in omens or the other impious practices and prophecies which were mentioned above. Thus, you will place all your hope in God, seeing that you never return to those abominable evils which are included above: with the help of our Lord Jesus Christ, to whom is honor and might for ever and ever. Amen.

3
Isidore of Seville: *Etymologies*, Book VIII, Chapter 9

Isidore (ca. 560–636), bishop of Seville (600–636), was the most widely learned churchman in early seventh-century Iberia, theological adviser of the Visigothic kings of Spain, and the author of a number of influential works, particularly the twenty books of *Etymologies*, a virtual encyclopedia of everything that was known in the Roman world in his lifetime, based on the theory that the meaning of everything could be explained by examining the origins of its name. Isidore's work immediately became and remained immensely popular (a manuscript of the *Etymologies* was copied in Ireland within a century of his death) and the work constituted a sort of "Encyclopedia Britannica" for medieval Europe. A close reader of the works of Augustine and possibly those of Caesarius of Arles, Isidore demonstrated a broader interest in the non-religious aspects of Greco-Roman thought than either, and his treatment of magic in Book VIII of the *Etymologies* both echoes and goes beyond those of Augustine.

Among Isidore's references in the text given here are several (VIII.9.2; VIII.9.10) to the great poem of the Roman poet Lucan, the *Pharsalia*, especially Book VI, one of the classic texts in Latin literature dealing with sorcery; to Exodus 7–8, the story of Moses and the magicians of Pharaoh (VIII.9.4); to Circe in Homer's *Odyssey*, Book X (VIII.9.5), whose image in Latin literature was closer to that of a sorceress than a goddess; to Vergil's *Aeneid*, Book IV (VIII.9.6); to the "witch" of En-dor in 1 Samuel 28 (VIII.9.7); to the fourth-century Latin Christian poet Prudentius (VIII.9.8); to the Roman encylopedist Varro (VIII.9.13). To Isidore, all these testimonies appear to have equal value, whether of pagan, Hebrew, or Christian origin.

SOURCE: Ernest Brehaut, *An Encyclopedist of the Dark Ages: Isidore of Seville* (New York, 1912; rprt. New York, 1964), 200–203, revised from *Isidori Hispalensis Episcopi Etymologiarum sive Originum Libri XX*, ed. W. M. Lindsay (Oxford, 1911), VIII.ix.1–31: Lat. rev. E. P. Some terms for which there are no modern English equivalents are here left in Latin.

FURTHER READING: Roger Collins, *Early Medieval Spain: Unity in Diversity, 400–1000* (New York, 1983), 60–67; J. N. Hillgarth, "Popular Religion in Visigothic Spain," in *Visigothic Spain: New Approaches*, ed. Edward James (Oxford, 1980), 3–60; the classic work remains in French: Jacques Fontaine, *Isidore de Séville et la culture classique dans l'Espagne wisigothique*, 3 vols., 2nd ed. (Paris, 1983). See also Flint, *The Rise of Magic*, 50–57, and for some later uses of Isidore, Jan Veenstra, *Magic and Divination*, 154–60.

Chapter 9. On the magi.

1. The first of the magi was Zoroaster, king of the Bactrians, whom Ninus, king of the Assyrians, slew in battle, and of whom Aristotle writes that on the evidence of his works it is clear that he composed 2,000,000 verses.

2. This art was enlarged by Democritus many centuries later when Hippocrates was famous for his knowledge of medicine. Among the Assyrians there was much practice of the magical arts, as [the poet] Lucan says [Lucan, *Pharsalia*, VI.427–29]: "Who could read the future by means of entrails, interpret birds' flight, or search out the lightnings of heaven or scrutinize stars by means of Assyrian lore."

3. And so this vanity of the magic arts flourished during many generations in the whole world by the teaching of the bad angels, through a certain knowledge of the future and the summoning up of infernal spirits. Their inventions are divinations, auguries, the so-called oracles, and necromancy.

4. And there is no miracle in the feats of the magicians, whose arts of wickedness reached such perfection that they actually resisted Moses by wonders very like his, turning twigs to serpents and water to blood.

5. It is said that there was a very famous magician, Circe, who turned Ulysses' companions into beasts. We also read of a sacrifice which the Arcadians of-

fered to their god Lycaeus when all who ate of it were changed to the shapes of beasts.

6. And it is plain that the famous poet wrote of a certain woman who excelled in the magic arts: "She promises to soothe by her charms the minds of whomsoever she wishes, and to cause others cruel anxieties; to stay the current in the stream, to turn the stars back. She summons the spirits of the dead at night; you shall hear the earth bellow beneath your feet and see the ash trees come down the mountain side."

7. Why should I tell further of the sorceress—if it is right to believe it—how she summoned the soul of the prophet Samuel from the secret places of hell and presented him to the gaze of the living—if we are to believe that it was the soul of the prophet and not some fantastic deceit created by the trickery of Satan.

8. Prudentius, too, tells of Mercury: "It is said that he recalled the souls of the dead to the light by the power of the wand he held, and others he condemned to death." And a little later he adds: "The wicked art can summon unsubstantial forms with its magic murmur and utter incantations over sepulchral ashes, and others it can deprive of life."

9. The magi are they who are usually called *malefici* because of the greatness of their guilt. They throw the elements into commotion, disorder men's minds, and without any draught of poison they kill by the mere virulence of a charm.

10. Whence Lucan says [*Pharsalia*, VI.657]: "Even when polluted by no awful drink of poison, the mind is killed by enchantments." They summon demons, and dare to work such juggleries that each one slays his enemies by evil arts. They use blood also, and victims, and often touch dead bodies.

11. Necromancers are they by whose incantations the dead appear to revive and prophesy and answer questions. *Nekros* in Greek means dead, while *manteia* means divination. To summon them blood is thrown on a corpse; for they say demons love blood, and therefore as often as necromancy is practiced blood is mixed with water, that they may be more easily attracted owing to the color of blood.

12. The *hydromantii* are so named from water. For it is hydromancy to summon the shades of demons by looking into water and to see their likenesses or mockeries, and to be told some things by them, while the pretence is made that it is actually the dead who are being questioned by the aid of blood.

13. This sort of divination is said to have been introduced by the Persians. Varro says there are four kinds of divination, namely, by earth, air, water, fire; hence geomancy, hydromancy, aeromancy, pyromancy.

15. *Divini* (sooth-sayers) are so called as if they were *Deo pleni* (full of God); for they pretend that they are full of divinity and they guess men's future by a deceitful cleverness.

15. Those who act by the art of words are called enchanters.

16. *Arioli* are so called because they utter nefarious prayers before the altars of idols and offer funeral sacrifices, and because they receive answers from demons on account of these same rites.

17. *Haruspices* are so called because they investigate the hours: they take charge of those days and hours in which business and other works may be done and they understand what a man ought to observe at particular times. They inspect the swellings of cattle and predict the future.

18. *Augurs* are those who understand the cries and the flight of birds, or other signs or observations of things that predict what will happen to men. The same is the case with auspices. Auspices are observances made by those making a journey.

19. *Auspices* are said to be like the appearance of birds, and auguries like the chatter of birds, that is, the voices and tongues of birds. Augury is almost *avigerium*, what birds do.

20. There are two kinds of auspices: one pertaining to the eyes, the other to the ears. Flight pertains to the eyes; the voice of birds pertains to the ears.

21. The Pythoness is so called from the Pythian Apollo, because he was the creator of divination.

22. Astrologers are so called, because they perform auguries by reading the stars.

23. The *genethliaci* are so named because of their observance of natal days. They lay out men's nativities according to the twelve constellations of heaven, and by the course of the stars endeavor to foretell the characters, deeds, and fortunes of the new-born, that is, under what sign each has been born, and what result it has for the life of him who is born.

24. These are they whom the vulgar call *mathematici*; whose kind of superstition the Latins called Constellations, that is, the notion of the stars, which they observe in terms of when someone was born.

25. At first the interpreters of the stars were called *magi*, as is read of those who announced the birth of Christ in the Gospel; later they had only the name of *mathematici*.

26. A knowledge of this art was granted up to the time of the Gospel, that when Christ was born no one after that should read the nativity of anyone from heaven.

27. Horoscopers speculate on the hours of the nativity of men in terms of their different fates.

28. *Sortilegi* are those who, under the false name of religion, by means of things which are called the *sortes* of the saints, offer the science of divination, or what the future holds, by the investigation of some parts of scripture.

29. *Salsitores* are so called because by observing parts of their members leaping they predict the meaning of future happiness or sadness.

30. To these belong also the *ligatures*, with their accursed remedies, which medical science condemns, whether in charms or in signs or in suspending and binding articles.

31. In all these the demonic art has arisen from a pestilential association of men and bad angels. Whence all must be avoided by Christians and rejected and condemned with thorough-going malediction.

4

Halitgar of Cambrai: The "Roman" Penitential (ca. 830)

From the sixth to the eleventh centuries, much of the thought and energy of Christian clergy that dealt with ecclesiastical discipline was recorded in the canons of church councils and synods, communications from ecclesiastical leaders, saints' lives, and selections from earlier church fathers, particularly Augustine and Gregory the Great (pope 590–604). A church synod held around 800 in the area of Freising and Salzburg indicates the contemporary concerns:

> Concerning incantations, auguries, and divination, and of those things done by people who conjure up tempests and commit other similar crimes, it is pleasing to the holy council that, wherever they may be found, the archpriest of the diocese shall examine what they do and constrain them by the most careful examination and make them confess to their evils. But he should subject them to moderation in punishment so that they do not lose their lives, but should be confined in prison for their own salvation, until by the inspiration of God they spontaneously mend the ways of sinners.[1]

A diocesan statute issued by Gerbald, bishop of Liège, issued around the turn of the ninth century at the urging of Charlemagne, may serve as another example:

> Those who perform *sortilegium* should be inquired about, as should *aruspices* and those who observe months and seasons, who interpret dreams and wear certain phylacteries around their necks, with [strange] words written on them. Women should be inquired about who give out potions to other women in order to kill a fetus and who perform other divinations so that their husbands may have more love for them. All *malefici* who are denounced for any

---

1. Hubert Mordek and Michael Glatthaar, "Vom Wahrsagerinnen und Zauberern. Ein Beitrag zur Religionspolitik Karls des Grossen," *Archiv für Kulturgeschichte* 75 (1993): 33–64, at 42. Trans. E. P.

of these things are to be brought before us so that their cases may be discussed before us.[2]

Many of their concerns were devoted to the problem of penance, the remorse, satisfaction, and absolution for sin. Books called penitentials were produced for clerical use and lay guidance, and these are important sources for both ecclesiastical ideas and contemporary practices, although they must be used with caution.

Around 830 Archbishop Ebbo of Rheims asked Halitgar, bishop of Cambrai (d. 831), to compose a handbook for confessors that would be based on the church fathers and the canons and replace the many and varied penitentials circulating in Carolingian Europe. Halitgar was a learned and energetic prelate, and his compilation reflects both earlier collections of canon law and a sense of his own independent judgment. He called the penitential "Roman," but there is relatively little that is distinctively Roman about it, except for the marked influence of Gregory the Great. It is illustrative of the widespread concern for a normative ecclesiastical and sacramental order throughout the Carolingian empire in the generation following the death of Charlemagne in 814. The reigns of Louis the Pious (r. 814–840) and his son Charles the Bald (840–877) also witnessed widespread concern over the use of sorcery in court circles. From the Council of Paris in 829 through the royal assemblies at Metz in 859 and Quierzy in 873, rulers and their high ecclesiastical advisers all expressed a sense of immediate danger from these practices, making the ninth century what the historian Pierre Riché has called "the point of departure in European sorcery."

SOURCE: John T. McNeill and Helena M. Gamer, *Medieval Handbooks of Penance: A Translation of the Principal "Libri poenitentiales" and Selections from Related Documents* (New York, 1938; rprt. 1990), 305–6.

FURTHER READING: The best work is in German: Raymond Kottje, *Die Bussbücher Halitgars von Cambrai und des Hrabanus Maurus* (Berlin, 1980). See also Aron Gurevich, "Popular Culture in the Mirror of the Penitentials," in his *Medieval Popular Culture: Problems of Belief and Perception* (Cambridge, 1988), 78–103; Julia M. H. Smith, "Religion and Lay Society," chapter 24 of *The New Cambridge Medieval History*, ed. Rosamund McKitterick (Cambridge, 1995), 2:654–78; Robert Somerville and Bruce C. Brasington, *Prefaces to Canon Law Books in Latin Christianity: Selected Translations, 500–1245* (New Haven, 1998), 59–78.

---

2. Carlo De Clercq, *La législation religieuse franque*, 2 vols. (Louvain-Paris, Antwerp, 1936, 1958), 1:360. Trans. E. P.

Of Magic

31. If one by his magic causes the death of anyone, he shall do penance for seven years, three years on bread and water.

32. If anyone acts as a magician for the sake of love but does not cause anybody's death, if he is a layman he shall do penance for half a year; if a cleric, he shall do penance for a year on bread and water; if a deacon, for three years, one year on bread and water; if a priest, for five years, two years on bread and water. But if by this means anyone deceives a woman with respect to the birth of a child, each one shall add to the above six forty-day periods, lest he be accused of homicide.

33. If anyone is a conjurer-up of storms he shall do penance for seven years, three years on bread and water.

Of Sacrilege

34. If anyone commits sacrilege—(that is, those who are called augurs, who pay respect to omens), if he has taken auguries or [does it] by any evil device, he shall do penance for three years on bread and water.

35. If anyone is a soothsayer (those whom they call diviners) and makes divinations of any kind, since this is a demonic thing he shall do penance for five years, three years on bread and water.

36. If on the Kalends of January, anyone does as many do, calling it "in a stag," or goes about in [the guise of] a calf, he shall do penance for three years.

37. If anyone has the oracles which against reason they call "Sortes Sanctorum," or any other "sortes," or with evil device draws lots from anything else, or practices divination he shall do penance for three years, one year on bread and water.

38. If anyone makes, or releases from, a vow beside trees or springs or by a lattice, or anywhere except in a church, he shall do penance for three years on bread and water, since this is sacrilege or a demonic thing. Whoever eats or drinks in such a place, shall do penance for one year on bread and water.

39. If anyone is a wizard, that is, if he takes away the mind of a man by the invocation of demons, he shall do penance for five years, one year on bread and water.

40. If anyone makes amulets, which is a detestable thing, he shall do penance for three years, one year on bread and water.

41. It is ordered that persons who both eat of a feast in the abominable places of the pagans and carry food back [to their homes] and eat it subject themselves to a penance of two years, and so undertake what they must carry out; and [it is ordered] to try the spirit after each oblation and to examine the life of everyone.

42. If anyone eats or drinks beside a [pagan] sacred place, if it is through ignorance, he shall thereupon promise that he will never repeat it, and he shall do penance for forty days on bread and water. But if he does this through con-

tempt, that is, after the priest has warned him that it is sacrilege, he has communicated at the table of demons; if he did this only through the vice of gluttony, he shall do penance for the three forty-day periods on bread and water. If he did this really for the worship of demons and in honor of an image, he shall do penance for three years.

43. If anyone has sacrificed under compulsion [in demon worship] a second or third time, he shall be in subjection for three years, and for two years he shall partake of the communion without the oblation; in the third year he shall be received to full [communion].

II

Sorcery in Christendom,

900–1300

BETWEEN 900 AND 1300 thinkers and writers in several intellectual disciplines and important literary genres began to reflect a new clerical view of—and interest in—an increasingly broad spectrum of ecclesiastical discipline, including the problem of various forms of heterodox practice and belief. The chronicles of monastic houses and, later, of individuals, the compiling of increasingly systematic compendia of theological and legal treatises, and the considerable increase of collections of saints' lives and miracles and moral stories for the education of both clergy and laity provided curious Europeans with the largest and most varied body of literature since the flourishing of the Christian Roman Empire in the fourth and fifth centuries. It is from this literary "explosion" of the eleventh and twelfth centuries that we derive our knowledge of attitudes toward magic and sorcery for the period preceding the schematization of dogma and philosophy in the thirteenth century. The chroniclers were interested primarily, of course, in the fortunes of their chief subjects, their own monastic houses, their aristocratic protectors or enemies, or the great men—kings and popes—of their time. Nevertheless, they did not omit other subjects which crossed their paths, and since the events of the invisible world of both benevolent and malevolent spirits were at least as important as those of the material world of great powers, they recorded a wide variety of concerns and episodes.

The compilers of legal treatises—Gratian is an example—brought before their readers texts which ranged in date from the earliest days of the church to their own times. These they sought to systematize by grouping relevant texts around a number of key problems of law or theology. Whether these compendia were spare and precise—as was Gratian's *Decretum*—or diffuse and rambling—as seems Caesarius of Heisterbach's *Dialogue on Miracles* (although it is not)—they all served the function of assembling manageable collections of authoritative opinion of great scope for the benefit of their (mostly clerical) readers (Text 11).

It is from these materials that we draw our knowledge of clerical and lay attitudes toward diabolism, early ideas of heresy and witchcraft, and the occult as reflected in a wide and not always consistent variety of sources in general before the thirteenth and fourteenth centuries.

The texts of Regino of Prüm (Text 5), Burchard of Worms (Text 6), and Master Gratian (Text 9) are from three important collections of canon law, the last, which drew on earlier collections with great originality and principles of organization, became the standard teaching text on the subject for the next several centuries. The *Corrector, sive Medicus* of Burchard of Worms (Text 6), written around the year 1000, is a much more elaborate version, and in a sense the summation, of the tradition of penitentials. The autobiography of Guibert, abbot of the monastery of Nogent-sous-Coucy, is an important witness to both the monastic concern with the actual practice of sorcery in the late eleventh and early twelfth centuries and the increasing attribution to heretics of characteristics that later were applied to practitioners of diabolical sorcery (p. 74 below). Hugh of St. Victor (Text 7), the schoolmaster of the house of canons of St. Victor, on the left bank of the Seine just outside of Paris, is an important theoretician of the organization of knowledge and its place in a legitimate Christian educational program at the beginning of the renaissance of the twelfth century.

The episodes selected from the twelfth-century chronicles of William of Malmesbury (Text 8) and Ralph of Coggeshall (Text 11) are inserted in longer histories, partly as literary diversions for the benefit of the reader, and partly as singular, isolated episodes which reveal the chronicler's fascination with unusual and striking events rather than a systematic theory of diabolism and witchcraft. Ecclesiastical lawyers, too, lacked systematic categories of diabolism and occult powers. Before the thirteenth century, witchcraft, predicting the future, and the invocation of demonic powers to achieve private and purely material purposes remained in a traditional juridical framework of ecclesiastical criminal sin which did not attract the attention of either the greatest minds or the strongest civil authorities in early Europe. Generally these thinkers relied on the works of Augustine and later thinkers for understanding their own world. Before 1300, chroniclers, ecclesiastical lawyers, moralists, and high prelates could record episodes of—and old patristic texts and laws concerning—a number of activities collectively labeled *sortilegium*—magic—without regarding their occurrence as anything other than singular and episodic, one more manifestation of Satan's usually unsuccessful attempts to tempt mankind from orthodox belief and practice.

5
Regino of Prüm: A Warning to Bishops,
the *Canon Episcopi* (ca. 906)

The *Canon Episcopi* (so called because of its alleged origin in a fourth-century church council and the customary citation of conciliar canons by their opening word or words) purports to be a canonical decision handed down by the Council of Ancyra, an ecclesiastical assembly held in 314, chiefly because in Regino's collection it followed a genuine canon of Ancyra and later copiers and users of the text ascribed *Episcopi* to Ancyra as well. When examined closely, it is clear that the canon is a composite of two different texts: the first three sentences echo a number of late ninth-century expressions of concern over heterodoxy; the rest of the text, however, is quite different, an elaborate condemnation of false beliefs that raises the question of the reality of a practice that will later become the witches' sabbat. It is an important text in the history of European witchcraft because the well-known collection of ecclesiastical law through which it was passed down in later centuries, Gratian's *Decretum*, became after 1150 the primary body of teaching material for the study of canon law.[1] Moreover, this single text—to which the numerous commentators on Gratian's collection at first paid remarkably little attention—became the starting point for all systematic discussions of sorcery and witchcraft from the fourteenth century on.

The first known appearance of the *Canon Episcopi* was in the canonical collection of the early tenth century compiled by Regino of Prüm, and the text was repeated in the later canonical collections of Burchard of Worms and Ivo of Chartres. Finally, about 1140, the Bolognese monk Gratian incorporated it in his *Concordia discordantium canonum* (Harmony of Discordant Canons), or, as the work came popularly to be called the *Decretum* (Text 9).

Book II of Regino's collection deals with the ecclesiastical discipline of layfolk. Chapter 5.42–45, deals generally with "enchanters and sorcerers." Chapter 5.43 condemns those who make offerings at trees, fountains, or stones "as if at an altar"; chapter 5.44 condemns those who sing "diabolical songs" or enchantments over bread or herbs; chapter 5.45 states that clergy should inquire about "any woman, who by any *maleficia* or incantations says that she is able to change men's minds, that is, from hatred into love or from love into hatred, or that

---

1. For the history of medieval canon law and forms of citation, see James A. Brundage, *Medieval Canon Law* (London and New York, 1995).

she can take or damage the goods of men. And, if they find any woman who says that she belongs to a group which rides with demons transformed into the likenesses of women on certain beasts on certain nights," they are to expel them from their parish. This is the so-called "short version" of the *Canon Episcopi* printed below. In Book II, chapters 354–75, Regino elaborates further on these practices and others, citing texts from earlier church councils and church fathers, papal statements (chiefly from Gregory I), Roman law, and earlier penitentials. These texts condemn the invocation of demons for purposes of divination, causing injury to others, weather-making, worshiping at trees or stones (idolatry), sacrificing to demons, magical cures, or the making of love potions. Chapter 371 is the famous *Canon Episcopi*. The paragraph break indicates the two separate texts that Regino has combined here. Some key terms have been left in Latin.

A later tenth-century cleric, Ratherius of Verona, also considered at great length, particularly in the context of legitimate and illegitimate medical practice, both the power of demons over humans and the issue of night flight. He condemns "those persons who are today so deceived in such matters to the point of perdition of their souls that over those whom they call witches [Lat. *saganas*] they set up Herodias, the killer of Christ's [John the] Baptist, as a queen, or rather as a goddess, declaring that a third part of the whole world was given her . . . when rather they are devils who with such illusions deceive unhappy women and men—more execrable than women because most damned."

SOURCE: Henry Charles Lea, *Materials*, 1:179–80, with revisions from F. G. A. Wasserschleben, ed., *Reginonis Abbatis Prumiensis Libri duo de synodalibus causis et disciplinis ecclesiasticis*, II, chap. 371 (Leipzig, 1840), pp. 534–36. Lat. rev. E. P.

FURTHER READING: Russell, *Witchcraft*, 75–80, 291–3; Robert Somerville and Bruce C. Brasington, *Prefaces to Canon Law Books in Latin Christianity* (New Haven, 1998), 92–93; Flint, *Rise of Magic*, 122–26; John T. McNeill and Helena M. Gamer, *Medieval Handbooks of Penance* (New York, 1938; repr. 1990), 314–21; Josef Steinruck, "Zauberei, Hexen- und Dämonenglaube im Sendhandbuch des Regino von Prüm," in *Hexenglaube und Hexenprozesse im Raum Rhein-Mosel-Saar*, ed. Gunther Franz and Franz Irsigler (Trier, 1995), 3–18. The quotation from Ratherius is in *The Complete Works of Rather of Verona*, trans. Peter L. D. Reid (Binghamton, 1991), 32–33.

B<small>ISHOPS AND THE</small> officials and clergy of bishops must labor with all their strength so that the pernicious art of *sortilegium* and *maleficium*, which was invented by the devil, is eradicated from their districts, and if they find a man or woman follower of this wicked sect to eject them foully disgraced from their parishes. For the Apostle says, "Avoid the man that is a heretic after the first and second admonition" (Titus 3:10–11). Those who have been subverted and are held captive by the Devil, leaving their creator, seek the aid of the Devil. And so Holy Church must be cleansed of this pest.

It is also not to be omitted that some wicked women, who have given themselves back to Satan and been seduced by the illusions and phantasms of demons, believe and profess that, in the hours of night, they ride upon certain beasts with Diana, the goddess of pagans, and an innumerable multitude of women, and in the silence of the night traverse great spaces of earth, and obey her commands as of their lady, and are summoned to her service on certain nights. But if only they alone perished in their faithlessness, without drawing many other people with them into the destruction of infidelity. For an innumerable multitude, deceived by this false opinion, believe this to be true, and so believing, wander from the right faith and return to the error of the pagans when they think that there is anything of divinity or power except the one God. Because of this, the priests in all their churches should preach with all insistence to the people that they may know this to be in every way false and that such phantasms are imposed on the minds of infidels and not by the divine but by the malignant spirit. Thus Satan himself, who transfigures himself into an angel of light, when he has captured the mind of a miserable little woman and has subjugated her to himself by infidelity and incredulity, immediately transforms himself into the species and similitudes of different personages and deluding the mind which he holds captive and exhibiting things, whether joyful or mournful, and persons, whether known or unknown, leads it through devious ways, and while the spirit alone endures this, the faithless mind thinks these things happen not in the spirit but in the body. Who is there that is not led out of himself in dreams and nocturnal visions, and sees much when sleeping which he had never seen waking? Who is so stupid and foolish as to think that all these things which are only done in spirit happen in the body, when the Prophet Ezekiel saw visions of the Lord in spirit and not in the body, and the Apostle John saw and heard the mysteries of the Apocalypse in the spirit and not in the body, as he himself says "I was in the spirit" (Apoc. 4: 2)? And Paul does not dare to say that he was rapt in the body (2 Cor. 12: 2–5). It is therefore to be proclaimed publicly to all that whoever believes such things or things similar to these loses the faith, and he who has not the right faith in God is not of God but of him in whom he believes, that is, of the Devil. For of our Lord it is written "All things were made by Him" (John 1: 3). Whoever therefore believes that anything can be made, or that any creature can be changed or transformed to better or to worse or be transformed into another species or likeness, except by the Creator himself who made everything and through whom all things were made, is beyond doubt an infidel.

6
Burchard of Worms: The *Corrector, sive Medicus* (ca. 1008–1012)

Burchard, bishop of Worms from 1000 to his death in 1025, composed his *Decretum* early in the eleventh century for the use of the clergy in his own diocese. Because of Burchard's considerable skills as a canon lawyer, however, the work circulated, even though unofficially, far beyond his own diocese. Book XIX of the *Decretum* is a penitential called the *Corrector, or the Physician*. Burchard used Regino's collection, including both the long and the short versions of the *Canon Episcopi*, the latter in the form of a question—that is, as an example of the questions a confessor should ask a penitent about specific beliefs or practices.

SOURCE: McNeill and Gamer, *Medieval Handbooks of Penance*, 329–33, 337–40.

FURTHER READING: Flint, *The Rise of Magic*, 123–25; Russell, *Witchcraft*, 80–82; Somerville and Brasington, *Prefaces*, 99–104; Ludo Milis, ed., *The Pagan Middle Ages* (Woodbridge, 1998), 133–49; Cyrille Vogel, "Pratiques superstitieuses au début du XIe siècle d'après le *Corrector sive medicus* de Burchard, évêque de Worms (965–1025)," in Vogel, *En rémission des péchés: Recherches sur les systèmes pénitentiels dans l'Église latine*, ed. Alexandre Faivre (Aldershot and Brookfield, 1994), chap. 10.

60. Have you consulted magicians and led them into your house in order to seek out any magical trick, or to avert it; or have you invited according to pagan custom diviners who would divine for you, to demand of them the things to come as from a prophet, and those who practice lots or expect by lots to foreknow the future, or those who are devoted to auguries or incantations? If you have, you shall do penance for two years in the appointed fast days.

61. Have you observed the traditions of the pagans, which, as if by hereditary right, with the assistance of the devil, fathers have ever left to their sons even to these days, that is, that you should worship the elements, the moon or the sun or the course of the stars, the new moon or the eclipse of the moon; that you should be able by your shouts or by your aid to restore her splendor, or these elements [be able] to succour you, or that you should have power with them—or

have you observed the new moon for building a house or making marriages? If you have you shall do penance for two years in the appointed fast days; for it is written "All, whatsoever ye do in word and in work, do all in the name of our Lord Jesus Christ."

63. Have you made knots, and incantations, and those various enchantments which evil men, swineherds, ploughmen, and sometimes hunters make, while they say diabolical formulae over bread or grass and over certain nefarious bandages, and either hide these in a tree or throw them where two roads, or three roads, meet, that they may set free their animals or dogs from pestilence or destruction and destroy those of another? If you have, you shall do penance for two years on the appointed days.

64. Have you been present at or consented to the vanities which women practice in their woolen work, in their webs, who when they begin their webs hope to be able to bring it about that with incantations and with the beginning of these the threads of the warp and of the woof become so mingled together that unless they supplement these in turn by other counter-incantations of the devil, the whole will perish? If you have been present or consented, you shall do penance for thirty days on bread and water.

65. Have you collected medicinal herbs with evil incantations, not with the creed and the Lord's prayer, that is, with the singing of the "credo in Deum" and the paternoster? If you have done it otherwise [than with the Christian formulae mentioned] you shall do penance for ten days on bread and water.

66. Have you come to any place to pray other than a church or other religious place which thy bishop or your priest showed you, that is, either to springs or to stones or to trees or to crossroads, and there in reverence for the place lighted a candle or a torch or carried thither bread or any offering or eaten there or sought there any healing of body or mind? If you have done or consented to such things, you shall do penance for three years on the appointed fast days.

67. Have you sought out oracles in codices or in tablets, as many are accustomed to do who presume to obtain oracles from psalters or from the Gospels or from anything else of the kind? If you have, you shalt do penance for ten days on bread and water.

68. Have you ever believed or participated in this perfidy, that enchanters and those who say that they can let loose tempests should be able through incantation of demons to arouse tempests or to change the minds of men? If you have believed or participated in this, you shall do penance for one year on the appointed fast days.

69. Have you believed or participated in this infidelity, that there is any woman who through certain spells and incantations can turn about the minds of men, either from hatred to love or from love to hatred, or by her bewitchments can snatch away men's goods? If you have believed or participated in such acts, you shall do penance for one year in the appointed fast days.

70. Have you believed that there is any woman who can do that which some, deceived by the devil, affirm that they must do of necessity or at his command, that is, with a throng of demons transformed into the likeness of women, (she whom common folly calls the witch Hulda), must ride on certain beasts in special nights and be numbered with their company? If you have participated in this infidelity, you should do penance for one year on the appointed fast days. . . .

90. Have you believed or participated in this infidelity, that some wicked women, turned back after Satan, seduced by illusions and phantoms of demons, believe and affirm: that with Diana, a goddess of the pagans, and an unnumbered multitude of women, they ride on certain beasts and traverse many areas of the earth in the stillness of the quiet night, obey her commands as if she were their mistress, and are called on special nights to her service? But would that these only should perish in their perfidy and not drag many with them into the ruin of their aberration. For an unnumbered multitude, deceived by this false opinion, believe these things to be true, and in believing this they turn aside from sound faith and are involved in the error of the pagans when they think there is any divinity or heavenly authority except the one God. But the devil transforms himself into the form and likeness of many persons, deluding in sleep the mind which he holds captive, now with joy, now with sadness, now showing unknown persons, he leads it through some strange ways, and while only the spirit suffers this, the unfaithful mind thinks that these things happen not in the spirit but in the body. For who is not in night visions led out of himself, and who while sleeping does not see many things which he never saw while awake? Who then is so foolish and stupid that he supposes that those things which take place in the spirit only, happen also in the body? When the prophet Ezekiel saw and heard visions in the spirit, not in the body, he himself spoke thus: "Immediately," saith he, "I was in the spirit." And Paul does not venture to say that he was "caught up" in the body. Therefore it is to be openly announced to all that he who believes such things loses the faith; and he who has not sound faith in God is not His, but [belongs to him] in whom he believes, that is, the devil. For it is written of our Lord: "All things were made by him, and without him was made nothing." If you have believed these vanities, you shall do penance for two years on the appointed fast days.

91. Have you observed funeral wakes, that is, been present at the watch over the corpses of the dead when the bodies of Christians are guarded by a ritual of the pagans; and have you sung diabolical songs there and performed dances which the pagans have invented by the teaching of the devil; and have you drunk there and relaxed your countenance with laughter and, setting aside all compassion and emotion of charity, have you appeared as if rejoicing over a brother's death? If you have, you shall do penance for thirty days on bread and water. . . .

149. Have you believed what some are wont to believe? When they make any

journey, if a crow croaks from their left side to their right, they hope on this account to have a prosperous journey. And when they are worried about a lodging place, if then that bird which is called the mouse-catcher, for the reason that it catches mice and is named from what it feeds on, flies in front of them, across the road on which they go, they trust more to this augury and omen than to God. If you have done or believed these things, you should do penance for five days on bread and water.

150. Have you believed what some are wont to believe: when they have occasion to go out somewhere before daylight, they dare not go, saying that it is the morrow and it is not permitted to go out before cock crow and that it is dangerous because the unclean spirits have more power to harm before cock crow than after and that the cock by his crowing is more potent to banish and allay them than that divine mind that is in a man by his faith and the sign of the cross. If you have done or believed this, you should do penance for ten days on bread and water.

151. Have you believed what some are wont to believe, either that those who are commonly called the Fates exist, or that they can do that which they are believed to do? That is, that while any person is being born, they are able even then to determine his life to what they wish, so that no matter what the person wants, he can be transformed into a wolf, that which vulgar folly calls a werewolf, or into any other shape. If you believe what never took place or could take place, that the divine image can be changed into any form or appearance by anyone except almighty God, you should do penance for ten days on bread and water.

152. Have you believed what some are wont to believe, that there are women of the wilds, called "the sylvan ones" who they say are in bodily form, and when they wish show themselves to their lovers and, they say, have taken delight with these, and then when they wish they depart and vanish? If you so believe, thou shalt do penance for ten days on bread and water.

153. Have you done as some women are wont to do at certain times of the year? That is, have you prepared the table in your house and set on the table your food and drink, with three knives, that if those three sisters whom past generations and old-time foolishness called the Fates should come they may take refreshment there; and have you taken away the power and name of the Divine Piety and handed it over to the devil, so, I say, as to believe that those whom you call "the sisters" can do or avail aught for you either now or in the future? If you have done or consented to this, you shall do penance for one year on the appointed days.

167. Have you drunk the holy oil in order to annul a judgment of God or made or taken counsel with others in making anything in grass or in words or in wood or in stone or in anything foolishly believed in, or held them in your mouth, or had them sewn in your clothing or tied about you, or performed any kind of

trick that you believed could annul the divine judgment? If you have, should do penance for seven years on the appointed days. . . .

170. Have you believed what many women, turning back to Satan, believe and affirm to be true, as you believ in the silence of the quiet night when you have gone to bed and your husband lies in your bosom, that while you are in bodily form you can go out by closed doors and are able to cross the spaces of the world with others deceived by the like error and without visible weapons slay persons who have been baptized and redeemed by the blood of Christ, and cook and eat their flesh and in place of their hearts put straw or wood or anything of the sort and when they are eaten make them alive again and given an interval of life? If you have believed this, you shall do penance for forty days, that is, a "carina," on bread and water, and in the seven succeeding years [perform a similar penance]. . . .

175. Have you done what some women filled with the discipline of Satan are wont to do, who watch the footprints and traces of Christians and remove a turf from their footprint and watch it and hope thereby to take away their health or life? If you have done or consented to this, you should do penance for five years on the appointed days. . . .

180. Have you done what some women do at the instigation of the devil? When any child has died without baptism, they take the corpse of the little one and place it in some secret place and transfix its little body with a stake, saying that if they did not do so the little child would arise and would injure many? If you have done, or consented to, or believed this, you should do penance for two years on the appointed days.

181. Have you done what some women, filled with the boldness of the devil are wont to do? When some woman is to bear a child and is not able, if when she cannot bear it she dies in her pangs, they transfix the mother and the child in the same grave with a stake [driven] into the earth. If you have done or consented to this, you should do penance for two years on the appointed days.

7

Hugh of St. Victor: The *Didascalicon*
VI.15 (Appendix B) (ca. 1120)

Hugh (d. 1141) was a canon and schoolmaster at the Augustinian house of St. Victor just outside Paris, which had been founded in 1108 by William of Champeaux (ca. 1070–1121), a former master at the cathedral school of Notre Dame and opponent of Peter Abelard. Throughout most of the twelfth century the school of St. Victor was one of the most influential in France, since its members ministered chiefly to the large and diverse student population of the city. Hugh's *Didascalicon* was written in the 1120s and was essentially an orientation to the different branches of legitimate learning, that is, to the organization of knowledge and a discussion of the books that students should read in each of the branches of knowledge.

The passage printed here is a later appendix that Hugh evidently intended to include toward the end of the work. Hugh's discussion of magic, partly derived from Augustine and Isidore of Seville, is important because it reflects the continuity of the earlier tradition, suggests that there was considerable interest in the subject in early twelfth-century Paris, and links, while condemning, learned magic and ordinary sorcery (and even illusionism), identifying all of these, no matter how exalted their claims to scientific prestige, to the cult of demons, forbidden rites, and crime.

In Hugh's case, the problem of learned magic is crucial. Although Augustine had dismissed professedly learned magic as a form of idolatry, the twelfth and thirteenth centuries witnessed a resurgence of claims that some forms of magic and divination did not involve demons and were therefore valid and not heretical. Moreover, stories of certain figures in the past, notably the earlier figures of Cyprian the Magician (Text 12) and Theophilus, the love-struck youth who sold his soul to the devil and later repented and was saved (Fig. 1), and the more recent and controversial figure of Gerbert of Aurillac, later Pope Sylvester II (999–1003), whose vast learning began by the late eleventh century to be considered a kind of diabolical magic, greatly increased suspicion of anyone claiming the ability to exercise magical powers, even the most learned. This problem became even more pressing in the thirteenth and fourteenth centuries, when even stronger claims were made on behalf of nondiabolical, "natural," or "ritual" magic. Hugh, following Augustine and Isidore of Seville, represented only one side of a debate that ranged from the twelfth through the sixteenth centuries and links even learned magic with necromancy and sorcery.

SOURCE: *The "Didascalicon" of Hugh of St. Victor: A Medieval Guide to the Arts*, trans. Jerome Taylor (New York, 1961), 154–55.

FURTHER READING: Marcia L. Colish, *Medieval Foundations*, 175–225; Peters, *The Magician, the Witch, and the Law*, 63–70; Richard Kieckhefer, *Magic in the Middle Ages*, 140–50; the best study of Gerbert is in Italian, Massimo Oldoni, *Fantasmi e fantasia nel medioevo: Gerberto e il suo doppio* (Naples, 1986).

T HE FIRST DISCOVERER of magic is believed to have been Zoroaster, king of the Bactrians, whom some say is none other than Cham the son of Noah with his name changed. He was afterwards killed by Ninus, king of the Assyrians, who had conquered him in war and who also caused his books, filled with the arts of evil-doing, to be destroyed by fire. Aristotle writes of this man that his books had preserved for the remembrance of posterity as many as two million two hundred thousand verses on the art of magic, dictated by himself. Subsequently, Democritus elaborated this art at the time when Hippocrates was enjoying fame in his practice of medicine.

Magic is not accepted as a part of philosophy, but stands with a false claim outside it: the mistress of every form of iniquity and malice, lying about the truth and truly infecting men's minds, it seduces them from divine religion, prompts them to the cult of demons, fosters corruption of morals, and impels the minds of its devotees to every wicked and criminal indulgence. As generally received, it embraces five kinds of sorcery: *mantiké*—which means divination, vain mathematics, fortunetelling, enchantments, and illusions. *Mantiké*, moreover, contains five sub-species, of which the first is necromancy, which means divination by means of the dead; for "*necros*" in Greek means "dead," and "necromancy" is derived from it. Divination in this case is achieved through the sacrifice of human blood, for which the demons thirst and in which they delight when it is spilled. The second is geomancy, or divination by means of earth; the third, hydromancy, or divination by means of water; the fourth, aeromancy, is divination by means of air; and the fifth is divination by fire, which is called pyromancy. For Varro declared that four were the elements in which divination consisted—earth, water, fire, and air. The first, therefore, namely necromancy, would seem to belong to hell—the second to earth, the third to water, the fourth to air, and the fifth to fire.

[False] mathematics is divided into three types: soothsaying, augury, and horoscopy. *Aruspices* (soothsayers) are so called as being *horuspices*, that is, inspectors of times (*horarum inspectores*), who observe the times in which things should be done; or they are called *aruspices* as being examiners of altars (*aras inspicientes*), who observe the future from the entrails and viscera of sacrificial animals. Augury, or *auspicium*, sometimes pertains to the eye, and is called *auspicium* as being *avispicium* (the watching of birds) because it concerns itself with the movement and flight of birds; sometimes it pertains to the ears, and then it is called *augurium* for *garritus avium* (the chattering of birds), which is heard by ear. Horoscopy, which is also called constellation, consists in seeking the fates of men in the stars, as do the *genethliaci*, who observe births and were once especially called *magi*, of whom we read in the Gospel.

Fortunetellers are those who seek divinations by lots. Sorcerers are those who, with demonic incantations or amulets or any other execrable types of remedies, by the cooperation of devils and by evil instinct, perform wicked things. Performers of illusions are those who with their demonic art make sport of human senses through imaginative illusions about one thing's being turned into another.

All in all, therefore, there are eleven parts of magic: under *mantiké*, five—necromancy, geomancy, hydromancy, aeromancy, and pyromancy; under [false] mathematics, three—soothsaying, augury, and horoscopy; then there are three others—fortunetelling, sorcery, and performing illusions.

Mercury is reported the first discoverer of illusions; the Phrygians discovered auguries; Tages first gave soothsaying to the Etruscans; hydromancy first came from the Persians.

8
William of Malmesbury:
The Sorceress of Berkeley (ca. 1140)

William of Malmesbury (d. 1142) wrote two important chronicles dealing with the history of England from the fifth to the twelfth century. He is one of the greatest chroniclers of the Middle Ages, and according to the principles of rhetorical historiography his histories often include anecdotal material as both a literary diversion and a moral message. The episode of the sorceress of Berkeley later circulated widely outside William's chronicle and was illustrated in the sixteenth century. The story, the authenticity of which William attests by praising the character of the person from whom he heard it (whether secondhand testimony was trustworthy was a lively point of discussion in twelfth-century historiography), interrupts an account of the critical events in England preceding the Norman Conquest in 1066. It is part of a series of moral exemplary stories dealing with the theme of the unquiet grave, among other topics. The year of the event discussed below was presumably 1065.

SOURCE: *William of Malmesbury's Chronicle of the Kings of England*, trans. J. A. Giles (London, 1847), 230–32.

FURTHER READING: Peters, *The Magician, the Witch, and the Law*, 29–33; John O. Ward, "Some Principles of Rhetorical Historiography in the Twelfth Century," in *Classical Rhetoric and Medieval Historiography*, ed. Ernst Breisach (Kalamazoo, 1985), 103–65; Rodney Thomson, *William of Malmesbury* (Woodbridge and Wolfeboro, 1987), 22–23; Antonia Gransden, *Historical Writing in England, c. 550 to c. 1307* (Ithaca, 1974), 166–85.

A~T THE SAME TIME~ something similar occurred in England, not by divine miracle, but by infernal craft; which when I shall have related, the credit of the narrative will not be shaken, though the minds of the hearers should be incredulous; for I have heard it from a man of such character, who swore he had seen it, that I should blush to disbelieve. There resided at Berkeley a woman addicted to sorcery, as it afterwards appeared, and skilled in ancient augury: she was excessively gluttonous, perfectly lascivious, setting no bounds to her debaucheries, as she was not old, though fast declining in life. On a certain day, as she was regaling, a jack-daw, which was a very great favourite, chattered a little more loudly than usual. On hearing which the woman's knife fell from her hand, her countenance grew pale, and deeply groaning, "This day," said she, "my plough has completed its last furrow; to-day I shall hear of, and suffer, some dreadful calamity." While yet speaking, the messenger of her misfortunes arrived; and being asked, why he approached with so distressed an air? "I bring news," said he, "from the village," naming the place, "of the death of your son, and of the whole family, by a sudden accident." At this intelligence, the woman, sorely afflicted, immediately took to her bed, and perceiving the disorder rapidly approaching the vitals, she summoned her surviving children, a monk, and a nun, by hasty letters; and, when they arrived, with faltering voice, addressed them thus: "Formerly, my children, I constantly administered to my wretched circumstances by demoniacal arts: I have been the sink of every vice, the teacher of every allurement: yet, while practising these crimes, I was accustomed to soothe my hapless soul with the hope of your piety. Despairing of myself, I rested my expectations on you; advanced you as my defenders against evil spirits, my safeguards against my strongest foes. Now, since I have approached the end of my life, and shall have those eager to punish, who lured me to sin, I entreat you by your mother's breasts, if you have any regard, any affection, at least to endeavour to alleviate my torments; and, although you cannot revoke the sentence already passed upon my soul, yet you may, perhaps, rescue my body, by these means: sew up my corpse in the skin of a stag; lay it on its back in a stone coffin; fasten down the lid with lead and iron; on this lay a stone, bound round with three iron chains of enormous weight; let there be psalms sung for fifty nights, and masses said for an equal number of days, to allay the ferocious attacks of my adversaries. If I lie thus secure for three nights, on the fourth day bury your mother in the ground; although I fear, lest the earth, which has been so often burdened with my crimes, should refuse to receive and cherish me in her bosom." They did their utmost to comply with her injunctions: but alas! vain were pious tears, vows, or entreaties; so great was the woman's guilt, so great the devil's violence. For on the first two nights, while the choir of priests was singing psalms around the body, the devils, one by one, with the utmost ease bursting open the door of the church, though closed with an immense bolt, broke asunder the two outer chains; the middle one being more laboriously wrought, remained entire. On the third night, about cock-crow, the whole monastery seemed to be overthrown from its very foundation, by the clamour of the approaching enemy. One devil, more terrible in appearance than the rest, and of loftier stature, broke the gates to shivers by the violence of his attack. The priests grew motionless with fear; their hair stood on end, and they became speechless. He proceeded, as it appeared, with haughty step towards the coffin, and calling on the woman by name, commanded her to rise. She replying that she could not on account of the chains: "You shall be loosed," said he, "and to your cost" and directly he broke the chain, which had mocked the ferocity of the others, with as little exertion as though it had been made of flax. He also beat down the cover of the coffin with his foot, and taking her by the hand, before them all, he dragged her out of the church. At the doors appeared a black horse, proudly neighing, with iron hooks projecting over his whole back; on which the wretched creature was placed, and, immediately, with the whole party, vanished from the eyes of the beholders—her pitiable cries, however, for assistance, were heard for nearly the space of four miles. No person will deem this incredible, who has read St. Gregory's *Dialogues;* who tells, in his fourth book, of a wicked man that had been buried in a church, and was cast out of doors again by devils. Among the French also, what I am about to relate is frequently mentioned. Charles Martel, a man of renowned valour, who obliged the Saracens, when they had invaded France, to retire to Spain, was, at his death, buried in the church of St. Denis; but as he had seized much of the property of almost all the monasteries in France for the purpose of paying his soldiers, he was visibly taken away from his tomb by evil spirits, and has nowhere been seen to his day. At length this was revealed to the bishop of Orleans, and by him publicly made known.

9

Master Gratian: The *Decretum* (ca. 1140)

Master Gratian's *Concordance of Discordant Canons,* popularly known as the *Decretum,* was a vast compendium of canon law that was arranged, not according to the chronology of texts, nor under general headings, as earlier collections had been, but according to topical questions whose apparent contradictions are resolved by dialectical reasoning and the citation of appropriate and authoritative statements by earlier ecclesiastical authorities as individual texts known as canons (in all, 3,945) from a very wide range of earlier legislation and authoritative opinion, as well as by Gratian's comments on these. Gratian includes the *Canon Episcopi* as *Causa* 26, question 5, canon 12. *Causae* 23–26 are generally known as the *causae* of the heretics because they contain most of what Gratian has to say about heresy. *Causa* 26 concludes these with a discussion of sorcery. Most of Gratian's texts and commentary are taken from earlier popes and church councils, Augustine, and Isidore of Seville, the latter two either at first hand or, more commonly, from earlier treatises or collections of canon law that cited or paraphrased the relevant excerpted texts. In the case of Augustine these were the work of Hrabanus Maurus in the ninth century, in that of Isidore, those of Burchard of Worms and Ivo of Chartres.

Causa 26 presents the case of, "A certain priest who was a magician and diviner [*sortilegus et divinus*], who was investigated by his bishop, refused to stop his activities, and was excommunicated. Later, at the point of death, the priest was given the last rites by another priest without his bishop having been consulted." Gratian uses the case to ask seven questions of law, ranging from a definition of *sortilegium* (q. 1), whether it is a sin (q. 2), what divination is (qq. 3–4), and whether excommunication is a proper way of dealing with unrepentant magicians and diviners (q. 5). Questions 6 and 7 deal with the problem of whether last rites should be given to condemned and unrepentant sinners and have nothing to do with magic or divination. Question 5, canon 12 is the text of *Episcopi*. The skepticism expressed in *Episcopi* thus entered canon law. It was echoed by John of Salisbury (Text 10) and at the end of the thirteenth century by the poet and scholar Jean de Meung, the continuator of the long allegorical poem *The Romance of the Rose* (discussed below, Text 30).

Also of great importance is the long excerpt from the ninth-century work of Hrabanus Maurus, *De magicis artibus*, a paraphrase of a number of texts by Augustine and others, *Nec mirum*, a text cited nearly as often as *Episcopi* by later writers, including Martin Luther in the sixteenth century (Text 40).[1] This long text begins by citing the evil sorcery of the magicians of Pharaoh in Exodus 7, then the powers of Circe in Homer's *Odyssey* (which Hrabanus knew only at second or third hand), then the Roman poet Lucan, whose *Pharsalia* contained one of the best-known scenes of women performing sacrilegious sorcery, a long list, partly derived from Isidore of Seville, of the kinds of magical arts, and concludes with a discussion of 1 Samuel 28, the case of the "witch" of En-dor. The *casus*, or the summing up of the case by a law teacher or commentator, is translated here.

In *Causa* 33, however, one of an important group of texts concerning marriage, Gratian also takes up the problem of sexual impotence and

---

1. On Hrabanus's sources for the passage, see Flint, *The Rise of Magic*, 54 n. 57. Gratian's sources attributed the text to Augustine, and Gratian indicates that it came from Augustine's *The City of God*. Although the text echos some of Augustine's observations in that work, it is not found there.

the dissolution of marriage. The range of the causa is wide, however, considering both natural and magical causes of impotence, and only one canon deals directly with *maleficium*. Although his primary canon (C. 33 q. 1 c. 4) is a text from an imperial divorce case in the ninth century, which Gratian took from an important earlier twelfth-century canonist, Ivo of Chartres, his handling of it reflects twelfth-century academic law and its extensive concerns about the nature of marriage.

Gratian's academic treatment of sexual impotence as an impediment to marriage may be compared to the well-known autobiography of Guibert of Nogent (ca. 1055–1125), the *Monodiae*. In Book I Guibert tells that his mother and father had been unable to consumate their marriage for seven years because a woman had resorted to evil spells in order to prevent the marriage. Guibert's point is his mother's virtuous steadfastness in the face of temptations to take a lover, but he notes that, "Eventually an old woman put an end to these evil charms," and takes no further notice. The matter of reversing magically induced sexual impotence in marriage received much more serious attention from Gratian and, later, Thomas Aquinas (Text 15). Guibert also wrote on other kinds of sorcery in connection with his anti-Judaic sentiments as well as in connection with the alleged behavior of heretics at their secret assemblies.

Gratian's text was soon commented upon by law teachers and students, and the standard commentary, the ordinary gloss, was taught with the text itself, although the gloss did not deal with every term in the text. The words glossed are printed here underlined; the gloss material itself is printed in *italics*; the translator's comments are in square brackets. One of the great strengths of the work of Gratian and his earliest commentators was the structure of the *Decretum*, which allowed teachers to cross-reference other relevant parts of the text, a feature that brought canon law to the level of revived Roman law.

SOURCE: *Decretum Gratiani . . . Una cum glossis*, Vol. 3 (Venice, 1595), *Causa 26, quaestio 5, canon 14, Nec mirum (casus)*, pp. 1375–76; *Causa 33, quaestio 1, canon 4, Si per sortiarias*, pp. 1537–40. The original Latin text is in PL 110: 1097C–1101C. [Trans. E. P.]

FURTHER READING: Peters, *The Magician, the Witch, and the Law*, 71–78; Flint, *The Rise of Magic*, 50–58, 290–301, esp. in reference to Gratian's use of Hincmar, 292 n. 114; James A. Brundage, "The Problem of Impotence," in Vern L. Bullough and James A. Brundage, eds., *Sexual Practices and the Medieval Church* (Buffalo, 1982), 135–48; Brundage, *Law, Sex, and Christian Society in Medieval Europe* (Chicago,

1987), 163–64, 201–2, 290–92, 376–78; Brundage, *Medieval Canon Law* (London–New York, 1995), esp. 44–69, 190–94. On Guibert, see *A Monk's Confession: The Memoirs of Guibert of Nogent*, trans. Paul J. Archambault (University Park, 1996). On Jean de Meung, see *The Romance of the Rose by Guillaume de Lorris and Jean de Meun*, trans. Harry W. Robbins, ed. Charles W. Dunn (New York, 1962), 389–94.

[THE CAUSA BEGINS with a general statement of the case, the *casus*, from which a number of questions of law were then identified. Although the cases are constructed so as to allow for the raising of particular legal questions, they need not be considered as purely hypothetical.]

A. Causa 26, quaestio 1, canon 4 Nec mirum (casus)

This chapter is divided into three parts. Augustine [Gratian and his source attributed the text to Augustine directly rather than to Hrabanus Maurus] *teaches three things. He first teaches that it is not a wonder that magicians should turn their staffs into serpents* [the reference is to Moses and the magicians of Pharaoh] *or water into blood, even with the resistance of Moses, because Circe performed similar acts, and Mercury as well. These things appeared to be, rather than were, the work of magicians. The second thing Augustine teaches is the many kinds of magicians and enchanters and how their names were derived. The third thing Augustine teaches is how such powers are given to demons so that they thus seduce men so that they are deceived into rejecting the truth, and that this is not done without the permission of God, and he tells why those magicians* [of Pharaoh] *turned their staffs into serpents.*

In the second part of the chapter are contained several objections addressed by Augustine concerning the pythoness [of En-dor: 1 Samuel 28] *and her divination and whether it stemmed from the error of magical arts and how the pythoness raised the spirit of Samuel to speak with Saul. To which objection Augustine responds that it was not the spirit of Samuel, but a demon. . . . In the third part Augustine responds thus: those who call themselves diviners or perform incantations possess no virtue or power of their own and therefore no one ought to believe them. Since health can be seen to replace illness, it must be that God hears and sees these things and that devotion must be given to God. And this is proved by the authority of Deuteronomy* [Deut. 13].

B. Causa 33, quaestio 1, canon 4, Si per sortiarias (casus)

A certain man was prevented by sorcery from rendering the debt [of sexual intercourse] to his wife. Meanwhile, another man corrupted her in secret, and she then married him who had corrupted her. Separated from her first husband, she then married the man who had corrupted her. This crime, which she admitted, she then sincerely confessed to God. The capacity of [sexual intercourse] with her then returned to her first husband, who took back his wife. The wife having been taken back, the husband, in order that his prayers might be heard and that he might receive communion in a pure state, vowed himself to continence. His wife, however, did not give her consent.

A certain man: *Gratian has spoken above about the impediment to matrimony that proceeds from spiritual causes and then about that which proceeds from the spirit and the body in conjunction. Now in this causa he speaks of that which proceeds from the body alone.*

[The first two canons of question 1 deal with natural impotence, and the third deals with the problem of conflicting claims between a husband and wife who had been married for some time, more than two months, says the gloss, as to whether sexual intercourse had taken place between them, stating that in such a dispute the word of the husband is to be believed, because "the man is the head of the woman." The fourth canon raises the problem of sexual impotence caused by *maleficium*.]

Canon 4

If sexual intercourse cannot be performed, whether because of concealed sortilaria or maleficia, but never by an unjust permission of God, and with the devil aiding, those to whom this happens should be urged, with a contrite heart and a humble spirit, to make a humble confession of all their sins to God and the priest. With profuse tears [of contrition], extensive charitable donations, prayers, and fasting, they may satisfy God. By exorcisms and other ecclesiastical practices, the ministers of the church may help them find health, just as the house of Abimelech was purified by the prayers of Abraham [Gen. 20: the women of the house of Abimelech had been unable to conceive]. If these do not work, however, the couple may be legitimately separated. But, even if the power of having sexual intercourse returns to them, they may not marry others.

Whether because of concealed: *This says that if someone who has had sorcery performed on him marries a woman and is therefore unable to have sexual intercourse with her, he should try to be cured by penitence and exorcisms, as is shown by the example of the lord Abimelech. And if such cures to not work the couple may be separated. But the couple may not thereafter remarry others, even if the possibility of sexual intercourse returns to them after they have been separated.*

Sortiarias: *and maleficias.* [the gloss then cites a cross-reference to C. 23 q. 4 c. 23 on the need to suffer evil and the inscrutability of the divine will]

Abimelech: *The king of Gerar.* [the gloss then cites a cross-reference to C. 32 q. 4 c. 4 on the sinfulness of adultery]

Separated: *unless the wife herself is said to have obtained the maleficum.*

Power: *that is, with others, not with the first spouses, since maleficium may not be permanent.*

Not: *this is said rather concerning ignorance than knowledge, since* [another earlier canonist said that] *no maleficium can be permanent. Others argue against this.*

10
John of Salisbury: The *Policraticus* (1154)

Episodes of the kind described by William of Malmesbury (Text 8) were precisely the kind of beliefs that Gratian intended to refute by including the *Canon Episcopi* (above, Text 5) in his compilation of church law. John of Salisbury (d. 1180) was a widely traveled and learned English cleric who had been a protégé and secretary of St. Thomas Becket, witnessed Becket's murder, and died as bishop of Chartres. His compendium on manners, morals, and politics, the *Policraticus*, dealt with a wide range of topics, including the interpretation of dreams and visions, from his discussion of which this selection is taken. John's skepticism of witches' night-rides echoes that of the texts in Regino, Ratherius, and Gratian and may help to cross-illuminate the selections from William of Malmesbury, Ralph of Coggeshall, and Pope Gregory IX.

SOURCE: C. C. J. Webb, ed., *Ioannis Saresberiensis Episcopi Carnotensis Policratici* (Oxford, 1909), vol. 1, book 11, chap. 17, pp. 100–101. Trans. E. P.

FURTHER READING: Hans Liebeschütz, *Mediaeval Humanism in the Life and Writings of John of Salisbury* (London, 1950); Michael Wilks, ed., *The World of John of Salisbury*, Studies in Church History, Subsidia 3 (Oxford, 1984); Colish, *Medieval Foundations*, 77–78; for John on another kind and context of magic, Peters, *The Magician, the Witch, and the Law*, 45–62.

THE EVIL SPIRIT, with God's permission, inflicts the excesses of his malice on certain people in such a way that they suffer in the spirit things which they erroneously and wretchedly believe they experience in the flesh. It is in this sense that they claim that a *noctiluca* or Herodias or a witch-ruler of the night convokes nocturnal assemblies at which they feast and riot and carry out other rites, where some are punished and others rewarded according to their merits. Moreover, infants are set out for *lamias* and appear to be cut up into pieces, eaten, and gluttonously stuffed into the witches' stomachs. Then, through the mercy of the witch-ruler, they are returned [in one piece] to their cradles. Who could be so blind as not to see in all this a pure manifestation of wickedness created by sporting demons? Indeed, it is obvious from this that it is only poor old women and the simpleminded kinds of men who enter into these beliefs.

11

Ralph of Coggeshall: The Heretics of Rheims
(1176–80)

Ralph, from 1207 to 1218 abbot of Coggeshall, a Cistercian monastery in England, wrote his chronicle in the last quarter of the twelfth century. The episode described here at first seems to reveal clearly the similarity between popular (or folkloric) traditions of witchcraft and popular images of heretics. But Ralph's informant, Gervais of Tilbury, was one of the great intellectual adventurers and storytellers of his age, and the story itself echoes a number of distinct literary genres: the lyric account of attempted seduction of a rustic young woman by a suave young cleric, for one, the artful linking of this to alleged heretical beliefs and practices, and finally the implication of sorcery in the escape of the old woman. The vow of virginity in itself, of course, was not at all heretical (Text 12).

Monastic culture also produced other literary genres in which similar ideas circulated. In the *Dialogue on Miracles*, written by the Cistercian Caesarius of Heisterbach between 1220 and 1235, several stories serve as a means of introducing monastic novices to the full program of monastic life. One of these, which tells of how a skeptical knight was convinced of the reality of the devil, illustrates the means by which exemplary stories might serve to disarm skepticism in general in a lively and vivid manner. Caesarius's work remained popular for centuries, both inside and outside monastic circles. Indeed, the transfer of initially monastic texts to a wider public was one of the means of preserving these ideas and their functioning in a wider circle of hearers.

SOURCE: Walter L. Wakefield and Austin P. Evans, *Heresies of the High and Late Middle Ages: Selected Sources Translated and Annotated*, Records of Civilization, Sources and Studies 81 (New York, 1969), 251–54. For Caesarius, see Caesarius of Heisterbach, *The Dialogue on Miracles*, trans. H. Scott and C. C. Swinton Bland (London, 1929), Vol. I, Book V, ch. 1–2, pp. 313–17.

FURTHER READING: Peters, *The Magician, the Witch, and the Law*, pp. 33–45; Russell, *Witchcraft*, pp. 116–18.

IN THE TIME OF Louis, king of France, who fathered King Philip, while the error of certain heretics, who are called Publicans in the vernacular, was spreading through several of the provinces of France, a marvelous thing happened in the city of Rheims in connection with an old woman infected with that plague. For one day when Lord William, archbishop of that city and King Philip's uncle, was taking a canter with his clergy outside the city, one of his clerks, Master Gervais of Tilbury by name, noticed a girl walking alone in a vineyard. Urged by the curiosity of hot-blooded youth, he turned aside to her, as we later heard from his own lips when he was a canon. He greeted her and attentively inquired whose daughter she was and what she was doing there alone, and then, after admiring her beauty for a while, he at length in courtly fashion made her a proposal of wanton love. She was much abashed, and with eyes cast down, she answered him with simple gesture and a certain gravity of speech: "Good youth, the Lord does not desire me ever to be your friend or the friend of any man, for if ever I forsook my virginity and my body had once been defiled, I should most assuredly fall under eternal damnation without hope of recall."

As he heard this, Master Gervais at once realized that she was one of that most impious sect of Publicans, who at that time were everywhere being sought out and destroyed, especially by Philip, count of Flanders, who was harassing them pitilessly with righteous cruelty. Some of them, indeed, had come to England and were seized at Oxford, where by command of King Henry II they were shamefully branded on their foreheads with a red-hot key. While the aforesaid clerk was arguing with the girl to demonstrate the error of such an answer, the archbishop approached with his retinue and, learning the cause of the argument, ordered the girl seized and brought with him to the city. When he addressed her in the presence of his clergy and advanced many scriptural passages and reasonable arguments to confute her error, she replied that she had not yet been well enough taught to demonstrate the falsity of such statements but she admitted that she had a mistress in the city who, by her arguments, would very easily refute everyone's objections. So, when the girl had disclosed the woman's name and abode, she was immediately sought out, found, and haled before the archbishop by his officials. When she was assailed from all sides by the archbishop himself and the clergy with many questions and with texts of the Holy Scriptures which might destroy such error, by perverse interpretation she so altered all the texts advanced that it became obvious to everyone that the spirit of all error spoke through her mouth. Indeed, to the texts and narratives of both the Old and New Testaments which they put to her, she answered as easily, as much by memory, as though she had mastered a knowledge of all the Scriptures and had been well trained in this kind of response, mixing the false with the true and mocking the true interpretation of our faith with a kind of perverted insight. Therefore, because it was impossible to recall the obstinate minds of both these persons from the error of their ways by threat or persuasion, or by any arguments or scriptural texts, they were placed in prison until the following day.

On the morrow they were recalled to the archepiscopal court, before the archbishop and all the clergy, and in the presence of the nobility were again confronted with many reasons for renouncing their error publicly. But since they yielded not at all to salutary admonitions but persisted stubbornly in error once adopted, it was unanimously decreed that they be delivered to the flames. When the fire had been lighted in the city and the officials were about to drag them to the punishment decreed, that mistress of vile error exclaimed, "O foolish and unjust judges, do you think now to burn me in your flames? I fear not your judgment, nor do I tremble at the waiting fire!" With these words, she suddenly pulled a ball of thread from her heaving bosom and threw it out of a large window, but keeping the end of the thread in her hands; then in a loud voice, audible to all, she said "Catch!" At the word, she was lifted from the earth before everyone's eyes and followed the ball out the window in rapid flight, sustained, we believe, by the ministry of the evil spirits who once caught Simon Magus up into the air. What became of that wicked woman, or whither she was transported, the onlookers could in no wise discover. But the girl had not yet become so deeply involved in the madness of that sect; and, since she still was present, yet could be recalled from the stubborn course upon which she had embarked neither by the inducement of reason nor by the promise of riches, she was burned. She caused a great deal of astonishment to many, for she emitted no sigh, not a tear, no groan, but endured all the agony of the conflagration steadfastly and eagerly, like a martyr of Christ. But for how different a cause from the Christian religion, for which they of the past were slaughtered by pagans!

People of this wicked sect choose to die rather than be converted from error; but they have nothing in common with the constancy and steadfastness of martyrs for Christ, since it is piety which brings contempt for death to the latter, to the former it is hardness of heart. These heretics allege that children should not be baptized until they reach the age of understanding; they add that prayers should not be offered for the dead, nor intercession asked of the saints. They condemn marriages; they preach virginity as a cover for their lasciviousness. They abhor milk and anything made thereof and all food which is the product of coition. They do not believe that purgatorial fire awaits one after death but that once the soul is released it goes immediately to rest or to damnation. They accept no scriptures as holy except the Gospels and the canonical letters. They are countryfolk and so cannot be overcome by rational argument, corrected by scriptural texts, or swayed by persuasions. They choose rather to die than to be converted from this most impious sect. Those who have delved into their secrets declare also that these persons do not believe that God administers human affairs or exercises any direction or control over earthly creatures. Instead, an apostate angel, whom they call Luzabel, presides over all the material creation, and all things on earth are done by his will. The body is shaped by the devil, the soul is created by God and infused into the body; whence it comes about that a persistent struggle is always being waged between body and soul. Some also say that in their subterranean haunts they perform execrable sacrifices to their Lucifer at stated times and that there they enact certain sacrilegious infamies.

12
Jacobus de Voragine: The Life of St. Justina, from *The Golden Legend* (1270)

In his vast collection of nearly two hundred saints' lives, recounted in the sequence of the ecclesiastical calendar, Jacobus de Voragine (James of Varazze, or *a Varagine*) systematically brought not only the sacred times of the year but the lives of the saints of the early and later church to the attention of his readers and hearers. His collection also made the issues of saints' lives in some ways contemporary with the lives of his audience, and in it the preacher or confessor could find materials on the magic of the Magi (1: 78–84), the identification of sorcery with demons (1: 108–13, 129, 152–53, 318–21, 340–50; 2: 3–10, 106–8, 192–95, 260–65), and a late thirteenth-century perspective on the entire course of church history and the festivals of the ecclesiastical calendar. The work survives in more than a thousand manuscripts (and in more pre-1500 printed editions than the Bible), and it was quickly translated into a number of European vernacular languages. In one way or another, it reached nearly everyone in Europe.

One episode from *The Golden Legend* that became widely cited in the fifteenth and sixteenth centuries, particularly in the context of what had by then become classical witchcraft theory and particularly in that of the question as to whether witches really went from one place to another at night, occurred in the life of the fifth-century St. Germanus, bishop of Auxerre:

Once when [Germanus] was a guest in a certain house, after the evening meal he noticed that preparations were made for another meal. Germanus wondered about this and asked for whom the preparations were made. He was told that some nice women came at night, and Saint Germanus decided to stay awake that night. He did and saw a troop of demons coming to the table in the guise of men and women. Germanus ordered them to stay where they were, then awakened the family and asked them whether they recognized the visitors. They answered yes, that they were all neighbors. Then, after telling the demons not to go away, he sent to the neighbors' houses and they were all found at home and in their beds. Finally, at his command, the visitors admitted that they were demons and that this was the way they fooled humans. (2:107)

Other stories from the *Golden Legend* illustrated other aspects of magic and sorcery. Early Christian legends of sorcerers like the convert Cyprian (Figs. 2–4) and the magician Hermogenes and his contest with St. James the Greater thus returned to wide familiarity in an age that understood them very differently from that in which they were first written and circulated. The *Golden Legend* and its local and vernacular adaptations were the main sources for hagiographical knowledge in the fourteenth, fifteenth, and sixteenth centuries, and they were used as material for sermons, in the celebration of individual saints' cults, and for general edification. Indeed, some saints virtually acquired cults because of the stories told about them in the *Golden Legend*.

Nearly a century earlier, the reformer and critic Gerald of Wales had included several of these stories in his *Gemma Ecclesiastica* around 1190, including the stories of St. James and Hermogenes and the sorcerer Cyprian. In Cyprian's case, the story can be traced from Gerald, through the mid-thirteenth-century encyclopedist Vincent of Beauvais, to Jacobus de Voragine and into the demonological tract of Nicholas Jacquier in the fifteenth century (Text 31).

SOURCE: Jacobus de Voragine, *The Golden Legend: Readings on the Saints*, trans. William Granger Ryan (Princeton, 1993), 2:192–95.

FURTHER READING: Alain Boureau, *La Légende dorée: Le système narratif de Jacques de Voragine († 1298)* (Paris, 1984); Sherry L. Reames, *The "Legenda aurea": A Reexamination of Its Paradoxical History* (Madison, 1985); André Vauchez, *Sainthood in the Later Middle Ages* (Cambridge, 1997); Eamon Duffy, *The Stripping of the Altars: Traditional Religion in England, c.1400–c.1580* (New Haven, 1992), 155–206; R. N. Swanson, *Religion and Devotion in Europe, c. 1215–c. 1515* (Cambridge, 1995), 145–72. On Gerald of Wales, see *The Jewel of the Church: A Translation of "Gemma Ecclesiastica" by Giraldus Cambrensis*, trans. John J. Hagen (Leiden, 1979).

T HE NAME JUSTINA is derived from *justitia*, justice; and Saint Justina showed her justice by giving to every person what was due to the person—to God, obedience; to the prelate her superior, reverence; to her equals, harmonious relations; to her inferiors, instruction; to her enemies, patience; to the poor and afflicted, compassion and help; to herself, holiness; and to her neighbor, love.

The virgin Justina was born in Antioch, the daughter of a pagan priest. Sitting at her window every day, she listened to the deacon Proclus reading the Gospel and in time was converted by him. Her mother told her father about this as they lay in bed, and when they had fallen asleep, Christ, accompanied by angels, appeared to them and said: "Come to me, and I will give you the kingdom of heaven!" As soon as they were awake, they had themselves baptized with their daughter.

This virgin Justina had long been pursued by a certain Cyprian, and in the end she converted him to the faith. Cyprian had been a magician from childhood: when he was seven years old, his parents consecrated him to the devil. He practiced the arts of magic, often being seen to change women into beasts of burden and performing many other marvels. He became enamored of Justina, and put his magic to work in order to have her for himself or for a man named Acladius, who also lusted after her. He therefore invoked the demon to come to him and enable him to win the virgin. The demon came and asked him: "Why did you call me?" Cyprian answered: "I love a maiden who is of the Galilean sect. Can you make it possible for me to have her and work my will with her?" The demon: "I was able to throw man out of paradise; I induced Cain to kill his brother; I caused the Jews to put Christ to death; I have brought every kind of disorder among men! How could I not be able to let you have one mere girl and do what you please with her? Take this lotion and sprinkle it around the outside of her house, and I will come and set her heart afire with love for you, and compel her to consent to you."

The following night the demon came to Justina and tried to awaken an illicit love in her heart. Sensing what was happening, she devoutly commended herself to the Lord and covered her whole body with the sign of the cross. Seeing that sign, the devil fled in terror and went and stood before Cyprian. "Why haven't you brought that maiden to me?" Cyprian asked. "I saw a certain sign on her," the demon answered, "and I weakened and all power left me." Cyprian dismissed that demon and called for a stronger one. This one told Cyprian: "I heard your orders and I saw why that other could do nothing, but I will do better and will carry out your will. I will go to her and wound her heart with lustful love, and you will enjoy her as you wish to." So the devil went to Justina and did his best to win her over and inflame her soul with sinful desire. But Justina again devoutly commended herself to God and dispelled all temptation with the sign of the cross, then blew upon the devil and drove him away. The spirit departed in confusion and fled to Cyprian. Cyprian: "Where is the virgin I sent you after?" The demon: "I admit I'm beaten, and I'm afraid to say how! I saw a certain terrible sign on her and at once lost all my strength!"

Cyprian scoffed at him and sent him away. Then he summoned the prince of demons and, when he came, said to him: "What is this power of yours that's so low, that a mere girl can overcome it?" Said the devil: "I will visit her and disturb her with various fevers. I will inflame her spirit with hotter passion and spread hot spasms throughout her body. I'll get her in a frenzy and put fearful phantasms before her eyes. And in the middle of the night I will bring her to you!"

Then the devil gave himself the appearance of a young woman and went to Justina, saying: "I come to you because I want to live in chastity with you; but tell me, I beg of you, what will be the reward of our effort?" The holy virgin answered: "The reward is great, the labor light." "Then," said the devil, "what about God's command to increase and multiply and fill the earth? I fear, my good friend, that if we persist in virginity, we shall nullify God's word. By being disdainful and disobedient we shall bring grievous judgment upon ourselves, and while we expected a reward, we will incur torment!" The virgin began to have serious doubts, induced by the devil, and she felt more strongly stirred by the heat of concupiscence, so much so that she rose and was on the verge of going out. But then she came to herself and recognized who it was that was speaking to her, so she shielded herself with the sign of the cross, then blew on the devil, causing him to melt like a candle. Thereupon she felt herself freed of all temptation.

Next the devil transfigured himself into a handsome young man and came into the room where Justina was lying in bed. Shamelessly he leapt into her bed and tried to envelop her in his embrace. This made Justina recognize the presence of a malignant spirit, so she quickly made the sign of the cross, and again the devil melted away. Then, God permitting, the demon sapped her strength with fevers, and killed many people along with their herds and flocks. He also made possessed persons predict that a great wave of death would seep through Antioch unless Justina consented to marry. For that reason the entire citizenry, beset as they were with disease, gathered at her parents' door and demanded that Justina be given in marriage so that the city could be delivered of this great peril. But Justina absolutely refused, and all were under the threat of death, but in the seventh year of the plague she prayed for them and drove out the pestilence.

Now the devil, seeing that he was making no headway, changed himself to look like Justina in order to besmirch her good name, and deceived Cyprian, boasting that he would bring Justina to him. Then, but this time looking like the virgin, he came running to Cyprian as if languishing with love for him and wanting to kiss him. Cyprian, thinking of course that it was Justina, was overwhelmed with joy and said: "Welcome, Justina, loveliest of women!" But the minute he pronounced the name of Justina, the devil could not bear it and vanished in a puff of smoke.

Cyprian, aggrieved at having been fooled, yearned the more ardently for

Justina and took to watching at her door. Sometimes he changed himself by magic into a woman, sometimes into a bird, but when he came close to that door, he no longer looked like a woman or a bird: he was Cyprian. Acladius, too, was changed by diabolic art into a sparrow and flew to the virgin's windowsill, but as soon as she looked at him, he was no longer a sparrow but Acladius, and he felt trapped and frightened because he could neither fly nor jump from such a height. Justina feared that he might fall and break to pieces, so she had him brought down by a ladder, and warned him to give up his mad adventure or be punished for breaking the law against trespass.

All these apparitions, of course, were nothing but devilish artifices, and none of them served the devil's purpose; so, defeated and confused, he went back and stood before Cyprian. Cyprian said to him: "So you too are beaten! What kind of power do you have, you wretch, that you can't overcome a simple girl or have any control over her? To the contrary, she defeats all of you and lays you low! But tell me one thing, I beg of you: where does her greatest strength come from?" The demon answered: "If you will swear never to desert me, I will reveal to you the power behind her victory." Cyprian: "What shall I swear by?" The demon: "Swear to me by my great powers that you will never desert me!" Cyprian: "By your great powers I swear to you that I will never desert you."

Now the devil, being reassured, told Cyprian: "That young woman made the sign of the cross, and at once all my strength ebbed away. I could do nothing, and like wax melting at a fire I melted away." Cyprian: "Therefore the Crucified is greater than you?" The demon: "Greater than all! And all of us and all those we deceive he turns over to be tormented in the fire that never dies out!" Cyprian: "Therefore I too should become a friend of the Crucified, so as not to incur so awful a punishment!" The devil: "You swore to me by the power of my army, by which no one can swear falsely, that you would never desert me!" Cyprian answered: "I despise you and all your devils, and I arm myself with the saving sign of the Crucified!" Instantly the devil fled in confusion.

Then Cyprian went to the bishop. When the bishop saw him, he supposed that he had come to lead Christians into error, and said to him: "Be satisfied, Cyprian, with misleading those who are not of the faith! You can do nothing against the Church of God, for the power of Christ is unconquerable." Cyprian: "I am sure that Christ's power cannot be conquered." And he told the bishop all that had happened to him, and had the bishop baptize him. Thereafter Cyprian made great progress both in knowledge and in holiness of life, and when the bishop died, Cyprian was ordained to take his place. He established the holy virgin Justina in a monastery and made her the abbess over many holy virgins. Saint Cyprian often sent letters to the martyrs and strengthened them in their struggles.

The prefect of that region heard of the renown of Cyprian and Justina and had them brought before him. He asked them if they were willing to sacrifice to the idols. When they persisted firmly in the faith of Christ, he ordered them to be put in a heated caldron filled with wax, pitch, and fat, but this only refreshed them and inflicted no pain. Then a priest of the idols said to the prefect: "Command me to stand in front of the caldron, and I will outdo all their power!" He went close to the caldron and said: "Great are you, O god Hercules, and you, Jupiter, father of the gods!" And behold, fire poured out and consumed the priest. Cyprian and Justina were taken out of the caldron, sentenced, and beheaded together. Their bodies were thrown to the dogs and lay for seven days, then were transported to Rome, and now, we are told, repose in Piacenza. They suffered under Diocletian, on the twenty-sixth day of September, A.D. 280.

III

Thomas Aquinas on Sorcery
and the Nature of Evil

T HOMAS AQUINAS (CA. 1225–74)
was a Dominican and a professor of theology at the University of Paris and
elsewhere from 1256 and traveled widely among the academic and religious
centers of Christendom during his mature years. In the early part of his academic career he produced a *Commentary on the Sentences of Peter Lombard*,
an explication of a work which had become the standard textbook of theology in
the late twelfth and early thirteenth centuries (Text 16). Another work, the
Summa contra gentiles (Text 13), is a vast attempt to reveal the rational bases of
Catholic dogma, not only for the benefit of the "Gentiles" (primarily Muslims),
but for those who hold different philosophical views as well. The *Summa theologiae* (Text 14) is an immense handbook for those setting out to learn theology—in 512 questions, 2,669 articles, and more than 10,000 objections, only 5
questions of which deal directly with sorcery and divination.

Taken together, these works constitute a great philosophical system, perhaps the most complete and detailed system in European history. Although
both *summae* were considered extremely controversial in their own day, they
later became the foundation of much Catholic thought and were even revived in
the nineteenth century. The selections from these works and from the *Quaes-
tiones quodlibetales* (Questions Dealing with All Kinds of Topics, Text 15) have
been chosen to illustrate a particular application of Aquinas's systematic ontology, which formed the basis, particularly when only the demonological
texts were extracted and quoted entirely out of context, of later demonologists'
theories.

Aquinas completed in his vast works of theology the long process of sum-
marizing and explicating in infinite detail the character of the relations between
man and God, the definition of which had been begun in earnest in the twelfth
century. Strongly influenced by both Plato and Aristotle, Aquinas gave a formal

structure to Christian philosophy and theology. In his elaborately detailed description of the universe and the powers it contains, he dealt with the problem
of evil, with the demons, and with demonic intervention in human affairs.
Unlike the chroniclers, moralists, and ecclesiastical lawyers cited earlier in this
book, Aquinas's task was to explain precisely how it was possible for demons to
influence human actions. The selections below reveal his method: the careful
step-by-step description of the nature of reality by constant reference to dogma
and to other parts of his elaborately structured work. The excerpts from the
Summa contra gentiles deal with the powers of magic in the natural world.
Those from the *Summa theologiae* deal with the assaults on man made by
demons. The brief excerpts which end the selections deal with the effects of
sorcery on marriage (Text 15) and the necessity of God's permission for the
sorcerer to affect man (Text 16). It may be noted that the rigorous logic and the
details of the view of the universe found in his work give, as it were, a legitimate
intellectual superstructure to the random accounts of chroniclers and the detailed legalism of lawyers. After Thomas, such incidents as those cited above
(see Texts 9, 11) could be regarded not as isolated events to wonder at, but as
manifestations of certain truths about the nature of reality which found their
explanation in a systematic exposition of Christian dogma.

But the work of theologians was not homogeneous, and they disputed
with each other as vigorously as they collectively disputed with Muslims, Jews,
and dissenters. One key reason for this was the very structure of their dialectical
reasoning itself. That form of reasoning attributed great authority to scripture,
ecclesiastical tradition, and the words of the church fathers. When authorities
appeared to contradict each other, theologians had to find a satisfactory means
of reconciling those apparent contradictions. That means became the basis of
scholastic logic (that is, the logic of the schools, later the universities).

When a theologian had arrived through study at a conclusion concerning a
point of doctrine, he first had to list all of the objections, including apparently
authoritative texts, which might conceivably be made against it. And these objections could not be merely weak arguments; they had to be the strongest possible arguments against his position. After listing these, the theologian would
then use a single authoritative text that appeared to contradict the first set of
texts and was used to serve as the hinge that turned the argument toward his
own position. This text was usually introduced with the phrase *sed contra*, "but
against these arguments . . ." Having turned toward his own position, the theologian then listed the authorities that supported him, his *solutio*, making his
point at the end of these. Finally, he then had to demonstrate how his own position overcame the counterarguments listed at the beginning of his discussion.

Because of this format, all conceivable arguments for and against any position or point of doctrine had to be addressed continually. This technique of ex-

position meant that not only doctrine, but also counterdoctrine was discussed and argued. The consequences of this method for later theological and philosophical development were considerable. Specifically in later debates about various aspects of witchcraft, the form of scholastic disputation, particularly its dependence on the *sed contra* argument, required that objections to witchcraft beliefs had to be given as well as the positions of those arguing for the full spectrum of those beliefs.[1]

For example, in his commentary on Book II, distinction 7, question 3, article 2 of Peter Lombard's *Sentences*, which asks whether it is permitted to Christians to seek the aid and advice of the demons, Aquinas begins by saying that is seems permissible to do so since St. Paul (in 1 Cor. 5: 5) says that fornicators are to be handed over to Satan for the destruction of the flesh so that the spirit may be saved—but he does not call them sinners.[2] Therefore, seeking the aid of demons seems permitted. Further, since it is permitted to accept help from sinners, in matters of charity, for example, and since the demons have only two parts—nature, which is good, and sin—it would seem to be permitted to accept aid from them just as one would be permitted to accept charity from a sinful person. Aquinas lists two more arguments in favor of the position that accepting aid and advice from demons is permitted.

Then comes the *sed contra*: in Deuteronomy 18: 10–12, God commands that all *incantatores et maleficos* be killed. And Augustine says that all divinations are to be avoided; although physical death ought not to be inflicted without grave cause. Therefore it is clear that they who deal with demons sin greatly.

Aquinas's *solutio* says that those things that are above nature and the capacity of human faculties are to be asked only from God. And anyone who attributes to a creature by a cult of idolatry that which is God's, is a sinner. Those who ask from demons that which should only be asked of God sin gravely. And one of these ways is to ask about the future, since Isaiah says "Should not a people consult the gods . . ." (Isa. 8:19), and the same is true of other magical operations, "because in these there is always apostasy from the faith by virtue of the pact made with the demon, verbally if the demon was invoked, or by deed if some sacrifice was performed." Aquinas then responds to the original four objections to his own thesis in turn.

It is important to note that in the course of a routine discussion in academic theology, Aquinas mentions in passing that all communication with demons requires a pact, which constitutes apostasy from the true faith. From

1. There is a good example of the consequences of this form of logical disputation in later demonological debates in Clark, *Thinking with Demons*, 179–94.
2. *Sancti Thomae Aquinatis Commentum super Quattuor Libros Sententiarum Magistri Petri Lombardi* (Parma, 1857), 451.

Aquinas, the argument about pacts involving both magicians and later witches derived much of its theological authority.[3]

13
From the *Summa contra gentiles*: Sorcery and the World of Nature

SOURCE: St. Thomas Aquinas, *The Summa contra gentiles*, third book (part 2, chaps. 104–6), literally translated by the English Dominican Fathers from the latest Leonine edition (London, 1928), pp. 67–75.

FURTHER READING: M.-D. Chenu, *Toward Understanding Saint Thomas*, trans. A. M. Landry and D. Hughes (Chicago, 1964), esp. 126–202, the best general introduction to Aquinas's thought and method; St. Thomas Aquinas, *On Evil*, trans. Jean Oesterle (Notre Dame, 1995), the most comprehensive work of Aquinas on the general subject; Jean-Pierre Torrell, *Saint Thomas Aquinas*, vol. 1 (Washington, D.C., 1996), esp. 212–16; Colish, *Medieval Foundations*, 265–301.

*That the works of magicians result not only from
the influence of heavenly bodies.*

Some there were who averred that such works as seem wonderful to us, being wrought by the magic art, are done, not by certain spiritual substances, but by the power of the heavenly bodies. This would seem to be indicated by the fact that those who practice works of this kind, observe the position of the stars: and are assisted by the employment of certain herbs and other corporeal things, for the purpose, as it were, of preparing matter of lower degree to receive the influence of the celestial power.

But this is in contradiction with the apparitions (in the works of magicians). For as it is impossible that an intellect be formed from corporeal principles, as we proved above, it is impossible for effects that are caused exclusively by the intellectual nature, to be produced by the power of a heavenly body. Now in these works of magicians, things appear that are exclusively the work of a rational nature; for instance, answers are given about stolen goods, and the like, and this could not be done except by an intelligence. Therefore it is not true that all such effects are caused by the mere power of a heavenly body.

Further. Speech is an act proper to the rational nature. Now in these works people appear to men and speak to them on various matters. Therefore such things cannot be done by the mere power of heavenly bodies. If, however, some-

3. There is still much of value in the study of Charles Edward Hopkin, *The Share of Thomas Aquinas in the Growth of the Witchcraft Delusion* (Philadelphia, 1940; rprt. New York, 1982).

one says that these apparitions are present, not to the sensorial organ, but only to the imagination:—this is, in the first place, apparently untrue. For imaginary forms do not seem real to anyone, unless his external senses be suspended: since it is not possible for a person to look on a likeness as a reality, except the natural judgements of the senses be tied. Now these conversations and apparitions are addressed to those who have free use of their external senses. Therefore these apparitions and speeches cannot be imaginary.

Besides, no imaginary forms can lead a person to intellectual knowledge beyond the natural or acquired faculty of his intellect: this is evident in dreams; since even if they contain some indication of the future, it is not every dreamer that understands the meaning of his dreams. Now, in these apparitions and speeches that occur in the works of magicians, it frequently happens that a person obtains knowledge of things surpassing the faculty of his intelligence, such as the discovery of hidden treasure, the manifestation of the future, and sometimes even true answers are given in matters of science. Either, therefore, these apparitions or speeches are not purely imaginary; or at least it is the work of some higher intelligence, and not only of a heavenly body, that a person obtain the aforesaid knowledge through these imaginings.

Again. That which is done by the power of heavenly bodies is a natural effect: since they are natural forms that are caused in this lower world by the powers of heavenly bodies. Hence that which cannot be natural to anything, cannot be caused by the power of the heavenly bodies. And yet some such things are stated to be caused, by the aforesaid works: for instance, it is averred that at the mere presence of a certain person all doors are unlocked, that a certain man becomes invisible, and many like occurrences are related. Therefore this cannot be done by the power of heavenly bodies.

Further. The reception, through the power of heavenly bodies, of that which follows, implies the reception of what precedes. Now movement of its very nature is the result of having a soul: since it is proper to animate things to move themselves. Therefore it is impossible for an inanimate being to be moved by itself, through the power of a heavenly body. Yet it is stated that by the magic art an image is made to move of itself, or to speak.

Therefore it is not possible for the effects of the magic art to be caused by a celestial power.

And if it be said that the image in question is endowed with some vital principle by the power of the heavenly bodies, this is impossible. For the principle of life in all living things is the substantial form, because, as the Philosopher says (2 *De Anima*, iv.) *in living things to be is to live.* Now, it is impossible for anything to receive anew a substantial form, unless it lose the form which it had previously, since *the generation of one thing is the corruption of another* (3 *Phys.* viii.). But in the making of an image no substantial form is discarded, and there is only a change of shape which is an accident: since the form of copper or something of the kind remains. Therefore the image in question cannot possibly be endowed with the vital principle.

Further. If anything is moved by a principle of life it necessarily has sensation, for the principle of movement is sensation or understanding. But understanding is not found without sensation in things that come to be and pass away. Now there cannot be sensation where there is not the sense of touch; nor the sense of touch without an organ of mean temperature. Such a temperature, however, is not found in the stone or wax or metal out of which the statue is made. It is not possible, therefore, that statues of this sort should be moved by a principle of life.

Besides. Perfect living things are generated not only by a celestial power, but also from seed: for *man and the sun generate man* (2 *Phys.* ii.): and such as are generated by a celestial power alone without seed, are animals formed by putrefaction, and such belong to a lower grade than the others. Accordingly if these images be endowed with the vital principle by a celestial power alone, so as to move themselves, it follows that they belong to the lowest grade of animals. And yet this would be false if they worked by an intrinsic principle of life: since among their operations some are of a high degree, for they give answers about hidden things. Therefore it is not possible that their operations and movements proceed from a principle of life.

Again. We find sometimes a natural effect produced by the power of heavenly bodies without the operation of art: thus, although one may produce frogs, or something of the kind by means of some artifice, frogs do happen to be produced without any artifice. Consequently if these images that are made by necromancy are endowed with the vital principle by the power of heavenly bodies, it will be possible for them to be formed without the operation of art. But this is not the case. Therefore it is evident that such images have not the principle of life, nor are they moved by the power of heavenly bodies.

Hereby we refute the opinion of Hermes who, according to Augustine (8 *De Civ. Dei* xxiii.) expressed himself thus: *As God is the cause of the heavenly gods, so man fashions the gods that reside in temples, being satisfied to live near men. I refer to those animal images, endowed with sense and spirit, that do great and wonderful things, images gifted with knowledge of the future, and who foretell by dreams and many other things; who afflict men with ailments and heal them, who bring sorrow and joy to them according to their merits.*

This opinion is also refuted by divine authority. For it is said in the Psalm (cxxxiv. 15 *seqq.*): *The idols of the Gentiles are silver and gold, the works of men's hands. They have a mouth but they speak not . . . neither is there any breath in their mouths.*

Yet seemingly we must not absolutely deny the possibility of some kind of efficacy being in these things through the power of the heavenly bodies: but only for such effects as certain lower bodies are able to cause by the power of the heavenly bodies.

Whence the works of magicians derive their efficacy.

It remains for us to inquire whence the magic arts derive their efficacy: a question that will present no difficulty if we consider their mode of operation.

For in the practice of their art they make use of certain significative words in order to produce certain definite effects. Now, words, in so far as they signify something, have no power except as derived from some intellect; either of the speaker, or of the person to whom they are spoken. From the intellect of the speaker, as when an intellect is of such great power than it can cause things by its mere thought, the voice serving to convey, as it were, this thought to the things that are to be produced. From the intellect of the person to whom the words are addressed, as when the hearer is induced to do some particular thing, through his intellect receiving the signification of those words. Now, it cannot be said that these significative words uttered by magicians derive efficacy from the intellect of the speaker. For since power follows essence, diversity of power indicates diversity of essential principles. Moreover, man's intellect is invariably of such a disposition that its knowledge is caused by things, rather than that it is able by its mere thought to cause things. Consequently if there be any men that are able of their own power to transform things by words expressive of their thoughts, they will belong to another species, and it would be an equivocation to call them men.

Further. By learning we acquire, not the power to do a thing, but the knowledge of how to do it. Yet some, by learning, are rendered able to perform these magic works. Therefore they must have not only knowledge but also the power to produce these effects.

If someone say that these men, by the influence of the stars, are born with the aforesaid power, while others are excluded from it; so that however much the others, who are born without this power, may be instructed, they cannot succeed in performing these works; we reply, first that, as shown above, heavenly bodies cannot make an impression on the intellect. Therefore a man's intellect cannot, through the influence of the stars, receive a power whereby the vocal expression of its thoughts is productive of something.

And if it be said that the imagination produces an effect in the utterance of significative words, and that heavenly bodies can work on the imagination, since its operation is performed by a bodily organ:—this does not apply to all the results produced by this art. For we have shown (ch. civ.) that these effects cannot all be produced by the power of the stars. Neither, therefore, can anyone by the power of the stars receive the power to produce those effects. Consequently it follows that these effects are accomplished by an intellect to whom the discourse of the person uttering these words is addressed. We have an indication of this in the fact that the significative words employed by the magician are *invocations, supplications, adjurations,* or even *commands* as though he were addressing another.

Again. Certain characters and definite figures are employed in the observances of this art. Now a figure cannot be the principle of either action or passion; else, mathematical bodies would be active and passive. Therefore, matter cannot, by definite figures, be disposed to receive a certain natural effect. Therefore magicians do not employ figures as dispositions. It remains, then, that they employ them only as signs, for there is no third solution. But we make signs only to other intelligent beings. Therefore the magic arts derive their efficacy from another intelligent being, to whom the magician's words are addressed.

And if someone says that certain figures are appropriate to certain heavenly bodies; and so the lower bodies are determined by certain figures to receive the impressions of certain heavenly bodies:—seemingly this is an unreasonable statement. For the patient is not directed to receive the impression of the agent, except through being in potentiality. Hence those things alone determine it to receive a particular impression, that cause it to be somehow in potentiality. Now figures do not cause matter to be in potentiality to any particular form, because a figure, as such, abstracts from all matter and sensible forms, since it is something mathematical. Therefore a body is not determined by figures or characters to receive the influence of a heavenly body.

Besides. Certain figures are appropriate to heavenly bodies as the effects thereof; for the figures of the lower bodies are caused by heavenly bodies. Now, the aforesaid arts do not use characters or figures as produced by heavenly bodies, in fact they are produced by man in the practice of the art. Therefore the appropriateness of figures to certain heavenly bodies has nothing to do with the question.

Further. As we have shown, matter is nowise disposed to form by means of figures. Hence the bodies on which these figures are impressed are as capable of receiving the influence of heavenly bodies as other bodies of the same species. Now, that a thing act on one rather than another of several equally disposed, by reason of something appropriate to be found in it, is a mark of its operating not by natural necessity, but by choice. Hence it is clear that these arts which employ figures in order to produce certain effects, derive their efficacy, not from something that acts by nature, but from some intellectual substance that acts by intelligence. This is also proved by the very name of *character* which they apply to these figures: for a character is a sign. Whereby we are given to understand that they employ these figures merely as signs shown to some intellectual nature.

Since, however, in the products of art figures are like specific forms, someone might say that there is no reason why, through the influence of a heavenly body, some power should not shape the figure that gives an image its species, not indeed as a figure, but as specifying the product of art, which acquires this power from the stars. But as to the letters that form an inscription on an image, and other characters, nothing else can be said of them, but that they are signs:

wherefore they are directed to an intelligence only. This is also proved by the sacrifices, prostrations and other similar practices, which can be nothing else than signs of reverence shown to an intellectual nature.

That the intellectual substance which gives efficacy to the practices of
magic is not good according to virtue.
We must furthermore inquire what is this intellectual nature by whose power these works are done.

And in the first place it is plain that it is not good and praiseworthy: for it is the mark of an ill-disposed mind to countenance things contrary to virtue. Now this is done in these arts: for they are often employed in order to further adultery, theft, murder and like malefices, wherefore those who practise these arts are called *malefics*. Therefore the intellectual nature on whose assistance these arts depend is not well disposed according to virtue.

Again. It is not the mark of a mind well disposed according to virtue, to befriend and assist men of evil life, rather than every upright man. Now those who practise these arts are often men of evil life. Therefore the intellectual nature from whose assistance these arts derive their efficacy is not well disposed according to virtue.

Further. It is the mark of a well-disposed mind to guide men towards those goods that are proper to man, namely the goods of reason. Consequently to lead men away from these, and to draw men to goods of the least worth, shows a mind of evil disposition. Now by these arts men progress, not in the goods of reason, which are science and virtue, but in goods of least account, such as the discovery of stolen goods, the capture of thieves, and so forth. Therefore the intellectual substances whose assistance these arts employ are not well disposed according to virtue.

Moreover. There is a certain deception and unreasonableness in the works of these arts: for they require a man indifferent to lustful pleasure, whereas they are frequently employed to further lustful intercourse. But there is nothing unreasonable or contradictory in the work of a well-disposed mind. Therefore these arts do not employ the assistance of an intellect that is well disposed as to virtue.

Besides. It is an ill-disposed mind that is incited by the commission of crime to lend his assistance to another. But this is done in these arts: for we read of innocent children being slain by those who practise them. Therefore the persons by whose assistance such things are done have an evil mind.

Again. The proper good of the intellect is truth. Since therefore it belongs to good to lead others to good, it belongs to any well-disposed intellect to lead others to truth. In the works of the magicians, however, many things are done by which men are mocked and deceived. The intellect whose help they use, therefore, is not morally well disposed.

Further. A well-disposed intellect is allured by truth in which it takes delight, but not by lies. The magicians, however, in their invocations make use of various lies, whereby they allure those whose help they employ; for they threaten certain impossible things, as for instance that, unless the one who is called upon gives help, he who invokes him will shatter the heavens or displace the stars, as Porphyry narrates in his *Letter to Anebolites. Those* intellectual substances, therefore, with whose help the works of the magicians are performed do not seem to be intellectually well disposed.

Moreover. That a superior should be subject as an inferior to one that commands him; or that an inferior should allow himself to be invoked as a superior, would seem to indicate a person of an ill-disposed mind. Now, magicians call upon those whose assistance they employ, as though these were their superiors: and as soon as they appear they command them as inferiors. In no way therefore are they seemingly of a well-disposed mind.

Hereby we refute the error of pagans who ascribed these works to the gods.

14
From the *Summa theologiae*:
The Demons Tempt Man

This passage from the *Summa theologiae* offers an excellent example of the distinctive method of academic argument and exposition of a thesis, or what is commonly called the "scholastic" method. The method consists of stating a problem, usually in the form of a question ("Whether . . ."), stating the strongest possible arguments against the position one will take oneself ("Objection 1, 2, 3," and so on), citing a single authoritative text that speaks against the objections always in the form "But against these . . ." (*Sed contra . . .*), stating one's own response to the question, and finally explaining how one's own response overcomes the initial objections. The method forced the theologian or philosopher to consider all possible perspectives on a particular question and to deal with the most formidable arguments against his own position. The method also required the writer to list, and hence inform his audience about, positions diametrically opposed to his own and potentially to dogmatic orthodoxy.

The technical references are to the second part of the second part (*secunda secundae*) of the *Summa*. The *Summa* itself is divided into questions, which are in turn divided into articles. Questions 94 to 96 deal most broadly with the general problem of superstition, under which Aquinas discusses demonology and idolatry, the underlying theological and legal category into which sorcery and witchcraft fall.

SOURCE: *The "Summa Theologica" of St. Thomas Aquinas*, literally translated by Fathers of the English Dominican Province, second part of the second part, question 94 (XCIV) (London, 1912), pp. 496–505.

FURTHER READING: Thomas Franklin O'Meara, *Thomas Aquinas Theologian* (Notre Dame, 1997); Leonard E. Boyle, "The *Summa Confessorum* of John of Freiburg and the Popularization of the Moral Teaching of St. Thomas and Some of His Contemporaries," in *St. Thomas, 1274–1294*, ed. Armand A. Maurer (Toronto, 1974), 2: 245–68; Charles Edward Hopkin, *The Share of Thomas Aquinas in the Growth of the Witchcraft Delusion* (Philadelphia, 1940; repr. New York, 1982); Russell, *Witchcraft*, 142–48; Cohn, *Europe's Inner Demons*, 174–79; Veenstra, *Magic and Divination*, 157–60.

Of the assaults of the Demons. (in Five Articles.)
We now consider the assaults of the demons. Concerning this we have five points of inquiry: (1) Whether men are assailed by the demons? (2) Whether to tempt is proper to the devil? (3) Whether all the sins of men are to be set down to the assaults or temptations of the demons? (4) Whether they can work real miracles for the purpose of leading men astray? (5) Whether the demons who are overcome by men, are hindered from making further assaults?

First Article

Whether men are assailed by the demons?
We proceed thus to the First Article:
Objection 1. It seems that men are not assailed by the demons. For angels are sent by God to guard man. But demons are not sent by God: for the demons' intention is the loss of souls; whereas God's is the salvation of souls. Therefore demons are not deputed to assail man.

Objection 2. Further, it is not a fair fight, for the weak to be set against the strong, and the ignorant against the astute. But men are weak and ignorant, whereas the demons are strong and astute. It is not therefore to be permitted by God, the author of all justice, that men should be assailed by demons.

Objection 3. Further, the assaults of the flesh and the world are enough for man's exercise. But God permits His elect to be assailed that they may be exercised. Therefore there is no need for them to be assailed by the demons.

On the contrary. The Apostle says (Eph. vi. 12): *Our wrestling is not against flesh and blood; but against principalities and powers, against the rulers of the world of this darkness, against the spirits of wickedness in the high places.*

I answer that, Two things may be considered in the assault of the demons—the assault itself, and the ordering thereof. The assault itself is due to the malice of the demons, who through envy endeavour to hinder man's progress; and through pride usurp a semblance of Divine power, by deputing certain ministers to assail man, as the angels of God in their various offices minister to man's salvation. But the ordering of the assault is from God, Who knows how to make orderly use of evil by ordering it to good. On the other hand, in regard to the angels, both their guardianship and the ordering thereof are to be referred to God as their first author.

Reply to Objection 1. The wicked angels assail men in two ways. Firstly by instigating them to sin; and thus they are not sent by God to assail us, but are sometimes permitted to do so according to God's just judgments. But sometimes their assault is a punishment to man: and thus they are sent by God; as the lying spirit was sent to punish Ahab, King of Israel, as is related in 3 Kings (xxii. 20). For punishment is referred to God as its first author. Nevertheless the demons who are sent to punish, do so with an intention other from that for which they are sent; for they punish from hatred or envy; whereas they are sent by God on account of His justice.

Reply to Objection 2. In order that the conditions of the fight be not unequal, there is as regards man the promised recompense, to be gained principally through the grace of God, secondarily through the guardianship of the angels. Wherefore (4 Kings [2 Kings] vi. 16), Eliseus said to his servant: *Fear not, for there are more with us than with them.*

Reply to Objection 3. The assault of the flesh and the world would suffice for the exercise of human weakness: but it does not suffice for the demon's malice, which makes use of both the above in assailing men. But by the Divine ordinance this tends to the glory of the elect.

Second Article

Whether to tempt is proper to the devil?
We proceed thus to the Second Article:

Objection 1. It seems that to tempt is not proper to the devil. For God is said to tempt, according to Genesis xxii. 1, *God tempted Abraham.* Moreover man is tempted by the flesh and the world. Again, man is said to tempt God, and to tempt man. Therefore it is not proper to the devil to tempt.

Objection 2. Further, to tempt is a sign of ignorance. But the demons know what happens among men. Therefore the demons do not tempt.

Objection 3. Further, temptation is the road to sin. Now sin dwells in the will. Since therefore the demons cannot change man's will, as appears from what has been said above, it seems that it is not in their province to tempt.

On the contrary, It is written (1 Thess. iii. 5): *Lest perhaps he that tempteth should have tempted you:* to which the gloss adds, *that is, the devil, whose office it is to tempt.*

I answer that, To tempt is, properly speaking, to make trial of something. Now we make trial of something in order to know something about it: hence the immediate end of every tempter is knowledge. But sometimes another end, either good or bad, is sought to be acquired through that knowledge; a good end, when, for instance, one desires to know of someone, what sort of a man he is as to knowledge, or virtue, with a view to his promotion; a bad end, when that knowledge is sought with the purpose of deceiving or ruining him.

From this we can gather how various beings are said to tempt in various ways. For man is said to tempt, sometimes indeed merely for the sake of knowing something: and for this reason it is a sin to tempt God; for man, being uncertain as it were, presumes to make an experiment of God's power. Sometimes too he tempts in order to help, sometimes in order to hurt. The devil, however, always tempts in order to hurt by urging man into sin. In this sense it is said to be his proper office to tempt: for though at times man tempts thus, he does this as a minister of the devil. God is said to tempt that He may know, in the same sense as that is said to know which makes others to know. Hence it is written (Deut. xiii. 3): *The Lord your God trieth you, that it may appear whether you love Him.*

The flesh and the world are said to tempt as the instruments or matter of temptations; inasmuch as one can know what sort of a man someone is, according as he follows or resists the desire of the flesh, and according as he despises worldly advantages and adversity: of which things the devil also makes use in tempting.

Thus the reply to the first objection is clear.

Reply to Objection 2. The demons know what happens outwardly among men; but the inward disposition of man God alone knows, Who is the *weigher of spirits* (Prov. xvi. 2). It is this disposition that makes man more prone to one vice than to another: hence the devil tempts, in order to explore this inward disposition of man, so that he may tempt him to that vice to which he is most prone.

Reply to Objection 3. Although a demon cannot change the will, yet, as stated above, he can change the inferior powers of man, in a certain degree: by which powers, though the will cannot be forced, it can nevertheless be inclined.

Third Article

Whether all sins are due to the temptations of the devil?
We proceed thus to the Third Article:

Objection 1. It seems that all sins are due to the temptation of the devil. For Dionysius says (*Div. Nom.* iv.) that *the multitude of demons is the cause of all evils, both to themselves and to others.* And Damascene says (*De Fide Orth.* ii.) that *all malice and all uncleanness have been devised by the devil.*

Objection 2. Further, of every sinner can be said what the Lord said of the Jews (John viii. 44): *You are of your father the devil.* But this was in as far as they sinned through the devil's instigation. Therefore every sin is due to the devil's instigation.

Objection 3. Further, as angels are deputed to guard men, so demons are deputed to assail men. But every good thing we do is due to the suggestion of the good angels; because the Divine gifts are borne to us by the angels. Therefore all the evil we do, is due to the instigation of the devil.

On the contrary, It is written (*De Eccl. Dogmat.*): *Not all our evil thoughts are stirred up by the devil, but sometimes they arise from the movement of our freewill.*

I answer that, One thing can be the cause of another in two ways; directly and indirectly. Indirectly as when an agent is the cause of a disposition to a certain effect, it is said to be the occasional and indirect cause of that effect: for instance, we might say that he who dries the wood is the cause of the wood burning. In this way we must admit that the devil is the cause of all our sins; because he it was who instigated the first man to sin, from whose sin there resulted a proneness to sin in the whole human race: and in this sense we must take the words of Damascene and Dionysius.

But a thing is said to be the direct cause of something, when its action tends directly thereunto. And in this way the devil is not the cause of every sin: for all sins are not committed at the devil's instigation, but some are due to the free-will and the corruption of the flesh. For, as Origen says (*Peri Archon* iii.), even if there were no devil, men would have the desire for food and love and suchlike pleasures; with regard to which many disorders may arise unless those desires be curbed by reason, especially if we presuppose the corruption of our natures. Now it is in the power of the free-will to curb this appetite and keep it in order. Consequently there is no need for all sins to be due to the instigation of the devil. But those sins which are due thereto man perpetrates *through being deceived by the same blandishments as were our first parents,* as Isidore says (*De Summo Bono* iii.).

Thus the answer to the first objection is clear.

Reply to Objection 2. When man commits sin without being thereto instigated by the devil, he nevertheless becomes a child of the devil thereby, in so far as he imitates him who was the first to sin.

Reply to Objection 3. Man can of his own accord fall into sin: but he cannot advance in merit without the Divine assistance, which is borne to man by the ministry of the angels. For this reason the angels take part in all our good works: whereas all our sins are not due to the demons' instigation. Nevertheless there is no kind of sin which is not sometimes due to the demons' suggestion.

Fourth Article

Whether demons can lead men astray by means of real miracles?
We proceed thus to the Fourth Article:

Objection 1. It seems that the demons cannot lead men astray by means of real miracles. For the activity of the demons will show itself especially in the works of Antichrist. But as the Apostle says (2 Thess. ii. 9), his *coming is according to the working of Satan, in all power, and signs, and lying wonders.* Much more therefore at other times do the demons perform only lying wonders.

Objection 2. Further, true miracles are wrought by some corporeal change. But demons are unable to change the nature of a body; for Augustine says (*De Civ.* xviii.); *I cannot believe that the human body can receive the limbs of a beast by means of a demon's art or power.* Therefore the demons cannot work real miracles.

Objection 3. Further, an argument is useless which may prove both ways. If therefore real miracles can be wrought by demons, to persuade one of what is false, they will be useless to confirm the teaching of faith. This is unfitting; for it is written (Mark xvi. 20): *The Lord working withal, and confirming the word with signs that followed.*

On the contrary, Augustine says (*Qq.* 83): *Often by means of the magic art miracles are wrought like those which are wrought by the servants of God.*

I answer that, As is clear from what has been said above, if we take a miracle in the strict sense, the demons cannot work miracles, nor can any creature, but God alone: since in the strict sense a miracle is something done outside the order of the entire created nature, under which order every power of a creature is contained. But sometimes miracle may be taken in a wide sense, for whatever exceeds the human power and experience. And thus demons can work miracles, that is, things which rouse man's astonishment, by reason of their being beyond his power and outside his sphere of knowledge. For even a man by doing what is beyond the power and knowledge of another, leads him to marvel at what he has done, so that in a way he seems to that man to have worked a miracle.

It is to be noted, however, that although these works of demons which appear marvellous to us are not real miracles, they are sometimes nevertheless something real. Thus the magicians of Pharaoh by the demons' power produced real serpents and frogs. *And when fire came down from heaven and at one blow consumed Job's servants and sheep; when the storm struck down his house and with it his children—these were the work of Satan; not phantoms;* as Augustine says (*De Civ. Dei* xx.).

Reply to Objection 1. As Augustine says in the same place, the works of Antichrist may be called lying wonders, *either because he will deceive men's senses by means of phantoms, so that he will not really do what he will seem to do; or because, if he work real prodigies, they will lead those into falsehood who believe in him.*

Reply to Objection 2. As we have said above, corporeal matter does not obey either good or bad angels at their will, so that demons be able by their power to transmute matter from one form to another; but they can employ certain seeds that exist in the elements of the world, in order to produce these effects, as Augustine says (*De Trin.* iii.). Therefore it must be admitted that all the transformations of corporeal things which can be produced by certain natural powers, to which we must assign the seeds above mentioned, can alike be produced by the operation of the demons, by the employment of these seeds; such as the transformation of certain things into serpents or frogs, which can be produced by putrefaction. On the contrary, those transformations which cannot be produced by the power of nature, cannot in reality be effected by the operation of the demons; for instance, that the human body be changed into the body of a beast, or that the body of a dead man return to life. And if at times something of this sort seems to be effected by the operation of demons, it is not real but a mere semblance of reality.

Now this may happen in two ways. Firstly, from within; in this way a demon can work on man's imagination and even on his corporeal senses, so that something seems otherwise than it is, as explained above. It is said indeed that this can be done sometimes by the power of certain bodies. Secondly, from without: for just as he can from the air form a body of any form and shape, and assume it so as to appear in it visibly: so, in the same way he can clothe any corporeal thing with any corporeal form, so as to appear therein. This is what Augustine says (*De Civ. Dei* xviii.): *Man's imagination, which, whether thinking or dreaming, takes the forms of an innumerable number of things, appears to other men's senses, as it were embodied in the semblance of some animal.* This it not to be understood as though the imagination itself or the images formed therein were identified with that which appears embodied to the senses of another man: but that the demon who forms an image in a man's imagination, can offer the same picture to another man's senses.

Reply to Objection 3. As Augustine says (*Qq.* 83): *When magicians do what holy men do, they do it for a different end and by a different right. The former do it for their own glory: the latter, for the glory of God: the former, by certain private compacts: the latter by the evident assistance and command of God, to Whom every creature is subject.*

Fifth Article

Whether a demon who is overcome by man, is for this reason hindered from making further assaults?

We proceed thus to the Fifth Article:

Objection 1. It seems that a demon who is overcome by a man is not for that reason hindered from any further assault. For Christ overcame the tempter most effectively. Yet afterwards the demon assailed Him by instigating the Jews to kill Him. Therefore it is not true that the devil when conquered ceases his assaults.

Objection 2. Further, to inflict punishment on one who has been worsted in a fight, is to incite him to a sharper attack. But this is not befitting God's mercy. Therefore the conquered demons are not prevented from further assaults.

On the contrary, It is written (Matt. iv. 11): *Then the devil left Him, i.e.,* Christ who overcame.

I answer that, some say that when once a demon has been overcome he can no more tempt any man at all, neither to the same nor to any other sin. And others say that he can tempt others, but not the same man. This seems more probable as long as we understand it to be so for a certain definite time: wherefore (Luke iv. 13) it is written: *All temptation being ended, the devil departed from Him for a time.* There are two reasons for this. One is on the part of God's clemency; for as Chrysostom says (*Super Matt. Hom.* v.), *the devil does not tempt man for just as long as he likes, but for as long as God allows; for although He allows him to tempt for a short time, He orders him off on account of our weakness.* The other reason is taken from the astuteness of the devil. As to this, Ambrose says on Luke iv. 13: *The devil is afraid of persisting, because he shrinks from frequent defeat.* That the devil does nevertheless sometimes return to the assault, is apparent from Matthew xii. 44: *I will return into my house from whence I came out.*

From what has been said, the objections can easily be solved.

15
From *Quodlibet* XI:
Sorcery and Sexual Impotence

The *quodlibet* was another form of academic exposition in which students and professors debated on "whatever one wished" (*quodlibet*), in the form of scholastic questions, as in their longer works of exposition.

SOURCE: St. Thomas Aquinas, *Quodlibet* XI, *Quaestio* IX, *Art.* X, *Utrum maleficia impediant matrimonium,* from St. Thomas Aquinas, *Opera omnia,* vol. 9 (Parma, 1859), p. 618. Trans. E. P.

FURTHER READING: Above, literature cited in Text 9.

Question: Whether the effects of sorcery are an impediment to matrimony?

It would seem that they are not. Since the works of God are stronger than those of the Devil, matrimony being a work of God and sorcery being a work of the

Devil, matrimony is therefore stronger than sorcery, and sorcery may not in itself constitute an impediment.

On the other hand, it may be said that the Devil's power is greater than that of man. Since man may impede matrimony, therefore the Devil may also impede it.

I answer that matrimony is a kind of contract. Now by matrimony one person delivers the rights over his body to another for sexual intercourse. We may in fact contend that a contract concerning that which is impossible is no contract at all, since no one may obligate himself to perform the impossible. Hence, when someone obligates himself by matrimony to sexual intercourse, and sexual intercourse is impossible for him, then the marriage does not exist. But it must be noted that the impossibility of sexual intercourse from any intervening impediment may be considered in two ways. Either the impediment intervenes in a marriage which has already been consummated or in one which has not yet been consummated. If it intervenes after a marriage has already been consummated, then the marriage may not be dissolved. If it occurs before the marriage has been consummated, then the marriage may be dissolved.

One should note, moreover, that impediments of this kind may be either permanent or temporary. If they are permanent, then that marriage is absolutely impeded. If they are temporary, then that marriage is impeded only for a time. This is so in both cases in which the impediment precedes consummation.

Concerning sorcerers, it is known that some say that sorcery has no existence and that it comes simply from lack of belief or superstition, since they wish to prove that demons do not exist except insofar as they are the creatures of man's imagination; insofar as men imagine them to exist, these fantasies afflict the fearful. The catholic faith, on the other hand, insists that demons do indeed exist and that they may impede sexual intercourse by their works. These impediments then, if they precede consummation and are permanent, impede matrimony absolutely.

To the first point I respond that the Devil himself, as well as matrimony, is the work of God. And among the works of God some are stronger than others. One of them may be impeded by another which is stronger. Whence, since the Devil is stronger than matrimony, nothing prevents that through his agency matrimony may be impeded.

16
From the *Commentary on the Four Books of Sentences*: Sorcery and Exorcism

The *Four Books of Sentences* by the Paris theologian Peter Lombard (who may be considered the intellectual successor of Hugh of St. Victor) became the standard teaching text for students of systematic theology virtually from its first appearance in the mid-twelfth century. The commentary of Thomas Aquinas was only one of many; a commentary on Lombard's *Book of Sentences* was virtually the subject of every theologian's doctoral dissertation. Lombard discusses magic only briefly, characteristically for the period, and chiefly in Book II, distinction 7, chapter 6, where he states that the magical arts derive their power from the devil, with God's permission, either to confound the wicked or to warn or test the good, and he relies only on a single text, Augustine's *On the Trinity*, Book III.

SOURCE: St. Thomas Aquinas, *Commentary on the Four Books of Sentences* (Venice, 1481), *Distinctio* 34, art. 3 *ad* 3, unnumbered folios. Trans. E. P.

FURTHER READING: Marcia Colish, *Peter Lombard*, 2 vols. (Leiden and New York, 1994); Colish, *Medieval Foundations*, 282–86.

SORCERY IS THEREFORE to be considered permanent because remedy may not be had for it by human agency, although God may impose a remedy either by forcing the Devil or even against the resistance of the Devil. It is never proper that that which is accomplished by sorcery should be destroyed by yet other sorcery, as if sorcery were to testify to its own authenticity. If it were possible to find a remedy by sorcery, then the effects of sorcery would nonetheless continue to be permanent, so no one ought by any means to invoke the aid of a demon through sorcery. Likewise, it is not proper that if, on account of our sins, a certain power over our person is given to the demon, the power should cease when the sin ceases, because the punishment remains, although the sin has gone. Thus, even the exorcisms of the Church are not always efficacious in driving out demons, insofar as the divine judgment requires [them] for all punishments of the body. Exorcisms are always efficacious, however, against those specific infestations against which they were first instituted.

17
Jacopo Passavanti: *The Mirror of True Penitence* (ca. 1350)

Jacopo Passavanti (d. 1357) was a fourteenth-century Dominican theologian in Florence, whose manual for confessors, *Lo specchio della vera penitenzia*, "The Mirror of True Penitence," was immensely popular throughout Tuscany and beyond. Passavanti was recognized in his lifetime as a scholar of "exceptional learning in both human and divine letters" and of considerable eloquence. The book was first printed in 1495. In works like Passavanti's *Mirror* and in the slightly earlier *Summa confessorum* of John of Freiburg, the learned doctrines of theologians like Aquinas and others were adapted to suit the actual practice of advising—and teaching—confessors. In Passavanti's case the language used was Tuscan, making the text even more widely available than it might have been in Latin. The first excerpt translates the theologians' demonology to the confessor's level. The second considers a remarkable variety of allegedly magical practices, ranging from high learned magic, through fraud, down to the practices at the lowest levels of knowledge and society.

SOURCE: Jacopo Passavanti, *Lo specchio della vera penitenzia* (Florence, 1725), 236–39, 240–41, 242. Trans. E. P.

THE THIRD KIND OF knowledge is diabolical knowledge. And it is called diabolical knowledge in two senses. Either it is that kind of knowledge which the devil has of things that he knows [below: I], or it is the learning by which men know, or wish to know, what the devil knows, or to learn from the devil [below: II].

Concerning the Knowledge of Demons: I
The first kind of diabolical knowledge is that by which the devil knows what he knows, and this knowledge is very great because the devil, although having sinned and lost grace and glory, did not lose his natural knowledge, which God the creator placed in the angelic nature. Therefore, as the devil did not lose any of his natural and efficient substance, so he did not lose any of his natural knowledge, by virtue of which he is most excellently, more so than any man, whether by natural genius or by the most laborious study, competent in all of the sciences and the arts, having the clearest understanding and insight, not only in general, but specifically and singularly in all things natural, spiritual, and corporeal. Hence, the devil knows from God only that which natural understanding knows without the illumination of divine grace. He knows separate substances, namely the angels and their substance, their natural properties, their orders, and their offices and the virtue and extent of their natural powers. He knows the stars and planets and their places, spheres, and circles, their heights and quantities, their differences and properties, their courses, equations, conjunctions, and judgments, as well as their influences, virtues, inclinations, and varieties.

He also knows the nature and substance of the soul, its intellective, sensible, and appetitive potencies, both its proper operations independently of the body, and those that are performed in conjunction with the body. The devil also knows the nature and properties of the elements, the complexions of bodies, the nature and species of fishes, of birds and beasts, of trees, of nature, of the qualities of the virtues of herbs, and of precious stones, the manners of gold and of silver and of other metals, and, to put it briefly, he knows everything that it is possible to know, whether it is to be known naturally or by the exercise of any human intellect.

The Doctors, considering his vast knowledge, have asked whether he knows the thoughts of the human heart, and whether he knows those things that will come to pass in the future. And they respond first concerning the thoughts of the heart, and they say that these thoughts may be known in two ways. By one way they are knowable in their effects, which are perceptible from outside, and in this manner they may be known not from the devil, but from the observation of external signs of internal thought. Some men have a capacity for most subtle judgment, either by their own natural disposition or by their learning or by their experience of hidden things. Hence, not only by observation of external signs, but also by a semblance of perception, by changes of facial expression and suchlike these can see the thoughts and affections that are inside a man, as do expert physicians by examining the pulse or by other means recognizing the dispositions, thoughts, and passions, as well as the affections of the soul, such as love, fear, sadness, and many other passions.

The other means by which it is possible to recognize interior thoughts is according to the intellect or the affections, as much as to say according to the will or the heart. And according to this mode, no creature who is external to man is able to perceive, but only God, to whom the will and the heart of man are subject and manifest without the means of any intermediary, as St. Augustine proves in his book *On the Divination by Demons*, and so does St. Thomas in his *Summa*. This, God said by the Prophet Jeremiah: [In Latin] "Debased is the heart of man, and inscrutable, and who knoweth this? I, God, scrutinizing the heart." [In Tuscan] "The heart of man is deep and perverse, and it cannot be searched out. Who, then can search it out? I, who am the Lord, search out all hearts." . . . Therefore, the devil cannot know the thoughts and will of the human heart except in such a way as can be perceived by act or sign, or by something else that manifests itself externally. And from this it follows that the devil knows all that men say, and all that men do, and all that which men practice in whatever place and at whatever time, and in what way. And it also follows from this that the devil knows what men fantasize and imagine, and what they dream, insofar as the actions of imagination and dream are not closed within the human intellect or will, but are corporeal sentiments, and can be perceived by external signs.

Concerning the devil's knowledge of things which have not yet happened but will happen in the future, the Doctors say that he is able to know this in two ways. One way is by knowing their causes, and in this way the devil knows by a certain knowledge events that will happen in the future to the extent that they follow from necessity and will occur, as that the Sun will rise tomorrow, that the Sun will be obscured when the Moon rises, as is the case will all events that occur from necessity. But when those things which are to occur in the future do not follow from necessity, these things cannot be known with certainty, but by conjecture and sharp thought, as does the physician who knows the causes of health from the science of medicine, and because of having cured the sick, he can know and predict the future health of the sick patient.

But when events which are to come follow from unique causes, these things cannot be known. These are such things as happen at random or through chance or contingency or from such causes that do not lend themselves to rational understanding. Thus, one way of knowing the future is manifest and clear to the devil, just as it is to men, when they understand the causes of things more perfectly, as in the case of the physician, who understands subtly the causes of health and is able better and with greater certainty to predict the future state of the sick patient and the state of health which has yet to occur. But the devil does not have an understanding of random events. But sometimes his predictions about these things come true, and this is not because he has any particular understanding of them, but by some guessing, some information, as could be possible in the case of a man.

It sometimes happens that one finds people who favor the side of the devil and who say that the devil can indeed know random or particular things which have not yet happened and that he knows how to predict them. To these we respond that they do not speak the truth and that they lie, like him whose side they favor, who is, as Christ has said of him, A liar, and the father of lies. . . .

From the great understanding and knowledge on the part of the devil it follows that he has vast power and many abilities; that, as the Doctors say, all of the nature of corporeal things is subject to good angels and to the bad as well, who have a natural ability to move a thing from one place to another. Whence there is no great body, nor city, nor castle, nor mountain that the devil cannot move, and move quickly. And this is true also of other things, both major and minor. And because he knows every science and every art, he is able to join one thing to another, because all things must obey him, as far as concerns local motion. And he is able to do and to simulate marvelous things. I do not say, of course, that the devil is able to perform true miracles, but marvelous things, understanding by true miracles properly those things which we know to be above or outside of the true order of nature, such as raising a dead man or creating something out of nothing, or restoring sight to the blind, and things like these. And such miracles God alone can perform.

But I call marvels certain things which men do not understand and are unable to perform themselves, so that when men see them done, they marvel at them, because they do not understand their causes and the methods of doing them. And the devil can certainly perform many of these things; for example, he can quickly make many serpents appear, not because he has created them out of nothing, but because he can move them from some forest where they are, or from some other place. He can raise up tempests at sea and in the air. And he can cure a sick person, not instantly and without medicine, which would be a true miracle, but with appropriate medicines, the kind that he can make far better than any physician that there may be in the world. Or he can cure an illness that he himself has inflicted, by removing the causes that have brought about the disease, and thus he can make the sick person well so that it appears as if he has cured him.

But with all of his knowledge and all of his power, of which Scripture says, "There is nothing like it upon the earth," the devil cannot change the will of a human, concerning which, and concerning especially the intellective part, the devil has no rule and no force, properly speaking. Whence he cannot put a thought into the human heart, nor a desire, that the human does not already wish to have. Whence he cannot enter or work in the human heart or mind unless a man opens up his heart and mind to him, so that he is able to enter it. For if he could insert whatever he wishes into a human heart, considering his great malice and his obstinate will toward evil and the hateful envy that he bears toward humans, no one would be able to survive his attack. As a consequence he could deprive man of his will, and the man would be responsible neither for his good deeds nor for his sins. . . .

The devil can transform the imagination and fantasy and can make a sleeping man dream and he can make apparitions appear and make the sleeping man imagine figures, impressions, likenesses to certain fearful things, delights, terrible things, or even true things, or things which might be true. . . .

We read in the lives of the Holy Fathers of the relatives of a young girl who had turned into a horse. And in the books of the poets there are accounts of plenty of these transformations, as is shown in the *Metamorphoses* of Ovid and *The Golden Ass* of the Platonist Apuleius. And all of these things, as St. Augustine shows in his book called *The City of God* do not happen truly, but only appear to happen, since the devil plays and fascinates both by his intelligence and by his ability to control the eyes of those who see his wonders. Whence the Holy Father told the relatives of the young girl whom they thought had been transformed into a horse that he saw a young girl and not a horse. And he prayed, and praying to God, that their eyes might be opened and that the image of the terrible horse that the devil had put into their eyes might depart, they perceived their young relative in her true form, which had not been changed but only appeared to have been changed. The devil cannot change one thing substantively into another, transforming the nature of things, or creating something out of nothing, which is proper only to God, although he can make things appear to change (p. 202 below).

Concerning the Knowledge of Demons: II

The other kind of diabolical knowledge is that by which humans want to know and be able to do certain things which the devil can know and do. And they wish to learn to do these things from the devil. Whence it should be known how the devil, desiring always the perdition of men, has found certain ways by which he is able to lead them finally to perdition. Outside those ways to perdition that are common to all humans, the vices and sins, the devil has introduced into the world a new path to perdition, upon which many men have set their feet, and enter on it with great delight, not at all considering the great danger and final damnation to which it leads. And this consists of a certain science and art which the devil has taught and revealed to certain wicked men [*uomini malefici*] since the beginning of the world, and especially after the Flood. This is the knowledge of certain hidden things and by it to acquire the ability to perform certain acts that are normally impossible for humans to do, as were those of Zoroaster and Hermes Trismegistus and others, who wrote books by which this cursed art was taught to many, and it is called generally the magical art, although it also is of many different kinds, modes, observances, and rites which have special names in the art. All the things told and done according to this art are condemned by both God and the Church because they all require an express or tacit pact with the demons.

[Passavanti then lists the many varieties of magical practices from the lists of St. Augustine and Isidore of Seville, cites their condemnation in Scripture, including the strictures of Leviticus and Deuteronomy and the episode of the "witch" of En-dor, in human and canon law, in theologians like Aquinas, and then turns to what he regards as the equally dangerous practices of the unlearned.]

And although the aforementioned magical art has much power, according to the inscrutable will of God, who allows it because of the innumerable sins of the magicians who follow the rules and teachings transmitted by demons, sometimes it displays itself through certain persons of low condition, both men and women who do not understand the art and cannot use it, since in any case only a few people know how to use it. Nevertheless these low people adopt the art and find certain incantations, conjurations, writings, and ligatures which when used with certain observances seem to bear certain resemblances with the magical art but have nothing to do with it. Perhaps these people who do this believe and have faith that they are doing what the magicians do, with the advice and counsel of the devil and that what they do is efficacious by the working of the devil who favors every wicked deed, and takes command and gains power over such persons who, not in reality or in fact, but according to their intention, are magicians, believing that the things they do are the magical art of the devil. From which it is certain that they sin mortally. . . .

There are also certain other people, both men and women, who do not know the magical art, nor do they invoke it, nor do they conjure up demons, and are not fortune-tellers, but claim that they are enchanters and fortune-tellers out of vanity or for some other interest, and by these claims fool many simple people who are prone to believe in this kind of thing. And they claim that they see the dead and speak with them and that they go at night in company with witches [*streghe*]. Others say that they know incantations against diseases of the eye or of toothache, migraine, and other ills, and they write charms which people wear on themselves. . . . All of these people are frauds and tricksters, and they sin mortally. . . .

And so one finds that demons, assuming the likeness of actual men and women, travel in the night in company in a place where they are seen by other people who then believe that they are really the people whom they pretend to be. And in some places this is called the *tregenda*. And the demons do this in order to disseminate this error and to spread scandal and to make infamous those people whose likenesses they have adopted, showing them to have done certain dishonest things at the *tregenda*. And there are people, especially women, who claim that they themselves travel at night in company with this *tregenda* and who name the names of many in their company. And they say that the ladies of this group who lead the others are Herodias, who had John the Baptist killed, and Diana, the ancient goddess of the Greeks.

IV

Popes, Theologians, Preachers, Lawyers, and Judges, 1230–1430

THE COMPLEX MECHANISMS and ontology of the spiritual and material universe, which the writings of St. Thomas and his fellow scholastic philosophers (however much they may have disagreed with one another over questions of particulars) had described in overwhelming, persuasive, and above all, systematic detail, afforded thinkers of the thirteenth and fourteenth centuries a convincing and, indeed, irrefutable rationale and method for approaching systematically the problems of diabolism, heresy, and now diabolical sorcery. The papacy, the investigative institutions of the church—particularly bishops and the inquisitors of heretical depravity—and local preachers, confessors, and theologians, all drawing upon an increasingly common body of theory and experience, reflected in their writings the slow process by which isolated cases of sorcery, "witchcraft," and possession came to be conceived as being similar reflections of a systematic assault on humans by Satan and his followers, the demons, diabolical sorcerers, and, later, witches. Instrumental in his process were the developing concepts of idolatry and superstition, which could include both learned magic and practical sorcery. Equally important were the descriptions of imagined activities of heretics, many of which were derived from older Roman descriptions of the imagined activities of Christians (Text 1) and later adaptations of these to heretics.

The next major—and the first official (papally issued)—collection of canon law after Gratian was the *Liber extra* (that is, the Book that goes beyond [*extra*] Gratian), issued by Pope Gregory IX in 1234 and formally dispatched to the canon law faculty at the University of Bologna. In Book V, which concerned criminal law broadly conceived, title 21, three more texts were added concerning magic and divination, two of which concerned the clerical practice of nondiabolical divination, and the third of which (X.5.21.2 *Ex tuarum*) was a letter from Pope Alexander III to the Patriarch of Grado condemning a priest who had turned to magic in order to recover goods that had been stolen from a church, for which the priest had to undergo a penance.[1]

The institution of the office of inquisitor of heretical depravity in the 1230s, however, raised many questions of law and procedure in matters of ecclesiastical discipline that were not always fully thought out or categorically settled. One question that inquisitors logically raised (given the discussion in Gratian and the *Liber extra*) was whether or not they needed to take cognizance of sorcery and divination in their investigation of heresy. In 1258 some inquisitors asked Pope Alexander IV (1254–61) for permission to add sorcery to those matters of ecclesiastical discipline of which they could take judicial cognizance. Alexander refused the request, but he left an important opening for later action. In his decretal letter *Quod super nonullis* of the same year (Text 19), Alexander allowed that inquisitors could try sorcerers and witches only if there was evidence of manifest heresy in their cases.

In the next official collection of canon law, the *Liber sextus* (the sixth book that follows the five books of the *Liber extra*), issued by Pope Boniface VIII (1294–1303) in 1298, Boniface included the decretal of Alexander IV and added one of his own confirming it. The problem of the inquisitors and sorcery now became a matter for the law schools, and the problem had to be made legally precise. It remained for the inquisitors, theologians, professors, and canon lawyers to find the means of identifying sorcery and witchcraft with heresy (Johannes Andreae in Text 19) and for preachers and confessors to warn the faithful of their consequences.

In the 1320s Pope John XXII (1316–34) expressed a particular fear and horror of sorcerers and claimed that he feared for his own life at their hands. His and others' remarks concerning diabolical sorcery (Texts 20–21) reveal a widespread acceptance of the existence and danger of diabolical sorcery, whether performed by men or women—even the poet Dante Alighieri was not immune to John's suspicions—its association with the devil, and its relation to heresy.

Dante himself, in his *Inferno* devoted a canto (*Inf.* 20) to sorcery. The activities condemned in it may be said to reflect general understanding at the turn of the fourteenth century. Dante first condemns divination, embodied by figures from classical antiquity who walk with their heads turned facing backward (an appropriate punishment for those who professed to see into the future). He then condemns three figures from his own time and an earlier generation for learned magic. Finally, he condemns a group of women "who have left the needle, the spool, and the spindle" (that is, the appropriate domestic occupations for women) and instead have told fortunes and cast spells with herbs and images. Dante thus offers a range of those concerns about various forms of magic which probably interested his contemporaries and readers.

---

1. Other texts dealing with the same subject are translated in G. G. Coulton, *Life in the Middle Ages*, vol. 1, *Religion, Folk-Lore and Superstition* (Cambridge, 1930), 160–63.

Yet another approach was taken by the inquisitors themselves. In the literary genre known as inquisitors' handbooks, writers like Bernard Gui (ca. 1323) and Nicolau Eymeric laid down in painstaking detail the categories of heresy and the methods for discovering, judging, and disciplining it. Eymeric's *Directorium inquisitorum*, completed in 1376 (Text 22), reflects particularly the systematic and detailed assimilation of diabolical sorcery to biblical, patristic, and recent legal tradition, particularly to the problem of idolatry. Eymeric's text was widely circulated and printed early, and it was reprinted with a substantial commentary by the greatest sixteenth-century authority on the Holy Office, Francisco Peña, late in the sixteenth century.

By the late fourteenth century trials of people accused of diabolical sorcery—initially in a series of political trials in France, but later also in England and elsewhere in the famous case of the Order of Knights Templar from 1308 to 1316—became more frequent and more widely publicized, to such an extent that the faculty of theology of the University of Paris felt compelled to issue a general condemnation of all of its aspects (Text 23) in 1398.[2] Preachers, too, railed widely against these practices, increasingly focusing on women, particularly as did St. Bernardino of Siena in a famous sermon of 1427 (Text 24).

By the early fifteenth century, diabolical sorcery had been closely assimilated to traditional (since 1200) ideas of heresy, and traditional learned and half-learned magic had also been assimilated to diabolical sorcery. These offenses had been defined and acted against by the highest and most influential ecclesiastical and lay authorities of Christian Europe. They had also served as the grounds of accusation and conviction in a number of political and ecclesiastical trials. Diabolism, the still-debated sabbat, and the fear of a conspiracy motivated by an undeviating and collaborative hostility toward Christian society had become the mark of all diabolical sorcerers, just as all diabolical sorcerers had become the servants of Satan. It remained only for the sorcerer's parallel, the witch, to become considered in the same way.

18

Pope Gregory IX: *Vox in Rama* (1233)

The decretal letter *Vox in Rama* ("A Voice in Rama") of Pope Gregory IX (1227–41) is addressed to the archbishop of Mainz, the bishop of

---

2. On the political trials of the fourteenth and fifteenth centuries, see William R. Jones, "Political Uses of Sorcery in Medieval Europe," *Historian* 34 (1972): 670–87; H. A. Kelly, "English Kings and the Fear of Sorcery," *Medieval Studies* 39 (1977): 206–38; Edward Peters, *The Magician, the Witch, and the Law*; Veenstra, *Magic and Divination*. On the case of the Templars, see Malcolm Barber, *The Trial of the Templars* (Cambridge, 1978), and Peter Partner, *The Murdered Magicians: The Templars and Their Myth* (New York, 1982).

Hildesheim, and to Conrad of Marburg, a priest whom the archbishop of Mainz had deputed to seek out heretics in his large archdiocese. The opening of the letter, ringing with biblical imagery and echoes, describes the woes that have befallen the church, among them the problem of pestilential heresy. Gregory IX's information on the behavior of some of the heretics, printed here, probably came from Conrad of Marburg himself; although this text never became part of canon law, it illustrates papal acceptance of others' views of some aspects of heretical practices at a crucial moment in the early thirteenth century. The letter is an example of what Norman Cohn has termed "the demonization of medieval heretics," that is, the elaborate description of alleged heretical behavior in terms that later came to be attributed to practitioners of diabolical sorcery, as in the work of Guibert of Nogent and Ralph of Coggeshall (Text 11).[1] Once thought to be directed at a particular group of rebellious peasants, the Stedinger, in northern Germany, the letter is now acknowledged to deal with Rhineland heretics as these were characterized by Conrad of Marburg.

SOURCE: Malcolm Barber, "Propaganda in the Middle Ages: The Charges Against the Templars," *Nottingham Medieval Studies* 17 (1973): 42–57, at 45–46.

FURTHER READING: Russell, *Witchcraft*, 159–65; Cohn, *Europe's Inner Demons*, 22–31.

THE FOLLOWING RITES of this pestilence are carried out: when any novice is to be received among them and enters the sect of the damned for the first time, the shape of a certain frog appears to him, which some are accustomed to call a toad. Some kiss this creature on the hind-quarters and some on the mouth; they receive the tongue and saliva of the beast inside their mouths. Sometimes it appears unduly large, and sometimes equivalent to a goose or a duck, and sometimes it even assumes the size of an oven. At length, when the novice has come forward, he is met by a man of marvellous pallor, who has very black eyes and is so emaciated and thin that, since his flesh has been wasted, seems to have remaining only skin drawn over the bone. The novice kisses him and feels cold, like ice, and after the kiss the memory of the catholic faith totally disappears from his heart. Afterwards they sit down to a meal and when they have arisen from it, from a certain statue, which is usual in a sect of this kind, a black cat about the size of an average dog,

---

1. On one particularly important aspect, that of female sexuality, see Dyan Elliott, *Fallen Bodies: Pollution, Sexuality, and Demonology in the Middle Ages* (Philadelphia, 1999), chap. 2: "From Sexual Fantasy to Demonic Defloration: The Libidinous Female in the Later Middle Ages," 35–60.

descends backwards, with its tail erect. First the novice, next the master, then each one of the order who are worthy and perfect, kiss the cat on its hind-quarters; the imperfect, who do not estimate themselves worthy, receive grace from the master. Then each returns to his place and, speaking certain responses, they incline their heads toward the cat. "Forgive us," says the master, and the one next to him repeats this, a third responding and saying, "We know master"; a fourth says, "And we must obey."

When this has been done, they put out the candles, and turn to the practice of the most disgusting lechery, making no distinction between those who are strangers and those who are kin. Moreover, if by chance those of the male sex exceed the number of women, surrendering to their ignominious passions, burning mutually in their desires, men engage in depravity with men. Similarly, women change their natural function, which is against nature, making this itself worthy of blame among themselves. When these most abominable sins have been completed, and the candles have been lit again and each has resumed his place, from a dark corner of the assembly, which is not lacking in the most damned of men, a certain man emerges, from the loins upward gleaming more brightly than the sun, so they say, whose lower part is shaggy like a cat and whose light illuminates the whole place. Then the master, picking out something from the clothing of the novice, says to the shining figure, "This which has been given to me, I give to you," and the shining figure replies, "You have served me well and will serve more and better. I commit what you have given into your custody," and having said that at once disappears. They even receive the body of the Lord every year at Easter from the hand of a priest, and carrying it in their mouths to their homes, they throw it into the latrine in contempt of the savior. Furthermore, these most unhappy of wretches, blaspheming the Lord in Heaven with polluted lips, assert in their madness that the Lord violently and deceitfully against justice threw Lucifer down into the lower world. These wretches also believe in him and affirm that he is the creator of heaven, and will return there in his glory when the Lord has fallen, through which with him and not before him they hope that they will have eternal happiness. They acknowledge all acts which are not pleasing to the Lord, and instead do what he hates.

19
Pope Alexander IV: Sorcery and the Inquisitors (1258)

From the institution of the office in the 1230s, the inquisitors of heretical depravity (technically, papal judges subdelegate) had as their primary—and ostensibly exclusive—duty the detection and eradication of heresy. By the 1250s a number of inquisitors had raised the question of whether their charge included sorcery or magic, offenses normally within the pastoral and judicial jurisdiction of local bishops or of secular courts but increasingly associated with sorcery during the late twelfth and early thirteenth centuries. In 1258 Pope Alexander IV (1254–1261) stated that it did not, unless the act involved manifest heresy, that is, heterodoxy that was clearly heretical and known.

One result of the increasing use of the inquisitorial method of legal procedure from the early thirteenth century, particularly in the context of matters of heterodoxy, as well as the appearance of a growing body of specialist inquisitorial literature, was that the concept of "heresy" itself had grown more precise, and that methods for discovering and dealing with it had become more articulated. Although bishops and secular courts appear to have had routine jurisdiction over cases of sorcery and divination, the elaboration of the concept of heresy logically raised the question among inquisitors as to whether these offenses ought to come within their own jurisdiction. It is this problem that Alexander's letter addressed. Witchcraft

Although it may be argued that Alexander is speaking of ritual magic, and that he at least allows for some kinds of divination and sorcery that do not involve demons or heretics, the text is nevertheless an opening for inquisitorial activity, as well as for the association of sorcery and demonolatry with heresy. It was important enough for Pope Boniface VIII to reissue it under his own name in 1298. Alexander's concern in this text is the scope of inquisitorial powers, rather than the problem of demonology and sorcery. The very next text in the collection deals with the question of whether inquisitors should investigate usury.

SOURCE: Hansen, *Quellen*, *Liber sextus*, V.2.8 *Corpus Iuris Canonici*, ed. Emil Friedberg (Leipzig, 1877), vol. 2, cols. 1071–72. The ordinary gloss on this passage is in *Sextum Decretalium Liber* (Venice, 1567), pp. 339–41. Trans. E. P.

FURTHER READING: Russell, *Witchcraft*, 155–56; Kieckhefer, *Magic*, 191; Peters, *The Magician, the Witch, and the Law*, 98–102.

*R*UBRIC: THE INQUISITORS deputed to investigate heresy must not intrude into investigations of divination or sorcery without knowledge of manifest heresy involved.

It is reasonable that those charged with the affairs of the faith, which is the greatest of privileges, ought not thereby to intervene in other matters. The inquisitors of pestilential heresy, commissioned by the apostolic see, ought not intervene in cases of divination or sorcery unless these *clearly savor* of manifest heresy. Nor should they punish those who are engaged in these things, but leave them to other judges for punishment.

* witchcraf included in heresy if it is religiously affiliated

Ordinary Gloss: "clearly savor," *as to pray at the altars of idols, to offer sacrifices, to consult demons, to elicit responses from them . . . or if they* [sorcerers] *associate themselves publicly with heretics in order to predict the future by means of the Body and Blood of Christ, etc.*

20
William, Cardinal of Santa Sabina: Sorcery and the Inquisitors (1320)

The pontificate of John XXII (1316–34) witnessed a number of striking changes in the medieval church. Pope John, a trained lawyer rather than a theologian, was a brilliant organizer and administrator and had a taste for ruling. Since the death of Benedict XI in 1304, the popes had lived outside of Italy, and John settled his pontificate in the Angevin-ruled (and later papally acquired) city of Avignon (now in southern France). John, an ascetic and physically fragile man (he was seventy-two when elected pope), attempted to restore some of the prestige which the papacy and the church had lost in the preceding two decades, while facing a number of internal crises within the clergy, notably those of the Spiritual Franciscans and the problem of apostolic poverty, and in European diplomatic affairs, notably the conflict between Robert I of Naples and the emperor Louis of Bavaria. Yet John also experienced several attempts on his life, one of which appears to have been an attempted assassination by poison and sorcery; hence his and Cardinal William of Santa Sabina's letters denouncing a danger which both of them suddenly felt to be at once immediate and threatening, focusing especially on idolatry, pacts, and the abusive use of sacramentals. John also reinvigorated the inquisitorial office, although he insisted on legal discipline at the same time, and the letters translated here are important evidence that the renewed inquisitorial office was instructed from the highest levels of church government to investigate sorcery as a form of heresy.

SOURCE: William, cardinal of Santa Sabina, letter of 22 August 1320, to the inquisitors of Carcassonne and Toulouse. Latin text in Hansen, *Quellen*, 4–5. Trans. E. P.

FURTHER READING: Guillaume Mollat, *The Popes at Avignon, 1305–*

1378 (rprt. New York, 1965), 9–25; Peters, *The Magician, the Witch, and the Law*, 129–35; Russell, *Witchcraft*, 171–75; Cohn, *Europe's Inner Demons*, 192–97.

OUR MOST HOLY father and lord, by divine providence Pope John XXII, fervently desires that the sorcerers [the Latin uses the masculine gender], the infectors of God's flock, flee from the midst of the House of God. He ordains and commits to you that, by his authority against them who make sacrifice to demons or adore them, or do homage unto them by giving them as a sign a written pact or other token; or who make certain binding pacts with them, or who make or have made for them certain images or other things which bind them to demons, or by invoking the demons plan to perpetrate whatever sorceries they wish; or who, abusing the sacrament of baptism, themselves baptize or cause to be baptized an image of wax or some other material; and who themselves make these things or have them made in order to invoke the demons; or if knowingly they have baptism, orders, or confirmation repeated; then, concerning sorcerers and witches [Lat. *de sortilegiis et maleficis*, again using masculine gender], who abuse the sacrament of the eucharist or the consecrated host and other sacraments of the church by using them or things like them in their witchcraft and sorcery, you can investigate and otherwise proceed against them by whatever means available, which are canonically assigned to you concerning the proceeding against heretics. Indeed, our same lord amplifies and extends the power given to inquisitors by law as much as the office of the inquisition against heretics and, by his certain knowledge, likewise the privileges in all and singular cases mentioned above.

21

Pope John XXII: Sorcery and the Inquisitors (1326)

SOURCE: Pope John XXII, the Decretal *Super illius specula*. Latin text in Hansen, *Quellen*, 5–6. Trans. E. P.

FURTHER READING: Other letters of John XXII are translated in Montague Summers, *The Geography of Witchcraft* (rprt. London, 1978), 526–32, although the book is entirely unreliable on all points except translations.

GRIEVINGLY WE OBSERVE . . . that many who are Christians in name only . . . sacrifice to demons, adore them, make or have made images, rings, mirrors, phials, or other things for magic purposes, and bind themselves to demons. They ask and receive responses from

them and to fulfill their most depraved lusts ask them for aid. Binding themselves to the most shameful slavery for the most shameful of things, they ally
themselves with death and make a pact with hell. By their means a most pestilential disease, besides growing stronger and increasingly serious, grievously
infests the flock of Christ throughout the world. By this edict we warn in perpetuity, guided by the sound counsel of our brothers, all and singular who have
been reborn at the baptismal font. In virtue of holy obedience and under threat
of anathema we warn them in advance that none of them ought dare to teach or
learn anything at all concerning these perverse dogmas, or, what is even more
execrable, to use any of them by whatever means for whatever purpose. . . . We
hereby promulgate the sentence of excommunication upon all and singular who
against our most charitable warnings and orders presume to engage in these
things, and we desire that they incur this sentence ipso facto.

22
Nicolau Eymeric: The *Directorium inquisitorum* (1376)

Encouraged by the opening of sorcery to their jurisdiction left by Alexander IV and its clarification by the letter of Boniface VIII and subsequent teaching commentary on it, as well as by the concerns of
John XXII, inquisitors of heretical depravity after 1320 began to include discussions of sorcery in the manuals of procedure their members produced. At first, these said little that was new, including the
well-known manual of Bernard Gui of 1324.[1] But a number of cases in
the course of the fourteenth century suggest a far greater interest in
sorcery on the part of inquisitors. The treatise on heresy by the jurist
Ugolino Zanchini (d. 1340) marks an important stage in the transition
from limited to intensified inquisitorial concern with sorcery and divination, far more extensive than that of Gui just a decade or so earlier.
Zanchini draws on both Roman law (*Code* 9.18) and canon law (especially *Causa* 26 of Gratian's *Decretum*), for example: "It is heretical to
believe that anything is divine except God, or that anything may be
created or transformed by some other cause than God, who is the creator of all things, as is shown in scripture, especially in the first chapter

---

1. The sections of Gui's manual concerning sorcery are translated in John Shinners, *Medieval
Popular Religion 1000–1500: A Reader* (Peterborough, Ontario, 1997), 457–59, and for the context of the work, see the selections translated in Walter L. Wakefield and Austin P. Evans,
Heresies of the High Middle Ages (New York, 1969), 373–445 (the sorcery materials are on
pp. 444–45).

of the Gospel of John, and as is shown in *Episcopi* and in the chapter *Nec mirum*. Nor is it licit to adore demons or to receive responses from them, as in C. 26 q. 2 and other places."[2]

During the course of the fourteenth century it is possible to see the shift in inquisitorial interest in a number of cases. One of the best known of these was the case of Alice Kyteler in Kilkenny, Ireland, in 1324–25.[3] Kyteler was tried by a continentally trained local bishop, Richard Ledrede, who turned a family and property dispute into a trial for sorcery, in which a servant of Alice, Petronilla of Meath, became the first person executed for sorcery. Striking in the case were the accusations that Alice and her accomplices formed a sect, performed injurious and erotic magic, that Alice had a familiar demon, and that Ireland was full of diabolical heretics. Although the trial led to no further cases, it illustrates the possibilities that the aligning of sorcery with heresy offered at the end of the first quarter of the fourteenth century. The work of Nicolau Eymeric should be read in the light of the long transition from Bernard Gui through Zanchini and cases like that of Kyteler.

Nicolau Eymeric became the inquisitor of the kingdom of Aragon in 1356. "Trained in varied learning, and incessant in industry . . . he systematized the procedure of his beloved institution [i.e., the Inquisition], giving the principles and details which should guide the inquisitor in all his acts. The book [the *Directorium inquisitorium*] remained an authority to the last, and formed the basis of all subsequent compilations."[4] Eymeric's handbook for inquisitors became the most influential and widely used text of its kind until the seventeenth century. It was reprinted late in the sixteenth century with an extended commentary by Francisco Peña, the greatest authority on the Roman Inquisition. Eymeric had earlier written a separate treatise on sorcery, perhaps as early as 1359, which he reworked for the *Directorium*.

SOURCE: Nicolau Eymeric, *Directorium inquisitorium*, 1376. Latin text in the edition of Rome, 1587, part 2, *Quaestio XLII De Sortilegis et Divinatoribus*, pp. 335–36; *Quaestio XLIII De Invocantibus Daemones*, pp. 338–43. Trans. E. P.

---

2. Hansen, *Quellen*, 59–63 at 60–61. See also Henry Charles Lea, *Inquisition of the Middle Ages*, 3: 449–50; Antoine Dondaine, "Le Manuel de l'Inquisiteur (1230–1330)," rprt. in Dondaine, *Les hérésies et l'Inquisition, XIIe–XIIIe siècles* (Aldershot, UK, 1990), 2: 85–194, at 121–25. Trans. E. P.

3. L. S. Davidson and John O. Ward, ed. and trans., *The Sorcery Trial of Alice Kyteler* (Binghamton, 1993; rprt., Ashville, N.C., 1998); Cohn, *Europe's Inner Demons*, 198–204.

4. Lea, *Inquisition of the Middle Ages*, abr. Margaret Nicholson (New York, 1961), 354–55.

FURTHER READING: Edward Peters, "Editing Inquisitors' Manuals in the Sixteenth Century: Francisco Peña and the *Directorium Inquisitorum* of Nicholas Eymeric," *Library Chronicle* 60 (1974); *Bibliographical Studies in Honor of Rudolf Hirsch*, ed. William E. Miller and Thomas G. Waldman, with Natalie D. Terrell, 95–107; and Gary Macy, "Nicholas Eymeric and the Condemnation of Orthodoxy," in *The Devil, Heresy and Witchcraft in the Middle Ages: Essays in Honor of Jeffrey Burton Russell*, ed. Alberto Ferreiro (Leiden, Boston, Cologne, 1998), 369–81.

THE FORTY-SECOND question asks whether magicians and diviners are to be considered heretics or as those suspected of heresy and whether they are to be subjected to the judgment of the inquisitor of heretics. To this we answer that there are two things to be seen here, just as there are really two things asked in this question. The first is, whether magicians and diviners are subject to the judgment of the inquisitor of heretics. The second, posed thusly, is whether they are to be considered as heretics or as those suspected of heresy.

The first thing to be considered, just as in the last *Quaestio* different kinds of blasphemers were distinguished, is that diviners and magicians must be distinguished; that is, there are two kinds of diviners and magicians.

Some are to be considered magicians and diviners just as are those who act purely according to the technique of chiromancy, who divine things from the lineaments of the hand and judge natural effects and the condition of men from this. . . .

Some others, however, are magicians and diviners who are not pure chiromantics, but are contracted to heretics, as are those who show the honor of *latria* or *dulia* to the demons, who rebaptize children and do other similar things.[5] And they do these things in order to foresee the future or penetrate to the innermost secrets of the heart. These people are guilty of manifest heresy.

5. *Latria* is that form of adoration which must be shown only to God; hence, *idolatria* is worship that is only appropriate for God but is shown to idols. *Dulia* is a form of veneration to be shown only to saints, holy men, and God's vicars on earth. Several historians have pointed out that a shift in confessional practice in the thirteenth and fourteenth centuries gradually supplanted the central role played by the category of the Seven Deadly Sins (in which either pride or avarice was the chief) by the Ten Commandments, in which idolatry (of which sorcery and diabolical witchcraft were examples) became the worst sin. The classic exposition is John Bossy, "Moral Arithmetic: Seven Sins into Ten Commandments," in *Conscience and Casuistry in Early Modern Europe*, ed. Edmund Leites (Cambridge, 1988), 214–34.

And such magicians and diviners do not evade the judgment of the inquisitor, but are punished according to the laws pertaining to heretics.

The Forty-third question asks whether those who invoke demons, either magicians or heretics or those suspected of heresy, are subject to the judgment of the inquisitor of heretics. . . .

It appears to the inquisitors from the above-mentioned books and from other books that certain invokers of demons manifestly show the honor of *latria* to the demons they invoke, inasmuch as they sacrifice to them, adore them, offer up horrible prayers to them, vow themselves to the service of the demons, promise them their obedience, and otherwise commit themselves to the demons, swearing by the name of some superior demon whom they invoke. They willingly celebrate the praises of the demon or sing songs in his honor and genuflect or prostrate themselves before him. They observe chastity out of reverence for the demon or abstain upon his instructions or they lacerate their own flesh. Out of reverence for the demon or by his instructions they wear white or black vestments. They worship him by signs and characters and unknown names. They burn candles or incense to him or aromatic spices. They sacrifice animals and birds, catching their blood as a curative agent, or they burn them, throwing salt in the fire and making a holocaust in this manner. All of these things and many more evil things are found in consulting and desiring things from demons, in all of which and in whichever the honor of *latria*, if the above things are considered intelligently, is clearly shown to the demons. If, note well, the sacrifices to God according to the old and the new law are considered, it is found there that these acts are true sacrifices only when exhibited to God, and not to the demons. This, then, is the case with the first category of those who invoke or speak on behalf of demons. . . . And by this manner the priests used to invoke Baal, offering their own blood and that of animals, as one reads in 4 [2 Kings] Kings 18.

   Certain other invokers of demons show to the demons they invoke not the honor of *latria*, but that of *dulia*, in that they insert in their wicked prayers the names of demons along with those of the blessed or the saints, making them mediators in their prayers heard by God. They bow down before images of wax, worshiping God by their names or qualities. These things and many other wretched things are found described in the aforementioned books in which the honor of *dulia* is shown to demons. If, indeed, the means of praying to the saints which the church has diligently instituted are considered, it will clearly be seen that these prayers are to be said, not to demons, but only to the saints and the blessed. This, then, is the case of the second category of those who invoke demons. And in this manner the Saracens invoke Mohammed as well as God and the saints and certain Beghards invoke Petrus Johannis and others condemned by the church.

Yet certain other invokers of demons make a certain kind of invocation in which it does not appear clearly that the honor either of *latria* or *dulia* is shown to the demons invoked, as, in tracing a circle on the ground, placing a child in the circle, setting a mirror, a sword, an amphora, or something else in the way before the boy, holding their book of necromancy, reading it, and invoking the demon and other suchlike, as is taught by that art and proved by the confessions of many. This, then, is the third way of invoking demons. And by this means Saul invoked the spirit of the python through the pythoness. In Saul's invocation, it is seen, no honor was done, neither *dulia* nor *latria*, as one reads in 1 [1 Kings] Samuel 26.

It seems, therefore, that the means of invoking demons vary in three ways. These conclusions pose in turn three cases or conclusions according to which the invokers of demons ought to be distinguished from one another in three ways.

First, the case or conclusion is that if the invokers of demons show to the demons they invoke the honor of *latria* by whatever means and if they are clearly and judicially convicted of this, or if they confess, then they are to be considered by the judgment of the church not as magicians, but as heretics, and if they recant and abjure heresy they are to be perpetually imprisoned as penitent heretics. If, however, they do not wish to desist or if they say they wish to desist and repent but do not wish to abjure, or if they do abjure and afterwards relapse, they are to be relinquished to the secular arm, and punished by the ultimate torture according to all the canonical sanctions which judge other heretics.

This conclusion may be deduced in three ways: first from the sayings of the saints and doctors of theology, second from the sayings of the doctors of canon law, and third from the decisions of the church.

First, from the sayings of the theologians, blessed St. Augustine in Book 10 of *The City of God*, speaking of sacrifices shown only to God and not to demons, says this: "We see that it is observed in each republic that men honor the highest leader by a singular sign which, if it is offered to someone else, would be the hateful crime of *lèse-majesté*. And thus it is written in the divine law under pain of death to those who offer divine honors to others. Exterior deeds are signs of interior deeds, just as spoken words are the signs of things; we direct our voices signifying prayers or praises to him, to whom we offer the same things in our hearts which we say, so we know that in sacrificing a visible sacrifice is to be offered to him to whom in our hearts we ought to offer ourselves as an invisible sacrifice. . . ."

By these words Augustine shows clearly that such sacrifice ought to be offered to God alone, and when it is offered to another than God, then by that deed one shows oneself to believe that that person is higher than God, which is heresy. Whoever, therefore, offers sacrifice to demons considers the demon as God and shows himself to believe the demon to be the true God by offering external signs. By which deeds they are to be considered heretics. . . .

Superstition is a vice opposed to the Christian religion or Christian worship. Therefore, it is heresy in a Christian, and as a consequence those who sacrifice to demons are to be considered heretics.

St. Thomas, in a commentary on Isaiah (Isaiah 1, 3) . . . poses the question whether it is illicit to seek the future through augury, and at the end of his commentary says, concerning demonology and what the demons are able to know, that it is always a sin to inquire of them as well as an apostasy from faith. As says Augustine, so says blessed Thomas.

The same St. Thomas [in his commentary on Peter Lombard's] *Sentences*, in Book II, *distinctio* 7, asks whether it is a sin to use the aid of a demon and answers . . . that that which is beyond the faculties of human nature is to be asked only of God, and, just as they sin gravely who, through the cult of *latria* to an idol, impute that which is only God's to a creature of God, so indeed do they gravely sin who implore the aid of a demon in those things which are only to be asked of God. And in this way is seeing into the future [to be considered]. . . .

Indeed, the same is to be said of other magical works in which the accomplishment of the task is anticipated by the aid of the devil. In all these there is apostasy from the faith because of the compact made with the demon or because of a promise if the compact is already in existence or by any other deed, even if sacrifice is not performed. Man may not serve two masters, as says St. Matthew in Chapter 8, and St. Thomas. From these things it is shown clearly that to invoke and consult demons, even without making sacrifice to them, is apostasy from the faith and, as a consequence, heresy. It is much worse if a sacrifice is involved. . . .

Peter of Tarentaise, who later was Pope Innocent V, holds . . . that although a man may be asked about a book which is lost, a demon may not, because the demon, when asked about such things, will not respond unless a pact is made with him, or illicit veneration, adjuration, or invocation. . . .

Our conclusion is also proved by the sayings of the canon lawyers. . . .

Thirdly, our conclusion is also proved by the decisions of the church. Indeed, *Causa* 26 q. 5 c. [12] *Episcopi* says this: "Bishops and their officials should labor with all their strength. . . ."[6]

And from this it appears that those who share and exercise the magical art are to be considered heretics and avoided. . . .

And from this it appears that the said evil women, persevering in their wickedness, have departed from the right way and the faith and the devils

---

6. Eymeric here quotes the *Canon Episcopi* (above, Text 5).

delude them. If, therefore, these same women, concerning whom it is not contested that they offer sacrifices to the demons they invoke, are perfidious and faithless and deviate from the right way as the said canon from the Council of Ancyra [*Episcopi*] makes clear, then, as a consequence, if they have been baptized they are to be considered heretics; since for a Christian to deviate from the right way and faith and to embrace infidelity is properly to hereticize. How much more, then, are Christians, who show the honor of *latria* to demons and sacrifice to the demons they invoke, to be said and considered to be perfidious, deviants from the right way, and faithless in the love of Christians, which is heresy—and by consequence to be considered heretics? ...

Indeed, the further a creature is separated from divine perfection, the greater the fault it is to show him the honor of *latria*. And since the demons (not on account of their nature, but on account of their guilt) are the most separated from God of all creatures, so much the worse is it to adore them. And to number them among the angels is wicked heresy. Those who count angels among the heretics show manifest heresy by so counting them, adoring them, or by any way sacrificing to them. And as a consequence, those who perpetrate this kind of wickedness are to be judged as heretics by the church.

The constitution of Pope John XXII against magicians and magical superstitions. ...[7]

Whoever invokes the aid of Mohammed, even if he does nothing else, falls into manifest heresy. So does anyone who in his honor constructs an altar to him. In similar cases the same thing may be said of invoking any demon, building him an altar, sacrificing to him, etc. These are the acts of *latria*, which ought to be given only to God. ...

In the second case the conclusion is that if those who invoke the demons do not show to the demons they invoke the honor of *latria*, but do show them the honor of *hyperdulia* or that of *dulia* in the manner described before and have clearly confessed to this judicially or have been convicted of it, such are to be considered by the judgment of the church not magicians, but heretics, and as a consequence if they recant and abjure heresy they are to be perpetually imprisoned as penitent heretics. If, however, they do not recant, they are to be treated as impenitent heretics; likewise if they abjure and then relapse, they are to suffer punishment like other heretics.

... *Dulia* may be expressed in two ways, or rather in two kinds of case. The first is as a sign indicating sanctity. This is the case of Abraham, Lot [and others]. ... This case is that of angels and saints who are in the heavenly fatherland and are adored by us and celebrated by the honor of *dulia*.

The second case is a sign of governance, jurisdiction, and power. This is the case with the prophet Nathan, and Bathsheba, the mother of Solomon who

7. Eymeric here quotes the decretal of Pope John XXII (above, Text 21).

adored David the King, as it says in 1 Kings 1. This is also the case with popes, kings, and others who lawfully wield power, as vicegerents of God in authority and rule. If, therefore, anyone should show to them the honor of *dulia* then he shows himself to believe that person to whom he displays the honor of *dulia* to be a saint and a friend of God, or a governor or a rector duly constituted by God, and thus that God ought to be honored in him, his vicar. Now when the honor of *dulia* is shown to a saint, God is principally adored by the honor of *latria* through the saint. And when a pope, king, or any other person who wields power is revered by the honor of *dulia*, God is venerated by the honor of *latria* through his vicar. And thus by these kinds of honors which are shown to the saints and to the rectors of the church and to the princes of this world, it is not themselves, but God in them who is principally venerated. Therefore, showing the honor of *dulia* to a demon who has been invoked by these means and by exterior actions, is to reveal oneself in heart and mind as believing inwardly that the demon is above the saints and the friend of God and is to be venerated as if saintly, or that he is above the rectors of this world and the governors duly constituted by God and therefore is to be revered as having jurisdiction and power. In both senses this is heretical and perverse, since it is contrary to the holy scriptures and against the decisions of the church. The demon is neither a saint nor the friend of God, chiefly since he is obstinate in his sin and wickedness. Nor is he one of God's governors in this world duly constituted, but he is the captured slave, the falsifier and deceiver, as the sacred canons and all that we have said above clearly shows. Therefore, those who are convicted of showing the demon the honor of *dulia* are to be treated not as magicians, but as heretics.

23

The Theology Faculty of the University of Paris Condemns Sorcery (1398)

One of the strongest claims made on behalf of the Latin Christian church was its authority to teach—its *magisterium*. Institutionally this authority was grounded in the offices of pope, councils, and bishops, and instrumentally from the twelfth century on in the great corporate institutions of the universities. In matters of theology, whether biblical, moral, or speculative, that authority came more and more to be located in the faculties of theology, most notably in the faculty of theology of the University of Paris.[1]

1. A good recent account is *A History of the University in Europe*, ed. Walter Rüegg, vol. 1, *Universities in the Middle Ages*, ed. Hilde De Ridder-Symeons (Cambridge, 1992). In this volume, see especially Monika Asztalos, "The Faculty of Theology." In addition, see Colish, *Medi-*

The theology faculty of the University of Paris was also particularly close to the French crown. King Philip IV of France had asked the opinion of the Paris theologians in his case against the Templars in 1308; in 1333 the faculty even publicly criticized a theological error on the part of Pope John XXII, and in 1414 King Charles VI said that the members of the faculty "hold the first rank in the science of sacred letters." Thus, when the theology faculty issued its condemnation of magical practices in 1398, its rulings were heard and respected. And they had the backing of the crown.

The condemnation of 1398 did not, however, result merely from the abstract deliberations of academic theologians. Events in France during the last quarter of the fourteenth century brought a number of very practical issues before both the crown and the faculty. The turmoil of the Hundred Years' War, the intermittent insanity of Charles VI, and a growing concern over what theologians and reformers termed "superstitious practices" (as with the Romans, a much stronger term than is indicated by modern meanings of "superstition") made the condemnation of 1398 of immediate interest and widespread influence. Decisions made at Paris were heard throughout Europe.

In the 1390s a number of trials for various kinds of sorcery were held in France, several at Paris. Some of these cases involved practices of sorcery aimed at causing—or curing—the madness of Charles VI.[2] These trials echo some of the issues raised in the trials for political sorcery at the beginning of the fourteenth century in France and the papal court. But France also saw trials for private acts of sorcery, and both kinds troubled rulers and theologians at the end of the fourteenth century and, of course, later.

The condemnation of 1398 is not exclusively directed at "learned" magic. By broadly categorizing many different kinds of activities as deriving from idolatry and superstition, the theology faculty was con-

eval Foundations, 265–318; Guy Fitch Lytle, "Universities as Religious Authorities in the Late Middle Ages and the Reformation," in *Reform and Authority in the Medieval and Reformation Church*, ed. Guy Fitch Lytle (Washington, D.C., 1981), 69–97; Jacques Le Goff, "The Universities and Public Authorities in the Middle Ages and the Renaissance," in Le Goff, *Time, Work, and Culture in the Middle Ages*, trans. Arthur Goldhammer (Chicago, 1980), 135–49, and J. M. M. H. Thijssen, *Censure and Heresy at the University of Paris, 1200–1400* (Philadelphia, 1998). For the European context of Paris around 1400, see Arno Borst, "Crisis and Reform in the Universities of the Late Middle Ages," in Borst, *Medieval Worlds*, 167–94.

2. For the background, see the brilliant study of Veenstra, *Magic and Divination* as well as Ronald C. Famiglietti, *Royal Intrigue: Crisis at the Court of Charles VI, 1392–1420* (New York, 1986). For England, see Hilary M. Carey, *Courting Disaster: Astrology at the English Court and University in the Later Middle Ages* (London, 1992).

tinuing the linking of elaborate magical practices with unlearned practice of diabolical sorcery for private and usually shameful ends.

SOURCE: Lynn Thorndike, *University Records and Life in the Middle Ages* (New York, 1944), 261–66.

FURTHER READING: Veenstra, *Magic and Divination*; Cohn, *Europe's Inner Demons*, 196–97; Russell, *Witchcraft*, 199–220.

CONSIDERING THE FEAT or principal operation and its makeup in itself and all its accompanying circumstances, namely, the great circle conscribed with divers unknown names and marked with various characters, the little wooden wheel raised on four wooden feet and a stake in the midst of the same great circle and the bottle placed upon the said wheel, above which bottle on a little paper scroll were written certain names, whose meaning is unknown to us, forsooth Garsepin, Oroth, Carmesine, Visoc, with the sign of the cross and certain characters interposed between the said names, and also thrones, earthen pots, a fire kindled, suffumigations, lights, swords and many other characters and figures and divers names and unknown words and also the naming or writing of four kings on four small paper wheels, forsooth, king Galtinus of the north, king Baltinus of the east, king Saltinus of the south, king Ultinus of the west, with certain characters written in red interposed between the names of the said kings; considering also the time and the suspect place and the behavior of those who were present at the said work and participated in it and the things they did after oaths had been taken by them many times as to making a legal division of the treasures to be found, also repeated after the declaration of the said work by the principal actor of that artifice, as appears from their confessions, from which it is learned that in a certain room in which were the said instruments, superstitious in themselves, with lights lit and suffumigrations about the bottle and circles, in which were the said inscriptions and said characters, the said co-workers, stripped to the waist in their smallclothes, holding swords by their hilts each one before a throne, sometimes fixing the points in the earth and sometimes circling about with the said swords near the thrones and circles and bottle, raising the points of the swords to the sky, and sometimes placing their hands together with the hand of the protagonist over the bottle, which he called holy and in which, as they said, should come the spirit who would reveal and make known hidden treasures; in view of all the aforesaid and their accompaniments our deliberate conclusion is as follows, that not only those who use such figments and sorceries to find hidden treasure or learn and know things secret and occult, but also all professed Christians in possession of reason who voluntarily operate and employ such things in such manner are to be held superstitious in the Christian religion, are to be deemed idolaters, are to be deemed invokers of demons and strongly suspect in the faith.

To all devotees of the orthodox faith the chancellor of Paris and the faculty of theology in the dear university of Paris, our mother, with full honor of divine worship, to have hope in the Lord and not look upon vanities and false insanities. From olden darkness a foul flood of errors newly emerging has warned us to recall, that often catholic truth which escapes others is quite clear to those studious in sacred writ, since certainly every art has this property of being clear to those trained in it, so that thence comes that maxim, "Believe the man who is skilled in his art." Hence that line of Horace which Jerome quotes writing to Paulinus, "Physicians utter what is medical, smiths handle tools." To this in the case of sacred writ is added something special which neither experience nor sense can give as in the other arts, nor can readily be apprehended by eyes wrapped in the mist of sin. For their malice has blinded them, says indeed the Apostle, so that from avarice many have erred from the faith. Moreover it is not irrationally named by the same the service of idols. Others from ingratitude, who, "although they have known God, have not glorified Him as God," have fallen, as he too relates, into all impiety of idolatry. Furthermore, unbridled pleasure led Solomon to idols; Dido, to magic arts. Others have been turned astray by proud curiosity and the dire desire to investigate the occult. Others, finally, wretched timidity, hanging breathless on the morrow, has driven into most superstitious and impious observances, as is noted in Lucan of the son of Pompey the Great and in the historians of many more. Thus it happens that the sinner withdrawing from God falls into vanities and false insanities and turns unto him who is the father of falsehood, finally imprudently and openly apostasizing. Thus Saul, abandoned by the Lord, consulted the witch whom he had previously opposed; thus Ochozias spurning the God of Israel sent to consult the god Acharon; thus in fine it needs be that all those, who in faith or works are without the true God, should be deluded by a false god.

Perceiving, therefore, that the nefarious, pestiferous and monstrous abomination of false insanities with its heresies has developed more than usual in our times, lest perchance the monster of such horrid impiety and pernicious contagion avail to infect our most Christian realm, which once was free and by God's protection shall be free from monsters, desirous of checking every attempt, mindful besides of our profession and burning with zeal for the faith, we have decreed to brand with the cautery of damnation a few articles bearing on this matter, lest henceforth they deceive unawares, recalling among innumerable others that saying of the most sapient doctor Augustine concerning superstitious observances, that those who believe in these or go to their houses or introduce them into their own homes or question them, should know that they have belied their Christian faith and baptism and become pagans and apostates, that is backsliders, and enemies of God, and have incurred the wrath of God gravely for eternity, unless, corrected by ecclesiastical penance, they are reconciled to God. Such his words. Not that it is our intention in any way to derogate from lawful and true traditions, sciences and arts, for it will keep us busy to extirpate and uproot, in so far as we may, the insane and sacrilegious errors of the foolish and fatal rites that harm, contaminate, infect the orthodox faith and Christian religion, and to restore its due honor to sincere truth.

Moreover, the first article is that by magic arts and sorceries and nefarious invocations to seek the intimacy and friendship and aid of demons is not idolatry. An error.

Second article, that to give or offer or promise to demons such-and-such a thing in order that they may fulfill a man's desire, or in their honor to kiss or carry something, is not idolatry. Error.

Third article, that to enter on a pact with demons, tacit or express, is not idolatry or a species of idolatry and apostasy. Error.

Fourth article, that to try by magic arts to include, coerce and bind demons in stones, rings, mirrors, images, consecrated in their name or rather execrated, or to wish to make these alive, is not idolatry. Error.

Fifth article, that it is licit to use for a good end magic arts or other superstitions forbidden by God and the church. Error.

Sixth article, that it is licit or even permitted to repel sorcery by sorcery. Error.

Seventh article, that anyone may give anyone a dispensation in any such case, so that he may employ such rites licitly. An error.

Eighth article, that magic arts and like superstitions and their observance are prohibited by the church irrationally. Error.

Ninth article, that God is induced by magic arts and sorcery to compel demons to obey invocations. An error.

Tenth article, that incensings and suffumigrations, which are performed in the exercise of such arts and sorceries, are to the honor of God and please Him. An error and blasphemy.

Eleventh article, that to use such things in such wise is not to sacrifice or immolate to demons and consequently not damnable idolatry. An error.

Twelfth article, that holy words and certain devout prayers and fasts and ablutions and bodily continence in boys and others, and the celebrating mass and other works of a good sort, which are performed in carrying on such arts, excuse these from evil and do not rather accuse them. An error.

Thirteenth article, that the holy prophets and others made their prophecies by such arts and performed miracles and expelled demons. An error and blasphemy.

Fourteenth article, that God himself directly or through good angels revealed such sorceries to holy men. An error and blasphemy.

Fifteenth article, that it is possible by such arts to force the free will of a man to the will or desire of another. An error.

Sixteenth article, that on this account the said arts are good and from God and that it is licit to observe them, because sometimes or often it happens through them, as those employing them seek or predict, or because good sometimes comes from them. An error.

Seventeenth article, that demons are really forced and coerced by such arts and do not pretend to be compelled in order to seduce men. An error.

Eighteenth article, that by such arts and impious rites, by sortilege, by incantations, by invocation of demons, by certain glances and other sorcery, no effect ever follows by aid of demons. An error.

Nineteenth article, that good angels are shut up in stones, and that they consecrate images or vestments, or do other things which are comprised in those arts. An error and blasphemy.

Twentieth article, that the blood of a hoopoe or kid or other animal, or virgin parchment or lionskin and the like have efficacy to compel and repel demons by the aid of arts of this sort. An error.

Twenty-first article, that images of copper or lead or gold or white or red wax or other material baptized, exorcized and consecrated, or rather execrated, according to the said arts and on certain days, have marvelous virtues which are recited in the books of such arts. An error in faith, in natural philosophy, and in true astrology.

Twenty-second article, that to use such and believe in them is not idolatry and infidelity. An error.

Twenty-third article, that some demons are good, some benign, some omniscient, some neither saved nor damned. An error.

Twenty-fourth article, that suffumigations which are performed in operations of this sort are converted into spirits, or that they are due to them. An error.

Twenty-fifth article, that one demon is king of the east and by his especial merit, another of the west, another of the north, another of the south. An error.

Twenty-sixth article, that the intelligence which moves the heaven influences the rational soul just as the body of the heaven influences the human body. An error.

Twenty-seventh article, that our intellectual cogitations and inner volitions are caused immediately by the sky, and that by a magic tradition such can be known, and that thereby it is licit to pass certain judgment as to them. An error.

Twenty-eighth article, that by certain magic arts we can reach the vision of the divine essence or of the holy spirits. An error.

Done are these and, after mature and frequent examination between us and our deputies, concluded in our general congregation at Paris at St. Mathurin in the morning specially set aside for this, September 19, 1398. In testimony of which thing we have decreed to append the seal of the said faculty to the present letters.

24
Bernardino of Siena Preaches Against
Women Sorcerers (1427)

Bernardino of Siena (1380–1444), one of the most successful Franciscan preachers of the fifteenth century, was particularly concerned with
those sins that threatened to call down the wrath of God on entire
communities if they were not punished. Prominent among these were
sorcery, infanticide, sodomy, and toleration of Jews. Although Bernardino's antisemitism has long been known, only recently have scholars
studied the other major topics of his sermons. Here, Bernardino illustrates the state of the problem from the perspective of a much-traveled
preacher already inclined to take sorcery and witchcraft very seriously,
although his depiction of the women sorcerers' activities is not yet that
of the "classic" witches of the later fifteenth and sixteenth centuries.
Bernardino was also a reader of Jacopo Passavanti and thus a link between the popularizing theology of the confessor's manual and the
ideas and technical tools of the popular preacher.

Although Bernardino had had considerable success in a case of the
execution of women sorcerers in Rome in 1424, which he refers to in
his sermon printed here, he did not have comparable success in his
own hometown in 1427.[1] Nor did his sense of urgent alarm concerning
women and sorcery, which he probably acquired on his preaching jour-
neys throughout northern Italy, reflect public opinion in the cities of
fifteenth-century Tuscany.

SOURCE: John Shinners, ed., *Medieval Popular Religion, 1000–1500:
A Reader* (Peterborough, Ontario, 1997), 242–45.

FURTHER READING: Bernadette Paton, " 'To the Fire, To the Fire! Let
Us Burn a Little Incense to God': Bernardino, Preaching Friars and
Maleficio in Late Medieval Sienna," in Charles Zika, ed., *No Gods
Except Me: Orthodoxy and Religious Practice in Europe, 1200–1600*
(Melbourne, 1991), 7–36; Paton, *Preaching Friars and the Civic Ethos:
Sienna, 1380–1480* (London, 1992), and especially Franco Mormando,
The Preacher's Demons: Bernardino of Siena and the Social Under-

---

1. The burnings in Rome in 1424 were apparently widely known. They are also mentioned in
Buch aller verbotenen Kunst, Unglaubens, und der Zauberei (Book of Forbidden Arts, Unbelief,
and Magic) by the Munich physician Johannes Hartlieb in 1456, who says that he was in Rome
and witnessed the burnings in 1424. Hartlieb discusses them immediately after his consideration of magical flight, thus linking the two originally unrelated actions. Hartlieb's text is in
Hansen, *Quellen*, 130–33, discussed in Lea, *Materials*, 1: 275. See Richard Kieckhefer, *Forbidden Rites: A Necromancer's Manual of the Fifteenth Century* (University Park, 1998), 32–34,
with further references.

world of Early Renaissance Italy (Chicago, 1998). For Florence in this period, see Gene Brucker, "Sorcery in Early Renaissance Florence," *Studies in the Renaissance* 10 (1963): 7–24. There is an important study of a trial at Todi in 1428 in Domenico Mammoli, *The Record of the Trial and Condemnation of a Witch, Matteuccia di Francesco, at Todi, 20 March 1428* (Rome, 1972). For a similar reaction in Venice a century or so later, Ruth Martin, *Witchcraft and the Inquisition in Venice, 1550–1650* (Oxford and New York, 1989).

GOD FORBID THAT A fearful judgment should overtake you because of your sin, for I know well that you have blasphemed and that daily you do blaspheme God and the saints. Your land will be laid waste and fire will light upon your city, Siena, and your country will fall under the rule of the enemy and be sacked of all the good things found in it. Then it will be desolate of those who dwelled there, and abandoned by those who used to till it, and the soldiers will possess it, and the daughter of Sion will be like an empty shadow, like the vine when it is stripped of its fruit. God will say, "Until now I have used oil, I have allured you with sweet promises to make you return to me. Now you will be in greater peril than you ever have been, for now you will become like the shadow of a vine." Did you not know that after the vintage, only the phantom of the vine remains? So will it be with your vines: they will be like shadows, since, because of the wars, it will be impossible to till the vineyards, and even if they were tilled, their fruit will be plundered. The soldiers will leave your houses without floor or windows or doors. Here will lie a house half in ruins; the beams of another's ceiling will have fallen to the ground. O how then shall [Siena] be called when she is so devastated? She shall be called a shadow. Mark me! Have you noticed that when they build the little hut for the man who guards the melons, it is always a habitable shelter while there are melons? But when these are gone, then it stands there like a hovel. Ah, citizen, give heed to him who has seen such things with his own eyes! I have come upon a place which, because of the wars raged there, had been abandoned, so that only three or four friars were left there. Wild beasts dwelled there as if there had always been a forest there. Where once lived so many men of high estate, now there lived wild beasts. Alas, woe is me! City of Siena, beware! You had better beware! When the house of your neighbor is on fire, have you never heard these words: "Hasten with water to your own house?" O my fellow citizens, have you not eyes? If you have them, open them a little! O city of Siena, open your eyes and amend yourself now so far as you can, so that you won't become a hovel or a shadow. Enough! I want this to suffice now regarding the sin of blasphemy. What is this sermon called, O women? This is a sermon about truth.

Another sin which derives from pride is the sin concerning charms and divinations, because of which God many times sends his scourges into cities. I realize that I spoke about this once before, and I said so much about it that he who heard me and understood what I was talking about must have been struck with fear. For I spoke so plainly and clearly about it that I thought nothing more needed to be said. Here is someone who [for health] measures by a span of the palm, another with parchment talismans [brevi], another with charms, another with sorceries, another with divinations. Some have visited the enchanter or diviner if they have been robbed of five cents. Do you know what you have done? You have caused men to renounce God, and you have caused the devil to be adored. O me, O me! The Lord of Heaven and Earth has been debased, and to think that the devil is adored through such a great iniquity. And this man says, "Really, I don't know what the matter is; I find that I've been told the truth." And I say to you that you do not perceive how you have been deceived, and that you were shown one thing for another. Alas! you who are so blinded, have you never comprehended his snares and deceits, how he has always deceived us, and has struggled to do so? Go look at the beginning of the book of Genesis, when he began to tempt Eve and Adam; how, persuading them to break God's commandment, he said, Eritis sicut dii, scientes bonum et malum—"You shall be as gods, knowing good and evil" [Gen. 3: 5] if you eat the fruit. And so he caused them to fall. O you who have cast lots, what a great evil you do, and how many people have trusted in them and followed them! How well they teach you the truth! And have they never told you nothing that would make you see that they lie? And despite this have you been willing to forsake them? Woe unto you! O you who have used the charm of the three good brothers [against wounds], what a great evil you do. O you who have used the charm for broken bones, to you, and to him or her who says that she is bewitched, and who makes you believe she is—to all these I say, take heed! For the first to feel the strokes from God's scourges will be those who have trusted in these enchantments and followed them; and next vengeance will overtake those who have not brought them to justice. Have you never noticed in the Old Testament how God condemned this? Solely because it was displeasing to God, and he made this plain and clear. Know that she or he who claims to have the power to break a charm knows as well, be assured, how to work one. When such people say that they wish to cure anyone, do you know what you should do? There is nothing better to do than cry "To the fire! To the fire! To the fire!" Woe is me! Don't you know what happened at Rome while I was preaching there? I wish I could make it happen here too! Come, let us offer a little incense here at Siena to the Lord God. I want to tell you what happened at Rome.

I had preached about these charms and about witches and sorceries to them, but they seemed to think that I had dreamed it all up. Finally it occurred to me to say that whoever knew of a man or woman doing such things and did not accuse them would be guilty of the selfsame sin. . . . And after I had preached, a multitude of witches and enchanters were accused. And due to the very great number of those accused, a guardian of the monastery came to me and said, "Are you aware that one and all of them are going to the flames?" I asked him, "What then? What is this? What is this? A great number of men and women have been accused." Finally, seeing how the matter stood, he took counsel with the Pope, and it was determined that the most important of these women—that is, those who had done the worst—would be taken into custody. One of them told and confessed, without being put to torture, that she had killed thirty children by sucking their blood; she also said that she had let sixty go free. She said that every time she let one of them go free, she had to sacrifice a limb to the devil, and she used to offer the limb of an animal. She had done this for a long time. Yet she confessed more, saying that she had killed her own little son, and had made a powder out of him, which she gave people to eat in these practices of hers. And because it seemed beyond belief that any creature could have done so many wicked things, they wished to prove whether this was indeed true. Finally she was asked whom she had killed. She said who they were, and whose children they were, and in what way and when she had killed them. Going there, they sought proof from the father of the children who had been killed: "Did you ever have a little son who at such and such a time began to pine away and then die?" Finally, since he replied this was so, and since the day and the hour and the manner in which this had happened all agreed, it was proved to be no more or less than what she had said. And she told how she used to go before dawn up to the piazza of St. Peter's, and there she had certain jars or unguents made of herbs which were gathered on the feasts of St. John and on the feast of the Ascension. (Do you know this, witch? Do you understand me? Are you present here? Are there here as well perhaps even some of those accursed ones who are in league with the devil?) Finally, I got hold of these unguents, and when I put them to my nose, they stank with so foul a stench that they seemed in truth to be of the devil, as they were. And they said that they anointed themselves with these, and when they were anointed, they seemed to be cats (though this was not so, for their bodies did not change form—but it seemed to them that they did). . . . At length she was condemned to be burned at the stake. And she was burned so that nothing remained but her ashes. There was also another woman taken who confessed that she had done like deeds, and she was as well condemned to be burned, but she died in another manner: for she was not strangled before she was put upon the pyre, and the fire was kindled there while she was alive, and nothing more was seen of her but her ashes. What was done to them should be done wherever one of them is found. And therefore I would give you this caution and warn you that wherever one may be, and whoever may know him or her, in any place whatsoever inside or outside the city, straightaway accuse her before the Inquisitor. Whether within the city or outside its walls, accuse her—every witch, every wizard, every sorcerer or sorceress, or worker of charms and spells.

Do what I tell you in order that you will not be called upon to answer for it on the Day of Judgment, having been able to prevent so great an evil which might have been prevented if you had accused her. And I tell you another thing: if any man or woman shall be accused of such things and if any person shall go to their aid, the curse of God will light upon his house and he will suffer for it in his goods and in his body, and afterwards also in his soul. Oh! Answer me: does it really seem to you that someone who has killed twenty or thirty little children in such a way has done so well that when finally they are accused before the *Signoria* you should go to their aid and beg mercy for them? If it had happened that she killed one of your little children, what would you think about the matter then? From your own feelings take thought for another. Think of another and greater fact: has it not occurred to you that such enchanters, every time they have worked any charms or spells have denied God by doing so? How great a sin does it seem to you to deny God, eh?

Figure 1. Theophilus becomes the servant of the devil (top) by kneeling before him, signing a contract, and placing his hands in those of the demon. He later repents (bottom) and is saved by the intercession of the virgin. From an early thirteenth-century French Psalter of Ingeborg of Denmark. The story is the prototype of later theories of the pact between humans and the demon (Text 12). Musée Condé, Chantilly.

Figure 2. St. James and Hermogenes. Left panel, probably from a late fifteenth-century diptych or portable altarpiece, by a follower of Hieronymus Bosch, showing part of the story of St. James the Greater and the sorcerer Hermogenes. From the apocryphal *Apostolic History* attributed to Abdias and transmitted in several collections down to the sixteenth century. Musée Valenciennes, Valenciennes.

Figure 3. St. James and Hermogenes. Pieter Breugel the Elder's 1564 engraving of the same scene as in Figure 2 suggests the associations that the image of the sorcerer who opposes the apostle had acquired on the eve of the great prosecutions for witchcraft. Bibliothèque Nationale, Paris.

Figure 4. St. James overthrows Hermogenes. Breugel, The fall of Hermogenes by the power of St. James and the overthrow of all his magical works. As in the image in Figure 3, Breugel was commissioned to rework an earlier Bosch picture for current tastes. Bibliothèque Nationale, Paris.

Figure 5. The devil begets Antichrist on a human woman. From *Der Entchrist*, Germany, 1475. This and other similar stories helped justify the demonologists' arguments that demons could have sexual intercourse with human beings. University of Pennsylvania.

Figure 6. Sano di Pietro. San Bernardino preaching in the public square in Siena, 1427. Preaching was one of the major sources of both religious instruction and communications in late medieval Europe. Duomo, Siena, Scala.

Figure 7. Vaudois, heretical sorcerers, and witches adoring the devil in the form of a goat. From a mid-fifteenth-century illuminated manuscript of Johannes Tinctoris's treatise against the sect and its alleged activities. Bibliothèque Royale Albert I, Brussels.

Figure 8. The first known illustration of women flying on broomsticks. From a mid-fifteenth-century manuscript with marginal illustrations of Martin Le Franc's poem, *Le Champion des dames* (Text 30). Bibliothèque Nationale, Paris.

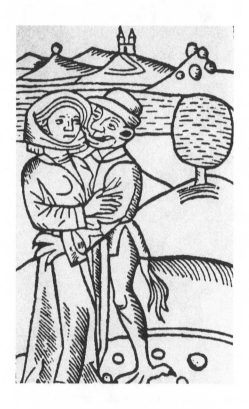

Figure 9. An early illustration of a witch causing weather magic, one of the most feared activities of witches in a largely agricultural society. Woodcut, *Wetterzauber*, from Johannes Vintler, *Buch der Tugend* (Augsburg, 1486). University of Pennsylvania.

Figure 10. A witch embracing her demon lover. Woodcut from Ulrich Molitor, *Des Sorcières et des devineresses* (*On Witches*), 1487, the first book illustrated with a set of pictures. Because demons were considered incapable of perfect imitation of God's creation, the human form assumed here has clawed feet and a tail. University of Pennsylvania.

Figure 11. The archer witch, whose magical arrows injure her neighbors. From Molitor, *On Witches*. University of Pennsylvania.

Figure 12. Witches partly transformed into beasts riding to the sabbat. From Molitor, *On Witches*. University of Pennsylvania.

Figure 13. The scene in Figure 12 reworked in the treatise *Tractatus von den bosen Weibern* (*Treatise Against Evil Women Called Witches*) (Ulm, 1490). Molitor's illustrations were often copied. University of Pennsylvania.

V

The Sect of Diabolical Witches,

1430–60

Scholarly research during the past three decades has greatly increased our knowledge, not only of the early and diverse antecedents of the classical concept of the witch, but also of the later large- and small-scale prosecutions of people for the crime of diabolical witchcraft and the growth of new credulous and skeptical attitudes toward it. One of the chief results of some of this scholarship has been to make more specific the period in which earlier ideas that associated sorcery with heresy and heresy with diabolism were combined by a number of thinkers, including jurists and writers, recognizing that the key years were 1430–60. Recent research has also defined the places where the process occurred earliest, particularly in the area of what is now northwestern Italy, southeastern France, central and western Switzerland, and southwestern Germany. Some of the most significant records of the "flash point" produced by this research are included in this chapter.

Although a vast series of natural and man-made disasters struck Europe from 1315 until well into the fifteenth century—the great famine of 1315–17, the successive waves of plague from 1348 on, large-scale increasingly destructive warfare, and both financial collapse across Europe and a transformation of traditional market economies that affected local areas, as well as the papal schism and the conciliar movement—it is also generally accepted by historians that in no case can a direct causal connection be made between these events and the transformation of the ideas of diabolical sorcery and heresy into witchcraft. Nor is there a direct connection between conventional and traditional Christian European misogyny and the furious misogyny that marked much, but not all, of the new idea of the witch.

More influential was the deep-seated awareness on the part of pastoral theologians in the late fourteenth and fifteenth centuries of the need for widespread reform in ecclesiastical and devotional life and their fear of the consequences for Christian Europe if reform were not accomplished to root out what they termed abuses and "superstitions," the latter becoming the governing category for diabolical sorcery and witchcraft as well as other and—to us, at least—less urgent and obvious offenses. The greater the urgency for and frustration of reform, the worse appeared the evils that reform was needed to combat. In the process, the devil's plan to ruin Christian society came to be regarded as having other new components—the diabolical sorcerer and the assembly of witches.

As Pierette Paravy, one of the most distinguished historians of the problem and period, has said of the years 1430–60:

> It is this fundamental distinction [that of the *Canon Episcopi* between the fantasy of night-flight and its reality] that disappears. The diverse worlds of throwers and raisers of *sortes*, of men and women who cure illnesses, are uniformly included without mercy in a single condemnation, to the extent that every kind of magic, when investigated, reveals a member of the devil's sect. . . . None of these elements is new, and all of them are attested in a complex intellectual and psychological heritage that unified pagan Mediterranean and [northern] Germanic traditions. What was new was the rigorous tie that bound and combined these elements with each other, coordinating them in a system that was at the same time fantastic and coherent.[1]

Another influential element was the slowly increasing use of learned law by the magistrates of ambitious state-building powers—that is, the historian of the subject must look at the context and, where possible, the personnel of particular courts that tried particular cases as well as the familiarity on the part of writers of demonological treatises and books on witchcraft with one set of trials or another. One of the most striking features of the texts produced in the period 1430–60 is the close relation of many of them to actual cases tried in known places, recently, by known judges. As Arno Borst has said, "We have . . . to attend to the dirty details of the first witchcraft trials and put them into the historical context of their specific locations, instead of spending time on religious and social history at large."[2]

One feature of the ecclesiastical and juridical thought of the fourteenth century had been the idea that sorcery, like heresy, must be collaborative, that the individual sorcerer, of course, should be apprehended and punished, but the sorcerer (increasingly assumed to be a member of a sect of sorcerers) also ought to be forced to reveal other members of the group. The letter of Pope Alexan-

---

1. Pierette Paravy, "Faire croire: Quelques hypothèses de recherche basées sur l'étude des procès de sorcellerie du Dauphiné au XVe siècle," in *Faire croire: Modalités de la diffusion et de la réception des messages religieux du XIIe au XVe siècle*, Collection de l'École française de Rome 51 (Rome, 1981), 121, 124.

2. Arno Borst, "The Origins of the Witch-Craze in the Alps," in Borst, *Medieval Worlds: Barbarians, Heretics, and Artists*, trans. Eric Hansen (Chicago, 1992), 104.

der V to the Franciscan inquisitor Pontus Fougeyron of 1409 (Text 25) explicitly mentions new sects and links various sorts of practitioners of sorcery to them. In 1437 Pope Eugenius IV, also a correspondent of Pontus Fougeyron, indicated the growing attitude that the threat from diabolical sorcerers was increasing (Text 26).

Around the same time a book on many aspects of ecclesiastical reform, including some of the earliest specific evidence of classical witchcraft, the *Formicarius* (The Ant-Colony), by the Dominican theologian Johannes Nider (Text 27), offered a wealth of anecdotes about sorcery trials Nider had heard of, based on his own conversations with the judges who had presided over them. Nider's work in this respect was not that of a speculative theologian—he derived his ideas about diabolical sorcery practiced by both men and women from conversations with real judges and inquisitors concerning real cases that they had tried personally, and he may have circulated some of the ideas in his book at the ecclesiastical Council of Basel (1431–49) in 1435–37, the largest assembly and exchanging-point of ideas in all of fifteenth-century Europe.[3] It was at the council, for example, that Nider first heard of the trial of Joan of Arc in 1431 from a fellow Dominican from the Sorbonne, and Nider immediately connected Joan's case to the problem of diabolical sorcery he had learned of nearer home just a few years earlier.[4]

Other secular judges did more than try witches and tell legal anecdotes to inquisitive local theologians. Claude Tholosan, a judge in the district of Briançonnais in the Dauphiné, wrote a remarkable treatise justifying the role of secular judges in such prosecutions (Text 29). At the same time, an anonymous inquisitor from the same area circulated a treatise called the *Errores Gazariorum* (Errors of the Cathars), which said little about Cathar heretics, but a great deal about activities attributed to new sects of devil-worshipers, which are virtually identical to the classical figure of the witch (Text 31). In 1440 the poet Martin Le Franc, provost of the cathedral of Lausanne, who believed firmly in many of the accusations against diabolical sorcerers, wrote a long poem called *The Defender of Ladies* in which his spokesman denied at least the reality of

3. On this immensely important church council, now recognized as closely associated with several texts on the new kind of witchcraft, see Joachim W. Stieber, *Pope Eugenius IV, the Council of Basel and the Secular and Ecclesiastical Authorities in the Empire* (Leiden, 1987); Michael Bailey, "Heresy, Witchcraft, and Reform: Johannes Nider and the Religious World of the Late Middle Ages" (Ph.D. diss., Northwestern University, 1998); Margaret Aston, *The Fifteenth Century: The Prospect of Europe* (London and New York, 1968). Some relevant texts are translated in Christopher M. D. Crowder, *Unity, Heresy, and Reform, 1378–1460: The Conciliar Response to the Great Schism* (New York, 1977), 146–65.

4. On the circulation of reports on the trial of Joan at Basel, see Thomas Heinz, "Jeanne la Pucelle, das Basler Konzil und die 'Kleinen' der 'Reformatio Sigismundi,'" *Francia* 11 (1981): 319–39.

flight to the sabbat against some vehement evidence in favor of its reality by his opponent in the poetic debate (Text 30). In 1458 the inquisitor Nicholas Jacquier circulated his *Flagellum haereticorum fascinariorum* (Scourge for heretical witches, Text 31), a formal attack on such skeptics as the Defender in Le Franc's poem, as well as an important and influential refutation of the *Canon Episcopi* as applying to Jacquier's own time.

Some evidence also suggests that the areas in which Fougeyron, Nider, Tholosan, and Le Franc worked were not the only places troubled by the apparently new phenomenon—a recently discovered royal pardon issued by King Charles VII of France in 1460 illustrates the case of a local man in southwestern France who killed a "witch-finder" who had accused the man's female relatives of sorcery and witchcraft (Text 32).

By the middle of the fifteenth century, witchcraft as diabolical sorcery had been fully assimilated to heresy and pronounced against in the public record by the highest and most powerful ecclesiastical and lay authorities. It served as the grounds of accusation and conviction in a number of trials that had been held in known, nearby places, by known judges (as well as in more widely publicized political and inquisitorial trials), and news of them circulated at the Council of Basel and from there throughout the rest of western Europe. Apostasy, diabolism, collective action against the human race, the still-debated sabbat, and undeviating hostility toward Christian society had now become the characteristics of all witches—and all witches had become the collaborative servants of Satan.

25
Pope Alexander V to Pontus Fougeyron on New Sects (1409)

One of the most distinctive features of the "new" concept of diabolical witchcraft was its collaborative character; that is, theologians and jurists tended to see those who were brought before them and charged with sorcery of one kind or another not simply as accused individuals who acted alone but as members of a larger conspiracy directed by Satan against humanity. Although individual pacts with the demon forced the witch to renounce his or her Christian baptism (thereby committing the terrible sin of apostasy) and to pay idolatrous homage to the devil instead of God (the even more terrible sin of idolatry, the sin against the First Commandment) and to be deserving of execution for these individual crimes, the individual witch only became understandable when considered as a member of a group devoted to the harm and eventual destruction of the human race. This may be one of the reasons why the idea of the witches' sabbat was developed out of the earlier idea of the heretical assembly as well as out of the old "delusion" of women flying at night with Diana in the *Canon Episcopi*—it was a visible sign of the witches' collective role in the devil's assault on humanity. The idea of entirely new heretical sects is reflected early in the fifteenth century in a letter from Pope Alexander V (1409–10) to the Franciscan Pontus Fougeyron, an energetic and dedicated inquisitor whose career is well known from other contemporary sources. Although the term "new heresy" was used as early as the ninth century and relatively frequently after the late twelfth—therefore cautioning against taking Alexander V's phrase as being as original as some scholars have—the concern nevertheless shows that Alexander certainly thought that something unprecedented was occurring.

SOURCE: Hansen, *Quellen*, pp. 16–17. Trans. E. P.

To PONTUS FOUGEYRON, nominated as inquisitor of heretical depravity in Avignon, in Arles [and elsewhere] . . . We have recently and sadly heard that some Christians and perfidious Jews within the boundaries of your jurisdiction have founded new sects and perform rites that are repugnant to the Christian religion. They also often teach hidden doctrines, preaching and affirming them. And we have also heard that there are within the boundaries of your jurisdiction many Christians and Jews who are sorcerers, diviners, invokers of demons, enchanters, conjurers, superstitious people, augurs, practitioners of nefarious and forbidden arts, and that all of these stain and pervert the Christian people, or at least the simpler-minded of them. [Pontus is to cooperate with diocesan officials against these people right up to the point of issuing a definitive sentence against them, and, if the work requires, to invoke the aid of the secular arm.]

26
Pope Eugenius IV: Two Letters on the
Pressing Danger (1434–37)

Pope Eugenius IV (1431–47) was an austere and devout prelate whose pontificate was troubled by his bad relations with the Council of Basel (on the Council of Basel, see below, also above, p. 151) and his opposition to the council's elected antipope Felix V. During his pontificate, the ecclesiastical reform movement which had been begun in Bohemia by John Hus had turned into a major civil war, and the city of Rome itself was troubled by rebellion and opposition to the pope. It was in the troubled early years of his pontificate that Pope Eugenius turned his attention to the problem of witchcraft, a question that troubled him particularly because of his intense and genuine piety and his ambition for the reform of the clergy.

In March 1440, addressing the members of the Council of Basel and denoucing Amadeus VIII/Felix V, Eugenius claimed that in the duchy of Savoy Amadeus had tolerated the existence of "men and women who in the vulgar tongue are called *'stregule'* or *'stregonos'* or *'Waudenses'* of whom it is said that there are many in his territories."[1] The usage implies that the term "Waldenses," or *vaudois*, no longer referred strictly to the older Waldensian heretics, but to the new *stregule*, or witches. In the same sense, the term Cathars had been used interchangeably with Waldensians since the late fourteenth century (Text 28).

SOURCE: Hansen, *Quellen*, 17–18. Trans. E. P.

A. A Letter to the Inquisitor Pontus Fougeyron, 1434

Among many heretics there are found also many Christian and Jewish magicians, diviners, invokers of demons, enchanters [*carminatores*], conjurers, superstitious people, augurs, those who use nefarious and forbidden arts, through whose efforts the Christian people, or at least a numerous and simple-minded part of them, are stained and perverted.

B. A Letter to All Inquisitors of Heretical Depravity, 1437

The news has reached us, not without great bitterness of spirit, that the prince of darkness makes many who have been bought by the blood of Christ partakers in his own fall and damnation, bewitching them by his cunning arts in such a way that these detestable persuasions and illusions make them members of his sect. They sacrifice to demons, adore them, seek out and accept responses from them, do homage to them, and make with them a written agreement or another kind of pact through which, by a single word, touch, or sign, they may perform whatever evil deeds or sorcery they wish and be transported to or away from wherever they wish. They cure diseases, provoke bad weather, and make pacts concerning other evil deeds. Or, so that they may achieve these purposes, the reckless creatures make images or have images made in order to constrain the demons, or by invoking them perpetrate more sorcery. In their sorcery they are not afraid to use the materials of baptism, the eucharist, and other sacraments. They make images of wax or other materials which by their invocations they baptize or cause to be baptized. Sometimes they make a reversal of the Holy Cross, upon which our Savior hanged for us. Not honoring the mysteries, they

1. Hansen, *Quellen*, 18–19. Trans. E. P.

sometimes inflict upon the representations and other signs of the cross various shameful things by execrable means.

27
Johannes Nider: The *Formicarius* (1435–38)

Johannes Nider (1380/85–1438), was born in southern Swabia and entered the Dominican Order shortly after 1402. After studying at the universities of Vienna and Cologne, he attended the Council of Constance in 1415–18 and was prior of the Dominican convent at Nuremberg in 1426/7–29. Extremely supportive of the reforming wing of the order, as well as a supporter of church reform broadly conceived, Nider became prior of the convent at Basel from 1429 to 1436 and served in several diplomatic capacities in the service of the Council of Basel from 1431 to 1434. Probably in 1435 he returned to the University of Vienna as professor of theology and was elected dean of the theological faculty in 1436. He died in Vienna in 1438.

Nider had written a number of works of theology earlier, and he wrote his best-known work, the long treatise on theology and moral and ecclesiological reform, the *Formicarius* (The Ant-Colony; the title is based on Proverbs 6: 6 and holds up the disciplined ant colony as a model for human society, with each book connecting a feature of human life to some real or imagined feature of the ant community), as the best recent scholar, Michael Bailey, estimates, between 1435 and 1438.

The work takes the form of a dialogue between a theologian and a doubter, and its format is highly anecdotal. The first two books deal with good works and revelations, the third with falsities and wicked acts, and the fourth with the deeds of virtuous people. The fifth book deals with the nature and practice of witchcraft under the general heading of works of evildoers and deceivers. But Nider does not simply reinterpret earlier theological and inquisitorial models. He cites his informants: the Bernese patrician Peter von Greyerz, who had worked as judge in the Simme Valley between 1392 and 1407; a monk at Vienna named Benedict, who had earlier been active in the peripheral world of sleight-of-hand tricks, court entertainments, and, as Nider says, necromancy;[1] and an inquisitor from Autun. Whether or not Nider reinterprets their earlier accounts of events from the end of the fourteenth

1. It is important to note that sleight-of-hand tricks, including juggling, since they deliberately aimed at deceiving the senses, the most vulnerable part of the human intellective apparatus, were regarded with both suspicion and fascination from antiquity well into the early modern period.

century to accord with the new assumptions about witchcraft that characterized Nider's 1430s—that is, into something that his informants had not intended—is a matter of debate. But Nider's stories gained great credibility from the specificity of their sources and the records of them that could be checked.

SOURCE: Burr, *The Witch Persecutions*, 6–7, rev. E. P., from the edition printed at Helmstedt, 1692, book 5, chap. 3. Burr's translation is based on the Latin edition of Augsburg, 1476.

FURTHER READING: Borst, "The Origins of the Witch-Craze in the Alps," 101–22; Michael Bailey, "The Medieval Concept of the Witches' Sabbath," *Exemplaria* 8 (1996): 419–39; Bailey, "Heresy, Witchcraft, and Reform: Johannes Nider and the Religious World of the Late Middle Ages" (Ph.D. diss., Northwestern University, 1998), esp. 214–74. There is a summary of the discussion of witchcraft in Nider's earlier work *Praeceptorium Divinae Legis*, in Lea, *Materials* 1:265–72, 260–65.

[THE BEGINNING OF THE fifth book links the different colors of ants to the color symbolism of vices and virtues. The *Piger*—the "sluggard" in the dialogue who takes his designation from Proverbs 6:6—asks the Theologian about *malefici et superstitiosi*. The Theologian responds that demons find it easy to deceive humans, trapped as they are in sense-perceptions, confined in the prison of the body, and possessing a tendency to melancholia. The first chapter then goes on to discuss visions of warfare and apparitions of ghosts. Throughout the work the Theologian responds with a few citations of traditional authorities, but the bulk of the responses consists of stories, skillfully chosen and told. The second chapter deals with demonic invasions of domestic households. The third chapter turns to sorcery and witchcraft, citing Isidore of Seville (Text 3) and first discussing erotic magic and its causes.]

I will relate to you some examples, which I have learned in part from the teachers of our faculty, in part from the experience of a certain upright secular judge, worthy of all faith, who from the torture and confessions of witches and from his experiences in public and private life has learned many things of this sort—a man with whom I have often discussed this subject broadly and deeply—to wit, Peter, a citizen of Bern, in the diocese of Lausanne, who has burned many witches of both sexes, and has driven others out of the territory of Bern. I have also conferred with one Benedict, a monk of the Benedictine order, who, although now a very devout cleric in a reformed monastery in Vienna, was, a decade ago while still in the world, a necromancer, juggler, buffoon, and strolling player, well known as an expert among the secular nobility. I have likewise heard certain of the following things from the inquisitor of heretical depravity at Autun, who was a devoted reformer of our order in the convent at Lyons, and has convicted many of witchcraft in the diocese of Autun.

There are, or there very recently were (as both the same inquisitor and Lord Peter have told me, and as is well known among the public) in the territory of Bern, a great many witches of both sexes who greatly hated human nature and assumed the likenesses of various kinds of beasts, especially those kinds that devour children.

In the town of Boltingen in the diocese of Lausanne there lived a man named Stadelin, a great witch, who was arrested by the same Lord Peter, the judge of the district. Stadelin had entered a house where a man and wife lived and by his witchcraft killed seven successive infants in her womb. In the same household he killed the foetuses of sheep, so that for seven years no sheep was born to them. When he was asked how this was done, he said that he placed a certain kind of lizard under the threshold of the house and if he removed it fecundity would be restored to them. When anyone tried to look for the serpent and did not find it, this was because it had been reduced to a powder, and the powder was sprinkled on the earth beneath the threshold, and when it was removed, in the same year fertility was restored to all the animals of the household. These confessions were drawn from him by torture and were not spontaneously given. And he was sent to the fire by the same judge.

The same inquisitor told me that in the duchy of Lausanne certain witches even devoured their own children. The witches gathered in a certain place, and when their deeds were done they saw the demon visibly appear in the form of a man. The disciples then had to deny Christianity, promise never to adore the Eucharist, and to trample the crucifix underfoot.

It was also known in the community. The judge Peter told me that in Bernese territory thirteen infants were devoured by witches in a very short time. Public justice grew harsh toward these parricides. When Peter asked a captured witch how they devoured these infants, she answered that the method is this: with unbaptized infants, or even with infants already baptized if they are not protected by the sign of the cross and by prayers, we kill by our ceremonies in their cradles, or when they are lying in bed beside their parents, so that they are thought to have been crushed [overlain by their parents] or to have died some other natural way. We then remove them secretly from their graves and cook them in a cauldron until their flesh, cooked and separated from the bones, is made into a powerful liquid. From the solids of this material we make a certain unguent that is useful for our desires, arts, and transformations. From the liquids we fill a container, and from this, with a few additional ceremonies, anyone who drinks immediately becomes a member and master of our sect.

The same procedure was more clearly described by another young man, arrested and burned as a witch, although, as I believe, truly, penitent, who had earlier, together with his wife, a witch invincible to persuasion, escaped the clutches of the aforesaid judge, Peter. The aforesaid youth, being again indicted at Bern, with his wife, and placed in a different prison from hers, declared: "If I can obtain absolution for my sins, I will freely lay bare all I know about witch-craft, for I see that I have death to expect." And when he had been assured by the scholars that, if he should truly repent, he would certainly be able to gain abso-lution for his sins, then he gladly offered himself to death, and disclosed the methods of the primeval infection.

The ceremony, he said, of my seduction was as follows: First, on a Sunday before the holy water is consecrated, the future disciple with his masters must go into the church, and there in their presence must renounce Christ and his faith, baptism, and the church universal. Then he must do homage to the *ma-gisterulus*, that is, to the little master (for so, and not otherwise, they call the devil). Afterward he drinks from the aforesaid flask; and, this done, he forthwith feels himself to conceive and hold within himself an image of our art and the chief rites of this sect. After this fashion was I seduced; and my wife also, whom I believe of so great pertinacity that she will endure the flames rather than confess the least whit of truth, but, alas, we are both guilty. What the young man had said was found in all respects the truth. For, after confession, the young man was seen to die in great contrition. His wife, however, though convicted by the testimony of witnesses, would not confess the truth even under the torture or in death; but, when the fire was prepared for her by the executioner, she uttered in most evil words a curse upon him, and so was burned.

[Piger then asks whether witchcraft should be driven out. The Theologian re-sponds that the ancients thought not, but that today it should. Chapter 4 deals with necromancy, the raising of the dead, duly noting the case of the witch of En-dor and the necessity of a pact with the devil, and recounting stories told him by the Benedictine monk who had himself been a necromancer. Nider then tells the history of witchcraft in the Simme Valley, also obtained from Peter von Greyerz.]

The person who began this witchcraft was a man called Scavius [the scabby man], who publicly used to glory in his art, saying that whenever he wished he could transform himself into a mouse and thereby escape from the hands of his en-emies. And he had done this often. But divine justice wished to put an end to his wickedness. When he was sitting by the window at an inn looking carefully around him, but having no suspicion of immediate danger, his enemies broke through the window and transfixed him with swords and spears so that he died miserably.

This man left behind a disciple named Hoppo, who made Stadelin into a master of witchcraft. These two knew how, whenever it pleased them, to take the manure, grains, and fruits or whatever they wanted from the field of a neigh-bor, seen by no one, and move them to their own field. They could cause im-mense hailstorms and poison winds with lightning, cause sterility in humans and animals, injure their neighbors in body and property, drive horses mad when their wealthy riders mounted them, and travel through air wherever they wished to go. . . . When judge Peter sent his servants to capture the said Stadelin, their hands were struck by a great tremor and a terrible odor assailed them so that they gave up hope of capturing him. But the judge told them to lay hands on the wretched man because he would lose all his powers when once touched by the hand of justice. And they were then able to take him. . . . The judge asked Stadelin how he was able to cause hailstorms and tempests. The criminal answered that he stood in a field saying certain words and begged the most powerful of all demons to send him a lesser demon to strike whatever Stadelin wished. When the demon arrived, he obeyed, and immediately the storms began, not always in the place designated by Stadelin, but where God permitted this to happen.

The judge asked Stadelin whether or not the storms contrived by him and the demon could be averted in any way. Stadelin answered that they could by saying these words: "I order you, hailstorms and winds, by the three divine nails of Christ, which wounded Him in hands and feet, and by the four evangelists, Saints Matthew, Mark, Luke, and John, that you turn into falling rain."

[The remaining eight chapters deal with erotic magic and ligatures (chap. 5), its cures (chap. 6), and related matters (chap. 7). In chapter 8 Nider tells the story of Joan of Arc, at least as he heard and understood it. Nider says that he heard the story from a certain Brother Nicholas, a licentiate in theology, who was a delegate from the University of Paris to the Council of Basel. Joan, he says, was determined by the most learned men to have had a malignant spirit and was burned at the stake by public justice. Chapter 8 continues to discuss both wicked and good women. Chapter 9 deals with incubi and succubi, a discussion continued in chapter 10. Chapter 11 deals with demonic possession, and the last chapter deals with demon-inspired insanity and its cures.]

28
The *Errores Gazariorum* (1437)

The anonymous *Errores Gazariorum* (Errors of the Cathars, although Cathars, originally dualist heretics, here means witches) was written by an inquisitor in the same general area as the authors of the texts above, probably in Savoy. The two extant manuscripts of the work both contain material from the Council of Basel, and one at least convincingly dates the text to the late 1430s. It reflects many of the same ideas that are found in the letters of Eugenius IV (Text 26), the tract of Nider (Text 27), the treatise of Claude Tholosan (Text 29), and the Adversary's position in Martin Le Franc's *Defender of Ladies* (Text 30); that is, these five texts are important testimony to the revolution in thought about sorcery and witchcraft that occurred in the 1430s. The text also illustrates the further elaboration in the early fifteenth century of the alleged activities of heretics found earlier in Roman anti-Christian literature (Text 1) and in later medieval characterizations of heretical assemblies (Text 18).

SOURCE: Hansen, *Quellen*, 118–22. Trans. E. P.

FURTHER READING: Lea, *Materials*, 1:273–75; Richard Kieckhefer, "Avenging the Blood of Children: Anxiety over Child Victims and the Origins of the European Witch Trials," in *The Devil, Heresy and Witchcraft in the Middle Ages: Essays in Honor of Jeffrey Burton Russell*, ed. Alberto Ferreiro (Leiden, Boston, Cologne, 1998), 91–109; Michael Bailey, "The Medieval Concept of the Witches' Sabbat."

FIRST, WHEN A PERSON of either sex is seduced by the persuasion of the enemy of the human race, the seducer, precipitating the seduced person into the abyss of the evil ones [the repetition of different forms of *seduce* is in the Latin text], makes him first swear to whatever is required of him and is given a container for the journey to the synagogue, filled with the ointment pertaining to this, and he teaches him how to anoint the staff as well as anything else he needs.

Further, when all are assembled at the synagogue, seduced by the devil, the enemy of every rational creature, the seduced person is presented, to whom the enemy appears sometimes as a black cat and at other times in the appearance of a man, but not a perfect man, or in the appearance of another animal, but most commonly in the shape of a black cat, by whom the seduced person is interrogated as to whether or not he wishes to be and to remain and to persist in that community for his benefit, and he responds yes, that he does. When the devil has heard and accepted the oath of fidelity from the seduced person, this is what is said first: he swears that he will be faithful to the master who presides over the whole society; second, that he will assemble with the society; third, that he will not reveal the secrets of the said sect, not even until death. Fourth, that he will kill all of those children he is able to injure or kill and will take them to the synagogue, and by this is to be understood children under three years old. Fifth, that he will hurry to the synagogue whenever he is called upon to do so. Sixth, that he will impede sexual intercourse in every marriage that he is able to, using *sortilegia* and *maleficia*. Seventh, that he will avenge all injuries to the sect or any act that may impede or divide it.

These things having been promised and sworn to, the poor seduced person adores the presiding devil and pays homage to him; and as a sign of homage kisses the devil, whether the devil appears as a human or some kind of animal, on the anus or the ass, giving the devil as tribute a member from his own body after death. These things having been done, that pestiferous sect rejoices together and dines at the reception of the new heretic who is now one of them, and murdered children are devoured by them. This most evil of banquets having been completed, the presiding devil cries out that the lights be extinguished and yells "Mestlet, mestlet." After they have heard this command they join themselves carnally, a single man with a woman or a single man with another man, and sometimes father with daughter, son with mother, brother with sister, and the natural order is little observed. When the unspeakable abominations are over and the lights are relit they eat and drink for the journey home. . . . When some were asked why they did this, they responded that they did this to vilify and show disrespect to the sacrament of the Eucharist. Then, all these things done, they returned to their homes.

After the seduced person pays homage to the presiding devil, he is given a jar full of ointment and a staff and certain other things with which the seduced man must go to the synagogue, and the demon teaches him how and in what ways to anoint the staff. That unguent is made by a mystery of diabolic malignancy out of the fat of small children who have been cooked, and with other things, as will be seen.

Further, when the unguent made of the said fat of children has been combined with the most poisonous of animals such as serpents, toads, lizards, and spiders, which are all mixed mysteriously as said above, and if a person is touched once with this unguent he immediately dies by an evil death, sometimes for a time in a persisting illness, sometimes dying quickly.

Further, they make powders for killing human beings. These powders are made from the internal parts of the children mixed with parts of poisonous animals, and all of this is scattered through the air by a member of that society on a cloudy day. Those touched by that powder either die or suffer serious and lingering illness. And this is the reason why in some villages of a region there is great mortality, and in other areas there is much bad weather.

Further, when they are able, they capture a red-haired man, not a member of the sect, but a good Catholic, and expose him naked, bound with cords, so that he can move neither hand nor foot. To the bound man they bring poisonous animals which bite him, by the actions of these most merciless and cruel members of the sect, so that the poor man, tortured by these torments expires and dies, overcome by the poisons. When he is dead, they suspend him by the feet, placing a glass or earthen container of some sort beneath his mouth so as to catch the distilled poisons that have killed him. And mixing these drippings from the dead man on the gallows with the inner parts of dead children and those of poisonous animals, they make another ointment with the help of the devil, of which the touch alone can kill people. . . .

Further, some convicted members of the sect who have already been burned confessed that storms and bad weather have been commanded by many devils together on the top of a mountain to break up ice. . . . They say that some of them and not all do this, because not all have the power or audacity to do this, carrying the ice during a period of stormy weather through the air with the help of the devil, using their staffs to destroy the crops of their enemies or of certain neighbors.

Further, according to the depositions of some, everyone who enters this sect does so for three reasons: first, there are some who are unable to live peacefully with others and therefore make many enemies, and their hand is raised against all, and the hands of all against them, living like the descendants of Ishmael, seeing that they are unable to wreak vengeance upon all of their enemies, ask the devil to avenge their hurts. . . .

There are some who wish to live luxuriously and, having consumed all their own goods, and still wishing to live luxuriously, and the devil as above persuades these to enter his synagogue. . . .

The third cause for someone to enter this damned society is that there are some who take most delight in the venereal act, and since they can indulge in their sexual passions at will, etc. . . .

Further, according to the confession of Johannes de Stipulis and other members of the sect now burned, when a new member enters the sect and has sworn his faith and paid homage, the devil pricks his left hand with an instrument and draws blood from it, with which he writes a certain writing on a deed, which he then keeps, and many have seen this, as many have testified to.

Further, when they want to strangle children while their father and mother are sleeping, in the dark of night with the silent help of the devil they enter the houses of the parents and grasp the child by the throat or the sides and strangle him until he is dead. In the morning, when he is taken for burial the man or woman or group who have killed the child appear at the burial and lament the death with the mourning parents and friends. But the next night they open the grave and take the body, sometimes leaving the head, and they never take hands and feet unless they need to make some magic with the hand. When they have taken the corpse of the child and filled the grave again, they carry it to the synagogue, where it is cooked and eaten, as has previously been said.

And note, that there are some of them who have killed their own sons and daughters and devoured them at the synagogue, as is seen in the case of Johanna Vacanda, who was burned at Chambéry on St. Lawrence's day and had confessed before the whole people that she had eaten the son of her daughter and killed him, with another woman whom she named at her trial.

29

Claude Tholosan:
Ut magorum et maleficiorum errores
(1436–37)

The most remarkable recent discovery of a previously unknown text from the period 1430–1630, already acknowledged to be the key decades in the formation of the idea of the diabolical witch, was Pierette

Paravy's publication in 1979 of her edition of a treatise on the offense of witchcraft and the punishment of witches by the lay magistrate Claude Tholosan, senior judge in the Briançonnais (Dauphiné), written in 1436 or 1437.[1] What made Tholosan's treatise distinctive was the fact that its author was not a pope, theologian, inquisitor, ruler, or poet, but a lay magistrate who had tried more than one hundred cases of witchcraft in his career and had obviously thought hard about the nature of the crime, the justification for criminalizing the offense, and the punishment that the crime deserved. By 1500 the Dauphiné had witnessed more than 360 executions for witchcraft, 71 percent of them, 268, occurring between 1425 and 1450, making it, with Savoy and western Switzerland, one of the major centers of the movement that spread through Europe after the Council of Basel in 1437. Tholosan's treatise is found in the *Quintus liber fachueriorum*, one of an otherwise lost series of registers of the *Chambre des comptes*, the accounting office of the principality. Hansen and Lea knew some of the cases from the register, but neither of them knew of the existence of the treatise.

Tholosan was a licentiate in civil (that is, Roman, or Ius Commune) law, a skill which "places him in that progressively enlarged section of the laity which attended universities in order to acquire that legal science which they dedicated to the service of a prince."[2] The first fourteen chapters of the treatise deal with acts attributed to witches, chapters 15–19 with the problem of jurisdictional competence, and chapters 20–34 with a series of consultations that Tholosan had made with other professional jurists from the schools—law professors—and with the legitimate powers and responsibilities of the prince to eradicate pestilential witchcraft.

Tholosan relies chiefly on canon law, since the offense of witchcraft is fundamentally a violation of canon law, in conjunction with which he draws heavily upon scripture, but he also cites other authorities, including Ugolino Zanchini (p. 120 above), and he brings stories of saints

---

1. Pierette Paravy, "À propos de la genèse médiévale des chasses aux sorcières: Le traité de Claude Tholosan, juge dauphinois (vers 1436)," *Mélanges de l'École française de Rome, Moyen-Age-Temps modernes* 91 (1979): 333–79. Paravy discussed the treatise and its implications further in "Faire croire: Quelques hypothèses de recherche basées sur l'étude des procès de sorcellerie du Dauphiné au XVe siècle," in *Faire croire: Modalités de la diffusion et de la réception des messages religieux du XIIe au Xve siècle*, Collection de l'École française de Rome 51 (Rome, 1981), 119–30, and in her extensive study, *De la chrétienté romaine à la Réforme en Dauphiné: Évêques, fidèles et déviants*, 2 vols., Collection de l'École française de Rome 183 (Rome, 1993), esp. 2:771–905.
2. Paravy, "À propos de la génèse médiévale," 335.

to bear on his argument, especially those of St. Germanus and St. Justina (Text 12).

Tholosan approaches the problem of witchcraft as that of a sect, involving apostasy and idolatry, with its own beliefs and rites, although he also believes that bodily transport to the sabbat is a demonic illusion (just as did Regino of Prüm and Gratian, Texts 5 and 9). He also accepts the ideas of sexual orgies and cannibalism. Tholosan's work is important because it is firsthand, unmediated by any second party (as had been Nider's reports on Boltingen, Text 27).

SOURCE: Pierette Paravy, "À propos de la génèse médiévale de la chasse aux sorciéres," 354–79. Trans. E. P. The numbered paragraphs are those in Paravy's edition. We have translated only the chief statements of each paragraph—the entire text is twenty-five printed pages.

JHESUS

1. *In order that the erroneous teachings of magicians and those who commit maleficia be made clear to the ignorant,* as St. Augustine says in *The City of God:* those erronerous teachings, Oh how terribly sad, so many and so great, and chiefly in the land of faithful Christians, having there for a long time won many believers, as I personally have learned.[3] I have decided to tear out these wild beliefs and the terrible sect of sorcerers by setting forth my understanding of them in a comprehensive treatise, based on the consistent testimony of respectable witnesses and many suitable arguments. . . .

3. Further, at the instigation of their master, these people swear that those who enter their sect deny God, whom they call the *Prophet;* they put a vase into which the devil has pissed in the middle of a circle they have drawn on the ground, and then they drink from this and bow so that they will completely withdraw from the faith of Christ. Then they raise their hands or some other thing and swear to renounce the laws of God and their faith, no longer believing in the articles of faith or the sacraments of the church. Then they turn their naked asses to heaven, in order to show their scorn for God, drawing a cross on the ground, spitting on it and treading it underfoot, as it is said, in contempt of God, whom they call the *Prophet.* . . .

4. Further, after they perform these ceremonies they kneel and kiss the devil, who appears in the form of a man and of different animals, and they kiss him on the mouth, giving him their bodies and souls and one of their children, usually the firstborn, whom they immolate and sacrifice. They offer him these things

3. As Paravy points out, Tholosan is not quoting Augustine directly, but rather Gratian's canon *Nec mirum,* C. 26 q. 5 c. 14 (Text 9), which Gratian took from Hrabanus Maurus's paraphrase of Augustine.

on bended knee; they hold the child, naked, under the arms and kill him, and then exhume him after burial and make a powder out of the body. . . .

6. Further, they imagine in dreams that they travel bodily at night, most often on Thursdays and Sundays, in the company of the devil, in order to suffocate children and strike them with sickness. They then extract the fat of the dead children and devour it and go to a certain place where they hold the synagogue of the region. They carry a banner with the picture of the devil on it and tell the devil of the evils they have done and bring new members into the sect. . . .

7. Further, they compound poisonous powders with poisons they get from an apothecary, mixed with the devil's piss and many other poisonous ingredients and, with the devil's help, they give these to their enemies. . . . And this powder works, with the help of the devil and according to the quantity given, so that there is no possibility of a medical cure, working as a lingering illness or sudden death. . . .

8. Further, with a long thistle and the piss of the devil, as well as the egg of a chicken and certain other ingredients, they prevent conception in women and render men insane, and with menstrual blood, contact with which can kill trees, they make an ointment with the help of the devil that makes men wild with sexual passion. And with the sacrament of the altar and the body of Christ they perform witchcraft, and also with the fat extracted from the bodies of children, preferably unbaptized children, which children they call "virgins." And they make an image with the powder of those whom they wish to make stressful and to torture. . . .

12. All of the above things I myself have heard from witches and, Oh how terrible, more than a hundred of them, and from people upon whom they worked their magic, I, Claude Tholosan, licentiate in law, senior judge of the district of the Briançonnais in the Dauphiné.

13. [Tholosan here inserts an extract from a letter of Pope Gregory I (590–604) to Brunhilde, queen of the Franks, on the responsibility of rulers to root out evils, taken from Gratian, C. 23, q. 4, c. 47]

15. [Tholosan now turns to forms of punishment, noting that the question is complex, since episcopal jurisdiction is primary; he then cites the treatise of Ugolino Zanchini to the effect that inquisitors can only intervene in it when there is a question of manifest heresy involved.]

16. The secular authority may intervene in those cases that involve corporal punishment and the confiscation of the property of the convicted. . . .

18. Nor does this combining of punishments constitute double jeopardy, since one punishment begins the process and the other completes it. . . .

19. [Tholosan here inserts a letter written by Peter of Blois, chancellor of Richard, archbishop of Canterbury (1173–1184), stating the obligation of secular princes to administer justice and serve the church in its spiritual mission. Tholosan's citation of this letter and that of Gregory I are interesting, since

neither was commonly cited at the time, indicating the literary sources at the disposal of a fifteenth-century lay magistrate.]

[The remainder of the treatise deals with forms of punishment, stating the arguments for and against the death penalty (which Tholosan favors), the confiscation of the property of the convicted, and finally the legitimate power and responsibilities of the prince and his officers, citing several professors of law whom Tholosan has consulted.]

35. And so the problem appears to me, Claude Tholosan, publicly licentiated in civil law and senior judge of the Briançonnais in the Dauphiné, unless I am corrected by those more learned in this subject than I.

30
Martin Le Franc,
The Defender of Ladies (1440)

Martin Le Franc (1410–61), one of the most influential French-language poets of the fifteenth century, was also a clerical official of Amadeus VIII, Duke of Savoy, who was later elected pope by the Council of Basel as Felix V.[1] Le Franc attended the Council of Basel in the service of Amadeus VIII, and Felix later made Le Franc provost of the cathedral at Lausanne. Pope Nicholas V later made him administrator of the monastery of Novalese. *The Defender of Ladies* was written in 1440 and dedicated to Philip the Good, duke of Burgundy, the most prominent European prince of his age. The poem is 24,384 lines long, of which 823 deal with witchcraft, and it forms part of an important literary and moral debate that raged from the late fourteenth through the sixteenth century concerning the character of women, centered on the allegedly mysogynistic portraits of women created by Jean de Meung in *The Romance of the Rose*. One of the best-known participants in the debate was Christine de Pizan. The general dispute has conventionally been characterized as "The debate over the *Romance of the Rose*," and it forms an important theme in the literature of misogyny (and philogyny) in late medieval and renaissance Europe.[2]

In the course of the poem the "Adversary" (= adversary of women)

---

1. On Amadeus VIII, see *Amédée VIII–Félix V: Premier duc de Savoie et pape (1383–1451)*, ed. Bernard Andenmatten and Agostino Paravicini Bagliani, with Nadia Pollini (Lausanne, 1992).

2. The early stages of the debate have been studied by Eric Hicks, *Le débat sur le Roman de la Rose* (Paris, 1977), and the whole problem in *Rethinking the "Roman de la Rose": Text, Image, Reception*, ed. Kevin Brownlee and Sylvia Huot (Philadelphia, 1992). Jean Gerson's contribution to the debate has been translated into English: Jean Gerson, *Early Works*, trans. Brian Patrick McGuire (New York and Mahwah, 1998), 378–98.

attacks both the character and achievements of women and is answered by Franc Vouloir (Free Will), the "champion" (defender) of the
poem's French title. In Book IV, ll. 17377–18200, the Adversary raises
the question of witchcraft and is answered by the Defender. Both sides
of the argument are important, since Le Franc puts into the Adversary's
accusations and the Defender's defense not only conventional misogyny, but some very new and recent elements of the charge of diabolical
sorcery, particularly idolatry, flight to the sabbat, the sabbat itself, the
demonic instruction of witches in evil magic at the sabbath, weather-
magic, and sexual criminal acts, citing recent cases and the confessions
of condemned women. The discussion slowly shifts from the activities
of witches to the nature of demonic power and finally to the Defender's
criticism of the clergy for allowing such beliefs to circulate. Although
the Defender may be assumed to triumph over the Adversary (his final
point is that it is far easier for the devil to tempt men than to tempt
women), Le Franc's arguments are important illustrations of the new
constellation of witchcraft beliefs that circulated not only among theologians, lay magistrates, inquisitors, and canon lawyers, but now also
among a literary elite.

Le Franc's discussion of witchcraft was first noted in this context by
the great Cologne archivist Joseph Hansen at the turn of the twentieth
century and later shrewdly discussed by Johan Huizinga in *The Autumn of the Middle Ages* in 1919.

A Paris manuscript of Le Franc's poem contains a marginal illustration of women flying on broomsticks, the first such illustration in the
pictorial history of witchcraft (Fig. 8).

SOURCE: Martin Le Franc, *Le Champion des dames*, ed. Robert Des-
chaux, vol. 4 (Paris, 1999), 113–46 (Middle French; trans. E. P.).

FURTHER READING: Lea, *Materials*, 1: 177; Johan Huizinga, *The Autumn of the Middle Ages*, trans. Rodney Payton and Ulrich Mammitzsch (Chicago, 1996), 286–93; L. Barbey, *Martin Le Franc, prévôt de
Lausanne et avocat de l'amour et de la femme au XVe siècle* (Fribourg,
1985).

[THE DEFENDER HAS described the
achievements of several illustrious women of antiquity and later ages in met-
alwork, painting, and other arts. The Adversary abruptly interrupts, insisting
that the Defender confront women's sorcery, flight, and cannibalism. The Defender argues that men invented sorcery and that the rest is a delusion.]

(l. 17441) The Adversary brightened up a little, responding, You'll surely change
your mind when you've heard this case related. It's true. I've heard it. I believe it,

that not just two or three old women, but more than three thousand, go together to hidden places to seek out their familiar demons. (l. 17449) This is no joke; this isn't fooling. I'm not trying to lie to you in speaking of this sorcery. When you once learn of their whorishness you'll want all of them burned up, because there's no persuasion in this world that could turn them from their tricks and farces. (l. 17457) I tell you that I've seen in a written trial record where an old woman confessed how, since the time when she was just sixteen years old that on certain nights she flew on a broomstick from Valpute and went directly to the awful synagogue of devils. (l. 17465) Ten thousand old women in a troop were there, as in a great assembly in the shapes of cats or goats, approaching the devil courteously, kissing him openly on his ass as a sign of their obedience, denying God quite openly and all of His great power. (l. 17473) There, they all do different things—some were instructed in their arts and perverse sorceries from the devil himself, by which they later committed many evils. Still others pleased themselves in dancing, others still in banqueting and booze. They found there all these things; you wouldn't believe their abundance. (l. 17481) Then the devil praised them all, but those who wanted to repent he sternly punished, beating them without stopping. But to all those who consented he gave whatever they wished. He promised them, and was not lying, the sum of everything they wanted. (l. 17489) This devil, now in the form of a cat, walked up and down the earth. Like a judge or lawyer, he listened to all requests. Each person paid him the respect that one would pay to God; thus the deceitful being enjoyed the praise and approving looks of all. (l. 17497) And know that when they all departed [from the sabbat] each man took any woman sexually. And if any woman had no man, a devil would do the service for her.

Then each returned home, like the wind, upon her broomstick—so much power had Satan given her, that wretched thief of souls. (l. 17505) For instance, one old hag told us that when she paid homage to the devil he gave her an ointment made out of awful, varied poisons, with which she made any man impotent, and thus made more than one hundred, and she ruined many fine young innocents that way. (l. 17513) And further, that wicked beast of a woman created whirlwinds and raised storms that destroyed both grain and vine, leveled trees and bushes, wasting entire lands. If anyone protested, he was instantly tempested. (l. 17521) More than six hundred have deposed to these crimes without having been put to torture that they've raised hailstorms, wind and rain, all against Nature. They've flung these elements wherever they wished, and done many other wicked things by the power of the devils. (l. 17529) Then she said more emphatically (about which I shudder to speak) that the devil made himself into a man and had his lustful way with her. Oh God, what horror! Oh God, such coupling is awful—Oh Lord Jesus what a sin! The woman's married to the devil! (l. 17537) I didn't want to believe all this, and said it's just a dizzy head, when another confessed witch whom I saw one day said, "I've seen Sohier and Quotin [at sabbat] dancing and leading the festivities, and I know that both Greeks and Latins attend our awful synagogue."

(l. 17545) Listen to what I say in answer, said Free Will. There's no old woman so stupid who's done even the least of these things. But in order to have her hanged or burned, the enemy of humankind, who knows well how to set traps to make the mind deceive itself, has made her mind fool itself. (l. 17553) There are no broomsticks or rods by which anyone could fly. But when the devil can fool the mind, they *think* they fly to some far place where they take their pleasure and do whatever it is they wish. They've even been heard to speak of Rome, without ever having been there.

[The Adversary then points out (ll. 17561–76) that Simon Magus flew in the air and that the devil can move anyone anywhere at all. The Defender responds that the devils are all chained up in Hell and can't get out by any means (ll. 17577–84). Not so, says the Adversary, because when Lucifer and the rebel angels fell God punished them in different ways, and some of them dwell in the air, making storms, while others tempt ordinary folk (ll. 17585–600). The Adversary then says (ll. 17601–16) that wherever we go the wicked enemy follows. If one temptation doesn't succeed, he'll try another, since he has no other purpose in this world:]

(l. 17617) Thus, when the devil sees the wicked *sorcière* who lacks both law and faith, he thinks he can convert her to his service. He promises her this and that and tells her how to overcome her enemies. And so she says, "Fie on you, Jesus Christ, and all your power." (l. 17625) The devil has her on a string and does whatever she asks of him, tying her up even tighter. Then he refuses what she asks until she submits to him. Then he bears her off, condemned to the fire. Then the *sorcière* curses the day she was born.

31
Nicholas Jacquier: *A Scourge for Heretical Witches* (1458)

Nicholas Jacquier served as a Dominican inquisitor in Tournai in 1465, in Bohemia from 1466 to 1468, and in Lille from 1468 until his death in 1472. In 1458 he wrote his *Scourge for Heretical Witches*, printed in 1581, both an attack on skeptics whose objections impeded the work of the inquisitors and a powerful argument that the *Canon Episcopi* (Text 5) did not apply to what Pope Alexander V in 1409 had already called the "new sect" of witches (Text 19), and that witches really were bodily transported to the sabbat.

In 1450 the Carcassonne inquisitor Jean Vineti had argued that the *Canon Episcopi*'s (Text 5) denial of the reality of flight with Diana did not apply to the "new sect" of heretics (Text 35, headnote). Six years later, the Munich physician Johannes Hartlieb had stated emphatically much the same argument in favor of bodily flight in his *Buch aller verbotenen Kunst, Unglaubens, und der Zauberei* (Book of All Forbidden Arts, Unbelief, and Magic):

> On flying through the air. In the wicked art of *nigromancia* [which Hartlieb had earlier called "the first forbidden art and is called by men the black art" (*schwartzen kunst*)] there is a great foolishness, when people think that witches with magical potions make a horse which then enters their houses, and if they wish they sit upon him and ride many miles in a very short time. And when they want to get off the horse they pull on the bridle, and when they wish to mount again they grasp the bridle and the horse returns. This horse is in reality the devil.[1]

That is, witches really do move bodily, not under their own power, but that of the devil.

In Jacquier's elaborate argument (the printed edition is 183 pages in small octavo and 12-point font), he had to range across a wide number of contemporary concerns—the sabbat, sexual impotence and ligatures, apostasy, idolatry, desecration of the cross, infanticide, the case of Gilles de Rais, the rationale for divine permission for devils to tempt human beings in these ways, and on whether penance should be imposed on convicted witches (rather than execution). His important denial of the applicability of the *Canon Episcopi* is translated here.

The printed edition also deserves some notice. The 1581 Frankfurt first edition is printed in a single volume, edited by the Frankfurt Carmelite Johannes Minzenberg, that also contains the 1564 *De veneficiis* of Lambert Daneau (Text 42), Joachim Camerarius's letter on Plutarch's *On the Failure of Oracles*, Martin of Arles's treatise on superstitions (first printed in 1517; Hansen, *Quellen*; Lea, *Materials*, 1: 296–98), the *Questions on Witchcraft* by the early sixteenth-century learned magician Johannes Trithemius (Hansen, *Quellen*, 291–96), the teacher of Agrippa of Nettesheim (see Text 47), and the Zwinglian physician and theologian Thomas Erastus's treatise on witches of the mid-sixteenth century. That is, by 1581, a year after Jean Bodin's treatise *On the Demon-Mania of Witches* (Text 48) effectively signaled the beginning of the greatest wave of witchcraft prosecutions in European history, a Frankfurt printer thought that Jacquier's 1458 treatise properly be-

---

1. Hansen, *Quellen*, 130–31; Lea, *Materials*, 1: 275.

longed in the company of the works on similar subjects by other early and later sixteenth-century writers.[2]

SOURCE: Hansen, *Quellen*, 133–45; Lea, *Materials*, 1:276–85; *Flagellum haereticorum fascinariorum, autore F. Nicolao Jaquerio, Ordinis Praedicatorum & olim Haereticae pravitatis Inquisitore* (Frankfurt, 1581). Trans. E. P.

SINCE THE IMPEDIMENTS to the prosecution of *fascinarii*, that is heretics, by the office of inquisition frequently occur, I, brother Nicholas Jacquier, of the Order of the brothers Preachers, will draw in a plain style out of scripture and the teachings of the saints, by which the whip drives out of the temple of God, that is the church of the faithful, perverse dogmas and erroneous assertions . . . that do great injury to the catholic faith and pose great prejudice and dangerous scandal to the faithful.

[Jacquier begins by discussing the nature of illusions (chap. 1), and then allows that the devils can send illusions to humans (chap. 2) about food, drink, and sex, citing (and thereby setting up early) the *Canon Episcopi* (Text 5) as an example of precisely those illusions sent in sleep. The demons send good illusions as well as evil ones (chap. 3). Chapters 4–6 continue the discussion of illusions and the demons' methods of inducing them, and he distinguishes these sharply from the real thing, citing a recent case, that of William Adeline in 1453, who had confessed spontaneously to the activities of the modern witches. Chapter 7, however, is Jacquier's real turning point. Here, he distinguishes between the "modern heretics" (that is, witches) and those delusioned old women of whom the *Canon Episcopi* speaks, first by addressing common objections to his own conclusions and then going on the attack.]

On the Difference between the sect and heresy of modern witches and the illusions of those women of whom c. Episcopi *speaks*

First, as experience makes clear, venereal practices and the passions of carnal voluptuousness cannot be accomplished or consummated by sleeping people,

2. On these, see Part VIII below, as well as the discussions of many of them in Clark, *Thinking with Demons*, and Lea, *Materials*. There has been very little study of composite works of this type, although the *Malleus Maleficarum* was also printed in later editions with addition material. For example, in 1580, a year before the first printing of Jacquier, a Frankfurt printer, probably the same one, Nicholas Basseus, issued the *Malleus* in a single volume edited by the same Frankfurt Carmelite Johannes Minzenberg, who the next year edited the work of Jacquier and others, that also included the 1489 *De lamiis et Pythonicis* of Ulrich Molitor (Text 38, headnote), Jean Gerson's early-fifteenth-century treatise on the testing of spiritual aparitions (Hansen, *Quellen*, 86; Lea, *Materials*, 1: 133–36), the 1482 treatise on magic and witchcraft by Bernard Basin (Hansen, *Quellen*, 236–38), and Thomas Murner's treatise on divination of 1499 (Hansen, *Quellen*, 254).

even if their sleep is interrupted by illusions or turpitudinous fantasies. Since the members of all the heresies and sects of the witches or *fascinarii* assert that in those assemblies in which they practice the cult of the demon they engage so voluptuously in such inordinate and vehement carnality that for several days afterward many of them remain afflicted, exhausted, and debilitated, it is clear that these apparitions are real, not those of sleeping people, but of people who are fully awake. . . . This is very different from those of whom the *Canon Episcopi* speaks. . . .

Second, in that illusory congregation mentioned in the *Canon Episcopi* there are only some women who imagine that they ride in obedience to Diana or the Herodiades, which is nothing but a fable or a poetical fiction. In this modern sect or synagogue of witches, not only women, but also men, and, which is even worse, clerics and religious visibly stand before the demons and speak with them. . . . There is nothing at all about this in that fantastic congregation and illusory association of Diana mentioned in the *Canon Episcopi*. . . .

Third, there seems to be a great difference between that fantastic illusion of women of which the *Canon Episcopi* speaks and the new sect and heresy of the witches and *fascinarii*, in which the said heretics assemble in reality and bodily with the demons, appearing visibly and really speaking. . . .

Fourth, [since the new heretics are obliged to perform actual homage to the devil and actually renounce their baptismal oaths and deny God] None of these preparations and oblations are done by those deluded, sleeping women of whom *Episcopi* speaks.

32
Jehan de la Case Is Pardoned for Killing a Witch-Finder (1460)

Although individuals who professed the ability to discover witches appeared frequently in the late sixteenth- and early seventeenth-century hunts and trials, the following case is unusual for its early date and for the light it sheds on some aspects of rural life of the time in the southwestern corner of France in the Pyrenees. Particularly interesting here is the mysterious character of Master Jehan the witch-finder, the anger and danger that such accusations could instill, the willingness of Jehan de la Case's family (and the parish priest) to appeal for royal clemency, and the king's perhaps calculated extension of the image of his benevolence in a territory in which royal presence had been relatively slight.

Some historians have argued that the concerns of John XXII (Texts 20 and 22) had led to a heightened concern about sorcery in the area of southwestern France and the Pyrenees, the old center of activity of the

Cathar heretics. If this was the case, little evidence has survived for the region in the interim, and much of it has been demonstrated to have been a nineteenth-century forgery.[1] But in 1450 the Dominican inquisitor of Carcassonne, Jean Vineti, in his *Treatise Against Those Who Invoke Demons*, argued that the mythical flight described in the *Canon Episcopi* (Text 5) had no bearing on the activities of modern (fifteenth-century) heretics (witches), thus anticipating the argument of Jacquier: "From this it appears that the said *Canon Episcopi* does not refer to modern heretics, who invoke demons, adore them, seek and accept responses from them, pay them tribute, and, exceeding the savagery of ferocious beasts, offer their own children and frequently the children of others as burnt offerings to the demons, [like dogs], returning to their own vomit."[2] Although few records have survived from the region, it is likely that the ideas in Vineti's treatise help to explain the concerns expressed by Jehan de la Case when his female relatives were accused of witchcraft by the "witch-finder."

SOURCE: Pierre Braun, "Un connaisseur de sorciers de l'an 1459," in *Histoire des faits de la sorcellerie: Actes de la Huitième Rencontre d'Histoire Religieuse tenue à Fontevraud les 5 et 6 Octobre 1984* (Angers, 1985), 9–24, at 22–24. Trans. E. P.

May, 1460, Tours

Remission for Jehan de la Case, called Asseline, who mortally wounded a certain Master Jehan, discoverer of witches and accuser of two of [Jehan de la Case's] close female relatives, and then also wounded one of the representatives of authority in order to avoid arrest. [National Archives JJ 190, fol. 49, number 90.]

Remission for Jehan de la Case otherwise known as Asseline [in Latin]

Charles [VII], by the grace of God king of France, makes known to all present and in the future that we have received a humble supplication from Jehan de la Case, otherwise known as Asseline, a poor laboring man responsible for the maintenance of a wife and six or seven small children, regarding the following events:

That, after some time, a certain Master Jehan, who called himself a physician, came to live in Vinhec in the Aure Valley in the seneschalsy of Toulouse. The said Master Jehan, as people said, used sortilege and divinations, saying that he could easily recognize those people who involved themselves with sorcery. He

1. Cohn, *Europe's Inner Demons*, 126–38, referring to Text 15 in the first edition of this book, corrected in subsequent printings. Thus, the discussions in Hansen and Lea must be disregarded.
2. Lea, *Materials*, 1:272–73; Hansen, *Quellen*, 125.

did much abuse, under the guise of medicine and divination, throughout the territory. Among others, he accused two women, close relatives of the said Jehan de la Case, of being witches. This accusation having come to the attention of the said suppliant, [Jehan de la Case] told Master Jehan that he did wrong to accuse the two women of such a crime and that he ought to withdraw his accusation. The same Master Jehan responded that Jehan de la Case had not spoken well and that he would not withdraw the accusation. This done, Master Jehan went to a hostel in Vielle de Loron, where there was assembled a large company of people, and behaving incontinently among them, repeated his accusation that the two women were witches and continued to speak in the same manner. The said suppliant repeated that Master Jehan had wrongly spoken ill, and they then exchanged insulting words. At that point, Master Jehan took a spear in his hand and struck the suppliant with it, and would have killed him had not some of those present prevented it, because Master Jehan tried to strike Jehan de la Case many times in the chest.

After this, on many occasions the two exchanged heated words about this matter. One day in the month of last October, shortly after their first violent encounter, the suppliant was at Mont de Loron in a tavern, and the said Master Jehan was also present, although they were in different rooms. After they had each taken a great deal to drink, the said Master Jehan left the room where he had been and moved toward the suppliant, and the suppliant, without saying a word, came against him with a striking weapon [*gisarme*] that he carried with him and struck the said Master Jehan a great blow on the head, so that he fell straight to the floor unconscious. The bailiff of the place or his lieutenant and others followed in order to lay hands on the attacker, but he flailed about him with his *gisarme* and wounded one of the officers in defending himself so that he was not taken and no one was able to take him into arrest, and he then fled the realm. The following night Master Jehan departed this life.

Because of this affair, the said suppliant, Jehan de la Case, doubting the fairness of justice in his case, did not dare to return, unless our grace and mercy were extended to him in this matter. Therefore he begged of us most humbly that, since the said Master Jehan had been nothing but an abuser who traveled around the territory like a vagabond, using divinations and sortileges, committing many evils and making exactions from people, no one even knew where he came from, nor whether he had been a Jew or a Christian. It was supposed that he had not been a Christian, since the parish priest where he had lived for three or four years stated in testimony when he was asked whether Master Jehan had been excommunicated that he did not know whether he was a Jew or a Christian. He said this because he knew that he had not performed the duties of a Christian and did not receive the sacraments of Holy Church, as every Christian was obliged to do each year.

The said suppliant was also sufficiently moved and angered to strike Master

Jehan for the great injuries that the deceased had inflicted on his two female relatives, who were women of good standing and good Catholics. He also stated that since he had killed Master Jehan he had lived well and gently, without having done or committed any other violent act that was blamable or reproachable. It therefore pleases us [the king] to impart to him our grace and mercy.

This is the reason why we, having considered these matters, and preferring clemency to the rigor of justice, have acquitted, remitted, and pardoned, and quit, remit, and pardon by our special grace, full power, and royal authority, the said suppliant in the said case by this document. The deed and the aforementioned case are pardoned of all bodily punishment, affliction, and offense, both criminal and civil to which he might be liable because of the aforementioned offense to our laws and our justice. And we have restored and do restore to him his good name and reputation in the territory and to all of his goods that have not been confiscated as civil satisfaction to the party injured. And on this matter we impose perpetual silence upon our royal procurator in both the present and the future.

We give and send by these same presents to _____ and to our other judicial officers, justices, or to their lieutenants present and future and to all who are associated with them, that our present grace, quittance, remission, and pardon are made, and that they should suffer and allow the said suppliant to enjoy, use openly and peacefully, without doing, placing, or giving him any difficulty, either now or in the future, in his body or his goods, nor otherwise prevent or disturb him in any manner whatsover. Therefore, if his body or any of his goods are, or might be, taken, seized, detained, or prevented, for this crime, they are to be returned to him without delay and openly.

Given at Tours in May 1460 [CCCC soixante] and of our reign the thirty-eighth [XXXVIII]. So signed, by the king in on the advice of counsel.

VI

The Hammer of Witches

THE GROWING APPREHENSION ON the part of high church officials, inquisitors, and the clergy in general that witchcraft was not only extant and dangerous but a clearly recognizable part of Satan's concerted attack on all mankind produced at the end of the fifteenth century two remarkable documents which, from all sides, represent the climax of earlier witch theories and the chief shaping force of later persecutions. In 1484, at the instance of two German inquisitors, Pope Innocent VIII issued his famous letter *Summis desiderantes affectibus* (Text 33), a document in which the fears of Pope John XXII and the activity of Pope Eugenius IV are brought to a summary conclusion, formalized, and accepted in their totality, and a plan of action against the worldwide conspiracy of the witches and Satan, their master, finally laid down. Three years later, as if to justify the letter's strong terms in retrospect, the same two Dominican inquisitors, Jacob Sprenger and Heinrich Kramer (Institoris) produced a book, somewhat on the model the earlier inquisitors' handbooks, solely on the subject of witchcraft, the *Malleus Maleficarum* (Hammer of Witches, Text 34). The *Malleus* instantly became the chief source of information about witches' activities and, to the surprise of no one, it was precisely those characteristics of witchcraft to which the *Malleus* paid most attention that appeared all over Europe during the sixteenth and seventeenth centuries. All later handbooks of witch theory, however, "scientific" or "anti-Catholic," looked back to the *Malleus* as their chief inspiration, as their "encyclopedia." The *Malleus* inspired additional papal activity, and the letter of Pope Alexander VI, a man not generally marked by excessive concern for the salvation of mankind, reflects the attack on the witches as a permanent aspect of papal policy after 1500 (Text 35).

The *Malleus* is divided into three parts. The first part establishes that disbelief in witches is manifest heresy, offers a kind of census of the effects of witchcraft, and explains why it is that women are witches more frequently than men. The second part offers a typology of witchcraft as well as a typology for its investigation. The third part treats in infinite detail the nature of the legal proceedings against witches, and justifies all its deviations from orthodox civil and ecclesiastical legal procedures with careful citations of Scripture, the church fathers, and more recent theologians and ecclesiastical lawyers. The excerpts from the *Malleus* given below are by no means an attempt to summarize or offer "highlights" of the work. It is a tightly knit book, each argument and dogma carefully drawn from the conclusions of the preceding arguments and dogmas, and it is excerpted only reluctantly. The force of the *Malleus* is its comprehensive character, and the selections made below offer only representative samplings of its intricate design. A reading of the whole work is well worth the effort, and it is only with this cautionary note that the editors have excerpted as much as they have.

33
Pope Innocent VIII: *Summis desiderantes affectibus* (1484)

Pope Innocent VIII (1484–1492) was moved by the complaints of two Dominican inquisitors, Heinrich Kramer and Jacob Sprenger, that local ecclesiastical authorities in Germany refused to aid them in their pursuit of heretical witchcraft. Sprenger and Kramer described some of their cases to the pope and elicited from him the famous bull called, from its opening Latin words, *Summis desiderantes*. The similarity in terminology of this and earlier papal letters on the subject is certainly striking, and its purpose is clearly to remove the juridical obstacles preventing Kramer and Sprenger from carrying out their witch-hunt. This document has traditionally been considered the "beginning" of the witch persecutions, but its likeness to other papal documents, its particular emphasis upon preaching, and its lack of dogmatic pronouncement on the subject of witchcraft place it squarely in the tradition of papal concern for heresy and disbelief. Its circulation with Sprenger and Kramer's later handbook, the *Malleus Maleficarum* (Text 37), gave it both a wider circulation and a more direct role in subsequent witch persecutions that it might otherwise have had.

SOURCE: Hansen, *Quellen*, 24–27. English translation from Burr, *The Witch Persecutions*, 7–10.

D ESIRING WITH SUPREME ardor, as pastoral solicitude requires, that the catholic faith in our days everywhere grow and flourish as much as possible, and that all heretical pravity be put far from the territories of the faithful, we freely declare and anew decree this by which our pious desire may be fulfilled, and, all errors being rooted out by our toil as with the hoe of a wise laborer, zeal and devotion to this faith may take deeper hold on the hearts of the faithful themselves.

It has recently come to our ears, not without great pain to us, that in some parts of upper Germany, as well as in the provinces, cities, territories, regions, and dioceses of Mainz, Cologne, Trier, Salzburg, and Bremen, many persons of both sexes, heedless of their own salvation and forsaking the catholic faith, give themselves over to devils male and female, and by their incantations, charms, and conjurings, and by other abominable superstitions and sortileges, offences, crimes, and misdeeds, ruin and cause to perish the offspring of women, the foal of animals, the products of the earth, the grapes of vines, and the fruits of trees, as well as men and women, cattle and flocks and herds and animals of every kind, vineyards also and orchards, meadows, pastures, harvests, grains and other fruits of the earth; that they afflict and torture with dire pains and anguish, both internal and external, these men, women, cattle, flocks, herds, and animals, and hinder men from begetting and women from conceiving, and prevent all consummation of marriage; that, moreover, they deny with sacrilegious lips the faith they received in holy baptism; and that, at the instigation of the enemy of mankind, they do not fear to commit and perpetrate many other abominable offences and crimes, at the risk of their own souls, to the insult of the divine majesty and to the pernicious example and scandal of multitudes. And, although our beloved sons Henricus Institoris and Jacobus Sprenger, of the order of Friars Preachers, professors of theology, have been and still are deputed by our apostolic letters as inquisitors of heretical pravity, the former in the aforesaid parts of upper Germany, including the provinces, cities, territories, dioceses, and other places as above, and the latter throughout certain parts of the course of the Rhine; nevertheless certain of the clergy and of the laity of those parts, seeking to be wise above what is fitting, because in the said letter of deputation the aforesaid provinces, cities, dioceses, territories, and other places, and the persons and offences in question were not individually and specifically named, do not blush obstinately to assert that these are not at all included in the said parts and that therefore it is illicit for the aforesaid inquisitors to exercise their office of inquisition in the provinces, cities, dioceses, territories, and other places aforesaid, and that they ought not to be permitted to proceed to the punishment, imprisonment, and correction of the aforesaid persons for the offences and crimes above named. Wherefore in the provinces, cities, dioceses, territories, and places aforesaid such offences and crimes, not without evident damage to their souls and risk of eternal salvation, go unpunished.

We therefore, desiring, as is our duty, to remove all impediments by which in any way the said inquisitors are hindered in the exercise of their office, and to prevent the taint of heretical pravity and of other like evils from spreading their infection to the ruin of others who are innocent, the zeal of religion especially impelling us, in order that the provinces, cities, dioceses, territories, and places aforesaid in the said parts of upper Germany may not be deprived of the office of inquisition which is their due, do hereby decree, by virtue of our apostolic authority, that it shall be permitted to the said inquisitors in these regions to exercise their office of inquisition and to proceed to the correction, imprisonment, and punishment of the aforesaid persons for their said offences and crimes, in all respects and altogether precisely as if the provinces, cities, territories, places, persons, and offences aforesaid were expressly named in the said letter. And, for the greater sureness, extending the said letter and deputation to the provinces, cities, dioceses, territories, places, persons, and crimes aforesaid, we grant to the said inquisitors that they or either of them, joining with them our beloved son Johannes Gremper, cleric of the diocese of Constance, master of arts, their present notary, or any other notary public who by them or by either of them shall have been temporarily delegated in the provinces, cities, dioceses, territories, and places aforesaid, may exercise against all persons, of whatsoever condition and rank, the said office of inquisition, correcting, imprisoning, punishing, and chastising, according to their deserts, those persons whom they shall find guilty as aforesaid.

And they shall also have full and entire liberty to propound and preach to the faithful the word of God, as often as it shall seem to them fitting and proper, in each and all the parish churches in the said provinces, and to do all things necessary and suitable under the aforesaid circumstances, and likewise freely and fully to carry them out.

And moreover we enjoin by apostolic writ on our venerable brother, the Bishop of Strasburg, that, either in his own person or through some other or others solemnly publishing the foregoing wherever, whenever, and how often soever he may deem expedient or by these inquisitors or either of them may be legitimately required, he permit them not to be molested or hindered in any manner whatsoever by any authority whatsoever in the matter of the aforesaid and of this present letter, threatening all opposers, hinderers, contradictors, and rebels, of whatever rank, state, decree, eminence, nobility, excellence, or condition they may be, and whatever privilege of exemption that may enjoy, with excommunication, suspension, interdict, and other still more terrible sentences, censures, and penalties, as may be expedient, and this without appeal and with power after due process of law of aggravating and reaggravating these penalties, by our authority, as often as may be necessary, to this end calling in the aid, if need be, of the secular arm.

And this, all other apostolic decrees and earlier decisions to the contrary notwithstanding; or if to any, jointly or severally, there has been granted by this apostolic see exemption from interdict, suspension, or excommunication, by apostolic letters not making entire, express, and literal mention of the said grant of exemption; or if there exist any other indulgence whatsoever, general or special, of whatsoever tenor, by failure to name which or to insert it bodily in the present letter the carrying out of this privilege could be hindered or in any way put off,—or any of whose whole tenor special mention must be made in our letters. Let no man, therefore, dare to infringe this page of our declaration, extension, grant, and mandate, or with rash hardihood to contradict it. If any presume to attempt this, let him know that he incurs the wrath of almighty God and of the blessed apostles Peter and Paul.

Given in Rome, at St. Peter's, in the year of Our Lord's incarnation 1484, on the nones of December, in the first year of our pontificate.

34
Heinrich Kramer and Jacob Sprenger:
The *Malleus Maleficarum* (1487)

The *Malleus Maleficarum* (Hammer of Witches), written in 1487 by the Dominican inquisitors Heinrich Kramer (more commonly called Institoris, the Latinized form of Kramer), and Jacob Sprenger, became the first encyclopedia of witch beliefs and was constantly cited in support of those beliefs by Catholics and Protestants down to the eighteenth century. Its form is similar to that of other works in the same genre; it springs from the handbook for investigating heretics, some examples of which were in fact called "Hammers of Heretics." Kramer and Sprenger were the inquisitors in Upper Germany; their book was prefaced by Pope Innocent VIII's bull *Summis desiderantes*, and contained as an appendix an alleged decision in its favor by the faculty of theology of the University of Cologne. With such claims to the sanction of authority, the *Malleus* exhaustively analyzed the entire problem of witch beliefs and set out meticulously the ways by which witches could be found, convicted, and executed. The unrelenting thoroughness of Kramer and Sprenger served, in a sense, to sum up the entire history of recent witch beliefs and to present Christian Europe with a complete, persuasive, massively documented, and apparently authorized description of the witches in its midst.

SOURCE: From the *Malleus Maleficarum*, trans. Montague Summers (London, 1928), pt. 1, qq. 6, 11; pt. 2, q. 1, chaps. 2, 4, 7; pt. 3, intro., qq. 5, 9, 10, 14, 15, 18, 31, 34 (pp. 41–47, 66, 99–101, 109–13, 118–22, 204, 209–10, 216–18, 222–30, 235, 258–61, 268–71).

Why it is that Women are chiefly addicted
to Evil Superstitions.
There is also, concerning witches who copulate with devils, much difficulty in considering the methods by which such abominations are consummated. On the part of the devil: first, of what element the body is made that he assumes; secondly, whether the act is always accompanied by the injection of semen received from another; thirdly, as to time and place, whether he commits this act more frequently at one time than at another; fourthly, whether the act is invisible to any who may be standing by. And on the part of the women, it has to be inquired whether only they who were themselves conceived in this filthy manner are often visited by devils; or secondly, whether it is those who were offered to devils by midwives at the time of their birth; and thirdly, whether the actual venereal delectation of such is of a weaker sort. But we cannot here reply to all these questions, both because we are only engaged in a general study, and because in the second part of this work they are all singly explained by their operations as will appear in the fourth chapter, where mention is made of each separate method. Therefore let us now chiefly consider women; and first, why this kind of perfidy is found more in so fragile a sex than in men. And our inquiry will first be general, as to the general conditions of women; secondly, particular, as to which sort of women are found to be given to superstition and witchcraft; and thirdly, specifically with regard to midwives, who surpass all others in wickedness.

Why Superstition is chiefly found in Women.
As for the first question, why a greater number of witches is found in the fragile feminine sex than among men; it is indeed a fact that it were idle to contradict, since it is accredited by actual experience, apart from the verbal testimony of credible witnesses. And without in any way detracting from a sex in which God has always taken great glory that His might should be spread abroad, let us say that various men have assigned various reasons for this fact, which nevertheless agree in principle. Wherefore it is good, for the admonition of women, to speak of this matter; and it has often been proved by experience that they are eager to hear of it, so long as it is set forth with discretion.

For some learned men propound this reason; that there are three things in nature, the Tongue, an Ecclesiastic, and a Woman, which know no moderation in goodness or vice; and when they exceed the bounds of their condition they reach the greatest heights and the lowest depths of goodness and vice. When they are governed by a good spirit, they are most excellent in virtue; but when they are governed by an evil spirit, they indulge the worst possible vices.

This is clear in the case of the tongue, since by its ministry most of the kingdoms have been brought into the faith of Christ; and the Holy Ghost appeared over the Apostles of Christ in tongues of fire. Other learned preachers also have had as it were the tongues of dogs, licking the wounds and sores of the dying Lazarus. As it was said: With the tongues of dogs ye save your souls from the enemy.

For this reason S. Dominic, the leader and father of the Order of Preachers, is represented in the figure of a barking dog with a lighted torch in his mouth, that even to this day he may by his barking keep off the heretic wolves from the flock of Christ's sheep.

It is also a matter of common experience that the tongue of one prudent man can subdue the wrangling of a multitude; wherefore not unjustly Solomon sings much in their praise, in *Proverbs* x: In the lips of him that hath understanding wisdom is found. And again, The tongue of the just is as choice silver: the heart of the wicked is little worth. And again, The lips of the righteous feed many; but fools die for want of wisdom. For this cause he adds in chapter xvi, The preparations of the heart belong to man, but the answer of the tongue is from the Lord.

But concerning an evil tongue you will find in *Ecclesiasticus* xxviii: A backbiting tongue hath disquieted many, and driven them from nation to nation: strong cities hath it pulled down, and overthrown the houses of great men. And by a backbiting tongue it means a third party who rashly or spitefully interferes between two contending parties.

Secondly, concerning Ecclesiastics, that is to say, clerics and religious of either sex, S. John Chrysostom speaks on the text, He cast out them that bought and sold from the temple. From the priesthood arises everything good, and everything evil. S. Jerome in his epistle to Nepotian says: Avoid as you would the plague a trading priest, who has risen from poverty to riches, from a low to a high estate. And Blessed Bernard in his 23rd Homily *On the Psalms* says of clerics: If one should arise as an open heretic, let him be cast out and put to silence; if he is a violent enemy, let all good men flee from him. But how are we to know which ones to cast out or to flee from? For they are confusedly friendly and hostile, peaceable and quarrelsome, neighbourly and utterly selfish.

And in another place: Our bishops are become spearmen, and our pastors shearers. And by bishops here is meant those proud Abbots who impose heavy labours on their inferiors, which they would not themselves touch with their little finger. And S. Gregory says concerning pastors: No one does more harm in the Church than he who, having the name or order of sanctity, lives in sin; for no one dares to accuse him of sin, and therefore the sin is widely spread, since the sinner is honoured for the sanctity of his order. Blessed Augustine also speaks of monks to Vincent the Donatist: I freely confess to your charity before the Lord our God, which is the witness of my soul from the time I began to serve God, what great difficulty I have experienced in the fact that it is impossible to find either worse or better men that those who grace or disgrace the monasteries.

Now the wickedness of women is spoken of in *Ecclesiasticus* xxv: There is no head above the head of a serpent: and there is no wrath above the wrath of a woman. I had rather dwell with a lion and a dragon than to keep house with a wicked woman. And among much which in that place precedes and follows about a wicked woman, he concludes: All wickedness is but little to the wickedness of a woman. Wherefore S. John Chrysostom says on the text, It is not good to marry (S. *Matthew* xix): What else is woman but a foe to friendship, an unescapable punishment, a necessary evil, a natural temptation, a desirable calamity, a domestic danger, a delectable detriment, an evil of nature, painted with fair colours! Therefore if it be a sin to divorce her when she ought to be kept, it is indeed a necessary torture; for either we commit adultery by divorcing her, or we must endure daily strife. Cicero in his second book of *The Rhetorics* says: The many lusts of men lead them into one sin, but the one lust of women leads them into all sins; for the root of all woman's vices is avarice. And Seneca says in his *Tragedies*: A woman either loves or hates; there is no third grade. And the tears of a woman are a deception, for they may spring from true grief, or they may be a snare. When a woman thinks alone, she thinks evil.

But for good women there is so much praise, that we read that they have brought beatitude to men, and have saved nations, lands, and cities; as is clear in the case of Judith, Debbora, and Esther. See also 1 *Corinthians* vii: If a woman hath a husband that believeth not, and he be pleased to dwell with her, let her not leave him. For the unbelieving husband is sanctified by the believing wife. And *Ecclesiasticus* xxvi: Blessed is the man who has a virtuous wife, for the number of his days shall be doubled. And throughout that chapter much high praise is spoken of the excellence of good women; as also in the last chapter of *Proverbs* concerning a virtuous woman.

And all this is made clear in the New Testament concerning women and virgins and other holy women who have by faith led nations and kingdoms away from the worship of idols to the Christian religion. Anyone who looks at Vincent of Beauvais (*in Spe. Histor.*, XXVI. 9) will find marvellous things of the conversion of Hungary by the most Christian Gilia, and of the Franks by Clotilda, the wife of Clovis. Wherefore in many vituperations that we read against women, the word woman is used to mean the lust of the flesh. As it is said: I have found a woman more bitter than death, and a good woman subject to carnal lust.

Others again have propounded other reasons why there are more superstitious women found than men. And the first is, that they are more credulous; and since the chief aim of the devil is to corrupt faith, therefore he rather attacks them. See *Ecclesiasticus* xix: He that is quick to believe is light-minded, and shall be diminished. The second reason is, that women are naturally more impressionable, and more ready to receive the influence of a disembodied spirit; and that when they use this quality well they are very good, but when they use it ill they are very evil.

The third reason is that they have slippery tongues, and are unable to conceal from their fellow-women those things which by evil arts they know, and, since they are weak, they find an easy and secret manner of vindicating themselves by witchcraft. See *Ecclesiasticus* as quoted above: I had rather dwell with a lion and a dragon than to keep house with a wicked woman. All wickedness is but little to the wickedness of a woman. And to this may be added that, as they are very impressionable, they act accordingly.

There are also others who bring forward yet other reasons, of which preachers should be very careful how they make use. For it is true that in the Old Testament the Scriptures have much that is evil to say about women, and this because of the first temptress, Eve, and her imitators; yet afterwards in the New Testament we find a change of name, as from Eva to Ave (as S. Jerome says), and the whole sin of Eve taken away by the benediction of Mary. Therefore preachers should always say as much praise of them as possible.

But because in these times this perfidy is more often found in women than in men, as we learn by actual experience, if anyone is curious as to the reason, we may add to what has already been said the following: that since they are feebler both in mind and body, it is not surprising that they should come more under the spell of witchcraft.

For as regards intellect, or the understanding of spiritual things, they seem to be of a different nature from men; a fact which is vouched for by the logic of the authorities, backed by various examples from the Scriptures. Terence says: Women are intellectually like children. And Lactantius (*Institutiones*, III): No woman understood philosophy except Temeste. And *Proverbs* xi, as it were describing a woman, says: As a jewel of gold in a swine's snout, so is a fair woman which is without discretion.

But the natural reason is that she is more carnal than a man, as is clear from her many carnal abominations. And it should be noted that there was a defect in the formation of the first woman, since she was formed from a bent rib, that is, a rib of the breast, which is bent as it were in a contrary direction to a man. And since through this defect she is an imperfect animal, she always deceives. For Cato says: When a woman weeps she weaves snares. And again: When a woman weeps, she labours to deceive a man. And this is shown by Samson's wife, who coaxed him to tell her the riddle he had propounded to the Philistines, and told them the answer, and so deceived him. And it is clear in the case of the first woman that she had little faith; for when the serpent asked why they did not eat of every tree in Paradise, she answered: Of every tree, etc.—lest perchance we die. Thereby she showed that she doubted, and had little faith in the word of God. And all this is indicated by the etymology of the word; for *Femina* comes from *Fe* and *Minus*, since she is ever weaker to hold and preserve the faith. And this as regards faith is of her very nature; although both by grace and nature faith never failed in the Blessed Virgin, even at the time of Christ's Passion, when it failed in all men.

Therefore a wicked woman is by her nature quicker to waver in her faith, and consequently quicker to abjure the faith, which is the root of witchcraft.

And as to her other mental quality, that is, her natural will; when she hates someone whom she formerly loved, then she seethes with anger and impatience in her whole soul, just as the tides of the sea are always heaving and boiling. Many authorities allude to this cause. *Ecclesiasticus* xxv: There is no wrath above the wrath of a woman. And Seneca (*Tragedies*, VIII): No might of the flames or of the swollen winds, no deadly weapon is so much to be feared as the lust and hatred of a woman who has been divorced from the marriage bed.

This is shown too in the woman who falsely accused Joseph, and caused him to be imprisoned because he would not consent to the crime of adultery with her (*Genesis* xxx). And truly the most powerful cause which contributes to the increase of witches is the woeful rivalry between married folk and unmarried women and men. This is so even among holy women, so what must it be among the others? For you see in *Genesis* xxi how impatient and envious Sarah was of Hagar when she conceived: how jealous Rachel was of Leah because she had no children (*Genesis* xxx): and Hannah, who was barren, of the fruitful Peninnah (I. *Kings* i): and how Miriam (*Numbers* xii) murmured and spoke ill of Moses, and was therefore stricken with leprosy: and how Martha was jealous of Mary Magdalen, because she was busy and Mary was sitting down (*S. Luke* x). To this point is *Ecclesiasticus* xxxvii: Neither consult with a woman touching her of whom she is jealous. Meaning that it is useless to consult with her, since there is always jealousy, that is, envy, in a wicked woman. And if women behave thus to each other, how much more will they do so to men.

Valerius Maximus tells how, when Phoroneus, the king of the Greeks, was dying, he said to his brother Leontius that there would have been nothing lacking to him of complete happiness if a wife had always been lacking to him. And when Leontius asked how a wife could stand in the way of happiness, he answered that all married men well knew. And when the philosopher Socrates was asked if one should marry a wife, he answered: If you do not, you are lonely, your family dies out, and a stranger inherits; if you do, you suffer perpetual anxiety, querulous complaints, reproaches concerning the marriage portion, the heavy displeasure of your relations, the garrulousness of a mother-in-law, cuckoldom, and no certain arrival of an heir. This he said as one who knew. For S. Jerome in his *Contra Iouinianum* says: This Socrates had two wives, whom he endured with much patience, but could not be rid of their contumelies and clamorous vituperations. So one day when they were complaining against him, he went out of the house to escape their plaguing, and sat down before the house; and the women then threw filthy water over him. But the philosopher was not disturbed by this, saying, "I knew that the rain would come after the thunder."

There is also a story of a man whose wife was drowned in a river, who, when he was searching for the body to take it out of the water, walked up the stream.

And when he was asked why, since heavy bodies do not rise but fall, he was searching against the current of the river, he answered: "When that woman was alive she always, both in word and deed, went contrary to my commands; therefore I am searching in the contrary direction in case even now she is dead she may preserve her contrary disposition."

And indeed, just as through the first defect in their intelligence they are more prone to abjure the faith; so through their second defect of inordinate affections and passions they search for, brood over, and inflict various vengeances, either by witchcraft, or by some other means. Wherefore it is no wonder that so great a number of witches exist in this sex.

Women also have weak memories; and it is a natural vice in them not to be disciplined, but to follow their own impulses without any sense of what is due; this is her whole study, and all that she keeps in her memory. So Theophrastus says: If you hand over the whole management of the house to her, but reserve some minute detail to your own judgment, she will think that you are displaying a great want of faith in her, and will stir up strife; and unless you quickly take counsel, she will prepare poison for you, and consult seers and soothsayers; and will become a witch.

But as to domination by women, hear what Cicero says in the *Paradoxes*. Can he be called a free man whose wife governs him, imposes laws on him, orders him, and forbids him to do what he wishes, so that he cannot and dare not deny her anything that she asks? I should call him not only a slave, but the vilest of slaves, even if he comes of the noblest family. And Seneca, in the character of the raging Medea, says: Why do you cease to follow your happy impulse; how great is that part of vengeance in which you rejoice? Where he adduces many proofs that a woman will not be governed, but will follow her own impulse even to her own destruction. In the same way we read of many women who have killed themselves either for love or sorrow because they were unable to work their vengeance.

S. Jerome, writing of Daniel, tells a story of Laodice, wife of Antiochus king of Syria; how, being jealous lest he should love his other wife, Berenice, more than her, she first caused Berenice and her daughter by Antiochus to be slain, and then poisoned herself. And why? Because she would not be governed, but would follow her own impulse. Therefore S. John Chrysostom says not without reason: O evil worse than all evil, a wicked woman, whether she be poor or rich. For if she be the wife of a rich man, she does not cease night and day to excite her husband with hot words, to use evil blandishments and violent importunations. And if she have a poor husband she does not cease to stir him also to anger and strife. And if she be a widow, she takes it upon herself everywhere to look down on everybody, and is inflamed to all boldness by the spirit of pride.

If we inquire, we find that nearly all the kingdoms of the world have been overthrown by women. Troy, which was a prosperous kingdom, was, for the rape of one woman, Helen, destroyed, and many thousands of Greeks slain. The kingdom of the Jews suffered much misfortune and destruction through the accursed Jezebel, and her daughter Athaliah, queen of Judah, who caused her son's sons to be killed, that on their death she might reign herself; yet each of them was slain. The kingdom of the Romans endured much evil through Cleopatra, Queen of Egypt, that worst of women. And so with others. Therefore it is no wonder if the world now suffers through the malice of women.

And now let us examine the carnal desires of the body itself, whence has arisen unconscionable harm to human life. Justly may we say with Cato of Utica: If the world could be rid of women, we should not be without God in our intercourse. For truly, without the wickedness of women, to say nothing of witchcraft, the world would still remain proof against innumerable dangers. Hear what Valerius said to Rufinus: You do not know that woman is the Chimaera, but it is good that you should know it; for that monster was of three forms; its face was that of a radiant and noble lion, it had the filthy belly of a goat, and it was armed with the virulent tail of a viper. And he means that a woman is beautiful to look upon, contaminating to the touch, and deadly to keep.

Let us consider another property of hers, the voice. For as she is a liar by nature, so in her speech she stings while she delights us. Wherefore her voice is like the song of the Sirens, who with their sweet melody entice the passers-by and kill them. For they kill them by emptying their purses, consuming their strength, and causing them to forsake God. Again Valerius says to Rufinus: When she speaks it is a delight which flavours the sin; the flower of love is a rose, because under its blossom there are hidden many thorns. See *Proverbs* v, 3–4; Her mouth is smoother than oil; that is, her speech is afterwards as bitter as absinthium. [Her throat is smoother than oil. But her end is as bitter as wormwood.]

Let us consider also her gait, posture, and habit, in which is vanity of vanities. There is no man in the world who studies so hard to please the good God as even an ordinary woman studies by her vanities to please men. An example of this is to be found in the life of Pelagia, a worldly woman who was wont to go about Antioch tired and adorned most extravagantly. A holy father, named Nonnus, saw her and began to weep, saying to his companions, that never in all his life had he used such diligence to please God; and much more he added to this effect, which is preserved in his orations.

It is this which is lamented in *Ecclesiastes* vii, and which the Church even now laments on account of the great multitude of witches. And I have found a woman more bitter than death, who is the hunter's snare, and her heart is a net, and her hands are bands. He that pleaseth God shall escape from her; but he that is a sinner shall be caught by her. More bitter than death, that is, than the devil: *Apocalypse* vi, 8, His name was Death. For though the devil tempted Eve to sin, yet Eve seduced Adam. And as the sin of Eve would not have brought death to our soul and body unless the sin had afterwards passed on to Adam, to which he was tempted by Eve, not by the devil, therefore she is more bitter than death.

More bitter than death, again, because that is natural and destroys only the body; but the sin which arose from woman destroys the soul by depriving it of grace, and delivers the body up to the punishment for sin.

More bitter than death, again, because bodily death is an open and terrible enemy, but woman is a wheedling and secret enemy.

And that she is more perilous than a snare does not speak of the snare of hunters, but of devils. For men are caught not only through their carnal desires, when they see and hear women: for S. Bernard says: Their face is a burning wind, and their voice the hissing of serpents: but they also cast wicked spells on countless men and animals. And when it is said that her heart is a net, it speaks of the inscrutable malice which reigns in their hearts. And her hands are as bands for binding; for when they place their hands on a creature to bewitch it, then with the help of the devil they perform their design.

To conclude. All witchcraft comes from carnal lust, which is in women insatiable. See *Proverbs* xxx: There are three things that are never satisfied, yea, a fourth thing which says not, It is enough; that is, the mouth of the womb. Wherefore for the sake of fulfilling their lusts they consort even with devils. More such reasons could be brought forward, but to the understanding it is sufficiently clear that it is no matter for wonder that there are more women than men found infected with the heresy of witchcraft. And in consequence of this, it is better called the heresy of witches than of wizards, since the name is taken from the more powerful party. And blessed be the Highest Who has so far preserved the male sex from so great a crime: for since He was willing to be born and to suffer for us, therefore He has granted to men this privilege.

*That Witches who are Midwives in Various Ways Kill the Child
Conceived in the Womb, and Procure an Abortion; or if they do not this
Offer New-born Children to Devils.*
Here is set forth the truth concerning four horrible crimes which devils commit against infants, both in the mother's womb and afterwards. And since the devils do these things through the medium of women, and not men, this form of homicide is associated rather with women than with men. And the following are the methods by which it is done.

The Canonists treat more fully than the Theologians of the obstructions due to witchcraft; and they say that it is witchcraft, not only when anyone is unable to perform the carnal act, of which we have spoken above; but also when a woman is prevented from conceiving, or is made to miscarry after she has conceived. A third and fourth method of witchcraft is when they have failed to procure an abortion, and then either devour the child or offer it to a devil.

There is no doubt concerning the first two methods, since, without the help of devils, a man can by natural means, such as herbs, savin for example, or other emmenagogues, procure that a woman cannot generate or conceive, as has been mentioned above. But with the other two methods it is different; for they are effected by witches. And there is no need to bring forward the arguments, since very evident instances and examples will more readily show the truth of this matter.

The former of these two abominations is the fact that certain witches, against the instinct of human nature, and indeed against the nature of all beasts, with the possible exception of wolves, are in the habit of devouring and eating infant children. And concerning this, the Inquisitor of Como, who has been mentioned before, has told us the following: that he was summoned by the inhabitants of the County of Barby to hold an inquisition, because a certain man had missed his child from its cradle, and finding a congress of women in the night-time, swore that he saw them kill his child and drink its blood and devour it. Also, in one single year, which is the year now last passed, he says that forty-one witches were burned, certain others taking flight to the Lord Archduke of Austria, Sigismund. For confirmation of this there are certain writings of John Nider in his *Formicarius*, of whom, as of those events which he recounts, the memory is still fresh in men's minds; wherefore it is apparent that such things are not incredible. We must add that in all these matters witch midwives cause yet greater injuries, as penitent witches have often told to us and to others, saying: No one does more harm to the Catholic Faith than midwives. For when they do not kill children, then, as if for some other purpose, they take them out of the room and, raising them up in the air, offer them to devils. But the method which they observe in crimes of this sort will be shown in the Second Part, which we must soon approach. But first one more question must be inquired into, namely, that of the Divine permission. For it was said at the beginning that three things are necessary for the effecting of witchcraft: the devil, a witch, and the Divine permission.

Of the Way whereby a Formal Pact with Evil is made.
The method by which they profess their sacrilege through an open pact of fidelity to devils varies according to the several practices to which different witches are addicted. And to understand this it first must be noted that there are, as was shown in the First Part of this treatise, three kinds of witches; namely, those who injure but cannot cure; those who cure but, through some strange pact with the devil, cannot injure; and those who both injure and cure. And among those who injure, one class in particular stands out, which can perform every sort of witchcraft and spell, comprehending all that all the others individually can do. Wherefore, if we describe the method of profession in their case, it will suffice also for all the other kinds. And this class is made up of those who, against every

instinct of human or animal nature, are in the habit of eating and devouring the children of their own species.

And this is the most powerful class of witches, who practise innumerable other harms also. For they raise hailstorms and hurtful tempests and lightnings; cause sterility in men and animals; offer to devils, or otherwise kill, the children whom they do not devour. But these are only the children who have not been re-born by baptism at the font, for they cannot devour those who have been bap-tized, nor any without God's permission. They can also, before the eyes of their parents, and when no one is in sight, throw into the water children walking by the water side; they make horses go mad under their riders; they can transport themselves from place to place through the air, either in body or in imagination; they can affect Judges and Magistrates so that they cannot hurt them; they can cause themselves and others to keep silence under torture; they can bring about a great trembling in the hands and horror in the minds of those who would arrest them; they can show to others occult things and certain future events, by the information of devils, though this may sometimes have a natural cause (see the question: *Whether devils can foretell the future*, in the *Second Book of Sen-tences*); they can see absent things as if they were present; they can turn the minds of men to inordinate love or hatred; they can at times strike whom they will with lightning, and even kill some men and animals; they can make of no effect the generative desires, and even the power of copulation, cause abortion, kill infants in the mother's womb by a mere exterior touch; they can at times bewitch men and animals with a mere look, without touching them, and cause death; they dedicate their own children to devils; and in short, as has been said, they can cause all the plagues which other witches can only cause in part, that is, when the Justice of God permits such things to be. All these things this most powerful of all classes of witches can do, but they cannot undo them.

But it is common to all of them to practise carnal copulation with devils; therefore, if we show the method used by this chief class in their profession of their sacrilege, anyone may easily understand the method of the other classes.

There were such witches lately, thirty years ago, in the district of Savoy, towards the State of Berne, as Nider tells in his *Formicarius*. And there are now some in the country of Lombardy, in the domains of the Duke of Austria, where the Inquisitor of Como, as we told in the former Part, caused forty-one witches to be burned in one year; and he was fifty-five years old, and still continues to labour in the Inquisition.

Now the method of profession is twofold. One is a solemn ceremony, like a solemn vow. The other is private, and can be made to the devil at any hour alone. The first method is when witches meet together in conclave on a set day, and the devil appears to them in the assumed body of a man, and urges them to keep faith with him, promising them worldly prosperity and length of life; and they recommend a novice to his acceptance. And the devil asks whether she will abjure the Faith, and forsake the holy Christian religion and the worship of the Anomalous Woman (for so they call the Most Blessed Virgin Mary), and never venerate the Sacraments; and if he finds the novice or disciple willing, then the devil stretches out his hand, and so does the novice, and she swears with upraised hand to keep that covenant. And when this is done, the devil at once adds that this is not enough; and when the disciple asks what more must be done, the devil demands the following oath of homage to himself: that she give herself to him, body and soul, for ever, and do her utmost to bring others of both sexes into his power. He adds, finally, that she is to make certain unguents from the bones and limbs of children, especially those who have been baptized; by all which means she will be able to fulfill all her wishes with his help.

We Inquisitors had credible experience of this method in the town of Breisach in the diocese of Basel, receiving full information from a young girl witch who had been converted, whose aunt also had been burned in the diocese of Strasburg. And she added that she had become a witch by the method in which her aunt had first tried to seduce her.

For one day her aunt ordered her to go upstairs with her, and at her command to go into a room where she found fifteen young men clothed in green garments after the manner of German knights. And her aunt said to her: Choose whom you wish from these young men, and I will give him to you, and he will take you for his wife. And when she said she did not wish for any of them, she was sorely beaten and at last consented, and was initiated according to the aforesaid ceremony. She said also that she was often transported by night with her aunt over vast distances, even from Strasburg to Cologne.

This is she who occasioned our inquiry in the First Part into the question whether witches are truly and bodily transported by devils from place to place: and this was on account of the words of the Canon (6, q. 5, *Episcopi*), which seem to imply that they are only so carried in imagination; whereas they are at times actually and bodily transported.

For when she was asked whether it was only in imagination and phantastically that they so rode, through an illusion of devils, she answered that they did so in both ways; according to the truth which we shall declare later of the manner in which they are transferred from place to place. She said also that the greatest injuries were inflicted by midwives, because they were under an obligation to kill or offer to devils as many children as possible; and that she had been severely beaten by her aunt because she had opened a secret pot and found the heads of a great many children. And much more she told us, having first, as was proper, taken an oath to speak the truth.

And her account of the method of professing the devil's faith undoubtedly agrees with what has been written by that most eminent Doctor, John Nider, who even in our times has written very illuminatingly; and it may be especially remarked that he tells us the following, which he had from an Inquisitor of the diocese of Edua, who held many inquisitions on witches in that diocese, and caused many to be burned.

For he says that this Inquisitor told him that in the Duchy of Lausanne certain witches had cooked and eaten their own children, and that the following was the method in which they became initiated into such practices. The witches met together and, by their art, summoned a devil in the form of a man, to whom the novice was compelled to swear to deny the Christian religion, never to adore the Eucharist, and to tread the Cross underfoot whenever she could do so secretly.

Here is another example from the same source. There was lately a general report, brought to the notice of Peter the Judge in Boltingen, that thirteen infants had been devoured in the State of Berne; and public justice exacted full vengeance on the murderers. And when Peter asked one of the captive witches in what manner they ate children, she replied: "This is the manner of it. We set our snares chiefly for unbaptized children, and even for those that have been baptized, especially when they have not been protected by the sign of the Cross and prayers" (reader, notice that, at the devil's command, they take the unbaptized chiefly, in order that they may not be baptized), "and with our spells we kill them in their cradles or even when they are sleeping by their parents' side, in such a way that they afterwards are thought to have been overlain or to have died some other natural death. Then we secretly take them from their graves, and cook them in a cauldron, until the whole flesh comes away from the bones to make a soup which may easily be drunk. Of the more solid matter we make an unguent which is of virtue to help us in our arts and pleasures and our transportations; and with the liquid we fill a flask or skin, whoever drinks from which, with the addition of a few other ceremonies, immediately acquires much knowledge and becomes a leader in our sect."

Here is another very clear and distinct example. A young man and his wife, both witches, were imprisoned in Berne; and the man, shut up by himself apart from her in a separate tower, said: "If I could obtain pardon for my sins, I would willingly declare all that I know about witchcraft; for I see that I ought to die." And when he was told by the learned clerks who were there that he could obtain complete pardon if he truly repented, he joyfully resigned himself to death, and laid bare the method by which he had first been infected with his heresy. "The following," he said, "is the manner in which I was seduced. It is first necessary that, on a Sunday before the consecration of Holy Water, the novice should enter the church with the masters, and there in their presence deny Christ, his Faith, baptism, and the whole Church. And then he must pay homage to the Little Master, for so and not otherwise do they call the devil." Here it is to be noted that this method agrees with those that have been recounted; for it is immaterial whether the devil is himself present or not, when homage is offered to him. For this he does in his cunning, perceiving the temperament of the novice, who might be frightened by his actual presence into retracting his vows, whereas he would be more easily persuaded to consent by those who are known to him. And therefore they call him the Little Master when he is absent, that through seeming disparagement of his Master the novice may feel less fear. "And then he drinks from the skin, which has been mentioned, and immediately feels within himself a knowledge of all our arts and an understanding of our rites and ceremonies. And in this manner was I seduced. But I believe my wife to be so obstinate that she would rather go straight to the fire than confess the smallest part of the truth; but, alas! we are both guilty." And as the young man said, so it happened in every respect. For the young man confessed and was seen to die in the greatest contrition; but the wife, though convicted by witnesses, would not confess any of the truth, either under torture or in death itself; but when the fire had been prepared by the gaoler, cursed him in the most terrible words, and so was burned. And from these examples their method of initiation in solemn conclave is made clear.

The other private method is variously performed. For sometimes when men or women have been involved in some bodily or temporal affliction, the devil comes to them, at times in person, and at times speaking to them through the mouth of someone else; and he promises that, if they will agree to his counsels, he will do for them whatever they wish. But he starts from small things, as was said in the first chapter, and leads gradually to the bigger things. We could mention many examples which have come to our knowledge in the Inquisition, but, since this matter presents no difficulty, it can briefly be included with the previous matter.

Here follows the Way whereby Witches copulate with those Devils known as Incubi.

As to the method in which witches copulate with Incubus devils, six points are to be noted. First, as to the devil and the body which he assumes, of what element it is formed. Second, as to the act, whether it is always accompanied with the injection of semen received from some other man. Third, as to the time and place, whether one time is more favourable than another for this practice. Fourth, whether the act is visible to the women, and whether only those who were begotten in this way are so visited by devils. Fifth, whether it applies only to those who were offered to the devil at birth by midwives. Sixth, whether the actual venereal pleasure is greater or less in this act. And we will speak first of the matter and quality of the body which the devil assumes.

It must be said that he assumes an aerial body, and that it is in some respects terrestrial, in so far as it has an earthly property through condensation; and this is explained as follows. The air cannot of itself take definite shape, except the shape of some other body in which it is included. And in that case it is not bound by its own limits, but by those of something else; and one part of the air continues into the next part. Therefore he cannot simply assume an aerial body as such.

Know, moreover, that the air is in every way a most changeable and fluid matter: and a sign of this is the fact that when any have tried to cut or pierce with a sword the body assumed by a devil, they have not been able to; for the divided parts of the air at once join together again. From this it follows that air is in itself a very competent matter, but because it cannot take shape unless some other terrestrial matter is joined with it, therefore it is necessary that the air which forms the devil's assumed body should be in some way inspissated, and approach the property of the earth, while still retaining its true property as air. And devils and disembodied spirits can effect this condensation by means of gross vapours raised from the earth, and by collecting them together into shapes in which they abide, not as defilers of them, but only as their motive power which gives to that body the formal appearance of life, in very much the same way as the soul informs the body to which it is joined. They are, moreover, in these assumed and shaped bodies like a sailor in a ship which the wind moves.

So when it is asked of what sort is the body assumed by the devil, it is to be said that with regard to its material, it is one thing to speak of the beginning of its assumption, and another thing to speak of its end. For in the beginning it is just air; but in the end it is inspissated air, partaking of some of the properties of earth. And all this the devils, with God's permission, can do of their own nature; for the spiritual nature is superior to the bodily. Therefore the bodily nature must obey the devils in respect of local motion, though not in respect of the assumption of natural shapes, either accidental or substantial, except in the case of some small creatures (and then only with the help of some other agent, as has been hinted before). But as to local motion, no shape is beyond their power; thus they can move them as they wish, in such circumstances as they will.

From this there may arise an incidental question as to what should be thought when a good or bad Angel performs some of the functions of life by means of true natural bodies, and not in aerial bodies; as in the case of Balaam's ass, through which the Angel spoke, and when devils take possession of bodies. It is to be said that those bodies are not called assumed, but occupied. See S. Thomas, II. 8, Whether Angels assume bodies. But let us keep strictly to our argument.

In what way is it to be understood that devils talk with witches, see them, hear them, eat with them, and copulate with them? And this is the second part of this first difficulty.

For the first, it is to be said that three things are required for true conversation: namely, lungs to draw in the air; and this is not only for the sake of producing sound; but also to cool the heart; and even mutes have this necessary quality.

Secondly, it is necessary that some percussion be made of a body in the air, as a greater or less sound is made when one beats wood in the air, or rings a bell. For when a substance that is susceptible to sound is struck by a sound-producing instrument, it gives out a sound according to its size, which is received in the air and multiplied to the ears of the hearer, to whom, if he is far off, it seems to come through space.

Thirdly, a voice is required; and it may be said that what is called Sound in inanimate bodies is called Voice in living bodies. And here the tongue strikes the respirations of air against an instrument or living natural organ provided by God. And this is not a bell, which is called a sound, whereas this is a voice. And this third requisite may clearly be exemplified by the second; and I have set this down that preachers may have a method of teaching the people.

And fourthly, it is necessary that he who forms the voice should mean to express by means of that voice some concept of the mind to someone else, and that he should himself understand what he is saying; and so manage his voice by successively striking his teeth with his tongue in his mouth, by opening and shutting his lips, and by sending the air struck in his mouth into the outer air, that in this way the sound is reproduced in order in the ears of the hearer, who then understands his meaning.

To return to the point. Devils have no lungs or tongue, though they can show the latter, as well as teeth and lips, artificially made according to the condition of their body; therefore they cannot truly and properly speak. But since they have understanding, and when they wish to express their meaning, then, by some disturbance of the air included in their assumed body, not of air breathed in and out as in the case of men, they produce, not voices, but sounds which have some likeness to voices, and send them articulately through the outside air to the ears of the hearer. And that the likeness of a voice can be made without the respiration of air is clear from the case of other animals which do not breathe, but are said to make a sound, as do also certain other instruments, as Aristotle says in the *de Anima*. For certain fishes, when they are caught, suddenly utter a cry outside the water, and die.

All this is applicable to what follows, so far as the point where we treat of the generative function, but not as regards good Angels. If anyone wishes to inquire further into the matter of devils speaking in possessed bodies, he may refer to S. Thomas in the *Second Book of Sentences*, dist. 8, art. 5. For in that case they use the bodily organs of the possessed body; since they occupy those bodies in respect of the limits of their corporeal quantity, but not in respect of the limits of their essence, either of the body or of the soul. Observe a distinction between substance and quantity, or accident. But this is impertinent.

For now we must say in what manner they see and hear. Now sight is of two kinds, spiritual and corporeal, and the former infinitely excels the latter; for it can penetrate, and is not hindered by distance, owing to the faculty of light of which it makes use. Therefore it must be said that in no way does an Angel, either good or bad, see with the eyes of its assumed body, nor does it use any bodily property as it does in speaking, when it uses the air and the vibration of the air to produce sound which becomes reproduced in the ears of the hearer. Wherefore their eyes are painted eyes. And they freely appear to men in these likenesses that they may manifest to them their natural properties and converse with them spiritually by these means.

For with this purpose the holy Angels have often appeared to the Fathers at the command of God and with His permission. And the bad angels manifest themselves to wicked men in order that men, recognizing their qualities, may associate themselves with them, here in sin, and elsewhere in punishment.

S. Dionysius, at the end of his *Celestial Hierarchy*, says: In all parts of the human body the Angel teaches us to consider their properties: concluding that since corporeal vision is an operation of the living body through a bodily organ, which devils lack, therefore in their assumed bodies, just as they have the likeness of limbs, so they have the likeness of their functions.

And we can speak in the same way of their hearing, which is far finer than that of the body; for it can know the concept of the mind and the conversation of the soul more subtly than can a man by hearing the mental concept through the medium of spoken words. See S. Thomas, the *Second Book of Sentences*, dist. 8. For if the secret wishes of a man are read in his face, and physicians can tell the thoughts of the heart from the heart-beats and the state of the pulse, all the more can such things be known by devils.

And we may say as to eating, that in the complete act of eating there are four processes. Mastication in the mouth, swallowing into the stomach, digestion in the stomach, and fourthly, metabolism of the necessary nutriment and ejection of what is superfluous. All Angels can perform the first two processes of eating in their assumed bodies, but not the third and fourth; but instead of digesting and ejecting they have another power by which the food is suddenly dissolved in the surrounding matter. In Christ the process of eating was in all respects complete, since He had the nutritive and metabolistic powers; not, be it said, for the purpose of converting the food into His own body, for those powers were, like His body, glorified; so that the food was suddenly dissolved in His body, as when one throws water on to fire.

How in Modern Times Witches perform the Carnal Act with Incubus Devils, and how they are Multiplied by this Means.

But no difficulty arises out of what has been said, with regard to our principal subject, which is the carnal act which Incubi in an assumed body perform with witches: unless perhaps anyone doubts whether modern witches practise such abominable coitus; and whether witches had their origin in this abomination.

In answering these two doubts we shall say, as to the former of them, something of the activities of the witches who lived in olden times, about 1400 years before the Incarnation of Our Lord. It is, for example, unknown whether they were addicted to these filthy practices as modern witches have been since that time; for so far as we know history tells us nothing on this subject. But no one who reads the histories can doubt that there have always been witches, and that by their evil works much harm has been done to men, animals, and the fruits of the earth, and that Incubus and Succubus devils have always existed; for the traditions of the Canons and the holy Doctors have left and handed down to posterity many things concerning them through many hundreds of years. Yet there is this difference, that in times long past the Incubus devils used to infest women against their wills; as is often shown by Nider in his *Formicarius*, and by Thomas of Brabant in his book on the *Universal Good*, or on *Bees*.

But the theory that modern witches are tainted with this sort of diabolic filthiness is not substantiated only in our opinion, since the expert testimony of the witches themselves has made all these things credible; and that they do not now, as in times past, subject themselves unwillingly, but willingly embrace this most foul and miserable servitude. For how many women have we left to be punished by secular law in various dioceses, especially in Constance and the town of Ratisbon, who have been for many years addicted to these abominations, some from their twentieth and some from their twelfth or thirteenth year, and always with a total or partial abnegation of the Faith? All the inhabitants of those places are witnesses of it. For without reckoning those who secretly repented, and those who returned to the Faith, no less than forty-eight have been burned in five years. And there was no question of credulity in accepting their stories because they turned to free repentance; for they all agreed in this, namely, that they were bound to indulge in these lewd practices in order that the ranks of their perfidy might be increased. But we shall treat of these individually in the Second Part of this work, where their particular deeds are described; omitting those which came under the notice of our colleague the Inquisitor of Como in the County of Burbia, who in the space of one year, which was the year of grace 1485, caused forty-one witches to be burned; who all publicly affirmed, as it is said, that they practised these abominations with devils. Therefore this matter is fully substantiated by eye-witnesses, by hearsay, and the testimony of credible witnesses.

As for the second doubt, whether witches had their origin from these abominations, we may say with S. Augustine that it is true that all the superstitious arts had their origin in a pestilent association of men with devils. For he says so in his work *On the Christian Doctrine*: All this sort of practices, whether of trifling or of noxious superstition, arose from some pestilent association of men with devils, as though some pact of infidel and guileful friendship had been formed, and they are all utterly to be repudiated. Notice here that it is manifest that, as there are various kinds of superstition or magic arts, and various societies of those who practise them; and as among the fourteen kinds of that art the species of witches is the worst, since they have not a tacit but an overt and expressed pact with the devil, and more than this, have to acknowledge a form of devil-worship through abjuring the Faith; therefore it follows that witches hold the worst kind of association with devils, with especial reference to the behaviour of women, who always delight in vain things.

Notice also S. Thomas, the *Second Book of Sentences* (dist. 4, art. 4), in the solution of an argument, where he asks whether those begotten in this way by devils are more powerful than other men. He answers that this is the truth, basing his belief not only on the text of Scripture in *Genesis* vi: And the same became the mighty men which were of old; but also on the following reason. Devils know how to ascertain the virtue in semen: first, by the temperament of him from whom the semen is obtained; secondly, by knowing what woman is most fitted for the reception of that semen; thirdly, by knowing what constellation is favourable to that corporeal effect; and we may add, fourthly, from their own words we learn that those whom they beget have the best sort of disposition for devils' work. When all these causes so concur, it is concluded that men born in this way are powerful and big in body.

Therefore, to return to the question whether witches had their origin in these abominations, we shall say that they originated from some pestilent mutual association with devils, as is clear from our first knowledge of them. But no one can affirm with certainty that they did not increase and multiply by means of these foul practices, although devils commit this deed for the sake not of pleasure but of corruption. And this appears to be the order of the process. A Succubus devil draws the semen from a wicked man; and if he is that man's own particular devil, and does not wish to make himself an Incubus to a witch, he passes that semen on to the devil deputed to a woman or witch; and this last, under some constellation that favours his purpose that the man or woman so born should be strong in the practice of witchcraft, becomes the Incubus to the witch.

And it is no objection that those of whom the text speaks were not witches but only giants and famous and powerful men; for, as was said before, witchcraft was not perpetrated in the time of the law of Nature, because of the recent memory of the Creation of the world, which left no room for Idolatry. But when the wickedness of man began to increase, the devil found more opportunity to disseminate this kind of perfidy. Nevertheless, it is not to be understood that those who were said to be famous men were necessarily so called by reason of their good virtues.

Whether the Relations of an Incubus Devil with a Witch are always accompanied by the Injection of Semen.
To this question it is answered that the devil has a thousand ways and means of inflicting injury, and from the time of his first Fall has tried to destroy the unity of the Church, and in every way to subvert the human race. Therefore no infalli-

ble rule can be stated as to this matter, but there is this probable distinction: that a witch is either old and sterile, or she is not. And if she is, then he naturally associates with the witch without the injection of semen, since it would be of no use, and the devil avoids superfluity in his operations as far as he can. But if she is not sterile, he approaches her in the way of carnal delectation which is procured for the witch. And should she be disposed to pregnancy, then if he can conveniently possess the semen extracted from some man, he does not delay to approach her with it for the sake of infecting her progeny.

But if it is asked whether he is able to collect the semen emitted in some nocturnal pollution in sleep, just as he collects that which is spent in the carnal act, the answer is that it is probable that he cannot, though others hold a contrary opinion. For it must be noted that, as has been said, the devils pay attention to the generative virtue of the semen, and such virtue is more abundant and better preserved in semen obtained by the carnal act, being wasted in the semen that is due to nocturnal pollutions in sleep, which arises only from the superfluity of the humours and is not emitted with so great generative virtue. Therefore it is believed that he does not make use of such semen for the generation of progeny, unless perhaps he knows that the necessary virtue is present in that semen.

But this also cannot altogether be denied, that even in the case of a married witch who has been impregnated by her husband, the devil can, by the commixture of another semen, infect that which has been conceived.

How, as it were, they Deprive Man of his Virile Member.
We have already shown that they can take away the male organ, not indeed by actually despoiling the human body of it, but by concealing it with some glamour, in the manner which we have already declared. And of this we shall instance a few examples.

In the town of Ratisbon a certain young man who had an intrigue with a girl, wishing to leave her, lost his member; that is to say, some glamour was cast over it so that he could see or touch nothing but his smooth body. In his worry over this he went to a tavern to drink wine; and after he had sat there for a while he got into conversation with another woman who was there, and told her the cause of his sadness, explaining everything, and demonstrating in his body that it was so. The woman was astute, and asked whether he suspected anyone; and when he named such a one, unfolding the whole matter, she said: "If persuasion is not enough, you must use some violence, to induce her to restore to you your health." So in the evening the young man watched the way by which the witch was in the habit of going, and finding her, prayed her to restore to him the health of his body. And when she maintained that she was innocent and knew nothing about it, he fell upon her, and winding a towel tightly round her neck, choked her, saying: "Unless you give me back my health, you shall die at my hands."

Then she, being unable to cry out, and with her face already swelling and growing black, said: "Let me go, and I will heal you." The young man then relaxed the pressure of the towel, and the witch touched him with her hand between the thighs, saying: "Now you have what you desire." And the young man, as he afterwards said, plainly felt, before he had verified it by looking or touching, that his member had been restored to him by the mere touch of the witch.

A similar experience is narrated by a certain venerable Father from the Dominican House of Speyer, well known in the Order for the honesty of his life and for his learning. "One day," he says, "while I was hearing confessions, a young man came to me and, in the course of his confession, woefully said that he had lost his member. Being astonished at this, and not being willing to give it easy credency, since in the opinion of the wise it is a mark of light-heartedness to believe too easily, I obtained proof of it when I saw nothing on the young man's removing his clothes and showing the place. Then, using the wisest counsel I could, I asked whether he suspected anyone of having so bewitched him. And the young man said that he did suspect someone, but that she was absent and living in Worms. Then I said: 'I advise you to go to her as soon as possible and try your utmost to soften her with gentle words and promises'; and he did so. For he came back after a few days and thanked me, saying that he was whole and had recovered everything. And I believed his words, but again proved them by the evidence of my eyes."

But there are some points to be noted for the clearer understanding of what has already been written concerning this matter. First, it must in no way be believed that such members are really torn right away from the body, but that they are hidden by the devil through some prestidigitatory art so that they can be neither seen nor felt. And this is proved by the authorities and by argument; although it has been treated of before, where Alexander of Hales says that a Prestige, properly understood, is an illusion of the devil, which is not caused by any material change, but exists only in the perceptions of him who is deluded, either in his interior or exterior senses.

With reference to these words it is to be noted that, in the case we are considering, two of the exterior senses, namely, those of sight and touch, are deluded, and not the interior senses, namely, common-sense, fancy, imagination, thought, and memory. (But S. Thomas says they are only four, as has been told before, reckoning fancy and imagination as one; and with some reason, for there is little difference between imagining and fancying. See S. Thomas, I, 79.) And these senses, and not only the exterior senses, are affected when it is not a case of hiding something, but of causing something to appear to a man either when he is awake or asleep.

As when a man who is awake sees things otherwise than as they are; such as seeing someone devour a horse with its rider, or thinking he sees a man transformed into a beast, or thinking that he is himself a beast and must associate with beasts. For then the exterior senses are deluded and are employed by the interior senses. For by the power of devils, with God's permission, mental images long retained in the treasury of such images, which is the memory, are drawn out, not from the intellectual understanding in which such images are stored, but from the memory, which is the repository of mental images, and is situated at the back of the head, and are presented to the imaginative faculty. And so strongly are they impressed on that faculty that a man has an inevitable impulse to imagine a horse or a beast, when the devil draws from the memory an image of a horse or a beast; and so he is compelled to think that he sees with his external eyes such a beast when there is actually no such beast to see; but it seems to be so by reason of the impulsive force of the devil working by means of those images.

And it need not seem wonderful that devils can do this, when even a natural defect is able to effect the same result, as is shown in the case of frantic and melancholy men, and in maniacs and some drunkards, who are unable to discern truly. For frantic men think they see marvellous things, such as beasts and other horrors, when in actual fact they see nothing. See above, in the question, Whether witches can turn the minds of men to love and hatred; where many things are noted.

And, finally, the reason is self-evident. For since the devil has power over inferior things, except only the soul, therefore he is able to effect certain changes in those things, when God allows, so that things appear to be otherwise than they are. And this he does, as I have said, either by confusing and deluding the organ of sight so that a clear thing appears cloudy: just as after weeping, owing to the collected humours, the light appears different from what it was before. Or by operating on the imaginative faculty by a transmutation of mental images, as has been said. Or by some agitation of various humours, so that matters which are earthy and dry seem to be fire or water: as some people make everyone in the house strip themselves naked under the impression that they are swimming in water.

It may be asked further with reference to the above method of devils, whether this sort of illusions can happen indifferently to the good and to the wicked: just as other bodily infirmities can, as will be shown later, be brought by witches even upon those who are in a state of grace. To this question, following the words of Cassian in his *Second Collation* of the Abbot Sirenus, we must answer that they cannot. And from this it follows that all who are deluded in this way are presumed to be in deadly sin. For he says, as is clear from the words of S. Antony: The devil can in no way enter the mind or body of any man, nor has the power to penetrate into the thoughts of anybody, unless such a person has first become destitute of all holy thoughts, and is quite bereft and denuded of spiritual contemplation.

This agrees with Boethius where he says in the *Consolation of Philosophy*:

We had given you such arms that, if you had not thrown them away, you would have been preserved from infirmity.

Also Cassian tells in the same place of two Pagan witches, each in his own way malicious, who by their witchcraft sent a succession of devils into the cell of S. Antony for the purpose of driving him from there by their temptations; being infected with hatred for the holy man because a great number of people visited him every day. And though these devils assailed him with the keenest of spurs to his thoughts, yet he drove them away by crossing himself on the forehead and breast, and by prostrating himself in earnest prayer.

Therefore we may say that all who are so deluded by devils, not reckoning any other bodily infirmities, are lacking in the gift of divine grace. And so it is said in *Tobias* vi: The devil has power against those who are subject to their lusts.

This is also substantiated by what we told in the First Part in the question, Whether witches can change men into the shapes of beasts. For we told of a girl who was turned into a filly, as she herself and, except S. Macharius, all who looked at her were persuaded. But the devil could not deceive the senses of the holy man; and when she was brought to him to be healed, he saw a true woman and not a horse, while on the other hand everyone else exclaimed that she seemed to be a horse. And the Saint, by his prayers, freed her and the others from that illusion, saying that this had happened to her because she had not attended sufficiently to holy things, nor used as she should Holy Confession and the Eucharist. And for this reason, because in her honesty she would not consent to the shameful proposal of a young man, he had caused a Jew who was a witch to bewitch the girl so that, by the power of the devil, he turned her into a filly.

We may summarize our conclusions as follows:—Devils can, for their profit and probation, injure the good in their fortunes, that is, in such exterior things as riches, fame, and bodily health. This is clear from the case of the Blessed Job, who was afflicted by the devil in such matters. But such injuries are not of their own causing, so that they cannot be led or driven into any sin, although they can be tempted both inwardly and outwardly in the flesh. But the devils cannot afflict the good with this sort of illusions, either actively or passively.

Not actively, by deluding their senses as they do those of others who are not in a state of grace. And not passively, by taking away their male organs by some glamour. For in these two respects they could never injure Job, especially the passive injury with regard to the venereal act; for he was of such continence that he was able to say: I have vowed a vow with my eyes that I shall never think about a virgin, and still less about another man's wife. Nevertheless the devil knows that he has great power over sinners (see *S. Luke* xi: When a strong man armed keepeth his palace, his goods are in peace).

But it may be asked, as to illusions in respect of the male organ, whether, granted that the devil cannot impose this illusion on those in a state of grace in a passive way, he cannot still do so in an active sense: the argument being that the man in a state of grace is deluded because he ought to see the member in its right place, when he who thinks it has been taken away from him, as well as other bystanders, does not see it in its place; but if this is conceded, it seems to be contrary to what has been said. It can be said that there is not so much force in the active as in the passive loss; meaning by active loss, not his who bears the loss, but his who sees the loss from without, as is self-evident. Therefore, although a man in a state of grace can see the loss of another, and to that extent the devil can delude his senses; yet he cannot passively suffer such loss in his own body, as, for example, to be deprived of his member, since he is not subject to lust. In the same way the converse is true, as the Angel said to Tobias: Those who are given to lust, the devil has power over them.

And what, then, is to be thought of those witches who in this way sometimes collect male organs in great numbers, as many as twenty or thirty members together, and put them in a bird's nest, or shut them up in a box, where they move themselves like living members, and eat oats and corn, as has been seen by many and is a matter of common report? It is to be said that it is all done by devil's work and illusion, for the senses of those who see them are deluded in the way we have said. For a certain man tells that, when he had lost his member, he approached a known witch to ask her to restore it to him. She told the afflicted man to climb a certain tree, and that he might take which he liked out of a nest in which there were several members. And when he tried to take a big one, the witch said: You must not take that one; adding, because it belonged to a parish priest.

All these things are caused by devils through an illusion of glamour, in the manner we have said, by confusing the organ of vision by transmuting the mental images in the imaginative faculty. And it must not be said that these members which are shown are devils in assumed members, just as they sometimes appear to witches, and men in assumed aerial bodies, and converse with them. And the reason is that they effect this thing by an easier method, namely, by drawing out an inner mental image from the repository of the memory, and impressing it on the imagination.

And if anyone wishes to say that they could go to work in a similar way, when they are said to converse with witches and other men in assumed bodies; that is, that they could cause such apparitions by changing the mental images in the imaginative faculty, so that when men thought the devils were present in assumed bodies, they were really nothing but an illusion caused by such a change of the mental images in the inner perceptions.

It is to be said that, if the devil had no other purpose than merely to show himself in human form, then there would be no need for him to appear in an assumed body, since he could effect his purpose well enough by the aforesaid illusion. But this is not so; for he has another purpose, namely, to speak and eat with them, and to commit other abominations. Therefore it is necessary that he should himself be present, placing himself actually in sight in an assumed body. For, as S. Thomas says, Where the Angel's power is, there he operates.

And it may be asked, if the devil by himself and without any witch takes away anyone's virile member, whether there is any difference between one sort of deprivation and the other. In addition to what has been said in the First Part of this work on the question, Whether witches can take away the male organ, it can be said that, when the devil by himself takes away a member, he does actually take it away, and it is actually restored when it has to be restored. Secondly, as it is not taken away without injury, so it is not without pain. Thirdly, that he never does this unless compelled by a good Angel, for by so doing he cuts off a great source of profit to him; for he knows that he can work more witchcraft on that act than on other human acts. For God permits him to do more injury to that than to other human acts, as has been said. But none of the above points apply when he works through the agency of a witch, with God's permission.

And if it is asked whether the devil is more apt to injure men and creatures by himself than through a witch, it can be said that there is no comparison between the two cases. For he is infinitely more apt to do harm through the agency of witches. First, because he thus gives greater offence to God, by usurping to himself a creature dedicated to Him. Secondly, because when God is the more offended, He allows him the more power of injuring men. And thirdly, for his own gain, which he places in the perdition of souls.

Introduction to Part III

Therefore in answer to the arguments, it is clear that witches and sorcerers have not necessarily to be tried by the Inquisitors. But as for the other arguments which seek to make it possible for the Bishops in their turn to be relieved from the trial of witches, and leave this to the Civil Court, it is clear that this is not so easy in their case as it is in that of the Inquisitors. For the Canon Law (c. *ad abolendam*, c. *uergentis*, and c. *excommunicamus utrumque*) says that in a case of heresy it is for the ecclesiastical judge to try and to judge, but for the secular judge to carry out the sentence and to punish; that is, when a capital punishment is in question, though it is otherwise with other penitential punishments.

It seems also that in the heresy of witches, though not in the case of other heresies, the Diocesans also can hand over to the Civil Courts the duty of trying and judging, and this for two reasons: first because, as we have mentioned in our arguments, the crime of witches is not purely ecclesiastical, being rather civil on account of the temporal injuries which they commit; and also because special laws are provided for dealing with witches.

Finally, it seems that in this way it is easiest to proceed with the extermination of witches, and that the greatest help is thus given to the Ordinary in the sight of that terrible Judge who, as the Scriptures testify, will exact the strictest account from and will most hardly judge those who have been placed in authority. Accordingly we will proceed on this understanding, namely, that the secular Judge can try and judge such cases, himself proceeding to the capital punishment, but leaving the imposition of any other penitential punishment to the Ordinary.

Whether Mortal Enemies may be Admitted as Witnesses.

But if it is asked whether the Judge can admit the mortal enemies of the prisoner to give evidence against him in such a case, we answer that he cannot; for the same chapter of the Canon says: You must not understand that in this kind of charge a mortal personal enemy may be admitted to give evidence. Henry of Segusio also makes this quite clear. But it is mortal enemies that are spoken of; and it is to be noted that a witness is not necessarily to be disqualified because of every sort of enmity. And a mortal enmity is constituted by the following circumstances: when there is a death feud or vendetta between the parties, or when there has been an attempted homicide, or some serious wound or injury which manifestly shows that there is mortal hatred on the part of the witness against the prisoner. And in such a case it is presumed that, just as the witness had tried to inflict temporal death on the prisoner by wounding him, so he will also be willing to effect his object by accusing him of heresy; and just as he wished to take away his life, so he would be willing to take away his good name. Therefore the evidence of such mortal enemies is justly disqualified.

But there are other serious degrees of enmity (for women are easily provoked to hatred), which need not totally disqualify a witness, although they render his evidence very doubtful, so that full credence cannot be placed in his words unless they are substantiated by independent proofs, and other witnesses supply an indubitable proof of them. For the Judge must ask the prisoner whether he thinks that he has any enemy who would dare to accuse him of that crime out of hatred, so that he might compass his death; and if he says that he has, he shall ask who that person is; and then the Judge shall take note whether the person named as being likely to give evidence from motives of malice has actually done so. And if it is found that this is the case, and the Judge has learned from trustworthy men the cause of that enmity, and if the evidence in question is not substantiated by other proofs and the words of other witnesses, then he may safely reject such evidence. But if the prisoner says that he hopes he has no such enemy, but admits that he has had quarrels with women; or if he says that he has an enemy, but names someone who, perhaps, has not given evidence, in that case, even if other witnesses say that such a person has given evidence from motives of enmity, the Judge must not reject his evidence, but admit it together with the other proofs.

There are many who are not sufficiently careful and circumspect, and consider that the depositions of such quarrelsome women should be altogether rejected, saying that no faith can be placed in them, since they are nearly always actuated by motives of hatred. Such men are ignorant of the subtlety and precautions of magistrates, and speak and judge like men who are colour-blind. But these precautions are dealt with in Questions XI and XII.

What is to be done after the Arrest, and whether the Names of the Witnesses should be made Known to the Accused.
This is the Fourth Action.

There are two matters to be attended to after the arrest, but it is left to the Judge which shall be taken first; namely, the question of allowing the accused to be defended, and whether she should be examined in the place of torture, though not necessarily in order that she should be tortured. The first is only allowed when a direct request is made; the second only when her servants and companions, if she has any, have first been examined in the house.

But let us proceed in the order as above. If the accused says that she is innocent and falsely accused, and that she wishes to see and hear her accusers, then it is a sign that she is asking to defend herself. But it is an open question whether the Judge is bound to make the deponents known to her and bring them to confront her face to face. For here let the Judge take note that he is not bound either to publish the names of the deponents or to bring them before the accused, unless they themselves should freely and willingly offer to come before the accused and lay their depositions in her presence. And it is by reason of the danger incurred by the deponents that the Judge is not bound to do this. For although different Popes have had different opinions on this matter, none of them has ever said that in such a case the Judge is bound to make known to the accused the names of the informers or accusers (but here we are not dealing with the case of an accuser). On the contrary, some have thought that in no case ought he to do so, while others have thought that he should in certain circumstances.

But, finally, Boniface VIII decreed as follows: If in a case of heresy it appears to the Bishop or Inquisitor that grave danger would be incurred by the witnesses or informers on account of the powers of the persons against whom they lay their depositions, should their names be published, he shall not publish them. But if there is no danger, their names shall be published just as in other cases.

Here it is to be noted that this refers not only to a Bishop or Inquisitor, but to any Judge conducting a case against witches with the consent of the Inquisitor or Bishop; for, as was shown in the introductory Question, they can depute their duties to a Judge. So that any such Judge, even if he be secular, has the authority of the Pope, and not only of the Emperor.

Also a careful Judge will take notice of the powers of the accused persons; for these are of three kinds, namely, the power of birth and family, the power of riches, and the power of malice. And the last of these is more to be feared than the other two, since it threatens more danger to the witnesses if their names are made known to the accused. The reason for this is that it is more dangerous to make known the names of the witnesses to an accused person who is poor, because such a person has many evil accomplices, such as outlaws and homicides, associated with him, who venture nothing but their own persons, which is not the case with anyone who is nobly born or rich, and abounding in temporal possessions. And the kind of danger which is to be feared is explained by Pope John XXII as the death or cutting off of themselves or their children or kindred, or the wasting of their substance, or some such matter.

Further, let the Judge take notice that, as he acts in this matter with the authority of the Supreme Pontiff and the permission of the Ordinary, both he himself and all who are associated with him at the depositions, or afterwards at the pronouncing of the sentence, must keep the names of the witnesses secret, under pain of excommunication. And it is in the power of the Bishop thus to punish him or them if they do otherwise. Therefore he should very implicitly warn them not to reveal the names from the very beginning of the process.

Wherefore the above decree of Pope Boniface VIII goes on to say: And that the danger to those accusers and witnesses may be the more effectively met, and the inquiry conducted more cautiously, we permit, by the authority of this statute, that the Bishop or Inquisitors (or, as we have said, the Judge) shall forbid all those who are concerned in the inquiry to reveal without their permission any secrets which they have learned from the Bishop or Inquisitors, under pain of excommunication which they may incur by violating such secrets.

It is further to be noted that just as it is a punishable offence to publish the names of witnesses indiscreetly, so also it is to conceal them without good reason from, for instance, such people as have a right to know them, such as the lawyers and assessors whose opinion is to be sought in proceeding to the sentence; in the same way the names must not be concealed when it is possible to publish them without risk of any danger to the witnesses. On this subject the above decree speaks as follows, towards the end: We command that in all cases the Bishop or Inquisitors shall take especial care not to suppress the names of the witnesses as if there were danger to them when there is perfect security; nor conversely to decide to publish them when there is some danger threatened, the decision in this matter resting with their own conscience and discretion. And it has been written in comment on these words: Whoever you are who are a Judge in such a case, mark those words well, for they do not refer to a slight risk but to a grave danger; therefore do not deprive a prisoner of his legal rights without very good cause, for this cannot but be an offence to Almighty God.

The reader must note that all the process which we have already described, and all that we have yet to describe, up to the methods of passing sentence (except the death sentence), which it is in the province of the ecclesiastical Judge to conduct, can also, with the consent of the Diocesans, be conducted by a secular Judge. Therefore the reader need find no difficulty in the fact that the above Decree speaks of an ecclesiastical and not a secular Judge; for the latter can take his method of inflicting the death sentence from that of the Ordinary in passing sentence of penance.

What Kind of Defence may be Allowed, and of the Appointment of an Advocate. This is the Fifth Action.

If, therefore, the accused asks to be defended, how can this be admitted when the names of the witnesses are kept altogether secret? It is to be said that three considerations are to be observed in admitting any defence. First, that an Advocate shall be allotted to the accused. Second, that the names of the witnesses shall not be made known to the Advocate, even under an oath of secrecy, but that he shall be informed of everything contained in the depositions. Third, the accused shall as far as possible be given the benefit of every doubt, provided that this involves no scandal to the faith nor is in any way detrimental to justice, as will be shown. And in like manner the prisoner's procurator shall have full access to the whole process, only the names of the witnesses and deponents being suppressed; and the Advocate can act also in the name of procurator.

As to the first of these points: it should be noted that an Advocate is not to be appointed at the desire of the accused, as if he may choose which Advocate he will have; but the Judge must take great care to appoint neither a litigious nor an evil-minded man, nor yet one who is easily bribed (as many are), but rather an honourable man to whom no sort of suspicion attaches.

And the Judge ought to note four points, and if the Advocate be found to conform to them, he shall be allowed to plead, but not otherwise. For first of all the Advocate must examine the nature of the case, and then if he finds it a just one he may undertake it, but if he finds it unjust he must refuse it; and he must be very careful not to undertake an unjust or desperate case. But if he has unwittingly accepted the brief, together with a fee, from someone who wishes to do him an injury, but discovers during the process that the case is hopeless, then he must signify to his client (that is, the accused) that he abandons the case, and must return the fee which he has received. This is the opinion of Godfrey of Fontaines, which is wholly in conformity with the Canon *de jud.* 1, *rem non novam*. But Henry of Segusio holds an opposite view concerning the return of the fee in a case in which the Advocate has worked very hard. Consequently if an Advocate has wittingly undertaken to defend a prisoner whom he knows to be guilty, he shall be liable for the costs and expenses (*de amin. tut.* 1, *non tamen est ignotum*).

The second point to be observed is that in his pleading he should conduct himself properly in three respects. First, his behaviour must be modest and free from prolixity or pretentious oratory. Secondly, he must abide by the truth, not bringing forward any fallacious arguments or reasoning, or calling false witnesses, or introducing legal quirks and quibbles if he be a skilled lawyer, or bringing counter-accusations; especially in cases of this sort, which must be conducted as simply and summarily as possible. Thirdly, his fee must be regulated by the usual practice of the district.

But to return to our point; the Judge must make the above conditions clear to the Advocate, and finally admonish him not to incur the charge of defending heresy, which would make him liable to excommunication.

And it is not a valid argument for him to say to the Judge that he is not defending the error, but the person. For he must not by any means so conduct his defence as to prevent the case from being conducted in a plain and summary manner, and he would be doing so if he introduced any complications or appeals into it; all which things are disallowed altogether. For it is granted that he does not defend the error; for in that case he would be more damnably guilty than the witches themselves, and rather a heresiarch than a heretical wizard. Nevertheless, if he unduly defends a person already suspect of heresy, he makes himself as it were a patron of that heresy, and lays himself under not only a light but a strong suspicion, in accordance with the manner of his defence; and ought publicly to abjure that heresy before the Bishop.

We have put this matter at some length, and it is not to be neglected by the Judge, because much danger may arise from an improper conducting of the defence by an Advocate or Procurator. Therefore, when there is any objection to the Advocate, the Judge must dispense with him and proceed in accordance with the facts and the proofs. But when the Advocate for the accused is not open to any objection, but is a zealous man and a lover of justice, then the Judge may reveal to him the names of the witnesses, under an oath of secrecy.

Of the Points to be Observed by the Judge before the Formal Examination in the Place of Detention and Torture.
This is the Eighth Action.
The next action of the Judge is quite clear. For common justice demands that a witch should not be condemned to death unless she is convicted by her own confession. But here we are considering the case of one who is judged to be taken in manifest heresy for one of the other two reasons set down in the First Question, namely, direct or indirect evidence of the fact, or the legitimate production of witnesses; and in this case she is to be exposed to questions and torture to extort a confession of her crimes.

And to make the matter clear we will quote a case which occurred at Spires and came to the knowledge of many. A certain honest man was bargaining with a woman, and would not come to terms with her about the price of some article; so she angrily called after him, "You will soon wish you had agreed." For witches generally use this manner of speaking, or something like it, when they wish to bewitch a person by looking at him. Then he, not unreasonably being angry with her, looked over his shoulder to see with what intention she had uttered those words; and behold! he was suddenly bewitched so that his mouth was stretched sideways as far as his ears in a horrible deformity, and he could not draw it back, but remained so deformed for a long time.

We put the case that this was submitted to the Judge as direct evidence of the fact; and it is asked whether the woman is to be considered as manifestly taken in the heresy of witchcraft. This should be answered from the words of S. Bernard which we have quoted above. For there are three ways in which a person may be judged to be so taken, and they not so closely conjoined as though it were necessary for all three to agree in one conclusion, but each one by itself, namely, the evidence of the fact, or the legitimate production of witnesses, or her own confession, is sufficient to prove a witch to be manifestly taken in that heresy.

But indirect evidence of the fact is different from direct evidence; yet though it is not so conclusive, it is still taken from the words and deeds of witches, as was shown in the Seventh Question, and it is judged from witchcraft which is not so immediate in its effect, but follows after some lapse of time from the utterance of the threatening words. Wherefore may we conclude that this is the case with such witches who have been accused and have not made good their defence (or have failed to defend themselves because this privilege was not granted them; and it was not granted because they did not ask for it). But what we are to consider now is what action the Judge should take, and how he should proceed to question the accused with a view to exorting the truth from her so that sentence of death may finally be passed upon her.

And here, because of the great trouble caused by the stubborn silence of witches, there are several points which the Judge must notice, and these are dealt with under their several heads.

And the first is that he must not be too quick to subject a witch to examination, but must pay attention to certain signs which will follow. And he must not be too quick for this reason: unless God, through a holy Angel, compels the devil to withhold his help from the witch, she will be so insensible to the pains of torture that she will sooner be torn limb from limb than confess any of the truth.

But the torture is not to be neglected for this reason, for they are not all equally endowed with this power, and also the devil sometimes of his own will permits them to confess their crimes without being compelled by a holy Angel. And for the understanding of this the reader is referred to that which is written in the Second Part of this work concerning the homage which they offer to the devil.

For there are some who obtain from the devil a respite of six or eight or ten years before they have to offer him their homage, that is, devote themselves to him body and soul; whereas others, when they first profess their abjuration of the faith, at the same time offer their homage. And the reason why the devil allows that stipulated interval of time is that, during that time, he may find out whether the witch has denied the faith with her lips only but not in her heart, and would therefore offer him her homage in the same way.

For the devil cannot know the inner thoughts of the heart except conjecturally from outward indications, as we showed in the First Part of this work where we dealt with the question whether devils can turn the minds of men to hatred or love. And many have been found who, driven by some necessity or poverty, have been induced by other witches, in the hope of ultimate forgiveness in confession, to become either total or partial apostates from the faith. And it is such whom the devil deserts without any compulsion by a holy Angel, and therefore they readily confess their crimes, whereas others, who have from their hearts bound themselves to the devil, are protected by his power and preserve a stubborn silence.

And this provides a clear answer to the question how it comes about that some witches readily confess, and others will by no means do so. For in the case of the former, when the devil is not compelled by God, he still deserts them of his own will, in order that by temporal unhappiness and a horrible death he may lead to despair those over whose hearts he could never obtain the mastery. For it is evident from their sacramental confessions that they have never voluntarily obeyed the devil, but have been compelled by him to work witchcraft.

And some also are distinguished by the fact that, after they have admitted their crimes, they try to commit suicide by strangling or hanging themselves. And they are induced to do this by the Enemy, lest they should obtain pardon from God through sacramental confession. This chiefly happens in the case of those who have not been willing agents of the devil; although it may also happen in the case of willing agents, after they have confessed their crimes: but then it is because the devil has been compelled to desert the witch.

In conclusion we may say that it is as difficult, or more difficult, to compel a witch to tell the truth as it is to exorcize a person possessed of the devil. Therefore the Judge ought not to be too willing or ready to proceed to such examination, unless, as has been said, the death penalty is involved. And in this case he must exercise great care, as we shall show; and first we shall speak of the method of sentencing a witch to such torture.

Of the Method of Sentencing the Accused to be Questioned: and How she must be Questioned on the First Day; and Whether she may be Promised her Life. The Ninth Action.
Secondly, the Judge must take care to frame his sentence in the following manner.

We, the Judge and assessors, having attended to and considered the details of the process enacted by us against you N. of such a place in such a Diocese, and having diligently examined the whole matter, find that you are equivocal in your admissions; as for example, when you say that you used such threats with no intention of doing an injury, but nevertheless there are various proofs which are sufficient warrant for exposing you to the question and torture. Wherefore, that the truth may be known from your own mouth, and that henceforth you may not offend the ears of the Judges, we declare, judge and sentence that on this present day at such an hour you be placed under the question and torture. This sentence was given, etc.

Alternatively, as has been said, the Judge may not be willing to deliver the accused up to be questioned, but may punish her with imprisonment with the following object in view. Let him summon her friends and put it to them that she may escape the death penalty, although she will be punished in another way, if she confesses the truth, and urge them to try to persuade her to do so. For very often meditation, and the misery of imprisonment, and the repeated advice of honest men, dispose the accused to discover the truth.

And we have found that witches have been so strengthened by this sort of advice that, as a sign of their rebellion, they have spat on the ground as if it were in the devil's face, saying, "Depart, cursed devil; I shall do what is just"; and afterwards they have confessed their crimes.

But if, after keeping the accused in a state of suspense, and continually postponing the day of examination, and frequently using verbal persuasions, the Judge should truly believe that the accused is denying the truth, let them question her lightly without shedding blood; knowing that such questioning is fallacious and often, as has been said, ineffective.

And it should be begun in this way. While the officers are preparing for the questioning, let the accused be stripped; or if she is a woman, let her first be led to the penal cells and there stripped by honest women of good reputation. And the reason for this is that they should search for any instrument of witchcraft sewn into her clothes; for they often make such instruments, at the instruction of devils, out of the limbs of unbaptized children, the purpose being that those children should be deprived of the beatific vision. And when such instruments have been disposed of, the Judge shall use his own persuasions and those of other honest men zealous for the faith to induce her to confess the truth voluntarily; and if she will not, let him order the officers to bind her with cords, and apply her to some engine of torture; and then let them obey at once but not joyfully, rather appearing to be disturbed by their duty. Then let her be released again at someone's earnest request, and taken on one side, and let her again be persuaded; and in persuading her, let her be told that she can escape the death penalty.

Here it is asked whether, in the case of a prisoner legally convicted by her general bad reputation, by witnesses, and by the evidence of the fact, so that the only thing lacking is a confession of the crime from her own mouth, the Judge can lawfully promise her her life, whereas if she were to confess the crime she would suffer the extreme penalty.

We answer that different people have various opinions on this question. For some hold that if the accused is of a notoriously bad reputation, and gravely suspected on unequivocal evidence of the crime; and if she is herself a great source of danger, as being the mistress of other witches, then she may be promised her life on the following conditions: that she be sentenced to imprisonment for life on bread and water, provided that she supply evidence which will lead to the conviction of other witches. And she is not to be told, when she is promised her life, that she is to be imprisoned in this way; but should be led to suppose that some other penance, such as exile, will be imposed on her as punishment. And without doubt notorious witches, especially such as use witches' medicines and cure the bewitched by superstitious means, should be kept in this way, both that they may help the bewitched, and that they may betray other witches. But such a betrayal by them must not be considered of itself sufficient ground for a conviction, since the devil is a liar, unless it is also substantiated by the evidence of the fact, and by witnesses.

Others think that, after she has been consigned to prison in this way, the promise to spare her life should be kept for a time, but that after a certain period she should be burned.

A third opinion is that the Judge may safely promise the accused her life, but in such a way that he should afterwards disclaim the duty of passing sentence on her, deputing another Judge in his place.

There seems to be some advantage in pursuing the first of these courses on account of the benefit which may accrue from it to those who are bewitched; yet it is not lawful to use witchcraft to cure witchcraft, although (as was shown in the First and Introductory Question to this Third Part) the general opinion is that it is lawful to use vain and superstitious means to remove a spell. But use and experience and the variety of such cases will be of more value to Judges than any art or text-book; therefore this is a matter which should be left to the Judges. But it has certainly been very often found by experience that many would confess the truth if they were not held back by the fear of death.

But if neither threats nor such promises will induce her to confess the truth, then the officers must proceed with the sentence, and she must be examined, not in any new or exquisite manner, but in the usual way, lightly or heavily according as the nature of her crimes demands. And while she is being questioned about each several point, let her be often and frequently exposed to torture, beginning with the more gentle of them; for the Judge should not be too hasty to proceed to the graver kind. And while this is being done, let the Notary write all down, how she is tortured and what questions are asked and how she answers.

And note that, if she confesses under torture, she should then be taken to another place and questioned anew, so that she does not confess only under the stress of torture.

The next step of the Judge should be that, if after being fittingly tortured she refuses to confess the truth, he should have other engines of torture brought before her, and tell her that she will have to endure these if she does not confess. If then she is not induced by terror to confess, the torture must be continued on the second or third day, but not repeated at that present time unless there should be some fresh indication of its probable success.

Let the sentence be pronounced in her presence in the following manner: We the aforesaid Judge, as above, assign to you N. such a day for the continuation of your questioning, that the truth may be heard from your own mouth. And the Notary shall write all down in the process.

And during the interval before that assigned time the Judge himself or other honest men shall do all in their power to persuade her to confess the truth in the manner we have said, giving her, if it seems expedient to them, a promise that her life will be spared.

The Judge should also take care that during that interval there should always be guards with her, so that she is never left alone, for fear lest the devil will cause her to kill herself. But the devil himself knows better than anyone can set down in writing whether he will desert her of his own will, or be compelled to do so by God.

Of the Continuing of the Torture, and of the Devices and Signs by which the Judge can Recognize a Witch; and how he ought to Protect himself from their Spells. Also how they are to be Shaved in those Parts where they use to Conceal their Devil's Masks and Tokens together with the due Setting Forth of Various Means of Overcoming their Obstinacy in Keeping Silence and Refusal to Confess. And it is the Tenth Action.

The Judge should act as follows in the continuation of the torture. First he should bear in mind that, just as the same medicine is not applicable to all the members, but there are various and distinct salves for each several member, so not all heretics or those accused of heresy are to be subjected to the same method of questioning, examination and torture as to the charges laid against them; but various and different means are to be employed according to their various natures and persons. Now a surgeon cuts off rotten limbs; and mangy sheep are isolated from the healthy; but a prudent Judge will not consider it safe to bind himself down to one invariable rule in his method of dealing with a prisoner who is endowed with a witch's power of taciturnity, and whose silence he is unable to overcome. For if the sons of darkness were to become accustomed to one general rule they would provide means of evading it as a well-known snare set for their destruction.

Therefore a prudent and zealous Judge should seize his opportunity and choose his method of conducting his examination according to the answers or depositions of the witnesses, or as his own previous experience or native wit indicates to him, using the following precautions.

If he wishes to find out whether she is endowed with a witch's power of preserving silence, let him take note whether she is able to shed tears when standing in his presence, or when being tortured. For we are taught both by the words of worthy men of old and by our own experience that this is a most certain sign, and it has been found that even if she be urged and exhorted by solemn conjurations to shed tears, if she be a witch she will not be able to weep: although she will assume a tearful aspect and smear her cheeks and eyes with spittle to make it appear that she is weeping; wherefore she must be closely watched by the attendants.

In passing sentence the Judge or priest may use some such method as the following in conjuring her to true tears if she be innocent, or in restraining false tears. Let him place his hand on the head of the accused and say: I conjure you by the bitter tears shed on the Cross by our Saviour the Lord Jesus Christ for the salvation of the world, and by the burning tears poured in the evening hour over His wounds by the most glorious Virgin Mary, His Mother, and by all the tears which have been shed here in this world by the Saints and Elect of God, from whose eyes He has now wiped away all tears, that if you be innocent you do now shed tears, but if you be guilty that you shall by no means do so. In the name of the Father, and of the Son, and of the Holy Ghost, Amen.

And it is found by experience that the more they are conjured the less are they able to weep, however hard they may try to do so, or smear their cheeks with spittle. Nevertheless it is possible that afterwards, in the absence of the Judge and not at the time or in the place of torture, they may be able to weep in the presence of their gaolers.

And as for the reason for a witch's inability to weep, it can be said that the grace of tears is one of the chief gifts allowed to the penitent; for S. Bernard tells us that the tears of the humble can penetrate to heaven and conquer the unconquerable. Therefore there can be no doubt that they are displeasing to the devil, and that he uses all his endeavour to restrain them, to prevent a witch from finally attaining to penitence.

But it may be objected that it might suit with the devil's cunning, with God's permission, to allow even a witch to weep; since tearful grieving, weaving and deceiving are said to be proper to women. We may answer that in this case, since the judgements of God are a mystery, if there is no other way of convicting the accused, by legitimate witnesses or the evidence of the fact, and if she is not under a strong or grave suspicion, she is to be discharged; but because she rests under a slight suspicion by reason of her reputation to which the witnesses have testified, she must be required to abjure the heresy of witchcraft, as we shall show when we deal with the second method of pronouncing sentence.

A second precaution is to be observed, not only at this point but during the whole process, by the Judge and all his assessors; namely, that they must not allow themselves to be touched physically by the witch, especially in any contact of their bare arms or hands; but they must always carry about them some salt consecrated on Palm Sunday and some Blessed Herbs. For these can be enclosed together in Blessed Wax and worn round the neck, as we showed in the Second Part when we discussed the remedies against illnesses and diseases caused by witchcraft; and that these have a wonderful protective virtue is known not only from the testimony of witches, but from the use and practice of the Church, which exorcizes and blesses such objects for this very purpose, as is shown in the ceremony of exorcism when it is said, For the banishing of all the power of the devil, etc.

But let it not be thought that physical contact of the joints or limbs is the only thing to be guarded against; for sometimes, with God's permission, they are able with the help of the devil to bewitch the Judge by the mere sound of the words which they utter, especially at the time when they are exposed to torture.

And we know from experience that some witches, when detained in prison, have importunately begged their gaolers to grant them this one thing, that they should be allowed to look at the Judge before he looks at them; and by so getting the first sight of the Judge they have been able so to alter the minds of the Judge or his assessors that they have lost all their anger against them and have not presumed to molest them in any way, but have allowed them to go free. He who knows and has experienced it gives this true testimony; and would that they were not able to effect such things!

Let judges not despise such precautions and protections, for by holding them in little account after such warning they run the risk of eternal damnation. For our Saviour said: If I had not come, and spoken to them, they would not have sin; but now they have no excuse for their sin. Therefore let the judges protect themselves in the above manner, according to the provisions of the Church.

And if it can conveniently be done, the witch should be led backward into the presence of the Judge and his assessors. And not only at the present point, but in all that has preceded or shall follow it, let him cross himself and approach her manfully, and with God's help the power of that old Serpent will be broken. And no one need think that it is superstitious to lead her in backwards; for, as we have often said, the Canonists allow even more than this to be done for the protection against witchcraft, and always say that it is lawful to oppose vanity with vanity.

The third precaution to be observed in this tenth action is that the hair should be shaved from every part of her body. The reason for this is the same as that for stripping her of her clothes, which we have already mentioned; for in order to preserve their power of silence they are in the habit of hiding some superstitious object in their clothes or in their hair, or even in the most secret parts of their bodies which must not be named.

But it may be objected that the devil might, without the use of such charms, so harden the heart of a witch that she is unable to confess her crimes; just as it is often found in the case of other criminals, no matter how great the tortures to which they are exposed, or how much they are convicted by the evidence of the facts and of witnesses. We answer that it is true that the devil can effect such taciturnity without the use of such charms; but he prefers to use them for the perdition of souls and the greater offence to the Divine Majesty of God.

This can be made clear from the example of a certain witch in the town of Hagenau, whom we have mentioned in the Second Part of this work. She used to obtain this gift of silence in the following manner: she killed a newly-born first-born male child who had not been baptized, and having roasted it in an oven together with other matters which it is not expedient to mention, ground it to powder and ashes; and if any witch or criminal carried about him some of this substance he would in no way be able to confess his crimes.

Here it is clear that a hundred thousand children so employed could not of their own virtue endow a person with such a power of keeping silence; but any intelligent person can understand that such means are used by the devil for the perdition of souls and to offend the Divine Majesty.

Again, it may be objected that very often criminals who are not witches exhibit the same power of keeping silence. In answer to this it must be said that this power of taciturnity can proceed from three causes. First, from a natural hardness of heart; for some are soft-hearted, or even feeble-minded, so that at the slightest torture they admit everything, even some things which are not true; whereas others are so hard that however much they are tortured the truth is not to be had from them; and this is especially the case with those who have been tortured before, even if their arms are suddenly stretched and twisted.

Secondly, it may proceed from some instrument of witchcraft carried about the person, as has been said, either in the clothes or in the hairs of the body. And thirdly, even if the prisoner has no such object secreted about her person, they are sometimes endowed with this power by other witches, however far they may be removed from them. For a certain witch at Issbrug used to boast that, if she had no more than a thread from the garments of any prisoner, she could so work that however much that prisoner were tortured, even to death, she would be unable to confess anything. So the answer to this objection is clear.

But what is to be said of a case that happened in the Diocese of Ratisbon? Certain heretics were convicted by their own confession not only as impenitent but as open advocates of that perfidy; and when they were condemned to death it happened that they remained unharmed in the fire. At length their sentence was altered to death by drowning, but this was no more effective. All were astonished, and some even began to say that their heresy must be true; and the Bishop, in great anxiety for his flock, ordered a three days' fast. When this had been devoutly fulfilled, it came to the knowledge of someone that those heretics had a magic charm sewed between the skin and the flesh under one arm; and when this was found and removed, they were delivered to the flames and immediately burned. Some say that a certain necromancer learned this secret during a consultation with a devil, and betrayed it; but however it became known, it is probable that the devil, who is always scheming for the subversion of the faith, was in some way compelled by Divine power to reveal the matter.

From this it may be seen what a Judge ought to do when such a case happens to him: namely, that he should rely upon the protection of God, and by the prayers and fasting of devout persons drive away this sort of devil's work from witches, in those cases where they cannot be made to confess under torture even after their clothes have been changed and all their hair has been shaved off and abraded.

Now in the parts of Germany such shaving, especially of the secret parts, is not generally considered delicate, and therefore we Inquisitors do not use it; but we cause the hair of their head to be cut off, and placing a morsel of Blessed Wax in a cup of Holy Water and invoking the most Holy Trinity, we give it them to drink three times on a fasting stomach, and by the grace of God we have by this means caused many to break their silence. But in other countries the Inquisitors order the witch to be shaved all over her body. And the Inquisitor of Como has informed us that last year, that is, in 1485, he ordered forty-one witches to be burned, after they had been shaved all over. And this was in the district and country of Burbia, commonly called Wormserbad, in the territory of the Arch-duke of Austria, towards Milan.

But it may be asked whether, in a time of need, when all other means of breaking a witch's silence have failed, it would be lawful to ask the advice in this matter of sorceresses who are able to cure those who are bewitched. We answer that, whatever may have been done in that matter at Ratisbon, it is our earnest admonition in the Lord that no one, no matter how great may be the need, should consult with sorceresses on behalf of the State; and this because of the great offence which is thereby caused to the Divine Majesty, when there are so many other means open to us which we may use either in their own proper form or in some equivalent form, so that the truth will be had from their own mouths and they can be consigned to the flames; or failing this, God will in the meantime provide some other death for the witch.

For there remain to us the following remedies against this power of silence. First, let a man do all that lies in his own power by the exercise of his own qualities, persisting often with the methods we have already mentioned, and especially on certain days, as will be shown in the following Question. See II. *Corinthians* ix: That ye may abound in all good works.

Secondly, if this should fail, let him consult with other persons; for perhaps they may think of some means which has not occurred to him, since there are various methods of counteracting witchcraft.

Thirdly, if these two fail, let him have recourse to devout persons, as it is said in *Ecclesiasticus* xxxvii: Be continually with a godly man, whom thou knowest to keep the commandments of the Lord. Also let him invoke the Patron Saints of the country. But if all these fail, let the Judge and all the people at once put their trust in God with prayers and fasting, that the witchcraft may be removed by reason of their piety. For so Josaphat prayed in II. *Paralipomenon* xx: When we know not what we should do, we have this one refuge, that we should turn our eyes to Thee. And without doubt God will not fail us in our need.

To this effect also S. Augustine speaks (26, q. 7, *non obseruabitis*): Whosoever observes any divinations or auguries, or attends to or consents to such as observe them, or gives credit to such by following after their works, or goes into their houses, or introduces them into his own house, or asks questions of them, let him know that he has perverted the Christian faith and his baptism and is a pagan and apostate and enemy of God, and runs grave danger of the eternal wrath of God, unless he is corrected by ecclesiastical penances and is reconciled with God. Therefore let the Judge not fail always to use the lawful remedies, as we have said, together with these following final precautions.

Of the Manner of Pronouncing a Sentence which is Final and Definitive.
In proceeding to treat of those cases in which the secular Judge by himself can arrive at a judgement and pronounce sentence without the co-operation of the Diocesan and Ordinaries, we necessarily presuppose that not only is it consistent with the protection of the faith and of justice that we Inquisitors should be relieved of the duty of passing sentence in these cases, but in the same sincerity of spirit we endeavour to relieve the Diocesans also from that duty; not in any desire to detract from their authority and jurisdiction, for if they should elect to exercise their authority in such matters, it would follow that we Inquisitors must also concur in it.

It must be remembered, also, that this crime of witches is not purely ecclesiastic; therefore the temporal potentates and Lords are not debarred from trying and judging it. At the same time we shall show that in some cases they must not arrive at a definitive judgement without the authorisation of the Diocesans.

But first we must consider the sentence itself; secondly, the nature of its pronouncement; and thirdly, in how many ways it is to be pronounced. With regard to the first of these questions, S. Augustine says that we must not pronounce sentence against any person unless he has been proved guilty, or has confessed. Now there are three kinds of sentence—interlocutory, definitive, and preceptive. These are explained as follows by S. Raymund. An interlocutory sentence is one which is given not on the main issue of the case but on some other side issues which emerge during the hearing of a case; such as a decision whether or not a witness is to be disallowed, or whether some digression is to be admitted, and such matters as that. Or it may perhaps be called interlocutory because it is delivered simply by word of mouth without the formality of putting it in writing.

A definitive sentence is one which pronounces a final decision as to the main issue of the case.

A preceptive sentence is one which is pronounced by a lower authority on the instruction of a higher. But we shall be concerned with the first two of these, and especially with the definitive sentence.

Now it is laid down by law that a definitive sentence which has been arrived at without a due observance of the proper legal procedure in trying a case is null and void in law; and the legal conduct of a case consists in two things. One concerns the basis of the judgement; for there must be a due provision for the hearing of arguments both for the prosecution and the defence, and a sentence arrived at without such a hearing cannot stand. The other is not concerned with the basis of the judgement, but provides that the sentence must not be conditional; for example, a claim for possession should not be decided conditionally upon some subsequent claim of property; but where there is no question of such an objection the sentence shall stand.

But in the case we are considering, which is a process on behalf of the faith against a charge of heresy (though the charge is a mixed one), the procedure is straightforward and summary. That heretic, and as truly such to be delivered and abandoned to the secular Court: wherefore by this sentence we cast you away as an impenitent heretic from our ecclesiastical Court, and deliver or abandon you to the power of the secular Court: praying the said Court to moderate or temper its sentence of death against you. This sentence was given, etc.

Of one Taken and Convicted, but Denying Everything.

The twelfth method of finishing and concluding a process on behalf of the faith is used when the person accused of heresy, after a diligent examination of the merits of the process in consultation with skilled lawyers, is found to be convicted of heresy by the evidence of the facts or by the legitimate production of witnesses, but not by his own confession. That is to say, he may be convicted by the evidence of the facts, in that he has publicly practised heresy; or by the evidence of witnesses against whom he can take no legitimate exception; yet, though so taken and convicted, he firmly and constantly denies the charge. See Henry of Segusio *On Heresy*, question 34.

The procedure in such a case is as follows. The accused must be kept in strong durance fettered and chained, and must often be visited by the officers, both in a body and severally, who will use their own best endeavours and those of others to induce him to discover the truth; telling him that if he does so and confesses his error, and abjures that vile heresy, he will be admitted to mercy; but that if he refuses and persists in his denial, he will in the end be abandoned to the secular law, and will not be able to escape temporal death.

But if he continues for a long time in his denials, the Bishop and his officers, now in a body and now severally, now personally and now with the assistance of other honest and upright men, shall summon before them now one witness, now another, and warn him to attend strictly to what he has deposed, and to be sure whether or not he has told the truth; that he should beware lest in damning another temporally he damn himself eternally; that if he be afraid, let him at least tell them the truth in secret, that the accused should not die unjustly. And let them be careful to talk to him in such a way that they may see clearly whether or not his depositions have been true.

But if the witnesses, after this warning, adhere to their statements, and the accused maintains his denials, let not the Bishop and his officers on that account be in any haste to pronounce a definitive sentence and hand the prisoner over to secular law; but let them detain him still longer, now persuading him to confess, now yet again urging the witnesses (but one at a time) to examine their consciences well. And let the Bishop and his officers pay particular attention to that witness who seems to be of the best conscience and the most disposed to good, and let them more insistently charge him on his conscience to speak the truth whether or not the matter was as he had deposed. And if they see any witness vacillate, or there are any other indications that he has given false evidence, let them attest him according to the counsel of learned men, and proceed as justice shall require.

For it is very often found that after a person so convicted by credible witnesses has long persisted in his denials, he has at length relented, especially on being truly informed that he will not be delivered to the secular Court, but be admitted to mercy if he confesses his sin, and he has then freely confessed the truth which he has so long denied. And it is often found that the witnesses, actuated by malice and overcome by enmity, have conspired together to accuse an innocent person of the sin of heresy; but afterwards, at the frequent entreaty of the Bishop and his officers, their consciences have been stricken with remorse and, by Divine inspiration, they have revoked their evidence and confessed that they have out of malice put that crime upon the accused. Therefore the prisoner in such a case is not to be sentenced hastily, but must be kept for a year or more before he is delivered up to the secular Court.

When a sufficient time has elapsed, and after all possible care has been taken, if the accused who has been thus legally convicted has acknowledged his guilt and confessed in legal form that he hath been for the period stated ensnared in the crime of heresy, and has consented to abjure that and every heresy, and to perform such satisfaction as shall seem proper to the Bishop and Inquisitor for one convicted of heresy both by his own confession and the legitimate production of witnesses; then let him as a penitent heretic publicly abjure all heresy, in the manner which we have set down in the eighth method of concluding a process on behalf of the faith.

But if he has confessed that he hath fallen into such heresy, but nevertheless obstinately adheres to it, he must be delivered to the secular Court as an impenitent, after the manner of the tenth method which we have explained above.

But if the accused has remained firm and unmoved in his denial of the charges against him, but the witnesses have withdrawn their charges, revoking their evidence and acknowledging their guilt, confessing that they had put so great a crime upon an innocent man from motives of rancour and hatred, or had been suborned or bribed thereto; then the accused shall be freely discharged, but they shall be punished as false witnesses, accusers or informers. This is made clear by Paul of Burgos in his comment on the Canon c. *multorum*. And sentence or penance shall be pronounced against them as shall seem proper to the Bishop and Judges; but in any case such false witnesses must be condemned to perpetual imprisonment on a diet of bread and water, and to do penance for all the days of their life, being made to stand upon the steps before the church door, etc. However, the Bishops have power to mitigate or even to increase the sentence after a year or some other period, in the usual manner.

But if the accused, after a year or other longer period which has been deemed sufficient, continues to maintain his denials, and the legitimate witnesses abide by their evidence, the Bishop and Judges shall prepare to abandon him to the secular Court; sending to him certain honest men zealous for the faith, especially religious, to tell him that he cannot escape temporal death while he thus persists in his denial, but will be delivered up as an impenitent heretic to the power of the secular Court. And the Bishop and his officers shall give notice to the Bailiff or authority of the secular Court that on such a day at such an hour and in such a place (not inside a church) he should come with his attendants to receive an impenitent heretic whom they will deliver to him. And let him make public proclamation in the usual places that all should be present on such a day at such an hour and place to hear a sermon preached on behalf of the faith, and that the Bishop and his officer will hand over a certain obstinate heretic to the secular Court.

On the appointed day for the pronouncement of sentence the Bishop and his officer shall be in the place aforesaid, and the prisoner shall be placed on high before the assembled clergy and people so that he may be seen by all, and the secular authorities shall be present before the prisoner. Then sentence shall be pronounced in the following manner:

We, N., by the mercy of God Bishop of such city, or Judge in the territories of such Prince, seeing that you, N., of such a place in such a Diocese, have been accused before us of such heresy (naming it); and wishing to be more certainly informed whether the charges made against you were true, and whether you walked in darkness or in the light; we proceeded to inform ourselves by diligently examining the witnesses, by often summoning and questioning you on oath, and admitting an Advocate to plead in your defence, and by proceeding in every way as we were bound by the canonical decrees.

And wishing to conclude your trial in a manner beyond all doubt, we convened in solemn council men learned in the Theological faculty and in the Canon and Civil Laws. And having diligently examined and discussed each circumstance of the process and maturely and carefully considered with the said learned men everything which has been said and done in this present case, we find that you, N., have been legally convicted of having been infected with the sin of heresy for so long a time, and that you have said and done such and such (naming them) on account of which it manifestly appears that you are legitimately convicted of the said heresy.

But since we desired, and still desire, that you should confess the truth and renounce the said heresy, and be led back to the bosom of Holy Church and to the unity of the Holy Faith, that so you should save your soul and escape the destruction of both your body and soul in hell; we have by our own efforts and those of others, and by delaying your sentence for a long time, tried to induce you to repent; but you being obstinately given over to wickedness have scorned to agree to our wholesome advice, and have persisted and do persist with stubborn and defiant mind in your contumacious and dogged denials; and this we say with grief, and grieve and mourn in saying it. But since the Church of God has waited so long for you to repent and acknowledge your guilt, and you have refused and still refuse, her grace and mercy can go no farther.

Wherefore that you may be an example to others and that they may be kept from all such heresies, and that such crimes may not remain unpunished: We the Bishop and Judges named on behalf of the faith, sitting in tribunal as Judges judging, and having before us the Holy Gospels that our judgement may proceed as from the countenance of God and our eyes see with equity, and having before our eyes only God and the glory and honour of the Holy Faith, we judge, declare and pronounce sentence that you standing here in our presence on this day at the hour and place appointed for the hearing of your final sentence, are an impenitent heretic, and as such to be delivered or abandoned to secular justice; and as an obstinate and impenitent heretic we have by this sentence cast you off from the ecclesiastical Court and deliver and abandon you to secular justice and the power of the secular Court. And we pray that the said secular Court may moderate its sentence of death upon you. This sentence was given, etc.

The Bishop and Judges may, moreover, arrange that just men zealous for the faith, known to and in the confidence of the secular Court, shall have access to the prisoner while the secular Court is performing its office, in order to console him and even yet induce him to confess the truth, acknowledge his guilt, and renounce his errors.

But if it should happen that after the sentence, and when the prisoner is already at the place where he is to be burned, he should say that he wishes to confess the truth and acknowledge his guilt, and does so; and if he should be willing to abjure that and every heresy; although it may be presumed that he does this rather from fear of death than for love of the truth, yet I should be of the opinion that he may in mercy be received as a penitent heretic and be imprisoned for life. See the gloss on the chapters *ad abolendam* and *excommunicamus*. Nevertheless, according to the rigour of the law, the Judges ought not to place much faith in a conversion of this sort; and furthermore, they can always punish him on account of the temporal injuries which he has committed.

Of the Method of passing Sentence upon a Witch who Annuls Spells
wrought by Witchcraft; and of Witch Midwives and Archer-Wizards.
The fifteenth method of bringing a process on behalf of the faith to a definitive sentence is employed when the person accused of heresy is not found to be one who casts injurious spells of witchcraft, but one who removes them; and in such a case the procedure will be as follows. The remedies which she uses will either be lawful or unlawful; and if they are lawful, she is not to be judged a witch but a good Christian. But we have already shown at length what sort of remedies are lawful.

Unlawful remedies, on the other hand, are to be distinguished as either absolutely unlawful, or in some respect unlawful. If they are absolutely unlawful, these again can be divided into two classes, according as they do or do not involve some injury to another party; but in either case they are always accompanied by an expressed invocation of devils. But if they are only in some respect unlawful, that is to say, if they are practised with only a tacit, and not an expressed, invocation of devils, such are to be judged rather vain than unlawful, according to the Canonists and some Theologians, as we have already shown.

Therefore the Judge, whether ecclesiastical or civil, must not punish the first and last of the above practices, having rather to commend the first and tolerate the last, since the Canonists maintain that it is lawful to oppose vanity with vanity. But he must by no means tolerate those who remove spells by an expressed invocation of devils, especially those who in doing so bring some injury upon a third party; and this last is said to happen when the spell is taken off one person and transferred to another. And we have already made it clear in a former part of this work that it makes no difference whether the person to whom the spell is transferred be herself a witch or not, or whether or not she be the person who cast the original spell, or whether it be a man or any other creature.

It may be asked what the Judge should do when such a person maintains that she removes spells by lawful and not unlawful means; and how the Judge can arrive at the truth of such a case. We answer that he should summon her and ask her what remedies she uses; but he must not rely only upon her word, for the ecclesiastical Judge whose duty it is must make diligent inquiry, either himself or by means of some parish priest who shall examine all his parishioners after placing them upon oath, as to what remedies she uses. And if, as is usually the case, they are found to be superstitious remedies, they must in no way be tolerated, on account of the terrible penalties laid down by the Canon Law, as will be shown.

Again, it may be asked how the lawful remedies can be distinguished from the unlawful, since they always assert that they remove spells by certain prayers and the use of herbs. We answer that this will be easy, provided that a diligent inquiry be made. For although they must necessarily conceal their superstitious remedies, either that they may not be arrested, or that they may the more easily ensnare the minds of the simple, and therefore make great show of their use of prayers and herbs; yet they can be manifestly convicted by four superstitious actions as sorceresses and witches.

For there are some who can divine secrets, and are able to tell things which they could only know through the revelation of evil spirits. For example: when the injured come to them to be healed, they can discover and make known the cause of their injury; as that it arose from some quarrel with a neighbour or some other cause; and they can perfectly know this and tell it to those who consult them.

Secondly, they sometimes undertake to cure the injury or spell of one person, but will have nothing to do with that of another. For in the Diocese of Speyer there is a witch in a certain place called Zunhofen who, although she seems to heal many persons, confesses that she can in no way heal certain others; and this is for no other reason than, as the inhabitants of the place assert, that the spells case on such persons have been so potently wrought by other witches with the help of devils that the devils themselves cannot remove them. For one devil cannot or will not always yield to another.

Thirdly, it sometimes happens that they know that they must make some reservation or exception in their cure of such injuries. Such a case is known to have occurred in the town of Speyer itself. An honest woman who had been bewitched in her shins sent for a diviner of this sort to come and heal her; and when the witch had entered her house and looked at her, she made such an exception. For she said: If there are no scales and hairs in the wound, I could take out all the other evil matter. And she revealed the cause of the injury, although she had come from the country from a distance of two miles, saying: You quarrelled with your neighbour on such a day, and therefore this has happened to you. Then, having extracted from the wound many other matters of various sorts, which were not scales or hairs, she restored her to health.

Fourthly, they sometimes themselves observe, or cause to be observed, certain superstitious ceremonies. For instance, they fix some such time as before sunrise for people to visit them; or say that they cannot heal injuries which were caused beyond the limits of the estate on which they live; or that they can only heal two or three persons in a year. Yet they do not heal them, but only seem to do so by ceasing to injure them.

We could add many other considerations as touching the condition of such persons: as that, after the lapse of a certain time they have incurred the reputation of leading a bad and sinful life, or that they are adulteresses, or the survivors from covens of other witches. Therefore their gift of healing is not derived from God on account of the sanctity of their lives.

Here we must refer incidentally to witch midwives, who surpass all other witches in their crimes, as we have shown in the First Part of this work. And the number of them is so great that, as has been found from their confessions, it is thought that there is scarcely any tiny hamlet in which at least one is not to be found. And that the magistrates may in some degree meet this danger, they should allow no midwife to practise without having been first sworn as a good Catholic; at the same time observing the other safeguards mentioned in the Second Part of this work.

Here too we must consider archer-wizards, who constitute the graver danger to the Christian religion in they they have obtained protection on the estates of nobles and Princes who receive, patronize, and defend them. But that all such receivers and protectors are more damnable than all witches, especially in certain cases, is shown as follows. The Canonists and Theologians divide into two classes the patrons of such archer-wizards, according as they defend the error or the person. They who defend the error are more damnable than the wizards themselves, since they are judged to be not only heretics but heresiarchs (24, quest. 3). And the laws do not make much special mention of such patrons, because they do not distinguish them from other heretics.

But there are others who, while not excusing the sin, yet defend the sinner. These, for example, will do all in their power to protect such wizards (or other heretics) from trial and punishment at the hands of the Judge acting on behalf of the Faith.

Similarly there are those in public authority, that is to say, public persons such as temporal Lords, and also spiritual Lords who have temporal jurisdiction, who are, either by omission or commission, patrons of such wizards and heretics.

They are their patrons by omission when they neglect to perform their duty in regard to such wizards and suspects, or to their followers, receivers, defenders and patrons, when they are required by the Bishops or Inquisitors to do this: that is, by failing to arrest them, by not guarding them carefully when they are arrested, by not taking them to the place within their jurisdiction which has been appointed for them, by not promptly executing the sentence passed upon them, and by other such derelictions of their duty.

They are their patrons by commission when, after such heretics have been arrested, they liberate them from prison without the license or order of the Bishop or Judge; or when they directly or indirectly obstruct the trial, judgement, and sentence of such, or act in some similar way. The penalties for this have been declared in the Second Part of this work, where we treated of archer-wizards and other enchanters of weapons.

It is enough now to say that all these are by law excommunicated, and incur the twelve great penalties. And if they continue obstinate in that excommunication for a year, they are then to be condemned as heretics.

Who, then, are to be called receivers of such; and are they to be reckoned as heretics? All they, we answer, who receive such archer-wizards, enchanters of weapons, necromancers, or heretic witches as are the subject of this whole work. And such receivers are of two classes, as was the case with the defenders and patrons of such.

For there are some who do not receive them only once or twice, but many times and often; and these are well called in Latin *receptatores*, from the frequentative form of the verb. And receivers of this class are sometimes blameless, since they act in ignorance and there is no sinister suspicion attaching to them. But sometimes they are to blame, as being well aware of the sins of those whom they receive; for the Church always denounces these wizards as the most cruel enemies of the faith. And if nevertheless temporal Lords receive, keep and defend them, etc., they are and are rightly called receivers of heretics. And with regard to such, the laws say that they are to be excommunicated.

But others there are who do not often or many times receive such wizards or heretics, but only once or twice; and these are not properly called *receptatores*, but *receptores*, since they are not frequent receivers. (Yet the Archdeacon disagrees with this view; but it is no great matter, for we are considering not words but deeds.)

But there is this difference between *receptatores* and *receptores*: those temporal Princes are always *receptatores* who simply will not or cannot drive away such heretics. But *receptores* may be quite innocent.

Finally, it is asked who are they who are said to be obstructors of the duty of Inquisitors and Bishops against such heretics; and whether they are to be reckoned as heretics. We answer that such obstructors are of two kinds. For there are some who cause a direct obstruction, by rashly on their own responsibility releasing from gaol those who have been detained on a charge of heresy, or by interfering with the process of the Inquisition by wreaking some injury to witnesses on behalf of the Faith because of the evidence they have given; or it may be that the temporal Lord issues an order that none but himself may try such a case, and that anyone charged with this crime should be brought before no one but himself, and that the evidence should be given only in his presence, or some similar order. And such, according to Giovanni d'Andrea, are direct obstructors. They who directly obstruct the process, judgement or sentence on behalf of the Faith, or help, advise or favour others in doing so, although they are guilty of great sin, are not on that account to be judged heretics, unless it appears in other ways that they are obstinately and willfully involved in such heresies of witches. But they are to be smitten with the sword of excommunication; and if they stubbornly endure that excommunication for a year, then are they to be condemned as heretics.

But others are indirect obstructors. These, as Giovanni d'Andrea explains, are those who give such orders as that no one shall bear arms for the capture of heretics except the servants of the said temporal Lord. Such are less guilty than the former, and are not heretics; but they, and also any who advise, help or patronize them in such actions, are to be excommunicated; and if they obstinately remain in that excommunication for a year, they are then to be condemned as if they were heretics. And here it is to be understood that they are in such a way to be condemned as heretics that, if they are willing to return, they are received back to mercy, having first abjured their error; but if not, they are to be handed over to the secular Court as impenitents.

To sum up, Witch-midwives, like other witches, are to be condemned and sentenced according to the nature of their crimes; and this is true also of those who, as we have said, remove spells of witchcraft superstitiously and by the help of devils; for it can hardly be doubted that, just as they are able to remove them, so can they inflict them. And it is a fact that some definite agreement is formed between witches and devils whereby some shall be able to hurt and others to heal, that so they may more easily ensnare the minds of the simple and recruit the ranks of their abandoned and hateful society. Archer-wizards and enchanters of weapons, who are only protected by being patronized, defended and received by temporal Lords, are subject to the same penalties; and they who patronize them, etc., or obstruct the officers of justice in their proceedings against them, are subject to all the penalties to which the patrons of heretics are liable, and are to be excommunicated. And if after they have obstinately endured that excommunication for a year they wish to repent, let them abjure that obstruction and patronage, and they can be admitted to mercy; but if not, they must be handed over as impenitents to the secular Court. And even if they have not endured their excommunication for a year, such obstructors can still be proceeded against as patrons of heretics.

And all that has been said with regard to patrons, defenders, receivers, and obstructors in the case of archer-wizards, etc., applies equally in respect of all other witches who work various injuries to men, animals, and the fruits of the earth. But even the witches themselves, when in the court of conscience with humble and contrite spirit they weep for their sins and make clean confession asking forgiveness, are taken back to mercy. But when they are known, those whose duty it is must proceed against them, summoning, examining, and detaining them, and in all things proceeding in accordance with the nature of their crimes to a definitive and conclusive sentence, as has been shown, if they wish to avoid the snare of eternal damnation by reason of the excommunication pronounced upon them by the Church when they deliberately fail in their duty.

35
Pope Alexander VI: The Pursuit of Witches in Lombardy (1501)

The increased attention which fifteenth-century popes had paid to the appearance of witchcraft cases in different parts of Christendom had culminated in Pope Innocent VIII's privilege to the Dominican inquisitors Kramer and Sprenger (Text 33) and the inquisitors' encyclopedia of witchcraft, the *Malleus Maleficarum* (Text 34). The papal privilege, printed as an introduction to the *Malleus* in all subsequent editions, offered a rationale for persecution by both ecclesiastical and civil tribunals. The privilege and the *Malleus*, however, applied primarily to southern Germany and Switzerland. Shortly after their publication, Pope Alexander VI issued the following letter to Angelo of Verona, the inquisitor of Lombardy; his concern was possibly inspired by the evils the *Malleus* had palpably demonstrated, and certainly by the notorious reluctance of northern Italian prelates to allow the authority of the inquisitors into their districts.

SOURCE: Pope Alexander VI, the bull *Cum acceperimus*, 1501. Latin text in Hansen, *Quellen*, 31. Trans. E. P.

SINCE WE HAVE learned that in the province of Lombardy many people of both sexes give themselves over to diverse incantations and devilish superstitions in order to procure many wicked things by their venery and vain rites, to destroy men, beasts, and fields, to spread great scandal, and to induce grievous errors, we decree, in order both to fulfill our pastoral office from our high commission and to restrain these evils, scandals, and errors, that they shall cease. That is the reason why we send to you, commit to you, and order you and your successors appointed in Lombardy our full confidence in the Lord, that you may seek out diligently those people of both sexes (either by yourself or with the aid of a company which you shall choose) and secure and punish them through the medium of justice. And so that you may be better able to fulfill this commission, we give to you against them full and sufficient powers, notwithstanding all other constitutions and apostolic orders, indulgences, and ordinary concessions which have been accorded at other times, and notwithstanding all other orders to the contrary of these, whatever they may be.

VII

Humanists, Sorcerers, Preachers, and Popes,

1500–1523

T HE FIRST HALF OF the sixteenth cen-
tury is generally not marked by a sustaining of the numbers of trials for witchcraft that had characterized the period 1430–1490, nor by a significant number of
treatises exploring the subject. But the issue was far from dead, neither in the
case of the "new sects" of witchcraft itself, nor in the general concerns about
demonic magic and sorcery, and it is very important in the history of the illustration of witchcraft. In a letter of 1501 the humanist scholar Desiderius Erasmus
describes an episode of sorcery detected at Orléans, a kind of sorcery that mis-
used the Christian sacraments and sacramentals in hideous rites and involved
magical books, but a case that also seems on the near periphery of witchcraft and
far from the learned magic whose most eloquent defenders, from Marsilio Ficino
on, were attempting to define as "natural" and distinct from diabolical sorcery
(Text 36).[1]

---

1. The best recent study along with that of Clark, *Thinking with Demons*, is William Ea-
mon, *Science and the Secrets of Nature* (Princeton, 1994). The classic work remains Frances
Yates, *Giordano Bruno and the Hermetic Tradition* (Chicago, 1964), 130–56. On Agrippa, see
Charles G. Nauert, *Agrippa and the Crisis of Renaissance Thought* (Urbana, Ill., 1965), and
Cornelius Agrippa, *De Occulta Philosophia Libri Tres*, ed. V. Perrone Compagni (Leiden–New
York–Cologne, 1992). See also Yates, *The Occult Philosophy in the Elizabethan Age* (London–
Boston, 1979), 37–71, and the collection, *Hermeticism and the Renaissance: Intellectual His-
tory and the Occult in Early Modern Europe*, ed. Ingrid Merkel and Alan G. Debus (London–
Toronto, 1988), particularly the essay by Paola Zambelli, "Scholastic and Humanist views of
Hermeticism and Witchcraft," 126–53; D. P. Walker, *Spiritual and Demonic Magic, from Ficino
to Campanella* (rept. Notre Dame, 1975), Brian Easley, *Witch Hunting, Magic and the New
Philosophy: An Introduction to the Debates of the Scientific Revolution, 1450–1750* (Atlantic
Highlands, N.J., 1980), and John M. Headley, *Tommaso Campanella and the Transformation of
the World* (Princeton, 1997). On Champier, see Brian P. Copenhaver, *Symphorien Champier and*

At the same time, preachers acquired new material from the literature and case archives of the late fifteenth century, particularly, but not exclusively, the *Malleus Maleficarum*, in order to stir their audiences into revulsion against witchcraft and other forms of "superstition" that a reform-minded clerical order continued to denounce vehemently. The sermons of Johann Geiler von Kaysersberg, delivered in 1508 and printed in 1517, with illustrations that may be by the Freiburg artist Hans Baldung Grien in later editions, represent an influential example of the genre (Text 37). Geiler also represents a link between the fifteenth-century beginnings of the witchcraft persecutions and their later states. He knew the work of Johannes Nider, and his sermons were well known to Martin Luther.

An articulate humanist believer in witchcraft, Gianfrancesco Pico della Mirandola wrote his lively Latin dialogue *Strix* in 1523 after attending inquisitorial trials and executions for witchcraft in Bologna in the same year (Text 38). The dialogue was translated twice into Italian, ensuring it a wide readership and carrying the new theme of diabolical witchcraft into the ranks of learned humanist readers and writers. Pico's knowledge of classical Latin and Greek literature contributed to the process by which that literature (like Jewish scripture in Hebrew) played a new role in sixteenth- and seventeenth-century debates over both the antiquity and reality of witchcraft.

Popes, too, continued to concern themselves with the phenomenon first identified as a new sect by Alexander V in 1409. Julius II (1503–13), the patron of Michelangelo, and the Florentine humanist Leo X (1513–21) both wrote to episcopal judges and inquisitors in a similar vein, and Hadrian VI (1522–23) virtually reissued their earlier letters in 1523 (Text 39), the same year as Pico's *Strix*.

These texts, along with a significant number of demonological treatises, continued the growing concerns with witchcraft and diabolical sorcery into the world of the reformations later in the sixteenth century.

36
Desiderius Erasmus: A Terrible Case of Sorcery in Orléans (1501)

Desiderius Erasmus of Rotterdam (1466–1536) was the greatest classical scholar of his age, a devout and influential editor of the Bible and the works of the church fathers, particularly Jerome, and a biting and

---

the Reception of the Occultist Tradition in France (The Hague, 1978), and Hansen, *Quellen*, 256–68; Lea, *Materials*, 1:354. For Cardanus, see Lea, *Materials*, 2:435–48, and Eamon, 278–81. See also Brian P. Copenhaver, "Astrology and Magic," in *The Cambridge History of Renaissance Philosophy*, ed. Chartes B. Schmitt, Quentin Skinner, Eckhard Kessler, and Jill Kraye (Cambridge, 1988), 264–300.

very public critic of contemporary abuses in both ecclesiastical circles and lay society. Letter 143, written to a patron, Antony van Bergen, abbot of the monastery of St. Bertin, tells of a case of sorcery around the turn of the sixteenth century for which we have no other evidence. Besides its value as evidence of some practices around the turn of the century, the letter also illustrates Erasmus's capacity for sarcasm about the Mendicant Orders, of the abuses of Christianity in his own age, and even for the erroneous Latin usage of medieval jurists.

SOURCE: *The Correspondence of Erasmus: Letters 142 to 297, 1501 to 1514*, trans. R. A. B. Mynors and D. F. S. Thomson, annotated by Wallace K. Ferguson (Toronto and Buffalo, 1974), 5–11.

FURTHER READING: James D. Tracy, *Erasmus of the Low Countries* (Berkeley, Los Angeles, London, 1996), 31, 226.

I WILL TELL YOU a tragic tale; quite modern, it is true, but so ghastly that in comparison the story of Medea or Thyestes or any other ancient tragedy would look like a comic theme.

Last year at Meung, a little town near Orléans, a dying sorcerer instructed his wife to hand over all his books of magic, and the other instruments of his cult, to a certain citizen of Orléans who would presently come to ask for them, since he had been his accomplice and partner in crime. This person took all the materials away to Orléans. Now for more than three years the sorcerer had at his own home been practising a wicked ritual, even more abominable than any kind of idolatry, with the connivance of his wife and the active assistance of his maiden daughter; so I shall give a brief account of the rites and ceremonies in which the blasphemous worship consisted, as I have been told them by most reliable informants.

He had placed the sacred body of Jesus our Redeemer in a kind of small wicker box and concealed it under the bedclothes. Oh, divine patience! As I relate this, "a shudder cold my limbs doth shake." Three years before he had purchased it from a starveling irreligious priest, a class too numerous hereabouts, for a smaller sum, I believe, than the Jews once paid for Christ, so that that wicked priest not only brought Judas back again but even outdid him, and it is said that he paid for his impious behaviour by a sudden death. Well then, whenever the sorcerer was about to perform his not holy but diabolical rites, the divine sacrament was brought out by profane hands, dug up from the bedclothes, stripped bare, and exposed to view. The daughter, a girl as yet unmarried, held up a naked sword (it being supposed that only a virgin could properly perform this function) and directed its point towards the sacred body in a threatening gesture. Next there was produced a kind of head, fashioned out of some substance or other, having three faces: of course, this represented the Three in One and One in Three. They swathed it in ninefold wrappings on which were a thousand representations of the letter *tau*, each inscribed with unknown angels' names; followed by as many decorated with the dreadful names of demons. When this had all been put together, the high priest of evil opened his books and, in accursed prayers dictated by Hecate, named first the Holy Trinity and a great number of angels, each in his proper company; and then hundreds of demons' names; and continued until the Devil himself arrived and answered his summons in person.

This abominable being provided, or at least pointed the way to, vast treasures; he had promised mountains of gold to his officiating priest, and even made him some gifts, but so disappointing were these that the latter began to repent of his three years' effort. Accordingly he used the customary formulae to call up the author of the promises made to him, and complained that for some considerable time he had been hoodwinked, and led on by nothing but hopes, without gaining anything worth while. The Devil, in reply, made excuses, saying that it was not his fault that it fell out so, but that there was something amiss in the ritual, for he must have an educated man there; and, if the man could find one, he himself would point the way to treasures richer than anyone hoped for. And when the other asked him whom he could best enlist for this purpose, the Devil urged him to approach the prior of a monastery of the order known as Preachers, which is behind the walls of Orléans, and cautiously sound him out. Now, this prior is what is called a *baccalarius formatus*; he has some repute among the vulgar, and is not the worst of preachers, as divines go nowadays at any rate; but, as it seemed to me afterwards and most men of the kind share this weakness, he is excessively hungry for notoriety. Yet I simply cannot even conjecture what the evil one was up to; was he trying to drive straight to ruin that priest of his, who was already thinking of quitting? Or did he seriously entertain the idea that the mind of a theologian could be bribed by the size of the reward offered to him? He was relying, I suppose, on the fact, superbly expressed by Virgil, that

Men's hearts to every ill incites
Th'accursed love of gold,

or again, as is claimed by those who have a closer acquaintance with men of this kind, that, hidden under those hoods, and under the most abject reputation for beggary, there sometimes lurk hearts ablaze with insufferable arrogance and an extraordinary lust for money.

But this is a question I leave undecided. Once he was duly persuaded, our hero went to meet the man. Thereupon, in order that he might gradually try out his attitude, he pretended to have some manuscripts at home that were of no use to him, since he was unlettered, but might be exceedingly serviceable to a man of education, and asked if he would like to purchase any of them. The theologian bade him produce the books, so that he might look at them; and he produced an Old Testament, popularly called the Bible, in a French translation. The theologian having expressed disdain for this book, and asking whether he had any others, the fellow produced, though with a show of unwillingness and reluctance, another one that lay concealed under his coat. When the other had turned the pages and observed that here was a master of illicit practices, he took a closer look—whether intrigued by its novelty, as frequently happens, or on purpose to investigate thoroughly what he began to suspect as an underlying scandal, I do not know. Therefore, asked what his decision was, he answered that it looked to him like a book of witchcraft. The other, pledging him to secrecy, said that he possessed several of the same sort at home but that they needed the help of a scholar. It was possible, however, that they might be worth a fortune. The theologian pricked up his ears at this, and begged him to bring those books also for him to see. He was, he said, deeply interested in the subject. He must certainly not neglect such a marvellous opportunity; and he was absolutely confident that it would come to a happy issue.

So they shook hands, and the poor wretch brought the rest of the books. The theologian continued his interrogation until the man, who by now trusted him completely, confessed the whole affair, even finally the matter of the body of Christ. Then the prior, appearing overjoyed, begged him to enact those momentous rites before him, and said he was now all agog to proceed quickly with the business. The man then took him home, and told his wife to bring out the aforesaid sacrament and the other instruments of witchcraft. These were produced and examined. The monk, completely concealing his purpose, as he himself recounts, went directly from the spot to the Official, as they call him—a man of the most unquestionable uprightness of life, with a high reputation for complete proficiency in civil and canon law, and a very good friend of mine. He, thereupon, acting on information laid by the theologian, instructed the royal constables to imprison the man together with his wife and daughter, deeming that an incident of so portentous a nature admitted of no delay. At once the house was forcibly entered, the holy sacrament brought forth with due reverence, and the remainder of that day and all the following night devoted to solemn hymns and prayers by the clergy and monks, who kept night-long vigil.

The next day a solemn supplication was decreed; the streets going to and coming from the church were hung with tapestries, and throughout the city the churches resounded with the ringing of holy bells. The entire body of clergy walked in procession, each carrying his relics, the whole city having turned out to view the spectacle; and the Eucharist, that had been removed from the house of sin, was conveyed with fitting solemnity to the church of Ste. Croix, where, before a larger congregation, they say, than had ever before been seen there, the theologian, not without suspicion of vainglory, gave an account of the whole affair, repeatedly appealing to the body of Christ which lay before him in the open air exactly as it had been brought from the sorcerer's house. He did likewise the following day, and was to have done so on consecutive days to come, announcing to the assembled multitude anything that the prisoners had mean-time confessed—I imagine because he thought it presented him with absolutely sure basis for winning immortality—had not the Official, who was no fool, silenced the theologian, already in full flight upon the windy chariot of fame. The prisoners were examined and heard, at some length, by theologians summoned from Paris for the purpose, with the assistance of two legal experts. I was informed by the Official that some amazing revelations were made by the man during the investigations, but that they could not yet be treated as reliable since the man's account was still not free of inconsistency; that the woman was terribly harassed by a demon at night—stabbed and beaten and pulled about until she almost fainted; but the girl was at peace with herself and not at all upset by the fear of punishment, since she stated that every morning at day-break she was visited by someone or other who consoled her and took all her grief away and bade her be calm in spirit. And at Meung the widow of the sorcerer, whom I mentioned above, is also detained in prison.

We may now proceed to regard the Medea and Thyestes and Nero of the poets as mere trifles, since the impiety of Christians has produced abomina-tions whereof the very names were unknown to the ancients. What name in-deed are we to give to such a horror as this? The names of Chaldeans, casters of horoscopes, astrologers, sorcerers, magicians, diviners, soothsayers, augurs, wizards, necromancers, geomancers, fortune-tellers, and enchanters are but trivial in my opinion, and inadequate for such deep-dyed wickedness as this. The augur notes the swift flight aloft of birds, and the favourable omen of the hungry chickens, while the soothsayer probes the configuration of the victim's entrails; the astrologer consults the stars, while the wizard collects herbs under a spell; the enchanter deals in prayers, the magician calls up departed spirits, and the palmist examines the wrinkles of the hand. These are terrible practices, and Christian ears can hardly bear to hear tell of them; but are they not vastly less so than this tragedy at Orléans? Did even Thessaly, that notorious haunt of witches, ever produce the like? Now the Jewish law visits the punishment of death upon those who commune with departed spirits, while the laws of the Roman Empire denounce in the strongest terms the superstitions of soothsay-ing and augury, referring to those who practise them as strangers to nature and enemies of the human race, worthy of punishment by the retributive sword, or burning, or being thrown to wild beasts (these are Constantine's own words), and prescribing that any who consult them are to be deprived of all their prop-erty and banished to an island; this is clear from the Code, in the title "Of Sorcerers and Astrologers," where there is an additional gloss that is indeed "noteworthy" (to use the language of Accorso's school), but deserves to be marked in black, inasmuch as it explains a "soothsayer" (haruspex) as one who watches heavenly movements and birds, and a "priest" (sacerdos) as one who professes necromancy, and some other instances of the kind of which it is hard to say whether their barbarity or their ignorance is greater. What is certain is their complete absurdity; yet I am by no means unfamiliar with such things, since monstrosities of this sort are of such frequent occurrence everywhere in the Digest that now that I am accustomed to them they do not even amuse me any longer, much less annoy me.

But to return to my point. The pontifical decrees, and also the letters known as Decretals, when they mention sorcery and damnable superstitions of the kind, do not even touch upon this kind of witchcraft, either because those bygone ages never suspected that such impiety was possible or because the authors of the written text considered that they had a duty to spare the ears of mankind. This novel and unprecedented abomination was the child, not of Night, mother of the Furies (as the poets' legend has it), but of greed, the parent of every crime; nor was it a single phenomenon, but a fusion of superstition, impiety, idolatry, and blasphemy, like the mingled brood of several different monsters. Are people then surprised if our modern generation is afflicted, now by wars, now by famine, now by pestilence, now by divers other evils, when, over and above those vices which have already well nigh ceased to appear as vices, so common are they, we are guilty of crimes that far outdo either the Giants, whom the thunderbolt confounded, or Lycaon's cruelty, for which the great flood itself hardly atoned? Are we ourselves surprised that new plagues come upon us every day, when each day, by fresh wickedness, we provoke the Lord our God and, as Horace says, "through our crimes will not permit/Heaven to lay its thunderbolts aside"?

37
Johann Geiler von Kaysersberg: *Die Emeis* (1508)

Johann Geiler von Kaysersberg (1445–1510) was one of the most prolific theologians and public preachers in pre-reformation Germany. He studied theology at Freiburg and Basel and became the preacher in the cathedral in Strassburg in 1478. His sermons in the vernacular are extremely lively and give an accurate impression of the power and appeal of a gifted preacher. In Lent of 1508 Geiler preached a series of sermons that were transcribed by a colleague and printed in 1516 as *Die Emeis* (The Ant-Colony, the title probably derived from Nider). Twenty-six of these sermons deal with witchcraft, and although Geiler does not accept every charge made against witches, he argues that those convicted of the crime should suffer the death penalty. Geiler's sermons are the first discussions of witchcraft in the German language since Johannes Hartlieb's work in 1456. The edition of 1516 contained a number of woodcut illustrations—several of them attributed to Hans Baldung Grien or someone from his workshop (Figs. 20–21)—that indicate the increasing importance of pictorial illustration in the late fifteenth and early sixteenth centuries. The sermons also explain the case of the witch milking an axe-handle (Fig. 21).

SOURCE: Hansen, *Quellen*, 284–91. Trans. E. P.

FURTHER READING: Lea, *Materials*, 1: 368–69.

On the Unholden, or the Witches (Hexen)

Now you ask me, what do you say, preacher, about those women who travel through the night and meet at assemblies? You ask me if there's something to all this. When they travel with Lady Venusberg, or the witches, when they go thus hither and yon, do they really travel, or do they remain? Or are they there in spirit? And what should I think about them? I will give you the answer to your questions.

Now to the first question, I say that they do travel hither and yon, but that they also remain where they are, because they dream that they travel, since the devil can create an impression in the human mind, and thus a fantasy, that they dream with others that they travel, and when they go with each other and see other women and dance, feast, and eat, and he can do all that to them (by an interior or exterior pact). And let us not be amazed that he can deceive them so completely that they dream that this happens. . . . Listen to this example [Geiler's example is taken from Nider]: I read that a preacher came into a village where there was a woman who said that she flew at night. The preacher came to her and asked about this, saying that if she believed it, she was deceived. She said, "If you won't believe it, then I will show you." And the preacher answered that he would indeed like to see it. When it was night, and she wished to go, she called him and then lay down on a bench of the kind they have in village houses. Then she sat down and anointed herself with oil and spoke a word that she was used to speaking, and she fell asleep sitting up. Then she began waving her hands and feet around so wildly that she fell off the bench and lay under it and bumped herself badly on her head.

You have heard the story of the saint, Germanus (Text 12) . . .

You ask, What should I believe about witches? Can they transform men into wolves, pigs, or birds? As we read in Saint Augustine's *City of God*, he writes about a well-known sorceress named Circe, who transformed the knight Ulysses into a pig or a sow. . . . As for your first question, I say that you must not believe that any man can be transformed into a wolf or a pig, that this is merely a ghost, or an appearance deceiving the eyes or created in the imagination [proof of this cited from the *Canon Episcopi*, Text 5]. I say that the devil cannot transform a man into a beast, nor can he transform one beast into another. But the devil can create beasts, the same beasts that nature can create. . . . And what nature cannot do by its own powers, neither can the devil do. . . . Can the devil transport people from one place to another against their will? I say yes, since good angels can do this, as we read in Habakkuk [Hab. 3] . . . and so can the evil spirit also, for, although God has withdrawn His grace from him, He has not taken from him his natural strength. . . . I say that what the witches or *Unholden* do is not a real thing . . . it is merely a sign; when the devil sees the sign and hears the word, he knows what they indicate; then he performs the act, and it is the devil who does this and not [the witches]. For the devil has made a pact with certain men and has given them certain words and signs. When they make the signs and use the words, the devil will do what they want, but it is the devil who does these things. So what the witches do is only a sign, not the deed itself. Take this example, so that you believe it: A witch who wishes to make storms or hail takes a staff and thrusts it into a stream and shakes some of the water with the staff over her head behind her, and then the hail falls. When she throws the water over her head and speaks the word, these things do not cause a hailstorm. But the devil, when he sees the sign and word, then works high above in the air and stirs the winds and brings down the hail. Yes, many men say that the witch has done this, but I believe that no witch can do this. It is not unreasonable that when someone sees this happen with his own eyes [that he thinks the witch does it], but she does not do it; she cannot do it—only the devil can do it, and he does it when she makes the signs and speaks the words that he has taught her. . . .

And why is the female sex more involved with witchcraft and the sorcery of the devil than the male? For every one man burnt for witchcraft, there are ten women burnt. William of Paris gives three reasons why women are more likely than men to be witches: because of their instability of spirit, because they are understood better by demons, and because of their talkativeness.

Now you will ask me to explain if witches can, when a cow can no longer give milk, draw milk from a tree or from an axe-handle [Fig. 21]. I say yes, with the help of the devil. How? Because it is a rule that the devil can transport a thing that can be moved from one place to another by the innate powers that he has from God. This is why an evil spirit can fly like a bird across a great mountain. Another evil spirit, who might wish to knock down a mountain, and who also had more power than the other, can move the thing from one place to another. This is how it comes about that a witch can sit on a pitchfork and anoint herself and speak the word that she is supposed to speak and then travel wherever she wishes. The pitchfork doesn't do this by itself; neither does the ointment do it; instead, when she anoints herself, the devil straightaway leads her on the pitchfork, once he sees the sign and word from the witch. And so it is with cows. The milk is a corporeal thing, and we have said that the devil can transport any corporeal thing if God allows him to, from one place to another. He takes the milk from a cow somewhere, if she wants milk, and transports it somewhere else when he sees the witch make the proper sign. And when the witch wants her milk, and she wants to milk an axe-handle, the devil can bring the milk there in a very short time.

As for the acts condemned in Deuteronomy 18, you must not believe in their powers, but you must also put those who do to death. Imperial law, too, commands this, that sorcerers and suchlike men should be put to death. But those who can be cured and made healthy ought not be put to death, but to a lesser punishment.

38
Gianfrancesco Pico della Mirandola: *Strix* (1523)

Gianfrancesco Pico della Mirandola (1469–1533), nephew of Giovanni Pico della Mirandola, the well-known philosopher of the late fifteenth century, was learned in Latin and Greek, defiantly anti-Aristotelian, and widely read in the classics, and so, technically, a humanist. But he was also highly suspicious about the pagan qualities of pagan learning, dubious about the validity of sense-perception, and hence extremely sensitive to the dangers of illusion (especially demonic illusion), and he brought his extensive reading in both classical and modern sources to bear in favor of belief in the reality of witchcraft and the need to rid Christian Italy of it.

Pico had been involved in 1512/13 in the defense of a devout young woman, Caterina de Racconigi, who had been accused of witchcraft, and in 1523 he was present at the trials of several witches in Bologna. The Bologna experience was the basis for the *Strix*.

Pico's ideas on the subject are expressed in a lively literary conversation in three scenes that he wrote in 1523, the *Strix sive de ludificatione daemonum* (Strix, or the deceptions of demons; the term *strix* itself comes from classical Latin and meant originally a screech owl and, by extension, a woman who transforms herself into a troublesome and dangerous bird). The Italian translation, *strega*, is rather more accurate, since it is sixteenth-century witches, with ancient examples only brought in to reinforce contemporary witchcraft beliefs, that concern the writer.

The literary dialogue—or conversation when it had more than two participants—was a popular form in fifteenth- and sixteenth-century Europe: Nider's *Formicarius* is a dialogue in rough form, while the Calvinist Lambert Daneau's *De veneficiis, quos olim sortilegos, nunc autem vulgo sortiarios vocant* (On witches, which were once called *sortilegi* but are now commonly called *sortiarii*), published in 1563, was another treatise against witchcraft in dialogue form (Text 42). In

1489 a legal counselor to the duke of Austria, Ulrich Molitor wrote a work in similar form in Latin, the *De lamiis*, specifically about belief in and skepticism toward witchcraft and the duke's obligation to search out and punish witches.[1] Molitor's little book, sometimes later printed with the *Malleus Maleficarum*, also included a series of elegant woodcut illustrations which continued the pictorial line begun by the Paris manuscript of Martin Le Franc (Fig. 10–12).

The conversation in Gianfrancesco Pico's *Strix* has four characters: Apistius (the name means "the man without faith"), a learned humanist skeptic who does not believe in the existence of witchcraft but is converted to belief in the course of the work; Phronimus (the name means "the prudent man"), his friend who does most of the converting; Dicaste (the name means "judge," here clearly an inquisitor); and Strix, the witch whom they interrogate. The views of Apistius are an early example of learned and articulated skepticism about growing witchcraft beliefs, but in the course of the conversation, which takes place over a two-day period, the skeptic is converted to belief. It is also a lively essay, in which the conversations are colloquial and dramatic, and perhaps all the more powerful for its literary qualities.

In part 1 Apistius and Phronimus argue about the reality of witchcraft with frequent and broadly learned references to classical sources; they argue (quite cordially, as the tone of all the conversations in the work) about the interpretation of Vergil, Seneca, Lucan, Homer, Plato, Iamblichus, Horace, Philostratus, Apuleius, and Lucian. At the end of part 1 Dicaste and the Strega appear, and in part 2, set the following day, Dicaste elicits from the Strega a confession of her and other witches' evil deeds. In part 3 Dicaste and Phronimus convince Apistius that he has been wrong about witchcraft, and at the very end Dicaste gives him a new name—Pistius, the man of faith.

Written originally in Latin (whence the title *Strix*), it was translated into Italian by Leandro Alberti in 1524, with a preface addressed to Pico's wife, Giovanna Caraffa, by the translator, and again by Turino Turini in 1555. Both translations are used here.

SOURCE: *Dialogo intitolato La Strega, o vero de gli Inganni de Demoni dell'illustre Signor Giovan Francesco Pico della Mirandola. Tradotto in Lingua Toscana per il Signor Abate Turino Turini da Pescia,* ed. Idi Li Vigni, *La Strega o vero de gli Inganni de Demoni* (Genoa, 1988). Trans. E. P. Material from Alberti's preface is in Hansen, *Quellen,* 324–26. The translation has been very much abbreviated.

FURTHER READING: Peter Burke, "Witchcraft and Magic in Renais-

---

1. On Molitor's work, see Lea, *Materials,* 1: 348–53, where there is an extensive summary.

sance Italy: Gianfrancesco Pico and His *Strix*," in Anglo, ed., *The Damned Art*, 32–52; Charles B. Schmitt, *Gianfrancesco Pico della Mirandola (1469–1533) and His Critique of Aristotle* (The Hague, 1967). See also Li Vigni's introduction to the 1988 edition.

Alberti's Preface to the Translation: To Giovanna Caraffa

There was discovered during the past year [in Bologna, 1523] a great wicked and cursed game of the Lady [witches' sabbat], where God was denied, blasphemed, and mocked, and the cross, that refuge of the Christian faithful and their battle-standard, was trampled upon, and where other most blasphemous works against our Christian faith were performed. These were investigated conscientiously and in detail and proceeded against by the censor and inquisitor of heretics, and many of the most wicked were consigned by him to the judge who, according to the requirements of the law, heaped up a great fire and burned them, both as a punishment for their sacrilege and as an example to others. . . .

Many people then began to say with injurious words that these people had been executed unjustly . . . and because these complaints increased from day to day, the illustrious lord Gian Francesco, your esteemed husband, a man certainly not lacking in Christian faith, learned and widely read, and free of all doubt in these matters, decided to undertake a detailed and most subtle examination of all that had taken place before the inquisitor [and interrogate the people involved] . . . in order to discover the insidious wiles of the demon and to spread everywhere the truth of the Christian faith, so that everyone would learn to guard himself against the frauds of our ancient enemy and also to see that everywhere such criminals are pursued. He then picked up his sharp pen and wrote three books against that wicked and perverse school of the demon [the *Strix*]. . . . He wrote this most praiseworthy, learned, and curious work, not a little profitable to the Christian religion. O may God will that every prince, like your own husband, that is, learned, should support learned men as faithful Catholics and true Christians.

Strix

I

Apistius: Phronimus, where are all these people running to?

Phronimus: I just met a few who told me where the mob's going . . . maybe they hope they'll see some novelty, the witch, and that's why they're all running there with their children.

Apistius: Oh, are there really witches around here? To see a real one I'd walk ten miles, at least.

Phronimus: Well, if you've never seen one, you can see one today.

Apistius: I'd really like to find a kind of bird that I've been searching for for a long time, but never found—a *strega*. . . . I'm telling you the truth and no fooling, for to see something that the ancients never saw ought to be an experience for anyone, especially for anyone who is curious. . . . Phronimus, I think you've made the same mistake that a lot of our friends have made, that is, assuming that what the mob says is the truth. I, for one, don't know that witches fly and are taken up by fantasies, that in the darkest night they devour the flesh of children.

Phronimus: Don't say that, because many learned men, experts, and certainly not part of the mob, all believe it, and have openly expressed their convictions. We cannot believe that they are mistaken.

Apistius: Sorry, but I have never found myself able to believe these things.

Phronimus: Why not?

Apistius: Because it has always seemed to me to be laughable, that, having drawn a circle and anointed the body with some ointment, I don't know in what way, and murmuring some gobbledygook, these people can mingle with demons and that this silly troop of riders through the night on whatever kind of stick that they've decorated, can ride on a goat or a ram, or that others are carried through the air by a force greater than any wind. And then they find themselves playing in the congregation of Diana or the Herodiades, eating, drinking, and creating unlawful pleasures.

Phronimus: Soon, however, what we've just been talking about will be made clearer to you. There's the Strega on the stairs of the church, talking with Dicaste.

Strega: Woe is me!

Dicaste: Keep up your spirits, speak without fear, and have no doubt that I'll see to it that no harm comes to you, just as I've promised, as long as you speak freely about all your activities.

Strega: I've already confessed. Why do you torment me further?

Dicaste: You must repeat, not just in the presence of two or three witnesses, but in that of many, and then before the whole people, if you want to escape the execution that the law commands. You've promised me to do everything I say, and I have promised you not to put you into the hands of the Podestà [the chief executive and judicial officer of the city], who will burn you according to ancient law. I don't require you to tell anything other than those things you've done with demons when you were with them, and about the game of Diana.

II

Strega: Why do you bother me? Why do you torment me so, after I've already confessed?

Apistius: Good lady, no one has brought you here to harm you. Phronimus here and I are here only to see and hear what you have to say and to help you in any way we can.

Dicaste: Tell them what you confessed to me yesterday and what the notary wrote down yesterday evening.

Apistius: Did you go off to the game of Diana, or that of Herodias?

Strega: Certainly I went to that game, and whether it was that of Diana or that of Herodias I don't know.

Dicaste: About this game of Diana or that of Herodias many papal decretal letters speak, as well as a conciliar canon [the *Canon Episcopi*] that says that they should be driven out.

Phronimus: Dicaste, do you believe that she did the same thing [as that described in *Episcopi*]?

Dicaste: Some say that it is the same thing [mentioned in the *Canon Episcopi*], while others believe that hers is rather a new heresy.

Phronimus: I think that it must be both, part ancient and partly a new superstition, as one would say, ancient in essence and new in accidents (to use the terminology of the modern theologians).

Dicaste: I've come across a good distinction by which we can resolve the many doubts that have arisen about this, whereby some think that these ladies are always carried off to the game [sabbat] only in the spirit and the imagination, and not in the body. But I think that sometimes the one happens, and sometimes the other.

Apistius: Why do you think that sometimes they are transported bodily and sometimes they only imagine that they are?

Dicaste: Sometimes it happens through a deception of the demon and sometimes by the choice of the witches. I remember that Henry and James [Kramer and Sprenger, the authors of the *Malleus Maleficarum*], German theologians, wrote about a certain witch who made the voyage now by one means, now by another, just as she pleased, that is, sometimes flying bodily, and at other times flying only in her imagination.

Apistius: You've answered our questions well, Witch, but now tell us whether you've murdered any infants.

Strega: That's enough!

Apistius: How did you murder them?

Strega: We entered the houses of our enemies by night, and when the parents were sleeping we stole the infants, carrying them to the fire where we pierced them with a needle and, putting our lips to the wounds, filled our mouths with their blood, and we put the bodies into a container so that we could make an ointment with which to anoint ourselves before we traveled to the game [sabbat].

Apistius: I'm still not sure I believe this. . . . But, just as I have always believed in the religion of true Christianity, I cannot conceive in any way that such crimes could possibly be pardoned.

III

Dicaste: [The ancient philosophers] thought that there were both good and evil demons, while we know that there are only evil demons, with names like Satan and the Devil; they are also called demons. And about them the prophet said, "All the gods of the Gentiles are demons . . ." [Psalm 95(6)]. Beyond this, no man of learning has doubted that the wickedness of incantations made on crops and those for other purposes, and making ligatures to torment marriages, and those acts that are outside of nature are not made by the art and practices of the demons, and from this come the commandments of ancient and modern theologians of holy scripture. In Deuteronomy [18:10–12] we read that sorcerers and enchanters are to be killed; in Leviticus [20:6] diviners and soothsayers; and the law commands that those who use the prophetic spirit are to be stoned. And many other things (as you can read in [*questions*] XXIV and XXVI of Gratian's *Decretum*.

Apistius: I don't deny that the demons exist and with their malice are able to commit many evils, but I would like someone to tell me how these things pertain to the issue at hand. If these women and men travel, or are transported to the game in the body, or whether they don't participate in the game only in the spirit and the imagination.

Dicaste: I think that they are sometimes transported bodily and sometimes are deceived into thinking that they are, because they have controlled the powers of the imagination very badly and are easily deceived. . . . But this isn't the thing I worry about most. It doesn't matter to us whether they go in the body or the spirit, on foot or on horseback. But to have renounced the faith to which they have sworn, scorned the sacraments and the Christian faith, to have adored the demon and committed many crimes, which is why we interrogate them. . . . This is condemned not only in the ancient laws of the church, but also in the new, and is particularly repeated by Innocent VIII [Text 33] first, and later by Julius II [Text 39, headnote], both among the greatest of popes. But nevertheless be careful not to believe that for the most part they are transported in the body. . . . Come here, Strega: swear on this holy scripture without lying in the least matter.

Strega: I've sworn.

Dicaste: Were you transported to the game in the body or in the spirit?

Strega: Both ways. In the body and in the spirit. I was raised up by touching with these same hands that demon known as Lodovico.

Dicaste: Did he appear like one of us?

Strega: No, more corpselike.

Dicaste: What sort of sexual intercourse did you have with a spirit-body?

Strega: I don't know anything about the body, but I know well that I had greater pleasure with it than with my husband.

Phronimus: [to Apistius]: Why don't you believe that demons desire to join themselves sexually with women under the appearance of men, and with men under the appearance of women?

Apistius: I have faith in your words.

Phronimus: Now, Dicaste, night falls and we must return home. Even if you haven't persuaded Apistius, you have clearly shown that both in antiquity and in our own time, this game is not a vain fable, but in essence most ancient and in its larger part made up of new things, changed according to the pleasure of the demon. And they will be changed further later, so great is the subtlety and power of deception possessed by the ancient enemy of mankind. You have shown that the circles, ointments, magical words, travel through the air, sexual relations with demons all occur as often in our own time as in the remote past.

Apistius: Yes, let's go home. I'm convinced.

Dicaste: You now believe these things?

Apistius: Yes, I believe them.

Dicaste: Really, or are you joking?

Apistius: Do you really think that I could joke about something upon which both ancients and moderns agree? Upon that which the poets, rhetoricians, Stoics, jurists, philosophers, theologians, wise and prudent men, soldiers, rustics, experimenters all agree?

Dicaste: And this discussion has changed your opinion?

Apistius: Without any doubt. And because I have changed the habit of my mind, from here on I wish also to change my name.

Dicaste: As you wish. And for the future you will be called Pistius [the man of faith].

39
Pope Hadrian VI, *On Diabolical Witchcraft* (1523)

Hadrian VI (1522–23), the only pope from the Low Countries, was a scholar of considerable influence, founder of the Collegium Trilingue (College of the Three Languages—Greek, Latin, and Hebrew) at the University of Louvain, and tutor of the future emperor Charles V, who engineered Hadrian's election to the papacy (the papal name Hadrian is also his own—Adriaan Florensz van Boeyens). Hadrian issued the bull translated here in 1523, echoing statements issued by his predecessors Julius II (1503–13) and Leo X (1513–21), and continuing a line of papal concern that dated in its modern form to Eugenius IV (Text 29).

SOURCE: Montague Summers, *The Geography of Witchcraft* (1927; rprt. London, 1978), 538–41.

T O OUR BELOVED SON Modesto Vincentino, of the Order of Preachers.

Yet a little while ago, as you did so clearly make known to Us, Our predecessor Pope Julius II of happy memory, learned, to his bitter sorrow and sore grief, from George de' Casali, Professor of the Order of Friars Preachers and accredited Inquisitor in the diocese of Cremona to punish heretical pravity, that in certain parts of Lombardy and especially in those districts in which the said George was accredited Inquisitor, there were found to be many persons of both sexes, who forgetful of their own souls' salvation and straying far from the Catholic Faith, made a certain sect, utterly denying the Faith which they received in Holy Baptism, spurning beneath their feet the Holy Cross and treating it with vilest contumely, above all abusing the Divine Sacrament of the Altar, taking the Devil to be their Lord and Master, promising him worship and obedience, and with accursed incantations, charms, sortilege, and other foul magic rites ever doing grave harm and hurt to men, animals, and the fruit of the earth, ensuing and wreaking numberless other abominations, enormities, and heinous crimes at the instigation of the Devil as aforesaid, to the deadly peril of their own souls, giving offence to the Divine Majesty of God, affording also an ill example and grave scandal to many. Yet when (as the aforesaid George declared) the Inquisitor, George de' Casali, in the course of his duties in the said districts to which he was accredited, would have proceeded against these wretches, some there were, clerics as well as lay folk of these parts, who seeking to know more than was their business most rashly and naughtily presumed to affirm that such offences did not fall under the jurisdiction of the Inquisitor George, attempting moreover to stir up hatred against him among the populace and to hinder his efforts, which indeed they did then hinder, wherefore the aforesaid persons who practised blasphemies and impieties remained unpunished and by their examples and precepts they kept continually inducing others to use like abominations which caused no small mischief and shame to the Faith, danger to immortal souls, and scandal to very many. Our predecessor accordingly being altogether loath that the execution of the Inquisitor's office should be hindered in any way at all and thuswise the poisonous taint of vile heresy be more widely spread, enjoined and commanded by a Brief addressed to the said George, that as Inquisitor he should take full cognizance of such infamies which fell within his jurisdiction and that he should exercise and employ to their uttermost his inquisitorial powers against all and sundry of whatsoever estate or rank they might happen to be, and that it was his duty, full power being assigned to him, to correct and punish the offences of all whom he might find guilty of the aforesaid enormities, the charges being heard by him and the Vicars of the local Ordinary, whensoever they wished to sit as assessors, and the judgements being delivered as is decreed in the case of other heretics according to the canon and civil law. Any persons who dared oppose this procedure were to be punished by ecclesiastical censures and other legal remedies. But those, who in regard to these matters lent him advice, help, or favour, Our predecessor decreed should gain and enjoy the same indulgences as those who bear the Cross against other heretics then gained and enjoyed according to the Apostolic indult conceded to them, as is more amply set forth in the particular Brief. To this We append a further declaration, that not only do impieties and crimes of this kind against the Catholic Faith and the Christian Religion come under the jurisdiction of the Inquisitor at Cremona, but in all other districts and dioceses they now come under the jurisdiction of the other Inquisitors of the Lombard congregation of the said Order. For inasmuch as they are the same offences they shall meet with the same treatment and punishment according to the tenor of the same letters. Wherefore you, who are, as you show Us, the accredited Inquisitor of these crimes in the city of Como, have in your own name as in the names of all other Inquisitors of heresy of this Order and Congregation wheresoever they be stationed or accredited, humbly made supplication that We would vouchsafe to extend unto you the aforesaid letter with certain additions and other provisions now conveniently to be made. We therefore lending a gracious ear to this your prayer, by Our Apostolic authority and by these presents extend the aforesaid letter with all that is contained therein in every clause and proviso to you as also to the other Inquisitors of the Order and Congregation, as well those who are now accredited as those who shall be accredited at some future date to all perpetuity, as if the letter were directed and delivered to you and to each several person of the aforesaid Inquisitors. This letter, then, with all the benefits thereby conferred We concede to you and to them. Notwithstanding any hindrance, let, or bar, which Our predecessor Julius in the aforesaid letter was minded should not hinder, let, or bar, and notwithstanding aught else whatsoever to the contrary. And because it would be indeed a hard task to convey the present letter to the several places, where perchance it might be necessary that the provisions thereof should be recognized and accepted, it is Our good pleasure and We decree by Our Apostolic authority that when it has been transcribed by the hand of any public notary and signed and sealed with the seal of some member of the Curia or some Dignitary of the Church as a token of surety, should such need arise, the same respect is thereto be shown as would be shown to these presents were they published or posted.

Given at Rome, at S. Peter's, under the Fisherman's Ring, 20 July, 1523, in the first year of Our Pontificate.

Figure 14. Albrecht Dürer's engraving *Witch Riding* shows a witch riding backward on a beast of composite nature, carrying a magical distaff, and performing weather magic. Dürer's source was probably an ancient cameo representing Aphrodite Pandemos; he worked the model into early sixteenth-century European motifs. Musée du Petit Palais, Paris, Cl. Giraudon.

Figure 15. In 1510 Dürer's disciple Hans Baldung Grien created this woodcut depicting the new theme of witches preparing to depart for the sabbat. The scene, largely because of its erotic implications, remained extremely popular for the next two centuries. Museum of Fine Arts, Boston.

Figure 16. Baldung Grien's 1523 *Weather Witches*. The figures are based on classical models, but their implements, the storm rising, and the beast beneath the draperies reflect contemporary concerns. Städtelisches Kunstinstitut, Frankfurt.

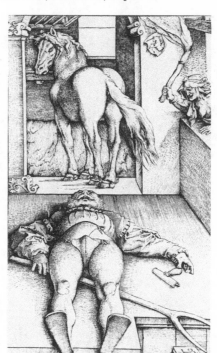

Figure 17. Baldung Grien's 1544 *Bewitched Groom* reflects a more somber and less specifically erotic concern on the artist's part. Städtelisches Kunstinstitut, Frankfurt.

Figure 18. Baldung Grien's 1514 *Three Witches*, possibly another version of the preparation for the sabbat, emphasizes the invertedness of the witches' universe. Albertina, Vienna.

Figure 19. Hans Schäuffelin illustrated the 1511 edition of Ulrich Tengler's *Der Neu Layenspiegel* (*Mirror for Layfolk*) with this composite illustration of the many different activities of witches. University of Pennsylvania.

Figure 20. A follower of Hans Baldung Grien created this image of witches preparing to depart for the sabbat as an illustration for the 1516 first printed edition of Johann Geiler von Kaysersberg's sermons, *The Ant Colony*. University of Pennsylvania.

Figure 21. The same artist used this woodcut to illustrate a point in Geiler von Kaysersberg's sermons concerning the devil's ability to transport milk instantly from a cow to a post so that the witch could demonstrate her magical powers. University of Pennsylvania.

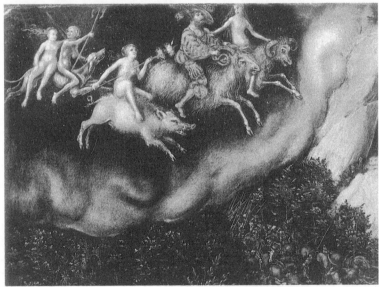

Figure 22. The Dutch artist Jacob Cornelisz van Oostsanen's *Saul and the Witch of Endor* depicts the "witch" of En-Dor in the mid-sixteenth century, pictorially linking the scriptural story to contemporary imagery of witchcraft. Rijksmuseum, Amsterdam.

Figure 23. Around 1530 Lucas Cranach the Elder painted several versions of the allegory of Melancholy (as had Dürer before him). This detail from *Melancholia* depicts witches and demons riding beasts, probably to the sabbat. Statens Museum for Kunst, Copenhagen.

Ein erschröckliche geschicht / so zu Derneburg in der Graffschafft Reinstein / am Hartz gelegen / von dreyen Zauberin / vnd zwayen
Mannen Hinrichtung tagen des Monats October Im 1555. Jare ergangen ist.

D Ie alte Schlang der Teuffel / hieweyl er Gott / vnd zuvoran den Sun Gottes / vnsern Herrn Jesum Christum / vnd das gantze menschliche geschlecht / sonderlich vmb vnsere Heerland Christi willen hasset / hat er sich bald im anfang / vnd kürtzlich nach der erschaffung vmb dz menschlich
bild / als vmb die / welcher same seinen Kopff zertretten solt / angewanten / die selbigen durch sein hinderlist vnd lugen / so ab dem jämmerlichen fall / dz sy in
zauberey vnd vngehorsame wider Gott gebracht / Darauff das gantz menschlich geschlecht / in einige vnd ewige verdamnuß in verderben kommen were / so Chri-
...

F Folget die geschicht / so zu Derneburg in der Graffschafft Reynstein am Hartz
gelegen / ergangen ist. Im October des 1555. Jare.

A Uff den Dienstag nach Michaelis / den ersten October / sind zwo Zauberin gebrandt worden / die eine Gödlische / die ander Osslersche genandt...

F Gedruckt zu Nürnberg bey Jörg Merckel / durch verleg Endres Zenckel Botten.

Figure 24. The 1567 edition of Olavus Magnus's great work *History of the Northern Peoples* contained a number of woodcuts illustrating matters discussed in the text. Here a witch draws in beasts to torment a sleeping man. University of Pennsylvania.

Figure 25. Broadsheet illustrating the execution of convicted witches at Derneburg in 1555. Such broadsheets (*Flugblatter*) were a primary means of circulating information and ideas about witches. University of Pennsylvania.

Figure 26. One method of determining whether a woman was a witch was to "swim" her, a survival of the older judicial ordeal. In theory, if the water rejected her (that is, if she didn't sink) then she was a witch. From Eberhard David Hauber, *Bibliotheca sive acta et scripta magica*. University of Pennsylvania.

187

TRACTAT

Von Bekanntnuß der Zau-
berer vnd Heren. Ob vnd wie viel
denselben zu glauben.

Anfänglich durch den Hochwürdigen Herrn
Petrum Binsfeldium, Trierischen Suffraganien/vnd
der H. Schrifft Doctorn/kurtz vnd summarischer
Weiß in Latein beschrieben.

Jetzt aber der Warheit zu stewr in vnser Teutsche Sprach
vertiret/durch den Wolgelerten M. Bernhart Vogel/deß löblichen
Stattgerichts in München/Assessorn.
EXOD. XXII. CAP.
Die Zauberer solt du nicht leben lassen.

Gedruckt zu München bey Adam Berg.

ANNO DOMINI M. D. XCII.
Mit Röm:Kay: May: Freyheit/nit nachzudrucken.

Figure 27. The title page of Peter Binsfeld's 1592 account of the trials at Trier illustrates a series of male and female witches' activities. Note the quotation from Exodus 22: 17, "Thou shalt not suffer a sorcerer to live." University of Pennsylvania.

VIII

The Problem of Sorcery and Witchcraft in the Age of the Reformation

THE CENTRAL THEOLOGICAL EVENTS of the sixteenth century were the Protestant and Roman Catholic Reformations. Their initial effect upon witchcraft belief, however, was surprisingly small. While Protestants on the whole were intensely critical of Catholic theology, the Catholic system of papal authority, the sacramental powers of the clergy, and the veneration of saints, and while they removed much jurisdiction from ecclesiastical courts and shifted persecution of the witch primarily to the civil criminal courts, Protestant theologians generally reaffirmed their belief in the presence and evil operations of fallen men and women in contractual service to Satan and shared with Catholics common ideas of the nature of the universe, material and spiritual causation, and some common points in the understanding of the authority of scripture. But they also denied that divine power worked through intermediary religious forms.[1]

Martin Luther (1483–1546), relying upon the literal interpretation of the scriptural texts for such belief, dramatically reasserted the reality of the devil in search of men's souls, citing his own personal encounters with the Evil One, and he warned that the world of the flesh and much of the world of the spirit was under Satan's sway. The "bewitchment" of which St. Paul spoke in his Epistle to the Galatians seemed to Luther to exist all around men and women in the contemporary world. Indeed, by suggesting not merely that witchcraft was a heresy, but that all heresy and false biblical interpreta-

---

1. On witchcraft and confessional differences in Reformation Europe, see Euan Cameron, "For Reasoned Faith or Embattled Creed? Religion for the People in Early Modern Europe," *Transactions of the Royal Historical Society* 6th ser., 7 (1998): 165–87. Cameron's essay should be read in conjunction with the argument in Clark, *Thinking with Demons*, 435–546.

tion was also a form of witchcraft, Luther extended the scope of persecution (Text 40).

John Calvin (1509–64) cited with equal assurance the scriptural warnings against Satan and his host of demons, and he attacked all attempts at metaphorical interpretation of man's relationships with the Powers of Darkness. Calvin insisted that the Bible had either literally described men and women possessed by or in service to Satan, or else it offered meaningless statements about the nature of God's universe; the latter possibility, of course, was unacceptable. Furthermore, Calvin's analysis of the will reaffirmed the concept of the voluntary surrender of a soul to the devil, a concept central to continued witchcraft belief and prosecution (Text 41).

Leading Catholic thinkers conceded nothing to the reformers in their commitment to ridding the world of Satan's legions. In 1580 Jean Bodin (1529–96) reminded princes that the crime of the witch was *lèse-majesté* against God, a crime infinitely more heinous than any earthly criminal act because it threatened to call down the wrath of God on any community or prince that refused to prosecute it. The laws against witches were divine, not secular, and no prince had the power to avoid prosecuting or to pardon such an offender. For Bodin, it was better that a few unfortunate innocents should burn than that a single witch should go unpunished (Text 45).

One purpose of Bodin's essay was to counter the arguments of one of the earliest works of the skeptical tradition, that of Johann Weyer (ca. 1515–88), in 1563 (Text 44), a work that admitted the reality of "infamous sorcerers" (*magi infames*) but denied both the existence and activities of witches.

In some Catholic areas of western Germany, witch persecutions reached new heights of intensity late in the second half of the sixteenth century. Contemporary accounts of witch-hunts and of the systematic crushing of opposition to such trials, such as those at the cathedral city of Trier, offer a remarkable account of the increased ardor of local officials and populaces (Text 47).

In many Protestant areas, the new religious fervor occasioned by the Reformation sometimes raised the fear of witches to a great pitch in areas where such phenomena had been relatively rare. Thus, in Scotland (Text 48) and in England (Text 46), the sixteenth century witnessed the beginning of major, although regional, persecutions that were to intensify well into the seventeenth century, when they reached their zenith.

By the end of the sixteenth century, the Lorraine judge Nicholas Rémy, systematically resynthesizing the components of witchcraft belief and vividly portraying for his readers the horrific evils effected by the witch, based on his own experience as a judge in Lorraine, spoke for a Europe, Catholic and Protestant, still singularly resolved upon its task of fulfilling its scriptural obligation, "Thou shall not suffer a witch to live" (Text 49).

40
Martin Luther: The Two Kinds of Sorcery
and the Reformation

Martin Luther (1483–1546) shattered forever the ostensible unity of
the Christian Church, ecclesiastical authority, and Christian theology
in Catholic Europe, but he shared and reinforced the witchcraft beliefs
of the culture that produced him. The great singularity in his demonological thought is his repeated insistence on the reality and presence
of the Devil and his assault on humans, and his detailed and frequent
testimonies of the Devil's physical and spiritual assaults upon himself
indicate how personal and intense a matter the work of Satan and his
hosts was for the great reformer. But Luther feared not only for himself,
but for an erring and sinful humanity. His sermon on the Gospel for the
Epiphany addresses both the attractiveness and the danger of seeking
knowledge from the dead, and he cites the case of Saul and the woman
of En-dor.[1] His commentary on St. Paul's Epistle to the Galatians elaborates on both physical and spiritual sorcery, and his sermon on the First
Commandment excerpted here (Text 40) lays out the dangers of sorcery
to each of the stages of human life. Luther's other theological writings
and his correspondence also make frequent reference to the evil and
harmful actions of witches, among which he often included the acts of
his opponents.

Luther's translation of the Bible into his native Saxon chancery German offers important examples of how the very different terminology
of ancient Hebrew and Greek became authoritative for contemporary
sixteenth-century beliefs concerning sorcery and witchcraft. Luther
translated Exodus 22: 17, "Thou shalt not suffer a witch to live," as
"Die Zauberinnen sollst du nicht leben lassen," using the word *Zauberinnen* (sorceresses), which had a very explicit sixteenth-century
meaning, quite distinct from the original Hebrew term *mekascheph*.[2]
He translated Leviticus 20: 27 as "When a man or woman is a *Wahrsager* or a *Zeichendeuter* [Hebrew: *ob, kosamim*], he or she should
suffer death. They should be stoned to death." Both these terms, as well
as the list of related terms in Deuteronomy 18: 10–12, again, had par-

1. *Luther's Works*, vol. 52, *Sermons* II, ed. Hans J. Hillerbrand and Helmut T. Lehmann, trans.
S. P. Hebart (Philadelphia, 1974), 177–83, at 180–83. Luther also discusses the woman of En-dor
in *D. Martin Luthers Werke. Kritische Gesammtausgabe. Tischreden*, vol. 4 (Weimar, 1916),
No. 4450, p. 319.
2. Luther commented on this text in his sermon on Exodus (*Predigten üben das 2. Buch Moses,
D. Martin Luthers Werke*, vol. 10 [Weimar, 1899]), 551–52.

ticular sixteenth-century meanings that had not been present in the original Hebrew or the later Greek or Latin Vulgate translations. Luther's translation of Deuteronomy 18: 10–12 also mentioned a *Zauberer* [sorcerer; Hebrew, *jideoni*]. The translation of 1 Samuel 28: 7–9 referred to the woman of En-dor and those like her as *Wahrsager* and *Zeichendeuter* (truth-teller and sign-reader). Thus, Luther's biblical translations validated sixteenth-century terminology by using it to translate authoritative scripture.[3]

Luther did not discuss these topics only in formal sermons and scriptural commentaries. His *Table Talk*, a vast group of collections of Luther's informal, domestic conversations with friends and disciples, offers a number of other important insights. In a passage in his *Table Talk* for 1533, one of his disciples records that:

Luther said many things about witchcraft [Lat. *fascinatio*], about asthma and nightmares [Ger. *von Hertzgespann und Elbe*], and how once his mother had been tormented by a neighbor woman who was a witch [Lat: *fascinatrix*]: "She was compelled to treat her neighbor with deference and to try to conciliate her, for the neighbor had through her practices caused her own children such sharp pain that they cried themselves to death. A certain preacher taxed her for this, though in general terms; he, too, was poisoned and had to die, for nothing could restore his health. She had taken the soil from his footsteps, had cast a spell over it (Ger: *damit gezaubert*], and had thrown it into the water. Without this soil he couldn't be healed." Then Luther was asked whether such things can also happen to godly people. He answered, "Yes, indeed. Our soul is subject to a lie. When it's freed, the body remains subject to murder. I believe that my illnesses aren't natural but are pure sorcery [Lat: *meras fascinationes*]. However, may God liberate his chosen ones from such evils."[4]

3. The most important (and far more nuanced than our remarks above) study of the entire question of Bible translation and witchcraft theory is that of Jörg Haustein, "Bibelauslegung und Bibelkritik. Ansäztze zur Überwindung der Hexenverfolgung," in *Das Ende der Hexenverfolgung*, ed. Sonke Lorenz and Dieter Bauer (Stuttgart, 1995), 249–67.

4. *Luther's Works*, vol. 54, *Table Talk*, ed. Theodore G. Tappert and Helmut T. Lehmann (Philadelphia, 1967), no. 2982b, p. 188. The Latin and German text is in *Werke. Tischreden*, vol. 3 (Weimar, 1914), No. 2982b, pp. 131–32. See the discussion and a slightly different translation in Heiko A. Oberman, *Luther: Man Between God and the Devil* (New Haven and London, 1983), 87–106. There is a selection of Luther's various remarks on these subjects in (a not always accurate) English translation in *The Table-Talk of Martin Luther*, trans. William Hazlitt (Philadelphia, n.d.), 310–29.

In another passage in the *Table Talk* from the year 1536, we learn that Luther, "mostly inveighed against love philters and incantations, the Devil's whores," and told the story of a witch who, in the form of a mouse, wanted to steal milk from a neighbor, who wounded the mouse and drove it away. The next day the witch-neighbor [Lat. *incantatrix*] came to the woman's door asking for oil to treat a wound, which was in the same place on her body as where the mouse had been wounded.[5] Luther used the phrase "the devil's whores" again in 1538: "On August 8 there was much talk about epicureans [skeptics] and despisers of God who have given themselves over to Satan, such as the witch [Ger. *Wettermacherin*, 'weather-maker'], the sorceress [Ger. *Milchdiebin*, 'milk-thief'] the devil's whores [Ger. *Teuffelshuren*] with whom Satan comes together."[6] Although Luther had total faith in the omnipotence of Christ over the Devil and his legions, he saw the power of witches as indeed awesome, and also in 1538, he said: "There is no compassion to be had for these women; I would burn all of them myself, according to the law, where it is said that priests began to stone criminals to death" (cf. Luther's translation of Leviticus 20: 27).[7]

SOURCE: *Decem praecepta Wittenbergensi praedicta populo. 1518*, in *D. Martin Luthers Werke. Kritische Gesammtausgabe*, vol. 1 (Weimar, 1883), 406–10. Trans. E. P.

FURTHER READING: Lea, *Materials*, 1: 417–23. Robert Herndon Fife, *The Revolt of Martin Luther* (New York, 1957), 10–12; Oberman, *Luther: Man between God and the Devil*; Jörg Haustein, *Martin Luthers Stellung zur Zauber- und Hexenwesen* (Stuttgart, 1990); Sigrid Brauner, *Fearless Wives and Frightened Shrews: The Construction of the Witch in Early Modern Germany* (Amherst, 1995), 51–68; Richard Marius, *Martin Luther: The Christian between God and Death* (Cambridge, Mass., 1999). Jörg Haustein has argued that Luther's early and powerful condemnations of witches became less severe after 1526, shifting to an argument for excommunication and exile rather than the death penalty. This seems to have become a general Lutheran view, at least in the case of Johann Weyer (Text 44). Jörg Haustein, "Martin Luther als Gegner des Hexenwahns," in Hartmut Lehmann and Otto Ulbricht, eds., *Vom Unfug des Hexenprozess. Gegner der Hexenvervolgungen von Johann Weyer bis Friedrich Spee* (Wiesbaden, 1992), 35–51.

---

5. *Tischreden*, vol. 3, no. 3491, pp. 355–56.

6. *Table Talk*, no. 3953, p. 298; *Tischreden*, vol. 4, no. 3953, pp. 31–32.

7. *Tischreden*, vol. 3, no. 3979, pp. 51–52. Cf. the fuller legal complaint that witches commit treason against God in *Tischreden*, vol. 6, no. 6836.

First Commandment:
Thou shalt not have strange gods before thee

All the sons of Adam are idolaters, and this is the first commandment of the law. And it must be understood that there are two kinds of idolatry, one exterior and one interior. Exterior idolatry is the worship of trees, stones, beasts, and stars, as is noted in the Old Testament and in the books of the Gentiles. This kind of idolatry proceeds from interior idolatry. Interior idolatry occurs when man, either through fear of punishment or love of what he desires, places his love and faith in something created. . . . This kind of idolatry is dominant in every man unless he is healed by grace in the faith of Jesus Christ, as Psalm 80 says, Hear, O my people. . . . [Luther then uses witchcraft as an example of idolatry, discussing the particular kinds of sorcery to which people tend to resort at different stages of life. In the period called *Adulescentia* (young adulthood), idolaters are inclined to use sorcery to make swords and other weapons stronger, to make women love them, to make themselves invulnerable to wounds, to observe the most propitious time to marry, to beget children, to avoid begetting children, or to find thieves. In the period called *Iuventus* (mature adulthood), to cure sick children, to protect their animals, to seek auguries, to observe "Egyptian" [unfavorable] days, or to practice astrology. The third age is Old Age, and the kinds of sorcery it favors are:]

By witchcraft eyesight may be injured or cured and healthy bodies made ill, blood drawn by arrows, images dedicated, and whomever they wish killed or consumed by an incurable disease. . . . Tempests may be raised, and thunder, destroying fruits, killing animals, and so forth. . . . People consult the Notary Art, or consult crystals or consecrated ointments or ivories to find hidden things. . . . Many believe that they ride on a broom or a goat, still others on other things, to some place, where they celebrate strange rites with others, which is not only forbidden to be done, but even to be believed in . . . or that old women are transformed into cats or other beasts and wander at night, and this, too, must not be believed.

Some believe that they follow a certain lady, others Herodias, others Lady Hulda, others Venus. . . . Some believe that they have demonic familiars. . . . The common folk call these *Vichtelen* or *Helekeppelin*, and they believe that the house that is occupied by these illusions of the demons will be the most fortunate, and they fear more to offend these demons than they fear God and the whole world. . . . They have unions with incubi and succubi of the demons. . . . I omit here mention of women's menstrual blood, used to make philtres of insane sexual passion, often made from the bodies of the dead.

No one should believe that witches and diviners, in order to stir up storms, kill bodies, kill animals, destroy property, &c., are the real causes of these things, nor to believe that creatures of God have this power, except through demons who have God's permission. . . . Except by the will of God no leaf falls from a tree to earth. Therefore, it is forbidden to Christians to think that these evils are caused by demons and witches and are thus ordained by God. God does good through himself, and evil through the evil ones.

Nor is it to be believed that old women are able to transform themselves into cats or other forms and to travel to banquets at night. And this is proved by [C.] xxvi, q. v, c. *Nec mirum* [Text 9]. These are the illusions of the devil, not true things. And this is shown well in an example told by Johannes Keysersperg [Text 39]. An old woman once, in order to deceive a preacher who claimed that her assertions were false, before his eyes anointed herself and sat on a bench and immediately fell asleep and moved her body wildly, whereupon she fell off the bench and injured her head. Later, returned to consciousness, she was convinced that this was an illusion. . . .

[Luther then tells the story of St. Germanus of Auxerre (Text 12) and turns in the sermon to a discussion of saints' cults.]

41
John Calvin: Witchcraft and the Reformation

John Calvin (1509–64) brought the remarkable rigor and logic of his mind, the clarity and forcefulness of his prose, and the total commitment of his soul to the service of the Protestant Reformation; these same qualities are all manifest in his treatment of demonology as well. The role and power of Satan is critical to the concept of witchcraft as it had evolved in Christian Europe, as is the concept of the pact between Devil and witch. Both of these areas are clarified by Calvin in a manner that more than justified the concern with witchcraft and the persecutions which the sixteenth century sustained and intensified. By elaborating the scriptural bases of demonological belief, and insisting on the equal validity of both testaments, Calvin insured that the Reformation would not tamper with church dogma on these matters. He frequently referred his readers to a passage of the New Testament, Ephesians 6:11–12, which starkly summed up his sense of the predicament: "Put on the whole armour of God, that ye may be able to stand against the wiles of the devil. For we wrestle not against flesh and blood, but against principalities, against powers, against the rulers of the darkness of this world."

In 1549 Calvin attacked both judicial astrology and witchcraft in his *Advertissement contre l'astrologie judiciaire*, a response to a defense of astrology by the poet Mellin de St. Gellais that had appeared anonymously in 1546: "Because arrogance is the direct root of all heresies, extravagant fantasies, and false and wicked opinions, it is not at all marvelous that God has let fall into so many delusions those who have not maintained a true disciplining of themselves in order to persevere in obedience to His truth, which is to humble oneself and to fear. . . . For a long time there has been an insane curiosity to attempt to judge by the stars all that will happen to men in the future."[1] Later in the same text Calvin comments on the "witch" of En-dor:

> It is true that all that comes from the devil is nothing but a lie, but God sometimes permits that deceivers may sometimes speak the truth when He wishes to punish unbelief and wickedness by this means. . . . Take, for example, the case of the witch of which Samuel speaks. That which she told Saul did indeed come to pass. Should we say, therefore, that hers was a science based on reason in order to predict hidden things? By no means. God, in His just vengeance by this means tightened the reins on Satan so that that unhappy king might be deceived, just as he deserved.[2]

Calvin's most powerful legacy is the thought and style of his *Institutes of the Christian Religion*, the most complete version of which was printed in 1559. But Calvin's immense literary output also contains many other references to sorcery and witchcraft, particularly in his sermons on Deuteronomy 18: 10–12. Although the meaning of the original Hebrew terms in Deuteronomy had long since become obscure (even as early as the time of the translators of the Septuagint, who had to approximate them with contemporary Greek terms), many sixteenth-century theologians, including Calvin, firmly believed that the original Hebrew corresponded exactly with their own ideas about demonology, sorcery, and witchcraft.

Sermon on Deuteronomy (1555)

SOURCE: *The Sermons of M. Iohn Calvin upon the Fifth Booke of Moses called Deuteronomie* (London, 1583; rprt. Carlisle, Pa., 1987), 668–71. Eng. rev. E. P.

FURTHER READING: Lea, *Materials*, 1: 428–30; William J. Bouwsma, *John Calvin: A Sixteenth-Century Portrait* (New York-Oxford, 1988); Alister E. McGrath, *A Life of John Calvin: A Study in the Shaping*

---

1. Jean Calvin, *Advertissement contre l'astrologie judiciaire*, ed. Olivier Millet (Geneva, 1985), 51.

2. Ibid. 93. Calvin then goes on to cite Deuteronomy 18 and Leviticus 20, listing all forms of sorcery and witchcraft as abominations to God, "and for such iniquities, God has destroyed entire peoples" (94–95).

of Western Culture (Oxford-Cambridge, Mass., 1990). See also Jean
Calvin, *Institutes of the Christian Religion*, ed. John T. McNeill,
trans. Ford Lewis Battles, Library of Christian Classics 20 (Philadelphia, 1960), Book I, ch. XIV, 13–19, pp. 172–79; Book II, ch. IV, 1–2,
pp. 309–11.

The Cix. Sermon which is the third upon the eighteenth chapter
[vv.] 10. 11. 12. 13. 14. 15 There shall not anie bee found among you &c.
We have seen how our Lord, to make his word prevail among the Jews, has
willed them to put away all superstitions from among them. For indeed the
truth of God cannot be coupled with satan's [Calvin's English translator rarely
capitalizes Satan; we have reproduced all capitalization and italicizing in the
1583 edition] lies and corruptions: we must be either altogether the ones or
altogether the others. . . . [augury and divination are also forbidden, because,
"these are stark witcheries, forged by men out of their own fond curiosity, and
blown into their ears by satan." [As for other practices condemned in this passage from Deuteronomy,] Indeed a man might distinguish among them, as
many have labored to do; but it is enough for us to understand that mention is
made here of *Enchanters, Sorcerers, Calkers, workers with Familiars, and of
such as ask counsel of the dead.* As concerning Enchanters, they are not the
jugglers that confuse men's eyes with sleight of hand and make men believe that
they do the things which they do not do: but the devil has such dominion over
the unbelievers that although a thing may not be done in actual deed, yet the
illusion is such that it makes men believe that they see that which they do not
see. And so it is a kind of enchantment, that is to say of devilish illusion, when a
man shall be made to think that one is transformed into a wolf, or that he sees
the shape of a thing that has no actual substance or truth in fact. Now it is
demanded whether such things can be done or not. And why not? We have an
example in Pharaoh's sorcerers [Exodus 7–8], who made frogs come up as well as
Moses did: not that the devil has anything in his own power, for we must not
imagine that he can fight against God. We know that he is under God's hand
and can do nothing without [God's] leave or permission. He may well attempt
much, but yet he cannot stir one finger, as we would say. . . .
   And therefore let us mark (as experience also shows) devils may work many
illusions by enchantments. And truly such things are not done in the dark. For
as long as we are enlightened by God, we need not fear that a man shall seem a
wolf to us, or that such trishtrash shall get the upper hand of us. But if we are
faithless, it is a just reward for our quenching of the light that should have shone
into us and of our turning of our backs on God. And when we will not be ruled
by him, then we no longer discern between white and black, but men seem to us
to be wolves, and all things are out of order, and justly so. Therefore, whereas

mention is made here of such as misshape things by their enchantments, let us note that the law is not superfluous. For since the case stands so, it is to be concluded that such things may befall, of which we have examples.

But for all that, it is abominable before God, and so likewise are *Soothsayers*. It is a question whether it is possible for a man to foretell of things, for it is God's office to foreknow things to come; how then may it belong to the devil? It is certain, as Isaiah says [Is. 41: 23], that idols can foresee nothing. And as for Satan, he must always needs be the father of lies and deceive all who ask counsel of him. Yet notwithstanding all this, God does now and then allow satan to tell of things to come, and this is for the hardening of those who will not obey the truth . . . Yet it is true also that soothsayers lie more often than not, and by that means our Lord deludes them that seek counsel with satan after this fashion. And let us not think it strange, though enchanters, soothsayers, and such other like do now and then tell of things to come; for it is God's just patience so that they may be plunged into error more deeply. For as much as they would be willingly deceived, he lets them be so, that they may perish. Thus you see why the law was made concerning such people who prophesy of things to come.

Also he speaks of *Sorcerers*. And this sort has many types. For what a sin it is, that men should forsake God and give themselves over to Satan. Must they not fall into horrible confusion? Yes, for after Satan has possessed us once and stopped our eyes, and God has withdrawn his light from us, so that we are destitute of his holy spirit and devoid of all reason, then there follow infinite abuses without end or measure. And many sorceries come from this condition. Many incredible things are reported of Sorcerers. And truly when we hear them spoken of, we ought not only to dislike them, but also to be sorrowful in our hearts, yes, and the very hairs of our heads ought to stand up when we encounter them. But we must also keep in mind that they are the vengeances of God upon such as have forsaken him. And their state may be a reason for us to remain in awe and fear; let us learn not to tempt our God, nor to play with him, since we see men become so brutish after they have once turned away from the right path.

Truly, if there had been no more than two or three examples of this, it might well seem strange to us. But we know that in all ages and in all Nations Sorcery or witchcraft has held sway, and even greater sway because it has rejected God's truth. . . .

Also mention is made [in the Deuteronomy text] of those who have Familiars. Satan's illusions must indeed be horrible. But what? These have existed in all ages, and we see a notable example in the case of King Saul, when he went to the Witch [of En-dor: 1 Sam. 28]. He as king had earlier forbidden all enchantments and all kind of damnable crafts, and he had behaved virtuously in executing God's law. And yet in the end he became so wretched that he fell to running after a Witch. And what was the cause of this, if not that he despised God? Whereupon in the end he fell into despair and gave himself over altogether to Satan. For if you look advisedly into the matter, you will find that Satan's illusions get the upper hand on men when their wits are amazed because of sorrow that gnaws at them inwardly, and for that, instead of receiving some comfort from God's word, they become overwhelmed with such anguish that they fall into utter despair. When does Satan in bodily shape meet some man and entangle him in his snares? When that man is in some grief of mind, or some hatred against his neighbor, or when a woman is contemptuous of her husband. . . . Of these things we have a fair warning in Saul. . . . He went after Witches. Whereas he had punished enchanters before, now he goes to seek them. And what came of it? Samuel was shown to him in a shape, that is to say in a shadow and fantasy so that Saul thought that the prophet had indeed been raised up by the Witch. . . .

Finally Deuteronomy mentions those who *take counsel of the dead*. For it is not our Lord's will that we should have anything to do with the dead. Therefore, they who use such conjurations go about to pervert the whole order of nature. For let men do what they can, yet they cannot bring the living and the dead together, but the devil steps in between them and pretends to be the persons of the dead so that as to outward appearance the dead man himself seems to appear, whereas in truth it is the devil that works such illusions. . . . And thereby we see also that all the things that have ever been said of the coming up again of dead men's ghosts have been but sleights of satan, and when men have been beguiled by that it was the same as if they had yielded themselves to satan.

And it was held for great devotion in Poperie [Roman Catholicism]. The reason why they make pilgrimages and pay for Masses to be sung and their feast of all souls [November 2] to be kept once a year was that a devout Monk who had an idle head had a Revelation. He heard the cries of dead men's souls, and immediately the Papists [Roman Catholics] concluded that a solemn feast was to be kept for the dead and such and such things were to be done for them. It was nothing other than mere Witchery that men have invented service for the dead in Popedom [Roman Catholicism], the very thing that God so condemns in this text [of Deuteronomy] and utterly abhors. And all they have for their devotion after this fashion to pray for the dead are witches and sorcerers, for they believe in Satan's enchantments in despite of God. . . .

By all this we see that although other vices were to be pardoned, yet this one ought to be punished and utterly rooted out. Therefore, if we want to be taken for God's people, let us see what this word *abomination* signifies: namely, that we must beware of sorceries, enchantments, and other similar things. And indeed we see how such things have always been despised, even among the heathen. However much witchcraft has reigned . . . It is a monster, and a shameful thing. And even the heathens called it this. . . . It is true that in Poperie all are witches in their idolatries, for in the fifteenth [chapter] of the first book of Samuel [1 Sam. 15: 23] God couples those two things together, and I have told you already that the service of the dead is a kind of witchcraft. Yet notwithstanding, they [Roman Catholics] always condemn the term. And why? Because God has permitted it to become more inexcusable. So then let us take note that it is not for us to tolerate either enchanters or witches among us. And if these are forbidden, we must understand by this that all other kinds of Wizardry are deadly crimes before God. And if Judges and Magistrates do their duties, it is certain that they will no more tolerate them than they tolerate murderers. . . . Why? It is an overthrowing of God's service and a perversion of the order of nature. Is it not worthy of punishment, and punishment again, if the order of nature should be confounded between men and brute beasts? Is there any reason for so doing? And surely when men begin with such enchantments it is certain that they fall into a deeper and more dreadful dungeon than they would if they had given their bodies over to company with the brute beasts [that is, bestiality]. And yet we see the selfsame illusions wrought by satan upon all witches and sorcerers. And what is the original cause of this, but that they are turned away from God's truth. Although there might be no further evil in this than in attributing God's office to satan, yet it is a matter in no wise to be tolderated. . . .

Is it not making war on God if this is tolerated? Then, let us note that if we want to be taken for Christians, Witchcrafts, enchantments, and such other similar things must be no more tolerated among us than Robberies and Murders.

42
Lambert Daneau: *De veneficiis* (1564)

The Latin dialogue by the Calvinist preacher Lambert Daneau (1530–1590) was the second tract on witchcraft to be printed in England, and in English (1575). Daneau was a Huguenot pastor near Orléans, where he wrote the work in the literary form of a dialogue between two characters (possibly modeled on Gianfrancesco Pico's *Strix* [Text 38] or similar literary treatments of the subject) after hearing of a number of trials for witchcraft in Paris and encountering the skepticism with which some thinkers in France reacted to them. Daneau's work reflects the thought of Calvin and was first printed in the Calvinist city of Geneva, where Daneau lived after leaving Orléans. Daneau's biblical and classical learning is greatly in evidence in the dialogue, and his free citation of classical Greek and Latin poets illustrates a common sixteenth-century aspect of the revival of classical learning—it could also be brought anachronistically to bear in support of contemporary witchcraft beliefs. Daneau also liberally cites early Christian writers, Roman law, Gratian (Texts 5 and 9), and the condemnation of sorcery by the Paris theology faculty in 1398 (Text 23).

Daneau's dialogue appears to have been brought to England, along with a number of Calvinist ideas about witchcraft, by the returning Marian exiles, notable among whom was Bishop John Jewel, who also wrote on witchcraft, preached vigorously against it to Queen Elizabeth I herself, and, with others, introduced the Calvinist version of the offense and conviction of the reality of the crime to England, which had passed a statute against witchcraft in 1563. Daneau's work was used by later writers in support of witchcraft beliefs (although Daneau makes no statement about the gender of the witches and assumes that they are simply those people of both sexes who had once been termed sorcerers) and prosecutions and by Reginald Scot, the English skeptic (Text 60), in 1584 to denounce witchcraft beliefs.

SOURCE: Lambert Daneau, *A Dialogue of Witches in foretime commonly called Sorcerers* (Latin original, Geneva, 1564; English translation, 1575). Eng., rev. E. P.

FURTHER READING: Lea, *Materials*, 2: 545–47. There are other short excerpts from Daneau translated in P. G. Maxwell-Stuart, *The Occult in Early Modern Europe: A Documentary History* (New York, 1999), 173–74, 177.

Anthony: But many suppose this to be the stuff of fables, that any people should be termed witches or sorcerers, and they cannot persuade themselves that these people could harm anybody. Therefore they laugh at your opinion because it does not seem to be supported by reason.

Theophilus: I am not ignorant of this, Anthony, and truly I remember when I sojourned in Orléans upon Loire, that there was a man witch, not only taken and accused, but also after sufficient inquiry and lawful conviction of the fault by the magistrates of that city was condemned and appealed that sentence to the high court of Paris. The Senate reversed his conviction, and also laughed at and lightly regarded the crime, and in the end sent him home as accused of a frivolous matter. The man, however, continuing his accustomed wickedness, and having killed many people with his poisonous sorceries, at length was executed by the command of the magistrates of Orleans. . . .

Anthony: By what names then, I pray you, did the ancient authors of the pure Latin tongue term these witches?

Theophilus: They called men witches *maleficos*, and the women who were given to such arts they termed *veneficas*, *sagas*, *thesalas*, *magas*, *lamias*, and *strigas*, all which words may be observed in the good and pure writers of the Latin tongue, Horace, in the first book of verses the xviii Ode, in his Epodes the xvii Ode, and in the first book of sermons the viii satire. Such a one in his time was Canidia; such a one was Circe, of whom Homer writes in the tenth book of the Odyssey; such a one was Medea of whom Ovid speaks in the seventh book of the Metamorphoses. To be brief, such a one was she of whom Lucan writes in the sixth book of the Pharsalia, with many more, of whom mention is made in sundry histories. These writers just cited, although they were poets, yet neither made up nor devised anything beside the truth, since such things as they saw were known and frequented in their own times. . . .

Anthony: Can you show me the cause, Theophilus, why witchcraft should exist in our time?

Theophilus: Truly, it is the terrible judgment of God against us, the cause of which is unknown to us. For the judgments of God, although they are hidden from us, are yet just and holy. . . . How much more the world now shamefully and obstinately rejects the word of God and its revealed light than it ever did before. How much more men now show themselves unthankful towards God; therefore, the more just cause God has to forsake them and give them over to Satan to revenge their contempt of His name. . . . So in this our age, wherein by God's great and incomprehensible benefits towards mankind, as a special gift, He has revealed to us the light of His holy gospel, for very justice He will have it that more despisers of this revealed light, more now than before, fall into the snares of Satan and become sorcerers, that is to say, addicted to Satan. . . .

Anthony: How, Theophilus, can this kind of people cast their devilish poisons and intoxications upon men or brute beasts? What can they infect with their sorceries in the air, water, herbs, and make havoc upon all things, as they themselves plainly confess . . . ?

Theophilus: Inasmuch as these witches are devilish and very crafty, truly they can infect with their poison whatever is on the earth that is corruptible and mortal, unless it is prevented by God. And there is nothing in this inferior world which is not of that kind, that is, mortal and corruptible. Therefore we must confess that their art has power over all these inferior things.

Anthony: Theophilus, where have you learned all these terrible things?

Theophilus: From their confessions and from innumerable judgments pronounced against them. . . . Don't you believe, Anthony, that sorcerers meet together and are bodily present at their devilish conventicles and synagogues?

Anthony: Only mentally and under the illusions of the devil. . . .

Theophilus: I don't deny that this is a matter of great controversy . . . but the constant confessions of sorcerers themselves, along with other infinite testimonies are against you and your opinion . . . for they confess these things when they are near death and when they are condemned and led to execution for that offense, and when they are so tormented, when such talk can help them no longer. . . .

Anthony: I pray you tell me how a man may in the end escape the fury and mischief of these men?

Theophilus: Surely, Anthony, there is no medicine against them . . . saving this only, that we most earnestly commit ourselves, and our life, every day and every moment unto God our father, commending ourselves unto Him in most sincere prayer, both in the morning when we rise, and when we go to bed.

43
Martín de Castañega,
Tratado muy sotil y bien fundado (1529)

Martín de Castañega, a Franciscan, published his skeptical tract in 1529, after having witnessed a series of trials for witchcraft at Pamplona in 1527. Although Spanish concerns with sorcery and witchcraft had generally been secondary to the problems of Judaizing, and, later of Protestantism, there had been trials for witchcraft at Calahorra in 1507, and Spanish theologians had written on the subject of sorcery and witchcraft since the mid-fifteenth century—notably Juan de Torquemada and Friar Lopé de Barrientos around 1450. The latter mentions the sabbat, perhaps the earliest appearance of the term in Spain, as the *Aquelarre*, and says, "There are women who call themselves *brujas* and believe and say that they go in the night with Diana, goddess of the pagans, riding on beasts and going and passing over vast spaces of land."[1] But both writers agree with the *Canon Episcopi* (Text 5) that these are only illusions, as does the anonymous *Repertorium on the Depravity of Heretics* of 1494 when it calls these women *xorguinae*.[2]

Alfonso de Spina, whose *Fortalicium fidei*, written in 1458–60 and printed in 1494, in its discussion of demonology included a class of demons who deceived old women into thinking that they flew at night, apostasized from Christianity, and killed children.[3] Around the same time (the date is uncertain, since he mentions Nider, but neither the *Malleus Maleficarum* nor the Spanish Inquisition), Martín de Arles y Androsilla, a canon of Pamplona, wrote his *Treatise on Superstition*, first printed in 1517. Martín de Arles admits that injurious witchcraft really occurs, but he denies the reality of bodily flight to the sabbat, a common theme among Spanish demonologists until the sixteenth century.[4]

Castañega's treatise was followed in Spain in 1530 or 1531 by Pedro Ciruelo's *Reprobations of Superstitions and Witchcrafts*, a treatise

---

1. Hansen, *Quellen*, 124; Lea, *Materials*, 1: 191.
2. Lea, *Materials*, 1: 193.
3. Extensive discussion and paraphrase in Lea, *Materials*, 1: 285–92.
4. Discussion in Lea, *Materials*, 1: 297–98. There is an extract translated in Maxwell-Stuart, *The Occult in Early Modern Europe*, 188–89.

much more in agreement with contemporary beliefs and anxieties and one that circulated much more widely.[5]

SOURCE: David H. Darst, "Witchcraft in Spain: The Testimony of Martín de Castañega's Treatise on Superstition and Witchcraft (1529)," *Proceedings of the American Philosophical Society* 123 (1979): 298–322.

I

This is the way the devil nowadays procures simple Christians and curious folk not well versed in the faith, as well as those who are inordinately inclined to temporal riches, honors, and vanities, to licentious carnal delights, and to the vain investigations of occult matters: he deceives them as he did the first woman by promising them wisdom and knowledge of things that cannot be achieved through natural means, such as knowledge of secret events that occur in remote parts. Since all naturally are inclined to know—and especially about occult and other hidden matters—thus it happens that many curious and less intelligent persons are deceived either by a greed for abundant knowledge or by a cupidity for achieving and having those things they desire with an inordinate appetite. Seeing that their own efforts are not enough, they accept the aid of the devil, who as their lord, protector, and master promises those things. . . .

The devil also tempts and deceives those who desire and procure to know secret, occult, and future things, as happened with Saul (1 Samuel 28), who consulted that pythoness to learn who would win an upcoming battle.

No one should consider it strange that the devil tempts poor people who desire inordinately temporal things, since he did not hesitate to tempt even Christ by offering him worldly riches; yet he saw our Lord despise them all. We see every day in our own experience how poor women and needy clerics take up the office of conjurers, witches, necromancers, and diviners in order to maintain themselves and have enough to eat; and they always have their houses full of people. We read the same about the prophet Balaam (Numbers 22), a covetous and ambitious necromancer. In this way the devil has his disciples and following, and he attempts to create a congregation with them. . . .

IV. Who the Diabolical Church's Ministers Are

The ministers of these diabolical execrations are, according to John Gerson (in *De Erroribus Circa Artem Magicam*), all those consecrated and dedicated to the devil by an express or occult pact. To understand this one must note the following explanations. An express pact with the devil is of two kinds. One is so clear and express that with formal words, denying the Faith, they profess anew to the

5. Lea, *Materials*, 1: 413–15; *Pedro Ciruelo's A Treatise Reproving All Superstitions and Forms of Witchcraft*, trans. Eugene A. Maio and D'Orsay W. Pearson (Rutherford, N.J., 1977).

devil in his presence, who appears to them in any form and figure he desires to take. They give him complete obedience and offer him their body and soul.

I met some of these witches and saw some burned and reconciled. One man said that the devil made him deny God and the Faith, but the devil could never make him deny Our Lady. He was a small, old man, and he recognized his sin and was reconciled. I could say the same about many others with whom I spoke and conversed, and I heard from their own mouths and depositions the ways that they first fell into error.

Others have an express and explicit pact with the devil, not because they have once spoken to him or seen him in some well-known aspect, but because they make the pact with his disciples, who are other enchanters, witches, or sorcerers. These people take the same vows as the others; for, although they never speak to the devil and have never seen him in any figure, they themselves renounce their faith and make a pact to serve the devil. They do the same ceremonies that other witches do or those that the devil teaches them and inspires them to do. Both of these types of people are consecrated to the devil— by express pact and are commonly called witches (*brujos*) or *jorguinos* or *megos*, which are corrupt words. *Sorguino* (commonly pronounced *jorguino*) comes from the word *sortílego* (L., *sortilegus*, conjurer), and the word *mego* comes from *mago* (L., *magus*, magician), whose meanings are common and clear in the writings of the Scholastics and appear in various chapters of the *Decretum* (of Burchard of Worms) (Text 6). The name *bruja* is from the Italian (I. *bruciare*) and means to burn or to sear, because the punishment for such conjurers and magicians is burning at the stake; and thus the name was given to them, but with the Spanish pronunciation rather than the Italian.

An implicit or occult pact is also of two kinds. Some make an occult pact with the devil without either denying or renouncing the formalities of the Catholic faith, yet at the same time they believe and take part in diabolical ceremonies and invocations. These people have an occult and tacit pact with the devil because hidden within such execrations and ceremonies and superstitions is apostasy of the Christian faith; for he who has confidence in something other than Christ or who asks for aid from someone other than Christ is against Christ and his law. These people are commonly called witches (*hechíceros*). There are others who don't believe in any of these things, but sometimes they consent and practice them, assuming that any remedy will do to achieve bodily health or some other thing they need; and these people commit mortal sin and also have an occult pact, although not as serious as the other kinds.

V. Why the Devil Has More Female Disciples Than Male Ones
There are more women than men consecrated and dedicated to the devil. The first reason is because Christ forbade them to administer the sacraments, and therefore the devil gives them the authority to do it with his execrations. The

second reason is because women are more easily deceived by the devil, as is shown by the deception of the first woman, to whom the devil had recourse before going to the man (Genesis 3). The third reason is because women are more curious to know and investigate occult lore, since their nature denies them access to such matters. The fourth reason is because women are more talkative than men and can't keep a secret; and thus they teach others, which the men don't do as frequently. The fifth reason is because women are more subject to anger and are more vindictive. Since they have less strength and means to avenge themselves on people with whom they are angry, they procure and seek vengeance and favor of the devil. The sixth reason is because the spells that men cast are attributed to some science or art, and the common people therefore call them necromancers and not warlocks. Such were the evil sorcerers of the Pharaoh (Exodus 7), whom scholars call magicians. They made serpents to appear and disappear in the King's presence by means of the devil's ministry, counteracting thereby the true miracles that God did through Moses. Balaam (Numbers 22) was also a necromantic prophet. But women, since they don't have any art or science as an excuse, can't be called necromancers (although Juan de Mena called Medea a necromancer for poetic reasons in *El laberinto de la fortuna*), rather they are called *megas, brujas, hechiceras, jorguinas*, or *adevinas* (soothsayers), as was also that pythoness to whom Saul had recourse to learn if he would win or lose an upcoming battle against the Philistines (I Samuel 28). In truth, there are just as many warlocks consecrated to the devil who pass for necromancers as there are simple women, because the devil does not respond or aid the invocations and conjurations of the necromancer by reason of any power or efficacy that the magician's art has over the devil, for there is no such science or art unless the two have made a pact. Thus the real difference is not among the ministers of the devil but among the different manners the devil uses to deceive and contract familiarity with men; so he will be the best necromancer who best follows and complies with the devil's will, and not he who knows the most arts and formulas, as in a true science.

Most of the women are old and poor rather than rich and young, because they become old the men don't pay any attention to them. They therefore have recourse to the devil, who satisfies their appetites. This is especially the case if the women were inclined and given to vices of the flesh when they were young. The devil deceives this kind of old woman by promising to satisfy her appetites, and he actually keeps his word in a way that will be described in Chapter XI. There are also more poor and needy women because, as with the other vices, poverty is often the occasion for many misdeeds in people that don't have a strong will or much patience. Since they think the devil will tend to their needs or respond to their desires and appetites, old and poor women are more easily deceived than young girls are, for the devil promises them nothing will be lacking if they follow him. No one should marvel that the hags don't receive anything they can use, however, because God doesn't consent that the devils have so much power to deceive people. If Satan had permission to give gold and silver to his disciples, I don't think anyone could be found to punish the wayward ones. The devil therefore only shows them great treasures, which he would indeed give if God would permit it. That will happen at the time of the Antichrist, but at present it is all deceit.

VI. How Those Consecrated to the Devil Can Fly Through the Air

Many doubt that witches can fly through the air and walk on water, as some say; and many church doctors have denied it. Therefore the following rule must be stated: knowing that flying through the air is possible, that it has been seen several times, that it and similar things are proven by scripture, and that the very persons deceived by the devil confess it to be so, there is no reason why it should not be believed. We read that the angel carried Habacuc from Judaea to Babylon with the food that he was taking to the reapers so that Daniel, who was in the lion's den in Babylon, could eat (Daniel 14, Vulgate Edition). Scripture also reports that the angel pulled Habacuc off his horse by the hair to show thereby the angel's ability to carry away a man. We likewise read that during the temptation of Christ the devil carried him from the desert to the pinnacle of the temple in Jerusalem; and afterwards he carried him from there to a high mountain where he showed him all the kingdoms of the world (Luke 4, Matthew 4). It is also said that the enchanter Simon Magus tried to ascend to heaven while Saint Peter was preaching about Jesus Christ. He was carried through the air in everyone's presence by demons who transported him to another spot to deceive and make people believe he had been carried to heaven. His ruse would have worked except for the prayers and petitions of Saint Peter, which were so effective that the devils deserted Simon Magus and he fell from aloft, burst open, and died (from the apocryphal *Acts of St. Peter*).

One must assume that if Simon Magus attempted such a novelty in public he had flown through the air many times before, crossing large expanses in little time with the aid of the devil. Are we therefore supposed to doubt it, since the devil has the power and man the obedience to him if God permits it and gives permission for it to happen? And one should also believe that God permits the devil to carry his disciples through the air, for God let himself be carried thusly to the above mentioned places. It appears, then, that since it is possible and since the witches themselves confess they go to strange and remote lands, it ought to be believed; although sometimes it is fairly obvious that the witches were deluded.

It is necessary to remark, however, that as we read and discover how the devil and any other good or bad angel by natural powers and virtues can carry someone through the air and over water, God permitting it, we also read how people can be driven out of their senses, which the doctors call ecstasy. During these ecstasies they have revelations of great secrets and of things that occur in remote areas, and these people think they are there. Thus we read of Saint Paul, who says he was caught up to the third heaven (2 Corinthians 12: 2), which is the Empyrean; and he says he does not know how it happened, bodily or spiritually. It therefore appears that being out of his senses and not using them, *in extasi mentis* caught up, he saw secrets that he didn't have permission to describe, and he wasn't sure in what way he was in heaven, bodily or spiritually. The devil can in his own way disturb the human senses, especially during a heavy sleep, to make a person think he is in the place that the devil represents to him.

There are apparently two ways the devil ministers to his disciples. Some really go to faraway lands and remote places by the devil's aid; others, carried away out of their senses as in a heavy sleep, have diabolical revelations of remote and occult—and often false—things, whereby they many times affirm what is not true. These latter are deceived by the devil, yet take pleasure and delight in those things as if their bodies were really there. All disciples, whether of the first or the second kind, have an explicit and express pact with the devil and he with them, and they are called *brujos*.

Not even the Council of Ancyra in the *Canon Episcopi* is against what I say; and because so many are deceived by its statements I will state clearly what the *Canon* reprobated and condemned, summing it up in four conclusions. First, Diana and Herodias, as the *Canon* says, were two normal women killed and not resuscitated. To say that live women converse with the dead, as those wicked women affirmed, is an error, a public deceit, and an illusion of the devil. Second, Diana and Herodias were wicked and faithless women when they lived. To affirm they were goddesses or that there was some divinity, power, or grace in them is a manifest error and blasphemy. Third, it is false to believe that the devil, because he can appear in various shapes, forms, and natures, can actually convert things to other substances and natures, like converting a man into a fox or a goat or some similar thing and afterwards returning the person to his original form, as many evil persons have said and affirmed. Fourth, it is possible that when wicked people think they walk through the air they are only imagining it by the devil's deceit, as declared above. These are the errors that the *Canon* wishes to eliminate and condemn, but it doesn't deny the possibility of what I have explained above.

VII. How the Devil's Disciples Can Take Various Shapes
No one should doubt that the devil can feign various shapes as often as he likes to deceive or frighten people. Reason demonstrates this and experience is a good witness that it has often happened, for it is documented in the lives of the Egyptian church fathers. The devil can do the same thing for his disciples, whom also he can show and transport in the shape he desires without losing any of their substance and volume, so well can Satan make and feign a deceit for the

eyes of those that would see it. Some examples can be found in the lives of the saints, for such was the case in Saint Augustine's discussion about Ulysses' companions, whom that famous sorceress *mega* Circe transfigured into beasts (*City of God*, XVIII, 8).

The devil can also make himself and his disciples invisible or partially so. The reason is this: eyesight tires from the visible rays that proceed from the visible thing, as is demonstrated in perspective. The devil can cause those visible rays to become tied up in such a way that they represent the figure he desires; or he can divert the rays so they don't go straight to the eyes looking at it. Thus the thing would be invisible, since it would not be seen by the eyes looking at it. Christ appeared thusly in the guise of a pilgrim and a gardener, and another time he made himself invisible when he hid in the temple. By the same process the devil transports his disciples invisibly or in any desired shape without taking or changing any of the true substance, quantity, and volume that the person has, as is read of Simon Magus. But these people can't leave their houses except through windows or open doors, and if they are closed the devil opens them. They can't leave through a window or door smaller than their body either, because the devil can't take away or diminish the volume of the body, nor the body's necessity to occupy space; so they need the same size door or window a person of normal size and measure needs. Although they could leave in the apparent form of a bird or a cat or a fox, or totally invisible, they still couldn't leave through a space smaller than a normal body occupies. The devil's disciples themselves confess to this, and if someone should claim otherwise it would be a blatant lie. . . .

XXIV. A Catholic Exhortation Against Simpleminded and Superstitious Christians

Finally, I exhort and warn all Christians in the name of Jesus Christ to heed this doctrine, to note the difference between the two lords, the one true, who is Jesus Christ our Redeemer, Creator, and Glorifier, and the other a tyrant, the devil, condemned eternally, our first enemy and subtle deceiver. He who serves Satan most will be the least free, and will suffer the worst pains and torments. Contemplate the Catholic Sacrament of the Holy Mother Church, all saintly and clean, ordered and established by Christ for the remedy of our sins; and look with clear eyes at the filth, vanity, and foolishness that the diabolical execrations and bewitchments bring to deceive and condemn the devil's disciples and followers. Think about the mocking and ridicule that the devil heaps on those who follow him, and the honor that comes to those who follow and serve Jesus Christ, plus the glory and goods that await them in the other world. To free oneself from the ties and deceits of the devil, one should devoutly hear mass on all holy days, listening closely to the sermon, and as often as possible confess with good confessors when the church requires. For those who are most tempted by the devil, be obedient to all the Church's commandments, and fear incurring any excommunication, and don't go too many days without taking communion. Don't commit any frivolities that the Church forbids, nor say prayers or words the Church doesn't use; and when there is any doubt, speak to your priest or confessor. Simple women shouldn't cure children or other people, especially with words and things that they wouldn't want learned men to see and hear. Nor should you go to those inclined or dedicated to these cures. Procure to ignore things you don't need to know or that tax your brain; don't be curious about occult things, desiring to know what you can't naturally learn; and always live with fear of going against the faith of the Holy Mother Church and its commands, proposing never to part from the Catholic faith. Pray the Creed often where the articles of faith are stated when you get out of bed and at night before retiring. Make the sign of the cross, naming Jesus Christ often, and say the creed and the other prayers you know, especially the Lord's prayer and the Ave Maria. I beseech the preachers who visit these lands to teach and declare these things, for they are most necessary and profitable and more meritorious to those who preach than other vain and curious speculations. I also humbly suplicate all prelates and other religious men, by whose negligence their subjects fall into deceits and errors, that they watch over and order these remedies provided rather than attending to other things which are of civil and temporal interest, because the latter properly belong to civil investigators. The *Canon Episcopi* specifically orders this. Thereby freeing their sheep from the diabolical snares and guiding them along the true and sure road, they will merit double honor in this world and infinite glory in the next.

44
Johann Weyer:
De praestigiis daemonum (1563)

Although a number of demonologists had long debated the reality of one or another aspect of accusations made against witches, particularly the question of bodily flight to the sabbat, Johann Weyer (1515–88) was the first critic to deny the existence of witches altogether, arguing that it was not the witches who were recruited by the devil to harm mankind, but that the very belief that witches existed at all was a harmful diabolical invention.

Weyer studied with Heinrich Cornelius Agrippa von Nettesheim, a physician and student of learned magic (and also a critic of several early sixteenth-century witchcraft trials) and then at the universities of Paris and Orléans in 1534–37. He became the municipal physician of Arnhem in Gelderland in 1545 and in 1550 physician to the duke of Jülich-Berg and Cleves in the ducal capital of Düsseldorf. Weyer retired in 1578 and died in 1588.

Weyer published the *De praestigiis daemonum* in Latin in 1563 and published expanded editions in 1564, 1566, 1577, and 1583, as well as an abridged German translation by himself in 1566, which was reprinted in 1567 and 1578. In essence the book argued that although diabolical sorcerers did indeed exist and should be severely prosecuted, witchcraft as defined in the sixteenth century was an impossible crime, that no human agency could cause the acts witches were accused and convicted of, that no binding contract could exist between humans and demons (deriving his argument from the Roman law of contracts), and that witchcraft confessions were simply the products of (mostly) female senile dementia.

Weyer also turned on its head the sixteenth-century argument that scripture and ancient authors had described the same thing as sixteenth-century witch-hunters. The very claim that allowed prosecutors to escape the *Canon Episcopi*'s claims of illusion—that modern witches were not those spoken of by Gratian—allowed Weyer to argue that therefore they were unknown to the ancients, who spoke of no diabolical pact. Weyer's humane Lutheranism then used contemporary Hebrew scholarship to argue his point that none of the Old Testament instances so favored by (especially Calvinist) demonologists spoke of contemporary witchcraft (Text 41).[1] He then made a point of discussing cases of people falsely convicted of witchcraft.

Weyer's work is extremely long and detailed, and these excerpts do not do it justice. It aroused a furious controversy shortly after its publication and was attacked by virtually every later demonologist, Protestant and Catholic, notably Jean Bodin (Text 45) until well into the seventeenth century. It was also used by skeptics and critics of the witchcraft prosecutions.

SOURCE: *On Witchcraft: An Abridged Translation of Johann Weyer's "De praestigiis daemonum."* Ed. Benjamin G. Kohl and H. C. Erik Midelfort, trans. John Shea (Asheville, N.C., 1998), 44–49, 276–78.

---

1. This text is included here because it forms part of an important, but little studied aspect of the witchcraft debate in the sixteenth and seventeenth centuries—the validity of Hebrew and Greek terminology in considering sixteenth- and seventeenth-century people accused of witchcraft. Although he was no great Hebraist, Weyer argued against the Hebraism of Calvin and other writers who applied Old Testament instances and terms literally to the witchcraft of their own century. On the general question, see Haustein, "Bibelauslegung und Bibelkritik," 249–67.

FURTHER READING: Lea, *Materials*, 2: 490–545; Kohl and Midelfort, introduction to *On Witchcraft*, xv–xlvi, with further references.

A. Book 2, Chapter 1:
Old Testament Names Denoting Magicians of Ill Repute and Poisoners

When a question is raised or a discussion begun about the activities of witches, men soon offer the testimony of scriptural passages containing the term "magician," or "evil-doer," or "enchanter," or "poisoner," or even "juggler" (as some translate). They then affirm that these terms denote, without distinction of meaning, the women who are commonly called "witches" or "wise women." I find, however, that these monstrous persons with their arts, their illusions, and their forbidden forms of divination are represented in differing ways by the Rabbis and the Hebrew interpreters, that our Latin translators use different names to describe them, and that the Greek translation does not agree precisely with the Hebrew or with the Latin translation. This will be obvious if you carefully compare the Hebrew text with any version and examine attentively the judgments of the Rabbis and the interpreters on all of these passages in which there is any mention of such prodigies: Exod. 7, 8, 9, 22; Lev. 19, 20; Deut. 18; Jer. 27; Dan. 2; 4 Kings 21; 2 Paral. 33, and all the others. Because of such differences and disagreements among the interpreters, I have consulted, on the aforesaid passages, a man most learned in all respects and most skilled in languages, Doctor Andreas Masius, who has explained as follows seven Hebrew words relating to magic and employed in the passages in question.

The first word, *Chasaph*, I see constantly translated in the Vulgate as signifying that evil-doing whereby men who are maddened by the demon do harm (or at least think they do), through the evil arts, to cattle, to crops, and even to human beings. As a result of these misdeeds, they are called evil-doers, and the law of Moses would have them banished from life, by the decree of Exodus 22: 6 [18]. "Thou shalt not suffer an evil-doer [*malefica*, fem.] to live." The word *Mechassepha*, which the law employs here, is derived from *Chasaph*; and it is put into the feminine gender (as the interpreters say), not because the law wishes men to be unpunished, but because the female sex, on account of its innate simplicity, is more frequently susceptible to the demon's ambushes. Therefore, the Greek translation which we ascribe to the seventy elders [the Septuagint] translates this decree more freely: "You shall not allow poisoners to live" (by the Latin Masculine I mean to include both masculine and feminine). I observe moreover that the word in question *Chasaph* and its derivatives are hardly ever used in the aforementioned Greek translation except to indicate poisoning—that is, by the Greek words *pharmakos, pharmakeus, pharmaka*, and other words of the same root. Even the common people (not to mention our authors, both Greek and Latin) believe that those whom we call "evil-doers" practice and accomplish their nefarious arts with the help of drugs, poisons, and medications, But Ibn Ezra, a writer of great repute among the Hebrews, says that the word *Chasaph* refers properly to sleights, that is, to those illusions whereby things are presented to our eyes otherwise than they really are. Even if we should grant his point (although to me it certainly seems hard to demonstrate it from Sacred Scripture), still, we read in the second chapter of Daniel that among other interpreters of his dream, Nebuchadnezzar summoned *Mechassephim*. Now if you translate the word as "jugglers, illusionists," I do not know what they could have contributed by their art to the explaining of a dream, since that art is wholly deceptive and illusory. One commentator upon this passage, Levi, the son of Gerson and a most eminent Hebrew philosopher, therefore says that the *Mechassephim* are those who profess the art of astrology; that is, of bringing spirits [*Genii*] down from the sky and coaxing them into certain inscribed characters which have been formed and fashioned at specific times and during specific courses of the constellations. When they have been thus beguiled, the *Mechassephim* incite them to help or harm certain chosen individuals, and they compel them to other tasks of every description, such as that of giving signs and predictions about hidden matters. In Malach. 3:5, *mechassephim* and *memaphim* are joined together—that is, "evil-doers" and "adulterers." If you wish my opinion as well, I should think that the word has broad application and that it refers to every sort of magical art, and I see that the majority of the Hebrews are also of this opinion. Yet I see that the Syrians use the word as the equivalent of *leitourgein* "to perform a religious act or to be engaged in sacred rites," also "to pray humbly and devoutly." And since the Syrians employ the concept thus, it is likely that the ancient Hebrews also once so used it. For it often happens that some word which has been lost from its own language is found preserved in a neighboring language. Thus today the Ligurians call the lotus tree or its fruit "Greek bean," although Latin-speakers do not now know what "Greek bean" is.

The second word was *Kasam*. It seems to pertain especially to prognostications of the future. Therefore, in the Greek Bible it is everywhere rendered (so far as I know) by the word *mantheuesthai*, which means "prophesy": as in Deut. 18, Jerem. 27, and elsewhere. But in the Latin Bible (and I am speaking always of the Vulgate translation) it is sometimes translated by "to foretell by entrails" and sometimes by "to divine," as in the passages that I have cited. There is also a passage, however, in which it is taken in a good sense for one who, because of the keenness of his more subtle intelligence, can foresee or conjecture the future, and see clearly what actions must be taken. This is how Isaiah (3:2) uses the word when he includes such persons among those men of Jerusalem who might save the nation.

The third word *Onen*, in the Latin Bible is sometimes translated "to observe dreams" (as in Deut. 18 and 2 Paral. 33), sometimes "to take omens from birds" (as Jerem. 27), sometimes also "to divine" (as in Micah 5). And in the Greek Bible it is sometimes rendered *oionizesthai*, "to take omens from birds," and generally by *apophthengesthai*, "to give forth oracles" (Micah 5). The ancient Hebrews say that this word properly applies to those who observe superstitiously the minute divisions of time, designating some as favorable and others as unfavorable for enterprises.

The fourth word *Nahas* (Deut. 18 and 2 Paral. 33), is translated in Latin "to observe the omens from birds"; and in Greek the word (like the preceding word) commonly occurs in the Bible as *oionizesthai*. The Hebrews say that it is properly applied to those conjectures whereby, on the basis of an over-curious and perfectly deranged religion, we divine the status of things present and future from some chance occurrence, such as the flight of birds on the right or the left, or the sighting of some animal or other, or the twitching of a limb, a ringing in the ears, a fall, a sneeze, a sob, a song, the motion of a sieve, and a thousand other such superstitions vainly practiced by poor foolish women.

The fifth word *Habar*, is translated "to enchant," both in Latin (*incantare*) and in Greek (*epadein*). The Jews use it when certain secret words, thought to be wondrously effective, are murmured by the Magicians. Compare our own Virgil's verse: "The chill serpent in the meadow is burst asunder by incantation" [*Eclogae* 8.71].

I, too, have seen persons who by their words bring wild animals to a halt and constrain them to await the cast of the weapon. I have seen persons who, as soon as they have espied the loathsome domestic animal which we call the rat, compel it (whether by a mere glance or by enchantment) to stand motionless at some given place as though stunned and struck senseless, not stirring from the spot until they catch it (not by traps but by reaching out the hand) and throttle it. In fact, even David, in the case of the "Snake that stops its ears" which he mentions in Psalm 57 (or 58 according to the Hebrew codices) seems clearly to indicate that such wonders are effected through enchantment. In that Psalm he uses the very word *Habar*, and also the word *Lahas*, which means the same thing.

The sixth word *Ob*, is generally rendered "Python" in the Latin translation, or "Pythonic spirit" (Deut. 18, Isaiah 19, 1 Kings 28, 4 Kings 23), and frequently elsewhere. Sometimes also—but less appropriately, as it seems to me—it is translated "magician" (1 Paral. 33). In the Greek, however, it is almost always translated *engastrimythos*, "ventriloquist," except in 4 Kings 21 and 23 (and nowhere else, so far as I know) where it is rendered "soother, charmer." But, for the Hebrews, the word *Ob* signifies a bag or bottle. Therefore, the demons who gave responses in obscure voices from the more remote parts of the body, such as the armpits, or the pudenda of women, as though from a bag or bottle, were called *Ob* by the Hebrews, or in the plural *Oboth*. But the Greeks called them by the suitable name *engastrimythos* or *engastritai* because they spoke from the bellies of men. Some Latin writers have imitated this Greek term and called them, not inappropriately, ventriloquists. Now those words are applied properly to the evil spirits themselves, but sometimes also to the men who admit them. We know from Aristophanes, in *The Wasps*, that once upon a time a demon of this sort made a magician called Euricles famous among the Athenians. In the play Aristophanes says that he has brought much advantage to the state of Athens by comedies of his which were ascribed to others—the performance of which he engineered by entering into the bellies of other poets, in imitation of the behavior and the oracular pronouncements of Eurycles. Because of this Eurycles (as the most learned Greek commentaries point out), prophets of this sort were later called *eurykleitai* and *engastrimythoi* or *engastritai*. St. Augustine in his book *On Christian Doctrine* attests that the girl mentioned in Acts 16 was also a ventriloquist. But enough on this subject.

The last Hebrew word was *Iidoni*, which I think is derived from the Hebrew word *iada*, meaning "to know" and "to understand," although I am not unaware that the Hebrews adduce some nonsense about an earthborn animal, of human form, to which they give the name *Iadua*, and by the bone of which those who are called prophesy. The Hebrew race is extremely fatuous in making up and believing such old wives' tales. The word *Iidoni* is sometimes translated "divine" in Latin (as in Deut. 18, Levit. 20, and perhaps elsewhere), and sometimes "soothsayer" (as in Levit. 19, 4 Kings 23, and Isaiah 19). And in Greek it is sometimes translated *epaiodos* "enchanter" (2 Paral. 33; Levit. 19 and 20), but sometimes *gnostes*, "one who knows" (1 Kings 28; 4 Kings 21 and 23)—which is most in keeping with the etymology that I have given. However, there are passages where it is translated "he who cries from the earth" (Isaiah 8 and 19). But I do not know whether this refers to an oracle given from the earth or to spirits of the dead stirred from their graves, as is said to have been done at 1 Kings 28. Personally, I should think that this word *Iidoni* embraces the whole class of demons that prophesy and give responses, and that they are so called because of their professed understanding of all things. But the word just preceding (*Ob*) signifies a particular species of demon—those who speak forth in obscure voice from the belly, the armpits, or other hidden parts of the human body. This interpretation can be supported by the fact that in the whole Bible these last two terms are scarcely ever found written one without the other; certainly the last, *Iidoni*, is found nowhere whatsoever except soon after the second last. And so it will be the case that, of the seven words which we have mentioned, the first five seem to refer to superstitious vanities of men (or even to their acts of poisoning) by which they suppose that they can understand hidden things or accomplish miracles; while the last two refer to the actual oracles of evil demons or of "demoniacs" (if I may so call them).

We must not omit here the principal word referring to these monsters, namely *Hartummin*. Rabbi Levi says that this word is used of persons who work wonders by natural means or are thought to do so by those who do not carefully observe their dexterity. Ibn Ezra takes it to mean those who understand the secrets of the qualities of things and of nature. But clear fact shows that they were not such, since the effects that we read of in Exod. 7 and 8 could not have been produced by natural powers; because, in that case, the magicians would have been learned in natural things and pleasing to God, and would not have been stubbornly devising what would insult Him. The *Hartummin* in Exodus were magicians of ill repute, who, as servants of the Devil, attempted all they could by means of diabolical tricks, casting images before the eyes of the impious, in order to diminish the authority of Moses and Aaron, the representatives of God; they should rather have been called juggling deceivers. The word *Hartummin* comes from other nations and is strange and foreign to the Hebrew tongue, but nevertheless it is adopted by the Hebrews (e.g., Gen. 41: 8, 24; Exod. 7: 13, 24; Exod. 8: 7, 18; Exod. 9: 11; Daniel 1: 20; Daniel 2: 2). St. Jerome, in Genesis, translates "Seers"; in Exodus, "Evil-doers" or "Witches." And indeed in Exod. 7: 13, the same persons who are first called *Hachamin*, or "wise," and *Mechassephim*, or "Evil-doers" (as some would have it), are then called *Hartummin Mezeraim*, that is, "Egyptian enchanters"; from this we can infer the nature of the *Hartummin*. And in Daniel, Jerome translates "soothsayers." In the opinion of Rabbi Isaac Natar, the Jews used this name for any among the Gentiles who professed singular wisdom, especially wisdom pertaining to superstition.

Our fellow Germans use one and the same word *Zauberer* for the magician who is a professional deceiver and illusionist and often well educated, for the "wise woman" or witch who is deluded by the Devil because of her feeble-mindedness and corrupted imagination, and for the poisoner who makes studied use of his drugs or poisons. And so, when someone mentions witches or poisoners, German-speakers are deceived by the ambiguous German term, and soon bring up the subject of Pharaoh's magicians who are far removed from the activities of witches and poisoners. Accordingly, I am not ashamed to proclaim publicly that all the German writers whom I have so far chanced to read in the vernacular have stumbled badly in this sort of argument, even if they have affixed pretentious titles to the covers of their books and even if they appear to have adduced the evidence of Sacred Scripture. I am especially ready to express my view because I see that they assign too much power to witches—power to disturb the atmosphere or cause disease; and thus unwittingly these writers provide drawn sword and kindling for the savage executioners, who lack judgment, discretion, and any trace of pity. Amidst this variety of beliefs, lest a confusion of terminology obscure the issue, it has suited by purpose for many reasons to distinguish the infamous magician from the witch and the poisoner, so that in this debased age of ours, still so unlearned in matters of this sort, the specific characteristics may be made clear—which is the proper function of

terminology—and the persons of whom I speak may be recognized and distinguished. I do this also to show publicly where my considered opinion, based
firmly upon reason and Sacred Scripture, differs from the rooted beliefs unfortunately held by others. I would grant, however, that there are certain points in
common among the persons described and their arts.

B. Book 6, Chapter 15:
Examples of Poor Innocent Women Punished
Because They Were Suspected of Maleficium

Add to the above examples the case, well known to our countrymen, of the
official who had as many of these poor deluded women as possible arrested and
punished by burning, on the information given by a soothsayer. Finally, this
soothsayer or "Pythian prophet" promised the official privately that, if the latter
would not be offended, he would given information against one more woman
who was guilty of *maleficium*. The official readily agreed, and the informer
accused the official's wife, stating that he would give open demonstration of the
fact lest the man have any doubts about the matter. He set an hour in which her
husband might see for himself that she was present at the assembly and dances
of the other witches. The official agreed to this proposal, and he invited some
friends and relatives to dine at the same table with himself and his wife at a
certain appointed time; meanwhile he did not disclose the reason for the gathering. Then, at the hour indicated by the soothsayer, he rose from the table and
bade all his guests to remain with his wife and not move from their places before
he should return. Next, he was guided by the soothsayer to a spot of the latter's
choosing, and he thought that he could clearly see assembled witches, and
dances, and all sorts of allurements to pleasure—and his own wife among the
assembly, pursuing the same delights and folly as the others. Returning home at
once, he found his invited friends sitting happily at the table along with his
wife, just where he had left them. And when he anxiously inquired whether his
wife had left her seat, he was told by all of them at once that she had remained
fixed to the spot during his absence. And so the official revealed the whole
matter, repenting too late of the punishment that he had inflicted upon innocent women; if I recall correctly, he condemned the Pythian accuser to death.

A few years ago, at the castle called Raed in the district of Minden, certain
men were executed for *maleficium* on the accusation of a woman named Mar-
garetha von Minden, who had previously been incarcerated in the fortress of
Hausberg on the Weser. Being later summoned into the district and the city of
Verden, she accused a certain woman, with the stipulation that if this woman,
upon being put in chains, did not confess to *maleficium*, she would herself be
held guilty. And the outcome was certainly not a happy one. The jailed woman

continued to deny the crime, and, as it happened, she died in jail as a result of the severe torture to which she had been subjected; and her accuser was ordered to be hauled into chains. Furiously spewing out venom and fire, as it were, she terrified the torturer and everyone else and drove them back, until a certain record-keeper, who was more familiar with her tricks, laid hold of her and roused others to seize her. Finally subjected to questioning, she herself paid for the charge which she had brought upon the other woman, who resolutely denied it. A persistent rumor was circulated that she had falsely accused the woman who died in prison, as well as other women who had been burned earlier.

Within our own memory, when some vegetable gardens of Düren were destroyed by hail but the plants in a neighboring garden that belonged to a certain old woman were unharmed, as often happens in storms, the old woman was accused of *maleficium* and dragged off to jail. Tyrannically subjected to the most dreadful torments, she could not be driven to confess to a single charge. She most wisely stated that it was not in her power to raise tempests or disturb the air; this was the province of God alone. She was therefore suspended from a beam while being torn apart by heavy weights hanging from either side of her, and she was about to give up her spirit when the overseer, intending to leave her in her pain, invited the torturer to go for a drink with him, saying that the old woman would speak otherwise when they returned. Then in her wretched torment, she begged the overseer to summon a confessor before going for the drink; but he laughed at her and departed. Later, however, upon returning, he found her dead, still hanging in the same position; and he falsely reported that she had committed suicide while he was gone. Not much later, this tyrant fell into such madness that he tore his garments and smeared excrement upon his face and killed himself.

In another little town not far from here, when a poor woman who had been imprisoned on suspicion of *maleficium* could not be induced by any torture to confess to some crime, a priest approached her with coaxing words, urging that she not allow herself any longer to be thus torn asunder by torture. She should just confess quietly to some failing, and he promised that he would purify her from *maleficium* with holy water, and that he would restore her to God as good as new. Thus prompted by the priest and deceived by his blandishments, she admitted that she had perchance perpetrated some evils of this nature. She hoped that in this way she would escape as the priest had persuaded her. But on the grounds of such a confession, falsely and cunningly obtained by coaxing, she was sentenced to be sacrificed to Vulcan's fires. Hearing the unexpected sentence, the poor woman admonished the unhearing judges: "See how you are killing me."

About forty-two years ago, near the village of Elten, a half mile from Emmerich in the Duchy of Cleves, in a heath of the royal road, a demon used to beset travellers in various and wondrous ways, striking them and casting them down from their horses and overturning their chariots; nothing more was ever seen than the image of a hand. The people named this demon Eckerken. The unbelieving villagers, not realizing that this was the mocking activity of a demon, attributed the crimes to *maleficium*. They therefore laid hands upon a woman named Beel [Sibylla] Duiscops, who was bound in service to the count of Berg. When she was finally burned to death the assaults ceased, but not because she had been responsible for the deceptions, although to promote cruel torture or unbelief she might have been induced by the demon's illusions to confess to the deed. In fact, the Devil ceased voluntarily and even gladly from the harassment which he alone had brought on, so that by this cessation he might plunge men deeper into the abyss of unbelief, and so that he might render them guilty of a bloodthirsty sentence, which is what he eagerly desires, especially in the case of the innocent, since he is a murderer from the very beginning. If, in fact, a diligent investigation and skillful inquiry had been made at the very times at which this illusory image of a hand was seen, Sibylla would no doubt have been discovered sleeping at home on most of these occasions, or doing something else. If you insist upon the point that she confessed, I answer that the confession was extorted by the torturer or came from the poor woman's depraved imagination. How that imagination might be corrupted by the Devil I have described so often that further repetition would be tedious.

Seven judges from a city by the Moselle wished to interrogate a woman who was arrested on a charge of causing milk to become sticky and stringy. She was examined by me and pronounced innocent, and she was later released by the Most Reverend Bishop. At the same time, by common decree, they ordered the arrest of another woman from the city who had been suspected of *maleficium* for many years—taking no account of the dropsy which all but put her into agony, to the extent that a few days previously she had purified her soul with the usual rites and ceremonies of the Roman Church, desiring to render it up to God. And what came of the arrest? She was carried on a chair into the courtyard of the castle, and behold!—being at once overcome by the severity of her disease, she breathed her last. Nevertheless, the tyranny of the lowly-born judges continued, and she was denied burial in the common cemetery (the burial was finally granted as a favor). Hence it comes about that a just God also chooses sometimes to take vengeance upon the wrongful sentences of the magistrate and the foolish unbelief of the commoners and, very often, upon tyranny; as happened at just about this time (to wit, on 9 September 1574) and not far from this town (near Linz am Rhein), when about forty of those who had enjoyed the spectacle of a holocaust of *lamiae* were drowned in the Rhine while sailing home.

45
Jean Bodin: *On the Demon-Mania of Witches* (1580)

Jean Bodin (1529/30–96), professor of law at Toulouse, royal adviser to the king of France, and public prosecutor at Laon, is best known as the author of one of the most influential works in the history of political theory, *Six livres de la République* (1576). A study of the concept of sovereignty, this work went through twenty-eight editions within a generation, and ranked its author with Machiavelli as one of Europe's two leading political theorists in the sixteenth century. Bodin was also a philosopher of history and of pre-Cartesian science, a learned and humane scholar and political economist, and one of the earliest defenders of religious toleration in a century of religious hatreds and bloodshed.

On the subject of witchcraft, however, Bodin was an implacable enemy of all who would question the justice and legitimacy of the witch-hunt-and-execution. To his *Démonomanie des sorciers* (1580), one of the most widely read demonological treatises of his day, he appended a victorious and closely reasoned critique of Johann Weyer's assault upon contemporary views (Text 44). Bodin's treatise went through ten editions before 1604 and was translated into German by Johann Fischart, also the translator of Rabelais. So inconceivable was it to Bodin that an educated man could dissent from the clear theological and empirical truth of witchcraft that he accused Weyer of being a witch himself and called for his prosecution.

SOURCE: Jean Bodin, *On the Demon-Mania of Witches*, trans. Randy Scott; intro. Jonathan L. Pearl (Toronto, 1995), book 4, chap. 5, pp. 203–18.

FURTHER READING: Clark, *Thinking with Demons*, 668–92; Ann Blair, *The Theater of Nature: Jean Bodin and Renaissance Science* (Princeton, 1997); Christopher Baxter, "Jean Bodin's *De la Démono-manie des Sorciers*: The Logic of Persecution," in Anglo, *The Damned Art*, 76–105.

On the Punishment That Witches Merit

There are two ways in which states are maintained in their status and greatness: reward and punishment—the former for the good, the latter for the bad. And if there is a lapse in the distribution of these, one must expect nothing but the inevitable ruin of the states, though it is not necessary that every crime be punished. For there would not be enough judges to judge them, nor executioners to execute them. Out of ten crimes fewer than one is punished by magistrates. Usually one only sees poor scoundrels punished. Those who have friends or money most often escape from the hands of men. Indeed it is true that neither their friends nor their riches will save them from the hand of God. But those people greatly delude themselves who think that the penalties are only established to punish the crime. I maintain that it is the least benefit which accrues to the state. For the greatest and the chief one is to appease the anger of God, especially if the crime is directly against the majesty of God, as this one is. . . . The second benefit of the punishment is to obtain the blessing of God on the whole country. As it is written for example in the law of God, "After you have destroyed with fire and sword the city from amongst my people, and from amongst your brothers, which has left God to serve idols, and you have killed every living soul, both men and beasts, you shall erect a heap of stone, a memorial, in triumph, and then I will extend my great mercies upon you, and will shower you with my favours and blessings."

The third benefit one receives from punishment of the wicked, is to strike fear and terror into others; as it is described in the law of God, others having seen the punishment are afraid to commit offence. The fourth benefit is to preserve them from being infected and harmed by the wicked, as plague victims and lepers infect the healthy. The fifth effect is to reduce the number of the wicked. . . . The sixth is so that the good can live in security. The seventh aim is to punish the wicked.

I indeed want to enumerate the benefits and uses which result from the punishment of the wicked. Now if ever there was a way to appease the anger of God, to obtain His blessing, to dismay some by the punishment of others, to preserve some from the infection of others, to reduce the number of the wicked, to secure the safety of the good, and to punish the most despicable wickednesses that the human mind can imagine, it is to chastise witches with the utmost rigour. However, the word "rigour" is a misnomer, since there is no penalty cruel enough to punish the evils of witches, since all their wickednesses, blasphemies, and all their designs rise up against the majesty of God to vex and offend Him in a thousand ways. . . . Some people raise objections to burning witches, even witches who have a formal pact with Satan. For it is principally against those witches that one must seek vengeance with the greatest diligence and utmost rigour, in order to bring an end to the wrath of God, and His vengeance upon us. And especially since those who have written on it interpret a magic spell as heresy, and nothing more—although true heresy is the crime of treason against God, and punishable by the fire. It is necessary, however, to note the difference between this crime and simple heresy. For we showed initially that the first occupation of witches is to deny God and all religion. The law of God condemns that person who has left the true God for another to be stoned, which all the Hebrew commentators say is the most terrible form of execution. This point is very significant. For the witch whom I have described does not just deny God in order to change and take up another religion, but he renounces all religion, either true or superstitious, which can keep men in the fear of committing offence.

The second crime of witches is, after having renounced God, to curse, blaspheme and scorn Him, and any other god or idol which he feared. Now the law of God declares as follows, "Whoever curses his God shall bear his sin. He who blasphemes the name of the Lord shall be put to death." . . .

For it seems that God wants to show that those who blaspheme what they think is God, do blaspheme God, with respect to their intention, which is the foundation of the hearts and minds of men: like the witches described above who broke the arms and legs on crucifixes, which they thought were gods. They also offered toads the host to feed on. One sees then a double outrage of impiety with witches who blaspheme the true God, and anything they think has some divinity, so as to uproot all pious conviction and fear of offence.

The third crime is even more abominable. Namely, they do homage to the Devil, worship him, offer sacrifice, and the most despicable make a trench and put their face in the ground praying and worshiping him with all their heart. . . . This abomination surpasses any penalty that man can conceive, considering the formal text of the law of God, which requires that one who only bows down to pay honour to images, which the Greeks call "idols," be put to death. . . . Now witches are not content to worship, or only to bow down before Satan, but they offer themselves to Satan, pray to him and invoke him.

The fourth crime is even greater: many witches have been convicted, and have confessed to promising their children to Satan. The fifth is even worse; that is, that witches are frequently convicted by their confession of having sacrificed to the Devil their infant children before they are baptised. They raise them in the air, and then insert a large pin into their head, which causes them to die and is a crime more bizarre than the one before. In fact Sprenger relates that he had one burned who had killed forty-one of them in this way.

The sixth crime is even more horrible. For witches are not satisfied to offer their own children to the Devil and burn them as a sacrifice . . . but they even dedicate them right from the mother's womb . . . which is a double parricide with the most abominable idolatry imaginable.

The seventh and the most common is that witches make an oath and promise the Devil to lure as many as they can into his service, which they customarily do, as we showed earlier. Now the law of God states that that person who is called this way, must stone the one who tried to entice him.

The eighth crime is to call upon and swear by the name of the Devil as a mark of honour, as witches do having it always on their lips, and swearing only by him, except when they renounce God. This is directly against the law of God, which forbids swearing by anything other than the name of God. This, Scripture

says, gives glory to God. Thus judges said in taking the oath of parties or witnesses, "Glory be to God."

The ninth is that witches are incestuous, which is the crime they have been
charged with and convicted of from earliest times. For Satan gives them to
understand that there was never a perfect sorcerer or enchanter who was not
born from father and daughter, or mother and son. . . . All these impieties are
directly against God and His honour, which judges must avenge with the utmost rigour, and bring an end to God's wrath against us. As for the other crimes
of witches, they concern injuries done to men, which they will avenge whenever they can. Now there is nothing so displeasing to God as to see judges
avenge the smallest offences committed against themselves or others, but dis-
semble the horrible blasphemies against the majesty of God, such as those I
have cited about witches.

Let us continue then with the other crimes. The tenth is that witches make a
profession of killing people, and worse of murdering little children, then boiling
them to render their humours and flesh drinkable, which Sprenger says he
learned from their confessions; and the Neopolitan Battista della Porta writes
about it in his book on magic. And still another fact to underline, is that they
put children to death before they are baptised. These are four circumstances
which make the murder very much worse.

The eleventh crime is that witches eat human flesh, especially of little children, and of course drink their blood. . . . But one sees that it is a vile belief the
Devil puts into the hearts of men in order to make them kill and devour each
other, and destroy the human race. Again it must be noted that all witches
customarily make poisons, which is enough to justify the death sentence. . . .

Now murder, according to the law of God and the laws of men, merits death.
And those who eat human flesh, or have others eat it, also deserve death: as for
example, a baker in Paris who made a business of making pies from the flesh of
people hanged. He was burned, and his house razed to the ground. . . .

The twelfth is particular, killing with poisons or spells, which is distinct from
simple homicide. . . . For it is a much more serious offence to kill with poison
than with overt violence, as we shall presently point out; and even more serious
to cause death by sorcery than by poison. . . .

The thirteenth crime of witches is to kill livestock, something which is
customary. . . . The fourteenth is common, and recognised by law, namely,
killing crops and causing famine and sterility in an entire region. The fifteenth
is that witches have carnal copulation with the Devil, (and very often near their
husbands, as I remarked earlier), a wickedness they all confess to.

There then are fifteen detestable crimes, the least of which merits a painful
death. This does not mean that all witches are guilty of such evils, but it has
been well established that witches who have a formal compact with the Devil
are normally guilty of all or of most of these evil deeds. Now when there are

several crimes committed by one person, and through several acts, they must all be punished, and there can never be impunity for one crime because of the concurrence of another. It is necessary, as Bartolus states, to impose several separate penalties either according to laws and ordinances or arbitration of the judge. In such a case if several crimes are committed through the same act, even though the crimes are of the same category (for example, parricide is also homicide) nevertheless it will be governed only by the penalty for parricides. Now the law of God which prescribes the death penalty, does not set out in detail the evil acts of witches. But it is written only that the sorceress is not to live. . . . Not only does God show the magnitude of the crime, but also His will that swift and true justice be done regarding it; and particularly the law calls for the death sentence so that the penalty is not reduced for the female sex, as it is done for all other crimes in legal parlance. . . . And as for court sorcerers, since this vermin approaches as near to princes as it can, not only now but from earliest times, in order to ruin the whole state, they lure princes into it, who then later lure their subjects. The law here is noteworthy. For it is stated that if there is a sorcerer who follows the court, or magician, or soothsayer, or augurer or one interpreting dreams by divining art, of whatever rank and however great a lord he might be, he shall be exposed to torments and tortured without making allowances for his rank. This law should be engraved in gold letters on the doors of princes, for they have no more dangerous plague in their following. . . . And since the crime is more detestable, the penalty must be more severe. That is to say, stoning where the penalty is practised, or burning which is the normal penalty observed from earliest times throughout Christendom. . . .

If with the crime of witchcraft it is established, either by confession or by witnesses, or by factual evidence that the witch caused someone's death, the crime is even greater, especially if it is a child. And even should it happen that the spell cast by the witch to bring about the death of his enemy, made another person die, nevertheless it is punishable by death. If she caused someone's death while trying to make him fall in love, she also deserves death, even though she may not be a witch, as the law says. But with one who is not a witch, the penalty ought to be lightened.

The difficulty, however, very often lies solely with the proof, and judges find themselves hampered only by that. If then there are no valid witnesses, or confessions by the accused, or factual evidence, which are the three proofs we have described on which a death sentence can be based, but there are only presumptions, one must distinguish whether the presumptions are weak or strong. If the presumptions are weak, one must not convict the person as a witch—nor acquit her either. Rather, one must declare that it will be more fully investigated, and in the meantime release the accused.

But if the presumptions are strong, one may consider imposing the death sentence because of the important difference which separates this crime from others. For where other crimes are concerned one must not sentence anyone to death on a presumption, however strong it may be. But those who cannot be condemned receive other penalties, such as the galleys, the lash, or some fine according to the rank of the persons and the weight of the proof. So it seems that in so abominable a crime as this, one ought to hand down the death sentence if the presumptions are strong. Nevertheless, I do not recommend that because of strong presumptions one pass sentence of death—but any other penalty except death. . . . One must be very sure of the truth to impose the death sentence. Here someone will say that one must either acquit or convict. If the case is valid, death is not enough. If it is not valid one must acquit him, or at the most declare that it will be more fully investigated, in the meantime releasing the prisoner with the proviso that he appear again when required to do so, etc. Nor is one to employ corporal punishment, or strip anyone of their honour because of presumptions. . . .

Proof for good and compelling reasons is enough, as Baldus says. . . . And for the same reason the proof of household witnesses is admissible for things done secretly in the home, which otherwise would not be admissible.

Now the wickedness of witches is usually done at night, in a deserted place, away from people, and by means one could never suppose or think of. It is sufficient, therefore, to have strong presumptions to impose corporal punishment in such a revolting case, and up to but not including bodily death. That is to say, beatings, amputations, brandings, life imprisonments, fines, confiscations, and other such penalties except banishment, unless the witch is confined to a particular place. For it is a normal thing with witches to move from one place to another when they have been discovered, carrying the plague elsewhere. And if they are obliged not to move from a place, they no longer dare to do anything, realizing they are watched and suspected. As for life imprisonment, although it is forbidden in ordinary law, canon law, however, has made more provision for it, especially in the present case. For there is nothing that witches fear more than prison, and it is one of the best ways to make them confess the truth and bring them to repentance. But one must not separate them from other prisoners who are not witches. For it has been found by experience that when they are alone the Devil makes them persist in their wickedness, and sometimes helps them to end their lives.

If then a witch is seized in possession of toads, lizards, communion wafers, or other strange bones and ointments, and if she is rumoured to be a witch, such presumptions are very strong and compelling. Or if in the past she was brought before the courts, and never cleared, it is an extremely compelling presumption. Or if she has been seen coming out of the stable or sheepfold of her enemy, and then later the livestock of the sheepfold dies. Or if those whom she threatened have died afterward or fallen into a languor, especially if there were several of them, it is a most powerful presumption. Because of these presumptions, even

though there was no other proof from confession or witnesses, one must however pronounce sentence according to the above mentioned penalties, up to and
excluding death. This is the rule that we must adhere to, setting aside the death
penalty, and softening the rigour of the laws when one proceeds upon presumption. And one must not be governed by those who claim that judges must not
sentence anyone to corporal punishment on presumptions, however strong they
may be. . . .

   After the trial is carried out and completed on strong presumptions, such as
we have described, one must prescribe a sentence of corporal punishment: otherwise there will never be punishment for wicked deeds if one punishes only the
crimes for which one has obvious proof. This is a difficulty which the juriscon-
sult has addressed in order to make a conviction, even though there may be
uncertainty when several have transgressed which one ought to be punished.
And although it is only then a question of damages, nonetheless the reason for
financial penalty in a civil suit is comparable to corporal punishments in a
criminal action, and especially in outrageous crimes like the one in question. So
that Baldus clearly argues that one ought to impose sentences of corporal punishment based on presumptions. . . . I certainly admit that it is better to acquit
the guilty than to condemn the innocent. But I say that one who is convicted on
acute presumptions is not innocent: for example the one who was discovered
with his bloody sword near the murder victim with no one else around, plus
other conjectures which we have pointed out. . . . How much more necessary it
is then, to prescribe corporal punishments when the presumptions against
witches are strong. And when there is factual evidence one must impose capital
punishment: for example, if the one accused of witchcraft was found in possession of human members, especially of little children, one must not hesitate to
pronounce the death sentence. For there is concrete factual evidence. If the one
accused of witchcraft, in order to cure someone invokes the Devil openly, or
with his face to the ground prays to his "little master," as they say, there is
concrete factual evidence. One must not have misgivings about imposing the
death penalty, as did Mr. Jean Martin who condemned to the flames a witch
from Sainte Preuve, who was accused of making the mason of Sainte Preuve
stooped and impotent. She had him take a bath, and gave him three lizards
wrapped in a handkerchief, enjoining him to throw them into the bath, and to
utter, "Go in the name of the Devil." For the invocation of the Devil is a hateful
idolatry, and this point alone was enough to convict her even though she did not
confess anything, and there was no proof of her having made the mason impotent. For many remove the charm and the illness given by other witches. One
must also proceed against them if one sees that the remedies they apply are not
natural or fitting (such as the three lizards, which were never found afterward in
the bath; or for example the witch of Angers, whom we have mentioned, who to
effect a cure used cat's brain, which is a strong poison, and crows' heads and

other filth) and with other presumptions and information, one must impose corporal punishment.

If it happens that a witch invokes or calls on the Devil, one must without doubt pronounce sentence of death, for the reasons stated above; and not only of death, but one must condemn such monsters to be burned alive, according to the general custom observed from earliest times in all Christendom. The judge must never deviate or depart from this custom and general law, or reduce the penalty unless there is an important and compelling reason. For the law states that it is one and the same to reduce or remit the penalty at all. And moreover, the law deems guilty a judge who remits or reduces the penalty of the law. . . . Indeed it goes even further. For it brands a judge with infamy for this reason. And that poses no problem in terms of law. Furthermore, the law requires that one punish with confiscation anyone who remits or reduces the prescribed penalty—and sometimes with exile and other penalties according to the difference in the cases, including punishing the judges with the same penalties that the guilty and convicted person would be punished with, as the law states. . . . And if it is true that the judge is guilty and must suffer the penalty for treason, who remitted or reduced the penalty for treason, as the law states, how much more guilty is the judge who remits or reduces the penalty of someone who is guilty of treason against God? . . . As much may be said of those who send witches away acquitted (even though they are guilty) and give as their only excuse that they cannot believe what is said about them: they deserve death. For it calls into doubt the law of God, and all human laws and histories, and countless executions carried out against this for two or three thousand years, and grants impunity to all witches. If someone tells me that all sentences in this realm are discretionary, I grant it, unless the death penalty is restricted by decree or by custom. Now according to very ancient custom, witches in all of Europe are condemned to be burned alive.

We have spoken chiefly about witches who have a sworn compact and a formal partnership with the Devil. But there are other kinds of witches whom we have treated at length in the second book, who are not so loathsome, but who still have partnership with the Devil in diabolical acts, such as those who tie codpieces, which is an abominable wickedness. And although there are some who do it without having a formal agreement or partnership with the Devil, nonetheless the act in itself is diabolical and deserves capital punishment. For one who practises it cannot deny that he is a transgressor of the law of God and of nature, preventing the consequence of marriage ordained by the law of God. For the result of it is that it is necessary to dissolve the marriages, or at the least it binds them in sterility, which in plain terms is a sacrilege. Nor can he deny either that it is murder—for one is not less a murderer who prevents the procreation of children than if he had cut their throats. In the third place he removes the mutual friendship of marriage, which is the sacred hearth of nature and of human society, and he puts there a great hatred. For normally these codpiece tiers instill a violent hatred between the two partners. Fourthly, this tying is done at the very instant the minister pronounces the holy words, and when everyone ought to have his mind fixed on God. The person who ties comes and mixes in diabolic words and mysteries, which is a hateful impiety. In the fifth place he is the cause of the adulteries and debaucheries which ensue. For those who are bound, burning with lust beside each other, go and commit adultery. In the sixth place many murders also result, committed against the person of those suspected of having done it, who very often had never thought of doing it. . . . It is therefore necessary, since this crime is multiplying rapidly, and these are the beginnings and the foundations of witches, to impose capital punishments for this crime which is directly against the law of God and nature. . . . As for the other kinds of sorceries, which are performed to learn future events, as is Geo-mancy, and other such things, which we alluded to in the second book, given that all these kinds of divination are diabolical and inventions of the Devil, forbidden by the word of God, all those who have been involved in it, and have been convicted for the first time must be sentenced to fines and reparations; then on the second time to the lash, and branded; and the third time hanged.

There are also those who profess to cure by removing a spell, as they claim, or by diabolical means drive off a storm, and prevent rains and hail. The law does not demand that they be punished, but I maintain that such doctors ought to be questioned and examined to learn whether they are witches, and until proof is found, they must be forbidden on pain of corporal punishments to dabble with medicines, and a close eye kept on them.

With respect to Chiromancy which is practised by those who meddle in for-tune telling by hand lines, I recommend that they who make it their occupation, as some do, on the first occasion be forbidden to practise it ever again, upon suitable penalty. The books of Chiromancy and Geomancy, furthermore, which are sold everywhere should be burned, and printers and book-sellers prohibited to print or display any for sale, with penalty for those who have been discovered with any in their possession to be exacted the first time by fines, and the second by public amends. And so that no one plead ignorance it would certainly be necessary to specify the authors in detail, and to enjoin all judges to burn on the spot any books of magic which have been found in inspecting inventories. . . .

Now it is indisputable that conjurers and charmers have a formal compact with the Devil, as well as all those who practise Necromancy, Psychagogy, Goety, and other such things. With regard to natural Astrology and its knowl-edge, since through it are known the marvels of God, the courses of the celestial lamps, the years, and the seasons—plus the fact that it is necessary for doctors and for the use of meteoric instruments, it must not be mixed with the others. But one must prevent the abuses of those who profess to divine the situation and the life of people, which brings with it a distrust of God and impiety. This is why the finest science in the world has been maligned, so that the words, "Astrologus," "Mathematicus" and "Chaldeus" in laws are often taken to mean "sorcerers." But excellent sciences must not be rejected because of their abuse. Otherwise one would have to condemn all the arts and sciences in the world, even the law of God. . . . In all matters where the human mind is frightened by superstitious fear, or cut-off from faith in the one, sole God, cleaving to vanities of whatever sort, God is offended by it, and it is true idolatry. For this reason pagans themselves proclaimed a heavy penalty against them. . . . One must pay careful heed to the distinctions between spells, in order to weigh their heinousness and gravity, distinguishing between witches who have a formal agreement with the Devil, and those who employ ligatures and other arts of sorcery. For there are some things which cannot be suppressed or punished by magistrates, such as the superstition of many people about not walking through the fields, which the pagans feared, as they feared bleeding from the left nostril, or meeting a pregnant woman before dining. But it is a much greater superstition to carry rolls of paper hung around the neck, or the consecrated host in one's pocket. This is what Judge Gentil did, who was found in possession of a host by the executioner who hanged him at Montfaucon. And other similar superstitions . . . which are strictly forbidden by the law of God and the prophets because of the distrust toward God, and the idolatry toward creatures. It cannot be corrected except by the word of God—but certainly the magistrate must chastise the charlatans and notebearers who sell that filth, and banish them from the country. . . .

Now it is a double impiety in the person of those who are priests and pastors. But the impiety is much greater when the priest or pastor has a pact with Satan and he converts a sacrifice into a despicable sorcery. . . . How much more punishable then is the sorcerer-priest who, instead of consecrating, blasphemes execrably. This is why Plato makes foremost among his laws one which requires that the sorcerer-priest be put to death without remission. For the indecency of the sorcery is much more atrocious in one who handles sacred things. Because instead of sanctifying them he pollutes, he soils, he blasphemes execrably. As did the curate of Soissons whom Froissart tells about, who baptised a toad, and gave it the consecrated host. He was burned alive without observance of canon laws which only excommunicate sorcerer-priests. It is true that one can say it is the ecclesiastical penalty, which does not prejudice the penalties of lay magistrates. Now just as proportionally in harmonic justice the penalty is greater and the crime more serious because of the station of the people, such as the doctor who poisons, the teacher who violates his pupil, the judge who wrongs someone, the notary who commits falsehood, the goldsmith who makes counterfeit money, the vassal who betrays his lord, the citizen who sells his country, the subject who kills his prince, the prince who breaks faith are much more worthy of punishment, and generally all those who fall short of their office: thus the sorcerer-priest is not only more wicked than all of them, but also more despicable than all other witches who are not priests. For this person deserts his God to abandon himself to the Devil, and betrays sacred things which he ought above all to have kept holy and inviolable. Thus the priest . . . who has been charged and convicted of setting spells with mirrors, or rings, or axes, or sieves, or other such things which are performed even without formal invocation of the Devil merits death, and the others banishment. In other crimes, save for spells and sacrileges, it is not proper that a priest be punished so severely. Rather the dignity of his person ought to diminish the penalty. And one who gives offence to the priests and ministers of God must be punished more severely than for all others: inasmuch as his dignity is greater and his person must be sacred and inviolable. But also when he so forgets himself as to dedicate himself to Satan, the punishment cannot be great enough. For it has been found in countless trials that witches very often are priests, or they have secret dealings with priests. And by money or by favours they are induced to say masses for witches, and they accommodate them with hosts, or they consecrate blank parchment, or they place rings, inscribed blades or other such things on the altar, or beneath the altar cloths as has often been discovered. Not long ago a curate was caught in the act, and he escaped since he had a good protector, who had given him a ring to place beneath the altar cloths when he said his Mass.

After the priests and ministers of God, the magistrates who are guardians and depositories of justice must be investigated, and if necessary, punished should any be found. For if there is a magistrate involved he will always let witches escape, and will maintain in this way the reign of Satan. And the first presumption against the magistrate who is a witch is when he makes a joke of such witchcraft. For under the pretense of laughter he brews his fatal poison. . . . And not without cause did the law seek rigorously to punish court sorcerers: for it takes only one witch-courtier to taint all the princes and ladies who follow the court and to infect the sovereign prince, because of the curiosity of great lords to see and learn the conjuring tricks of sorcerers, thinking that in this way they will achieve great things. Thus Satan holds nothing in higher recommendation than to entice princes—for as soon as they are steeped in it they execute the will of Satan, make mockery of all religion, give an example to their subjects of every lewdness, incest, parricide, cruelty, and exaction; provoke seditions among their subjects or civil wars to see the spilling of blood, and make sacrifice to the Devil, to whom nothing is more pleasing than innocent blood. For he wishes to preserve the wicked. . . .

But what penalty does one merit who pledged himself to Satan in order to be cured of an incurable illness, although we have shown above that out of ten there is scarcely one who gets better, and even then only from spells? In this case the ignorant person would to some degree be excusable from capital punishment, but not an educated man, although ignorance has no place in this crime. For no one can say that through error he mistakenly denied God his Creator in order to give himself to the Devil. Thus one sees in every trial that Satan desires a free will. But indeed the error may be excusable only with such persons, among the illicit workings of spells, who do not have a sworn agreement with Satan, such as the sorcery of rings, mirrors, sieves and other such things which some do because of having seen it performed, just as we explained above. And yet they must not remain without some penalty for the first offence, and for the second they must receive corporal punishment, and for the third death, since even a purse snatcher is normally sentenced to death for the third offence, as is almost the universal custom.

What shall we say then of those who have invoked evil spirits and performed the mysteries to attract Satan, but he did not come (although he never fails to, even though he did not answer, as he mimics the sly bawds who make one implore them)? One cannot say that it is only an attempt, but a detestable, accomplished and perfected witchcraft. Thus capital punishment is called for, and a reduction of the penalty for attempts which produced no effect has no place in this case. . . . That is, to have invoked and beseeched Satan, which also is a direct renunciation of God. Thus it is an abuse of both divine and human laws to pardon a penitent witch, under the pretext that the laws and canons require one to pardon repentant heretics. . . . For one who recognises something contrary to the law of God, even though he may be a heretic, nonetheless after he has revised this view his conscience remains intact. But one who worships Satan or denies God (although the one cannot be without the other) has set into effect something which cannot be undone. . . . And as for those who did not renounce God, but who made use of characters, circles and invocations, which they found written in some forbidden books, and though the "familiar spirit," as they say, did not come, one must distinguish the rank of the persons. If it is an ignorant joker who does not think that such familiar spirits are devils, he must be punished by stiff fines. . . . And if the person who made such an invocation is an educated man and of sound judgment, he merits death. For it cannot be denied in this case that he knowingly invoked Satan. And if the one who is sentenced to make amends for such wickedness is stubborn, and he refuses to obey justice, he must be sentenced to death. . . .

It is not within the power of princes to pardon a crime that the law of God punishes with death, such as the crimes of witchcraft. Moreover, princes do a great offence to God to pardon such horrible wickednesses committed directly against His majesty, since the smallest prince avenges his injuries with capital punishment. So those who let witches escape or who do not carry out their punishment with utmost rigour, can be assured that they will be abandoned by God to the mercy of witches. And the country which tolerates them will be struck by plagues, famines, and wars—but those who take vengeance against them will be blessed by God, and will bring an end to His wrath. This is why one who is charged and accused of being a witch must never be simply let off and acquitted, unless the calumny of the accuser or informer is clearer than the sun. Since the proof of such wickednesses is so hidden and so difficult, no one would ever be accused or punished out of a million witches if parties were governed, as in an ordinary trial, by a lack of proof. This is why the ordinance does not permit judges to do so in crimes unless the matter allows it. . . .

I recall having read in the *Malleus maleficarum*, that the plague did not stop in the region of Constance until they had exhumed a witch and reduced her body to ashes. As in a similar case there was a woman in the village of Verigny who was charged and accused of many evil spells, and because of the difficulty of the proof, released. Later I learned from the inhabitants that a countless number of livestock and people had died. She died in April, 1579. Since her death all the inhabitants of Verigny and their livestock have been at peace and no longer die as before. This shows clearly that with the end of the chief cause, comes the end of the effects, even though God brings down afflictions on those whom He pleases.

46

The Confessions of the Chelmsford Witches: England (1566)

Sorcery and witchcraft had been made offenses against the common law by a statute of Henry VIII in 1542. The statute was repealed (with a number of others dealing with criminal matters) under Edward VI in 1547, and a new statute was passed early in the reign of Elizabeth I in 1563. This statute in turn was repealed by a more severe statute under James VI and I in 1604, which remained in effect until 1736. Although there is evidence for a growing concern with various forms of sorcery (especially political prophecy) in sixteenth-century England (among both Protestants and Catholics), it is also possible that the 1563 statute was at least partly the result of a new concern with the subject specifically on the part of clerics and scholars who had been exiles from England during the reign of Mary (1553–58) and had familiarized themselves with contemporary continental witchcraft theory. John Jewel, later bishop of Salisbury and a prominent preacher at the royal court, spoke of witches before Elizabeth in 1559 or 1560:

> This kind of people (I mean witches and sorcerers) within these last few years are marvelously increased within this your grace's realm. These eyes have seen most evident and manifest marks of their wickedness. Your grace's subjects pine away even unto death, their colour fadeth, their flesh rotteth, their speech is benumbed,

their senses are bereft. Wherefore your poor subjects' most humble petition unto your highness is, that the laws touching such malefactors may be put in due execution.[1]

The act of 1563 introduced the death penalty for murder committed by sorcery and prescribed a year's imprisonment and the pillory for non-deadly witchcraft.

In 1566 at Chelmsford in Essex County three women were tried and convicted of witchcraft. The trial not only resulted in the first punishments and executions for witchcraft in England, but it also inspired the first of many pamphlets on both the subject of witchcraft and particular trials that constitute an important source for witchcraft beliefs.

The trials at Chelmsford were the first of a series of trials for witchcraft (including others at Chelmsford in 1579 and 1589) that generated a large pamphlet literature and new longer treatises on the subject.[2] The first substantial treatise was the work of the skeptic Reginald Scot in 1584 (Text 60), followed by the treatises supporting the prosecutions by Henry Holland in 1590, George Gifford in 1587 and 1593, William Perkins in 1608, John Cotta and Alexander Roberts in 1616, Thomas Cooper in 1617, and Richard Bernard in 1627. Although the first treatises used chiefly continental evidence, after the work of Gifford, English writers had substantial English trial evidence on which to draw.[3]

What proved the efficacy of the witch persecutions above all else was the success of the courts in England and on the Continent in securing confessions from so many of the accused, especially in cases in which torture was not used. Here was tangible proof of the intentions, the diabolical pact, and the unnatural powers of the witch (or, conversely, those of the devil working through the witch), uttered by his or her own tongue and signed by his or her own hand. Why did they confess? Was it simply a question of torture and the fear of torture? Did the courts strike some sense of guilt whereby the "witch" was led to see herself as the prosecutor and her accusers described her? Did the accused actually believe herself to possess these traits and powers before being brought to trial and call attention to herself by her subsequent actions? The data from which to construct answers to these questions are pain-

---

1. Wallace Notestein, *A History of Witchcraft in England from 1558 to 1718* (Washington, D.C., 1911; rprt. New York, 1965), 16–17 (for the 1566 Chelmsford trials, pp. 33–40). The first treatise on the subject in English was that of Francis Coxe, *A short treatise declaringe the detestable wickednesse of magicall sciences, as necromancie, conjurations of spirits, curiouse astrologie and such lyke* of 1561. The second was the translation of Lambert Daneau (Text 42) in 1575.

2. The trials of 1589 generated a pamphlet with a well-known picture.

3. On Gifford, see Alan Macfarlane, "A Tudor Anthropologist: George Gifford's *Discourse* and *Dialogue*," in Anglo, *The Damned Art*, 140–55.

fully inadequate to the task. The effect of the confessions, however, is less unclear: they spread both fear of the witch and confidence in the courts, and they could be cited effectively against skeptics.

SOURCE: Charles Williams, *Witchcraft* (London, 1941; repr. Wellingborough, UK, 1980), 194–201. Williams modernized the English and abbreviated the text of the pamphlet *The examination and confession of certaine wytches at Chensford* [sic] *the xxvi. daye of July 1566* (London, 1566), either from the surviving copy at Lambeth or from H. Beigel's edition printed for the Philobiblon Society, London, 1864–65. See *A Short-Title Catalogue of Books Printed in England, Scotland, and Ireland and of English Books Printed Abroad, 1475–1640*, first compiled by A. W. Pollard and G. R. Redgrave; 2nd ed., rev. begun by W. A. Jackson and F. S. Ferguson, completed by Katharine F. Pantzer, vol. 2, I–Z (London, 1976), no. 19869.5, p. 235. Williams's editorial comments are printed in italics.

FURTHER READING: James Sharpe, *Instruments of Darkness: Witchcraft in Early Modern England* (Philadelphia, 1997); Marion Gibson, *Reading Witchcraft: Stories of Early English Witches* (London and New York, 1999). Two important older works are Alan Macfarlane, *Witchcraft in Tudor and Stuart England: A Regional and Comparative Study* (London, 1970), and Keith Thomas, *Religion and the Decline of Magic* (New York, 1971). Important recent perspectives may be found in *Witchcraft in Early Modern Europe*. There are lists of indictments and trials in Notestein, *History of Witchcraft in England*, and in C. L'Estrange Ewen, *Witch Hunting and Witch Trials: The Indictments for Witchcraft from the Records of 1373 Assizes Held for the Home Circuit, A.D. 1559–1736* (London, 1929).

Elizabeth Francis, the first to be examined, deposed as follows:
"First she learned this art of witchcraft at the age of twelve years of her grandmother, whose name was Mother Eve of Hatfield Peverel, deceased. Item, when she taught it her, she counselled her to renounce God and his word and to give of her blood to Satan (as she termed it), which she delivered her in the likeness of a white spotted cat, and taught her to feed the said cat with bread and milk, and she did so, also she taught her to call it by the name of Satan and to keep it in a basket.

"When this Mother Eve had given her the Cat Satan, then this Elizabeth desired first of the said Cat (calling it Satan) that she might be rich and to have goods, and he promised her she should—asking her what she would have, and she said sheep (for this Cat spake to her as she confessed in a strange hollow voice, but such as she understood by use) and this Cat forthwith brought sheep into her pasture to the number of eighteen, black and white, which continued with her for a time, but in the end did all wear away she knew not how.

"Item, when she had gotten these sheep, she desired to have one Andrew Byles to her husband, which was a man of some wealth, and the Cat did promise she should, but that he said she must first consent that this Andrew should abuse her, and she so did.

"And after when this Andrew had thus abused her he would not marry her, wherefore she willed Satan to waste his goods, which he forthwith did, and yet not being contented with this, she willed him to touch his body which he forthwith did whereof he died.

"Item, that every time that he did anything for her, she said that he required a drop of blood, which she gave him by pricking herself, sometime in one place and then in another, and where she pricked herself there remained a red spot which was still to be seen.

"Item, when this Andrew was dead, she doubting herself with child, willed Satan to destroy it, and he bade her take a certain herb and drink it, which she did, and destroyed the child forthwith.

"Item, when she desired another husband he promised her another, naming this Francis whom she now hath, but said he is not so rich as the other, willing her to consent unto that Francis in fornication which she did, and thereof conceived a daughter that was born within a quarter of a year after they were married.

"After they were married they lived not so quietly as she desired, being stirred (as she said) to much unquietness and moved to swearing and cursing, wherefore she willed Satan her Cat to kill the child, being about the age of half a year old, and he did so, and when she yet found not the quietness that she desired, she willed it to lay a lameness in the leg of this Francis her husband, and it did in this manner. It came in a morning to this Francis' shoe, lying in it like a toad, and when he perceived it putting on his shoe, and had touched it with his foot, he being suddenly amazed asked of her what it was, and she bad him kill it and he was forthwith taken with a lameness whereof he cannot be healed.

"After all this when she had kept this Cat by the space of fifteen or sixteen years, and as some say (though untruly) being weary of it, she came to one Mother Waterhouse her neighbour (a poor woman) when she was going to the oven and desired her to give her a cake, and she would give her a thing that she should be the better for so long as she lived, and this Mother Waterhouse gave her a cake, whereupon she brought her this cat in her apron and taught her as she was instructed before by her grandmother Eve, telling her that she must call him Satan and give him of her blood and bread and milk as before, and at this examination would confess no more."

Agnes Waterhouse, who was said to have received the cat, was presently examined "before Justice Southcote and M. Gerard the Queen's attorney." She was a woman of sixty-four; her daughter Joan was examined also, and the chief evidence against them was that of a child of twelve. The account is as follows:

The Confession of Agnes Waterhouse the xxvii day of July in
Anno 1566 at Chelmsford before Justice Southcote and
M. Gerard the Queen's attorney.

"First being demanded whether that she were guilty or not guilty upon her arraignment of the murdering of a man, she confessed that she was guilty, and then upon the evidence given against her daughter Joan Waterhouse, she said that she had a white Cat, and willed her Cat that he should destroy many of her neighbours' cattle, and also that he should kill a man, and so he did, and then after she must go two or three miles from her house, and then she took thought how to keep her Cat, then she and her Cat concluded that he the said Cat would become a Toad, and then she should keep him in a close house, and give him milk, and so he would continue till she came home again, and then being gone forth, her daughter having been at a neighbour's house there by, required of one Agnes Brown, of the age of twelve years or more, a piece of bread and cheese, and the said Agnes said that she had none, and that she had not the key of the milkhouse door, and then the said Joan went home and was angry with the said Agnes Brown and she said that she remembered that her mother was wont to go up and down in her house and to call Satan Satan she said she would prove the like, and then she went up and down the house and called Satan, and then there came a black Dog to her and asked her what she would have, and then she said she was afraid and said, I would have thee to make one Agnes Brown afraid, and then he asked her what she would give him and she said she would give him a red cock, and he said he would have none of that, and she asked him what he would have then, and he said he would have her body and soul, and so upon request and fear together she gave him her body and soul (and then said the queen's attorney *How wilt thou do before God?* O my Lord, I trust God will have mercy upon me, and then he said *thou sayest well*), and then he departed from her, and then she said that she heard that he made the said Agnes Brown afraid.

"The said Agnes Brown was then demanded and called for, and then she came in, and being asked what age she was of she said she thought she was twelve years old, and then the queen's attorney asked her what she could say, and then she said that at such a day, naming the day certain, she was churning of butter and there came to her a thing like a black Dog with a face like an ape, a short tail, a chain and a silver whistle (to her thinking) about his neck, and a pair of horns on his head, and brought in his mouth the key of the milkhouse door, and then my lord she said, I was afraid, for he skipped and leaped to and fro, and sat on the top of a nettle, and then I asked him what he would have, and he said he would have butter, and I said I had none for him and then he said he would have some or he went, and then he did run to put the key into the lock of the milkhouse door, and I said he should have none, and he said he would have some, and then he opened the door and went upon the shelf, and there upon a new cheese laid down the key, and being a while within he came out again, and locked the door and said that he had made flap butter for me, and so departed, and then she said she told her aunt of it, and then she sent for the priest, and when he came he bade her to pray to God, and call on the name of Jesus, and so the next day my lord he came again to me with the key of our milkhouse door in his mouth, and then I said in the name of Jesus what hast thou there, and then he laid down the key and said that I spake evil words in speaking of that name, and then he departed, and so my aunt took up the key, for he had kept it from us two days and a night, and then we went into the milkhouse and there we did see the print of butter upon the cheese, and then within a few days after he came again with a bean pod in his mouth, and then the queen's attorney asked what that was, and so the other justices declared, and then she said my lord I said in the name of Jesus what hast thou there, and so then he laid it down and said I spake evil words and departed and came again by and by with a piece of bread in his mouth, and I asked him what he would have, and he said butter it was that he would have, and so he departed, and my lord I did not see him no more till Wednesday last, which was the 28th day of July, why said the queen's attorney was he with thee on Wednesday last, yes she said, what did he then to thee said he, my lord said she he came with a knife in his mouth and asked me if I were not dead, and I said No I thanked God, and then he said if I would not die that he would thrust his knife to my heart but he would make me to die, and then I said in the name of Jesus lay down thy knife, and he said he would not depart from his sweet dame's knife as yet, and then I asked of him who was his dame, and then he nodded and wagged his head to your house Mother Waterhouse, then the queen's attorney asked of the said Agnes Waterhouse what she said to it, then she demanded what manner knife that it was and Agnes Brown said that it was a dagger knife, there thou liest said Agnes Waterhouse, why, quoth the queen's attorney, marry my lord (quoth she) she saith it is a dagger knife and I have none such in my house, but a great knife, and therein she lieth, yea yea, my lord quoth Joan Waterhouse she lieth in that she saith it had a face like an ape, for this that came to me was like a dog, well said the queen's attorney, well, can you make it come before us now, if ye can we will dispatch you out of prison by and by, no faith said Agnes Waterhouse I cannot, for in faith if I had let him go as my daughter did I could make him come by and by, but now I have no more power over him, then said the queen's attorney, Agnes Waterhouse when did thy Cat suck of thy blood never said she, no said he, let me see, and then the jailer lifted up her kerchief on her head, and there was divers spots in her face and one on her nose, then said the queen's attorney, in good faith Agnes when did he suck of thy blood last, by my faith my lord said she, not this fortnight, and so the jury went together for that matter."

*The end and last confession of mother Waterhouse at her death, which
was the 29th day of July, Anno 1566.*

"First (being ready prepared to receive her death) she confessed earnestly that ·
she had been a witch and used such execrable sorcery the space of fifteen years,
and had done many abominable deeds, the which she repented earnestly and
unfeignedly, and desired almighty God's forgiveness in that she had abused his
most holy name by her devilish practises, and trusted to be saved by his most
unspeakable mercy. And being demanded of the bystanders, she confessed that
she sent her Satan to one Wardol, a neighbour of hers, being a tailor (with whom
she was offended) to hurt and destroy him and his goods. And this her Satan
went thereabout for to have done her will, but in the end he returned to her
again, and was not able to do this mischief, she asked the cause, and he answered because the said Wardol was so strong in faith that he had no power to
hurt him, yet she sent him divers and sundry times (but all in vain) to have
mischieved him. And being demanded whether she was accustomed to go to
church to the common prayer or divine service, she said yea, and being required
what she did there she said she did as other women do, and prayed right heartily
there, and when she was demanded what prayer she said, she answered the
Lord's prayer, the Ave Maria, and the Belief, and then they demanded whether in
Latin or in English, and she said in Latin, and they demanded why she said it not
in English but in Latin, seeing that it was set out by public authority and according to God's word that all men should pray in the English and mother tongue
that they best understand, and she said that Satan would at no time suffer her to
say it in English, but at all times in Latin: for these and many other offences
which she hath committed, done and confessed, she bewailed, repented, and
asked mercy of God, and all the world forgiveness, and thus she yielded up her
soul, trusting to be in joy with Christ her Saviour, which dearly had bought her
with his most precious blood. Amen."

47

The Prosecutions at Trier (1581–93)

Witch fears and witch persecutions of great intensity flared sporadi-
cally throughout Europe in the late sixteenth century.[1] One of the most
striking lasted for almost twelve years, with varying degrees of activity, in the lands of the elector-archbishop of Trier, centered in the

---

1. One of the most meticulous studies of the outbreak of prosecutions in a particular region
during the 1580s is Wolfgang Behringer, *Witchcraft Persecutions in Bavaria: Popular Magic,
Religious Zealotry and Reason of State in Early Modern Europe*, trans. J. C. Grayson and David
Lederer (Cambridge, 1997), 116–211.

cathedral city of Trier. Sporadic trials and executions had begun in the jurisdiction of the elector-archbishop as early as 1572, and other trials took place in the region in 1582, the latter under the direction of the senior judge of the civil court at Trier, vice-governor of the city, rector of the university, and later the highest-ranking victim of any witchcraft trial in Europe, Dietrich Flade.[2]

In the annual report of the Jesuit college at Trier for 1585 (Text 47A) a young boy testified to having been taken to the sabbat. In 1586 another Jesuit report stated that "In this year and in those next following, feminine duplicity mocked the public distress by witchcraft; and Satan himself trumped up here another Circe, as it were, to wreak cruel woes on mortals, to bewitch to death the cattle, to ruin the harvests, and to stir up tempests by her arts. And what carried the infamy of the horrible thing to the uttermost, was that both rich and poor, of every rank, age, and sex, sought a share in the accursed crime."[3] As the prior of the Carthusian convent at Cologne observed, "Among the inhabitants of Trier the evil spirit seems to have set up his throne."[4] These years were years of meteorological and economic disaster for the region, and when, in 1587, witches were accused of having made an attempt on the life of the elector-archbishop himself (Text 47B), one of the accused named Dietrich Flade (Text 47C). In June 1587 a woman convicted of witchcraft also named Flade, as did others, and in 1588 Flade was named as one of the leaders of the sect of witches. After unsuccessfully protesting his innocence, Flade fled from Trier in October 1588, but was captured and then appealed to the elector. This appeal along with a letter from the elector was submitted to the theological faculty of the university of Trier (Text 47D). Flade was arrested and imprisoned. His trial began in August 1589, and in September Flade confessed to the charges and was sentenced to death and executed (Text 47E).

Flade's case became widely known throughout Europe. The Louvain demonologist Martín Del Rio described it in his own treatise (Text 50), and the suffragan bishop of Trier, Peter Binsfeld, wrote a justification of the Trier prosecutions for witchcraft, *Treatise on the Confessions of*

---

2. The case is recounted by George Lincoln Burr, "The Fate of Dietrich Flade," in *George Lincoln Burr: His Life and Selections from His Writings*, ed. Lois Oliphant Gibbons (Ithaca, N.Y., 1943), 190–233, and "On the Loos Manuscript," 147–55.

3. Burr, "The Fate of Dietrich Flade," 202–3.

4. Andreas Heinz, "'Bei den Trieren scheint der Böse Geist seinen Sitz aufgeschlagen zu haben: Ein bisher unbekannter Bericht des Kölner Kartäuserpriors Johannes Reckschenkel (1526–1611) über Hexenverfolgungen im Trierer Land," in *Hexenglaube und Hexenprozesse im Raum Rhein-Mosel-Saar*, ed. Gunther Franz and Franz Irsigler (Trier, 1995), 449–57.

Sorcerers and Witches, also in 1589 (Fig. 27), an immensely influential work that was translated into German in 1591 and printed in Munich in 1592.[5]

Binsfeld's text was answered by the Dutch professor of theology at Trier, Cornelius Loos (1546–1595), a close reader of Johann Weyer (Text 44), who wrote a treatise *On True and False Magic* denouncing the Trier trials and the beliefs that underlay them. But his text was confiscated before it could be printed, and Loos was imprisoned in the Trier monastery of St. Maximin (ironically, the burial place of Regino of Prüm [Text 5]), and in 1593 he was forced by Binsfeld to recant his accusations and other beliefs, the process narrated some years later by the canon Linden of Trier. Despite its brevity, Linden's account (Text 47F) offers a wealth of illuminating details: the involvement of notables as well as commoners, the pervasiveness of the fear, the severity of the judicial process, and the ability of men to profit from the agonies of their brothers.

A persecution such as that at Trier demands a population that believes in the efficacy of the process by which the witches are identified and exterminated. Skeptics were dangerous dissenters, intolerable to those who saw the need to mobilize a region against the servants of evil. When such a skeptic arose at Trier in the person of Cornelius Loos, he not only had to be silenced, but, in the end, brought to add his voice to the consensus for persecution.

SOURCE: Burr, "The Fate of Dietrich Flade," 200–201, 205–6, 209, 216–17, 221–22; Burr, *The Witch Persecutions,* 13–18.

FURTHER READING: *Hexenglaube und Hexenprozesse im Raum Rhein-Mosel-Saar,* ed. Gunther Franz and Franz Irsigler, vol. 1 of *Trierer Hexenprozesse: Quellen und Darstellungen* (Trier, 1995).

A

"Often have our priests been summoned to the witches, whose number here is very great, and have attended them even to the place of punishment; and through God's goodness it has been brought about that with great grief for their sins they have died piously even amid the torments of the flames." And they add an anecdote which not only suggests the whereabouts of their activity, but for him who will read between the lines has a more direct bearing upon our story. "Among these witches, there was one who had beguiled by her arts a boy of eight, and was wont to take him to the place where at night they gave themselves up to their devilish doings, in order that while they danced together he

5. Behringer, *Witchcraft Persecutions in Bavaria,* 140–42.

might beat the drum; and he was often present when they were plotting witch-craft against others. This boy the Archbishop ordered to be brought to Trier, that he might be taught his catechism by us (for he was completely ignorant of Christian teaching, not even knowing the Lord's prayer). And while our priest was testing his mind in various ways, he noticed that the cord of the sacred waxen image of *Agnus Dei* which he had hung about the boy's neck had been twisted and tied with knots as if broken. Asking the reason, he learned that the Devil had visited the boy in the night, had scolded him sharply for letting himself be so easily won over, and had bid him fling away the thing hanging on his neck, unless he wished to be flogged. The frightened boy had done his bid-ding, and of a sudden had been snatched away to the walls of the city. There he found a black goat, and, mounting it, was borne in briefest space to the wonted spot of the vile sport of the witches; and, when all was at length over, was brought back to the palace. Many things the boy revealed which the confessions of witches have since proved true. So the Governor of the city, in the name and by the authority of the Archbishop, asked that the boy might be taken into our school until he should be properly instructed in religion, so that afterward, living at the palace, but attending the sacraments with us, he might be safe from the wiles of demons; and this was done."

B

"Through the cunning enemy of mankind, was also misled a certain youth of fifteen years—a rustic, but keen of wit—who went several times to the places where the witches have their meetings and perpetrate their horrid dances, their feasts, and the rest of their crimes. He had not, indeed, yet renounced God and the virgin Mother of God (as is prescribed by their ritual), and been initiated into the diabolic mysteries; but, having taken a cat's brain at the feast, he contracted (especially as it was in the wane of the moon) a great imbecility of his own brain. He was at length arrested by the Governor and brought to this city, which he had before seen but had never entered (a thing seemingly due less to accident than to the artfulness of the Devil, who wished his followers to be through him brought into danger), and quartered in the Electoral palace, in order that, being kept in a secluded place, he might the better be taught by our priests and escape his wretched bondage. But, when he was tormented at night by the witches and the Devil, and even cruelly beaten, and when the waxen figure of consecrated *Agnus Dei*, which had been hung about his neck, was torn off, and he was urged with many threats to go on with what he had begun, then by order of the Archbishop he was brought to our college. And not even there was he safe from this persistent annoyance, until the bedchamber in which he was had been purged by exorcisms, and freed from all molestation of the Devil by the benedic-tions of the Church. Later, when he was exorcised in our sanctuary according to the Catholic ritual, he kept his eyes constantly fixed on the window nearest the altar; and when asked, 'What are you looking at?' he concealed what afterward he confessed—that he saw his master Sambuco (for in this way is given charge of each witch a special demon whom the witches call master) sitting behind that window and threatening him through the window-slit if he should break the pact he had made with himself. When questioned by the examiner, the boy narrated (what afterward he confessed to the Archbishop himself) that, among those whom he was denouncing by his testimony, was one who had boasted at the witch-sabbath, that on a certain night he had administered to the sleeping Archbishop, in whose service he held an office of great importance, a deadly potion, His Grace being accessible, because contrary to his habit he had on going to bed laid on the table the amulet of sacred wax which he wore about his neck; but that, there being not enough of the drug, the Elector would this time escape death. Nor was the story false or doubtful; for the Archbishop, on awaking, although ignorant of the matter, felt himself so ill that for several days his life was in danger, until his physician expelled the dire poison by a health-giving draught. And, when, as the lad went on to tell other things of this sort, it was not easy to put faith in what he said, he turned to the Governor of the city: 'Nay, your life too,' he said, 'has been twice plotted against; but the little locket you wear, which has two engraved figures cut in it, and holds something consecrated (he meant *Agnus Dei*), and which you have been wont to hang on your bed, was a hindrance to them, so that they could not carry out what they planned.' And the Governor himself admitted the truth of these statements."

C

"Inasmuch as a young boy named Matthias, born at Weisskirch, led by others into witchcraft, was accused thereof by other executed persons, and was alleged also to have been present at the witch-sabbath, he was, by order of the Governor of Trier, brought to this city in custody; and, being examined, did at once, without torture, freely confess that he had through the seduction of the Devil several times been present at the sabbath,—that there he had seen a great number of richly-clad people, and among the rest two grandees in showy array. Now these, being described by him as to the clothing they then wore and their bodily figure, correspond entirely with Dr. Flade and another, both in their physical proportions and in all other details; and the aforesaid description was afterward confirmed by the fact that, when once the lad followed with others to see a criminal flogged out of the city, and Dr. Flade fell under his eyes, he at once recognized him, and afterward openly declared that he had seen the Meier of Trier (meaning Dr. Flade, the Judge) at the witch-sabbath, and had met him at the expulsion of the criminal."

D

"It has doubtless long ago come to your knowledge," he writes, "into what general suspicion of witchcraft our Judge at Trier, Dr. Dietrich Flade, has fallen, and what has since taken place as to his flight. Now, although at first, when he was accused by only one or two of the persons executed for witchcraft, we thought the matter hardly worthy of notice, and therefore for a while, on account of his rank, let the matter drift; yet afterward the scandal grew ever greater, and the accusations of the witches, both old and young, men and women, became so frequent that we were led to have the trials, in so far as they related to him, excerpted, and find that twenty-three executed men and women have confessed against him, and persisted firmly in the assertion to their end that he was with and among them at their witch-sabbaths, took the lead in evil suggestions, and helped personally to carry them out. And these confessions come not from one court alone, but from many different ones—from Trier, Maximin, Paulin, Euren, Esch, St. Matthias, Pfalzel, Saarburg, and elsewhere; and the suspicion is increased by the fact that others accused by these same persons have been found guilty and have confessed—among them some of considerable respectability, except that partly through avarice, partly through unchastity and other devilish impulses, they have fallen into this wretchedness. All this you will learn from the enclosed *Extract*, and especially what a young boy who was misled into such witch-doings confessed freely and without constraint against him, Flade, though he had never before known him, with description of his person, rank, and appearance, and now, seeing him by chance at an execution, he immediately, without anybody's suggestion, pointed him out and said that he was the one who had been always at the witch-sabbaths. Well known to you, moreover, is what afterwards occurred in connection with his second attempt at flight. And we send you also herewith the petition the said Dr. Flade wrote us, wherein at the end he almost betrays himself, desiring us to allow him to enter the monastic life, and offering us the disposition of his property; a thing which surely, if he were not conscious of guilt, was not likely to be done by him, a man notoriously avaricious and, as shown by an investigation heretofore made, of such character that by reason of his avarice justice was almost ill-administered, so that we perhaps already had cause enough to dismiss him from his office. When we bethink us, however, of the position of honor he has so long held, and remember too that among scholars there are current all sorts of objections as to the confessions that this one or that has been seen at the witch-sabbath, we have wished, for the sake of further information, and especially because witchcraft is counted among the ecclesiastical crimes, and it has heretofore been customary for such cases to be first submitted to ecclesiastical judges, and then after their finding to be remitted to the lay judge, not to omit to consult in this matter the theological faculty as well as the jurists, so that nobody, whether of high or of low degree, may have rights to complain, and that in the administration of justice we may fall into no error. Therefore it is our gracious will," concludes the Elector, "that you of the theological faculty come together privately and consider this matter as its importance demands, and immediately let us know in writing how you find it, according to the canon law and the unanimous opinion of the theologians, that we may take such further steps as it behooves, and that Justice may be left to her course without respect of persons."

E

"Thus, as a criminal and dishonored, he heard his sentence from the very court whose severity he himself as judge had for many years restrained. As he went to the place of execution, whither, though he was in declining years and was worn out by his troubles, he insisted on going afoot, the whole city, stirred by the novel sight, followed after. And yet, with such lofty spirit did he bear himself that to not one of all those who beheld his self-control in that terrible humiliation did he utter a word of complaint for himself or his fall or the infamy of his ignominious death. When the stake was reached he addressed the thronging crowd in words suited to the occasion and with unbroken spirit, exhorting them to learn from the example of his mournful fate to shun the deceits and wiles of the arch-enemy Satan. Thus by word and deed the criminal mitigated the atrocity of his crime, yet justified to his townsmen his death."

F

Inasmuch as it was popularly believed that the continued sterility of many years was caused by witches through the malice of the Devil, the whole country rose to exterminate the witches. This movement was promoted by many in office, who hoped wealth from the persecution. And so, from court to court throughout the towns and villages of all the diocese, scurried special accusers, inquisitors, notaries, jurors, judges, constables, dragging to trial and torture human beings of both sexes and burning them in great numbers. Scarcely any of those who were accused escaped punishment. Nor were there spared even the leading men in the city of Trier. For the judge, with two Burgomasters, several Councilors and Associate Judges, canons of sundry collegiate churches, parish-priests, rural deans, were swept away in this ruin. So far, at length, did the madness of the furious populace and of the courts go in this thirst for blood and booty that there was scarcely anybody who was not smirched by some suspicion of this crime.

Meanwhile notaries, copyists, and innkeepers grew rich. The executioner rode a blooded horse, like a noble of the court, and went clad in gold and silver; his wife vied with noble dames in the richness of her array. The children of those convicted and punished were sent into exile; their goods were confiscated; plowman and vintner failed—hence came sterility. A more dire pestilence or a more ruthless invader could hardly have ravaged the territory of Trier than this inquisition and persecution without bounds: many were the reasons for doubting that all were really guilty. This persecution lasted for several years, and some of those who presided over the administration of justice gloried in the multitude of the stakes, at each of which a human being had been given to the flames.

At last, though the flames were still unsated, the people grew impoverished, rules were made and enforced restricting the fees and costs of examinations and examiners, and suddenly, as when in war funds fail, the zeal of the persecutors died out.

And, finally, as I have made mention of Losaeus Callidius [Loos], who tried by a thousand arts to make public the book which he had written in defence of the witches (and some fear that even yet some evil demon may bring this about), I have brought for an antidote the Recantation signed by him. Its authentic and so-called original copy is in the possession of a devout and most honorable man, Joannes Baxius, J. U. Lic. (whose energy and zeal against this nefarious heresy God will some day reward), from whom I have received the following transcript, certified by a notary:

I, Cornelius Losaeus Callidus, born at the town of Gouda in Holland, but now (on account of a certain treatise *On True and False Witchcraft*, rashly and presumptuously written without the knowledge and permission of the superiors of this place, shown by me to others, and then sent to be printed at Cologne) arrested and imprisoned in the Imperial Monastery of St. Maximin, near Trier, by order of the Most Reverend and Most Illustrious Lord, the Papal Nuncio, Octavius, Bishop of Tricarico: whereas I am informed of a surety that in the aforesaid book and also in certain letters of mine on the same subject sent clandestinely to the clergy and town council of Trier, and to others (for the purpose of hindering the execution of justice against the witches, male and female), are contained many articles which are not only erroneous and scandalous, but also suspected of heresy and smacking of the crime of treason, as being seditious and foolhardy, against the common opinion of theological teachers and the decisions and bulls of the Supreme Pontiffs, and contrary to the practice and to the statutes and laws of the magistrates and judges, not only of this Archdiocese of Trier, but of other provinces and principalities, I do therefore revoke, condemn, reject, and repudiate the said articles, in the order in which they are here subjoined.

1. In the first place, I revoke, condemn, reject, and censure the idea (which both in words and writing I have often and before many persons pertinaciously asserted, and which I wished to be the head and front of this my disputation) that the things which are written about the bodily transportation or translation

of witches, male and female, are altogether fanciful and must be reckoned the figments of an empty superstition; [and this I recant] both because it smacks of rank heresy and because this opinion partakes of sedition and hence savors of the crime of treason.

2. For (and this in the second place I recant), in the letters which I have clandestinely sent to sundry persons, I have pertinaciously, without solid reasons, alleged against the magistracy that the [aerial] flight of witches is false and imaginary; asserting, moreover, that the wretched creatures are compelled by the severity of the torture to confess things which they have never done, and that by cruel butchery innocent blood is shed and by a new alchemy gold and silver coined from human blood.

3. By these and by other things of the same sort, partly in private conversations among the people, partly in sundry letters addressed to both the magistracies, both lay and spiritual, I have accused of tyranny to their subjects the superiors and the judges.

4. And consequently, inasmuch as the Most Reverend and Most Illustrious Archbishop and Prince-Elector of Trier not only permits witches, male and female, to be subjected in his diocese to deserved punishment, but has also ordained laws regulating the method and costs of judicial procedure against witches, I have with heedless temerity tacitly insinuated the charge of tyranny against the aforesaid Elector of Trier.

5. I revoke and condemn, moreover, the following conclusions of mine, to wit: that there are no witches who renounce God, pay worship to the Devil, bring storms by the Devil's aid, and do other like things, but that all these things are dreams.

6. Also, that magic (*magia*) ought not to be called witchcraft (*maleficium*), nor magicians (*magi*) witches (*malefici*), and that the passage of Holy Scripture, "Thou shalt not suffer a witch to live" (*Maleficos non patieris vivere* [Exodus 22: 18]) is to be understood of those who by a natural use of natural poisons inflict death.

7. That no compact does or can exist between the Devil and a human being.

8. That devils do not assume bodies.

9. That the life of Hilarion written by St. Jerome is not authentic.

10. That there is no sexual intercourse between the Devil and human beings.

11. That neither devils nor witches can raise tempests, rain-storms, hailstorms, and the like, and that the things said about these are mere dreams.

12. That spirit and form apart from matter cannot be seen by man.

13. That it is rash to assert that whatever devils can do, witches also can do through their aid.

14. That the opinion that a superior demon can cast out an inferior is erroneous and derogatory to Christ [Luke 11].

15. That the Popes in their bulls do not say that magicians and witches perpetrate such things (as are mentioned above).

16. That the Roman Pontiffs granted the power to proceed against witches, lest if they should refuse they might be unjustly accused of magic, just as some of their predecessors had been justly accused of it.

These assertions, all and singular, with many calumnies, falsehoods, and sycophancies, toward the magistracy, both secular and ecclesiastical, spitefully, immodestly, and falsely poured forth, without cause, with which my writings on magic teem, I hereby expressly and deliberately condemn, revoke, and reject, earnestly beseeching the pardon of God and of my superiors for what I have done, and solemnly promising that in future I will neither in word nor in writing, by myself or through others, in whatsoever place it may befall me to be, teach, promulgate, defend, or assert any of these things. If I shall do to the contrary, I subject myself thenceforward, as if it were now, to all the penalties of the law against relapsed heretics, recusants, seditious offenders, traitors, backbiters, sycophants, who have been openly convicted, and also to those ordained against perjurers. I submit myself also to arbitrary correction, whether by the Archbishop of Trier or by any other magistrates under whom it may befall me to dwell, and who may be certified of my relapse and of my broken faith, that they may punish me according to my deserts, in honor and reputation, property and person.

In testimony of all which I have, with my own hand, signed this my recantation of the aforesaid articles, in presence of notary and witnesses.

(*Signed*) CORNELIUS LOOSAEUS CALLIDIUS

(*and attested*)

Done in the Imperial Monastery of St. Maximin, outside the walls of Trier, in the abbot's chamber, in presence of the Reverend, Venerable, and Eminent Sirs, Peter Binsfeld, Bishop of Azotus, vicar-general in matters spiritual of the Most Reverend Archbishop of Trier, our most clement lord; and Reinerus, abbot of the said monastery; Bartholomaeus van Bodeghem, of Delft, J. U. L., Official of the Ecclesiastical Court of Trier; Georgius von Helffenstein, Doctor of Theology, Dean of the Collegiate Church of St. Simeon in the city of Trier, and Joannes Colmann, J. U. D., Canon of the said church and Seal-Bearer of the Court of Trier, etc., in the year of Our Lord 1592 *more Trev.*, on Monday, March 15th, in the presence of me the notary undersigned and of the worthy Nicolaus Dolent and Daniel Maier, secretary and copyist respectively of the Reverend Lord Abbot, as witnesses specially called and summoned to this end.

(*Signed*) ADAMUS HEC TECTONIUS, Notary

(*And below*)

Compared with its original and found to agree, by me the undersigned Secretary of the town of Antwerp,

G. KIEFFEL

Here you have the Recantation in full. And yet afterwards again at Brussels, while serving as curate in the church of Notre Dame de la Chapelle, he [Loos] was accused of relapse, and was released only after a long imprisonment, and being again brought into suspicion (whence you may understand the pertinacity of his madness) escaped a third indictment through a premature death; but (much the pity!) left behind not a few partisans, men so imperfectly versed in medicine and sound theology as to share this stupid error. Would that they might be wise, and seriously realize at last how rash and noxious it is to prefer the ravings of a single heretic, Weyer, to the judgment of the Church!

48
The Prosecutions in Scotland (1591)

As was true in the fourteenth and fifteenth centuries and as is true in our own time, individual criminal cases—especially those involving prominent political figures—could excite the public interest and contribute to popular conceptions as much as any general considerations of crime and the nature of the criminal. The first statute concerning witchcraft in Scotland was passed in 1563, the same year as the Elizabethan statute in England. Isolated trials and convictions followed, but not until the years 1590–93 was there a group of witchcraft trials whose results were widely publicized, because they touched on the person of the king and queen themselves.

In 1 Samuel 15: 23 it is stated that "the sin of rebellion is as the sin of witchcraft," and in the heavily biblical culture of late sixteenth-century western Europe, that maxim carried considerable weight. It carried even greater weight when particular rulers perceived themselves to be personally threatened by witchcraft, as did King James VI of Scotland, whose experience with the trials of 1590–1593 and their role in the attack on the king by the earl of Bothwell in 1591 led to the writing of James's own treatise on the subject, the *Daemonologie*, in 1597. Although James VI and I showed himself relatively moderate in dealing with witchcraft both before and after the years 1591–1597, the statute of 1563 and the trials described here laid the groundwork for the later prosecution of witchcraft in Scotland and perhaps for the later English statute of 1604 (Text 46).

The following account of the trial for witchcraft of Agnes Sampson, Dr. Fian, and others was circulated in a contemporary pamphlet, *Newes from Scotland* (1591). Of particular interest is the denunciation of one alleged witch extracted under torture from another accused witch, indicating by what means a persecution could grow and flour-

ish. Of the tortures mentioned in the text, the "pilliwinkes" were similar to a thumbscrew; the "bootes" were sheaths for the lower leg,
mounted with wedges, which, when driven by a large hammer increased pressure on the shin and ankle bones, eventually crushing
the leg.

SOURCE: Burr, *The Witch Persecutions*, 19–23.

FURTHER READING: Christina Larner, *Enemies of God: The Witch
Hunt in Scotland* (London, 1981); Larner, "Two Late Scottish Witchcraft Tracts: *Witch-Craft Proven* and *The Trial of Witchcraft*," in Anglo, *The Damned Art*, 227–45; Larner, *Witchcraft and Religion* (Oxford, 1984). On the interests of James VI (after 1603 James I of England)
in witchcraft and his own work, the *Daemonologie* of 1597, see Stuart
Clark, "King James's *Daemonologie*: Witchcraft and Kingship," in Anglo, *The Damned Art*, 156–81; Clark, *Thinking with Demons*, 619–33;
P. G. Maxwell-Stuart, "The Fear of the King Is Death: James VI and the
Witches of East Lothian," in *Fear in Early Modern Society*, ed. William G. Naphy and Penny Roberts (Manchester and New York, 1997),
209–25. On torture, see Edward Peters, *Torture* (1985; expanded ed.
Philadelphia, 1996).

Within the towne of Trenent, in
the kingdome of Scotland, there dwelleth one David Seaton, who, being deputie
bailiffe in the said towne, had a maid called Geillis Duncane, who used secretlie
to absent and lie forth of hir maister's house every other night: This Geillis
Duncane tooke in hand to helpe all such as were troubled or grieved with anie
kinde of sicknes or infirmities and in short space did perfourme many matters
most miraculous; which things, for asmuche as she began to do them upon a
sodaine, having never done the like before, made her maister and others to be in
great admiration, and wondered thereat: by means whereof, the saide David
Seaton had his maide in great suspition that shee did not those things by naturall and lawful wayes, but rather supposed it to bee done by some extraordinarie
and unlawfull meanes.

Whereupon, her maister began to grow verie inquisitive, and examined hir
which way and by what means shee was able to performe matters of so great
importance; whereat shee gave him no aunswere: nevertheless, her maister, to
the intent that hee might the better trie and finde out the truth of the same, did
with the help of others torment her with the torture of the pilliwinkes upon her
fingers, which is a grievous torture; and binding or wrenching her head with a
cord or roape, which is a most cruell torment also; yet would she not confess
anie thing; whereuppon, they suspecting that she had beene marked by the
Devill (as commonly witches are), made diligent search about her, and found
the enemies mark to be in her fore crag, or fore part of her throate; which being

found, she confessed that al her doings was done by the wicked allurements and entisements of the Devil, and that she did them by witchcraft. After this her confession, she was committed to prison, where shee continued a season, where immediately shee accused these persons following to bee notorious witches, and caused them forthwith to be apprehended, one after another, viz. Agnes Sampson the eldest witche of them all, dwelling in Haddington; Agnes Tompson of Edenbrough; Doctor Fian alias John Cuningham, master of the schoole at Saltpans in Lowthian, of whose life and strange acts you shal heare more largely in the end of this discourse. These were by the saide Geillis Duncane accused, as also George Motts wife, dwelling in Lowthian; Robert Grierson, skipper; and Jannet Blandilands; with the potter's wife of Seaton: the smith at the Brigge Hallis, with innumerable others in those parts, and dwelling in those bounds aforesaid; of whom some are alreadie executed, the rest remaine in prison to receive the doome of judgment at the Kinges Majesties will and pleasure.

The saide Geillis Duncane also caused Ewphame Mecalrean to bee apprehended, who conspired and performed the death of her godfather, and who used her art upon a gentleman, being one of the Lordes and Justices of the Session, for bearing good will to her daughter. Shee also caused to be apprehended one Barbara Naper, for bewitching to death Archibalde lait Earle of Angus, who languished to death by witchcraft, and yet the same was not suspected; but that hee died of so straunge a disease as the Phisition knewe not how to cure or remedie the same. But of all other the said witches, these two last before recited, were reputed for as civill honest women as anie that dwelled within the cittie of Edenbrough, before they were apprehended. Many other besides were taken dwelling in Lieth, who are detayned in prison untill his Majesties further will and pleasure be knowne. . . .

As touching the aforesaide Doctor Fian alias John Cunningham, the examination of his actes since his apprehension, declareth the great subtletie of the Divell, and therefore maketh thinges to appeare the more miraculous; for beeing apprehended by the accusation of the saide Geillis Duncane aforesaide, who confessed he was their Regester, and that there was not one man suffered to come to the Divels readings but onely hee: the saide Doctor was taken and imprisoned, and used with the accustomed paine provided for those offences, inflicted upon the rest, as is aforesaide. First, By thrawing of his head with a rope, whereat he would confess nothing. Secondly, Hee was perswaded by faire meanes to confesse his follies, but that would prevaile as little. Lastly, Hee was put to the most severe and cruell paine in the worlde, called the bootes who after he had received three strokes, being inquired if he would confesse his damnable actes and wicked life, his toong would not serve him to speake, in respect whereof the rest of the witches willed to searche his toong, under which was founde two pinnes, thrust up into the heade; whereupon the witches did say, Now is the charme stinted; and shrewed, that those charmed pinnes were the cause he could not confesse any thing: Then was he immediately released of the bootes, brought before the King, his confession was taken, and his own hand willingly set thereunto. . . .

Thus, all the daie, this Doctor Fian continued very solitarie, and seemed to have a care of his owne soule, and would call uppon God, shewing himselfe penitent for his wicked life; neverthless, the same night, he found such meanes that he stole the key of the prison doore and chamber in which he was, which in the night hee opened and fled awaie to the Saltpans, where hee was always resident, and first apprehended. Of whose sodaine departure, when the Kings Majestie had intelligence, hee presently commanded diligent inquirie to bee made for his apprehension; and for the better effecting thereof, hee sent publike proclamations into all partes of his lande to the same effect. By meanes of whose hot and harde pursuite he was agayn taken, and brought to prison; and then, being called before the Kings Highnes, hee was re-examined, as well touching his departure, as also touching all that had before happened. But this Doctor, notwithstanding that his owne confession appeareth, remaining in recorde under his owne hande writting, and the same thereunto fixed in the presence of the Kings Majestie and sundrie of his Councell, yet did he utterly denie the same.

Whereupon the Kings Majestie, perceiving his stubborne willfulnesse, conceived and imagined, that in the time of his absence, hee had entered into newe conference and league with the Devill his maister; and that hee had beene again newly marked, for the which he was narrowly searched; but it coulde not in anie waie be founde; yet for more tryall of him, to make him confesse, hee was commaunded to have a most strange torment, which was done in this manner following. His nailes upon all his fingers were riven and pulled off with an instrument called in Scottish a Turkas, which in England wee call a payre of pincers, and under every nayle there was thrust in two needels over even up to the heads. At all which torments notwithstanding, the Doctor never shronke anie whit; neither woulde he then confesse it the sooner, for all the tortures inflicted upon him. Then was hee, with all convenient speede, by commandement, convaied againe to the torment of the bootes, wherein hee continued a long time, and did abide so many blowes in them, that his legges were crusht and beaten together as small as might be; and the bones and flesh so brused, that the bloud and marrow spouted forth in great abundance; whereby, they were made unserviceable for ever. And notwithstanding all these grievous paines and cruell torments, he would not confesse anie things; so deeply had the Devill entered into his heart, that hee utterly denied all that which he before avouched; and would saie nothing thereunto, but this, that what hee had done and sayde before, was onely done and sayde, for fear of paynes which he had endured.

Upon great consideration, therefore, taken by the Kings Majestie and his Councell, as well for the due execution of justice uppon such detestable malefactors, as also for example sake, to remayne a terrour to all others heerafter, that shall attempt to deale in the lyke wicked and ungodlye actions as witch-craft, sorcerie, conjuration, and such lyke; the saide Doctor Fian was soon after arraigned, condemned and adjudged by the law to die, and then to be burned according to the lawe of that lande provided in that behalfe. Whereupon hee was put into a carte, and beeing first strangled, hee was immediately put into a great fire, being readie provided for that purpose, and there burned in the Castle Hill of Edenbrough, on a Saterdaie, in the ende of Januarie last past, 1591.

49
Nicholas Rémy: *Demonolatry* (1595)

From the treatises by Jean Bodin (Text 45) and Peter Binsfeld (Fig. 27) to that of Pierre de Lancre in 1612, a new series of treatises on demonology with a particular emphasis on witchcraft appeared in western Europe and effectively supplemented, if they did not supplant entirely, the older *Malleus Maleficarum* (which was itself reprinted and supplemented with additional texts during these years). Although several of these were written by ecclesiastics, whether inquisitors or not, a number were written by laymen, usually judges themselves, who cited known cases and confessions, thereby giving their works substantial authority. One of the most interesting of these was the treatise by Nicholas Rémy, *Demonolatry*, of 1595.

Rémy (1530–1612), statesman, jurist, and man of letters, was privy councillor to the duke of Lorraine and after 1591 the attorney general of the duchy, and a judge involved in witchcraft cases for more than fifteen years. When an epidemic in 1592 drove him from the court at Nancy to a country estate where he enjoyed a long stretch of leisure time, Rémy compiled a demonological treatise based primarily upon his own courtroom experience. It enjoyed a great reputation, being reprinted eight times, including two German translations. Rémy dealt learnedly and systematically with the formal confessions of his victims, producing a book that seemed irrefutable both as sound Christian scholarship and for its clear natural evidence.

Particularly important is Rémy's argument that magistrates and judges are immune to witchcraft by virtue of their legitimate office and the divine sanction of princely rule. This idea had been developed in the fifteenth century, and in the work of Claude Tholosan (Text 29) and later legal writers on the subject it became a major theme—the magistrate in the course of duty rendered the power of witches and demons useless against himself and his servants.

SOURCE: Nicolas Rémy, *Demonolatry*, trans. E. A. Ashby (London, 1930), bk. 1, chaps. 1–3, pp. 1–7.

FURTHER READING: Robin Briggs, *Witches and Neighbors: The Social and Cultural Context of European Witchcraft* (New York, 1996); Clark, *Thinking with Demons*.

The Inducements by which Men may first be led astray by Demons, and so falling become Dealers in Magic.

Experience itself, to our own great loss and bane, affords us sad proof that Satan seizes as many opportunities of deceiving and destroying mankind as there are different moods and affections natural to the human character. For such as are given over to their lusts and to love he wins by offering them the hope of gaining their desires: or if they are bowed under the load of daily poverty, he allures them by some large and ample promise of riches: or he tempts them by showing them the means of avenging themselves when they have been angered by some injury or hurt received: in short, by whatever other corruption or luxury they have been depraved, he draws them into his power and holds them as it were bound to him. But it is not our purpose to discuss here what are those blind passions and desires by which men may be led into sin; for it would be a waste of time and an abuse of learning to involve ourselves in the much-worn controversy between Prometheus and Epimetheus, reason and appetite. That we pass by, and say that Satan assails mankind not only through their secret and domestic affections and (if I may so express it) by burrowing into their very hearts, but also openly and in declared warfare, as it is called. For he openly addresses them by word of mouth, and appears in visible person to converse with them, as he did when he contended with the Saviour in the wilderness (Matthew 4). But this he does the more easily when he finds a man weakened by the hardships and cares of life; for then he suggests to the man that he is grieved at his misfortunes and is willing to come to help him. But not even so can he aid and assist any man unless that man has broken his baptismal pledge and agreed to transfer his allegiance to him and acknowledge him as his Master.

But if he cannot gain his object in this way by mere persuasion, then Satan employs those allurements and temptations which I have already mentioned: he fabricates some fair and delectable body and offers it for a man's enjoyment: or he can do much by means of a false display of riches: or by providing drugs to poison those upon whom a man wishes to be avenged, or to heal those to whom a man owes a debt of gratitude: often, indeed, the Demons forcibly drive and compel men into compliance by fierce threats and revilings, or by the fear of the lash or prison. For men may just as easily be led by violence to practise sorcery as by coaxing and blandishment, though I shall not here adduce examples to substantiate this statement, since this matter will be considered more fully in its due place: for the present I am content to say that I have found it to be the rarer case for a sorcerer to be driven by force into his abominable practices.

The truth is that, when Satan cannot move a man by fair words, he compels him by fear and threats of danger. When Claude Morèle, who was convicted of witchcraft at Serre (5th Dec., 1586), was asked what was the chief inducement that had first led him to give himself to the Demon, he answered that he had withstood the temptation of all the Demon's fair words, and had only yielded when Satan had threatened to kill his wife and children. At Guermingen, 19th Dec., 1589, Antoine Welch no longer dared to oppose the Demon in anything after he had threatened to twist his neck unless he obeyed his commands, for he seemed on the very point of fulfilling his threat. At Harécourt, 10th Nov., 1586, when he could by no promises persuade Alexée Driget to dedicate herself to him, the Demon at last threatened to destroy the house in which she lived; and this misfortune indeed befell her not long afterwards; but it will be more convenient to discuss elsewhere whether he was the actual cause of it, or whether he merely foresaw that it would happen. Certainly there are many examples in the pagan histories of houses being cast down, the destruction of the crops, chasms in the earth, fiery blasts and other such disastrous tempests stirred up by Demons for the destruction of men for no other purpose than to bind their minds to the observance of some new cult and to establish their mastery more and more firmly over them.

Therefore we may first conclude that it is no mere fable that witches meet and converse with Demons in very person. Secondly, it is clear that Demons use the two most powerful weapons of persuasion against the feeble ills of mortals, namely, hope and fear, desire and terror; for they well know how to induce and inspire such emotions.

How Demons prepare, for those whom they have won, by their Cunning, Drugged Powders, Wands, Ointments and Various Venoms of the sort: some of which cause Death, some only Sickness, and some even Healing. And how these things are not always, or for all Men, poisonous: since there may be found some who are uninjured by frequent Applications of them, notably they whose Office and Business it is to condemn Witches to Death.

From the very beginning the Devil was a murderer (John 8), and never has he ceased to tempt the impious to commit slaughter and parricide. Therefore it is no wonder that, once he has caught men in his toils, his first care is to furnish them with the implements and instruct them in the practices of witchcraft. And lest the business should be delayed or hindered through lack of poison or difficulty in administering it, he provides them at the very first with a fine powder which must infallibly cause the sickness or death of those against whom it is used: nor does its harmfulness of necessity depend upon its being mingled with a man's food or drink, or applied to his bare flesh; for it is enough if but his clothes be lightly dusted with it. The powder which kills is black; that which only causes sickness is ashen, or sometimes reddish in colour. And since witches are often led by fear or bribery, and sometimes even by pity (of which they claim that they are not entirely destitute), to heal those who have been stricken in this manner, they are not without a remedy to their hand; for they are given a third powder, white in colour, with which they dust the sick, or mix it with their food or drink, and so the sickness is dispersed. And these drugs of varying properties and virtue are distinguishable only by their colour. Claude Fellet (at Mazières, 9th Nov., 1584), Jeanne le Ban (at Masmunster, 3rd Jan., 1585), Colette Fischer (at Gerbeville, 7th May, 1585), and nearly all the women of their fellowship, record that they always found the effects of their powders such as we have said. But this distinction in the colours is not so much to ensure the selection of the required poison (for the drugs owe their potency to the Demon, not to any inherent properties of their own), as a visible sign of the pact between the witch and the Demon, and a guarantee of faith. Matteole Guilleraea (at Mazières, 4th Dec., 1584) and Jeanne Alberte (at S. Pierre-Mont, 8th Nov., 1581) add that although the ashen-coloured powder does not as a rule cause a fatal sickness, it has nevertheless the power to kill when it is first received by witches after their enlistment in that army of wickedness; for that initial step has a kind of preference.

But it is a matter of no small wonder that witches not only impregnate with such poisons articles of which the purpose and use is to drive away Demons, but even make use of them during the very time of prayer and the performance of the Sacraments. At Seaulx, 11th Oct., 1587, Jacobeta Weher was envious of the lover of the daughter of her fellow-countryman Pétrone, but could not injure her as she wished; for the girl had emphatically bidden her beware of trying to harm her. But at last, under pretext of doing something else, she infected an asperge with the poison powder and sprinkled the girl with it as she was praying in church: and at once she was stricken with a mortal sickness and soon after died. At Blainville, 16th Jan., 1587, the whole neighbourhood, except Alexée Belheure, had been invited to a feast given by a noble knight named Darnielle on the occasion of his son's baptism. Ill brooking this slight, she evaded the observation of those who were carrying the newly baptized child and, sprinkling it with a poison powder of this kind, killed it.

And since it is not convenient for them always to keep this powder ready in their hand to throw, they have also wands imbued with it or smeared with some unguent or other venemous matter, which they commonly carry as if for driving cattle. With these they often, as it were in joke, strike the men or the cattle which they wish to injure: and that this is no vain or innocent touch is testified by the confessions of François Fellet (at Mazières, 19th Dec., 1583). Marguereta Warner (at Ronchamp, 1st Dec., 1586), Matteole Guilleret (at Pagny-sur-Moselle, 1584), and Jacobeta Weher whom I have just mentioned.

Yet there are those who, thanks to some singular blessing from Heaven, are immune from such attacks; for witches have not always unlimited power against all men, as Jeanne Gransaint (at Condé-sur-l'Escaut, July, 1582) and Catharina Ruffe (at Ville-sur-Moselle, 28th July, 1587) have recorded that they were more than once informed by their Demons. I remember questioning that woman of Nancy called Lasnier (Asinaria, from her husband the ass-driver [asinarius]), upon the statements of the witnesses, and especially concerning this particular point; and she spoke with great indignation as follows: "It is well for you Judges that we can do nothing against you! For there are none upon whom we would more gladly work our spite, than you who are always harrying us folk with every torture and punishment."

Jaqueline Xaluëtia (at Grand-Bouxières-sous-Amance, 29th April, 1588), freely and without any previous questioning, acknowledged the same. This woman, having long been suspected of witchcraft, was put in chains; but after a little she was liberated by order of the Judge, because she had endured all the torture of her questioning in an obstinate silence. After much turning of the matter over in her mind, she could not rest until she had worked some evil upon the Judge who had treated her with such severity; for the filthy rabble of witches is commonly desirous of revenge. Therefore she ceased not to pester her Demon to find some safe and easy way for her to vent her spite: but he, knowing her folly towards herself in this matter, kept pleading different excuses for postponing the affair and inventing reasons why he should not comply with her wish. But at length, since Xaluëtia did not cease to importune him, he told her in shame and grief that, in place of that fortune which he had often foretold for her, her own folly and impotence would be exposed and would betray her. "I have always, my Xaluëtia," he said, "endured very hardly the unbridled severity of those executioners towards you, and often in the past have I had a mind to be revenged: but I openly admit that all my attempts come to nothing. For they are in His guardianship and protection who alone can oppose my designs. But I can repay these officers for their persecutions by causing them to share in a common disaster, and will strike the crops and the fields far and wide with a tempest and lay them waste as much as I am able."

This is not unlike the statement of Nicole Morèle (at Serre, 24th Jan., 1587), that Demons are impregnated and seared with an especial hatred towards those who put into operation the law against witches, but that it is in vain that they attempt or seek to wreak any vengeance against them. See how God defends and protects the authority of those to whom He has given the mandate of His power upon earth, and how He has therefore made them partakers of His prerogative and honour, calling them Gods even as Himself (Ps. 82): so that without doubt they are sacrosanct and, by reason of their duty and their office, invulnerable even to the spells of witches. Indeed they are not even bound in the least by the commands of the Demons themselves, even though they may have previously vowed allegiance to them and have been touched with the stain of that oath. For that witches benefit by the protection of the sanctity of a magistrate's office (at least for as long as they hold such office), so that they are free from all the most importunate complaints and instigations of their Little Masters, who testified by Didier Finance (at Saint-Dié, 14th July, 1581), who said that during the whole period of his magistracy he never once saw his familiar spirit, who at all other times had been his most sedulous adviser on every occasion.

Therefore let the Magistrate undertake his duties with confidence, knowing that he is pursuing a vocation in which he will always have God as his champion and protector. By reason of a like sanctity Marcus, in the [treatise] *On the Operation of Demons* of [Michael] Psellus, tells that his Demon uttered no sound upon the days when the Crucifixion and Resurrection are commemorated, although he strove his utmost to do so. Moreover, the poisons which Demons give to witches are thus harmless only to those Judges whom I have just mentioned: for there can be no doubt that the poisons which they gather and concoct with their own hands are equally injurious to all men else and are imbued with equal venom against all. It has, moreover, often been proved by experience that witches also have their own laboratories stuffed full of animals, plants and metals endowed with some natural poison; and these are so numerous and various that they may be reckoned as many as those which Agamede in Homer (*Iliad*, xi. 741) is said to have known:

Who knew all poisons that the wide earth breeds.

For they are in the discipline and service of that Master who is ignorant of nothing which has power to destroy men.

But I would rather that such matters remain hidden in the bosom of Nature than that, through my naming them, they should come to any man's knowledge. And it is for this reason that I have always been led, whenever I have found such things written down in the examination of prisoners, to have them altogether suppressed: or at least I would advise, or rather admonish, the actuary to omit them when he reads out such examinations in public. For in Lorraine it is the custom to refer the judgement of capital crimes to the votes of the ignorant and excited multitude, giving them full power, and having no regard to the provocation caused by a public exhibition of the accused; although this is contrary to the recommendation of the Duumvirs of Nancy, to whom the whole matter should first be referred. Would that these matters were not now so publicly known! But it has indeed come to pass after the wont of mankind, who with impetuous rashness thrust into the light those matters which should more particularly be kept hidden; and the memory of such things lives longer and is often more curious and pleasant to dwell upon than that of natural human happenings. In this way the Scholiast of Theocritus wrote that after many ages he saw with wonder at Mount Selinus in Sicily the very mortars in which Circe and Medea brewed their poisons. And if men have so prized the mere implements, as if they were the earthen lamp of Epictetus, what must we think they would have done if they had found the actual poisons, or the secret rule of compounding them inscribed upon some monument?

That Witches can with safety anoint their Hands and their entire Bodies with their Magic Ointments: yet if they but touch the Edge of a Person's Garment it will at once prove fatal to such a one, provided that it is the Witch's intent to Hurt. For otherwise such Contact is harmless and does not injure.

Witches have another most treacherous manner of applying their poison; for, having their hands smeared with it, they take hold of the very ends of a man's garment as it were to entreat and propitiate him. Thus it is hardly possible for you to be on your guard and avoid them, since the action has an appearance of kindness rather than of injury. Nevertheless, it is a most instant poison to the body, as has been made manifest by frequent experience: and it is the more marvellous because the witch's bare hand endures with complete safety the poison which thus penetrates even several folds of clothing. You may say that there have been men who have transmitted the infection of the plague to others although they themselves were free from it; but this is not a parallel case. For, as will be explained elsewhere, this touch of a witch is noxious and fatal only to those whom the witch wishes to injure: whereas the infection of the plague strikes those whom you least wish to harm. And this forces me to believe that, in the case we are considering, something is due to the hidden ministry of the Demon, which does not appear but works in secret; and that the unguent is merely the outward symbol of the wretched witch's complicity in the crime under the guidance and advice of the Demon. Indeed we know from experience that the poison can with impunity be handled and touched by anybody after the witches have been thrown into prison and have renounced their partnership with the Demon; and the officers who are sent to search for their boxes of poison are able to bring them back in their hands with safety.

This was proved not long since (2nd Sept., 1589) at Furscheim, a village in German Lorraine. Marie Alberte and Catharina Praevotte, just before they were sentenced for witchcraft, were asked to say whether they had left any of their evil poisons at home, so that after they were dead these venoms might not be a danger to any. They at once told where the poison could be found; and the searchers brought two earthenware vessels containing bitumen spotted with yellow and white and glistening here and there with specks of metal. Otillia Kelvers and Anguel Yzarts (6th and 7th Aug., 1589) of the same town, and several other witches in other towns, were found to have done the same. Some may think that the witches give such information in order to curry favour with their Judges, and that they cunningly indicate some unguent which they have prepared for some other and ordinary domestic use instead of the true poison;

but this is not the case, and there are many clear proofs that there is no pretence or simulation in this matter.

For, in the first place, if these unguents are put upon the fire they flare and splutter and glitter as nothing else can. Jeanne Michaëlis of Etival (2nd June, 1590) has testified to this fact. Again, there have been seen cases of witches who as soon as the Judge has given them permission to rub or anoint themselves with the unguent, have at once been carried aloft and have disappeared. Lucius Apuleius (Bk. III, *The Golden Ass*) tells of Pamphile that she in the same way applied such an unguent to herself and, after a few tentative leaps from the ground, flew up and away in full flight. And however much witches may differ concerning other matters, they are all, when questioned, agreed about the magic use, properties and powers of this ointment. They are even particular in describing its colour; and this provides further proof that the matter is no dream, but visible and perceptible to the eyes. At St. Dominique, 2nd Dec., 1586, Jeanne Gallée tells that the Demon gave it to her wrapped in oak leaves, and that its colour was white: and that she nearly always had her hands smeared with it that she might never be without the means of doing an injury on any occasion. At Haraucourt, 2nd Nov., 1586, Alexée Drigie agrees with this, except that she declared hers was reddish in colour: and she adds that when, at the instigation of the Demon, she anointed with it her husband, who was lying asleep by her side, he very soon died in great agony, writhing and contorting all his limbs.

IX

Witchcraft Prosecutions in the

Seventeenth Century

THE SEVENTEENTH CENTURY wit-
nessed new and larger groups of trials for witchcraft, a new interest in the representation of witchcraft, in both pictorial sources and on the dramatic stage, and
a substantial demonological literature that effectively replaced the older *Malleus Maleficarum*. Many of the new witchcraft trials occurred in places that had
never seen such trials before. The literature of the seventeenth century also produced a steady stream of old and new rationales for them, one of the most influential of which was the *Disquisitiones magicarum* of the Louvain Jesuit Martín
Del Rio (Text 50), who suggested that Muslims, then heretics, and finally Protestants were responsible for the history of diabolical sorcery and witchcraft in
Europe. Ben Jonson's *The Masque of Queens* (Text 51), based on Jonson's extensive reading of contemporary witchcraft literature, brought witches visibly onto
the English court stage.

The opening of the secular courts to witch persecutions, which the authors of the *Malleus Maleficarum* had urged, had occurred in the second half
of the sixteenth century, placed the proceedings in the hands of judges who
were often far less learned jurists than their ecclesiastical counterparts and
far more susceptible to local pressures. Both individual trials in courts unfamiliar with the proper procedure to be used in witchcraft cases—like that
of Marie Cornu in 1611 (Text 52), and in the dramatic regional persecutions
at Bamberg (No. 53), Würzburg (Text 54), and—perhaps—Bonn (Text 55) were
spectacular examples of wholesale extermination. The striking individual case
of Urbain Grandier and the Devils of Loudun (Text 56) and the small-scale
persecution involving the case of Suzanne Gaudry (Text 57) illustrate the fact
that accusations of witchcraft could also flare up suddenly and in relative iso-
lation. The letter of Father Surin, the exorcist in the Loudun affair, and the

crudeness of the judges of Suzanne Gaudry reveal the varieties of spiritual and psychological extremes which the persecutions of the seventeenth century produced.

In the second half of the century, the witch-fears spread to the British colonies in North America, and Cotton Mather's sermon on witchcraft (Text 58) indicates the intellectual and emotional temper which soon led to the trials at Salem Village (now Danvers), Massachusetts Bay Colony in 1692. Theoretical demonological and witchcraft studies continued to affirm and develop the traditional concepts, even in the last decades of the seventeenth century, as is demonstrated by Richard Bovet's *Pandaemonium* of 1684, the evidence supporting witchcraft continued to be accumulated, as is shown by the essay of Joseph Glanvill (Text 59). Glanvill and More, among the most highly respected thinkers of the seventeenth century, maintained a philosophical spiritualism which predisposed them not only to belief in witchcraft, but also to affirmation of its existence by the presentation of "natural data" that offer tantalizing views of social as well as intellectual history.

50
Martín Del Rio: *Disquisitiones magicarum*
(1603)

Martín Del Rio (1551–1608) was an immensely learned scholar and servant of the Supreme Council of Brabant who became a Jesuit at the age of thirty and wrote his *Disquisitiones magicarum* in Louvain, where he certainly knew of and cited the trials at Trier and the cases of Dietrich Flade and Cornelius Loos. The work, which deals with many other things besides witchcraft, evidently became the most widely cited defense of the prosecution of the crime of witchcraft in the seventeenth century, displacing the *Malleus Maleficarum* and even the work of Nicholas Rémy.

In the excerpt here, Del Rio asserts an etiology of witchcraft beliefs and practices that begins with the European attraction to Arab learning, initially in Spain, then follows with the emergence of heresies, and then of Protestantism. Del Rio refers to his former teacher at the Sorbonne, Juan Maldonado, who was also a teacher of Pierre de Lancre and perhaps of Jean Filesac, as a great authority.

SOURCE: *The Occult in Early Modern Europe*, ed. and trans. P. G. Maxwell-Stuart (New York, 1999), 164–67.

FURTHER READING: Lea, *Materials*, 2:640–46; Clark, *Thinking with Demons*.

Proloquium

I have read that magic increased in the footsteps of the Saracen filth throughout Spain to such an extent that there was in that country thereafter the greatest lack and ignorance of all good literature. Hardly anything except the demonic arts was taught openly in Toledo, Seville and Salamanca. While I was living in the last of these (now the mother of good arts) I was shown a very deep crypt, the remains of an unholy school, which that woman of virile mind, Queen Isabella, wife of Ferdinand the Catholic, had ordered blocked up with rubble and rocks scarcely a hundred years before.

First the Hussites invaded Bohemia, then the Lutherans Germany, and Sprenger and Nider, investigators of heretic depravity, have told us that the Hussites were followed by a great force of workers of maleficent magic, while the Lutherans know what torrents of witches they have poured into the lands of the North, which have become paralysed with fear, as though frozen by Arctic cold. For in these places there is scarcely anything unharmed or free from—I scarcely know what to call them—these animals disguised as humans, these evil spirits. Most of the older ones in the territory of Trier, not only upon the rack but after questioning as well, confessed to the judges that they were first drenched with this disastrous stain when that foul, hellish support of Lutheranism, himself well known for magic, Albert of Brandenburg, plundered and ravaged that province with fire and sword. However, many inhabit the Alpine territory next to Switzerland in which they know a few women expert in malefice, most of them celebrated for one crime. Nor does any truer or more visible cause occur than that which, right up to the present moment, nefarious remnants of the Waldenses have secretly adhered to there in caves.

Nothing has spread this plague further and more quickly through England, Scotland, France and Belgium than the dread pestilence of Calvinism. Before, in a few places, an unreliable rumour was scattered about a few (and then only the common) people. Now, with this heresy, as in the case of the frenzy of a fever, it has invaded very many people all over the place (and openly), who are famous for their nobility, learning, wealth and dignity. Thus the insatiable Behemoth "who draws the Jordan into his mouth" (*Job* 40.18) and "the food of his pasture is carefully selected" (*Habbakuk* 1.16) hopes, since he has already swallowed the sea, to ravage the very sphere of the Lord. What? Does Daneau, a Calvinist minister, tell us that there is a regular convention of witches in Geneva near the cathedral, and in that city within the space of three months more than 500 people were sentenced to death by the judges? In answer to my question, why does magic regularly accompany heresy, I am reminded of the reasons very clearly advanced by my late friend Dr. Juan Maldonato SJ, a priest and a very learned and holy man, when he gave public lectures in Paris on evil spirits. He gave five reasons as follows:

1. Evil spirits dwell in heretics as once they did in idols. Jerome quite rightly is accustomed to say that the Devil, since he has seen the idols in which he used to live thrown down, has made worse idols from the divine writings themselves in the minds of heretics. . . . So it follows that, just as when a war is over, the soldiers are spread in all directions and become robbers and lay siege to every road, so evil spirits, when heresies are driven off or destroyed, which before were flourishing, as if the temples in which they were worshipped have been overturned, seek new dwellings in other people. For when evil spirits are compelled to come out of a person in whom they had lodged, they are accustomed to arrange that those people who are tired out by the siege are compelled to hand over the citadel which they were holding. They seek by way of an agreement that they be allowed to retreat into another place. This we understand by the example of that Legion which asked Christ to allow them to occupy pigs.

2. All heresy is aggressive and very violent, but cannot stay at the same pace, especially because divine providence does not allow that, and nature herself also is so constructed that error cannot imitate truth for long. Therefore all heresy must, unless it revert in good time to that religion whence it came, either degenerate into magical arts or into the final extremity of atheism, since there are above all two reasons by which heretics are actuated. One is the arrogance of an intellectual running riot and believing nothing unless in all circumstances it may be seen with the eyes. The other is an intemperate curiosity and eagerness for novelty. It becomes an absolute necessity that those who have become heretics through pride, just as they came to the conclusion that they had embraced the light all in a moment during the first flush of their discovery in that sect, so when that same flush grows cold they discover that the light is darkness and, despairing of finding the truth elsewhere, they believe absolutely nothing. Those whom curiosity has pushed into heresy, when that which at first seemed to be novel little by little has become familiar, are impelled by that same curiosity to enter upon a close companionship with evil spirits and to learn and exercise their demonic arts.

3. It seems to be so arranged by nature that just as plague follows famine, so various types of meddlesome arts follow heresy. For heresy is "a famine of the Word of God" (*Amos* 8.11); and as in a lack of corn-supply people are compelled to eat food which is not healthy, whence it happens that plague arises from the corrupted humours: so, while heresy flourishes, while people used the corrupted meanings of Scripture, at length they have recourse to the magical arts which are like diseases of the soul.

4. Evil spirits are accustomed to use heretics as though they were beautiful prostitutes to draw people into error. For it is clear that in Scripture heresy is called a prostitute. *Isaiah* 1.21, "How is the faithful city become an harlot?" Therefore, like bawds who, when the body of the harlot has been deflowered,

make a brothel-keeper of her: so evil spirits when the first type of heresy has perished, so that in some smaller degree people may be charmed into error, make magicians out of heretics.

5. In my opinion, the fifth cause is the negligence of those who rule the Church. For just as in uncultivated fields locusts are accustomed to be born, so from a lack of the Word of God are born the arts of trickery. For locusts also signify evil spirits in Scripture, *Apocalypse* 9.3. Therefore what Joel said seems to connect with the present time: "That which the palmerworm hath left hath the locust eaten" (1.4). For what the heretics had made a shell, witches despoil by the art of evil spirits, and what witches leave behind, atheists destroy. . . .

How I wish these things had not intruded upon our eyes! We have seen the once flourishing Gueux of Belgium devouring everything with Calvinism, Lutheranism and Anabaptism, like caterpillars. We have seen these "three unclean spirits coming out of the mouth of the dragon, out of the mouth of the Beast, and out of the mouth of the false prophet" (*Apocalypse* 16.13). Now that these are withering away and almost expiring through the passage of time, we see various swarms of locust-witches ravaging the whole of the North. We see elsewhere the number of atheists or politicians increasing with the result that since so few true and fervent Catholics remain, none can be seen distinctly because their numbers are so small.

51
Ben Jonson: *The Masque of Queens* (1609)

Representations of sorcery and witchcraft existed not only in demonological treatises and court records, but increasingly in the late sixteenth and early seventeenth centuries on the dramatic stage. England at the beginning of the seventeenth century was ruled by James I (1603–1625), who had himself published his *Daemonologie* in 1597, an attack on the sceptical theories of Reginald Scot (Text 60), that went through two English editions in 1603, was translated into Latin for continental circulation in 1608, and was echoed by the influential treatise of William Perkins, *A Discourse on the Damned Art of Witchcraft* in 1609. The best known stage representation of witchcraft during James's reign was, of course, Shakespeare's *Macbeth*, probably first performed in 1606 and several times thereafter.[1]

1. Act I, scenes 1 and 3; Peter Stallybrass, "*Macbeth* and Witchcraft," in *Focus on Macbeth*, ed. John Russell Brown (London and Boston, 1982), 189–209. On representations of the sorcerer in dramatic literature, see Barbara Traister, *Heavenly Necromancers: The Magician in English*

Ben Jonson's *The Masque of Queens* was performed in 1609 and is remarkable not only for its reflections of contemporary witchcraft beliefs, but for the extensive and learned reading notes that Jonson wrote to accompany the depiction of the witches in the first part of the masque. These reveal Jonson's considerable familiarity with contemporary witchcraft theory, citing Nider, the *Malleus Maleficarum*, Cornelius Agrippa von Nettesheim, Bartolomeo Spina, Bodin, Rémy, James VI & I, Martín Del Rio, and other recent (and many ancient Greek and Roman) writers on the subject. But Jonson's uses of sources and his depiction of the witches in the text included here is instrumental—the witches are plainly said to represent those evil qualities that besmirch the reputations of good, indeed heroic women, the real subject of the masque. The masque was mounted by Inigo Jones and the ballets choreographed by Jerome Herne.

The Masque of Queens was followed in 1615/16 by Thomas Middleton's *The Witch* (which includes two female witches named Stadlin and Hoppo, originally the male witches of Johann Nider's *Formicarius* [Text 27]), and in 1634 by Thomas Heywood and Richard Brome's *The Late Lancashire Witches*.[2] Both the courtly and the popular theater century are important sources, not unmediatedly for witchcraft beliefs, but, like pictorial representations, of the novel opportunities they offered to stagecraft and artistic techniques.

The theme of witchcraft also appeared in dramas elsewhere and in other literary forms, spectacularly in Torquato Tasso's epic poem *Jerusalem Delivered* of 1575, and Cervantes's "The Dogs' Colloquy" of 1613, as well as in sixteenth- and seventeenth-century versions of older Greek and Latin literary works.[3]

Renaissance Drama (Columbia, Missouri, 1984), and Edward Peters, "*Rex curiosus*: A Preface to Prospero," *Majestas* 4 (1996): 61–84.

2. Edward J. Esche, *A Critical Edition of Thomas Middleton's "The Witch"* (New York and London, 1993); Thomas Middleton, *The Witch*, ed. Elizabeth Schafer (New York, 1994); Laird H. Barber, *An Edition of "The Late Lancashire Witches" by Thomas Heywood and Richard Brome* (1962; rprt. in *Renaissance Drama: A Collection of Critical Editions*, ed. Stephen Orgel, New York and London, 1979); Peter Corbin and Douglas Sedge, eds., *Three Jacobean Witchcraft Plays* (Manchester, 1986). The transgendering of Nider's male witches to Middleton's female witches appears to have come from their inclusion in Reginald Scot's *Discoverie of Witchcraft* of 1584 (Text 61), a skeptical work that inspired James VI's *Daemonologie* and was certainly read by Middleton.

3. Stuart Clark, "Tasso and the Literature of Witchcraft," in *The Renaissance in Ferrara and Its European Horizons*, ed. J. Salmons (Swansea, 1984), 3–21; Gareth Roberts, "The Descendants of Circe: Witches and Renaissance Fictions," in *Witchcraft in Early Modern Europe*, 183–206; Julia M. Kisacky, *Magic in Boiardo and Ariosto* (New York, 2000). On the German moralizing

SOURCE: Ben Jonson, *Selected Masques*, ed. Stephen Orgel (New Haven and London, 1970), 80–99, 348–370.

FURTHER READING: Stephen Orgel, *The Jonsonian Masque* (1965; rprt. New York, 1981), 130–46.

[*THE MASQUE OPENS onto the scene of* "an ugly hell, which flaming underneath, smoked to the top of the roof. . . . Witches, with a kind of hollow and infernal music, came forth. . . . First one, then two, and three and more until their number increased to eleven, all differently attired. . . . The eleven witches beginning to dance (which is a usual ceremony at their convents or meetings, where sometimes also they are vizarded and masked) on the sudden one of them missed their chief, and interrupted the rest with this speech."[4]]

> Sisters, stay, we want our *Dame*;   1
> Call upon her by her name,
> And the charm we use to say,
> That she quickly *anoint*, and come away.   4
>   CHARM 1
> Dame, Dame, the watch is set:
> Quickly come, we all are met.
> From the lakes and from the fens,
> From the rocks and from the dens,

---

drama *Hexenwahn*, by Thomas Birck of Tübingen of 1600, see H. C. Erik Midelfort, *Witch Hunting in Southwestern Germany, 1562–1684* (Stanford, 1972), 46–47.

4. [This and the following notes are Jonson's. I have included the relevant text, lines 40–326, but not all the notes.] See the king's majesty's book (our sovereign) [James I] of *Demonology*. Bodin [Text 45]. Remigius [Text 49]. Del Rio [Text 50], the *Malleus Maleficarum* [Text 34], and a world of others in the general; but let us follow particulars.

1. DAME Amongst our vulgar witches, the honor of Dame (for so I translate it) is given, with a kind of preëminence, to some special one at their meetings. Which del Rio insinuates, *Disquisitiones Magicae* II, question ix [B], quoting that of Apuleius, *The Golden Ass* I.[8], "concerning a certain woman tavern keeper, a queen of sorceresses," and adds, "that you may know that even then some were honored by them with this title." Which title Master Philip Ludwig Elich, *Daemonomagia* [Frankfurt, 1607], question x [p. 140], doth also remember.

4. ANOINT When they are to be transported from place to place they use to anoint themselves, and sometimes the things they ride on. Beside Apuleius' testimony, see these later: Remy, *Daemonolatria* I.xiv. Del Rio, *Disquisitiones Magicae* II, question xvi [C]. Bodin, *Demonomanie* II.iv. Bartolomeo Spina, *Quaestio de Strigibus* [(Rome, 1576, etc.) chapter xviii]. Philip Ludwig Elich, [*Daemonomagia*] question x [p. 141]. Paracelsus in *De Magna et Occulta Philosophia* teacheth the confection: "an ointment from the flesh of newborn infants, cooked like a sauce, and with sleep-inducing herbs, such as poppy, nightshade, hemlock," etc. And Giovanni Battista della Porta, *Magia Naturalis* [Naples, 1558, etc.] II.xxvi.

From the woods and from the caves,
From the churchyards, from the graves,
From the dungeon, from the tree
That they die on, here are we.
       Comes she not yet?
       Strike another heat.

              CHARM 2

The weather is fair, the wind is good;
Up, Dame, o' your horse of wood;
Or else tuck up your gray frock,
And saddle your goat or your green cock,
And make his bridle a bottom of thread
To roll up how many miles you have rid.
Quickly come away,
For we all stay.
       Nor yet? Nay, then,
       We'll try her again.

              CHARM 3

The owl is abroad, the bat and the toad,
       And so is the cat-a-mountain;
The ant and the mole sit both in a hole,
       And frog peeps out o' the fountain;
The dogs they do bay, and the timbrels play,
       The spindle is now a-turning;
The moon it is red and the stars are fled,
       But all the sky is a-burning;
The *ditch* is made, and our nails the spade,   75

---

75. DITCH This rite also of making a ditch with their nails is frequent with our witches; whereof see Bodin, Remy, del Rio, [Sprenger and Krämer] *Malleus Maleficarum*, [Johann Georg] Godelmann, *De Lamiis* [i.e. *Tractatus De Magis, Veneficis, et Lamiis*, Frankfurt, 1591, etc.] II; as also the antiquity of it most vively expressed by Horace, *Satires* I.viii.[26ff.], where he mentions the pictures, and the blood of a black lamb, all which are yet in use with our modern witchcraft: "Then they (speaking of Canidia and Sagana) began to dig up the earth with their nails, and to tear a black lamb to pieces with their teeth; the blood was all poured into a trench so that from it they might draw forth the spirits, souls that would give them answers. One image there was of wool, and one of wax," etc. And then, by and by [34ff.], "You might see serpents and hell-hounds roaming about, and the blushing moon, that she might not witness such deeds, hiding behind the tall tombs." Of this ditch, Homer makes mention in Circe's speech to Ulysses, *Odyssey* X about the end [516ff.]. And Ovid, *Metamorphoses* VII.[243–45], in Medea's magic: "Then nearby she dug two ditches in the earth and performed her rites; plunging her knife into the throat of a black sheep, she drenched the open ditches with its blood." And of the waxen images, in Hyp-

With pictures full, of wax and of wool;
Their livers I stick with needles quick;
There lacks but the blood to make up the flood.
> Quickly Dame, then, bring your part in,
> Spur, spur upon little Martin,
> Merrily, merrily make him sail,
> A worm in his mouth and a thorn in's tail,
> Fire above, and fire below,
> With a whip i' your hand to make him go.
>> O, now she's come!
>> Let all be dumb.

[*Dame.*]   Well done, my hags. And come we fraught with spite   87
To overthrow the glory of this night?
Holds our great purpose?

Hag.   Yes.

Dame.   But wants there none
Of our just number?

Hag.   Call us one by one,
And then our Dame shall see.

Dame.   First, then, advance,
My drowsy servant, stupid Ignorance,
Known by thy scaly vesture, and bring on
Thy fearful sister, wild Suspicion,
Whose eyes do never sleep; let her knit hands
With quick Credulity, that next her stands,

---

sipyle's epistle to Jason [*Heroides* VI.91–2], where he expresseth that mischief also of the needles: "She vows to their doom the absent persons, fashions the waxen image, and into its wretched heart drives the slender needle." Bodin, *Demonomanie* II.viii, hath (beside the known story of King Duff, out of Hector Boethius) much of the witches' later practice in that kind, and reports a relation of a French ambassador's, out of England, of certain pictures of wax found in a dunghill near Islington, of our late queen's; which rumor I myself (being then very young) can yet remember to have been current.

87. DAME This Dame I make to bear the person of Ate, or mischief (for so I interpret it) out of Homer's description of her, *Iliad* IX.[505–12], where he makes her swift to hurt mankind, strong, and sound of feet; and *Iliad* XIX.[91–94], walking upon men's heads; in both places using one and the same phrase to signify her power, "harming men." I present her barefooted, and her frock tucked, to make her seem more expedite, by Horace his authority, *Satires* I.viii.[23–24]: "My own eyes have seen Canidia walk with black robe tucked up, her feet bare, her hair dishevelled . . ." But for her hair, I rather respect another place of his, *Epodes* V.[15–16], where she appears, "Canidia, her locks entwined with short snakes, and her hair dishevelled." And that of Lucan, [*Pharsalia*] VI.[654ff.], speaking of Erictho's attire: "She wore a motley robe such as the furies wear, and revealed her face by throwing back her hair, and wreathed her bristling locks with a garland of vipers." For her torch, see Remy, II.iii.

Who hath but one ear, and that always ope;
Two-facèd Falsehood follow in the rope;
And lead on Murmur, with the cheeks deep hung;
She Malice, whetting of her forkèd tongue;
And Malice Impudence, whose forehead's lost;
Let Impudence lead Slander on, to boast
Her oblique look; and to her subtle side,
Thou, black-mouthed Execration, stand applied;
Draw to thee Bitterness, whose pores sweat gall;
She flame-eyed Rage; Rage, Mischief.

Hag.   Here we are all.

Dame.   Join now our hearts, we faithful opposites
To Fame and Glory. Let not these bright nights
Of honor blaze thus to offend our eyes;
Show ourselves truly envious, and let rise
Our wonted rages; do what may beseem
Such names and natures: Virtue else will deem
Our powers decreased, and think us banished earth,
No less than heaven. All her antique birth,
As Justice, Faith, she will restore, and, bold
Upon our sloth, retrieve her Age of Gold.
We must not let our native manners thus
Corrupt with ease. Ill lives not but in us.
I hate to see these fruits of a soft peace,
And curse the piety gives it such increase.
Let us *disturb* it then, and blast the light;   134 (5)
Mix hell with heaven, and make Nature fight

---

134. DISTURB These powers of troubling nature are frequently ascribed to witches, and challenged by themselves wherever they are induced by Homer, Ovid, Tibullus, Petronius Arbiter,
Seneca, Lucan, Claudian, to whose authorities I shall refer more anon. For the present, hear
Socrates in Apuleius' *The Golden Ass* I.[8] describing Meroë the witch: "Verily, she is a magician, and of divine might, which hath power to bring down the sky, to bear up the earth, to turn
the waters into hills and the hills into running waters, to call up the terrestrial spirits into the
air, to pull the gods out of the heavens, to extinguish the planets, and to lighten the very
darkness of hell." And book II.[5], Byrrhena to Lucius, of Pamphile: "For she is accounted the
most chief and principal magician and enchantress of every necromantic spell: who, by breath-
ing out certain words and charms over boughs and stones and other frivolous things, can throw
down all the light of the starry heavens into the deep bottom of hell, and reduce them again to
the old chaos." As also this later of Remy, in his most elegant arguments before his *Daemonolatria*: "How they may overturn the universe from its very foundations, and mingle the
shades below with the gods above, this is their sole concern." And Lucan [*Pharsalia* VI.437]:
"they whose art is to do whatever is thought impossible. . . ."

	Within herself; loose the whole hinge of things,
	And cause the ends run back into their springs.
Hag.	What our Dame bids us do
	We are ready for.
Dame.	Then fall to.
	But first relate me what you have sought,
	Where you have been, and what you have brought.
1st Hag.	I have been all day looking after 142
	A raven feeding upon a quarter,
	And soon as she turned her beak to the south,
	I snatched this morsel out of her mouth.
2nd Hag.	I have been gathering wolves' hairs,
	The mad dogs' foam and the adders' ears,
	The spurging of a dead man's eyes,
	And all since the evening star did rise.
3rd Hag.	I last night lay all alone
	O' the ground to hear the mandrake groan,
	And plucked him up, though he grew full low,
	And as I had done, the cock did crow.
4th Hag.	And I ha' been choosing out this skull
	From charnel houses that were full,
	From private grots and public pits,
	And frighted a sexton out of his wits.
5th Hag.	Under a cradle I did creep
	By day, and when the child was asleep
	At night I sucked the breath, and rose
	And plucked the nodding nurse by the nose.
6th Hag.	I had a dagger: what did I with that? 162
	Killed an infant to have his fat.

142. IST HAG For the gathering pieces of dead flesh, Cornelius Agrippa, *De Occulta Philosophia* III.xlii and IV, last chapter [*Opera* ("Lyons," n.d.) I.452 (Ff2v)], observes that the use was to call up ghosts and spirits with a fumigation made of that (and bones of carcases) which I make my witch here not to cut herself, but to watch the raven, as Lucan's Erictho, [*Pharsalia*] VI.[55off.]: "Whenever any corpse lies exposed on the ground, she sits by it before beast or bird can come; but she will not mangle the limbs with the knife or her bare hands; she waits for the wolves to tear it, and means to snatch the prey from their unwetted throats," as if that piece were sweeter which the wolf had bitten or the raven had picked, and more effectuous; and to do it at her turning to the south, as with the prediction of a storm. Which, though they be but minutes in ceremony, being observed make the act more dark and full of horror.

162. 6TH HAG Their killing of infants is common, both for confection of their ointment (whereto one ingredient is the fat boiled, as I have showed before out of Paracelsus and Porta) as also out of a lust to do murder. Sprenger in *Malleus Maleficarum* [part II, question I, chapter 13] reports that a witch, a midwife in the diocese of Basel, confessed to have killed above forty infants, ever as

> A piper it got at a church-ale,
> I bade him again blow wind i' the tail.

7th Hag. A murderer yonder was hung in chains,   166
> The sun and the wind had shrunk his veins;
> I bit off a sinew, I clipped his hair,
> I brought off his rags that danced i' the air.

8th Hag. The scritch-owl's eggs and the feathers black,
> The blood of the frog and the bone in his back
> I have been getting, and made of his skin
> A purset to keep Sir Cranion in.

9th Hag. And I ha' been plucking, plants among,
> Hemlock, henbane, adder's tongue,
> Nightshade, moonwort, libbard's bane,
> And twice by the dogs was like to be ta'en.

10th Hag. I from the jaws of a gardener's bitch
> Did snatch these bones, and then leaped the ditch;
> Yet went I back to the house again,
> Killed the black cat, and here's the brain.

----

they were newborn, with pricking them into the brain with a needle, which she had offered to the devil. See the story of the three witches in Remy, *Daemonolatria* II.iii, about the end of the chapter. And Master Philip Ludwig Elich, [*Daemonomagia*] question vii [pp. 97–8]. And that it is no new rite, read the practice of Canidia, Horace, *Epodes* V, and Lucan, [*Pharsalia*] VI.[554ff.], whose admirable verses I can never be weary to transcribe: "Nor is she slow to take life, if such warm blood is needed as gushes forth at once when the throat is slit, nor does she scorn murder if her rites demand live blood, and if her ghoulish feast demands still palpitating flesh. In the same way she pierces the pregnant womb and delivers the child by an unnatural birth in order to place it on the fiery altar, and whenever she requires the service of a bold, bad spirit, she takes life with her own hand. Every man's death serves her turn."

166. 7TH HAG The abuse of dead bodies in their witchcraft both Porphyry and [Michael] Psellus [the younger] are grave authors of. The one, *De Sacrifiis et Diis atque Daemonibus* [Venice, 1497, etc.], [last] chapter, "De Vero Cultu. . . ." The other, *De Daemonibus* [i.e. *De Operatione Daemonum*, Paris, 1577, etc.], which Apuleius toucheth too, *The Golden Ass* II.[21–2]. But Remy, who deals with later persons, and out of their own mouths, *Daemonolatria* II.iii, affirms, "it is the way of evildoers in our time too to do this, especially if the body of someone who has been executed is made an example and raised on a cross. For not only from the corpse do they procure material for their soothsaying, but also from the very instruments of execution, the rope, the stake, the irons, since in the common opinion there is in these things a certain force and efficacy for magical incantations." And to this place I dare not, out of religion to the divine Lucan, but bring his verses from the same book [VI.543–49]: "She breaks with her teeth the fatal noose, and mangles the carcass that dangles on the gallows, and scrapes the cross of the criminal; she tears away the rain-beaten flesh and the bones calcined by exposure to the sun. She purloins the nails that pierced the hands, the clotted filth, and the black humor of corruption that oozes over all the limbs; and when a muscle resists the teeth, she hangs her weight upon it."

11th Hag.　I went to the toad breeds under the wall,
　　　　　I charmed him out and he came at my call;
　　　　　I scratched out the eyes of the owl before,
　　　　　I tore the bat's wing; what would you have more?
Dame.　Yes, I have brought, to help our vows,
　　　　　Hornèd poppy, cypress boughs,
　　　　　The fig-tree wild that grows on tombs,
　　　　　And juice that from the larch tree comes,
　　　　　The basilisk's blood and the viper's skin:
　　　　　And now, our orgies let's begin.

　　　　　　　　　.　.　.

　　　　　You fiends and furies, if yet any be
　　　　　Worse than ourselves, you that have quaked to see
　　　　　These knots untied, and shrunk when we have charmed,
　　　　　You that to arm us have yourselves disarmed,
　　　　　And to our powers resigned your whips and brands
　　　　　When we went forth, the scourge of men and lands;
　　　　　You that have seen me ride when *Hecatè*　　222
　　　　　Durst not take chariot, when the boisterous sea
　　　　　Without a breath of wind hath knocked the sky,
　　　　　And that hath thundered, Jove not knowing why;
　　　　　When we have set the elements at wars,
　　　　　Made midnight see the sun, and day the stars;
　　　　　When the winged lightning in the course hath stayed,
　　　　　And swiftest rivers have run back, afraid
　　　　　To see the corn remove, the groves to range,
　　　　　Whole places alter, and the seasons change;
　　　　　When the pale moon at the first voice down fell
　　　　　Poisoned, and durst not stay the second spell;
　　　　　You that have oft been conscious of these sights,
　　　　　And thou three-formèd star, that on these nights
　　　　　Art only powerful, to whose triple name
　　　　　Thus we incline, once, twice and thrice the same:
　　　　　If now with rites profane and foul enough
　　　　　We do invoke thee, darken all this roof

222. THREE-FORMED Hecate, who is called *trivia* and *triformis*, of whom Virgil, *Aeneid* IV.[511]: "threefold Hecate, the three faces of the virgin Diana." She was believed to govern in witchcraft, and is remembered in all their invocations. See Theocritus in *Pharmaceutria* [*Idylls* II.14]: "Hail, frightful Hecate," and Medea in Seneca [*Medea*, 750–51]: "Now, summoned by my sacred rites, do you, orb of the night, put on the most evil face and come, threatening in all your forms." And Erictho in Lucan [*Pharsalia* VI.700ff.]: "[I cry] to Persephone, and to her, the third incarnation of our patron Hecate," etc.

With present fogs. Exhale earth's rott'nest vapors,
And strike a blindness through these blazing tapers.
Come, let a murmuring charm resound
The whilst we bury all i' the ground.
But first see every foot be bare,
And every knee.

Hag.   Yes, Dame, they are.

CHARM 4

Deep, O deep, we lay thee to sleep;
We leave thee drink by, if thou chance to be dry,
Both milk and blood, the dew and the flood.
We breathe in thy bed, at the foot and the head;
We cover thee warm, that thou take no harm;
And when thou dost wake,
    Dame earth shall quake,
    And the houses shake,
    And her belly shall ache
    As her back were brake
    Such a birth to make
    As is the blue drake,
    Whose form thou shalt take.

Dame. Never a star yet shot?
Where be the ashes?

Hag.   Here i' the pot.

Dame. Cast them up, and the flintstone
Over the left shoulder bone
Into the west.

Hag.   It will be best.

CHARM 5

The sticks are a-cross, there can be no loss,
The sage is rotten, the sulfur is gotten
Up to the sky that was i' the ground.
Follow it then with our rattles, round,
Under the bramble, over the briar;
A little more heat will set it on fire;
Put it in mind to do it kind,
Flow water, and blow wind.
Rouncy is over, Robble is under,
A flash of light and a clap of thunder,
A storm of rain, another of hail.
We all must home i' the egg shell sail;

The mast is made of a great pin,
The tackle of cobweb, the sail as thin,
And if we go through and not fall in—

Dame. *Stay!* All our charms do nothing win 268
Upon the night; our labor dies!
Our magic feature will not rise,
Nor yet the storm! We must repeat
More direful voices far, and beat
The ground with vipers till it sweat.

CHARM 6

Bark dogs, wolves howl,
Sea roar, woods roll,
Clouds crack, all be black
But the light our charms do make.

Dame. Not yet? My rage begins to swell;
Darkness, devils, night and hell,
Do not thus delay my spell!
I call you once and I call you twice,
I beat you again if you stay my thrice;
Through these crannies where I peep
I'll let in the light to see your sleep,
And all the secrets of your sway
Shall lie as open to the day
As unto me. Still are you deaf?
Reach me a bough that ne'er bare leaf
To strike the air, and aconite
To hurl upon this glaring light;
A rusty knife to wound mine arm,
And as it drops I'll speak a charm
Shall cleave the ground as low as lies
Old shrunk-up Chaos, and let rise

268. STAY This stop, or interruption, showed the better by causing that general silence which made all the following noises enforced in the next charm more direful. First imitating that of Lucan [*Pharsalia* VI.725–27]: "Erictho marvelled that fate had power to linger thus. Enraged with death, she lashed the motionless corpse with a live serpent." And then their barking, howling, hissing and confusion of noise, expressed by the same author in the same person [685–93]: "And lastly her voice, more powerful than any drug to bewitch the powers of Lethe, first uttered indistinct sounds, sounds untunable and far different from human speech. The dog's bark and the wolf's howl were in that voice; it resembled the complaint of the restless owl and the night-flying screech-owl, the shrieking and roaring of wild beasts, the serpent's hiss, the beat of waves dashing against rocks, the sound of forests, and the thunder that issues from a rift in the cloud: in that one voice all these things were heard." See Remy too, *Daemonolatria* I.xix.

Once more his dark and reeking head
To strike the world and nature dead
Until my magic birth be bred.

CHARM 7

Black go in, and blacker come out;
At thy going down we give thee a shout.
        Hoo!
At thy rising again thou shalt have two,
And if thou dost what we would have thee do,
Thou shalt have three, thou shalt have four,
Thou shalt have ten, thou shalt have a score.
        Hoo! Har! Har! Hoo!

CHARM 8

A cloud of pitch, a spur and a switch
To haste him away, and a whirlwind play
Before and after, with thunder for laughter
And storms for joy of the roaring boy,
His head of a drake, his tail of a snake.

CHARM 9

About, about and about,
Till the mist arise and the lights fly out;
The images neither be seen nor felt;
The woolen burn and the waxen melt;
Sprinkle your liquors upon the ground
And into the air, around, around.
        Around, around,
        Around, around,
        Till a music sound
        And the pace be found
        To which we may dance
        And our charms advance.

52
The Trial of Marie Cornu (1611)

The following court record from what is now northern France (but at
the time was under the jurisdiction of the Spanish Netherlands) in the
year 1611 is a useful text for understanding one perspective on the
crime of witchcraft during the height of the persecutions. The court

record is meticulous, and this may well have been the first (and possibly the only) case of the kind it had tried. The bailiff who tried the case has consulted with the authorities of the higher court at Mons, and the finished character of the record suggests that the advice of the superior court was very carefully followed. Long suspicion, accusation by others, confession of pact and sexual relations with the demon, and the rest of the classic signs of witchcraft are all present here, but the record also tells us the story of, as Robert Muchembled described her, "a child of misery." Records of witchcraft trials do not tell us only about witchcraft.

SOURCE: Achieves départementales du Nord, à Lille (AND) 10 H 54: Fenain, Nord, arr. Douai, canton Marchiennes. Robert Muchembled, ed., *Le roi et la sorcière: l'Europe des bûchers (XVe–XVIIIe siècle)* (Paris, 1993), 132–34. The year is 1611. Trans. E. P.

FURTHER READING: Robert Muchembled, *Sorcières: Justice et société aux seizième et dix-septième siècles* (Paris, 1987), 116–201.

THIS IS A CRIMINAL trial held before us, Quintin Legambe, squire, lord of Autreulle, bailiff of the lands and lordships of Marchiennes, Fenain, etc., in the case of Marie Cornu, popularly called La Rousse, having been married three times and presently widow after her third marriage of the good Quintin de Ligny, charged and accused of being a *scorcière*, and following the depositions which, by reason of this, have been made about her, informations following upon this and held by us about her reputation and general good name, by which we have found that for many long years she has been vehemently suspected of having exercised *sorcellerie* and by this means has committed many grave and enormous crimes, according to which it is amply apparent to us, as much by virtue of accusations against her made by many accomplices and by the confessions of the said Marie Cornu, here present, and often repeated, so that it appears more than sufficient for the holding and procedure of this trial.

In the first place, she, having found herself attainted and convicted of having renounced and denied God, our Creator and Redeemer, and having adored and vowed herself forever to the devil, ancient and eternal enemy of the human race, and having also renounced her baptism and her share in paradise in the presence of the said devil, which she has declared to have been her lover and named Belzebub, having given him her soul and suffered that he rebaptize her, giving her the name Malavisée, and that she gave him as a token some hair which she had taken and removed from her shameful parts, and afterwards permitted and suffered that the said Belzebub put a mark on her right shoulder, from which he drew some blood, with which she signed a document and gave it to the said devil.

Also she permitted the said devil to carry her an infinite number of times during the night to nocturnal dances and assemblies, as often in Fenain as in other places, in the company of that devil and of many men, women, and young girls, who she has declared were present and well known to her. And there she danced, assisted at table, and there adored the said Belzebub, prince of the devils, being in the form of a black and stinking he-goat, and of being placed on her knees and of having kissed his posterior and of having attached a black candle to his horn, saying "I adore you, Belzebub"; requesting help from him against those who have offended her or refused her something, and toward these ends having received from him a powder, so that by his help and counsel she might make both beasts and people languish and die, and of having, with the said Belzebub, committed the sin of sodomy and against nature; all of which are detestable crimes, and directly committed and perpetrated in despite and scorn of our God.

And to come to the crimes and *maléfices* committed and performed by her for the thirty-six years or thereabouts for which she has confessed to having been a *sorcière*, upon many persons and beasts, and of having been married three times and that her first husband, named Baltazar Bauduin, of whom she has confessed having murdered by putting a gray powder (which the said devil Belzebub delivered to her) into a tart of boiled milk which she then gave him to eat, and that she did this because the said husband gave more caresses in the household to a daughter of his named Julie Bauduin, presently the wife of Robert Menez, whom her late husband had had from a preceding marriage to another woman, than to her, who was his present wife. She has also confessed to having caused the death of Pierre Hélo, her second husband, having given to him a meal of pike prepared with butter, on which she had sprinkled the gray powder, because the said Hélo, her husband, treated a daughter of hers named Marguerite badly, a daughter she had had by her first husband, Baltazar Bauduin. Having also confessed to having killed her third husband, Quintin de Ligny, having put the same powder into a tart which she gave him to eat, because the said husband was always scolding [*grondait toujours*] her. And she also, by *maléfice* caused the nose to fall off Anne Leurien, wife of Michel Richart, by having put a powder in her drink, because Anne had been the cause that she did not marry Adrien Leurien, father of the said Anne. In addition, she caused to languish a child of Jehan Herlin, having put some powder on a slice of bread, because the said child had quarreled with her, when she was working in the house of the said Herlin, the child since having become lame. And she confessed to having killed a cow of the said Michel Richart by having put the powder near the soil of the stable, because the wife of the said Richart had refused to give her some milk.

Confessing also to having once held a nocturnal assembly in her own house and of having there danced with the said affectionate Belzebub. And there were present at this assembly Jenne Olivier, wife of Jehan Maughuier, Antoinette

Solbreucq, widow of the good Michiel Wague, Jacqueline Piedana, wife of Michiel Damet, and others whom she could not at present name, according that they had all confessed, where there were on the table black bread and black butter.

And finally, she confessed to have caused the deaths of two of her own children whom she had by the said Pierre Hélo, her second husband, one of four years or thereabouts and the other about a month old, by having put the said powder in the boiled milk that she gave them to drink; afterwards when the child was buried in the cemetery of Fenain, she dug up its body with the help of the said Belzebub, because she had given the infant to him when it had been in her womb. She carried the corpse to a nocturnal assembly and dance very near to Fenain, where she devoured a part of its heart, and the wife of Jehan Maughuier, also present, devoured another part, and that the devils made a powder of the rest to give it to the women and enable them to commit evil acts, killing and other things, both people and animals, as they should find it convenient to do.

For these reasons, We, the above-named bailiff, after having taken advice about all of this from many counsellors and advocates of the court at Mons, and having communicated to the jurymen of this court, having been present at the instruction of the said trial, and having the fear of God before our eyes, have, by this, our definitive sentence, condemned and condemn the said Marie Cornu, prisoner here before the court (preferring mercy to the rigor of justice), to be put to the last punishment until her death, by fire, but being strangled first.

Pronounced at Fenain, 14 February 1611.

53
The Prosecutions at Bamberg (1628)

The archives of the municipal library of the cathedral city of Bamberg contain the minutes of a very famous trial in the history of European witchcraft, that of the burgomaster, or mayor, himself, Johannes Junius. This trial is of particular interest not only because of the light it sheds on the process of accusation, but also because included among its documents is the letter which Junius smuggled out of prison to his daughter, indicating that the official court documents upon which we so depend for our understanding of witchcraft can cover a multitude of virtues and sufferings that are too often unseen in our histories.

SOURCE: Burr, *The Witch Persecutions*, 23–28.

FURTHER READING: Wolfgang Behringer, *Witchcraft Persecutions in Bavaria*, trans. J. C. Grayson and David Lederer (Cambridge, 1997), 194–206; 224–29. There is a reproduction of Junius's letter to his daughter in Rossell Hope Robbins, *The Encyclopedia of Witchcraft and Demonology* (New York, 1959), 291.

On WEDNESDAY, JUNE 18, 1628, was examined without torture Johannes Junius, Burgomaster at Bamberg, on the charge of witchcraft: how and in what fashion he had fallen into that vice. Is fifty-five years old, and was born at Niederwaysich in the Wetterau. Says he is wholly innocent, knows nothing of the crime, has never in his life renounced God; says that he is wronged before God and the world, would like to hear of a single human being who has seen him at such gatherings [the witch-sabbaths]. Confrontation of Dr. Georg Adam Haan. Tells him to his face he will stake his life on it, that he saw him, Junius, a year and a half ago at a witch-gathering in the electoral council-room, where they ate and drank. Accused denies the same wholly.

Confronted with [the servant] Hopffens Elsse. Tells him likewise that he was on Haupts-moor at a witch-dance; but first the holy wafer was desecrated. Junius denies. Hereupon he was told that his accomplices had confessed against him and was given time for thought.

On Friday, June 30, 1628, the aforesaid Junius was again without torture exhorted to confess, but again confessed nothing, whereupon, since he would confess nothing, he was put to the torture, and first the Thumb-screws were applied. Says he has never denied God his Saviour nor suffered himself to be otherwise baptized; will again stake his life on it; feels no pain in the thumb-screws.

Leg-screws. Will confess absolutely nothing; knows nothing about it. He has never renounced God; will never do such a thing; has never been guilty of this vice; feels likewise no pain.

Is stripped and examined; on his right side is found a bluish mark, like a clover leaf, is thrice pricked therein, but feels no pain and no blood flows out.

Strappado. He has never renounced God; God will not forsake him; if he were such a wretch he would not let himself be so tortured; God must show some token of his innocence. He knows nothing about witchcraft. . . .

On July 5, the above named Junius is without torture, but with urgent persuasions, exhorted to confess, and at last begins and confesses:

When in the year 1624 his law-suit at Rothweil cost him some six hundred florins, he had gone out, in the month of August, into his orchard at Friedrichsbronnen; and, as he sat there in thought, there had come to him a woman like a grass-maid, who had asked him why he sat there so sorrowful; he had answered that he was not despondent, but she had led him by seductive speeches to yield him to her will. . . . And thereafter this wench had changed into the form of a goat, which bleated and said, "Now you see with whom you have had to do. You must be mine or I will forthwith break your neck." Thereupon he had been frightened, and trembled all over for fear. Then the transformed spirit had seized him by the throat and demanded that he should renounce God Almighty, whereupon Junius said, "God forbid," and thereupon the spirit vanished through the power of these words. Yet it came straightway back, brought more people with it, and persistently demanded of him that he renounce God in Heaven and all the heavenly host, by which terrible threatening he was obliged to speak this formula: "I renounce God in Heaven and his host, and will henceforward recognize the Devil as my God."

After the renunciation he was so far persuaded by those present and by the evil spirit that he suffered himself to be otherwise baptized in the evil spirit's name. The Morhauptin had given him a ducat as dower-gold, which afterward became only a potsherd.

He was then named Krix. His paramour he had to call Vixen. Those present had congratulated him in Beelzebub's name and said that they were now all alike. At this baptism of his there were among others the aforesaid Christiana Morhauptin, the young Geiserlin, Paul Glaser, [and others]. After this they had dispersed.

At this time his paramour had promised to provide him with money, and from time to time to take him to other witch-gatherings. . . .

Whenever he wished to ride forth [to the witch-sabbath] a black dog had come before his bed, which said to him that he must go with him, whereupon he had seated himself upon the dog and the dog had raised himself in the Devil's name and so had fared forth.

About two years ago he was taken to the electoral council-room, at the left hand as one goes in. Above at a table were seated the Chancellor, the Burgomaster Neydekher, Dr. Georg Haan, [and many others]. Since his eyes were not good, he could not recognize more persons.

More time for consideration was now given him. On July 7, the aforesaid Junius was again examined, to know what further had occurred to him to confess. He confesses that about two months ago, on the day after an execution was held, he was at a witch-dance at the Black Cross, where Beelzebub had shown himself to them all and said expressly to their faces that they must all be burned together on this spot, and had ridiculed and taunted those present. . . .

Of crimes. His paramour had immediately after his seduction demanded that he should make away with his younger son Hans Georg, and had given him for this purpose a gray powder; this, however, being too hard for him, he had made away with his horse, a brown, instead.

His paramour had also often spurred him on to kill his daughter, and because he would not do this he had been maltreated with blows by the evil spirit.

Once at the suggestion of his paramour he had taken the holy wafer out of his mouth and given it to her. . . .

A week before his arrest as he was going to St. Martin's church the Devil met him on the way, in the form of a goat, and told him that he would soon be imprisoned, but that he should not trouble himself—he would soon set him free. Besides this, by his soul's salvation, he knew nothing further; but what he had spoken was the pure truth; on that he would stake his life. On August 6, 1628, there was read to the aforesaid Junius this his confession, which he then wholly ratified and confirmed, and was willing to stake his life upon it. And afterward he voluntarily confirmed the same before the court.

[Junius was thus convicted and was quickly burned at the stake. But on July 24, 1628, Junius had smuggled out of prison a letter to his daughter, Veronica, in which he stated that everything he had confessed was the result of the unbearable torture inflicted upon him. So severely crippled were his hands that it took him several days to write the letter.]

Many hundred thousand good-nights, dearly beloved daughter Veronica. Innocent have I come into prison, innocent have I been tortured, innocent must I die. For whoever comes into the witch prison must become a witch or be tortured until he invents something out of his head and—God pity him—bethinks him of something.

I will tell you how it has gone with me. When I was the first time put to the torture, Dr. Braun, Dr. Kötzendörffer, and two strange doctors were there. Then Dr. Braun asks me, "Kinsman, how come you here?" I answer, "Through falsehood, through misfortune." "Hear, you," he says, "you are a witch; will you confess it voluntarily? If not, we'll bring in witnesses and the executioner for you." I said "I am no witch, I have a pure conscience in the matter; if there are a thousand witnesses, I am not anxious, but I'll gladly hear the witnesses." Now the chancellor's son was set before me ... and afterward Hoppfens Elsse. She had seen me dance on Haupts-Moor. . . . I answered: "I have never renounced God, and will never do it—God graciously keep me from it. I'll rather bear whatever I must." And then came also—God in highest Heaven have mercy—the executioner, and put the thumb-screws on me, both hands bound together, so that the blood ran out at the nails and everywhere, so that for four weeks I could not use my hands, as you can see from the writing. . . . Thereafter they first stripped me, bound my hands behind me, and drew me up in the torture. Then I thought heaven and earth were at an end; eight times did they draw me up and let me fall again, so that I suffered terrible agony. . . .

And this happened on Friday, June 30, and with God's help I had to bear the torture. . . . When at last the executioner led me back into the prison, he said to me: "Sir, I beg you, for God's sake confess something, whether it be true or not. Invent something, for you cannot endure the torture which you'll be put to; and, even if you bear it all, yet you will not escape, not if you were an earl, but one torture will follow after another until even you say you are a witch. Not before that," he said, "will they let you go, as you may see by all their trials, for one is just like another. . . ."

And so I begged, since I was in wretched plight, to be given one day for thought and a priest. The priest was refused me, but the time for thought was given. Now, my dear child, see in what hazard I stood and still stand. I must say that I am a witch, though I am not,—must now renounce God, though I have never done it before. Day and night I was deeply troubled, but at last there came to me a new idea. I would not be anxious, but, since I had been given no priest with whom I could take counsel, I would myself think of something and say it. It were surely better that I just say it with mouth and words, even though I had not really done it; and afterwards I would confess it to the priest, and let those answer for it who compel me to do it. . . . And so I made my confession, as follows; but it was all a lie.

Now follows, dear child, what I confessed in order to escape the great anguish and bitter torture, which it was impossible for me longer to bear. . . .

[Junius paraphrases the confession above.]

Then I had to tell what people I had seen [at the witch-sabbath]. I said that I had not recognized them. "You old rascal, I must set the executioner at you. Say—was not the Chancellor there?" So I said yes. "Who besides?" I had not recognized anybody. So he said: "Take one street after another; begin at the market, go out on one street and back on the next." I had to name several persons there. Then came the long street. I knew nobody. Had to name eight persons there. Then the Zinkenwert—one person more. Then over the upper bridge to the Georgthor, on both sides. Knew nobody again. Did I know nobody in the castle—whoever it might be, I should speak without fear. And thus continuously they asked me on all the streets, though I could not and would not say more. So they gave me to the executioner, told him to strip me, shave me all over, and put me to the torture. "The rascal knows one on the market-place, is with him daily, and yet won't name him." By that they meant Dietmayer: so I had to name him too.

Then I had to tell what crimes I had committed. I said nothing. . . . "Draw the rascal up!" So I said that I was to kill my children, but I had killed a horse instead. It did not help. I had also taken a sacred wafer, and had desecrated it. When I had said this, they left me in peace.

Now, dear child, here you have all my confession, for which I must die. And they are sheer lies and made-up things, so help me God. For all this I was forced to say through fear of the torture which was threatened beyond what I had already endured. For they never leave off with the torture till one confesses something; be he never so good, he must be a witch. Nobody escapes, though he were an earl. . . .

Dear child, keep this letter secret so that people do not find it, else I shall be tortured most piteously and the jailers will be beheaded. So strictly is it forbidden. . . . Dear child, pay this man [the jailer bribed to carry the letter out to Junius's daughter] a dollar. . . . I have taken several days to write this: my hands are both lame. I am in a sad plight. . . .

Good night, for your father Johannes Junius will never see you more. July 24, 1628.

[The next passage was written on the margin of the letter.]

Dear child, six have confessed against me at once: the Chancellor, his son, Neudecker, Zaner, Hoffmaisters Ursel, and Hoppfens Elsse—all false, through compulsion, as they have all told me, and begged my forgiveness in God's name before they were executed. . . . They know nothing but good of me. They were forced to say it, just as I myself was. . . .

54
The Prosecutions at Würzburg (1629)

In the 1620s, a particularly intensive witch-hunt developed in the area in and around the cathedral city of Würzburg under the prince-bishop Philipp Adolf von Ehrenburg. This contemporary account was written in August, 1629, by the prince-bishop's chancellor in a letter to a friend. It is preserved in the municipal library in Munich. As in the persecutions at Trier (Text 47), the victims included notables, and the terror was apparently all-pervasive. As Wolfgang Behringer points out, the prosecutions at Würzburg, Bamberg (Text 53), Ellwangen, and Eichstätt were the most severe and extensive prosecutions in all of south Germany.

SOURCE: Burr, *The Witch Persecutions*, 28–29.

FURTHER READING: Behringer, *Witchcraft Prosecutions in Bavaria*, 224–29.

As TO THE AFFAIR of the witches, which Your Grace thinks brought to an end before this, it has started up afresh, and no words can do justice to it. Ah, the woe and the misery of it—there are still four hundred in the city, high and low, of every rank and sex, nay, even clerics, so strongly accused that they may be arrested at any hour. It is true that, of the people of my Gracious Prince here, some out of all offices and faculties must be executed: clerics, electoral councilors and doctors, city officials, court assessors, several of whom Your Grace knows. There are law students to be arrested. The Prince-Bishop has over forty students who are soon to be pastors; among them thirteen or fourteen are said to be witches. A few days ago a Dean was arrested; two others who were summoned have fled.

The notary of our Church consistory, a very learned man, was yesterday arrested and put to the torture. In a word, a third part of the city is surely involved. The richest, most attractive, most prominent, of the clergy are already executed. A week ago a maiden of nineteen was executed, of whom it is everywhere said that she was the fairest in the whole city, and was held by everybody a girl of singular modesty and purity. She will be followed by seven or eight others of the best and most attractive persons. . . . And thus many are put to death for renouncing God and being at the witch dances, against whom nobody has ever else spoken a word.

To conclude this wretched matter, there are children of three and four years, to the number of three hundred, who are said to have had intercourse with the Devil. I have seen put to death children of seven, promising students of ten, twelve, fourteen, and fifteen. Of the nobles—but I cannot and must not write more of this misery. There are persons of yet higher rank, whom you know, and would marvel to hear of, nay, would scarcely believe it; let justice be done. . . .

P.S. Though there are many wonderful and terrible things happening, it is beyond doubt that, at a place called the Fraw-Rengberg, the Devil in person, with eight thousand of his followers, held an assembly and celebrated mass before them all, administering to his audience (that is, the witches) turnip-rinds and parings in place of the Holy Eucharist. There took place not only foul but most horrible and hideous blasphemies, whereof I shudder to write. It is also true that they all vowed not to be enrolled in the Book of Life, but all agreed to be inscribed by a notary who is well known to me and my colleagues. We hope, too, that the book in which they are enrolled will yet be found, and there is no little search being made for it.

55
The Prosecutions at Bonn (ca. 1630)

This letter from Pastor Duren of the village of Alfter, near Bonn, to Count Werner von Salm purports to describe the witch persecutions in that city. But the authenticity of this document is unverifiable because the putative manuscript source is no longer extant, and the events it describes are corroborated by no other documents or references. George Lincoln Burr translated and reprinted it in his *Witch Persecutions*, and thus it has been made a well-known part of that small body of "primary sources" with which the English-speaking student of the history of witchcraft is familiar. What Burr apparently overlooked, however, was the remarkable similarity of this "'Bonn letter" to the authenticated letter of the chancellor of the prince-bishop of Würzburg of August 1629, describing the prosecutions in that city (Text 54). Thus, the chief interest of this document is historiographical rather than historical. The problem of fraudulent accounts of witch persecutions has not yet received historians' full attention. In some cases, possibly including this one at Bonn, the derivative character of our only source raises the question of the reliability of the data it contains. Yet its circulation no doubt contributed to current popular fears, and hence it does offer insights into one aspect of the witch literature of the seventeenth century.

SOURCE: Burr, *The Witch Persecutions*, 18–19.

THOSE BURNED ARE MOSTLY male witches of the sort described. There must be half the city implicated: for already professors, law-students, pastors, canons, vicars, and monks have here been arrested and burned. His Princely Grace has seventy wards who are to become pastors, one of whom, eminent as a musician, was yesterday arrested; two others were sought for, but have fled. The Chancellor and his wife and the Private Secretary's wife are already executed. On the eve of Our Lady's Day there was executed here a maiden of nineteen who bore the name of being the fairest and the most blameless of all the city, and who from her childhood had been brought up by the Bishop himself. A canon of the cathedral, named Rotenhahn, I saw beheaded and burned. Children of three or four years have devils for their paramours. Students and boys of noble birth, of nine, ten, eleven, twelve, thirteen, fourteen years, have here been burned. In fine, things are in such a pitiful state that one does not know with what people one may talk and associate.

56
The Devils of Loudun (1636)

No single witchcraft trial of any individual is better known to us today, in all its details, than that of Urbain Grandier, a priest of Loudun, France, convicted of witchcraft, tortured, and burned at the stake in 1636 for having bewitched the local convent of Ursuline nuns. The context, machinations, pathology, and ultimate tragedy of the case have been clearly and movingly portrayed in Aldous Huxley's *The Devils of Loudun*. The sentence of the Royal Commissioners is noteworthy for its dramatic and well-staged effects, calculated to impress upon all minds the gravity of the crimes of this priest convicted of bewitching a convent.

More remarkable is the letter of Father Surin who, sent to exorcise the demons Grandier was accused of summoning, found himself possessed as well, and offered, in a rambling letter to his friend and spiritual adviser, a startling description of the symptomology of witchcraft in terms meaningful to a devout Christian of the seventeenth century.

SOURCE: J. Aubin, *Les Diables de Loudun* (Amsterdam, 1693), 154–55, 218–21. Trans. A. C. K.

FURTHER READING: Robert Rapley, *A Case of Witchcraft: The Trial of Urbain Grandier* (Manchester, 1999).

Sentence of the Royal Commissioners
Against Urbain Grandier (1636)

We have decreed and shall decree the said Urbain Grandier duly arraigned and convicted of the crime of Wizardry, Sorcery and Possessions occurring by his deed, in the persons of several Ursuline Nuns of this town of Loudun, and other members of the Secular Clergy; together with other incidents and crimes resulting from this. For expiation of which, we have condemned and shall condemn this Grandier to make honorable repentance, bare-headed, a rope around his neck, bearing in his hand a burning torch weighing two pounds, before the main door of the Church of Saint Pierre du Marché, and before that of Saint Ursula of this said town, and there, upon his knees, to ask pardon of God, of the King and of justice; and this accomplished, to be taken to the public square of Sainte Croix, to be attached to a stake upon a pyre, which will be constructed at the said square for this purpose, and there to be burned alive with the pacts and the signs of Sorcery lying on the pyre, together with his Manuscript Book against priestly celibacy, and his ashes scattered to the wind. We have decreed and shall decree each and every of his possessions to be acquired and confiscated by the King, out of which the sum of one-hundred and fifty *livres* initially will be taken, to be used to purchase a copper lamp, upon which extracts of this present Sentence will be engraved, this being installed in a prominent place in the said Church of the Ursulines, to remain there in perpetuity. And prior to proceeding to the execution of the present Sentence, we order that the said Grandier will be subjected to ordinary and extraordinary Torture. . . . Pronounced at Loudun before the said Grandier, and executed the eighteenth of August, 1636.

Letter of Father Surin, Jesuit, exorcist of the Ursuline
Sisters of Loudun, to his Friend Father Datichi, Jesuit,
at Rennes; written from Loudun, May 3, 1635.

Pax Christi.

To my Reverend Father,

There is scarcely anyone to whom it is more of a pleasure to relate my adventures than to your Reverence, who hears them willingly, and who formulates thoughts on them that do not come easily to other men, who do not know me as you do. Since my last letter I have fallen into a state of things far beyond my foresight, but most in conformity with the Providence of God for my soul:

I am no longer at Marennes, but at Loudun, where I have just received your letter. I am in perpetual conversation with the Devils, in which I have had encounters which would be too lengthy to elaborate for you, and which have given me more reasons to know and admire the goodness of God than I have ever had. I want to tell you something, and I would tell you more of it if you were more close-mouthed.

I have entered into combat with four of the most powerful and malicious Demons of Hell. Me, I say, whose infirmities you know; God has permitted the combats to be so violent, and the contacts so frequent, that the least of the battlefields was the exorcism, for the enemies have announced themselves under cover, day and night, in a thousand different ways. You can imagine what a pleasure there is in finding oneself at the mercy of God alone. I will not say more on it; it is enough that knowing my state, you decide to pray for me. All the more because for three and a half months, I am never without a Devil at my side, exerting himself. Things have gone so far that God has permitted, for my sins, I think, something never seen, perhaps, in the Church: that during the exercise of my ministry, the Devil passes from the body of the possessed person, and coming into mine, assaults me and overturns me, shakes me, and visibly travels through me, possessing me for several hours like an energumen. I would not know how to explain to you what occurs inside of me during this time, and how this Spirit unites with mine, without depriving me either of the knowledge or the liberty of my soul, while nevertheless making himself like another me, and how it is as if I had two souls, one of which is deprived of its body, of the use of its organs, and stands apart, watching the actions of the one which has entered. The two Spirits battle on the same field, which is the body, and the soul is as if it were divided; following one part of itself, it is the subject of diabolical impressions; following the other, of movements which are its own, or which God gives to it. At the same time, I feel a great peace, under the absolute will of God; and without my knowing how, there comes an extreme rage, and aversion to Him, which becomes almost violent trying to separate itself from the other feeling, which astounds those who see it; on the one hand a great joy and *douceur*, and on the other, a sadness which reveals itself by lamentations and cries similar to those of the Demons: I feel the state of damnation and am frightened by it, and I feel as if I were pierced by sharp points of despair in this foreign soul which seems to be mine, and the other soul, which is full of confidence, makes light of such feelings, and in full liberty curses the one which causes them; verily, I feel that the same cries which leave my mouth come equally from these two souls, and I am hard-pressed to discern if it is the mirth which produces them, or the extreme fury which fills me. The tremblings which overcome me when the Holy Sacrament is bestowed upon me come equally, it seems to me, from horror at its presence, which is unbearable to me, and from a sweet and gentle reverence, without my being able to attribute them more to one than to the other, and without its being in my power to restrain them. When one of these two souls moves me to want to make the sign of the cross on my mouth, the other turns my hand away with great speed, and seizes my finger with my teeth, in order to gnaw on it in a rage. I almost never find prayer easier and more tranquil than during these agitations; while my body rolls on the ground, and the Ministers of the Church speak to me as if to a Devil, and accuse me of maledictions, I could not tell you the joy that I feel, having become a Devil not out of rebellion to God, but by virtue of the distress which depicts ingenuously for me the state to which sin has reduced me; so that appropriating to myself all of the maledictions which are offered to me, my soul has cause to sink in its nothingness.

When the other possessed persons see me in this state, it is a pleasure to see their triumph, and how the Devils make fun of me, saying, Doctor, heal thyself, and go preach now from the pulpit; how nice it will be to see him preach, after he has rolled on the ground; *Tentaverunt, subsannaverunt me subsannatione, frenduerunt super me dentibus suis.* What a cause of benediction to see oneself made the Devil's plaything, and how the Justice of God in this world makes sense of my sins! what a blessing to experience the state from which Jesus Christ has drawn me, no longer by heresay, but by the sensation of that very state; and how good it is to have at one and the same time the ability to enter into that misery and to give thanks to the goodness which has delivered us from it with so many efforts!

That is how things stand with me at this time, almost every day. Great disputes are emerging over this, and *factus sum magna quaestio,* if it is a Possession or not, if it is possible that Ministers of the Gospel come to such great harm. Some say that it is a chastisement from God upon me, as punishment for some illusion; others say something quite different; as for me, I hold fast where I am, and would not exchange my fate for anyone's, being firmly convinced that there is nothing better than to be reduced to such great extremities. The one in which I find myself is such that I have few free actions: when I want to speak, my words are blocked; at Mass, I am paralyzed; at the table, I cannot carry a bite to my mouth; at Confession, I suddenly forget my sins; and I feel the Devil come and go inside of me as if it were his home. From the moment I awake, he is there: at prayer, he snatches my thought away whenever he wants; when my heart begins to swell with God, he fills it with fury; he puts me to sleep when I want to stay awake; and publicly, out of the mouth of the Possessed Woman, he boasts that he is my master: to which I have nothing to retort. Having the reproach of m conscience, and the sentence pronounced upon sinners on my head, I must submit to it, and worship the order of Divine Providence, to which every creature must submit.

There is not just one Demon who works on me, but two ordinarily; one of them is Leviathan, the opposite of the Holy Ghost, inasmuch as they have said here that they have a Trinity in Hell that the Witches worship: *Lucifer, Beelzebub,* and *Leviathan,* who is the Third Person of Hell, and several authors have written and remarked on this heretofore. Now, the actions of the false Paraclete are completely the opposite of the true one, and they impart a desolation that one could never describe adequately. He is the leader of the entire group of our Demons, and he is the supervisor of the whole affair, which is one of the strangest that perhaps has ever been seen. In this same location, we see Paradise and Hell; nuns who are, taken in one sense, like St. Ursulas, and, taken in another, worse than the most damned in all sorts of dissoluteness, obscenity, blasphemy and frenzy.

I do not want your Reverence to make my letter public, if it please you. You are the sole person, outside of my Confessor and my Superiors, to whom I have wanted to tell so much, and only in order to provide some communication which helps us to glorify God, in Whom I am your most humble servant,

Jean-Joseph Surin

57
The Trial of Suzanne Gaudry (1652)

The trial of Suzanne Gaudry, preserved in the oddly meticulous and syntactically disordered court records, offers a view of a case close to the modern age's traditional stereotype of witchcraft persecutions: the pathetic and illiterate old woman, the sabbath, the nocturnal flights, the carnal love of the devil, the effective use of terror and torture to obtain a confession, the recantation and burning at the stake, all brought together in a judicial atmosphere composed half of orderly interrogation and half of frightful insinuation and contradiction. The "leading questions," drawn from the "experience" of past centuries, show how a local secular court coordinated its activities to the more general traditions, and make clearer how the content of confessions remained so constant throughout the period of persecutions. The trial took place in territories under Spanish jurisdiction.

SOURCE: J. Français, *L'Eglise et la sorcellerie* (Paris, 1910), 236–51. Trans. A. C. K.

At Ronchain, May 28, 1652. . . . Interrogation of Suzanne Gaudry,
prisoner at the court of Rieux.
Questioned about her age, her place of origin, her mother and father.
—Said that she is named Suzanne Gaudry, daughter of Jean Gaudry and Marguerite Gerné, both natives of Rieux, but that she is from Esgavans, near Ode-

narde, where her family had taken refuge because of the wars, that she was born the day that they made bonfires for the Peace between France and Spain, without being able otherwise to say her age.

Asked why she has been taken here.

—Answers that it is for the salvation of her soul.

—Says that she was frightened of being taken prisoner for the crime of witchcraft.

Asked for how long she has been in the service of the devil.

—Says that about twenty-five or twenty-six years ago she was his lover, that he called himself Petit-Grignon, that he would wear black breeches, that he gave her the name Magin, that she gave him a pin with which he gave her his mark on the left shoulder, that he had a little flat hat; said also that he had his way with her two or three times only.

Asked how many times she has been at the nocturnal dance.

—Answers that she has been there about a dozen times, having first of all renounced God, Lent and baptism; that the site of the dance was at the little marsh of Rieux, understanding that there were diverse dances. The first time, she did not recognize anyone there, because she was half blind. The other times, she saw and recognized there Noelle and Pasquette Gerné, Noelle the wife of Nochin Quinchou and the other of Paul Doris, the widow Marie Nourette, not having recognized others because the young people went with the young people and the old people with the old. And that when the dance was large, the table also was accordingly large.

Questioned what was on the table.

—Says that there was neither salt nor napkin, that she does not know what there was because she never ate there. That her lover took here there and back.

Asked if her lover had never given her some powder.

—Answers that he offered her some, but that she never wanted to take any, saying to her that it was to do with what she wanted, that this powder was gray, that her lover told her she would ruin someone but good, and that he would help her, especially that she would ruin Elisabeth Dehan, which she at no time wanted to do, although her lover was pressing her to do it, because this Elisabeth had battered his crops with a club.

Interrogated on how and in what way they danced.

—Says that they dance in an ordinary way, that there was a guitarist and some whistlers who appeared to be men she did not know, which lasted about an hour, and then everyone collapsed from exhaustion.

Inquired what happened after the dance.

—Says that they formed a circle, that there was a king with a long black beard dressed in black, with a red hat, who made everyone do his bidding, and that after the dance he made a . . . [the word is missing in the text], and then everyone disappeared. . . .

Interrogated on how long it has been since she has seen Grignon, her lover.

—Says that is has been three or four days.

Questioned if she has abused the Holy Communion.

—Says no, never, and that she has always swallowed it. Then says that her lover asked her for it several times, but that she did not want to give it to him.

After several admonitions were sent to her, she has signed this

Mark
X
Suzanne Gandry

Second Interrogation, May 29, 1652, in the presence of the aforementioned

This prisoner, being brought back into the chamber, was informed about the facts and the charges and asked if what she declared and confessed yesterday is true.

—Answers that if it is in order to put her in prison it is not true; then after having remained silent said that it is true.

Asked what is her lover's name and what name has he given himself.

—Said that his name is Grinniou and that he calls himself Magnin.

Asked where he found her the first time and what he did to her.

—Answers that it was in her lodgings, that he had a hide, little black breeches, and a little flat hat; that he asked her for a pin, which she gave to him, with which he made his mark on her left shoulder. Said also that at the time she took him oil in a bottle and that she had thoughts of love.

Asked how long she has been in subjugation to the devil.

—Says that it has been about twenty-five or twenty-six years, that her lover also then made her renounce God, Lent, and baptism, that he has known her carnally three or four times, and that he has given her satisfaction. And on the subject of his having asked her if she wasn't afraid of having a baby, says that she did not have that thought.

Asked how many times she found herself at the nocturnal dance and carol and whom she recognized there.

—Answers that she was there eleven or twelve times, that she went there on foot with her lover, where the third time she saw and recognized Pasquette and Noelle Gerné, and Marie Homitte, to whom she never spoke, for the reason that they did not speak to each other. And that the sabbat took place at the little meadow. . . .

Interrogated on how long it is since she saw her lover, and if she also did not see Marie Hourie and her daughter Marie at the dance.

—Said that it has been a long time, to wit, just about two years, and that she saw neither Marie Hourie nor her daughter there; then later said, after having asked for some time to think about it, that it has been a good fifteen days or three weeks [since she saw him], having renounced all the devils of hell and the one who misled her.

Asked what occurred at the dance and afterwards.

—Says that right after the dance they put themselves in order and approached the chief figure, who had a long black beard, dressed also in black, with a red hat, at which point they were given some powder, to do with it what they wanted; but that she did not want to take any.

Charged with having taken some and with having used it evilly.

—Says, after having insisted that she did not want to take any, that she took some, and that her lover advised her to do evil with it; but that she did not want to do it.

Asked if, not obeying his orders, she was beaten or threatened by him, and what did she do with this powder.

—Answers that never was she beaten; she invoked the name of the Virgin [and answered] that she threw away the powder that she had, not having wanted to do any evil with it.

Pressed to say what she did with this powder. Did she not fear her lover too much to have thrown it away?

—Says, after having been pressed on this question, that she made the herbs in her garden die at the end of the summer, five to six years ago, by means of the powder, which she threw there because she did not know what to do with it.

Asked if the devil did not advise her to steal from Elisabeth Dehan and to do harm to her.

—Said that he advised her to steal from her and promised that he would help her; but urged her not to do harm to her; and that is because she [Elisabeth Dehan] had cut the wood in her [Suzanne Gaudry's] fence and stirred up the seeds in her garden, saying that her lover told her that she would avenge herself by beating her.

Charged once more with having performed some malefice with this powder, pressed to tell the truth.

—Answers that she never made any person or beast die; then later said that she made Philippe Cornié's red horse die, about two or three years ago, by means of the powder, which she placed where he had to pass, in the street close to her home.

Asked why she did that and if she had had any difficulty with him.

—Says that she had had some difficulty with his wife, because her cow had eaten the leeks.

Interrogated on how and in what way they dance in the carol.

—Says that they dance in a circle, holding each others' hands, and each one with her lover at her side, at which she says that they do not speak to each other, or if they speak that she did not hear it, because of her being hard-of-hearing. At which there was a guitarist and a piper, whom she did not know; then later says that it is the devils who play.

After having been admonished to think of her conscience, was returned to prison after having signed this

Mark

X

Suzanne Gaudry

Deliberation of the Court of Mons—June 3, 1652

The undersigned advocates of the Court of Mons have seen these interrogations and answers. They say that the aforementioned Suzanne Gaudry confesses that she is a witch, that she has given herself to the devil, that she has renounced God, Lent, and baptism, that she has been marked on the shoulder, that she has cohabited with him and that she has been to the dances, confessing only to have cast a spell upon and caused to die a beast of Philippe Cornié; but there is no evidence for this, excepting a prior statement. For this reason, before going further, it will be necessary to become acquainted with, to examine and to probe the mark, and to hear Philippe Cornié on the death of the horse and on when and in what way he died. . . .

Deliberation of the Court of Mons—June 13, 1652

[The Court] has reviewed the current criminal trial of Suzanne Gaudry, and with it the trial of Antoinette Lescouffre, also a prisoner of the same office.

It appeared [to the Court] that the office should have the places probed where the prisoners say that they have received the mark of the devil, and after that, they must be interrogated and examined seriously on their confessions and denials, this having to be done, in order to regulate all this definitively. . . .

Deliberation of the Court of Mons—June 22, 1652

The trials of Antoinette Lescouffre and Suzanne Gaudry having been described to the undersigned, advocates of the Court of Mons, and [the Court] having been told orally that the peasants taking them to prison had persuaded them to con-fess in order to avoid imprisonment, and that they would be let go, by virtue of which it could appear that the confessions were not so spontaneous:

They are of the opinion that the office, in its duty, would do well, following the two preceding resolutions, to have the places of the marks that they have taught us about probed, and if it is found that these are ordinary marks of the devil, one can proceed to their examination; then next to the first confessions, and if they deny [these], one can proceed to the torture, given that they issue from bewitched relatives, that at all times they have been suspect, that they fled to avoid the crime [that is to say, prosecution for the crime of witchcraft], and that by their confessions they have confirmed [their guilt], notwithstanding that they have wanted to revoke [their confessions] and vacillate. . . .

Third Interrogation, June 27, in the presence of the aforementioned

This prisoner being led into the chamber, she was examined to know if things were not as she had said and confessed at the beginning of her imprisonment.

—Answers no, and that what she has said was done so by force.

Asked if she did not say to Jean Gradé that she would tell his uncle, the mayor, that he had better be careful . . . and that he was a Frank.

—Said that this is not true.

Pressed to say the truth, that otherwise she would be subjected to torture, having pointed out to her that her aunt was burned for this same subject.

—Answers that she is not a witch.

Interrogated as to how long she has been in subjection to the devil, and pressed that she was to renounce the devil and the one who misled her.

—Says that she is not a witch, that she has nothing to do with the devil, thus that she did not want to renounce the devil, saying that he has not misled her, and upon inquisition of having confessed to being present at the carol, she insisted that although she had said that, it is not true, and that she is not a witch.

Charged with having confessed to having made a horse die by means of a powder that the devil had given her.

—Answers that she said it, but because she found herself during the inquisition pressed to say that she must have done some evil deed; and after several admonitions to tell the truth:

She was placed in the hands of the officer of the *haultes oeuvres* [the officer in charge of torture], throwing herself on her knees, struggling to cry, uttering several exclamations, without being able, nevertheless, to shed a tear. Saying at every moment that she is not a witch.

The Torture

On this same day, being at the place of torture.

This prisoner, before being strapped down, was admonished to maintain herself in her first confessions and to renounce her lover.

—Said that she denies everything she has said, and that she has no lover. Feeling herself being strapped down, says that she is not a witch, while struggling to cry.

Asked why she fled outside the village of Rieux.

—Says that she cannot say it, that God and the Virgin Mary forbid her to; that she is not a witch. And upon being asked why she confessed to being one, said that she was forced to say it.

Told that she was not forced, that on the contrary she declared herself to be a witch without any threat.

—Says that she confessed it and that she is not a witch, and being a little stretched [on the rack] screams ceaselessly that she is not a witch, invoking the name of Jesus and of Our Lady of Grace, not wanting to say any other thing.

Asked if she did not confess that she had been a witch for twenty-six years.

—Says that she said it, that she retracts it, crying Jésus-Maria, that she is not a witch.

Asked if she did not make Philippe Cornié's horse die, as she confessed.

—Answers no, crying Jésus-Maria, that she is not a witch.

The mark having been probed by the officer, in the presence of Doctor Bouchain, it was adjudged by the aforesaid doctor and officer truly to be the mark of the devil.

Being more tightly stretched upon the torture-rack, urged to maintain her confessions.

—Said that it was true that she is a witch and that she would maintain what she had said.

Asked how long she has been in subjugation to the devil.

—Answers that it was twenty years ago that the devil appeared to her, being in her lodgings in the form of a man dressed in a little cow-hide and black breeches.

Interrogated as to what her lover was called.

—Says that she said Petit-Grignon, then, being taken down [from the rack] says upon interrogation that she is not a witch and that she can say nothing.

Asked if her lover has had carnal copulation with her, and how many times.

—To that she did not answer anything; then, making believe that she was ill, not another word could be drawn from her.

As soon as she began to confess, she asked who was alongside of her, touching her, yet none of those present could see anyone there. And it was noticed that as soon as that was said, she no longer wanted to confess anything.

Which is why she was returned to prison.

Verdict

July 9, 1652

In the light of the interrogations, answers and investigations made into the charge against Suzanne Gaudry, coupled with her confessions, from which it would appear that she has always been ill-reputed for being stained with the crime of witchcraft, and seeing that she took flight and sought refuge in this city of Valenciennes, out of fear of being apprehended by the law for this matter; seeing how her close family were also stained with the same crime, and the perpetrators executed; seeing by her own confessions that she is said to have made a pact with the devil, received the mark from him, which in the report of *sieur* Michel de Roux was judged by the medical doctor of Ronchain and the officer of *haultes oeuvres* of Cambrai, after having proved it, to be not a natural mark but a mark of the devil, to which they have sworn with an oath; and that following this, she had renounced God, Lent, and baptism and had let herself be known carnally by him, in which she received satisfaction. Also, seeing that she is said to have been a part of nocturnal carols and dances. Which are crimes of divine lèse-majesté:

For expiation of which the advice of the undersigned is that the office of Rieux can legitimately condemn the aforesaid Suzanne Gaudry to death, tying her to a gallows, and strangling her to death, then burning her body and burying it there in the environs of the woods.

At Valenciennes, the 9th of July, 1652. To each [member of the Court] *4 livres, 16 sous.* . . . And for the trip of the aforementioned Roux, including an escort of one soldier, 30 *livres.*

58

Cotton Mather: "A Discourse on Witches" (1689)

In 1689, the Reverend Cotton Mather (1663–1728) preached a sermon in Boston entitled "A Discourse on Witchcraft," which was then printed and circulated in Massachusetts as a part of a larger collection, Mather's *Memorable Providences Relating to Witchcraft and Possessions* (Boston, 1689). Three years later, the witch scare erupted in Salem Village.

A vast literature exists on the trials for witchcraft in New England, and the subject has become a common component of the study of North American colonial history. Mather's sermon is given here, however, to show the consistency of North American ideas with those of contemporary thinkers in England. The records of the North American trials are all readily available in print elsewhere.

SOURCE: Burr, *The Witch Persecutions,* 2–5.

FURTHER READING: Paul Boyer and Stephen Nissenbaum, *Salem Village Witchcraft: A Documentary Record of Local Conflict in Colonial New England* (Belmont, Calif., 1972; rprt. Boston, 1993); Boyer and Nissenbaum, *Salem Witchcraft Papers: Verbatim Transcripts of the Legal Documents of the Salem Witchcraft Outbreak,* 3 vols. (1977); David D. Hall, *Witch-Hunting in Seventeenth-Century New England: A Documentary History, 1638–1692* (Boston, 1991). There is a substantial body of scholarship, most recently Richard Godbeer, *The Devil's Dominion: Magic and Religion in Early New England* (Cambridge, 1992); Elizabeth Reis, *Damned Women: Sinners and Witches in Puritan New England* (Ithaca and London, 1997); Reis, ed., *Spellbound: Women and Witchcraft in America* (Wilmington, Del., 1998); Bryan F. Le Beau, *The Story of the Salem Witch Trials* (Upper Saddle River, N.J., 1998). A careful critique is that of Bernard Rosenthal, *Salem Story: Reading the Witch Trials of 1692* (Cambridge, 1993).

SUCH AN HELLISH THING there is as Witchcraft in the World. There are Two things which will be desired for the advantage of this Assertion. It should first be show'd

WHAT Witchcraft is;

My Hearers will not expect from me an accurate Definition of the vile Thing; since the Grace of God has given me the Happiness to speak without Experience of it. But from Accounts both by Reading and Hearing I have learn'd to describe it so.

WITCHCRAFT is the Doing of Strange (and for the most part Ill) Things by the help of evil Spirits, Covenanting with (and usually Representing of) the woful children of men.

This is the Diabolical Art that Witches are notorious for.

First. Witches are the Doers of Strange Things. They cannot indeed perform any proper Miracles; those are things to be done only by the Favourites and Embassadours of the Lord. But Wonders are often produced by them, though chiefly such Wonders as the Apostle calls in 2 Thes. 2, 9. Lying wonders. There are wonderful Storms in the great World, and wonderful Wounds in the little World, often effected by these evil Causes. They do things which transcend the ordinary Course of Nature, and which puzzle the ordinary Sense of Mankind. Some strange things are done by them in a way of Real Production. They do really Torment, they do really Afflict those that their Spite shall extend unto. Other Strange Things are done by them in a way of Crafty Illusion. They do craftily make of the Air, the Figures and Colours of things that never can be truly created by them. All men might see, but, I believe, no man could feel, some of the Things which the Magicians of Egypt exhibited of old.

Secondly. They are not only strange Things, but Ill Things, that Witches are the Doers of. In this regard also they are not the Authors of Miracles: those are things commonly done for the Good of Man, alwaies done for the Praise of God. But of these Hell-hounds it may in a special manner be said, as in Psal. 52, 3. Thou lovest evil more than good. For the most part they labour to robb Man of his Ease or his Wealth; they labour to wrong God of His Glory. There is Mention of Creatures that they call White Witches, which do only Good-Turns for their Neighbours. I suspect that here are none of that sort; but rather think, There is none that doeth good, no, not one. If they do good, it is only that they may do hurt.

Thirdly. It is by virtue of evil Spirits that Witches do what they do. We read in Ephes. 2, 2. about the Prince of the power of the air. There is confined unto the Atmosphere of our Air a vast Power, or Army of Evil Spirits, under the Government of a Prince who employs them in a continual Opposition to the Designs of GOD: The Name of that Leviathan, who is the Grand-Seigniour of Hell, we find in the Scripture to be Belzebub. Under the Command of that mighty Tyrant, there are vast Legions & Myriads of Devils, whose Businesses & Accomplishments are not all the same. Every one has his Post, and his Work; and they are all glad of an opportunity to be mischievous in the World. These are they by whom Witches do exert their Devillish and malignant Rage upon their Neighbours:

And especially Two Acts concur hereunto. The First is, Their Covenanting with the Witches. There is a most hellish League made between them, with various Rites and Ceremonies. The Witches promise to serve the Devils, and the Devils promise to help the witches; How? It is not convenient to be related. The Second is, their Representing of the Witches. And hereby indeed these are drawn into Snares and Cords of Death. The Devils, when they go upon the Errands of the Witches, do bear their Names; and hence do Harmes too come to be carried from the Devils to the Witches. We need not suppose such a wild thing as the Transforming of those Wretches into Bruits or Birds, as we too often do.

It should next be proved THAT Witchcraft is.

The Being of such a thing is denied by many that place a great part of their small wit in derideing the Stories that are told of it. Their chief Argument is, That they never saw any Witches, therefore there are none. Just as if you or I should say, We never met with any Robbers on the Road, therefore there never was any Padding there.

Indeed the Devils are loath to have true Notions of Witches entertained with us. I have beheld them to put out the eyes of an enchaunted Child, when a Book that proves, There is Witchcraft, was laid before her. But there are especially Two Demonstrations that evince the Being of that Infernal mysterious thing.

First. We have the Testimony of Scripture for it. We find Witchcrafts often mentioned, sometimes by way of Assertion, sometimes by way of Allusion, in the Oracles of God. Besides that, We have there the History of diverse Witches in these infallible and inspired Writings. Particularly, the Instance of the Witch at Endor, in 1 Sam. 28. 7. is so plain and full that Witchcraft it self is not a more amazing thing, than any Dispute about the Being of it, after this. The Advocates of Witches must use more Tricks to make Nonsense of the Bible, than ever the Witch of Endor used in her Magical Incantations, if they would evade the Force of that famous History. They that will believe no Witches, do imagine that Jugglers only are meant by them whom the Sacred Writ calleth so. But what do they think of that law in Exod. 22. 18. Thou shalt not suffer a Witch to live? Methinks 'tis a little too hard to punish every silly Juggler with so great Severity.

Secondly. We have the Testimony of Experience for it. What will those Incredulous, who must be the only Ingenious men, say to This? Many Witches have like those in Act. 19. 18. Confessed and shewed their deeds. We see those things done, that is impossible any Disease or any Deceit should procure. We see some hideous Wretches in hideous Horrours confessing. That they did the Mischiefs. This Confession is often made by them that are owners of as much Reason as the people that laugh at all Conceit of Witchcraft: the exactest Scrutiny of skilful Physicians cannot find any Distraction in their minds. This Confession is often made by them that are apart One from another, and yet they agree in all the Circumstances of it. This Confession is often made by them that at the same time will produce the Engines and Ensignes of their Hellish Trade, and give the standers-by an Ocular Conviction of what they do, and how. There can be no Judgment left of any Humane Affairs, if such Confessions must be Ridiculed: all the Murders, yea, and all the Bargains in the World must be meer Imaginations if such Confessions are of no Account.

59

Joseph Glanvill,
Sadducismus Triumphatus (1689)

Joseph Glanvill (1636–80), with his colleague Henry More (1614–87), was one of the most important controversialists in the seventeenth-century debate over the question of spiritual causation. Both Glanvill and More were philosophers of immense erudition and culture associated with the movement in seventeenth-century English thought known as Cambridge Platonism. Both thinkers accepted a fundamental spiritual reality in the natural as well as the supernatural world, and both saw a great danger to religious and specifically Christian beliefs caused by the inroads of an antispiritualist mechanism and materialism that they identified with the thought of Descartes, Hobbes, and Spinoza. It is in this context that their writings on witchcraft must be understood.

If one could prove the existence of evil spirits, one would thereby demonstrate the reality of spiritual causes and agents in the natural world, and witchcraft offered for More and Glanvill such a proof. Predisposed to seeing spirits, evil and good, all about them in the world, More and Glanvill readily compiled case histories of witchcraft, utilizing these "well-attested" tales as empirical evidence for the reality of spirit in the lives of men. Glanvill himself witnessed and publicized the activities of the "Demon of Tedworth," and he and More became a virtual clearinghouse for similar relations by other men. Adding such empirical data to the scriptural sources of witchcraft belief, they felt that they had completed a compelling case for witchcraft from both a traditional and a progressive, more scientific point of view.

SOURCE: Joseph Glanvill, *Sadducismus Triumphatus, Or full and plain Evidence concerning Witches and Apparitions. . . The Third Edition with Additions, The Advantages whereof, above the former, the reader may understand out of Dr. H. More's account prefixed thereunto* (London, 1700), Part I.

FURTHER READING: Richard Bovet, *Pandaemonium,* trans. Montague Summers (Aldington, Kent, 1951) of 1684 also reflects ideas similar to those of More and Glanvill.

Dr. Henry More, his Letter with the Postscript to Mr. Joseph Glanvil,
minding him of the great Expedience and Usefulness of his new
intended edition of the Daemon of Tedworth . . .

And forasmuch as such course-grained Philosophers as those Hobbians and Spinozians, and the rest of the Rabble, slight Religion and the Scriptures, because there is such express mention of Spirits and Angels in them, things that their dull Souls are so inclinable to conceit to be imposable—I look upon it as a special piece of Providence, that there are ever and anon such fresh Examples of Apparitions and Witchcraft as may rub up and awaken their benumbed and lethargic Minds into a suspicion at least, if not assurance that there are other intelligent Beings besides those that are clad in heavy Earth or Clay; in this I say, methinks the divine Providence does plainly outwit the Powers of the dark Kingdom, permitting wicked Men and Women, and Vagrant Spirits of that Kingdom to make Leagues or Covenants one with another, the Confession of Witches against their own Lives being so palpable an Evidence, besides the miraculous Feats they play, that there are bad Spirits, which will necessarily open a door to the belief that there are good ones, and lastly that there is a God.

Wherefore let the small Philosophick Sir-Foplings of this present Age deride them as much as they will, those that lay out their pains in committing to writing certain well attested Stories of Witches and Apparitions, do real service to true Religion and sound Philosophy, and the most effectual and accommodate to the confounding of Infidelity and Atheism, even in the Judgement of the Atheists themselves, who are as much afraid of the truth of those Stories as an Ape is of a Whip, and therefore force themselves with might and main to disbelieve them, by reason of the dreadful consequence of them as to themselves. The Wicked fear where no fear is, but God is in the Generation of the Righteous; and he that fears God and has his Faith in Jesus Christ, need not fear how many Devils there be, nor be afraid of himself or of his Immortality; and therefore it is nothing but a foul dark Conscience within, or a very gross and dull constitution of Blood that makes Men so averse from these truths.

But however, be they as averse as they will, being this is the most accommodate Medicine for this Disease, their diligence and care of mankind is much to be commended that make it their business to apply it, and are resolved, though the peevishness and perverseness of the Patients makes them pull off their Plaster, as they have this excellent one of the Story of the Dæmon of Tedworth by decrying it as an Imposture, so acknowledged by both yourself and Mr. Mompesson, are resolved I say with Meekness and Charity to bind it on again, with the addition of new filletting. I mean other Stories sufficiently fresh and very well attested and certain. This worthy design therefore of yours, I must confess I cannot but highly commend and approve, and therefore wish you all good success therein; and so commit you to God, I take leave and rest,

Your affectionate Friend to serve you,

H.[enry] M.[ore]

Joseph Glanvill, Sadducismus Triumphatus
An Introduction to the Proof of the Existence of Apparitions, Spirits, and
Witches: To the great usefulness and seasonableness of the present
Arguent, touching Witches and Apparitions in subserviency to Religion.
The Question, whether there are Witches or not, is not matter of vain Speculation, or of indifferent Moment; but an Inquiry of very great and weighty Importance. For, on the resolution of it, depends the Authority and just Execution of some of our Laws; and which is more, our Religion in its main Doctrines is nearly concerned. There is no one, that is not very much a stranger to the World but knows how Atheism and Infidelity have advanced in our days, and how openly they now dare to show themselves in Asserting and Disputing their vile Cause. Particularly the distinction of the Soul from the Body, the being of Spirits, and a Future Life are Assertions extremely despised and opposed by the Men of this sort, and if we lose those Articles, all Religion comes to nothing. They are clearly and fully Asserted in the Sacred Oracles, but those Wits have laid aside these Divine Writings. They are proved by the best Philosophy and highest Reason; but the Unbelievers, divers of them are too shallow to be capable of such proofs, and the more subtle are ready to Scepticize away those grounds.

But there is one Head of Arguments that troubles them much, and that is, the Topic of Witches and Apparitions. If such there are, it is a sensible proof of Spirits and another Life, an Argument of more direct force than any Speculations, or Abstract reasonings, and such an one as meets with all the sorts of Infidels. On which account they labour with all their might to persuade themselves and others, that witches and Apparitions are but Melancholic Dreams, or crafty Impostures; and here it is generally, that they begin with the young men, whose understanding they design to Debauch.

They expose and deride all Relations of Spirits and Witchcraft, and furnish them with some little Arguments, or rather Colours against their Existence. And youth is very ready to entertain such Opinions as will help them to fancy that they are wiser than the generality of Men. And when they have once swallowed this Opinion, and are sure there are no Witches, nor Apparitions, they are prepared for the denial of Spirits, a Life to come, and all the other Principles of Religion. So that I think it will be a considerable and very seasonable service to it, fully to debate and settle this matter, which I shall endeavour in the following sheets, and I hope so, as not to impose upon myself or others, by empty

Rhetorications, fabulous Relations, or Sophistical Reasonings, but treat on the Question with that freedom and plainness, that becomes one that is neither fond, fanciful nor credulous.

II: The true stating of the Question by defining what Witch and Witchcraft is.

The Question is whether there are Witches or not. Mr. Webster accuseth the Writers on the Subject of defect, in not laying down a perfect description of a Witch or Witchcraft, or explaining what they mean.[1] What his perfect description is, I do not know; but I think I have described a Witch or Witchcraft in my Considerations, sufficiently to be understood, and the Conception which I, and I think, most Men have is, That a Witch is one, who can do or seems to do strange things, beyond the Power of Art and ordinary Nature, by virtue of a Confederacy with Evil Spirits. Strange Things, not Miracles; these are the extraordinary Effects of Divine Power, known and distinguished by their circumstances, as I shall show in due place. The strange things are really performed, and are not all Impostures and Delusions. The Witch occasions, but is not the Principal Efficient; she seems to do it, but the Spirit performs the wonder, sometimes immediately as in Transportations and Possessions, sometimes by applying other Natural Causes, as in raising Storms, and inflicting Diseases, sometimes using the Witch as an Instrument, and either by the Eyes or Touch conveying Malign Influences: And these things are done by virtue of a Covenant, or Compact betwixt the Witch and an Evil Spirit. A Spirit, viz. an Intelligent creature of the Invisible World, whether one of the Evil Angels called Devils, or an inferiour Demon or Spirit, or a wicked Soul departed; but one that is able and ready for mischief, and whether altogether Incorporeal or not, appertains not to this Question.

III. That Neither the Notation of the Name that signifies indifferently, nor the false Additions of others to the Notion of a Witch can any way dissettle the Author's definition.

This I take to be a plain Description of what we mean by a Witch and Witchcraft: What Mr. Webster and other Advocates for Witches, talk concerning the words whereby these are expressed, that they are improper and Metaphorical, signifying this, and signifying that, is altogether idle and impertinent. The word *Witch* signifies originally a Wise Man, or rather a Wise Woman. The same doth *Saga* in the Latin, and plainly so doth Wizard in English signify a Wise Man, and they are vulgarly called cunning Men or Women. An Art, Knowledge, Cunning

---

1. Glanvill refers here disparagingly to the skeptic John Webster, an influential representative of the current of skepticism discussed in the next chapter of this book. See Thomas Harmon Jobe, "The Devil in Restoration Science: The Glanvill-Webster Debate," *Isis* 72 (1981): 343–56.

they have that is extraordinary; but it is far from true Wisdom, and the word is degenerated into an il sense, as *Magia* is.

So when they are called, and we need to look no further, it is enough, that by the Word, we mean the thing and person I have described, which is common meaning; and Mr. Webster and the rest prevaricate when they make it signify an ordinary Cheat, a Cozener, a Poisoner, Seducer, and I know not what. Words signify as they are used, and in common use, Witch and Witchcraft, do indeed imply these, but they imply more, viz. Deluding, Cheating and Hurting by the Power of an Evil Spirit in Covenant with a wicked Man or Woman: This is our Notion of a Witch.

Mr. Webster I know will not have it to be a perfect Description. He adds to the Notion of the Witch he opposeth, carnal Copulation with the Devil, and the real Transformation into an Hare, Cat, Dog, Wolf; the same doth Mr. Wagstaff.[2] Which is, as if a Man should define an Angel to be a Creature in the shape of a Boy with Wings, and then prove there is no such Being. Of all Men I would not have Mr. Webster to make my Definitions for me; we ourselves are to have the leave to tell what it is that we affirm and defend. And I have described the Witch and Witchcraft, that sober Men believe and assert. Thus briefly for Defining.

IV: What things the Author concedes in this Controversy about Witches and Witchcraft.
I shall let the Patrons of Witches know what I allow and grant to them;

First, I grant, That there are some Witty and Ingenious Men of the opposite Belief to me in the Question. Yea, it is accounted a piece of Wit to laugh at the belief of Witches as silly Credulity. And some men value themselves upon, and pride them in their supposed Sagacity of seeing the Cheat that imposeth on so great a part of Believing Mankind. And the Stories of Witches and Apparitions afford a great deal of Subject for Wit, which it is pity that a witty Man should lose.

Secondly, I own that some of those who deny Witches have no design against, nor a disinclination to Religion, but believe Spirits, and a Life to come, as other sober Christians do, and so are neither Atheists, Sadducees and Hobbists.

Thirdly, I allow that the great Body of Mankind is very credulous, and in this matter so, that they do believe vain impossible things in relation to it. That carnal Copulation with the Devil, and the real Transmutation of Men and Women into other Creatures are such. That people are apt to impute the extraordinaries of Art, of Nature to Witchcraft, and that their Credulity is often abused by subtle and designed Knaves through these. That there are Ten thousand silly lying Stories of Witchcraft and Apparitions among the vulgar. That infinite such have been occasioned by Cheats and Popish Superstitions, and many invented and contrived by the Knavery of Popish Priests.

---

2. Wagstaffe, like Webster, wrote against contemporary witchcraft beliefs.

Fourthly, I grant that Melancholy and Imagination have very great force, and can beget strange persuasions. And that many Stories of Witchcraft and Apparitions have been but Melancholy fancies.

Fifthly, I know and yield, that there are many strange natural Diseases that have odd Symptoms, and produce wonderful and astonishing effects beyond the usual course of Nature, and that such are sometimes falsely ascribed to Witchcraft.

Sixthly, I own, the Popish Inquisitors, and other Witch-finders have done much wrong, that they have destroyed innocent persons for Witches, and that watching and Torture have extorted extraordinary Confessions from some that were not guilty.

Seventhly and Lastly, I grant the Transactions of Spirits with Witches, which we affirm to be true and certain, are many of them very strange and uncouth, and that we can scarce give any account of the Reasons of them, or well reconcile many of those passages to the commonly received Notion of Spirits, and the State of the next World.

If these Concessions will do mine Adversaries in this Question any good, they have them freely. And by them I have already spoiled all Mr. Webster's and Mr. Wagstaff's and the other Witch-Advocates' Books, which prove little else than what I have here granted. And having been so free in Concessions, I may expect that something should be granted me from the other party. . . .

V: *The Postulata which the Author demands of his Adversaries as his just right.*

The demands that I make are: That whether Witches are or are not, is a question of Fact. For it is in effect, whether any Men or Women have been, or are in Covenant with Evil Spirits, and whether they by the Spirits' help, or the Spirits on their account perform such or such things.

Secondly, That matter of Fact can only be proved by immediate Sense, or the Testimony of others Divine or Humane. To endeavour to demonstrate Fact by abstract reasoning and speculation, is, as if a Man should prove that Julius Caesar founded the Empire of Rome by Algebra or Metaphysics. So that what Mr. Webster saith, That the true and proper mediums to prove the actions of Witches by, are Scripture and sound Reason and not the improper way of Testimony . . . is very Nonsense.

Thirdly, That the History of the Scripture is not all Allegory, but generally hath a plain literal and obvious meaning.

Fourthly, That some Humane Testimonies are credible and certain, viz. That they be so circumstantiated as to leave no reason of doubt. For our senses sometimes report truth, and all Mankind are Liars, Cheats and Knaves, at least they are not all Liars, when they have no Interest to be so.

Fifthly, That which is sufficiently and undeniably proved, ought not to be denied, because we know not how it can be, that is, because there are difficulties in the conceiving of it. Otherwise Sense and Knowledge is gone as well as Faith. For the Modus of most things is unknown, and the most obvious in Nature have inexplicable difficulties in the Speculation of them, as I have shown in my *Scepsis Scientifica*.

Sixthly and lastly, we are much in the dark, as to the Nature and Kinds of Spirits, and the particular condition of the other World. The Angels', Devils', and Souls' happiness and misery we know, but what kinds are under these generals, and what actions, circumstances and ways of Life under those States we little understand. These are my Postulata or demands, which I suppose will be thought reasonable, and such as need no more proof.

The Collection of Relations. Relation VIII: The Narrative of Mr. Pool, a Servant and Officer in the Court to Judge Archer in his Circuit, concer ing the Trial of Julian Cox for Witchcraft—who being himself then present, an Officer in the Court, noted as follows, viz.

Julian Cox, aged about 70 Years, was Indicted at Taunton in Somersetshire, about Summer Assizes, 1663, before Judge Archer, then Judge of Assize there, for Witchcraft, which she practiced upon a young Maid, whereby her Body languished, and was impaired of Health, by reason of strange Fits upon account of the said Witchcraft.

The Evidence against her was divided into two Branches: First, to prove her a Witch in general: Secondly, to prove her Guilty of the Witchcraft contained in the Indictment.

For the proof of the first Particular: The first Witness was a Huntsman, who Swore that he went out with a Pack of Hounds to Hunt a Hare, and not far from Julian Cox her House, he at last started a Hare. The Dogs hunted her very close, and the third Ring hunted her in view, till at last the Huntsman perceiving the Hare almost spent, and making toward a great Bush, he ran on the other side of the Bush to take her up, and preserve her from the Dogs; but as soon as he laid Hands on her, it proved to be Julian Cox, who had her head groveling on the ground, and her Globes (as he expressed it) upward: He knowing her, was so affrighted that his Hair on his Head stood on end; and yet spake to her, and asked her what brought her there; but she was so far out of Breath, that she could not make him any Answer: His Dogs also came up with full Cry to recover the Game, and smelled at her, and so left off Hunting any farther. And the Hunts-man with his Dogs went home presently, sadly affrighted.

Secondly, Another Witness Swore, That as he passed by Cox her Door, she was taking a Pipe of Tobacco upon the Threshold of her Door, and invited him to come in and take a Pipe, which he did, and as he was Smoking, Julia said to him, Neighbour, look what a pretty thing there is: He looked down and there was a monstrous great Toad betwixt his Legs, staring him in the Face: He endeavoured to kill it by spurning it, but could not hit it: Whereupon Julian bade him forbear, and it would do him no hurt; but he threw down his Pipe and went home (which was about two Miles off of Julian Cox her House) and told his Family what had happened, and that he believed it was one of Julian Cox her Devils.

After, he was taking a Pipe of Tobacco at home, and the same Toad appeared betwixt his Legs: He took the Toad out to kill it, and to his thinking, cut it in several pieces, but returning to his Pipe, the Toad still appeared: He endeavoured to burn it, but could not: At length he took a Switch and beat it; the Toad ran several times about the Room to avoid him, he still pursuing it with Correction: At length the Toad cried, and vanished, and he was never after troubled with it.

Thirdly, Another Swore, That Julian passed by his Yard while his Beasts were in Milking, and stooping down, scored upon the ground for some small time; during which time, his Cattle ran Mad, and some ran their Heads against the Trees, and most of them died speedily: Whereupon concluding they were Bewitched, he was after advised to this Experiment, to find out the Witch, viz. to cut off the Ears of the Bewitched Beasts and burn them, and that the Witch should be in misery, and could not rest till they were plucked out; which he tried, and while they were burning, Julian Cox came into the House, raging and scolding, that they had abused her without cause, but she went presently to the Fire, and took out the Ears that were burning, and then she was quiet.

Fourthly, Another Witness Swore, That she had seen Julian Cox fly into her own Chamber-window in her full proportion, and that she very well knew her, and was sure that it was she.

Fifthly, Another Evidence, was the Confession of Julian Cox herself, upon her Examination before a Justice of Peace, which was to this purpose: That she had been often tempted by the Devil to be a Witch, but never consented. That one Evening she walked out about a Mile from her own House, and there came riding towards her 3 Persons upon 3 Broom-staves, born up about a Yard and a half from the ground; 2 of them she formerly knew, which was a Witch and a Wizard that were Hanged for Witchcraft several Years before. The third Person she knew not; he came in the Shape of a black Man, and tempted her to give him her Soul, or to that effect, and to express it by pricking her Finger, and giving her Name in her Blood in token of it, and told her, that she had Revenge against several Persons that had wronged her, but could not bring her purpose to pass without his help, and that upon the Terms aforesaid he would assist her to be revenged against them; but she said, she did not consent to it. This was the sum of the general Evidence to prove her a Witch.

But now for the second Particular, to prove her guilty of the Witchcraft upon the Maid, whereof she was Indicted, this Evidence was offered.

It was proved that Julian Cox came for an Alms to the House where this Maid was a Servant, and that the Maid told her, she should have none, and gave her a cross Answer that displeased Julian; whereupon Julian was angry, and told the Maid she should repent it before a Night, and so she did; for before Night she was taken with a Convulsion Fit, and that after that left her, she saw Julian Cox following her, and cried out to People in the House to save her from Julian.

But none saw Julian but the Maid, and all did impute it to her Imagination only, And in the Night she cried out of Julian Cox, and the black Man, that they came upon her Bed and tempted her to Drink something they offered her, but she cried out, She defied the Devil's Drenches. This also they imputed to her Imagination, and bade her be quiet, because they in the same Chamber, with her, did not see or hear any thing, and they thought it had been her Conceit only.

The Maid the next Night expecting the same Conflict she had the Night before, brought up with her a Knife, and laid it at her Bed's head. About the same time of the Night as before, Julian and the black Man came again upon the Maid's Bed, and tempted her to Drink that which they brought, but she refused, crying in the audience of the rest of the Family, that she defied the Devil's Drenches, and took the Knife and stabbed Julian, and as she said, she wounded her in the Leg, and was importunate with the Witness to ride to Julian Cox's House presently to see if it were not so. The Witness went and took the Knife with him. Julian Cox would not let him in, but they forced the Door open, and found a fresh Wound in Julian's Leg, as the Maid had said, which did suit with the Knife, and Julian had been just Dressing it when the Witness came. There was Blood also found upon the Maid's Bed.

The Next Morning the Maid continued her Out-cries, that Julian Cox appeared to her in the House-wall, and offered her great Pins which she was forced to swallow: And all the Day the Maid was observed to convey her Hand to the House-wall, and from the wall to her Mouth, and she seemed by the motion of her Mouth, as if she did Eat something; but none saw anything but the Maid, and therefore thought still it might be her Fancy, and did not much mind it. But towards Night, the Maid began to be very ill, and complained, that the Pins that Julian forced her to Eat out of the Wall, did torment her in all parts of her Body that she could not endure it, and made lamentable Out-cries for pain: Whereupon several Persons being present, the Maid was undressed, and in several parts of the Maid's Body several great swellings appeared, and out of the heads of the swellings, several great Pins' points appeared; which the Witness took out, and upon the Trial there were about 30 great Pins produced in Court, (which I myself handled) all which were Sworn by several Witnesses, that they were taken out of the Maid's Body, in manner as is aforesaid.

Judge Archer, who Tried the Prisoner, told the Jury, That he had heard that a Witch could not repeat that Petition in the Lord's-Prayer, viz. (And lead us not into Temptation) and having this occasion, he would try the Experiment, and told the Jury, that whether she could or not, they were not in the least measure to guide their Verdict according to it, because it was not Legal Evidence, but that they must be guided in their Verdict by the former Evidences given in upon Oath only.

The Prisoner was called for up to the next Bar to the Court, and demanded if she could say the Lord's Prayer? She said she could, and went over the Prayer readily, till she came to that Petition; then she said, "And lead us into Temptation," or "And lead us not into no Temptation," though she was directed to say it after one that repeated it to her directly; but she could not repeat it otherwise than is expressed already, though tried to do it near half a score times in open Court. After all which the Jury found her Guilty, and Judgement having been given within 3 or 4 days, she was Executed without any Confession of the Fact.

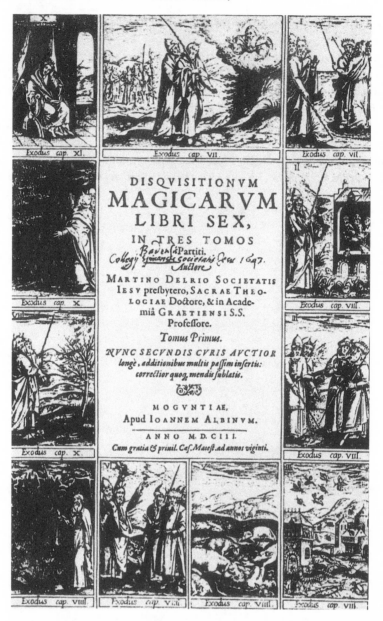

Figure 28. The title page of Martín Del Rio's 1603 *Disquisitiones magicarum* (*Disquisitions on Magic*) illustrates various biblical condemnations of sorcery and witchcraft as both Catholics like Del Rio and Protestants understood them. University of Pennsylvania.

Figure 29. Adrian Huberti's late sixteenth-century depiction of the preparation for the sabbat is one of many variations on Hans Baldung Grien's original design. University of Pennsylvania.

Figure 30. Francesco Maria Guazzo's 1610 *Compendium Maleficarum* was the most extensively illustrated of all tracts on demonology. Guazzo was insistent that men, women, and children might all be witches, showing them here coming before the demon to offer homage. University of Pennsylvania.

Figure 31. Jaspar Isaac's *Abomination des sorciers*, a composite picture from the first half of the seventeenth century, illustrates most of the commonplace features of popular and learned belief in witchcraft. Bibliothèque Nationale, Paris.

Figure 32. Frans Francken the Younger's *Sabbat de sorcières* represents the wider circulation of witches' sabbat pictures in the later sixteenth century. Kunsthistorisches Museum, Vienna.

Figure 33. David Teniers the Younger's 1633 *Scène de sabbat* depicts the preparation and departure for the sabbat in the form of the domestic interior, a familiar setting in seventeenth-century Dutch art. Musée de la Chartreuse, Douai.

Figure 34. The seventeenth-century painter Saint-Aubert's *La Première fois* depicts in considerable erotic detail the initiation of a young witch. Musée Municipal, Cambrai.

Figure 35. David Teniers the Younger, *Le Départ pour le sabbat*. Teniers repeatedly painted the departure for the sabbat in the context of a domestic interior, as in Figure 33. Bibliothèque Nationale, Paris.

Figure 36. Michael Herr, *Walpurgisnacht*, ca. 1650. This had become by then the standard image in German-speaking lands of the sabbat, usually thought to be celebrated on St. Walburga's night on a mountain called the Brocken. Germanisches Nationalmuseum, Nuremberg.

Mein Leſer! wilſt du noch den Zauber=Berg
verneinen?
Es ſtellt ja dieſes Blat dir ſolchë deutlich für/
Du ſiehſt der Hexen = Chor auff ſelbigen er=
ſcheinen.
Wiewohl ich irre mich ; Er ſteht nur auff
Pappier.

Figure 37. Frontispiece to Christian Thomasius's tract *On the Crime of Witchcraft*. The seated Thomasius writes a set of verses to the reader (see Text 69). University of Pennsylvania.

Figure 38. William Hogarth's engraving *Credulity, Superstition, and Fanaticism: A Medley* contains pictorial references to more than a dozen recent instances in England of belief in witchcraft and possession, as well as the puppet-figure of a witch riding a broom manipulated by the preacher-puppeteer.

Figure 39. In *Weird Sisters*, 1762, James Gillray, one of the greatest political cartoonists, depicts three of George III's ministers—Dundas, Pitt, and Thurlow—as the three witches in *Macbeth*, looking to the moon (the crescent and shadow, respectively profiles of Queen Charlotte and the slumbering George III). From *Fashionable Contrasts: Caricatures by James Gillray*, ed. Draper Hill (London: Phaidon Press, 1966), Plate 2.

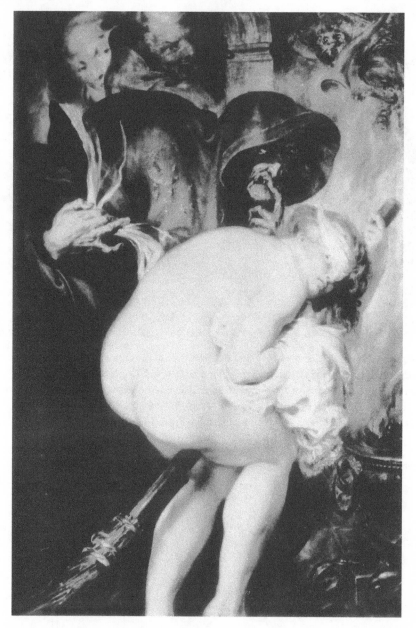

Figure 40. The early nineteenth-century Austrian painter Anton Wierz depicted the familiar scene of the initiation of a young witch, but in this case the subject is purely erotic.

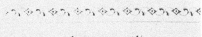

the SAbbath

the SAbbath

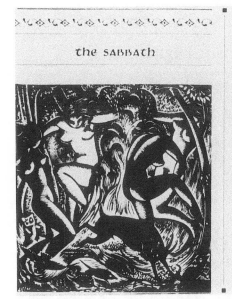

THE wild din of the Sabbath fills my brain.
White witches dance to tunes that wheel and whirl,
An eddying sea with many a foam-like curl,
And leap across the fires and back again.
Their flesh is flecked with many a splash and stain
Of fire and blood; their madding locks unfurl;
Stark hand in hand, stark naked girl and girl,
They scream and caper to the ghastly strain.
A tempest of shrill fifes and kettle-drums
Rings through the woods with streams of ruddy fire,
Fire flickering like a serpent's forked prong;
And ever anon, as the wild band thrums and strums
The deepling dance, the devilish desire
Rises to frenzy, and becomes a song.

Figure 41. Woodcut by John Buckland-Wright. This illustration from John Evelyn Barlas (Evelyn Douglas), *Yew Leaf and Lotus Petal* (1935) suggests the appropriation of some of the pictorial images in this book into modern art. University of Pennsylvania.

X

Belief, Skepticism, Doubt, and Disbelief in the Sixteenth, Seventeenth, and Eighteenth Centuries

By THE END OF THE SEVENTEENTH CENTURY, such defenders of demonological and witchcraft belief as Glanvill and More were engaged in a desperate struggle to halt the spread of skepticism and disbelief among the educated classes in Europe. The last decades of that century, however, witnessed the triumph of those who sought to end the active persecution of alleged witches and to alter the intellectual and theological systems whereby such persecution was deemed necessary and purposeful. Although occasional witch scares and executions continued in the more remote areas of Europe, by the early eighteenth century witchcraft had ceased to be an intellectual and legal concern of educated people, except insofar as legal reformers sought to remove the laws dealing with the subject from the books. By the end of the century, witchcraft had become a topic of historical rather than contemporary interest.

The decline of active witchcraft fear and belief can be studied with interest by a multitude of disciplines and from a multitude of explanatory perspectives, but it is, among other things, an intellectual event, and one reflected in the history of thought and philosophy. Europe's witches depended for their putative existence on specific systems of thought and modes of interpreting the natural and supernatural worlds; when people questioned or lost confidence in those systems or modes, or when new structures of inquiry and belief intervened, the credibility or assumed usefulness of the very existence of witches, and hence the witch-hunt, could no longer be justified. This is what had occurred by the eighteenth century.

The intellectual components of this decline are many and complex, but they can be grouped under several broad headings: the growth of antischolastic thought and the identification of the scholastic basis of contemporary witchcraft belief; a growing aversion to the "credulity" and "superstition" of the common people, and the desire of educated people to distinguish themselves from these; the growth of philosophical systems and attitudes that provided natural accounts of phenomena that had formerly demanded supernaturalist and demonological explanations. To these should be added an emerging critical spirit among thinking people, whereby the antiquity and pervasiveness of beliefs and practices no longer added a presumption in their favor, but rather constituted a cause for suspicion and doubt.

Examples of selective and systematic skepticism were manifest already in the sixteenth century. Reginald Scot believed in the reality of witchcraft, but saw as illusory many of the fears and beliefs associated with it, seeking to discredit, among other things, the concept of a witches' sabbath (Text 60). The criteria by which people disabused themselves of any particular aspect of witchcraft belief, however, were made available to investigators of other areas of the system as well. Montaigne, whose systematic skepticism was widely influential, demonstrated how easily men might deceive themselves when dealing with the unusual, and asked whether, in the face of the doubts he had raised, men dare consider themselves certain enough to kill a fellow man in the name of such tenuous beliefs (Text 61). The recantations of men who had themselves been involved in witch-hunts—from members of the Spanish Inquisition, Jesuit confessors of condemned witches, and the repentant Salem Village jurors in 1693—recantations and self-scrutinies arising from particular doubts concerning the signs and evidences of witchcraft, added to this growing legal and intellectual caution (Texts 63, 65, 67).

In opposition to scholastic modes of thought, the seventeenth century witnessed the rise of philosophies in which there was no place for spiritual or supernatural causes of the events of the natural world. Arising from Descartes's categorical separation of the realms of matter and spirit, from experimental and mathematical science, and from contrary strains of deductive rationalism and empirical naturalism, mechanistic modes of explanation increasingly replaced accounts of spirit acting upon matter as satisfactory accounts of events in men's minds. Hobbes's thoroughgoing materialism left no room for spirits, evil or good, and he engaged in an often ironic metaphorical reinterpretation of his culture's beliefs in such beings (Text 64). Spinoza's pantheistic monism and naturalist mechanism invalidated such beliefs as well, and he attributed all demonology to philosophical naïveté and to historically conditioned sectarian corruptions of our understanding of God and of the harmonious universe which manifests him (Text 62).

Mechanists, materialists, and pantheists all sought to change the intellectual paradigm upon which witchcraft belief depended. Few people, however, embraced the new systems of thought consistently and rigorously. Rather, most educated men lived within two worlds by the late seventeenth century, accepting much of traditional belief but adding to it a new awareness of the appeal of natural and mechanistic explanations where such were possible. The great skeptic and fideist Pierre Bayle never denied the theoretical bases of demonology and witchcraft; rather, he questioned the application of those beliefs in the particular, appealing to the critical intellect to avoid the superstitions of the vulgar and the uneducated, and he demonstrated how the same phenomena attributed to witchcraft could be accounted for by the natural operations of the imagination and the emotions of mankind (Text 68). Many increasingly felt that witchcraft was born of fear of and confusion about the created universe. Balthazar Bekker, a theologian and one of the most influential opponents of witchcraft belief, attacked the entire demonological system as a lack of confident faith in the goodness and wisdom of the God he saw as Creator of the universe, and he offered naturalistic explanations of the role of the imagination and the credulity of men in the formation and sustenance of witchcraft and demonology (Text 66). From this combination of decreasing anxiety about the structure of the inhabited world and increasing assurance of people's ability to understand that world in earthly terms, witchcraft, as a Western belief, was ultimately to founder.

60
Reginald Scot, *Discoverie of Witchcraft* (1584)

The last decades of the sixteenth century in England witnessed an increase in witchcraft trials, above all at the Assizes in Essex (Text 46). Confessions and testimony revealed a deep-seated fear of the awesome powers of the witch to perform unnatural harmful actions and a pervasive credulity among both the learned and the unlearned. In the face of this, a few voices raised themselves in skeptical opposition to increasingly widespread notions of the witch and her powers and to the general sense that the testimony of the trials was manifestly true. Among these skeptical voices were Johann Weyer (Text 44) and Reginald Scot (1538–99), whose *Discoverie of Witchcraft* (1584) called upon thinking men, especially churchmen, to reconsider their views of the witch and to reassess the nature of the judicial evidence.

Scot's is the second book on witchcraft originally written in English to have been printed in England. A country gentleman and, briefly, a member of Parliament, Scot was best known for his treatise *The Hop Garden*, of 1574, which urged the development of hop cultivation in his home area of Kent. Perhaps a group of local trials for witchcraft struck his interest—in any case, Scot was seriously read by later demonologists, both pro and con. Scot's treatise inspired an outraged King James VI of Scotland to write his own demonological treatise, the *Daemonologie*, in 1597, and especially in Anglophone circles Scot became a common target for defenders of both the concept of witchcraft and the persecution of witches.

SOURCE: Reginald Scot, *The Discoverie of Witchcraft* (1584), ed. Hugh Ross Williamson (Carbondale, Ill., 1964), bk. 1, chaps. 2, 5, 6, 9; bk. 2, chaps. 1, 9, 18–20; bk. 16, chaps. 1–3.

FURTHER READING: Anglo, "Reginald Scot's *Discoverie of Witch-craft*: Scepticism and Sadduceeism," in Anglo, *The Damned Art*: 106–39; Keith Thomas, *Religion and the Decline of Magic* (New York, 1971); James Sharpe, *Instruments of Darkness: Witchcraft in Early Modern England* (Philadelphia, 1997), 50–57.

What testimonies and witnesses are allowed to give evidence against reputed witches, by the report & allowance of the inquisitors themselves, and such as are speciall writers heerein.

Excommunicat persons, partakers of the falt, infants, wicked servants, and runnawaies are to be admitted to beare witnesse against their dames in this mater of witchcraft: because (saith Bodin the champion of witchmoongers) none that be honest are able to detect them. Heretikes also and witches shall be received to accuse, but not to excuse a witch. And finallie, the testimonie of all infamous persons in this case is good and allowed. Yea, one lewd person (saith Bodin) may be received to accuse and condemne a thousand suspected witches. And although by lawe, a capitall enemie may be challenged; yet James Sprenger, and Henrie Institor, (from whom Bodin, and all the writers that ever I have read, doo receive their light, authorities and arguments) saie enimie would have killed hir, and that hee hath both assaulted & wounded hir; otherwise she pleadeth all in vaine. If the judge aske hir, whether she have anie capitall en-imies; and she rehearse other, and forget hir accuser; or else answer that he was hir capital enimie, but now she hopeth he is not so: such a one is nevertheless admitted for a witnes. And though by lawe, single witnesses are not admittable; yet if one depose she hath bewitched hir cow; another, hir sow; and the third, hir butter: these saith (saith M[alleus]. Mal[eficarum]. and Bodin) are no single wit-nesses; because they agree that she is a witch.

The fifteene crimes laid to the charge of witches, by witchmongers, specialle by Bodin, in Demonomania [Text 45].

They denie God, and all religion.

Answere. Then let them die therefore, or at the least be used like infidels, or apostataes.

They cursse, blaspheme, and provoke God with all despite.

Answere. Then let them have the law expressed in Levit. 24. and Deut. 13 & 17.

They give their faith to the divell, and they worship and offer sacrifice unto him.

Ans. Let such also be judged by the same lawe.

They doo solemnelie vow and promise all their progenie unto the divell.

Ans. This promise proceedeth from an unsound mind, and is not to be regarded; because they cannot performe it, neither will it be prooved true. Howbeit, if it be done by anie that is sound of mind, let the cursse of Jeremie, 32.36. light upon them, to wit, the sword, famine and pestilence.

They sacrifice their owne children to the divell before baptisme, holding them up in the aire unto him, and then thrust a needle into their braines.

Ans. If this be true, I maintaine them not herein: but there is a lawe to judge them by. Howbeit, it is so contrarie to sense and nature, that it were follie to beleeve it; either upon Bodins bare word, or else upon his presumptions; speciallie when so small commoditie and so great danger and inconvenience insueth to the witches thereby.

They burne their children when they have sacrificed them.

Ans. Then let them have such punishment, as they that offered their children unto Moloch: Levit. 20. But these be meere devises of witchmoongers and inquisitors, that with extreame tortures have wroong such confessions from them; or else with false reports have beelied them; or by flatterie & faire words and promises have woon it at their hands, at the length.

They sweare to the divell to bring as manie into that societie as they can.

Ans. This is false, and so prooved elsewhere.

They sweare by the name of the divell.

Ans. I never heard anie such oth, neither have we warrant to kill them that so doo sweare; though indeed it be verie lewd and impious.

They use incestuous adulterie with spirits.

Ans. This is a stale ridiculous lie, as is prooved apparentlie hereafter.

They boile infants (after they have murthered them unbaptised) untill their flesh be made potable.

Ans. This is untrue, incredible, and impossible.

They eate the flesh and drinke the bloud of men and children openlie.

Ans. Then are they kin to the Anthropophagi and Canibals. But I beleeve never an honest man in England nor in France, will affirme that he hath seene any of these persons, that are said to be witches, do so; if they shuld, I beleeve it would poison them.

They kill men with poison.

Ans. Let them be hanged for their labour.

They kill mens cattell.

Ans. Then let an action of trespasse be brought against them for so dooing.

They bewitch mens corne, and bring hunger and barrennes into the countrie; they ride and flie in the aire, bring stormes, make tempests, &c.

Ans. Then will I worship them as gods; for those be not the works of man nor yet of witch: as I have elsewhere prooved at large.

They use venerie with a divell called Iucubus, even when they lie in bed with their husbands, and have children by them, which become the best witches.

Ans. This is the last lie, verie ridiculous, and confuted by me elsewhere.

Of foure capitall crimes objected against witches, all fullie answered and confuted as frivolous.

First therefore they laie to their charge idolatrie. But alas without all reason: for such are properlie knowne to us to be idolaters, as doo externall worship idols or strange gods. The furthest point that idolatrie can be stretched unto, is, that they, which are culpable therein, are such as hope for and seeke salvation at the hands of idols, or of anie other than God; or fixe their whole mind and love upon anie creature, so as the power of God be neglected and contemned thereby. But witches neither seeke nor beleeve to have salvation at the hands of divels, but by them they are onlie deceived; the instruments of their phantasie being corrupted, and so infatuated, that they suppose, confesse, and saie they can doo that, which is as farre beyond their power and nature to doo, as to kill a man at Yorke before noone, when they have beene scene at London in that morning, &c. But if these latter idolaters, whose idolatrie is spirituall, and committed onelie in mind, should be punished by death; then should everie covetous man, or other, that setteth his affection anie waee too much upon an earthlie creature, be executed, and yet perchance the witch might escape scotfree.

Secondlie, apostasie is laid to their charge, whereby it is inferred, that they are worthie to die. But apostasie is, where anie of sound judgement forsake the gospell, learned and well knowne unto them; and doo not onelie imbrace impietie and infidelitie; but oppugne and resist the truth erstwhile by them professed. But alas these poore women go not about to defend anie impietie, but after good admonition repent.

Thirdlie, they would have them executed for seducing the people. But God knoweth they have small store of Rhetorike or art to seduce; except to tell a tale of Robin good-fellow be to deceive and seduce. Neither may their age or sex admit that opinion or accusation to be just: for they themselves are poore seduced soules. I for my part (as elsewhere I have said) have prooved this point to be false in most apparent sort.

Fourthlie, as touching the accusation, which all the writers use herein against them for their carnall copulation with Incubus: the follie of mens credulitie is as much to be woondered at and derided, as the others vaine and impossible confessions. For the divell is a spirit, and hath neither flesh nor bones, which were to be used in the performance of this action. And since he also lacketh all instruments, substance, and seed ingendred of bloud; it were folie to staie over-long in the confutation of that, which is not the nature of things. And yet must I saie somewhat heerein, bicause the opinion hereof is so stronglie and universallie received, and the fables hereupon so innumerable; whereby M[alleus] Mal[eficarum], Bodin, Hemingiuss, Hyperius, Danaeus, Erastus, and others that take upon them to write heerein, are so abused, or rather seeke to abuse others; as I woonder at their fond credulitie in this behalfe. For they affirme undoubtedlie, that the divell plaieth Succubus to the man, and carrieth from him the seed of generation, which he delivereth as Incubus to the woman, who manie times that waie is gotten with child; which will verie naturallie (they saie) become a witch, and sucha one they affirme Merline was.

A conclusion, in manner of an epilog, repeating manie of the former
absurdities of witchmongers, conceipts, confutations thereof, and of the
authoritie of James Sprenger and Henrie Institor inquisitors and
compilers of M[alleus] Mal[eficarum].

Hitherto you have had delivered unto you, that which I have conceived and gathered of this matter. In the substance and principall parts wherof I can see no difference among the writers heereupon; of what countries, condition, estate, or religion so ever they be; but I find almost all of them to agree in unconstancie, fables, and impossibilities; scratching out of *M. Mal.* the substance of all their arguments: so as their authors being disapproved, they must coine new stuffe, or go to their grandams maids to learne more old wives tales, whereof this art of witchcraft is contrived. But you must know that James Sprenger, and Henrie Institor, whom I have had occasion to alledge manie times, were copartners in the composition of that profound & learned booke called *Malleus Maleficarum*, & were the greatest doctors of that art: out of whom I have gathered matter and absurditie enough, to confound the opinions conceived of witchcraft; although they were allowed inquisitors and assigned by the pope, with the authoritie and commendation of all the doctors of the universitie of Collen, &c: to call before them, to imprison, to condemne, and to execute witches; and finallie to seaze and confiscate their goods.

These two doctors, to mainteine their credit, and to cover their injuries, have published those same monsterous lies, which have abused all Christendome, being spread abroad with such authoritie, as it will be hard to suppresse the credit of their writings, be they never so ridiculous and false. Which although they mainteine and stirre up with their owne praises; yet men are so bewitched, as to give credit unto them. For proofe whereof I remember they write in one place of their said booke, that by reason of their severe proceedings against witches, they suffered intollerable assaults, speciallie in the night, many times finding needdels sticking in their biggens, which were thither conveied by witches charmes: and through their innocencie and holiness (they saie) they were never miraculouslie preserved from hurt. Howbeit they affirmie that they will not tell all that might make to the manifestation of their holines: for then should their owne praise stinke in their owne mouthes. And yet God knoweth their whole booke conteineth nothing but stinking lies and poperie. Which groundworke and foundation how weake and wavering it is, how unlike to continue, and how slenderlie laid, a child may soone discerne and perceive.

By what meanes the common people have beene made beleeve in the miraculous works of witches, a definition of witchcraft, and a description thereof.

The common people have beene so assotted and bewitched, with whatsoever poets have feigned of witchcraft, either in earnest, in jest, or else in derision; and with whatsoever lowd liers and couseners for their pleasures herein have invented, and with whatsoever tales they have heard from old doting women, or from their mothers maids, and with whatsoever the grandfoole their ghostlie father, or anie other morrow masse preest had informed them; and finallie with whatsoever they have swallowed up through tract of time, or through their owne timerous nature or ignorant conceipt, concerning these matters of hagges and witches: as they have so settled their opinion and credit thereupon, that they thinke it heresie to doubt in anie part of the matter; speciallie bicause they find this word witchcraft expressed in the scriptures; which is as to defend praieng to saincts, because *Sanctus, Sanctus, Sanctus* is written in *Te Deum*.

And now to come to the definition of witchcraft, which hitherto I did deferre and put off purposelie: that you might perceive the true nature thereof, by the circumstances, and therefore the rather to allow of the same, seeing the varietie of other writers. Witchcraft is in truth a cousening art, wherin the name of God is abused, prophaned and blasphemed, and his power attributed to a vile creature. In estimation of the vulgar people, it is a supernaturall worke, contrived betweene a corporall old woman, and a spirituall divell. The manner thereof is so secret, mysticall, and strange, that to this daie there hath never beene any credible witnes thereof. It is incomprehensible to the wise, learned or faithfull; a probable matter to children, fooles, melancholike persons and papists. The trade is thought to be impious. The effect and end thereof to be sometimes evill, as when thereby man or beast, grasse, trees, or corne, &c; is hurt: sometimes good, as whereby sicke folkes are healed, theeves bewraied, and true men come to their goods, &c. The matter and instruments, wherewith it is accomplished, are words, charmes, signes, images, characters, &c; the which words although any other creature doo pronounce, in maner and forme as they doo, leaving out no circumstance requisite or usuall for that action: yet none is said to have the grace or gift to performe the matter, except she be a witch, and so taken either by hir owne consent, or by others imputation.

Reasons to proove that words and characters are but babies, & that
witches cannot doo such things as the multitude supposeth they can,
their greatest woonders prooved trifles, of a yoong gentleman cousened.

That words, characters, images, and such other trinkets, which are thought so necessarie instruments for witchcraft (as without the which no such thing can be accomplished) are but bables, devised by couseners, to abuse the people withall; I trust I have sufficientlie prooved. And the same maie be further and more plainelie perceived by these short and compendious reasons following.

First, in that Turkes and infidels, in their witchcraft, use both other words, and other characters than our witches doo and also such as are most contrarie. In so much as, if ours be bad, in reason theirs should be good. If their witches can doo anie thing, ours can doo nothing. For as our witches are said to renounce Christ, and despise his sacraments: so doo the other forsake Mahomet, and his lawes, which is one large step to christianitie.

It is also to be thought, that all witches are couseners; when mother Bungie, a principall witch, so reputed, tried, and condemned of all men, and continuing in that exercise and estimation manie yeares (having cousened & abused the whole realme, in so much as there came to hir, witchmongers from all the furthest parts of the land, she being in diverse bookes set out with authorities registred and chronicled by the name of the great witch of Rochester, and re-puted among all men for the cheefe ringleader of all other witches) by good proofe is found to be a meere cousener; confessing in hir death bed freelie, without compulsion or inforcement, that hir cunning consisted onlie in delud-ing and deceiving the people: saying that she had (towards the maintenance of hir credit in that cousening trade) some sight in physicke and surgerie, and the assistance of a freend of hirs, called Heron, a professor thereof. And this I know, partlie of mine owne knowledge, and partlie by the testimonie of hir husband, and others of credit, to whome (I saie) in hir death bed, and at sundrie other times she protested these things; and also that she never had indeed anie mate-riall spirit or divell (as the voice went) nor yet knew how to worke anie super-naturall matter, as she in hir life time made men beleeve she had and could doo.

The like may be said of one T. of Canturburie, whose name I will not lit-terallie discover, who wonderfullie abused manie in these parts, making them thinke he could tell where anie thing lost became: with diverse other such practises, whereby his fame was farre beyond the others. And yet on his death bed he confessed, that he knew nothing more than anie other, but by slight and devises, without the assistance of anie divell or spirit, saving the spirit of cou-senage: and this did he (I saie) protest before manie of great honestie, credit, & wisedome, who can witnesse the same, and also gave him good commendations for his godlie and honest end.

Againe, who will mainteine, that common witchcrafts are not cousenages, when the great and famous witchcrafts, which had stolne credit not onlie from all the common people, but from men of great wisdome and authoritie, are discovered to be beggerlie slights of cousening varlots? Which otherwise might and would have remained a perpetuall objection against me. Were there not three images of late yeeres found in a doonghill, to the terror & astonishment of manie thousands? In so much as great matters were thought to have beene pretended to be doone by witchcraft. But if the Lord preserve those persons (whose destruction was doubted to have beene intended thereby) from all other the lewd practises and attempts of their enimies; I feare not, but they shall easilie withstand these and such like devises, although they should indeed be practised against them. But no doubt, if such bables could have brought those matters of mischeefe to passe, by the hands of traitors, witches, or papists; we should long since have beene deprived of the most excellent jewell and comfort that we enjoy in this world. Howbeit, I confesse that the feare, conceipt, and doubt of such mischeefous pretenses may breed inconvenience to them that stand in awe of the same. And I wish, that even for such practises, though they never can or doo take effect, the practisers be punished with all extremities: bicause therein is manifested a traiterous heart to the Queene, and a presumption against God.

But to returne to the discoverie of the aforesaid knaverie and witchcraft. So it was that one old cousener, wanting monie, devised or rather practised (for it is a stale devise) to supplie his want, by promising a yoong Gentleman, whose humor he thought would that waie be well served, that for the summe of fourtie pounds, he would not faile by his cunning in that art of witchcraft, to procure unto him the love of anie three women whome he would name, and of whome he should make choise at his pleasure. The yoong Gentleman being abused with his cunning devises, and too hastilie yeelding to that motion, satisfied this cunning mans demand of monie. Which, bicause he had it not presentlie to disbursse, provided it for him at the hands of a freend of his. Finallie, this cunning man made the three puppets of wax, &c: leaving nothing undone that appertained to the cousenage, untill he had buried them, as you have heard. But I omit to tell what a doo was made herof, and also what reports and lies were bruted; as what white dogs and blacke dogs there were seene in the night season passing through the watch, mawgre all their force and preparation against them, &c. But the yoong Gentleman, who for a litle space remained in hope mixed with joy and love, now through tract of time hath those his felicities powdered with doubt and despaire. For in steed of atchieving his love he would gladlie have obteined his monie. But bicause he could by no meanes get either the one or the other (his monie being in huckster's handling, and his sute in no better forwardnes) he revealed the whole matter, hoping by that meanes to recover his monie; which he neither can yet get againe, nor hath paied it where he borrowed. But till triall was had of his simplicitie or rather follie herein, he received some trouble himselfe hereabouts, though now dismissed.

61

Michel de Montaigne:
"Concerning Cripples" (1588)

In a sixteenth-century France torn apart by religious war and passionate, dogmatic hatreds, the tolerant and worldly Michel de Montaigne (1533–1595), fideistically rational and skeptically devout, called for an admission of ignorance by men and a moderation in their actions toward each other that challenged the right of the fanaticism of the hunt after witches and, indeed, after heretics in general. As his motto, Montaigne took the phrase "Que sais-je?"—"What do I know?" The answer was to be a humbling one for an honest man. Given how little one knew, and how uncertain the foundations of human judgment, how could a man kill another in the name of human knowledge and judgment? In his essay "Concerning Cripples," the implications of such a skeptical attitude for witchcraft persecutions are made clear.

SOURCE: Michel de Montaigne, *The Complete Works of Montaigne: Essays, Travel Journal, Letters* trans. Donald M. Frame (Stanford, Calif., 1958), 784–92.

FURTHER READING: M. A. Screech, *Montaigne and Melancholy: The Wisdom of the "Essays"* (London, 1983), 156–60; Clark, *Thinking With Demons*, 264–80. For the Corras case, see Natalie Zemon Davis, *The Return of Martin Guerre* (Cambridge, Mass., 1983).

I WAS JUST MUSING, as I often do, on how free and vague an instrument human reason is. I see ordinarily that men, when facts are put before them, are more ready to amuse themselves by inquiring into their reasons than by inquiring into their truth. They leave aside the cases and amuse themselves treating the causes. Comical prattlers!

The knowledge of causes belongs only to Him who has the guidance of things, not to us who have only the enduring of them, and who have the perfectly full use of them according to our nature, without penetrating to their origin and essence. Nor is wine pleasanter to the man who knows its primary properties. On the contrary, both the body and the soul disturb and alter the right they have to the enjoyment of the world by mixing into it the pretension to learning. Determining and knowing, like giving, appertains to rule and mastery; to inferiority, subjection, and apprenticeship appertains enjoyment and acceptance. Let us return to this habit of ours.

They pass over the facts, but they assiduously examine their consequences. They ordinarily begin thus: "How does this happen?" What they should say is: "But does it happen?" Our reason is capable of filling out a hundred other words and finding their principles and contexture. It needs neither matter nor basis; let it run on; it builds as well on emptiness as on fullness, and with inanity as with matter: Suited to give solidity to smoke. (Persius.)

I find that in almost every case we ought to say: "That is not so at all." And I would often use that reply, buy I dare not, for they cry out that it is an evasion produced by feeblemindedness and ignorance. And I am ordinarily obliged to play the fool for company's sake and discuss frivolous subjects and stories which I entirely disbelieve. Besides, it is truly a little rude and quarrelsome flatly to deny a statement of fact. And few people fail, especially in things of which it is hard to persuade others, to affirm that they have seen the thing or to cite witnesses whose authority stops us from contradicting. Following this custom, we know the foundations and causes of a thousand things that never were; and the world skirmishes amid a thousand questions of which both the pro and the con are false. *The false is so close to the true that the wise man should not trust himself in so dangerous a spot* [Cicero].

Truth and falsehood are alike in face, similar in bearing, taste, and movement; we look upon them with the same eye. I find not only that we are lax in defending ourselves against deception, but that we seek and hasten to run ourselves through on it. We love to embroil ourselves in vanity, as something in conformity with our being.

I have seen the birth of many miracles in my time. Even when they are smothered at birth, we do not fail to foresee the course they would have taken if they had lived out their full age. For it is only a matter of finding the end of the string, and we can unwind as much as we want. And there is more distance between nothing and the smallest thing in the world than there is between this and the biggest.

Now the first persons who are convinced of a strange initial fact, as they spread their story, feel from the opposition they meet where the difficulty of persuasion lies, and go and calk that place with some false patch. Besides, *by the innate desire in men to foster rumors diligently* [Livy], we naturally scruple to return what has been lent us without some interest and addition from our own stock. The private error first creates the public error, and afterward in turn the public error creates the private error. Thus this whole structure goes on building itself up and shaping itself from hand to hand; so that the remotest witness is better instructed about it than the nearest, and the last informed more convinced of it than the first. It is a natural progression. For whoever believes anything esteems that it is a work of charity to persuade another of it, and in order to do so does not fear to add out of his own invention as much as he sees to be necessary in his story to take care of the resistance and the defect he thinks there is in the other person's comprehension. . . .

There is nothing on which men are commonly more intent than on making a way for their opinions. Where the ordinary means fail us, we add command, force, fire, and the sword. It is unfortunate to be in such a pass that the best touchstone of truth is the multitude of believers, in a crowd in which the fools so far surpass the wise in number. *As if anything were so common as lack of sense!* [Cicero.] *A fine evidence of sanity is the multitude of the insane!* [Saint Augustine.] It is a difficult thing to set one's judgment against accepted opinions. The first conviction, taken from the subject itself, seizes the simple; from them it spreads to the able, under the authority of the number and antiquity of the testimonies. For my part, in a matter on which I would not believe one, I would not believe a hundred ones. And I do not judge opinions by their years. . . .

Many abuses are engendered in the world, or, to put it more boldly, all the abuses in the world are engendered, by our being taught to be afraid of professing our ignorance and our being bound to accept everything that we cannot refute. We talk about everything didactically and dogmatically. The style in Rome was that even what a witness deposed to having seen with his own eyes, and what a judge decided with his most certain knowledge, was drawn up in this form of speech: "It seems to me." It makes me hate probable things when they are planted on me as infallible. I like these words, which soften and moderate the rashness of our propositions: "perhaps," "to some extent," "some," "they say," "I think," and the like. And if I had had to train children, I would have filled their mouths so much with this way of answering, inquiring, not decisive—"What does that mean? I do not understand it. That might be. Is it true?"—that they would be more likely to have kept the manner of learners at sixty than to represent learned doctors at ten, as they do. Anyone who wants to be cured of ignorance must confess it. Iris is the daughter of Thaumas. Wonder is the foundation of all philosophy, inquiry its progress, ignorance its end. I'll go further: There is a certain strong and generous ignorance that concedes nothing to knowledge in honor and courage, an ignorance that requires no less knowledge to conceive it than does knowledge.

In my youth, I read about the trial of a strange case, which Corras, a counselor of Toulouse, had printed, about two men who impersonated one another. I remember (and I remember nothing else) that he seemed to me, in describing the imposture of the man he judged guilty, to make it so marvelous and so far surpassing our knowledge and his own, who was judge, that I found much rashness in the sentence that had condemned the man to be hanged. Let us accept some form of sentence which says "The court understands nothing of the matter," more freely and ingenuously than did the Areopagites, who, finding themselves hard pressed by a case that they could not unravel, ordered the parties to come back in a hundred years.

The witches of my neighborhood are in mortal danger every time some new author comes along and attests to the reality of their visions. To apply the examples that the Holy Writ offers us of such things, very certain and irrefragable examples, and bring them to bear on our modern events, requires greater ingenuity than ours, since we see neither their causes nor their means. It belongs perhaps only to that most powerful testimony to say to us: "This is a miracle, and that, and not this other." God must be believed in these things, that is truly most reasonable; but not, by the same token, one of us, who is astonished at his own narrative (and he is necessarily astonished unless he is out of his senses), whether he tells it about someone else or against himself.

I am sluggish and tend to hold to the solid and the probable, avoiding the ancient reproaches: *Men put greater faith in those things that they do not understand* [author unknown]. *By a twist of the human mind, obscure things are more readily believed* [Tacitus]. I see indeed that people get angry, and I am forbidden to doubt on pain of execrable insults. A new way of persuading! Thank God, my belief is not controlled by anyone's fists. Let them bully those who accuse them of holding a false opinion; I accuse them only of holding a difficult and rash one, and condemn the opposite affirmation, just as they do, if not so imperiously. *Let them appear as probable, or be affirmed positively* [Cicero].

He who imposes his argument by bravado and command shows that it is weak in reason. In a verbal and scholastic altercation these people may have as good an apparent case as their contradictors; but in the effective consequences they draw from them, the latter have much advantage.

To kill men, we should have sharp and luminous evidence; and our life is too real and essential to vouch for these supernatural and fantastic accidents. As for druggings and poisonings, I put them out of my reckoning; those are homicides, and of the worst sort. However, even in such matters they say that we must not always be satisfied with confessions, for such persons have sometimes been known to accuse themselves of having killed people who were found to be alive and healthy.

In those other extravagant accusations, I should be inclined to say that it is quite enough that a man, whatever recommendation he may have, should be believed about what is human; about what is beyond his conception and of supernatural effect, he should be believed only when some supernatural approbation has sanctioned him. This privilege that it has pleased God to give to some of our testimonies must not be cheapened and communicated lightly.

My ears are battered by a thousand stories like this: "Three people saw him on such-and-such a day in the east; three saw him the next day in the west, at such-and-such a time, in such-and-such a place, dressed thus." Truly, I would not believe my own self about this. How much more natural and likely it seems to me that two men are lying than that one man should pass with the winds in twelve hours from the east to the west! How much more natural that our understanding should be carried away from its base by the volatility of our untracked mind than that one of us, in flesh and bone, should be wafted up a chimney on a broomstick by a strange spirit!

Let us not look for outside and unknown illusions, we who are perpetually agitated by our own home-grown illusions. It seems to me that we may be pardoned for disbelieving a marvel, at least as long as we can turn aside and avoid the supernatural explanation by nonmarvelous means. And I follow Saint Augustine's opinion, that it is better to lean toward doubt than toward assurance in things difficult to prove and dangerous to believe.

A few years ago I passed through the territory of a sovereign prince, who, as a favor to me and to beat down my incredulity, did me the kindness of letting me see, in his own presence and in a private place, ten or twelve prisoners of this nature, and among others one old woman, indeed a real witch in ugliness and deformity, long very famous in that profession. I saw both proofs and free confessions, and some barely perceptible mark or other on this wretched old woman, and I talked and asked questions all I wanted, bringing to the matter the soundest attention I could; and I am not the man to let my judgment be throttled much by preconceptions. In the end, and in all conscience, I would have prescribed them rather hellebore than hemlock. *It seemed to be a matter rather of madness than of crime* [Livy]. Justice has its own corrections proper for such maladies. As for the objections and arguments that worthy men have brought up against me, both on this subject and often on others, I have not felt any that are binding and that do not admit of a solution more likely than their conclusions. It is true indeed that the proofs and reasons that are founded on experience and fact I do not attempt to disentangle; moreover they have no end to take hold of; I often cut them, as Alexander did his knot. After all, it is putting a very high price on one's conjectures to have a man roasted alive because of them.

62
Benedict de Spinoza: *The Political Works*

Benedict de Spinoza (1632–77) was an excommunicated Dutch Jew who articulated a rationalistic yet mystical pantheism in which the whole of reality was conceived of as a manifestation of the Divine, of the Perfect and Infinite Being of which all things that are were merely modes. In such a scheme there was no room for real evil, for Satan, for suspensions of natural (for Spinoza, divine) laws, that is to say, no room for the conceptions upon which witchcraft belief depends. If a man would clarify his theological concepts, Spinoza insisted, the existence of subsidiary agents of evil would appear contradictory to the reality that must flow from the nature of the Divine.

SOURCE: Benedict de Spinoza, *The Political Works*, ed. and trans. A. G. Wernham (Oxford, 1958), 269–71.

FURTHER READING: Benedict Spinoza, *Short Treatise on God, Man,*

and His Well-Being, in The Collected Works of Spinoza, ed. and trans.
Edwin Curley, vol. 1 (Princeton, 1985), II. 25, "Of Devils," p. 145; Margaret Gullan-Whur, Within Reason: A Life of Spinoza (London, 1998).

MOST MEN, HOWEVER, believe that
the unenlightened violate the order of nature rather than conform to it; they
conceive men in nature as a state within a state. They maintain, in fact, that the
human mind is not produced by natural causes at all, but is the direct creation of
God, and is so completely independent of every other thing that it has an absolute power to determine itself and use reason correctly. But experience teaches
us only too well that it is no more in our power to have a sound mind than to
have a sound body. Moreover, since everything does all it *can* do to preserve its
own being, we cannot have the slightest doubt that, if it *were* as much in our
power to live by the precept of reason as it is to be led by blind desire, all men
would be guided by reason, and *would* order their lives wisely; which is very far
from being the case. For everyone is captivated by his own pleasure. Nor do
theologians dispose of this difficulty by their dogma that the cause of this weakness is the vice or sin which arose in human nature through the fall of our first
ancestor. For if even the first man had as much power to stand as to fall, if his
mind was sound and his nature uncorrupted, how, with his knowledge and
foresight, could he possibly have fallen? Their answer is that he was deceived by
the Devil. Then who was it that deceived the Devil himself? Who, I ask, made
the very foremost of all intelligent creatures so insane that he wished to be
greater than God? For surely, if the Devil had a sound mind, he must have been
doing all he could to preserve himself and his own being? Again, if the first man
himself was sound in mind and master of his own will, how could he possibly
have allowed himself to be seduced and tricked? If he had the power to use
reason correctly, he could not have been deceived; for he must have done everything in his power to preserve his own being and his own sound mind. Now the
hypothesis is that he did have the power to use reason correctly: therefore he
must have preserved his sound mind, and could not have been deceived. This,
however, is shown to be false by the story told about him; and so we must admit
that the first man did not have it in his power to use reason correctly, but was
subject to passions like ourselves.

63
Alonso de Salazar Frias: A Spanish Inquisitor
on Witchcraft and Evidence (1610–14)

As more critical and cautious thought spread throughout learned Europe, and as educated men began to dissociate themselves from the beliefs and attitudes of the uneducated, skepticism about witchcraft persecutions and trial procedures increasingly made its presence felt among the officers of civil and ecclesiastical institutions. No more striking example of this could be found than the person of the Spanish inquisitor Alonso de Salazar Frias explaining the need to cease the dangerously self-fulfillng witch-hunts.

Salazar Frias (ca. 1564–1635) was appointed as third inquisitor to the regional inquisitorial tribunal of Logroño in northern Spain in 1609. He had obtained degrees in canon law at Salamanca and Sigüenza (the latter in 1588, when he was also ordained a priest) and spent the next twenty-one years in the service of several bishops, as well as in diplomatic service in Rome, after which he was appointed to the inquisitorial staff of the Logroño tribunal.

The hearings at Logroño resulted in widespread investigations and confessions to witchcraft, around 500 confessions, when Salazar began to express concern over the nature of the investigatory procedure and the inconclusive character of much of the evidence. Other Spanish clerics had also begun to express skepticism, and when Salazar was ordered by the Suprema, the central council of the Inquisition in Madrid, to make a visitation throughout the district of his tribunal, his eight-month investigation in 1611–1612 convinced him that the arrests, convictions, and executions for witchcraft were based on inadequate evidence and irregular legal procedure, in spite of the criticism he received from the other two members of the Logroño tribunal, Alonso Becerra and Juan Valle de Alvarado.

When Salazar Frias's final reports were read by the Suprema, the tribunal issued an *instrucción*, or command, for the future handling of witchcraft cases by the inquisitors that was based entirely on Salazar Frias's observations and recommendations. In effect, this stopped the prosecution of witches by the inquisitors in Spain.

SOURCE: Gustav Henningsen, *The Witches' Advocate: Basque Witchcraft and the Spanish Inquisition* (Reno, Nev., 1980), A.: 178–79, C.: 329–31, D.: 367–69, E.: 371–76; B.: H. C. Lea, *A History of the Inquisition in Spain*, vol. 4: 233–34.

FURTHER READING: H. C. Lea, *A History of the Inquisition in Spain*, 4: 224–41; Henningsen, *The Witches' Advocate*.

A. Salazar's Dissenting
Verdict in a Trial of 1610

Item, according to what scholars say of these phenomena, it is demonstrable that the witches go to the sabbaths many times in dreams [*spiritual y mental-*

mente; literally, spiritually and mentally], even though perhaps at other times they participate bodily [*corporalmente*]. This phenomenon is also described in the trial record of Fray Pedro de Arburu by the witnesses' statements concerning his alibi and his [deep] sleep. In spite of the great divergence in the methods of participating in the assemblies, to date none of the accused [i.e., the witches] have been able to distinguish between these two methods; on the contrary they maintain that they always participate personally and bodily.

But when they err on such a material point it is extremely probable that they are also in error with regard to those they name as their accomplices. It is all the more probable since the scholars say also that at the sabbaths the Devil can with the greatest ease conjure up figures [of innocent people] whom the witches believe are the authentic persons. The same phenomenon may also be seen to appear outside the witches' sabbaths. Thus some of the accused declare that an apparition replaces them in their beds when they are going to the sabbath; in particular María de Zozaya, Miguel de Goiburu, Mari Juanto, María de Echegui, Beltrana de la Fargua, and those to whom María de Echegui refers. This objection could very well be made to many of the most compromising witnesses' statements against the accused, for if, for instance, we take the evidence of witnesses against Juan de la Bastida [alias Lambert], there are some who maintain they have seen him at the *aquelarre* on the selfsame days and times when he was under lock and key in the Tribunal's secret prison.

Similarly [all] the witnesses are [also] mistaken in claiming that the miller Martín de Amayur gave María Presona a blow with a stick. In fact she denies this in all her interrogations during which she otherwise makes such frank confessions both with regard to herself and to the other witches.

Neither have definite proofs been produced by the things that outside witnesses have been brought to confirm, concerning the witches' assemblies, the ointments, the sexual intercourse with the Devil, and the other tangible witch phenomena. In part these investigations suffer from the same uncertainty as those discussed above; and also in the trial of María de Zozaya, the very opposite was proved [i.e., that the witches' requisites were not to be found].

B. Salazar's Second Report
to the Suprema, 1611

Considering the above with all the Christian attention in my power, I have not found even indications from which to infer that a single act of witchcraft has really occurred, whether as to going to *aquelarres*, being present at them, inflicting injuries, or other of the asserted facts. This enlightenment has greatly strengthened my former suspicions that the evidence of accomplices, without external proof from other parties, is insufficient to justify even arrest. Moreover, my experience leads to the conviction that, of those availing themselves of the

Edict of Grace, three-quarters and more have accused themselves and their accomplices falsely. I further believe that they would freely come to the Inquisition to revoke their confessions, if they thought that they would be received kindly without punishment, for I fear that my efforts to induce this have not been properly made known, and I further fear that, in my absence, the commissioners whom, by your command, I have ordered to do the same, do not act with due fidelity, but, with increasing zeal are discovering every hour more witches and *aquelarres*, in the same way as before.

I also feel certain that, under present conditions, there is no need of fresh edicts or the prolongation of those existing, but rather that, in the diseased state of the public mind, every agitation of the matter is harmful and increases the evil. I deduce the importance of silence and reserve from the experience that there were neither witches nor bewitched until they were talked and written about. This impressed me recently at Olague, near Pampeluna, where those who confessed stated that the matter started there after Fray Domingo de Sardo came there to preach about these things. So, when I went to Valderro, near Roncesvalles, to reconcile some who had confessed, when about to return the arcades begged me to go to the Valle de Ahescoa, two leagues distant, not that any witchcraft had been discovered there, but only that it might be honored equally with the other. I only sent there the Edict of Grace and, eight days after its publication, I learned that already there were boys confessing.

C. Becerra and Valle de Alvarado
Protest Salazar's Views (1613)

I have felt it right to inform Your Eminence of the matter of the witches on which we are at present working, for it looks as if the Devil is endeavoring to cloak the truth in every possible way. He is naturally very eager to bring souls to perdition, and unfortunately there is no shortage of people to help him realize his intentions.

The Council has commanded Dr. Alonso Becerra and me to send our opinion on the papers concerning *el licenciado* Alonso de Salazar's journey of visitation in the course of this month. But even though we are working every day of the week and on Sundays as well it will not be possible within such a short time to pronounce an opinion on such a momentous matter (from which [i.e., the visitation] he returned completely duped). It is true that we have completed the most important part of our report, which will be sent off in a week's time. We shall take the opportunity then of requesting more time in which to formulate the remainder. We are still completely convinced that when the Council reads our report with the thoroughness and consideration which are customary, it will be bound to realize as a clear and obvious fact supported by unassailable arguments that this sect is a reality. And this is in spite of all the delusions and deceits employed by the Devil, and which all purport to show that the witches do not exist. It will also be evident that the witches really do go to the sabbath and participate corporally in the meetings, and that they believe absolutely that their devil is God—as they state it in their confessions.

We have also collected a great many material proofs [*actos positivos*] which are completely unassailable, and I should be very glad to send a copy of this information to Your Eminence. For this subject has never been investigated and explored so thoroughly before, and moreover it will have to be acknowledged that the confessions of the accused agree on all points with what earlier authors have written regarding these matters.

I cannot understand how any sensible and intelligent person can bring himself to doubt this truth [i.e., the existence of the witches]. People have known about the sect for centuries in all neighbor countries and in all adjacent provinces, and its members have been punished with the greatest severity. In this very district the Inquisition has been aware of the existence of the sect for over a century, and *la Suprema* has held several meetings in order to subject the problem here to thorough investigation and consideration. It is therefore impossible to comprehend how anyone can dare to challenge these facts and misrepresent the truth that has been absolutely proved and acknowledged by all the scholars in Christendom, and how anyone dares to assert that it is the scholars and the Council of the Inquisition who have been in error and who have committed injustice for all this time—all this with no other basis than his [Salazar's] own whim, because from the very beginning (without knowing what he was doing) he clung to an erroneous interpretation. But now he is defending it tooth and nail. He is seeking to ally himself with persons who have no experience in these matters, and in particular he is leaning on that friend who used to live in this neighborhood [Venegas de Figueroa], who had espoused his case quite openly, and has done much to influence in his favor those superiors [in *la Suprema*] on whom he is continually exerting pressure.

All this grieves us [i.e., Becerra and Valle] deeply, and the only thing that relieves our pain is the knowledge that Your Eminence is on our side and is ready to defend this case of God. For Your Eminence has, like ourselves, understood the gravity of the matter and has realized what vile actions are rife in blaspheming God's Divine Majesty and sending so many souls to perdition. The very thought of it arouses horror and makes the heart bleed.

The long interruption in the legal proceedings as a result of the publication of the Edict of Grace has made the Devil and his witches bolder. The sect is spreading in all the districts where the Edict was read and is constantly acquiring more members, and those who are not witches [must look on helplessly while they] see their children taken to the *aquelarre*. So now they can only hope that the necessary steps will be taken [*todos están esperando el remedio*]. But when the case is brought up in the Council I am certain that the Noble Lords—

may God guide them—will make the decision that is needed, so that this fearful scourge may be eradicated.

Until that time I trust that Your Eminence will, with your indomitable courage, lend your aid and cast light on this matter, for if we are to serve God and defend His honor we must realize that this is the most momentous and grave case which has ever come up before the Inquisition. . . . [We can disregard the second part of the letter. It is a long attack on Salazar, who is depicted as a quarrelsome intriguer and indescribably arrogant.]

D. Salazar's Proposals
to the Suprema (1614)

[Henningsen paraphrases Salazar's clauses.]

1. The Holy Office is to make known its deep regret for the ill-treatment suffered by the accused at the hands of the district commissioners, their own relatives, or the local authorities. It is also to be announced that for the present the Inquisition is referring the punishment of the guilty to the High Court of Navarra, but that in the future, any persons who are guilty of inflicting such injustice will incur the severest penalties imposed by the Inquisition.

2. The Tribunal is to open proceedings against the commissioners who have been party to the abuses, and in addition to the penalty to which each of them is condemned the Tribunal must ensure that these people never again take any part in witchcraft cases. As obvious subjects for such "disciplinary enquiries" Salazar mentions specifically the commissioners at Vera, Maestu, and Larrea. . . .

3. Permission to revoke confessions of witchcraft is to be given out so effectively that all those who have hitherto held back may come forward without fear.

4. The parish priests are to be expressly ordered not to deny the sacraments to any of the accused, unless their guilt has been determined by the Tribunal.

5. All confessions and testimonies in the present witchcraft case are to be declared invalid, so that it will not be possible to institute proceedings against any person on the basis of these statements (unless new charges are preferred), and no suspect or his relatives will be debarred from the right to occupy honorable posts.

6. On account of the deficiencies of the trials, the *sambenitos* of the persons sentenced at the auto de fe of 1610 are not on any account to be displayed in the churches.

7. For the same reason the property that was sequestered is not to be confiscated.

8. The Tribunal is to discontinue the proceedings against those prisoners who died in prison before their trials were concluded. And their children and depen-

dents are to be summoned in order that they may be informed that these proceedings have not debarred them from honorable posts. These details are to be entered in their files.

9. The proceedings against Fray Pedro de Arburu and his cousin Juan de la Borda are to be quashed. Any part of their sentence still to be served is to be remitted, and they are to be informed that the proceedings have not excluded them from any honorable office.

10. The Tribunal is to publish an edict imposing silence regarding the whole question of witchcraft. Any person whose conscience may be troubling him in connection with these matters is to be enjoined not to discuss his problem with others but to go straight to one of the commissioners or to his own confessor, who can communicate the matter to the Tribunal. The same discretion is to be observed by persons who wish to accuse others of witchcraft.

11. Any persons who come of their own free will to confess anything about themselves or witness against others concerning these matters are to be freely admitted. Their statements are to be written down carefully with all the flaws and contradictions they may contain (as required by the ruling of the Inquisition); and if any testimony is made relating to accomplices, the witness is to be closely questioned so as to make plain what he in fact is able to witness.

12. No commissioner is to take evidence or make inquiries in these matters before he has informed the Tribunal and received express orders to proceed.

13. The commissioners are to be issued instructions on how to receive confessions of witchcraft. They are to be enjoined among other things to study the personal circumstances of those who come to confess and keep account of any details of background information that come to their notice. For these details will be of value when the Tribunal makes a decision regarding the confession. For their part, the inquisitors are to observe the greatest caution when appointing a commissioner to undertake further investigation of the case, and the inquisitors are to agree unanimously on the appointment.

14. Should fresh evidence be produced against any person previously under suspicion, his trial may be reopened, but the new evidence is to be entered as a continuation of his original case record, so that the question of his guilt may be resolved on the basis of both the old and the new testimonies. The vote may take place as soon as all three inquisitors are present, but before further action is taken the entire file with the inquisitors' vote and a copy of the new witchcraft instructions is to be remitted to *la Suprema*.

15. All voluntary *confitentes* who resort to the Tribunal are to have their cases dealt with mercifully, without delay. They are not to suffer imprisonment, confiscation of goods, or any other penalty. Those who make their confession to a commissioner are not to be summoned to the Tribunal. When their confessions have been examined by the inquisitors and their cases resolved,

their reconciliation or absolution may be entrusted to the commissioner, and unless the case presents particular problems it may be expedited by the Tribunal summarily without the advice of the Council.

16. In order to secure an entirely impartial treatment of these cases, in future the Tribunal is to commit the investigations to a commissioner from a different archdeaconry, so that examination of witnesses and other inquiries are never undertaken by the commissioner from the accused person's home district.

17. The cases of witches who confess to having relapsed are to be dealt with in the same manner as those of first offenders described above. Whether they confess before the Tribunal or to an inquisitorial secretary, the inquisitors are, whenever possible, to absolve them *ad cautelam* without consulting *la Suprema*, and under no circumstances are these cases to be delayed.

18. It has been ascertained that the clause relating to witches (*brujos y brujas*) is not incorporated in the Edict of Faith published by other inquisitorial tribunals. For the sake of uniformity this clause should be deleted from the Edict of Faith of the Logroño Inquisition.

19. All letters, instructions, and ordinances concerning the witch question that have in the course of time been received from *la Suprema* by the Tribunal are to be bound in chronological order into a volume, preceded by a copy of the new instructions, so that all this information will always be at hand should fresh cases of this nature arise, or if *la Suprema* should request to examine the papers.

20. All employees of the Tribunal in *el secreto* are to be made acquainted with the new instructions, a copy of which is to be included among the *cartas acordadas*. Each year, when the Tribunal forwards its *relación de causas*, a report is to be made on the progress of this matter, what results have been achieved, and what steps have been taken in individual cases.

E. The Instructions of the Suprema (August 29, 1614)

[Henningsen paraphrases the council's instructions.]

1. If the witches confess to murdering children or adults, the inquisitors are to ascertain (a) whether the victims died at the time referred to by the witches, (b) whether the deaths might have been from natural causes, and (c) whether there were any marks on the bodies or any other unusual circumstances concerning the deaths.

2. The inquisitors are also to seek to discover (a) how the witches got into the house and by what means they left it, and (b) whether they were admitted by anyone, or simply entered by way of an open door or window.

3. Concerning the meetings described by the witches in their confessions, the inquisitors are to find out (a) whether such meetings really took place, (b) by whom the witches were summoned to the gatherings, and (c) whether there

were any outside witnesses to the witches' sabbaths who saw them practicing their evil arts.

4. If the witches confess to killing cattle the owners are to be asked (a) whether the animals did in fact die, (b) how they died, and (c) whether marks were found on them.

5. If the witches confess to destroying crops, inquiries are to be made as to (a) whether the damage really was inflicted, and (b) whether at the time in question the fields had been exposed to hail, fog, gales, or frost which in themselves were sufficient to cause the loss of the crops.

6. If the witches confess to summoning up gales or hailstorms it must be determined whether these took place at a season when this kind of weather is a normal occurrence.

7. The inquisitors are to instruct the commissioners and the priests to explain to the people that damage to crops is sometimes the way God punishes us for our sins, and sometimes is a natural consequence of bad weather. These things occur everywhere whether there are witches present in the district or not, and it is therefore most undesirable for people to believe that the witches are always to blame.

8. In any concrete instance the inquisitors are to make efforts to verify whether the witches really did go to the *aquelarre* or in fact did not set foot outside the door on the nights when they maintain they had been to the gatherings. This can be ascertained by questioning those who live in the same house as the witch.

9. Whenever a person comes to make a confession of witchcraft or to denounce others, his entire statement is to be written down in the same words and style that he himself uses and with all the contradictions he may make. Afterwards he is to be expressly questioned regarding his motives for making the confession and whether he has been exposed to violence or coercion in this connection. If he testifies against others, attempts must be made to substantiate what he says and to discover whether there is enmity between him and those he accuses of witchcraft.

10. No commissioner is to institute inquiries into these matters, either on his own initiative or as the result of a denunciation. He is to confine himself to receiving statements from the delinquent or witness and to send this information on to the Tribunal, which will instruct him further.

11. When judging the confessions the inquisitors are to give particular attention to estimating whether any part of the confession can be proved by outside witnesses, or whether any of the things that the witch confesses have occurred outside the gatherings.

12. Whenever a witch or a witness comes to revoke his statement the revocation is to be accepted and entered as a continuation of the previous testimony. The inquisitors are to receive these people compassionately so that they may be free of the general and widespread fear of punishment after revocation. The

Tribunal is to see that the commissioners receive these orders with express instructions to follow them.

13. In the future, in the directives that the Tribunal may send to the commissioners for the examination of witnesses or for other investigations regarding witches, the rules and general practice of the Holy Office must be strictly adhered to. By issuing the directives in the manner they have done to date the witnesses' statements have been made valueless. For the commissioners—without putting the preliminary questions required by the standing instructions—have been reading the entire contents of the directives to the witnesses, thus giving them the opportunity to mention things of which they knew nothing.

14. Any person presenting himself in order to confess is to be received with compassion. When he has completed the confession of his errors he is to be asked whether he has held firm to Devil-worship even when outside the gatherings. He is to be questioned further on whether he anointed himself with the intention of going to the sabbath or when awake practiced other forms of apostasy. The cases are then to be decided according to the following general rules: *Adults* (women over twelve and men over fourteen) are to be reconciled only if they confess to having worshipped the Devil when awake. But because of the doubt prevailing in these cases this is to be enforced without confiscation of goods. The rest, who confess to having taken part in the *aquelarres*, but who have not persisted in apostasy when awake, are to be absolved *ad cautelam*. *Children* (girls under twelve and boys under fourteen) are without exception to be absolved *ad cautelam*.

Reconciliation and absolution may be administered by the commissioners so that there will be no need for the witches to present themselves to the Tribunal.

15. No person is to be imprisoned or sentenced solely on the basis of the witches' denunciations. If the witches in their confessions testify against others, the evidence is to be tested by means of investigations as stipulated in the present instructions, and only after these have provided confirmation may proceedings be initiated against the accomplices.

16. As soon as the secular or ecclesiastical courts discover that any case they have opened involves witchcraft, they are to assign it to the Holy Office. In such cases the inquisitors are to ascertain whether the accused persons or witnesses have been exposed to torture and if so what forms of torture were employed. They are further to establish on what grounds the case was opened and the evidence on which the charge was based. For if the evidence should not fulfill the legal requirements, the witches' confessions must be viewed with extreme care.

17. Those hitherto reconciled who may relapse are to be absolved *ad cautelam*. However, this is not applicable to persons who are reconciled from now on and later relapse. In such cases the Tribunal is to consult *la Suprema* and

remit the trial record with the inquisitors' vote, at the same time drawing the attention of the Council to the present instructions.

18. Since witchcraft is a difficult matter in which the judges may be easily deceived it is essential for all three inquisitors to be present when the Tribunal determines what investigations are to be made, and that all three inquisitors record their votes when this type of case is to be remitted to *la Suprema*.

19. All the evidence resulting from the present cases is to be suspended so that—unless fresh evidence materializes—no legal proceedings can be instituted on the basis of the old evidence, and the suspects are not to be debarred from holding posts in the Holy Office.

20. Should fresh evidence emerge against any person previously under suspicion, thus requiring the case to be reopened, the fresh evidence is to be added to the original testimony. And when the inquisitors vote on these cases they are to take both the old and the new evidence into consideration. If the inquisitors resolve to suspend the case they need not inform *la Suprema*. However, if they decide to continue the trial, the entire case along with the inquisitors' verdicts and a copy of the present instructions is to be remitted to the Council. However, until a decision is reached, the accused or suspected person is not to be regarded meanwhile as debarred from honorable office.

21. In order to make completely clear for future reference the degree of faith which can be placed in the testimonies and confessions hitherto received, the Tribunal is to examine the records and make additions regarding the precise circumstances of each individual case. Thus every detail relating to violence, coercion, or other conditions which diminish the reliability of the evidence is to be appended.

22. The cases of those persons who died during the trial are to be suspended and there will be no possibility for the *fiscal* of the Tribunal to reopen them (i.e., against the descendants of the accused). This is to be entered in the records, with a note to the effect that the descendants are not debarred from honorable office.

23. The special nature of witchcraft cases and in particular the circumstances prevailing during the present trials make it necessary for us to make the following stipulations: The *sambenitos* of those who were burned or reconciled at the auto de fe of 1610 are not to be displayed in the churches, and the Tribunal is not to confiscate the property that was then sequestered. This is to be entered into the records with a note to the effect that the trial does not debar the children of the accused from holding posts in the Holy Office or from any other honorable office.

24. For the same reason neither are those who received lesser penalties, or were absolved, to be debarred from any kind of honorable office, and this is to be entered in their records.

25. The Tribunal is to make a detailed list of the goods sequestered and the

fines paid in connection with these cases. A detailed memorandum is also to be drawn up showing all the costs incurred by the Tribunal in this matter. On the basis of this information *la Suprema* will decide what is to be done with the property received from the accused persons.

26. The inquisitors are to issue a prohibition stating that no persons are to threaten or coerce others into making confessions of witchcraft or into exposing any person to unpleasantness on account of confessions they may already have made to the Holy Office.

Also, the Tribunal is to summon the commissioners one at a time and instruct them to see that it is made known that the Inquisition—and in particular *la Suprema*—disassociates itself from the violence and abuses that have been inflicted, and deeply regrets that the local authorities (*los alcaldes de los lugares*) have, without any legal authority, exposed the suspects to such abuses in order to make them confess and witness against others.

Finally, the commissioners are to be instructed to inform the people that for the moment the Holy Office will allow the High Court of Navarra to punish the guilty, but that any person who commits such abuses in the future will be severely punished by the Holy Office.

27. The High Court is not to be prevented from examining these cases and punishing guilty persons. The Tribunal is not to intervene, neither are the inquisitors, to attempt to influence the High Court by private intercession.

28. Priests and confessors are to be supplied with the following instructions through the commissioners, if necessary in writing: If it comes to the knowledge of the priests, through the confessional or in any other way, that a person has employed the above methods of violence or coercion, they are to warn the person concerned that it is his duty to inform the Inquisition of the matter and that it is likewise his duty to report others he knows to have used these methods. The priests are to assure those concerned that the Inquisition will assume they have acted out of Christian zeal and that therefore no punishment will be meted out for acts of this nature committed to date. The persons concerned are further to be warned that they are bound to make their declarations, both in order to relieve their consciences, and so that those who have been exposed to scandal may have their good name and reputation restored to them. Finally, the priests are to admonish the persons concerned with the warning that they will incur the punishment of the Inquisition if they commit any similar offenses in the future.

29. When the Tribunal delivers these instructions to the commissioners they are to be notified verbally to proceed with moderation when dealing with this type of case, and to observe these instructions to the last detail.

30. The priests and confessors are to be instructed through the commissioners not to deny the sacraments to persons suspected of witchcraft unless expressly ordered to do so by the Inquisition.

31. Public discussion of the witch question has produced very undesirable consequences. It has divided the people into factions and caused private investigations to be carried out by self-appointed persons who sought to confirm their personal opinions. The Tribunal is therefore to issue an order imposing silence on these discussions. At the same time it must be announced that the matter may only be raised if anyone wishes to make a confession or statement to the Inquisition, and that the person concerned both before and after the hearing is under the usual obligation to preserve secrecy.

32. All the letters, instructions, and ordinances received to date from *la Suprema* concerning these matters are to be collected and bound together in chronological order. A copy of the present instructions is to be placed at the beginning of the volume. Thus all this material will always be at hand for the guidance of the inquisitors in future cases of this kind.

64

Thomas Hobbes: *Leviathan* (1651)

Thomas Hobbes (1588–1679) was a materialist and mechanist for whom the concepts of witchcraft—indeed, concepts involving spiritual agents of any kind—were philosophically inconceivable and insignificant. In book 4 of his great work of political philosophy, *Leviathan*, Hobbes interprets the meaning of scriptural passages concerning witchcraft as metaphorical, a device that men unwilling to admit the interaction of matter and spirit but unwilling to abandon scripture will utilize, less ironically than Hobbes, to reconcile their various intellectual and religious commitments.

SOURCE: Thomas Hobbes, *Leviathan* (London, 1651), bk. 4, chaps. 45–46.

FURTHER READING: Ian Bostridge, *Witchcraft and Its Transformations, c. 1650–c. 1750* (Oxford, 1997), 38–52.

Of Daemonology, and other Reliques of the Religion of the Gentiles.
The impression made on the organs of Sight, by lucide Bodies, either in one direct line, or in many lines, reflected from Opaque, or refracted in the passage through Diaphanous Bodies, produceth in living Creatures, in whom God hath placed such Organs, an Imagination of the Object, from whence the Impression proceedeth; which Imagination is called *Sight*; and seemeth not to bee a meer Imagination, but the Body it selfe without us; in the same manner, as when a man violently presseth his eye, there appears to him a light without, and before him, which no man perceiveth but himselfe; because there is indeed no such thing without him, but onely a motion in the interiour organs, pressing by

resistance outward, that makes him think so. And the motion made by this pressure, continuing after the object which caused it is removed, is that we call *Imagination*, and *Memory*, and (in sleep, and sometimes in great distemper of the organs by Sicknesse, or Violence) a *Dream*: of which things I have already spoken briefly, in the second and third Chapters.

This nature of Sight having never been discovered by the ancient pretenders to Naturall Knowledge; much lesse by those that consider not things so remote (as that Knowledge is) from their present use; it was hard for men to conceive of those Images in the Fancy, and in the Sense, otherwise, than of things really without us: Which some (because they vanish away, they know not whither, nor how,) will have to be absolutely Incorporeall, that is to say Immateriall, or Formes without Matter; Colour and Figure, without any coloured or figured Body; and that they can put on Aiery bodies (as a garment) to make them Visible when they will to our bodily Eyes; and others say, are Bodies, and living Creatures, but made of Air, or other more subtile and aethereall Matter, which is, then, when they will be seen, condensed. But Both of them agree on one generall appellation of them, *Daemons*. As if the Dead of whom they Dreamed, were not Inhabitants of their own Brain, but of the Air, or of Heaven, or Hell; not Phantasmes, but Ghosts; with just as much reason, as if one should say, he saw his own Ghost in a Looking-Glasse, or the Ghosts of the Stars in a River; or call the ordinary apparition of the Sun, of the quantity of about a foot, the *Daemon*, or Ghost of that great Sun that enlighteneth the whole visible world: And by that means have feared them, as things of an unknown, that is, of an unlimited power to doe them good, or harme; and consequently, given occasion to the Governours of the Heathen Common-wealths to regulate this their fear, by establishing that *Daemonology* (in which the Poets, as Principall Priests of the Heathen Religion, were specially employed, or reverenced) to the Publique Peace, and to the Obedience of Subjects necessary thereunto; and to make some of them Good *Daemons*, and others Evill; the one as a Spurre to the Observance, the other, as Reines to withhold them from Violation of the Laws.

What kind of things they were, to whom they attributed the name of *Daemons*, appeareth partly in the Genealogie of their Gods, written by *Hesiod*, one of the most ancient Poets of the Graecians; and partly in other Histories; of which I have observed some few before, in the 12. Chapter of this discourse.

The Graecians, by their Colonies and Conquests, communicated their Language and Writings into Asia, Egypt, and Italy; and therein, by necessary consequence their Daemonology, or (as St. Paul calles it) their Doctrines of Devils: And by that meanes, the contagion was derived also to the Jewes, both of Judaea, and Alexandria, and other parts, whereinto they were disposed. But the name of Daemon they did not (as the Graecians) attribute to Spirits both Good, and Evill; but to the Evill onely: And to the Good Daemons they gave the name of the Spirit of God; and esteemed those into whose bodies they entered to be

Prophets. In summe, all singularity if Good, they attributed to the Spirit of God; and if Evil, to some Daemon, but a *kakodaimon*, an Evill Daemon, that is, a Devill. And therefore, they called *Daemoniaques*, that is, *possessed by the Devill*, such as we call Mad-men or Lunatiques; or such as had the Falling Sicknesse; or that spoke any thing, which they for want of understanding, thought absurd: As also of an Unclean person in a notorious degree, they used to say he had an Unclean Spirit; of a Dumbe man, that he had a Dumbe Devill; and of John Baptist (Math. 11. 18.) for the singularity of his fasting, that he had a Devill; and of our Saviour, because he said, hee that keepeth his sayings should not see Death in *aeternum, Now we know thou hast a Devill; Abraham is dead, and the Prophets are dead*: and again, because he said (John 7. 20.) *They went about to kill him*, the people answered, *Thou bast a Devill, who goeth about to kill thee?* Whereby it is manifest, that the Jewes had the same opinions concerning Phantasmes, namely, that they were not Phantasmes, that is, Idols of the braine, but things reall, and independent on the Fancy.

Which doctrine if it be not true, why (may some say) did not our Saviour contradict it, and teach the contrary? nay why does he use on diverse occasions, such forms of speech as seem to confirm it? To this I answer, that first, where Christ saith, *A spirit hath not flesh and bone*, though hee shew that there by Spirits, yet hee denies not that they are Bodies: And where St. Paul saies, *We shall rise spirituall Bodies*, he acknowledgeth the nature of Spirits, but that they are Bodily Spirits; which is not difficult to understand. For Air and many other things are Bodies, though not Flesh and Bone, or any other grosse body, to bee discerned by the eye. But when our Saviour speaketh to the Devill, and commandeth him to go out of a man, if by the Devill, be meant a Disease, as Phrenesy, or Lunacy, or a corporeal Spirit, is not the speech improper? can Diseases heare? or can there be a corporeall Spirit in a Body of Flesh and Bone, full already of vitall and animal Spirits? Are there not therefore Spirits, that neither have Bodies, nor are meer Imaginations? To the first I answer, that the addressing of our Saviours command to the Madnesse, or Lunacy he cureth, is no more improper, then was his rebuking of the Fever, or of the Wind, and Sea; for neither do these hear: Or than was the command of God, to the Light, to the Firmament, to the Sunne, and Starres, when he commanded them to bee: for they could not heare before they had a beeing. But those speeches are not improper, because they signifie the power of Gods Word: no more therefore is it improper, to command Madnesse, or Lunacy (under the appellation of Devils, by which they were then commonly understood,) to depart out of a mans body. To the second, concerning their being Incorporeall, I have not yet observed any place of Scripture, from whence it can be gathered, that any man was ever possessed with any other Corporeall Spirit, but that of his owne, by which his body is naturally moved.

Our Saviour, immediately after the Holy Ghost descended upon him in the form of a Dove, is said by St. Matthew (Chapt. 4. 1.) to have been *led up by the Spirit into the Wildernesse*; and the same is recited (Luke 4.1.) in these words, *Jesus being full of the Holy Ghost, was led in the Spirit into the Wildernesse*: Whereby it meant that by *Spirit* there is meant the Holy Ghost. This cannot be interpreted for a Possession: For Christ and the Holy Ghost, are but one and the same substance; which is no possession of one substance, or body, by another. And whereas in the verses following, he is said *to have been taken up by the Devill into the Holy City, and set upon a pinnacle of the Temple*, shall we conclude thence that hee was possessed of the Devill, or carryed thither by violence? And again, *carryed thence by the Devill into an exceeding high mountain, who shewed him them thence all the Kingdomes of the world*: Wherein, wee are not to beleeve he was either possessed, or forced by the Devill; nor that any Mountaine is high enough, (according to the literall sense,) to shew him one whole Hemisphere. What then can be the meaning of this place, other than that he went of himself into the Wildernesse; and that this carrying of him up and down, from the Wildernesse to the City, and from thence into a Mountain, was a Vision? Conformable whereunto, is also the phrase of St. Luke, that hee was led into the Wildernesse, not *by*, but *in* the Spirit: whereas concerning His being Taken up into the Mountaine, and unto the Pinnacle of the Temple, hee speaketh as St. Matthew doth. Which suiteth with the nature of a Vision.

Again, where St. Luke sayes of Judas Iscariot, that *Satan entered into him and thereupon he went and communed with the Chief Priests, and Captaines, how he might betray Christ unto them*: it may be answered, that by the Entering of *Satan* (that is the *Enemy*) into him, is meant, the hostile and traiterous intention of selling his Lord and Master. For as by the Holy Ghost, is frequently in Scripture understood, the Graces and good Inclinations given by the Holy Ghost; so by the Entring of Satan, may bee understood the wicked Cogitations, and Designs of the Aversaries of Christ, and his Disciples. For as it is hard to say, that the Devill was entred into Judas, before he had any such hostile designe; so it is impertinent to say, he was first Christs Enemy in his heart, and that the Devill entred into him afterwards. Therefore the Entring of Satan, and his Wicked Purpose, was one and the same thing.

But if there be no Immateriall Spirit, nor any Possession of mens bodies by any Spirit Corporeall, it may again be asked, why our Saviour and his Apostles did not teach the People so; and in such cleer words, as they might no more doubt thereof. But such questions as these, are more curious, than necessary for a Christian mans Salvation. Men may as well aske, why Christ that could have given to all men Faith, Piety, and all manner of morall Vertues, gave it to some onely, and not to all: and why he left the search of naturall Causes, and Sciences, to the naturall Reason and Industry of men, and did not reveal it to all, or any man supernaturally; and many other such questions: Of which nevertheless there may be alleged probable and pious reasons. For as God, when he brought the Israelites into the Land of Promise, did not secure them therein, by subduing all the Nations round about them; but left many of them, as thornes in their sides, to awaken from time to time their Piety and Industry: so our Saviour, in conducting us toward his heavenly Kingdome, did not destroy all the difficulties of Naturall Questions; but left them to exercise our Industry, and Reason; the Scope of his preaching, being onely to shew us this plain and direct way to Salvation, namely, the beleef of this Article, *that he was the Christ, the Son of the living God, sent into the world to sacrifice himselfe for our Sins, and at his coming again, gloriously to reign over his Elect, and to save them from their Enemies eternally*: To which, the opinion of Possession by Spirits, or Phantasmes, are no impediment in the way; though it be to some an occasion of going out of the way, and to follow their own Inventions. If wee require of the Scripture an account of all questions, which may be raised to trouble us in the performance of Gods commands; we may as well complaine of Moses for not having set downe the time of the creation of such Spirits, as well as of the Creation of the Earth, and Sea, and of Men, and Beasts. To conclude, I find in Scripture that there be Angels, and Spirits, good and evill; but not that they are Incorporeall, as are the Apparitions men see in the Dark, or in a Dream, or Vision; which the Latines call *Spectra*, and took for *Daemons*. And I find that there are Spirits Corporeall, (though subtile and Invisible;) but not that any mans body was possessed, or inhabited by them; And that the Bodies of the Saints shall be such, namely, Spirituall Bodies, as St. Paul calls them.

Neverthelesse, the contrary Doctrine, namely, that there be Incorporeall Spirits, hath hitherto so prevailed in the Church, that the use of Exorcisme, (that is to say, of election of Devills by Conjuration) is thereupon built; and (though rarely and faintly practised) is not yet totally given over. That there were many Daemoniaques in the Primitive Church, and few Mad-men, and other such singular diseases; whereas in these times we hear of, and see many Mad-men, and few Daemoniaques, proceeds not from the change of Nature; but of Names. But how it comes to passe, that whereas heretofore the Apostles, and after them for a time, the Pastors of the Church, did cure those singular Diseases, which now they are not seen to doe; as likewise, why it is not in the power of every true Beleever now, to doe all that the Faithfull did then, that is to say, as we read (Mark 16. 17.) *In Christs name to cast out Devills, to speak with new Tongues, to take up Serpents, to drink deadly Poison without harm taking, and to cure the Sick by the laying on of their hands,* and all this without other words, but *in the Name of Jesus,* is another question. And it is probable, that those extraordinary gifts were given to the Church, for no longer a time, than men trusted wholly to Christ, and looked for their felicity onely in his Kingdome to come; and consequently, that when they sought Authority, and Riches, and trusted to their own Subtility for a Kingdome of this world, these supernaturall gifts of God were again taken from them. . . .

An *Image* (in the most strict signification of the word) is the Resemblance of some thing visible: In which sense the Phantasticall Formes, Apparitions, or Seemings of visible Bodies to the Sight, are onely *Images*; such as are the Shew of a man, or other thing in the Water, by Reflexion, or Refraction; or of the Sun, or Stars by Direct Vision in the Air; which are nothing reall in the things seen, nor in the place where they seem to bee; nor are their magnitudes and figures the same with that of the object; but changeable, by the variation of the organs of Sight, or by glasses; and are present oftentimes in our Imagination, and in our Dreams, when the object is absent; or changed into other colours, and shapes, as things that depend onely upon the Fancy. And these are the Images which are originally and most properly called *Ideas*, and *Idols*, and derived from the language of the Graecians, with whom the word *Eido* signifieth to *See*. They are also called *Phantasmes*, which is in the same language, *Apparitions*. And from these Images it is that one of the faculties of mans Nature, is called the *Imagination*. And from hence it is manifest, that there neither is, nor can bee any Image made of a thing Invisible.

It is also evident, that there can be no Image of a thing Infinite: for all the Images, and Phantasmes that are made by the Impression of things visible, are figured: but Figure is a quantity every way determined: And therefore there can bee no Image of God; nor of the Soule of Man; nor of Spirits; but onely of Bodies Visible, that is, Bodies that have light in themselves, or are by such enlightened.

Of Darknesse from Vain Philosophy, and Fabulous Traditions
By *Philosophy*, is understood the *Knowledge acquired by Reasoning, from the Manner of the Generation of any thing, to the Properties; or from the Properties, to some possible Way of Generation of the same; to the end to bee able to produce, as far as matter, and humane force permit, such Effects, as humane life requireth.* So the Geometrician, from the Construction of Figures, findeth out many Properties thereof; and from the Properties, new Ways of their Construction, by Reasoning; to the end to be able to measure Land, and Water; and for infinite other uses. So the Astronomer, from the Rising, Setting, and Moving of the Sun, and Starres, in divers parts of the Heavens, findeth out the Causes of Day, and Night, and of the different Seasons of the Year; whereby he keepeth an account of Time: And the like of other Sciences.

By which Definition it is evident, that we are not to account as any part thereof, that originall knowledge called Experience, in which consisteth Prudence: Because it is not attained by Reasoning, but found as well in Brute Beasts, as in Man; and is but a Memory of successions of events in times past, wherein the omission of every little circumstance altering the effect, frustrateth the expectation of the most Prudent: whereas nothing is produced by Reasoning aright, but generall, eternall, and immutable Truth.

Nor are we therefore to give that name to any false Conclusions: For he that Reasoneth aright in words he understandeth, can never conclude an Error:

Nor to that which any man knows by supernaturall Revelation; because it is not acquired by Reasoning:

Nor that which is gotten by Reasoning from the Authority of Books; because it is not by Reasoning from the Cause to the Effect, nor from the Effect to the Cause; and is not Knowledge, but Faith.

65
Friedrich Spee: *Cautio criminalis* (1631)

Friedrich Spee was a Jesuit and poet assigned the painful task of being confessor of witches condemned to death during the persecutions at Würzburg in the late 1620s (Text 54). Appalled by the method of the trials, Spee published an anonymous attack upon the persecution in 1631, the *Cautio criminalis*, which became celebrated later in the century, when the philosopher Leibniz revealed the identity of its author.

SOURCE: Burr, *The Witch Persecutions*, 30–35.

What, now, is the outline and method of the trials against witches
to-day in general use?—a thing worthy Germany's consideration.
I answer: . . .

1. Incredible among us Germans and especially (I blush to say it) among Catholics are the popular superstition, envy, calumnies, back-bitings, insinuations, and the like, which, being neither punished by the magistrates nor refuted by the pulpit, first stir up suspicion of witchcraft. All the divine judgments which God has threatened in Holy Writ are now ascribed to witches. No longer do God or nature do aught, but witches everything.

2. Hence it comes that all at once everybody is clamoring that the magistrates proceed against the witches—those witches whom only their own clamor has made seem so many.

3. Princes, therefore, bid their judges and counselors to begin proceedings against the witches.

4. These at first do not know where to begin, since they have no testimony or proofs, and since their conscience clearly tells them that they ought not to proceed in this rashly.

5. Meanwhile they are a second time and a third admonished to proceed. The multitude clamors that there is something suspicious in this delay; and the same suspicion is, by one busybody or another, instilled into the ear of the princes.

6. To offend these, however, and not to defer at once to their wishes, is in

Germany a serious matter: most men, and even clergymen, approve with zeal whatever is but pleasing to the princes, not heeding by whom these (however good by nature) are often instigated.

7. At last, therefore, the judges yield to their wishes, and in some way contrive at length a starting-point for the trials.

8. Or, if they still hold out and dread to touch the ticklish matter, there is sent to them a commissioner [inquisitor] specially deputed for this. And, if he brings to his task something of inexperience or of haste, as is wont to happen in things human, this takes on in this field another color and name, and is counted only zeal for justice. This zeal for justice is no whit diminished by the prospect of gain, especially in the case of a commissioner of slender means and avaricious, with a large family, when there is granted him as salary so many dollars per head for each witch burned, besides the fees and assessments which he is allowed to extort at will from the peasants.

9. If now some utterance of a demoniac or some malign and idle rumor then current (for proof of the scandal is never asked) points especially to some poor and helpless Gaia, she is the first to suffer.

10. And yet, lest it appear that she is indicted on the basis of rumor alone, without other proofs, as the phrase goes, lo a certain presumption is at once obtained against her by posing the following dilemma: Either Gaia has led a bad and improper life, or she has led a good proper one. If a bad one, then, say they, the proof is cogent against her; for from malice to malice the presumption is strong. If, however, she has led a good one, this also is none the less a proof; for thus, they say, are witches wont to cloak themselves and try to seem especially proper.

11. Therefore it is ordered that Gaia be haled away to prison. And lo now a new proof is gained against her by this other dilemma: Either she then shows fear or she does not show it. If she does show it (hearing forsooth of the grievous tortures wont to be used in this matter), this is of itself a proof; for conscience, they say, accuses her. If she does not show it (trusting forsooth in her innocence), this too is a proof; for it is most characteristic of witches, they say, to pretend themselves peculiarly innocent and wear a bold front.

12. Lest, however, further proofs against her should be lacking, the Commissioner has his own creatures, often depraved and notorious, who question into all her past life. This, of course, cannot be done without coming upon some saying or doing of hers which evil-minded men can easily twist or distort into ground for suspicion of witchcraft.

13. If, too, there are any who have borne her ill will, these, having now a fine opportunity to do her harm, bring against her such charges as it may please them to devise; and on every side there is a clamor that the evidence is heavy against her.

14. And so, as soon as possible, she is hurried to the torture, if indeed she be not subjected to it on the very day of her arrest, as often happens.

15. For in these trials there is granted to nobody an advocate or any means of fair defense, for the cry is that the crime is an excepted one, and whoever ventures to defend the prisoner is brought into suspicion of the crime as are all those who dare to utter a protest in these cases and to urge the judges to caution; for they are forthwith dubbed patrons of the witches. Thus all mouths are closed and all pens blunted, lest they speak or write.

16. In general, however, that it may not seem that no opportunity of defense has been given to Gaia, she is brought out and the proofs are first read before her and examined—if examine it can be called.

17. But, even though she then denies these and satisfactorily makes answer to each, this is neither paid attention to nor even noted down: all the proofs retain their force and value, however perfect her answer to them. She is only ordered back into prison, there to bethink herself more carefully whether she will persist in her obstinacy—for, since she has denied her guilt, she is obstinate.

18. When she has bethought herself, she is next day brought out again, and there is read to her the sentence of torture—just as if she had before answered nothing to the charges, and refuted nothing.

19. Before she is tortured, however, she is led aside by the executioner, and, lest she may by magical means have fortified herself against pain, she is searched, her whole body being shaved . . . ; although up to this time nothing of the sort was ever found. . . .

21. Then, when Gaia has thus been searched and shaved, she is tortured that she may confess the truth, that is to say, that she may simply declare herself guilty; for whatever else she may say will not be the truth and cannot be.

22. She is, however, tortured with the torture of the first degree, i.e., the less severe. This is to be understood thus: that, although in itself it is exceeding severe, yet, compared with others to follow, it is lighter. Wherefore, if she confesses, they say and noise it abroad that she has confessed without torture.

23. Now, what prince or other dignitary who hears this can doubt that she is most certainly guilty who thus voluntarily without torture confesses her guilt?

24. Without any scruples, therefore, after this confession she is executed. Yet she would have been executed, nevertheless, even though she had not confessed; for, when once a beginning has been made with the torture, the die is already cast—she cannot escape, she must die.

25. So, whether she confesses or does not confess, the result is the same. If she confesses, the thing is clear, for, as I have said and as is self-evident, she is executed: all recantation is in vain, as I have shown above. If she does not confess, the torture is repeated—twice, thrice, four times: anything one pleases is permissible, for in an excepted crime there is no limit of duration or severity

or repetition of the tortures. As to this, think the judges, no sin is possible which can be brought up before the tribunal of conscience.

26. If now Gaia, no matter how many times tortured, has not yet broken silence—if she contorts her features under the pain, if she loses consciousness, or the like, then they cry that she is laughing or has bewitched herself into taciturnity, and hence deserves to be burned alive, as lately has been done to some who though several times tortured would not confess.

27. And then they say—even clergymen and confessors—that she died obstinate and impenitent, that she would not be converted or desert her paramour, but kept rather her faith with him.

28. If, however, it chances that under so many tortures one dies, they say that her neck has been broken by the Devil. . . .

29. Wherefore justly, forsooth, the corpse is dragged out by the executioner and buried under the gallows.

30. But if, on the other hand, Gaia does not die and some exceptionally scrupulous judge hesitates to torture her further without fresh proofs or to burn her without a confession, she is kept in prison and more harshly fettered, and there lies for perhaps an entire year to rot until she is subdued.

31. For it is never possible to clear herself by withstanding and thus to wash away the aspersion of crime, as is the intention of the laws. It would be a disgrace to her examiners if when once arrested she should thus go free. Guilty must she be, by fair means or foul, whom they have once but thrown into bonds.

32. Meanwhile, both then and earlier, they send to her ignorant and headstrong priests, more importunate than the executioners themselves. It is the business of these to harass in every wise the wretched creature to such a degree that, whether truly or not, she will at last confess herself guilty; unless she does so, they declare, she simply cannot be saved, nor share in the sacraments.

33. The greatest care is taken lest there be admitted to her priests more thoughtful and learned, who have aught of insight or kindliness; as also that nobody visits her prison who might give her counsel or inform the ruling princes. For there is nothing so much dreaded by any of them as that in some way the innocence of any of the accused should be brought to light. . . .

34. In the meantime, while Gaia, as I have said, is still held in prison, and is tormented by those whom it least behooves, there are not wanting to her industrious judges clever devices by which they not only find new proofs against Gaia, but by which moreover they so convict her to her face (an't please the gods!) that by the advice of some university faculty she is then at last pronounced to deserve burning alive. . . .

35. Some, however, to leave no stone unturned, order Gaia to be exorcised and transferred to a new place, and then to be tortured again, in the hope that by this exorcism and change of place the bewitchment of taciturnity may perhaps be broken. But, if not even this succeeds, then at last they commit her alive to the

flames. Now, in Heaven's name, I would like to know, since both she who confesses and she who does not perish alike, what way of escape is there for any, however innocent? O unhappy Gaia, why hast thou rashly hoped? why hast thou not, at first entering prison, declared thyself guilty? why, O foolish woman and man, wilt thou die so many times when thou mightst die but once? Follow my counsel, and before all pain declare thyself guilty and die. Thou wilt not escape; for this were a disgrace to the zeal of Germany.

36. If, now, any under stress of pain has once falsely declared herself guilty, her wretched plight beggars description. For not only is there in general no door for her escape, but she is also compelled to accuse others, of whom she knows no ill, and whose names are not seldom suggested to her by her examiners or by the executioner, or of whom she has heard as suspected or accused or already once arrested and released. These in their turn are forced to accuse others, and these still others, and so it goes on: who can help seeing that it must go on without end?

37. Wherefore the judges themselves are obliged at least either to break off the trials and so condemn their own work or else to burn their own folk, aye themselves and everybody: for on all soon or late false accusations fall, and, if only followed by the torture, all are proved guilty.

38. And so at last those are brought into question who at the outset most loudly clamored for the constant feeding of the flames; for they rashly failed to foresee that their turn, too, must inevitably come—and by a just verdict of Heaven, since with their pestilent tongues they created us so many witches and sent so many innocent to the flames.

39. But now gradually many of the wiser and more learned begin to take notice of it, and, as if aroused from deep sleep, to open their eyes and slowly and cautiously to bestir themselves. . . .

46. From all which there follows this corollary, worthy to be noted in red ink: that, if only the trials be steadily pushed on with, there is nobody in our day, of whatsoever sex, fortune, rank, or dignity, who is safe, if he have but an enemy and slanderer to bring him into suspicion of witchcraft. . . .

66
Balthasar Bekker: *The Enchanted World* (1690)

Balthasar Bekker (1634–98) was a Dutch pastor and Cartesian rationalist who wrote what was in many ways the seventeenth century's most fundamental and influential critique of demonology and witchcraft belief, *The Enchanted World*, the first two volumes of which first appeared in Dutch in 1690 and were soon translated into French, German, and English. Within two months of its first Dutch publication, the first

two volumes of the work had sold four thousand copies in the Netherlands alone. Armed with an optimistic rational theology that challenged the powerful role given to the devil in witchcraft belief, an
abhorrence of inherited "superstition" that refused to elevate tradition
and folklore to the status of sound belief, and a mechanistic sense of
human "disorders" of the imagination, Bekker undertook to analyze
and to negate the components of Christian witchcraft belief. Putting his
critical reason to work in the areas of scriptural interpretation, formal
theology, natural history, and natural philosophy, and offering alterna-
tive explanations of generally accepted witchcraft incidents, Bekker
was one of a handful of seventeenth-century thinkers preparing the conceptual and intellectual path for a complete renunciation of the demonological beliefs that had stood the tragic test of time for centuries.

Bekker's work was both widely admired and criticized in its time,
and it cost Bekker his position as a Calvinist minister.

SOURCE: Balthasar Bekker, *Le monde enchanté*, 4 vols. (Amsterdam,
1691), vol. 3, chap. 3, art. 4–6; vol. 4, chap. 33, art. 1–9. Trans. A. C. K.

FURTHER READING: Robin Attfield, "Balthasar Bekker and the Decline of the Witch-Craze: The Old Demonology and the New Philosophy," *Annals of Science* 42 (1985): 383–95.

On alleged pacts between man and Satan

Leaving aside what concerns Scripture on this question, to make use of it in its
proper place, Reason teaches me enough to know that men's wills can never be
under compulsion; so that it is of no value to say that they do with its assent
that to which they are coerced. Of two necessary evils, there is one to be chosen;
and if that is done voluntarily, it is not in order to take one of them upon oneself,
but in order to avoid the other, when one cannot escape both of them. One does
not wish for either of these two evils, but rather for one less than the other.
Thus, the Devil must not imagine that he possesses the will of those men whom
he has obliged to sign the contract that exists between him and them. It is true
that they are not exempt from sin by virtue of this; on the contrary, they grievously trespass against God: first, by signing this contract, in which the will
chooses as the lesser of two evils that which is in reality the greater; secondly,
by being the occasion of all the evil that the Devil himself does, but by their
means, granted for the sake of argument that it occurs in such a way. But no one
can say, however, that he agrees of his own will to the Pact to which he is forced
by the Devil himself.

Now if God, after the perfidious rebellion of this evil Spirit, still gives him
permission to do harm, particularly to men, against their will, how would that
harmonize with the Justice of God, since this evil Enemy would be able to harm
man only by making use of the most infamous and cruel means imaginable? For

who would dare to say that the Devil is allowed to commit the greatest of crimes to prevent him from committing lesser ones? And who can deny that it is a much greater evil to bind oneself to the Devil, by a contract signed with one's own hand and with a vow, and to give oneself to him in body and soul by an express denial of God, than to sin simply by seduction and by weakness? And isn't it the same way, that to do evil unto man against his will, and to afflict him only on earth with temporal pains, as the Devil surely would do without the aid of this pact, if he could, is an infinitely lesser evil than to force him to obligate himself to do evil, and to sacrifice himself body and soul to this evil Spirit, in order to be damned eternally? You can see a little, thus, the good reason that these men [defending the concept of the voluntary pact] have invented, in order to make us believe that the Devil, without the aid of this Pact that they attribute to him, cannot effect any evil.

But leaving that aside, a man, they say, would not be able to avoid being tormented by the Devil, if this evil Spirit were not limited by being unable to harm anyone without the aid of such a Pact. For having as his goal nothing else but the doing of harm, what man is there who could escape from him, if he could effect it at his pleasure? There would be no one, thus (following their line of reasoning), who would be assured of his body, or his life, or of the salvation of his soul, what with this Spirit being on the watch over all things. I must admit, however, that I should expect these arguments only from persons who believed in no other Spirits except the Devils, who did not know even of a God, or a Savior, and who imagined that the world was filled entirely with evil Spirits. For me, since I believe that there are Spirits, I also believe that there are as many good ones for the preservation of men as there are evil ones for their ruin. And if it is granted that, on the other hand, the good Spirits, that is to say the holy Angels, or even the tutelary Spirits, following the ancient opinion of the Pagans, have as much inclination to secure the good for men as the others have a penchant for doing evil unto them, it follows necessarily that no one would be in dire peril of suffering or committing evil, because the good Angels not being limited in their power, their care for the preservation of men always would have its effect; and, moreover, that they would be as favorable to men as the Devils are opposed to them. Thus the affair would remain between the two, and the Devil would have no advantage.

That it is evident, from everything that has been said up to this point,
that there is nothing whatsoever, neither of illusions, nor of apparitions
of Spirits, nor of Divinations, nor of Magic, in the manner of which men
speak of these:
If I had been obliged to bring together all the examples [of witchcraft, apparitions, spells, and so on], not all of those which are extant, but only those which I have had in my hands, I should never have finished, so many are there in such

great quantity everywhere. But having chosen those which are the best known or the most famous, as well as those which have recently occurred close to us, and about which, as a consequence, one can best inquire, it seems to me that this should be sufficient to convince any person who is disinterested and who loves the truth. To wit, that no one has had any experience whatsoever of that Magic, whatever name one can give to it, which occurs through the contrivance or the operations of the Devil, or by virtue of a Pact contracted with him; nor any whatsoever of the least act of evil Spirits upon man or upon any thing of which man knows. Among all those I have cited, there is not a single example in which the chief circumstances are not incomplete, lacking something that would be necessary if one desired to draw conclusions from them; there is not one whose certainty is not doubtful, and which doesn't lack solid evidence; there is not one in which one doesn't have good cause to suspect that there is deception. Several of these have occurred, but simply by virtue of the imagination, and several to which far more scope was given than was theirs, by virtue of prejudice alone. And beyond that, all that is natural that is found in these is simply something unusual, of whose cause, for the most part, we are ignorant. There is, thus, no other Magic than that which is in the imagination of men; there are no Phantoms, no Divination, nor any obsession which is from the Devil.

In saying this, I limit my explanation to the exclusion of the Devil, without seeking to deny, by virtue of this, any kind of Magic, if one wants to give that name to it. For seeing how everything of which we have spoken has not been fabricated, nor forged only in the imagination, but rather, for the most part, has occurred in fact, we must say that experience teaches us that there truly is a Magic, and that more of the world is bewitched than is thought: namely, those who have been deceived by the cunning of others, or those to whom others have secretly done harm, or both. The people of Macon, of Tedworth, of Sainte Anne-berg, of Campen and of Beckington, certainly have been bewitched, that is to say, they have been pitifully deceived. In the two latter places, it was the war-locks and the witches themselves whom people thought bewitched. In the other places, the observations that should have been made were not made, because it was thought (or even it was said), that this was the Devil [before them]. The Priests and Nuns of Loudun had performed the Magic themselves, for which Grandier was burned at the stake, although he was innocent. And elsewhere, the Judges in a matter of Magic were themselves the Magicians. The Devils who made themselves seen and heard were in the brains of men; if not, they were made of flesh and bones. This Zachary, this Devil who hid himself in a ring, was a great Magician, since he duped so many people for so long a time. And if we turn to fact, this Catherine of Harlingen, of whom we spoke in Chapter Thirty-One [revealing her to be a fraud], was a Sorceress . . . in that same sense. . . .

But those who preserve the ordinary meaning [of magic, or witchcraft] make use of this expedient: they do not deny that many things attributed to the Devil occur following the proper but secret course of nature, or occur from the trickery of men, but deny that it follows from this that they are all of the same order. For let us suppose, they say (so that they are taken for men who make suppositions), that of a hundred adventures believed to be Sorcery, there are ninety-nine which are not, yet one must not infer from this that the hundredth could not so be. But I don't want to appear less stingy than they, and I will also say, if we suppose that out of a hundred tales that are called sorcery, it be proven that one of them is not, one must demonstrate why the other ninety-nine would be sorcery: for could there possibly be one of these that could be resolved with less difficulty [by a supposition of witchcraft] than this one out of a hundred was by natural means? And if I am now only one case away from the end of the hundred, it would take a great deal of difficulty to stop me from reaching my goal. Unless those persons show me one of the hundred which is so entirely above the ordinary forces of Nature, that there could be no other thing involved except these Spirits. . . .

There is no argument so absurd as that of attributing an unusual effect to an occult or unknown cause, but above all, to these sorts of [spiritual] intellects, as people want to do, in order to draw as a consequence that they have the power and the capacity to do such things. Why not rather investigate deeply into knowledge of Nature, in order to be able to unite things corporeal to things corporeal? For if I encounter something which has not yet been proven, but which nevertheless is of the same nature as something else, what reason do I have to look for another cause than that which I already have found at work in the other? Suppose that I see a new style of slippers that is beautiful, and such as I never have seen the likes of in the shop of any shoemaker, nor on anyone's feet: must I infer from this that it was neither a shoemaker nor his servant who made them, but rather a baker or a tinker? Nevertheless, it would not be so strange a thing that a baker or a tinker should have made a pair of slippers, since they have hands and feet just like other people, as it would be to say that a Spirit had done a corporeal thing, or, which is the same thing, that a body does spiritual things. It is simply that I have not yet been in all the shops; or perhaps that a former style is being revived that would not seem so strange to the old folks as it does to me. Moreover, I have not investigated the secrets of nature in such a way that I could know what she is yet capable of doing again, and I have not thumbed through books in such a way that there could not be in them certain things formerly known to be natural things, but that pass today for witchcraft.

I have been speaking here only of things that truly happen; what a greater vanity would it not be if I wanted to seek beyond nature the cause of things that do not happen? For if a thing said to have happened never occurred, it has no cause. Now we have seen in all the examples cited above, that the majority of things occur only by virtue of deception, or lack of knowledge, or inadvertence, or that by virtue of the imagination, they have been seen as other things than what they were. What wisdom can there be in all this to bother one's head over the question of what the Devil does or does not do, what he can and cannot do? Imaginary Theology goes even further, when details are missing from some affair that does not have its likeness in the ancient histories, as is the case with the wife of Abbekerk. Such a thing immediately gets attributed to the Devil, and the books of the Theologians and Philosophers are rummaged through [to find supporting evidence]. If it isn't found there, something is invented, so that the affair can still be attributed to the Devil, and the inference is made that he could well have done it. And when it is seen how much difficulty there is in reconciling these things with the laws of Divine Providence, to the extent that they are known to us, something must be said of this matter: either one has recourse to some Author who believed things to be as we want them, or else several passages of Scripture are twisted in order to favor such a view—but always while making the reservation that it was done by the permission of God or by his secret judgments.

How else would it be possible that such questions as our Voetius asked could have been posed?—*Voetius, part. I, pag. 944–971.*

I will cite several of these here to serve as samples of the others.

"If the Devil can appear in the form of a true believer, or of a saint, either dead or alive"—*pag. 944.*

"If the Devil cannot appear in the form of a Lamb or a Dove or even a Man, without some recognizable defect or deformity?"—*pag. 946.*

"If the Devil can act directly upon the rational memory?"—*pag. 965.*

"If the Devil's actions extend to the mental faculties not only of men awake, but also of sleepers?"—*pag. 965–66.*

"If there are no evil thoughts without a proximate and current inspiration from the Devil?"—*pag. 966.*

"If the Devil can act upon a thing which is distant from him, and by means of what quality which issues from him?" And several other questions of the same sort, which depend on this or follow from it—*pag. 967.*

"If the Devil can make the Elements flow more rapidly than they do, make them burn more quickly than they do, and make them softer or harder?"—*pag. 968.*

"If the Devil can produce, essentially, the Elements, or destroy them; for example, if he can change air into water, and vice-versa?"—*pag. 968.*

"If the Devil truly can eat, or if he only does so in appearance, like the charlatans?"—*pag. 970.*

There are many other such questions, but I limit myself to these. He asks "how the Devil can enter a solid place, when he has a body?"—*pag. 971.* I did not believe it worth the trouble to reveal his answers to the other questions, because it would take too long, but here I must do it. "Is it," he says, "because these bodies [that the Devil assumes] are ofttimes so subtle, that they penetrate as easily as light does, by means of the pores? Or because he forms these bodies, on the spot, from the light, or from some other substance that might be in the room? Or finally, because he opens and shuts the windows without being perceived, because these bodies are too heavy or dense? Or because he removes stones or beams from the wall or from the grating, and afterwards returns them to place?" What do you make of such an answer, Reader, which consists of three or four questions? Does it not increase the obscurity of the difficulty, rather than resolve it? But to speak of things as they are, he doesn't pose enough questions. For I would ask him how the body is seen when it appears, since it is more subtle than the air, which cannot be seen because of its subtlety? Secondly, who manifested more power or wisdom: either God, when He formed the body of Adam with visible and palpable substance, or His accursed creature, if it is true that he has always formed visible bodies from all kinds of substances that he finds. Finally, consider this infernal architect, who, in the winking of an eye, can break, remove, disassemble, replace and reconstruct, at his pleasure, the doors, windows, roof-tiles, lattices and stones of a house. That is how lost one becomes, when one goes beyond the limits of Nature, and when one wants to go beyond revelation. For where does Reason teach us anything of all that? Or where indeed is the Scripture which imputes such acts to the Devil? What does it serve man, thus, to believe what is said of all this? The prejudice which is thrown at him again and again makes it so easy for man to believe all of this, and superstition reinforces this case. That occurs because one hears it unceasingly shouted, by the so very ordinary practice of preaching and writing, in which it is asserted without end that the Devil involves himself in all sorts of things; and because of ignorance and lack of experience concerning the secrets of nature; and because of the desire men have to appear more savant in occult things than in things which are known. But above all, man is forced, as soon as he meets something which arrests his judgment, to throw it back upon the Devil. He can do this in all safety, and without being fearful of passing for idiotic, stupid, wicked or impious. But if he should happen to put into doubt, and even more, if he should deny that the Devil can be the author of the thing, he is called an Atheist, because he falls back upon a God, and he limits himself to only One, Who created, Who governs and Who maintains all things. What other reason could one find to convince Atheists, than to produce these examples of visions, phantoms, Magic and obsession? As if there had to be no God, if it were not true that the Devil acted upon men in all sorts of encounters? If you answer yes, why could He not do by means of his Angels the things which cannot be done naturally, or rather, by the force of Nature, of which man still does not know the thousandth part?

67
The Recantation of the Salem Village Jurors (1693)

In 1692 a series of witchcraft charges and a period of prosecution occurred in Salem Village (now Danvers, Massachusetts) in Massachusetts Bay Colony.[1] When the prosecutions ended in 1692, 156 people
had been imprisoned. Of these, nineteen were hanged, one was pressed
to death, and four died in prison. The trials at Salem Village represented
one of the last significant prosecutions in the Western world. The effect of the events at Salem, however, far from rekindling the active
hunt after sorcerers and witches, only further intensified a rapidly
growing skepticism—confessional as well as secular—concerning both
the possibility of the crime and the question of its criminal nature.

For, during the year following the trials, confinements, and executions, the jury that had convicted its fellow citizens formally recanted
the sentence and admitted the error of its actions. This recantation
does not in any way question the theology of witchcraft belief; rather,
it was as if the jurors had put to themselves Montaigne's challenge and
had failed to find the necessary inner conviction: Did we know enough
with certainty to put these men and women to death on the basis of our
conjectures? The Salem Village trials represented as much the crisis
of confidence in the validity of methods for identifying and trying
witches as it did any continuity of practice.

The jurors' recantation appeared at the same time as a significant
number of literary works that were highly critical in varying degrees of
both the trials and of the theology that had led to them, particularly
those of Robert Calef, John Hale, Thomas Maule, Ebenezer Turrell, and
Thomas Hutchinson.

Several of the surviving accused persons or the relatives of those who
had not survived went a step further. In April 1693, Philip English
petitioned the governor of Massachusetts Bay Colony for the return of
his goods seized by the Sheriff George Corwin. On September 13, 1710,
the claim of William Good for damages he had endured as a result of
the execution of his wife, Sarah, on July 19, 1692, suggests that the
Salem stories, having originated in a legal and theological worldview
applied to particular local circumstances, ended in a legal worldview in
which damages could be sought and expected from the authority of a

1. See the references to Text 58 above. To these should be added Richard Weisman, *Witchcraft,
Magic, and Religion in Seventeenth-Century Massachusetts* (Amherst, 1984), and David D.
Hall, *Worlds of Wonder, Days of Judgment: Popular Religious Belief in Early New England*
(New York, 1989), and especially David Harley, "Explaining Salem: Calvinist Psychology and
the Diagnosis of Possession," *American Historical Review* 101 (1996): 307–30.

mistaken and repentant court. The colonial assembly offered him thirty pounds.

SOURCE: *The Witchcraft Delusion in New England: Its Rise, Progress, and Termination*, with preface, introduction, and notes by Samuel G. Drake (Roxbury, Mass., 1866), 134–35.

FURTHER READING: See the references to Text 58.

WE, WHOSE NAMES are under written, being in the year 1692 called to serve as jurors in the court at Salem on trial of many, who were by some suspected guilty of doing acts of witchcraft upon the bodies of sundry persons:

We confess that we ourselves were not capable to understand, nor able to withstand, the mysterious delusions of the powers of darkness, and prince of the air; but were, for want of knowledge in ourselves, and better information from others, prevailed with to take up with such evidence against the accused, as, on further consideration and better information, we justly fear was insufficient for the touching the lives of any (Deut. xvii. 6) whereby we fear we have been instrumental, with others, though ignorantly and unwittingly, to bring upon ourselves and this people of the Lord the guilt of innocent blood; which sin the Lord saith, in scripture, he would not pardon (2 Kings xxiv. 4), that is, we suppose, in regard of his temporal judgements. We do therefore hereby signify to all in general (and to the surviving sufferers in special) our deep sense of, and sorrow for, our errors, in acting on such evidence to the condemning of any person; and do hereby declare, that we justly fear that we were sadly deluded and mistaken; for which we are much disquieted and distressed in our minds; and do therefore humbly beg forgiveness, first of God for Christ's sake, for this our error; and pray that God would not impute the guilt of it to ourselves, nor others; and we also pray that we may be considered candidly, and aright, by the living sufferers, as being then under the power of a strong and general delusion, utterly unacquainted with, and not experienced in, matters of that nature.

We do heartily ask forgiveness of you all, whom we have justly offended; and do declare, according to our present minds, we would none of us do such things again on such grounds for the whole world; praying you to accept of this in way of satisfaction for our offence, and that you would bless the inheritance of the Lord, that he may be entreated for the land.

Foreman, Thomas Fisk,	Th. Pearly, sen.
William Fisk,	John Peabody,
John Bachelor,	Thomas Perkins,
Thomas Fisk, jun.	Samuel Sayer,
John Dane,	Andrew Eliot,
Joseph Evelith,	Henry Herrick, sen.

68

Pierre Bayle: *Answer to the Questions of a Provincial* (1703)

Pierre Bayle (1647–1706) spent his intellectual life in a solemn dialec-
tic of reason and faith. He abhorred, above all, the arrogance of self-
confident dogmatism, and sought to demonstrate to his contemporaries the rational, empirical, and historical difficulties at the center of
the positions and theses they espoused with such assurance of their
own reasonableness, indicating, in his own mind, the necessity of a
tolerant faith respecting the rights of conscience. In his writings on
witchcraft, Bayle combined three vital strains of seventeenth-century
thought: a skepticism of popular and traditional opinion; a Cartesian
mechanism which sought simpler, wholly natural explanations of phenomena thought to be beyond the powers of nature; and a desire for
tolerance and peace that rejected the use of torture and stake for the
victims of religious enthusiasm.

Bayle never theoretically attacked the theological basis of witchcraft
belief; that would have been an unacceptable dogmatism for him.
Rather, he challenged the right of men to assign confidently certain
phenomena to the category of witchcraft and to maintain explanations
that contemporary wisdom ought to know enough to reject. He was, in
this sense, less an innovator than an upholder of the tradition of Weyer
and Montaigne.

SOURCE: Pierre Bayle, *Réponse aux questions d'un provincial*, 4
partes (1703), in *Oeuvres diverses de M. Pierre Bayle*, 4 vols. (La Haye,
1727), vol. 3, pt. 2, pp. 559–62. Trans. A. C. K.

YOU KNOW THAT in several provinces
of France, in Savoy, in the Canton of Bern, and in several other parts of Europe,
all one hears of is witchcraft, and that no town or hamlet is so small that it has
no one reputed to be a witch. Tales of apparitions and evil spells are endless in
number; the heads of little children are filled with them, and that makes them
completely credulous and timorous with regard to such things. You hear of
nothing else among the common people but that an illness has been given to
such and such persons by a witch, and that it has been cured either by the same
witch, or by one of his confreres. And the truth is that they go running to those
types as soon as they decide that an illness comes from a spell. It is moreover
true that several ill persons are cured by such means, but it is no less true that
these cures, and these illnesses, are an effect of the dominion that the imagination exercises over the other faculties of the body and the soul. This dominion is
sometimes so despotic that nothing can prevail against it. An imagination that
is alarmed by the fear of a witch's spell can overthrow the animal constitution,

and produce those extravagant symptoms that exasperate the most expert medical doctors. This same imagination, forearmed with confidence that the spell has been lifted, and that the witch has sworn to it, by virtue of several words that she babbled over some herbs, arrests the course of the disease. It was maintained by the anxieties of the mind and by the panic-stricken terrors of the soul; it ceases from the time that the person believes himself delivered from the charm. Tranquility of the heart and inward joy return, and allow the faculties to regain their interrupted functions.

I understand, thus, that it is very possible for a woman to persuade herself that someone has put the Devil into her body. All that is necessary for this is that she be asked if the witch whom she suspects made any grimaces near her, at the time that she believes she was put under a spell, and muttered several words which are preliminary to the evocation of the Demon that someone wants to make enter her. It is enough to tell her that he is a man who has put many other people under the possession of the Devil. She thereupon will believe herself a veritable possessed person, and will act in the way that she knows possessed people act; she will scream, she will jump up and down, and so on and on. . . .

A similar persuasion can easily enter the mind of those devout nuns who read many treatises filled with stories of temptations and apparitions. They attribute to the malice of Satan the wicked thoughts that come to them, and if they observe an obstinate strength in their temptations, they imagine that he persecutes them close at hand, that he haunts them, and finally that he lays hold of bodies. Angela de Fulgino, a great name among the Mystics, seems to me to be in good faith when she relates that the Devils, not content with inspiring her with evil desires, beat her terribly. The description that she gives of the pains that they made her suffer in her body and in her soul would inspire compassion in the most hardened of hearts. They excited such a flame of impurity in her body that she could not repress its force except by material fire; but her confessor forbade her this remedy. They chased all of the virtues from her soul, which caused her an unbelievable agony, and so furious an anger that she came very close to tearing herself apart, and sometimes it drove her to the point of beating herself horribly. "I suffered incessantly, from these demons, torments and passions of the spirit which were incomparably sharper and more numerous than those of the body. . . . When, in my soul, all virtues had been overthrown and had fled, and my soul could not oppose this, there was such a grief in my soul that anything could make it lament because of its desperate grief and anger. Indeed, I weep incessantly sometimes, and sometimes such great anger rises up in me that I am wholly torn to pieces. Sometimes I am not able to control myself, so that I strike myself horribly, and from this striking, my head sometimes swells up, as do my other members. . . . I perceive that I am given up to many demons who bring back to life those vices which I abhor and which were dead [in me], and they bring in [me] other vices which I never had." No more than with Job's body, there was no part of her body that the Devils had not struck. "There are numberless torments of the body inflicted by many demons many times. Indeed, I believe that the afflictions and passions which I have described now may be corporeal. For there is in me now no member which has not suffered horribly. Never am I without anguish, never do I rest without languor. I am broken and fragile, and filled with pain, so that it is possible only to lie prone. There is no member in me that has not been beaten, twisted and punished by the demons, and I am always ill and always swollen and full of pain in all my body. Only with immense pain may I move myself, and only with complete exhaustion may I rest. Nor indeed am I able to take enough food to keep myself alive." I would not dare to suspect her of any falsehood; I believe that she is speaking sincerely. But see what the imagination is capable of, once unhinged by too contemplative a life.

I have gone on a bit too much with the story of this woman, and I have quoted sections of it at too great a length, because I remembered that you did not put too much stock in what I wrote to you about the bitterness that accompanies the devout life. You have persisted in telling me that mystics seem to you to be the happiest men in the world. It was thus necessary to convince you by means of a great example that they do not always enjoy "those illapsus and those ineffable sweetnesses" that you have read in their writings.

It is not necessary for me to give you proofs of the force of the imagination: you will find enough of them in the books that have been published on this matter, and you are not unaware of what everyone says, that there is nothing more important to an ill person than having a full confidence in the skill of his doctor, and in the virtues of the medications. The fear of death inspires so much grief and so many worries in ill persons, even if they say nothing about it, that these increase their illness much more than remedies diminish it, and very often become great obstacles for the remedies to overcome. Remove this cause, give a full confidence to the ill person, and he will have a tranquil mind, and that will be his cure. It is thus that monks famous for their holiness and the gift of miracles and that sacred relics have been able to cure many men. It is thus that imposters have broken the fever of several persons into a sweat, persons to whom they had promised this operation by means of sympathetic properties. The internal agitation with which a person prepares himself for this effect in a warm bed is the true sudorific of those people. If credulous folks with an easily impressed imagination alone fell into the hands of these imposters, the latter almost never would be disparaged.

I beseech you not to accuse of fraud those who protest that phantoms have appeared to them, for the tales that they have read or heard told about these sorts of apparitions were able to leave so deep a mark upon their brain that the animal spirits cannot fall upon these marks without vigorously stimulating the idea of a specter. If a lively attention to those latter objects, accompanied by fear, unsettles the imagination, be assured that the action of the animal spirits upon this mark will be stronger than the action of light upon the optic nerves. The imagination thus will be stronger than sight, and will paint its objects as if they were present, in such a way that although a person may be awake he will believe that one sees a thing which is not present to the eyes, but only to the internal senses. Consider a bit what happens in our dreams. The most reasonable heads become extravagant while sleeping, and create chimeras more bizarre than those of the madmen whom one shuts up in the asylums. These objects of dreams appear as if they were present to the external senses: one believes that one sees Fauns and Satyrs, that one hears a tree or a river talking, etc. From whence does that come? From the fact that the action of the senses is interrupted, and the imagination rules. The same thing will happen in much the same way to those who are not asleep, if by the effect of some fear, or of some great internal emotion, the acts of the imagination have more force than those of sight, hearing, etc.

I could not restrain myself from making you recall something which is undoubtedly very common in your Province, and which visibly demonstrates what the imagination can accomplish. Several men are unable to consummate their marriage, and believe that this impotence is the effect of a spell. From then on, the newlyweds regard each other with an evil eye, and their discord at times descends into the most horrible enmity: the sight of one makes the other shiver. What I tell you here are not old wives' tales, but certain and incontestable facts which only too often come into the sight and ken of all the neighbors in the provinces, where much faith is put in the traditions of witchcraft. The common opinion is that the witches visit this evil service upon newlyweds by pronouncing certain words during the nuptial benediction; but it is also said that the witches must tie several knots in a ribbon, or in a rope, from which comes the vulgar expression "knotting the braid." They add that if the fiancés sleep together before the wedding, the spell is no longer to be feared. That is why there are some good mothers who consent to anticipating the wedding night in order to foil the witch. But I can tell you that there are examples of folks married for a long time who come to hate each other, and to believe that a witch has given them this mutual aversion.

There are also examples of an aversion incited among brothers, or among cousins, or among domestics of different sexes; I speak of that aversion whose features make people judge that witchcraft is involved in it. Thus one must not take as a general maxim what several authors say, that one cannot "knot the braid" with regard to concubines. I don't have to tell you that people are certain that if the witch undoes the knots of the rope he undoes the spell, and that if the rope falls into the hands of anyone who can untie it, all the wizardry disappears, and that there always are hailstorms if one restores it to its original state. Neither do I have to tell you that a witch is often begged to raise the spell, and offered some gift in payment. I must suppose that all these things are known to you.

But in order to show you that there is only imagination involved in these things, it would suffice to report to you a little adventure that I can guarantee is completely true. I knew a peasant who, having married a widow, and being unable to consummate his marriage, persuaded himself that the braid had been knotted, and had great trouble bearing this patiently. Several weeks passed without any change except that he became daily more dissatisfied, and his wife more displeased. They nevertheless went together to their work: now one day as they were working on their vines, it began to rain, and they took refuge in one of those huts of vine-shoots that are put up in the middle of vineyards to be used as refuges in case of rain. They were scarcely in there when it thundered and hailed. The good man then remembered the tradition that it hails every time the braid is unknotted for someone, and imagining that it was his being unknotted, he felt all his virility returning to life, and consummated his marriage on the spot. Wouldn't you say that he had the same auspices as Dido and Aeneas? He related the thing so naively when the occasion presented itself, that there was no room for doubt of his ingenuousness.

I am not so certain of another adventure told to me, which is about a man who found himself in the same situation as this peasant, and felt himself cured as soon as he was told that a small boy, who was looking for nests, had found a rope with several knots in a haystack, and that he had had the patience to untie all these knots, one after the other, and that while he worked a bit of hail fell. That was undoubtedly a pious fraud. This tale was told only to make the person believe that he was no longer under the spell.

M. Venette, Medical Doctor of La Rochelle, has published a fact which gives us here a more convincing proof. "About thirty-five years ago," he relates, "Pierre Burtel . . . working for my father in one of his country houses, told him something so unfavorable about me one day, that I was obliged the next day to say to Burtel, the cooper, that, to avenge myself, I would knot his braid when he married, which he was going to do in a little while with a servant from our neighborhood. This man truly believed what I said to him, and although I spoke only in jest, nevertheless these fake threats made so strong an impression on his mind, already preoccupied with spells, that after being married, he spent almost a month without being able to sleep with his wife. He felt desires to embrace her tenderly many times, but, when he had to execute what he was resolved upon, he found himself impotent; his imagination being thus overburdened with ideas of witchcraft. On the other side of this, the wife, who was well built, felt as much coldness toward him as he had toward her; and because this man did not caress her, hatred quickly took ahold of her heart, and she manifested for him the same repugnances that he had for her. It was thus a good game to hear them tell everyone that they were bewitched, and that I had knotted the braid for them. At this point I repented of having mocked so simple a man in such a way, and I did everything that one could do on this occasion to persuade them that this was not the case: but the more I protested to the husband that what I had said were only trifles to avenge myself on him, the more he abhorred me and believed that I was the author of all of his troubles. The curé of Notre-Dame, who had married them, even used all his wit and all his prudence to settle this affair. Finally, he succeeded better than I had in bringing this to an end, and by his efforts broke the spell after twenty-one days."

He uses this example to prove what he just had established, that the impotence that is alleged to be caused by witchcraft comes only from a susceptible imagination.

Let us cite as well Pierre Pigray, who strongly refutes those who suppose that the braid is knotted by "a certain ceremony that is performed by saying several sacred words." It is most notorious, he says, "that the least passion of the mind prevents and turns us away from this [sexual] pleasure: it is most certain that it can be knotted without any ceremony, that is to say, that the member of a cold, fearful, melancholy and apprehensive man can be rendered weak and puny, simply by telling him that it has been knotted for him; the fear and apprehension that he will have (the force of which suffices not only to trouble us in this act, but to make us fall into great and extreme illnesses) alone will render him for a time impotent and inept; but in the case of a sanguine, healthy, strapping man, without apprehension or any passion of the mind, it is impossible for all of the enchanters to benumb him, if he is alongside of a subject whom he loves, or to prevent him from doing well and executing his natural function. I saw an honorable personage, fallen into this difficulty, for whom it never had been thought to knot the braid; but from the fear of that alone, he fell into this impotence for some time. And the remedy used to cure this evil demonstrates well enough the abuse, namely (it is said), to make the woman pee into a ring, as if that had the power to cure the husband. It is true that it does not matter whatever the remedy be, provided that it removes and cures the passion of the mind."

There is hardly a superstition of greater antiquity than that which attributes to certain words the quality of bestowing or curing illnesses. Those who have understood that words cannot be the physical cause of such effects resort to upholding the position that they operate by an "explicit" or "implicit" pact with the Demon. But to refute them, it suffices to say that if those who used these words made use of others according to their fantasy, they would produce the same effects. I have read somewhat that Hemmingius, a most famous Theologian, quoted two barbarous verses in one of his sermons, and added, to amuse himself, that they could chase away fever. One of his listeners made the attempt on his valet, and cured him, and soon after, word of the remedy spread, and it happened that several feverish people found themselves well by virtue of it. Learning of that, Hemmingius felt obliged to say that he had spoken in that way in fun, and that it was only a witticism. From that moment on, the remedy was a failure; people no longer put any faith in it. In the second volume of the *Aventures d'Assouci*, you will see how cures that pass for supernatural can be effected without any magic.

69

Christian Thomasius: Witchcraft and the Law, 1702

Christian Thomasius (1655–1728) was a widely renowned and controversial jurist who was the first head of the University of Halle in Brandenburg, Prussia. His insistence on religious toleration, his criticism of judicial torture, and finally his arguments that demons could not cause material effects, that they could not assume bodily form, that they could have no sexual union with humans, and that no pact could be made between demons and humans—in effect, his denial of the crime of witchcraft—drew down on him the opposition of both theologians and other jurists, one of whom in 1698 described Thomasius's religious beliefs as "Thomasian atheism." His most important work on this subject was his 1701 *De crimine magiae* (On the crime of magic), translated into German two years later by his student Johann Reiche, himself a powerful critic of witchcraft beliefs.

Thomasius also wrote the *Historische Untersuchung vom Ursprung und Fortgang des Inquisitions Prozesses* (Historical investigation into the origins and continuation of the inquisitorial trial) in 1712, an astonishingly detailed and devastating critical consideration of virtually every known text, from the Bible to his own day, that had ever been cited in favor of witchcraft beliefs. In one sense the latter work offers a running commentary on many of the texts in this volume: those of scripture, Roman law, canon law, John of Salisbury (Text 10), Augustine (Text 1), Gervase of Tilbury (Text 11), Pope Alexander IV (Text 19), Thomas Aquinas (Texts 13–16), *The Golden Legend* (Text 12), the Paris statement of 1398 (Text 23), Nider (Text 27), Jacquier (Text 31), the *Malleus Maleficarum* (Text 34), Molitor, Erasmus (Text 36), Weyer (Text 44), Daneau (Text 42), Bodin (Text 45), Remy (Text 49), Del Rio (Text 50), James VI and I (Text 51), Spee (Text 65), Bekker (Text 66), and dozens of others. Thomasius's book was also responsible for circulating Leibniz's identification of Friedrich Spee as the author of the *Cautio criminalis* (Text 65).

The work translated here is a memorial, or vindication of his position against the criticism that assailed him as soon as the *De crimine magiae* appeared in 1701. It summarizes notes from his winter lectures in 1702.

Thomasius was criticized so strongly because he lashed out equally at both Catholic and Protestant theologians and jurists, dismissing the woman of En-dor (1 Samuel 28) as simply a ventriloquist and asking, "What judge would be so foolish as to believe a thousand women, if they unanimously confessed that they had been to heaven and danced with St. Peter and slept with his hunting-dogs, and yet the witches' confessions are more absurd than this?" Although he came down most severely against Catholicism, he also refused to give any quarter to Protestant theologians. He lashed out at contemporaries—a German translation of Glanvill's *Sadducismus Triumphatus* (Text 59) had appeared at Hamburg in 1701. He was responsible for the translation into German of English works critical of witchcraft beliefs—those of John Webster, originally written in 1673, and Francis Hutchinson, originally written in 1718—in association with the medical student Christian Weissbach, who had independently translated John Wagstaff's critical book into German in 1711. Thomasius died in 1728, coincidentally in the same year that the last woman was burned for witchcraft in Prussia.

SOURCE: Christian Thomasius, *Über die Hexenprozesse*, ed. Rolf Lieberwirth (Weimar, 1967), 221–24. The numbered statements of belief and disbelief are in Thomasius's text. Trans. E. P.

FURTHER READING: Lea, *Materials*, 3: 1394–1406.

Unfortunately, since I was forced to learn that someone has taken the opportunity to use my disputation *De crimine magiae* in order to incriminate me falsely of not believing in the devil, disregarding the opposite position which is to be read in open and clear words in the disputation itself, I have myself taken the opportunity to testify clearly, by means of the discourse of those Egyptian magicians, to my innocence and to report my opinion of witches more fully than I could in that disputation because of the shortness of time I had and the press of other affairs. Specifically, as I (1) believe in the devil, and (2) the devil is the original cause of evil, and it follows from this that (3) I hold that he is responsible for the first sinful fall of the first human beings [that is, original sin]. I also believe (4) that sorcerers and witches exist, and that they injure men and beasts in various ways.

I also believe (5) that there are crystal-gazers and exorcists and they are able to accomplish wonderful things by means of superstitious things and blessings. I allow (6) that by these people certain things are done which are not illusions or fraudulent and cannot be ascribed to the natural powers of bodies and natural elements, but must come from the devil, and that (7) certain things happen by these means, about which one can say nothing other than that they come from a greater power than that of man, and cannot be ascribed to God and his angels, as when, for example, there come forth from a human body things that are sometimes natural and sometimes artificial, such as threads, needles, potsherds, hair, pike's teeth, and in far greater number out of orifices that could not possibly contain them, for example, out of the ears. I also hold (8) that no one should permit crystal-gazers, exorcists, and conjurors to live in a well-ordered republic, but should expel them from it or when the opportunity arises to punish them in more severe ways. I hold that (9) those same sorcerers and witches who injure humans by these different means should be put to death, also when injuries are committed by otherwise unknown and secret powers of Nature, or even when no injuries resulted, but sorcerers and witches only tried to commit them by their spells and deceit.

But I deny most firmly and cannot believe (10) that the devil has horns, claws, or talons, or that he appears as a Pharisee, or a monk, or a monster as men depict him. I cannot believe (11) that he can take on a material body and appear to men in this or some other form. I also cannot believe (12) that the devil can enter into agreements with humans, cause them to give him written documents [that is, pacts], sleep [that is, have sexual intercourse] with them, or that he bears them off to the Blocksberg [sabbat] on a broom or a goat, and so forth. I believe (13) that all of these things are either the inventions of idle people or false stories told by those who wish to deceive others and through this to obtain some authority from them or to get money from them, or the result of melancholic illusions, or forced from people by an executioner [that is, a torturer].

I believe (14) that the commonly held opposite opinion gains nothing when I allow as well that through superstitions and exorcisms all kinds of wonderful things can really take place. For who does not know, for example, that Jews, when they throw a piece of bread on which are marked certain characters into a fire, or when they otherwise cast a spell on the fire, do cause the fire to burn no more? Who does not know that Gypsies can set fire to stables and barns and that nevertheless this does not cause injury? But I have never heard anybody claim that either Jews or Gypsies were witch-masters and had made pacts with the devil. I believe (15) that the commonly held opinion gains nothing when I now allow that some illnesses are caused by the devil and that some of them are brought about by magicians by the help of the devil. Holy men, by the power of God and through their strong faith, have certainly performed wonders, but they have not done this by making a pact with God, or signing a contract with Him. Why then should not the devil also work through the children of unbelief without such a pact? Or why cannot their wicked faith and strong impression and desire alone work evil through Satan's power? Just as God has revealed Himself ɔ the faithful and His prophets through visions, dreams, and voices, so the devil can reveal to his sorcerers and witches the harmful superstitious means to invisibility.

I hold (16) that since the procedure of the witch trials is inadequate, because jurists have made the pact with the devil the basis of the charge, a thing which is not possible in nature, that one has to proceed cautiously if people are to be convicted of having injured others through witchcraft. There must be many proofs, and the rules of evidence indicated in the Code of Criminal Law are not correct, as has been shown in my disputation. And (17) especially in the case of wonderful and supernaturally induced diseases, great investigation should be made in order to make certain that there are no deceptions involved, even when they are testified to by learned and trustworthy persons and even by doctors of medicine, because learned and trustworthy people can be as easily deceived as any others, if not more so. And I believe that (18) among these stated or supernaturally induced diseases, about which someone has compiled an entire book, most of them have been told about by deception and that among a hundred cases there is scarcely one that does not involve some hocus-pocus or some hasty action. The well-known deception involving the golden tooth shows how foolish deceptions often stand behind things that appear otherwise, about which the medical masters have written books and undertaken investigations. And I must also confess (19) that when I would, for example, see a bowl full of pike's teeth drawn from a man's ear, I myself would at first think that this was a thing that could only have been done with the help of the devil and witchcraft, but when the matter was really investigated further, I would not know exactly how I should answer him who would object. That man in no way can consider this a natural disease, because it contradicts human sense; man cannot grasp such things and in such great numbers. And the devil cannot bring about things that are self-contradicting either, because even the divine power, greater than all others, cannot bring about self-contradictory things. Thus I am led to the conclusion by further observations that even in this case I would rather say that I do not know how this happens, than that the devil does it. Because just as certainly as the fact that two times three is six, it is equally certain that I do not know what I do not know. If someone else says, however, this thing has been caused by the devil, even though he does not understand it, I will accept this, if that person will only permit me to remain in my learned ignorance.

But even if one postulated that this business came from the devil, I still don't see (20) how a trial for witchcraft could be based on it. For then the question becomes, who was the witch-master who inflicted this disease on the patient and how could any judge become certain of this. It is certainly no great problem to get an executioner [torturer] to extract a confession, but this is not enough. I am afraid that if someone tortures you or me, we will confess to everything that the torturer wants to demand. And if tortured further concerning the particulars of the case, we would lie about them because we knew what the judge wanted to hear and that this would get us out of the torture chamber.

In a word, I consider that witch trials are useless, that the bodily horned devil with his pitch-ladle and his mother is a pure fabrication of popish priests, and that it is their greatest secret in order to frighten people with such devils so that they will pay money for masses for their souls, contribute rich inheritances and money to the endowments of monasteries or other pious causes and treat innocent people who cry "Father, what do you do?" as if they were sorcerers. Christ did not convert sinners with such devils, nor did the Apostles by their preaching build any such systems in which the devil was a cornerstone which, when removed, would bring down with it the whole structure.

At that time it was said, Who denies Christ denies God. Today it is said, Who denies the horned and painted devil denies God. Even in the depths of darkest popery would it have been possible for such mischief to be conceived? Some time ago I heard a learned preacher whom I admire very much, say in a sermon that man should watch out for the devil, but not fear him. I must also watch out, for example, for my own vices as much as for the vices of those who take the devil's side, or for those of others, young and old, who might be at Wittenberg or here in Delitzsch, or somewhere else, but I do not fear for them. I take into consideration that I attribute to them no motive of devilry; that is blasphemy, but if they choose to blasphemize anyway, I let them diabolize as long as they want to, and I let them pass on, even if some mask themselves as an angel of light or others practice their abuses against me under the appearance of praying for me, and so forth.

Acknowledgments

Permission to reprint portions of previously published works is gratefully acknowledged.

Augustine, *De Doctrina Christiana*, ed. and trans. R. P. H. Green (Oxford: Clarendon Press, 1995). Copyright © 1995 R. P. H. Green, reprinted by permission of Oxford University Press.

Bernardino of Siena, from *Medieval Popular Religion, 1000–1500: A Reader*, ed. John Shinners (Peterborough, Ont.: Broadview Press, 1997). Copyright © 1997 John Shinners, reprinted by permission of Broadview Press.

Bodin, Jean, *On the Demon-Mania of Witches*, trans. Randy Scott, intro. Jonathan L. Pearl (Toronto: Centre for Reformation and Renaissance Studies, 1995). Reprinted by permision of Victoria University Centre for Reformation and Renaissance Studies.

Burchard of Worms, *Corrector, sive Medicus*, from *Medieval Handbooks of Penance: A Translation of the Principal "Libri poenitentiales" and Selections from Related Documents*, trans. John T. McNeill and Helena M. Gamer (New York: Columbia University Press, 1938, reprint 1965). Copyright Columbia University Press, reprinted by permission of Columbia University Press.

Caesarius of Arles, Sermon 54, from *Caesarius of Arles: Sermons, Volume I (1–80)*, trans. Mary Magdeleine Mueller (New York: Fathers of the Church, 1956).

"Confessions of the Chelmsford Witches," from Charles Williams, *Witchcraft* (1941, reprint Wellingborough: Aquarian Press, 1980).

Del Rio, Martín, *Disquisitiones magicarum*, from *The Occult in Early Modern Europe: A Documentary History*, ed. and trans. P. G. Maxwell-Stuart (New York: St. Martin's Press, 1999). Copyright © 1999 P. G. Maxwell-Stuart, reprinted by permission of St. Martin's Press.

Erasmus, Desiderius, "A Terrible Case of Sorcery in Orléans," from *The Correspondence of Erasmus: Letters 142–297, 1501–1514*, trans. R. A. B. Mynors and D. F. S. Ferguson (Toronto: University of Toronto Press, 1974). Copyright © 1979 University of Toronto Press, reprinted by permission of University of Toronto Press.

Gregory IX, *Vox in Rama*, from Malcolm Barber, "Propaganda in the Middle Ages: The Charges Against the Templars," *Nottingham Medieval Studies* 17 (1973): 42–57. Reprinted by permission of Nottingham Medieval Studies.

Hadrian IV, *On Diabolical Witchcraft*, from Montague Summers, *The Geography of Witchcraft* (1927; reprint London: Routledge, 1978). Reprinted by permission of Taylor & Francis Books.

Halitgar of Cambrai, " 'Roman' Penitential," from *Medieval Handbooks of Penance: A Translation of the Principal "Libri poenitentiales" and Selections from Related Documents*, trans. John T. McNeill and Helena M. Gamer (New York: Columbia University Press, 1938, reprint 1965). Copyright Columbia University Press, reprinted by permission of Columbia Press.

Hugh of St. Victor, *The Didascalicon of Hugh of St. Victor: A Medieval Guide to the Arts*, trans. Jerome Taylor (New York: Columbia University Press, 1961). Copyright © 1961 Columbia University Press, reprinted by permission of Columbia University Press.

Jacobus de Voragine, "The Life of St. Justina," from *The Golden Legend: Readings on the Saints*, trans. William Granger Ryan (Princeton, N.J.: Princeton University Press, 1993). Copyright © 1993 Princeton University Press. Reprinted by permission of Princeton University Press.

Martín de Castañega, *Tratado muy sotil y bien fundado*, from David H. Darst, "Witchcraft in Spain: The Testimony of Martín de Castañega's Treatise on Superstition and Witchcraft," *Proceedings of the American Philosophical Society* 123 (1979): 298–322. Reprinted by permission of the American Philosophical Society.

Montaigne, Michel de, "Concerning Cripples," from *The Complete Works of Montaigne: Essays, Travel Journal, Letters*, trans. Donald M. Frame (Stanford, Calif.: Stanford University Press, 1958). Copyright © 1958 Board of Trustees of the Leland Stanford Junior University, reprinted by permission of Stanford University Press.

Ralph of Coggeshall, "The Heretics of Rheims," from *Heresies of the High Middle Ages: Selected Sources Translated and Annotated*, ed. Walter L. Wakefield and Austin P. Evans (New York: Columbia University Press, 1969). Copyright © 1969 Columbia University Press, reprinted by permission of Columbia University Press.

Salazar Frias, Alonso de, from Gustav Henningsen, *The Witches' Advocate: Basque Witchcraft and the Spanish Inquisition, 1609–1614* (Reno: University of Nevada Press, 1980). Copyright © Gustav Henningsen, reprinted by permission of University of Nevada Press.

Spinoza, Benedict de, *The Political Works*, ed. A. G. Wernham (Oxford: Clarendon Press, 1958). Copyright © 1958 A. G. Wernham, reprinted by permission of Oxford University Press.

"The Theology Faculty of the University of Paris Condemns Sorcery," from Lynn Thorndike, *University Records and Life in the Middle Ages* (New York: Columbia University Press, 1944). Reprinted by permission of Columbia University Press.

Tholosan, Claude, *Ut magorum et maleficiorum errores*, from Pierrette Paravy, "À propos de la génèse médiévale des chasses aux sorcières," *Mélanges de l'École française de Rome: Moyen Âge, Temps modernes* 91 (1979): 354–79.

Weyer, Johann, *De praestigiis daemonum*, from *On Witchcraft: An Abridged Translation of Johann Weyer's "De praestigiis daemonum"*, ed. Benjamin G. Kohl and H. C. Erik Midelfort, trans. John Shea (Asheville, N.C.: Pegasus Press, 1998). Reprinted by permission of Pegasus Press.

CPSIA information can be obtained
at www.ICGtesting.com
Printed in the USA
JSHW020954210120
3719JS00001B/44